Letters from Africa 1914–1931

"I have a feeling that wherever I may be in the future, I will be wondering whether there is rain at Ngong."

Isak Dinesen in a letter to her mother, 26 February 1919

Isak Dinesen

Letters from Africa 1914-1931

Edited for the Rungstedlund Foundation by
FRANS LASSON

Translated by
ANNE BORN

THE UNIVERSITY OF CHICAGO PRESS

Chicago

This translation has been supported in part by a grant from the Danish Ministry for Cultural Affairs

ISAK DINESEN was the pen name of the Danish Baroness Karen Blixen of Rungstedlund (1885–1962). A gifted and original storyteller, she drew on her experiences in Africa and her earlier life in Europe to create tales in keeping with her belief that "without repeating life in imagination you can never be fully alive."

Originally published in two volumes as *Breve fra Afrika 1914–24* and *Breve fra Afrika 1925–31*,

The University of Chicago Press, Chicago 60637
 Published 1981
Printed in the United States of America
85 84 83 82 81 5 4 3 2 1

Library of Congress Cataloging in Publication Data

Blixen, Karen, 1885–1962.
Letters from Africa, 1914–1931.

"Originally published in two volumes as Breve fra Afrika 1914–24 and Breve fra Afrika 1925–31."
Includes bibliographical references and index.
1. Blixen, Karen, 1885–1962—Correspondence.
2. Authors, Danish—20th century—Correspondence.
I. Lasson, Frans. II. Title.
PT8175.B545Z5313 1981 839.8′1372 [B] 80–25856
ISBN 0–226–15309–6

Contents

The Rain at Ngong: An Introduction to the Letters of Isak Dinesen vii

Chronology by Frans Lasson xxvii

Translator's Note xli

Letters from Africa 1914–1931

1914 1

1915 29

1916 34

1917 36

1918 57

1919 95

1920 101

1921 106

1922 121

1923 143

1924 184

1925 228

1926 238

1927 298

1928 332

1929 398

1930 401

1931 415

Notes 433

Index 447

The Rain at Ngong

An Introduction to the Letters of Isak Dinesen (Karen Blixen)

In 1939, when Karen Blixen's reputation as a writer had been definitively established by a sizable Danish and an even larger foreign readership, she wrote, in a letter to a close relation who had expressed anxiety about her personal situation since the death of her mother in January of the same year:

> I'm going to start off by saying that if you think I find my position here at Rungsted this summer difficult,—Aunt Bess read me a letter from you which gave me the idea that this was what you were thinking,—then it is a misunderstanding, and I would like to put it right. To me everything here seems so lovely; it has really given me great happiness to have been able to stay here in completely unchanged conditions, and I think that this puts me in a far happier situation than Elle, for instance, who has to begin to cope with life in all its forms. The staff is so extremely good, and everything in the beloved old home seems to gather itself around me and protect me, and from day to day I feel as if Mother were here taking part in everything. You know how lovely it is here in springtime, the starlings sing outside my window in the mornings, the flowers are coming out in the garden just as in all the other years, and everything is still filled with Mother's peace and blessing. I just can't express all my gratitude for having been given this space of time in which to gather my thoughts and try to see clearly what I should do with my life. It seems as if even the uncertain conditions in the world around me fit in quite well with my being here and do not disquiet me, as they must do other poor people who have so much to look after and worry about; for I know that everything of mine belongs to the past, and must soon pass away; I have no need, like the others to struggle against the forces that are changing the world, and I feel that the amazing harmony that Mother took with her everywhere goes along with me too,—I think of Nietzsche's words: "I am a yea-sayer."
>
> So that what in reality is hard for me is not the loss of Mother, or of the others who are dead, but my relationship to life and the living, and my doubts as to whether I am still really able to take my place among them. When I came back from Africa I said to Mother that she was not to expect much from me, for half of me

was lying in the Ngong Hills,—and now I have the feeling that half of what was left is, well, not in the churchyard, but somehow in the past, or in the universe itself, having no connection with everyday life, or any of its demands. I do really think that, viewed purely objectively, it is a difficult proposition, for the second time in one's life, and when one is no longer young, to be faced with the task of creating a life for oneself. I don't mean from the purely financial point of view, or as regards such details as where one is to live, and how one is to manage, but something much deeper: How is one to live? But even to work that out for myself I have this period here to help me; I do not need to hurry, but can leave it to reveal itself to me as it comes. . . .

Severance, in human terms, and the strange calm in the middle of a storm that otherwise sweeps everything along with it—these were experiences that could no longer frighten Karen Blixen, for like so much else they were merely repetitions of what she had been through earlier in Africa. The fact that, eight years after her departure from the farm, and perhaps in fact for the rest of her life, she could feel that she really had no proper place among the living, in the present and the reality that were theirs, is unlikely to surprise any perceptive reader of *Out of Africa*. The enormous challenge about which she had dreamed since her earliest youth and later found in her life on the farm, had been irrevocably taken away from her, and now there remained to her only the choice between becoming "a piece of printed matter," as she expressed it in her more bitter moments, or being completely destroyed.

On her return to Denmark she told a close friend that she was giving herself six months in which to find out whether or not she would be able to live the life she had now been allotted—and if she found it was impossible she would quietly make her exit from life. In the spring of 1931, when she was still living in the ruins of her external world, she had the ability to mobilize her forces to meet a catastrophe, to draw up her personal accounts and reach a result that was somehow a profit. In a letter to her brother Thomas Dinesen on 10 April she writes:

> . . . it seems to me that it would in no way be terrible or sad if I, after in many ways having been more happy here than it is by far the majority of people's lot to be,—and there is not one single person I would change with,—were now calmly to retire from life together with everything that I have loved here. What I imagine a great many people would think of that: for instance, that it was terrible for Mother and so on, is something I cannot take into account. It may perhaps be just as hard for Mother to lose me as for

> me to lose Ngong; but when one comes to realize the whole nature of life, which is: that nothing lasts, and that in that very fact lies some of its glory, the sadness of this is really not so terrible. To me it would seem the most *natural* thing to disappear with my world here, for it seems to me to be to quite the same extent as my eyes, or as some or other talent I might have, vital parts of myself, and I do not know how much of me will survive losing it. Generally: the continuance of life is in my opinion often misunderstood, for how much of oneself does in fact go on living? How much is there left, under present circumstances, of that person that I, or you, were fifteen years ago?

There were times when Karen Blixen could despair over her immediate circumstances and rage against fate, but her nature urged her to be a yea-sayer, no matter what life faced her with. She regarded her life with the eye of a painter, well aware that the dark shadows in the picture were quite as essential as the light and the bright colors. Sorrows and adversities were as much a part of the pattern as the rare but never-to-be-forgotten spells of happiness that she had experienced; she may even perhaps have had a partly unconscious need of suffering, because she felt that more that anything else it could mature the artist in her. In this respect she was, to quote the words of Arndt to Malli from the story "Tempests," "both a riddle to herself, and a messenger of joy." She could call out to the pain and loss in her life as well, like Jacob in his struggle with the angel: "I will not let you go until you bless me!"

This alternation between light and darkness, between wholehearted acceptance of the circumstances of life and total rejection, was most likely a basic element in Karen Blixen's nature. This is clearly evident in the numerous, greatly varying contributions to the Memorial Anthology, but was not biographically substantiated until the publication of Thomas Dinesen's book, *Tanne (My Sister Isak Dinesen,* London, 1975), in which quotations from Karen Blixen's letters to her brother shed an entirely new light on her much mythicized personality. Nothing in *Tanne* contradicted her own description of her years on the farm; but the private letters brought the reader at one stroke so close to Karen Blixen that he could see her naked face beneath the mask and discover that behind the sure touch and consciously distanced presentation of the memoirs lay a reality of painful human experience that it had been beyond Karen Blixen's strength to reenact and weave into the pattern of the book when she came to write *Out of Africa.* Perhaps she had absolutely no wish for the reader to know anything of the most agonizing defeats of her personal life while she was still living. But in conversation she confided in both close friends and casual acquaintances, describing the blows that fate had dealt her, and when her life was drawing to its close she supplied future biographers with detailed information on her life. And yet, she could never bring herself to mention what had been the cause of her deepest suffering.

A biographical chronology has been specially compiled for the English-language edition of the *Letters,* which should prove useful for the reader's orientation. This survey of the exterior and interior events in Karen Blixen's life is on p. xxvii.

As editor of the planned memorial work on Karen Blixen, which resulted in 1974 in three separate books published in Denmark and written by Thomas Dinesen, Clara Svendsen, and Thorkild Bjørnvig, I had the opportunity at one point to read through number of the letters Karen Blixen wrote to her brother while she was living in Africa. As I have mentioned, quotations of various lengths from these letters were included in *Tanne.* The year following the publication of the three books I received permission to read the large, usually inaccessible collection of several hundred letters from Karen Blixen to her mother, Ingeborg Dinesen, which had been deposited at the Royal Library in Copenhagen, with unpublished manuscripts and a quantity of personalia, shortly after Karen Blixen's death. I immediately realized how greatly the publication of a large selection of letters would contribute to the understanding of Karen Blixen's character and development as a human being, viewed as the background to her artistic achievement. I set myself the aim—although for the time being it was a remote, apparently unattainable one—of arranging an edition of everything of essential interest in the letters written by Karen Blixen to her nearest relatives; it was a big project, but it had natural limitations, and the greater part of the correspondence appeared to be intact.

After having first put the idea to the literary executor, Clara Svendsen, I went over to Leerbæk in Jutland and talked to Thomas Dinesen about the projected plan. We had enjoyed a happy collaboration since I visited him for the first time in 1968 while tracking down photographs for the comprehensive pictorial biography of Karen Blixen that was published by Gyldendal a year later. It was a joy to see with what confidence he welcomed my new suggestion and I was soon able to proceed with my preparations with his full support, even though he made it clear to me from the outset that he was not prepared to allow the publication of any more of Karen Blixen's letters to himself. However, I elected to set that problem temporarily aside and meantime I had plenty to do for several months reading through the letters to Ingeborg Dinesen thoroughly, selecting what I considered should be included in the book, and arranging for careful transcriptions of the many handwritten letters in the collection.

In the summer of 1975 I was at Leerbæk again to look for family letters among Thomas Dinesen's private archives. The search revealed a quantity of letters from Karen Blixen to her mother, and also to her two sisters, Ea de Neergaard and Ellen Dahl; but the most important find was probably that of the letters to her mother's sister, Mary Bess Westenholz of Folehave. It became abundantly clear that these discussions, in themselves resembling intricately formulated articles and containing splendid contributions to the lifelong debate carried on between the two, regarding among other things the liberation of women, Victorianism, and sexual morality, ought to be published with the rest, in particular because this little collection seemed to be all that remained of Karen Blixen's many years of correspondence with "Aunt Bess."

At the same time the question of her unpublished letters to Thomas Dinesen and the passages in the letters quoted from, that for various reasons had not been included in *Tanne,* was raised again, and through the mediation of the author Ole Wivel, Thomas Dinesen was persuaded to entrust me with the complete collection, first for the purpose of reading it through again and then to include it chronologically in the manuscript among the letters to the other members of the family—not *in extenso,* but in a far larger selection than in *Tanne.* Respect was naturally paid to Thomas Dinesen's requests for certain sentences or sections of letters to be excised out of regard for people who are occasionally discussed in a manner that Karen Blixen would not have adopted outside the confines of the family. The very fact that these relatively inessential cuts in the letters to be published were comparatively few reveals the admirable courage and perspicacity that Thomas Dinesen, as the remaining representative of the siblings at Rungstedlund, manifested in consenting to this publication. Coming generations will be grateful to him for this.

It has thus been possible, with the aid of much helpful support, to produce an edition of letters that covers the whole period 1914–31, the seventeen years during which Karen Blixen made her home in Africa. The few lacunae in the collection occur because she spent a total of three and a half years on visits to her family in Denmark or in journeying to and from Kenya during the period concerned. In actual fact, when the time is calculated it can be seen that she spent only rather more than fourteen years in Africa, but there must be very few readers of *Out of Africa* who are aware of this. Karen Blixen intentionally concealed any possibility of dating the various events she describes in the book by omitting to give any dates; in this way she achieves an epically progressive homogeneity in her narrative that makes *Out of Africa* differ fundamentally from the majority of great memoirs. But the reader who returns to her book again and again will inevitably wonder now and then when some event or other took place. Among the questions to which these letters will in many cases provide the answers, is the dating of the experiences and daily occurrences described in *Out of Africa*. Innumerable incidents, observations, and reflections from the letters are reproduced in the memoirs; one cannot read many of the letters in the collection without recognizing that during the writing of her work on Africa Karen Blixen used her own letters to her mother as memoranda. But in her poetical reworking of the raw material of reality many of the evaluations in the letters have been unnoticeably altered, the attenuated perspective of present experience lengthened, and in the process numerous details have acquired an iridescence and luster that exactly matches Karen Blixen's feeling for the vital essence of the moment.

The background of reality to her African saga of "Barua a soldani"—the well-preserved, completely unspotted letter from King Christian X, that, as is documented in my postscript to Thorkild Bjørnvig's book, *The Covenant*, was discovered at Rungsted in 1969—is not the only evidence of Karen Blixen's artistic freedom of action regarding the so-called realities of everyday life. A consecutive reading of the letters and the book reveals countless such parallels. A single case is that of the modest bottle of beer that, according to the account sent to her mother on 12 February 1928, she gives the Swede Casparsson to take with him on his journey to Tanganyika, and that in the description of the refugee Emmanuelson in the memoirs is transformed into a bottle of genuine Chambertin 1906. As Karen Blixen writes: "I thought that it might well be his last drink in life."

Even in the letters, without any thought of publication, mention of the same event written on the same day to two different addresses, merely through an apparently trifling change of detail, can acquire this luster. In a passage, not included here, in the letter to Thomas Dinesen dated 12 August 1918, Karen Blixen recounts how at Kikuyu Station, a few days before Dusk's sad end, she only just managed to snatch her beloved dog away from the rails before a big locomotive came thundering through. Karen Blixen goes on: "At that moment I did not give any thought to the possible danger to myself,—afterwards Berkeley Cole, who was standing in the compartment, said: 'It was the bravest thing I have seen in my life!' " The event is described the same day in more detail in the letter to her mother included in this book: "At that moment I did not give a thought to whether I was in danger, but afterwards Lord Delamere, who was in the

carriage, said: 'It was the pluckiest thing I have seen in my life.' "
Naturally Karen Blixen had no idea that the statements in the two letters, sent respectively to the battlefront in France and to less eventful Rungsted, would ever be placed together for comparison. Nevertheless, the sudden transformation of the farmer Berkeley Cole into Lord Delamere, the most important man in British East Africa, has a great deal to say about Karen Blixen's instinctive feeling for publicity. Doubtless the letter to her brother contains the actual version of the story, the impression of the moment, without any attempt to change the color of the picture or add more weight to the situation than it previously had. But with an unerringly sure sense for the importance of background, in her account to her mother Karen Blixen lets her esteemed acquaintance Lord Delamere act as spectator and commentator; she knows that her letter will be shown to other near relatives in Denmark, and after all, a statement from the founder of the colony will have a greater effect on both them and her mother than a remark by her close friend Berkeley Cole.

This is merely one of many examples. The impression given by *Out of Africa* as writing based on reality is amply corroborated when one reads the letters; everyone can make his own observations, according to how familiar one is with the memoirs. To how great an extent Karen Blixen herself intended to provide a truthful, almost documentary description of her life in Kenya appears from something that Thomas Dinesen told me some years ago. He had visited her at Skagen, the northernmost place in Denmark, during the winter of 1936–37 while she was engaged in writing *Out of Africa,* and she had asked his advice about various things. I quote Thomas Dinesen:

> For instance, if she had been writing about a hunting expedition and read what she had written to me, I might suggest: "You ought to put in what Finch Hatton told you about!"—or whatever I might come to think of. "Well, but that isn't something that I experienced myself," Tanne would reply, "it is not something I can be certain about, because after all it is just a story. Everything that I write must be true. I must be able to vouch for every word!"

And Thomas Dinesen added:

> I feel that *Out of Africa* gives an accurate picture of the period, the Africans and the friends out there in every respect—but it is as if somehow the whole thing is seen through colored glass. Tanne gave light and shadow a deeper tone which casts a remarkable radiance over the reality she depicted. During my long stay in Kenya I received a clear impression of Africa and of the world that Tanne was living in, and when later on I read her book I was unable

> to point to a single detail that did not agree with what I remembered and knew about. There was nothing of all that I experienced as well that she did not take the greatest pains to describe exactly as she visualized it.

This is a crucial evaluation of undoubted reliability. But it does not alter the fact that the artist, the saga-writer, in Karen Blixen time and again overruled the objective author of memoirs. What Karen Blixen says about inspiration in a late Danish radio interview with Niels Birger Wamberg applies more than anything else to her work on *Out of Africa:* "To me it seems that inspiration is the whole thing gathered together into a unity; what usually has to be worked out suddenly becomes completely clear as a whole, as if it were bestowed on one like a gift." But the inevitable comparison between the respective statements in the letters and the memoirs about her experiences and adventures in Kenya will have no detrimental effect on the confidence that the reader is bound to place in the author of a book such as *Out of Africa,* provided that one merely bears in mind at the outset that Karen Blixen's most renowned work is a piece of *Dichtung und Wahrheit*—truth in a higher sense than the usual type of memoir, whose fidelity to reality in every smallest detail cannot compensate for its paucity of imagination. The quality of these memoirs resides precisely in the tautness of composition and meticulous selection of material; everything that Karen Blixen felt to be superfluous has been filtered away, all the threads are woven together in a sophisticatedly simple technique which is unique in the body of her work. It would be wrong, even given the presumed documentary truth-value of the letters, to demand full agreement between the view of situations and the features of reality in the private accounts, which were certainly not written with later publication in mind, and the finished work of art, whose aim is to provide a synthesis of the multitudinous impressions of life and the salient points of an acquired philosophy.

Karen Blixen's talented and beloved Aunt Bess, who regarded her niece with deep although anxious affection, despite the fact that in many ways she differed radically from her nature and whole way of thinking, in 1928 suggested the publication of the letters that through the years she had sent from Africa to Folehave in North Sealand. Karen Blixen's reply, of 30 March 1928, is characteristic of the uncertainty she still at that time felt with regard to her talents and potential as a writer:

> What a frightful idea of yours, to publish my letters; if I knew this was going to happen I think it would be impossible for me to write. I am really very grateful to you for taking pleasure in reading my

letters, and it interests me just as much to write to you as it has always done to discuss life's problems with you orally,—but I do not have sufficient self-confidence to feel that my observations can be of any interest except to someone who, like you, takes a benevolent interest in me for my own sake.

Now, half a century later, interest in Karen Blixen has undeniably increased, and the time may be said to be ripe for the publication of a large selection of her letters. The studies of her life and opinions produced during the last decade have prepared the ground—now after all the books about Karen Blixen it is only reasonable that her own voice should be heard. Naturally the value of such a publication will depend on the amount of fresh light it casts on the personality and human development of the letter-writer; in this respect the Karen Blixen correspondence must take its place among the most important in modern Danish literature. A comparison with the situation after the death of Hans Christian Andersen cannot be entirely inappropriate. As Paul V. Rubow writes in his foreword to the republication of Edvard Collin's book on the fairytale writer: "For the study of H. C. Andersen as a human being and writer, but not for the sake of his personal reputation, it has been an advantage that he died childless. People who have children can be assured that a thicker veil will be thrown over their posthumous reputation than over those who die without descendants." Or as Carl Roos has it in another connection: "The truth about an eminent person can only increase his importance. Life is better than legend." The value of the great three-volume edition of letters from and to H. C. Andersen, published 1877–78, and Collin's annotated selection of the writer's letters to the Collin family (1882), to an overall body of knowledge about Danish literature's most remarkable unicorn can hardly be overestimated. These four books opened the way to the intensive research on H. C. Andersen of this century.

The study of Blixen began a considerable time ago, but the work has been dispersed over many areas and seems to lack a concerted objective in which literary, psychological, and biographical investigations can, as it were, meet and cohere. Therefore the publication of Karen Blixen's letters to the nearest members of her family such a comparatively short time after her death must be regarded as a decisive step forward in the work of gaining a truer understanding of her inherited mental traits and psychological characteristics. The reader will quickly discover that in these letters Karen Blixen gives an even more fervent, more moving expression of what she was feeling when at the heights and depths of her experience than is to be found even in *Out of Africa*. The remorseless insistence with which she uncovers past mistakes and omissions in a ceaselessly unresting struggle to reach clarification and understanding of her self is unparalleled in modern Danish literature, at least on *her* artistic level. The letters that deal most closely with Karen Blixen's personal life and problems will provide a message of survival and an aid to people with many types of problems, including quite other difficulties than Karen Blixen's own.

To those who might raise doubts as to the moral justification of publishing such purely private self-revelations it may perhaps be requisite to cite Karen Blixen's own words to Thomas Dinesen in the long letter of 5 September 1926, in which she writes of one of the most testing crises of her life:

> I have often thought it desirable that someone should talk or write completely honestly to one; even if one had no special interest in him his life would be bound to be illuminating. When one is reading a book one often thinks: yes, it is all very well for it to go in such or such a way, or that it ends in this manner; but I don't believe it. And in life one thinks often: if only those who have been through something similar to my experience would tell me really honestly how it ended. . . .

If, after this statement by Karen Blixen herself, there should still be readers who consider that publishing a collection of letters such as this is an encroachment into an area where none but sender and receiver have the right to enter, it will be reasonable to quote what Karen Blixen—according to *The Covenant*—said on one occasion to Thorkild Bjørnvig during a conversation when she touched upon the promise he had given her—not to write about her until she was no longer alive:

> No, you are not to write about me until after my death. But then I wish you to. Then you must feel completely free and not obliged to give any thought to what I would think about it. If I were alive I wouldn't be able to stop myself interfering, and I would prefer to avoid that. Perhaps I might find I couldn't bear to read it, perhaps I might think it wonderful, but you must write just as your heart dictates, write as you have done about Nietzsche, that is what I would want you to do.

But here, in the letters, it is Karen Blixen who is writing about herself. It may be that she could not have borne to see her own letters in print; it may be that she would have thought it wonderful. The crux of the matter is that she was unable to bring herself to destroy them, even though she may have toyed with the idea; after all, they documented the life she had led, an irreplaceable witness to what she had been thinking and feeling at decisive moments in her African life, written from the heart. This is where the great differences between the letters and the memoirs lies. The letters contain almost all the current accounts and the provisional stock-taking en route right up to the final result, the summing-up of life's actives and passives in *Out of Africa*.

It is above all the letters to Thomas Dinesen that give the reader an impression of the efforts Karen Blixen expended in the struggle to become the personality and the woman she felt she could become. The crises she underwent as the years went by matured her view of life into a really effective protection against the outward adversity and private sorrows that afflicted her; the more her possibilities for worldly prosperity were narrowed down, on account of the constant financial problems of the farm, the more she consciolsy strove to extend the boundaries of her inner world. By her will to survive inevitable defeat on several fronts, during her last years in Africa Karen Blixen drew on certain mental resources that apparently could only be called forth by her desperate situation, and it was these resources that finally, when the whole of the life that had been hers lay in ruins, made her strong enough to bring to completion what had previously amounted to no more than scattered fragments and half-hearted attempts. Without the total bankruptcy in Africa it is probably doubtful whether *Seven Gothic Tales* would ever have seen the light of day.

The letters say little about Karen Blixen's artistic activities while she was living in Africa, but instead give a unique commentary on the development of a human being up to the point where the ground had been thoroughly prepared and all the necessary conditions obtained for the activating of inherited creative powers. At the same time they document what Karen Blixen always maintained later in life, that during the seventeen years on the farm she did not primarily dream of becoming a writer but strove first and foremost to consolidate her life in Kenya, as a natural center in the galaxy of English friends and acquaintances she had gathered around her when her marriage to Bror Blixen was in the process of dissolution.

Certain of the letters stand out as particularly telling evidence of the varying moods and situations in which she found herself. The reader is referred, for instance, to the letters from the autumn of 1921 or the two long letters to Thomas Dinesen, dated 1 April and 5 September 1926, that with glowing indignation and merciless self-accusation try to battle through the crises that arise by digging down to the very roots of the causes of her difficulties.

Three decisive factors in Karen Blixen's personal life that have hitherto been incompletely elucidated or completely obscured, can be clarified and documented through the letters or the commentaries provided. They consist of the case history of her illness, her friendship with Denys Finch Hatton and her reaction to the breakup of their relationship that according to absolutely reliable accounts took place some months before his sudden death in May, 1931.

Both Thorkild Bjørnvig's *The Covenant* and Thomas Dinesen's *Tanne* contain statements relating to Karen Blixen's illness and to her friendship with Denys Finch Hatton that—taken as first-hand knowledge—contribute to sustain the myth of Karen Blixen as a person who from her youth had been cut off from and who was by nature not particularly interested in living fully the life of a sexually normal woman. *The Covenant* states: "she turned back to the illness that had separated her from life even when young, first and foremost, definitively, from the erotic life."

In the third yearbook of The Karen Blixen Society *Blixeniana* 1978, Professor Mogens Fog, the Danish neurologist, meticulously described the course of Karen Blixen's illness on the basis of almost fifty years' material contained in medical notes, and his own neurological treatment of her case for many years, and this description provides unequivocal proof that already by 1915–16 the disease was so much under control that she was no longer infectious. The post-syphilitic spinal consumption (tabes dorsalis) that developed later was limited in extent and did not prevent her from having a physical relationship. The fact that she herself, in the letter to Thomas Dinesen of 5 September 1926, mentions the disease specifically by name, must—collated with Mogens Fog's irrefutable documentation of the type and course of the disease—finally put a stop to the creation of ridiculous myths around what is virtually a more tragic than piquant part of Karen Blixen's destiny. It is characteristic of her own view of the human condition that in the letters she herself mentions the disease as one of her lesser misfortunes in comparison with the real trials she was exposed to: the wreck of her marriage, the hopes that were shattered of achieving and becoming something, the constant shortage of money on the farm that she felt like a foreign body in her life incompatible with her true nature.

Several of the letters confirm that her friendship with Denys Finch Hatton was a fully consummated love relationship, although presumably with the emphasis on mental sympathy. That following her separation, after Bror Blixen had left the farm, Karen Blixen consciously disregarded the narrower bourgeois moral norms which undoubtedly prevailed in the more conventional society of a small country like Denmark than in British East Africa with its many settlers, clearly appears from the fact that for a time in 1922 she believed herself to be expecting Denys Finch Hatton's child and was in the depths of despair when this proved to be a false alarm. The idea of having a child by him must at one time have been quite natural to her even though she would have been aware that he was unlikely to want the tie of marriage. When in 1926, aged 41 and at a critical point in her life, she again believed herself to be pregnant—revealed in the letter mentioned above, dated 5 September, and the comments on it made at my request by Thomas Dinesen—she herself chose *not* to have the child she was possibly expecting, but for quite other reasons than one might expect, taking her age and frail health into consideration. This decision can justly be accounted as a dividing line in her life. As she herself formulates it in the letter to her brother: "I have always felt that this: to resort to 'living in one's children' after having oneself 'failed in life,'—and thus to have no faith or substance to give the children,—was one of the most pitiful things one could fall back on. . . ."

And the natural sequel to this idea follows in the unfinished letter to Thomas Dinesen of 1 April 1926:

> No, you see, I must *be myself,* be something in myself, have, own something that is really mine, achieve something that is mine and is me, in order to be able to live at all, and in order to be able to have, and hope to continue to have, the indescribable happiness in my life that my love for Denys is to me. And I do not have that here, now,—I have and am nothing at all; I have betrayed my angel Lucifer and sold my soul to the angels in Paradise, and yet I cannot live in it; I don't belong, I have no place to be anywhere in the world, and yet I must stay in it; I hate and dread each minute and yet they come, and if I came to hear about it I would not believe it possible to live in such a manner.
>
> You must not think that I am so spineless that I have not considered whether it would not be best if I were to take my life, and been prepared to do so if I really came to the conclusion that it was. Surely the greatest coward in the world would be prepared to do it to escape from such a life as I have now. But I do not think that it would help. For what I long for is after all life, and what I fear and take flight from is emptiness and annihilation,—and what else can one hope to achieve by dying? I want so terribly much to live, I want so terribly not to die.

With this resolution *not* to have a child Karen Blixen puts definitely behind her one of the possibilities for happiness that up to then she had never lost sight of—a renunciation that perhaps was forced upon her, but that was also a personal choice that compelled her nature to turn away from painful dependence on exterior circumstances: the threatened bankruptcy of the farm, her friendship with Denys, who wanted to be his own master, towards the final, all-important determination to disclose her inner reality in a work that was her true self, an enduring expression of her being.

In her comprehensive biography of Denys Finch Hatton, published in 1977, the English writer Errol Trzebinski relates that the relationship between him and Karen Blixen broke up during her final year on the African farm. The break was confirmed by several people and there is no reason to doubt the reliability of the sources. But the letters reveal nothing of Karen Blixen's own feelings about the situation. It was probably the hardest blow she had to suffer, an irremediable defeat, that she could not bring herself to mention to her family. No letters from Karen Blixen to her brother for the period between November 1928 and April 1931 have survived; it will always be difficult to determine, from a distance of fifty years, whether she did write any or not. In 1929 Karen Blixen was living at Rungsted with her mother for more than six months and thus had ample opportunity to discuss her problems with Thomas Dinesen.

All the letters to Ingeborg Dinesen from the final years on the farm seem to be extant, but nowhere is the break with Denys mentioned. However, there exists a first-hand account of how Karen Blixen's despair over yet once more seeing her hold over another human being fail her could lead to a desparate resolve to put an end to what at moments she saw as a completely abortive existence. In utter despair she tried to take her own life, and a handwritten note of apology to the people in whose house she made the suicide attempt was found among her posthumous papers more than thirty years later. This, probably dated, documentation of the event was meanwhile mislaid, but, in answer to my direct question, Thomas Dinesen confirmed that his sister did once tell him about her action "perfectly calmly"; she had wounded herself, "but before she had lost too much blood she had stopped it," he writes. He does not recollect when it took place, but it can most likely be dated to the period shortly after the breakup of the relationship with Denys Finch Hatton, when even the loss of the farm must very probably in her eyes have been a tangible outward sign that her life was over rather than the actual cause of her desperate action. The poignant letter to her brother of 10 April 1931, written one month before Finch Hatton's death, *can* be interpreted as a half-concealed cry for help in avoiding a repetition of the attempt—with so-called success. Even when she was involved in the most harrowing human crisis Karen Blixen battles to remain a yea-sayer: "I want so terribly much to live, I want so terribly not to die. . . . "

At Karen Blixen's funeral in 1962 Thomas Dinesen described how, shortly before his sister was obliged to leave the farm, she suffered an accident, was severely injured in the arm and nearly died from loss of blood. Later on he asked her: "What did you feel then, what did you think about?" "Can you remember," she said, "Bjørnson's poem about Arnljot Gelline? About the Battle of Stiklestad? King Olav has fallen, and his skalds fall around him one after the other. 'There fell Gissur also, that gold-flashing skald. Torfinn by his side, he sang: 'Now, King, I have given thee my best song, it runs red over thy name.' That is how I felt then."

Something in those words would seem to indicate that it was actually the suicide attempt that Thomas Dinesen was referring to on that occasion.

The incidents in Karen Blixen's biography recounted here, supported by letters and verbal information, could naturally be supplemented with further, equally important statements regarding other human experiences that helped to determine her view of life and her own potentialities. Suffice it to mention here her tragic sense of having lost a decisive battle that she had exerted all her strength in the attempt to win when Bror Blixen forced through their separation in 1921. It is *his* decision to start a new life in Africa without her that, together with the diappointment over not having a child with Denys Finch Hatton in the years to come, almost unnoticeably undermines Karen Blixen's relationship with Denys by a traumatic dread of—yet again—building her whole life around one single person, precisely because her feelings for *him* were so much deeper than those binding her to Bror Blixen. It may have been this fear that drove her in the end to demand more of Denys Finch Hatton than he with his need for independence was able to give her. It was this—that he disengaged himself from her grasp, even though he continued to support her with advice and practical help and still continued to visit her, that must have seemed to her to finally seal her fate as a woman: to be one who was unable to hold on to another person, and her efforts to achieve this later in life were merely more or less exaggerated repetitions of her experiences during the years in Africa.

It is fortunate for the study of Karen Blixen's development as a human being that this book contains such a large selection of all the existing letters to the nearest members of her family. This material gives information of both a practical and an intellectual nature relating to every aspect of her life. We learn of the collaboration between black and white people on the farm, of her close ties with the English colonies in Kenya, of seventeen years of financial struggle to keep the farm going, of the continual communication with the family in

Denmark, of her marriage and relationship with the men who mentally and erotically influenced her destiny, of the aesthetic and religious elements that came to mark her view of life. But also the letters are of historical interest reaching beyond the person of Karen Blixen. She arrived in Africa at the same time as the last wave of, in particular, English colonists in Kenya, but quickly established a personal, deeply involved relationship with the native population that was far in advance of her time. Only a generation after the publication of the book about the farm, the Africa it depicts has long since become part of history.

The letters provide, often from week to week, a close-up of Karen Blixen's African life that from now on will accompany and amplify the experience of reading her memoirs. It is precisely the interplay between the private letters and the strictly composed *Out of Africa* that will be a source of particular interest to the reader. What is missing in one book will be found in the other. I would like to testify here that in selecting the letters and making the necessary cuts in the vast quantity of material I have omitted no statement or important piece of information that would alter the overall impression of Karen Blixen that the book must necessarily give. The only aspect of her life that is little documented in the present selection is Karen Blixen's remarkably extrovert cultivation of social life during much of her time on the farm; she loved to have people around her and during the years in Kenya acquired innumerable friends, most of whom are mentioned briefly in the letters to her mother. In order to include what I felt to be the most important material within the appropriate limits there has been a considerable reduction in the gallery of characters mentioned, which might lead the uninformed reader to believe that for the most part of her time in Africa Karen Blixen was sequestered from the other Europeans in the colony.

The reduction of material has also affected another sphere, the financial history of the farm. This has been effected partly from the wish to avoid needless repetition and lengthy reports on harvest prospects and the possibility of loans, partly because in her letters home Karen Blixen was not the most objective judge of the financial sacrifices made by the family on the altar of the farm during the course of the years. As she herself could put it: "The others only gave money. I gave my health and my whole life!" There is no point in making public Karen Blixen's complaints about the attitude of the shareholders toward the extremely unprofitable Karen Coffee Company, in any case not before a serious researcher is given access to private archives and enabled to document to what lengths the family actually went in supporting Karen Blixen in what she herself interpreted as a

European cultural mission to Africa. To write a book on the financial background and development of the farm would undoubtedly be an enthralling assignment for the right person, but would require a knowledge of all existing documents on the subject. Such a book is bound to be written some day, but it is not the purpose of this edition of letters to provide material for it.

As it stands, there are sufficient topics for literary research to be found in *Letters from Africa*. A comparative study of the *Letters* and *Out of Africa* would provide documentation on how many features are common to the memoir-writer Karen Blixen and the storyteller Isak Dinesen. In addition, Karen Blixen's opinions on the liberation of women and the relationship between the sexes, that in numerous letters are the objects of penetrating and subtle analysis, contain more than sufficient material for a book. Doctorands *in spe* need only read this volume to find suitable subjects for their theses.

The index of names and subjects is at the end of the book, as are the notes (p. 433). The notes provide information on a choice of subjects felt to be of use to the reader as additional material but are not intended to provide complete annotation. An examination of the archives for the purpose of tracing the financial history of the farm was not feasible; therefore the notes give only occasional details of this.

Foremost among those to whom gratitude is due on the publication of this volume is the late Thomas Dinesen, Karen Blixen's brother, whose courtesy and helpfulness during the course of publication played a decisive part in the finished work. Not only did he place his large private collection of letters entirely at my disposal; in addition, most of the photographs that accompany the letters originate from the archives at Leerbæk. Readers who may wish to supplement the visual impression of life on the farm are referred to Frans Lasson's and Clara Svendsen's *The Life and Destiny of Isak Dinesen* (new American edition, Chicago, 1976), which contains a comprehensive selection of pictures from Karen Blixen's seventeen years in Africa.

As stated in the colophon to the Danish edition, these letters were first published for the Rungstedlund Foundation, and I owe a debt of gratitude to Ole Wivel for guidance, good advice and practical support. During the years that have passed since the commencement of the work I have received the benefit of his many-sided experience as head of a publishing house, member of the committee of management of the Foundation, and friend through many years of the Dinesen family. It is largely due to Ole Wivel's influence that Karen Blixen's letters to her brother were included in this book.

Most of the letters are preserved as typed by Karen Blixen herself (on the little Corona she continued to use right up until her death; she could never accustom herself to anything else), but all the letters from before 1918 are written in her beautiful and plastic, although not always decipherable, hand. A transcription for publication purposes requires much practice in interpreting Karen Blixen's characters, and I was aware that this was possessed by both Clara Svendsen and Mrs. Ulla Rask. As early as 1934 the latter was occupied at Rungsted in taking down in shorthand Karen Blixen's own translation of *Seven Gothic Tales* as she dictated it, and later helped in the typing of *Out of Africa, Winter's Tales* and *The Angelic Avengers,* among other things. Finally, I myself undertook various transcriptions in collaboration with the secretary of The Karen Blixen Society, Mrs. Aase Vahl. If the work had not been shared it would have been impossible to produce the manuscript ready for printing by the desired date.

The staff in charge of the Picture Archives and Manuscript Section of the Royal Library, Copenhagen, have as so often before been unfailingly helpful and I extend my most sincere thanks to all who were concerned. I am also grateful to Mr. R. G. Opondo, chief librarian at the McMillan Memorial Library in Nairobi for obtaining a great deal of invaluable information. Thomas Dinesen's youngest daughter, Mrs. Ingeborg Michelsen, as representative of the family, gave advice and practical help. Her powerful persuasion during the decisive phase of the negotiations regarding Karen Blixen's letters to her father contributed much to the successful outcome.

Last but not least I wish to thank René Herring, the librarian, who at the suggestion of Rektor Preben Kirkegaard, of the Danish School of Librarianship, volunteered to give practical aid in composing the notes and index, and in correcting proofs, etc. How much it meant to have a tireless and alert reader at one's side at a point when the dateline for delivery of the manuscript inexorably drew near will best be understood by those who, like me, have suffered nightmares about the work that still remained to be done.

Forty years on since the publication of *Out of Africa* these letters open a new door into Karen Blixen's world. She was never to forget what she had experienced in Africa; and in her book about the farm she made certain that it would not be forgotten as long as there are readers of her work. But in the letters we meet someone who is never mentioned in the memoirs: the young, inexperienced Karen Blixen, and we watch her personality unfolding like a flower. She knew from the start that the years on the farm marked a dividing line in her life. As she writes in a letter to her mother, dated 26 February 1919: "I have a feeling that wherever I may be in the future, I will be wondering whether there is rain at Ngong."

This was the thought that constantly possessed her when she was a world-famous writer living at Rungstedlund. Every single night before going to bed she would open the door on to the courtyard and stand still there for a few moments. Down there to the south, thousands of kilometers away, Denys Finch Hatton lay in his grave under the obelisk in the Ngong Hills, and to Karen Blixen it was as if the only life she really cared to live, was buried in the same grave. Since her return to Denmark she had been a spectator of life, indeed, even before her departure from Africa she had felt herself like one dead who must see the world continue on its course without her. In March 1931 she writes to her mother: "It is an irony of fate that we have had such good, early rains. When I think how often at this time of year I have gone outside gazing out for the rain that would not come, it is strange to lie and listen to it pouring down now, and know that it doesn't make the slightest difference."

Now, when Karen Blixen too has found her grave, beneath the great stone on Ewald's Hill, the door on to the south needs to be kept open. This is the reason for the publication of these letters. Through them the rain still streams down at Ngong and at night the roaring of the lions can be heard very close to the house. Not the lions that lay on Denys Finch Hatton's grave, but the lions in Karen Blixen's life—the challenge that she would offer everything to meet.

"No-one came into literature more bloody than I," Karen Blixen once said. The letters in this book confirm her words.

Frans Lasson

Chronology by Frans Lasson

1845 19 December: Birth of Karen Blixen's father, Wilhelm Dinesen, at Katholm, the country house in Jutland, as the second youngest of eight siblings. The Dinesens are an ancient Danish family of landed gentry. 1863: Wilhelm Dinesen is admitted as an officer cadet to the Military Academy in Copenhagen; with his father, Chamberlain A. W. Dinesen, experiences the defeat of Denmark in the war with Prussia in 1864, and later, as a French officer, the Prussian victory in the Franco-German war of 1870–71 (in 1872 writes his book, *Paris under the Commune*). 1872: "Mentally deranged," as he himself describes it, travels to North America and lives as a hunter among the Indians in Wisconsin. Returns to Denmark on account of his father's illness, but after the latter's death a year or two later again attempts—this time without success—to go to war, now as an officer (on the Turkish side) during the Russo-Turkish war of 1877–78. Spends the remainder of his life as a landowner in Denmark. 1879: purchases several country properties in the neighborhood of the fishing village of Rungsted in North Sealand, including "Rungstedlund" (the ancient village inn, where Denmark's greatest lyric poet, Johannes Ewald, lived from 1773 to 1775), and "Folehave," a few kilometers away. Writes and publishes several books, under his own name or under the pseudonym "Boganis," including two volumes of *Hunting Letters* (1889–92), still considered as classics of their genre in Denmark.

1856 5 May: Ingeborg Westenholz, Karen Blixen's mother, born at Matrup, the country house in Jutland, eldest daughter of the wealthy businessman, later finance minister, Regnar Westenholz (1815–66) and Mary Westenholz, "Mama" (1832–1915), daughter of the prosperous Copenhagen magnate, Councillor of State A. N. Hansen, whose English-born wife was the daughter of a clergyman on the Channel Island of Guernsey.

1857 13 August: Mary Westenholz (Aunt Bess) Ingeborg Westenholz's sister, born at Matrup.

1859 18 April: Aage Westenholz, Ingeborg Westenholz's brother (later to become an engineer, founder of the Siam Electric Corporation and chairman of the limited company, the Karen Coffee Company) born at Matrup.

1881 17 May: Wilhelm Dinesen and Ingeborg Westenholz marry and take up residence at Rungstedlund, while Mama and Mary (Bess) move from the Matrup estate to Folehave, although Matrup remains in the possession of the Westenholz family.

1883 2 April: Inger Benedicte (Ea) Dinesen, Karen Dinesen's elder sister, born at Rungsted.

1885 17 April: Karen Christentze Dinesen (Tanne) born at Rungstedlund.

1886 25 July: Baron Bror Blixen-Finecke, Karen Dinesen's second cousin and future husband, born at the country house Näsbyholm in southern Sweden, the younger twin son of the inheritor of the estate, Baron Frederik Blixen-Finecke and his wife Clara B.-F., sister of the greatest landowner in Denmark, Count Mogens Krag-Juel-Vind-Frijs of Frijsenborg Castle, whose mother was the sister of Wilhelm Dinesen's mother. 13 September: Ellen Alvilde (Elle) Dinesen, Karen Dinesen's younger sister, born at Rungstedlund.

1887 24 April: Denys Finch Hatton, Karen Dinesen's closest friend in Africa, born in London, second son of Henry Stormont, thirteenth earl of Winchilsea and eighth earl of Nottingham.

1892 9 August: Thomas Fasti Dinesen, Karen Dinesen's brother born at Rungstedlund. Wilhelm Dinesen becomes member of parliament for Grenaa in Jutland.

1894 8 May: Anders Runsti Dinesen, Karen Dinesen's younger brother, born at Rungsted.

1895 28 March: Karen Dinesen's father hangs himself in the Copenhagen boardinghouse where he stays when Parliament is in session. It is conjectured that his motive was induced by a political setback following on a long-standing period of depression brought about by the prospect of complete physical and mental disablement resulting from syphilis, contracted many years earlier and never cured. Now Ingeborg Dinesen, supported by Mama and Aunt Bess, is left with the task of bringing up the five young children at Rungstedlund. The daughters are not sent to school but are taught by a governess who—together with their female relations—gives them a somewhat unsystematic, in certain spheres inadequate but otherwise highly qualified cultural and linguistic education. But the absence of a masculine counterbalance to offset the dominating influence of pious and forceful women in the home already now instigates in Karen Dinesen a silent but fierce opposition to her elders' demands for respect towards such bourgeois virtues as thrift, modesty, and spotless moral conduct, and the Unitarian Christianity of the maternal side of the family, at least where Karen is concerned, seems to have fallen on stony ground. All three daughters show artistic talent, Ea and Elle chiefly in the field of music, while Karen has been both drawing and writing from her early childhood. Numerous notebooks containing drafts of youthful poems, plays, and stories are preserved.

1899 After the fire that destroyed the home farm, Ingeborg Dinesen and her daughters spend six months in Switzerland, where Karen attends a French school and improves her already extensive knowledge of the principal languages (with the exception of German).

1902 Karen Dinesen starts to attend drawing lessons regularly at the Misses Meldahl and Sode's Art School in Copenhagen, with the idea of learning to be a painter.

1903 Goes to a Unitarian congress in Holland with her sister Elle and Aunt Bess. On 30 November is enrolled in the preparatory class of the Academy of Art women's art college in Copenhagen.

1904 Attends the Academy of Art. Visits her mother's family in Scotland. Stays for a time with Professor Carlyle in Oxford in order to perfect her English.

1905 Stays in London for the first time. Elected vice-chairman of the art students' union at the Academy of Art.

1906 Admitted to the life class at the Academy of Art, but seems not to have availed herself of the instruction.

1907 Makes her debut as an author (under the pseudonym Osceola) with the story "The Hermits", published in the Copenhagen periodical *Tilskueren* in its August issue. "The Ploughman" appears (likewise pseudonymously) in the October number of the periodical *Gads danske Magasin*.

1909 The story "The de Cats Family" appears in the January issue of *Tilskueren*. None of these early stories attracts any particular attention, and because of the lack of encouragement Karen Dinesen loses the impulse to continue writing. During these artistically lean years she spends her time in the company of contemporary upper-class young people grouped around Frijsenborg, and at some point falls deeply but unhappily in love with her second cousin, Baron Hans Blixen-Finecke, twin brother to her future husband. Her feelings are not reciprocated, and she makes an abrupt and lengthy break with the aristocratic circle in order to avoid the risk of meeting Hans Blixen at one or other of the great houses.

1910 Driven by a feeling of emptiness and restless desperation Karen Dinesen—with her sister Ea—spends a few months in Paris attending a new college of art, but her efforts produce no results.

1912 Winter holiday in Norway with her brother Thomas, and a long stay in Rome in the company of her closest girlhood friend, Daisy Grevenkop-Castenskiold, one of the daughters at Frijsenborg. 23 December: announces her engagement to Baron Bror Blixen-Finecke of Näsbyholm.

1913 The engaged couple discuss future prospects with both Aage Westenholz and their mutual uncle Mogens Frijs of Frijsenborg. Bror Blixen goes out to British East Africa, which is being recommended as the land of the future for young people of initiative. A newly established family limited company in Denmark with Aage Westenholz as chairman and a considerable capital deposit mainly provided by Karen Dinesen's maternal relatives, make it possible for him to acquire the Swedish-owned coffee farm "MBagathi", and despite his limited knowledge of both agriculture and accountancy, the company appoints him manager of the farm—a fatal move. 2 December: Karen Dinesen leaves Denmark to travel, via Naples, to a new life in Africa.

1914 14 January: Karen Dinesen sails in to the port of Mombasa and is married the same day to Bror Blixen. She arrives at her new home just outside the government town of Nairobi in British East Africa bearing the title of baroness, much coveted in circles to which many of her friends belong. Shortly after the wedding she is obliged to consult a doctor and learns that her husband has infected her with syphilis. She is treated with mercury tablets, but this remedy later proves to have been ineffective. 1 August: outbreak of the first World War. In spite of their voluntary and courageous contribution to the allied war effort in acting as leaders of the despatch service and provision transports, Karen Blixen and her husband are for a time accused, completely without cause, of being pro-German, on account of their affiliation to the Swedish colony in British East Africa.

1915 After living on the farm for just over a year Karen Blixen is obliged to return to Denmark in April for expert medical treatment. For three months she is a patient in the National Hospital in Copenhagen, after which she goes to stay with her mother at Rungstedlund. 7 September: death of Mama, aged 83. While in Denmark Karen Blixen writes the poem, "Ex Africa", in which she gives a picture of the country she has had to leave so suddenly.

1916 Both Karen Blixen's sisters marry, Ea the Sealand landowner Viggo de Neergaard, Elle the wealthy Copenhagen barrister and businessman and later landowner, Knud Dahl. Her brother Thomas qualifies as an engineer, and on the death of his paternal uncle, Laurentzius Dinesen, is offered the inheritance of the estate of Katholm, the childhood home of Wilhelm Dinesen. However, because of economic reasons he does not accept. As beneficiary to the Dinesen family trust he is assured of economic independence for the rest of his life. The family company expresses assurance in the future success of the Karen Coffee Co. and purchases a larger, considerably more imposing farm outside Nairobi for the Blixens. In the summer Bror Blixen comes to Denmark and in November he and Karen Blixen return to Africa to take charge of the new farm.

1917 12 January: Karen Blixen's girlhood friend Daisy Grevenkop-Castenskiold dies suddenly in London, where her husband is the Danish ambassador. The threatened crisis in Karen Blixen's marriage becomes a reality. Bror Blixen proves completely unfitted to the post of farm manager on account of his unreliability over money. Karen Blixen's sister Ea de Neergaard gives birth to a daughter. Thomas Dinesen joins the Canadian Army as a volunteer, to fight against the Germans like his father and grandfather before him.

1918 5 April: Karen Blixen meets the English Army pilot, Denys Finch Hatton, at a dinner in Nairobi. Thomas Dinesen is awarded the British Victoria Cross for heroism during the Allied offensive on the French front.

1919 14 August: Karen and Bror Blixen travel via London to Denmark, arriving in November. Bror Blixen proceeds to visit his family in Sweden and in March of the following year returns to Kenya, as British East Africa is now called. The marriage is breaking up. Karen Blixen stays for more than a year with her mother at Rungstedlund. During this visit to Denmark she is ill for five months, suffering from Spanish influenza and blood poisoning.

1920 In November Karen Blixen goes out once again to Africa, this time with Thomas Dinesen; as the representative of the family company he is to assess the situation and assist in sorting out the finances of the farm, which are now in a completely chaotic state.

1921 Karen Blixen's maternal uncle, Aage Westenholz, chairman of the Karen Coffee Co., visits Kenya to make a decision on the future of the farm. His inspection results in the dismissal of Bror Blixen as manager and the appointment of Karen Blixen to run the farm, with the provision that Bror Blixen is to have nothing more to do with the plantation or the Karen Coffee Co. A serious crisis with the maternal side of the family arises following their denunciation of Bror Blixen. The couple separate, much against Karen Blixen's wishes. Although her old illness was prevented from developing a long time ago, its aftereffects now begin to be felt in earnest in the form of lengthy attacks of pain.

1922 Karen Blixen is disappointed in her expectations of pregnancy (by Denys Finch Hatton). 17 June: Ea de Neergaard dies in Denmark at the age of 39.

1923 2 March: after spending more than two years on the farm Thomas Dinesen leaves for home convinced that in the long view the state of affairs of the Karen Coffee Co. is such as to be past hope of recovery. Karen Blixen works on the composition of a lengthy essay on the institution of marriage past and present (printed in Danish in *Blixeniana,* the yearbook of the Karen Blixen Society, 1977).

1924 Finishes writing *Modern Marriage and Other Considerations* and sends it to Thomas Dinesen in Copenhagen. 3 November: Ingeborg Dinesen, now aged 68, goes to Kenya with Thomas and stays with her daughter on the farm for over two months.

1925 13 January: Karen Blixen's mother bids her farewell and starts on the homeward voyage to Denmark. Karen and Bror Blixen's divorce is made absolute. 5 March: Karen Blixen and Thomas Dinesen leave Mombasa en route by sea to Europe. Thomas disembarks at Aden, his sister continues her journey via Paris and arrives in Denmark in May. During the following eight months, spent with her mother at Rungstedlund, she makes several fruitless attempts at making literary contacts in Denmark. Her brother Anders takes over the estate of Leerbæk in Jutland, that has hitherto been run by Ingeborg Dinesen's second sister, Aunt Lidda, and her husband, the landowner Georg Sass. The poem "Ex Africa" is published in *Tilskueren.* Karen Blixen arranges a meeting with the influential Danish critic Georg Brandes, possibly to enlist his aid in getting some of her work published in Denmark.

1926 1 February: Karen Blixen leaves Denmark to return to the farm in Kenya. In April Thomas Dinesen marries Jonna Lindhardt. Karen Blixen's insecurity in her relationship with Denys Finch Hatton and her decision not to have the child that she believes she is expecting, bring about an acute personal crisis, through which she struggles to battle her way partly by analyzing its causes in detail in long letters to Thomas Dinesen. The marionette play, *The Revenge of Truth,* written in her youth, is published, doubtless through the good offices of Georg Brandes, in the May issue of *Tilskueren,* not pseudonymously as arranged but under the author's own name. The dreams of authorship receive fresh encouragement. Now Karen Blixen resumes the fiction-writing of her youth in earnest, while at the same time the collapse of the farm continues inevitably to approach. The first *Gothic Tales* are drafted in English. One of the completed tales, "Carnival" (published 1977) can probably be dated to this year.

1927 23 January: Karen Blixen's mother visits the farm for the second time and stays with her daughter for over three months.

1928 Bror Blixen marries Cockie Birkbeck. Karen Blixen finds herself in a difficult position socially in the English colony because of the presence of a new Baroness Blixen, who takes part with her husband in the royal safaris arranged during the official visit of the Prince of Wales to Kenya from October to December; with Denys Finch Hatton Bror Blixen is also engaged as white hunter to the prince. It is presumably Finch Hatton who sets the arrangements in motion for the prince, the heir apparent to the English throne, to dine at the farm on 9 November, in order to redress somewhat Karen Blixen's awkward position.

1929 Ingeborg Dinesen falls seriously ill in Denmark. Karen Blixen leaves at once for home and stays at Rungstedlund from 18 May until 25 December, only interrupting her visit for a trip to England to meet, among other people, Finch Hatton's family. Thomas Dinesen's memoirs from the front line in France, *No Man's Land,* published in Danish. Karen Blixen returns to the farm without any real hope of being able to salvage her African life. The rupture of her relationship with Denys Finch Hatton is impending.

1931 After several years of financial crisis the farm is sold by the company at a forced sale. Karen Blixen undertakes to wind up the enterprise, see to the harvesting of the last of the coffee and make arrangements for the future of her black employees before going back to Denmark. 14 May: Denys Finch Hatton, aged 44, is killed when his private airplane crashes in Tanganyika. 19 August: Karen Blixen arrives by boat from Mombasa at Marseilles, where she is met by Thomas Dinesen, who accompanies her on the journey through Europe. 31 August: she takes up residence with her mother at Rungstedlund, totally ruined at the age of 46. Ingeborg Dinesen and Thomas Dinesen provide her with financial support during the next three years to help her to make a start on a new life. She herself entertains grave doubts of being able to endure the style of life that she has now been forced to adopt; but with extraordinary willpower and self-control she sets out to write and complete a planned collection of stories, *Nine Tales*, in order to survive as a human being.

1932 After an intensive year's work on the book, which she writes in English, Karen Blixen begins to seek contacts with foreign publishers. Thomas Dinesen provides his sister with an introduction to the American author Dorothy Canfield Fisher, who reads the manuscript of some of the tales and immediately recommends her own publisher, Robert Haas in New York, to publish them. He acknowledges the great talent of the writer, but at first declines to publish a collection of short stories by an unknown European writer. Karen Blixen, undaunted, goes on with her work.

1933 Constant Huntington, of the English publishing firm of Putnam, categorically refuses to look at Karen Blixen's manuscript when she meets him during a visit to London and tells him about her book. Robert Haas reads two new stories that are sent to him and decides after all to publish the book in America. The number of tales in the book is restricted to seven and a new title is chosen. Karen Blixen insists on publishing *Seven Gothic Tales* under the pseudonym of Isak Dinesen, a decision that despite warnings the publisher is unable to make her retract.

1934 19 February: at Rungsted Karen Blixen receives a telegram from Robert Haas telling her that her as yet unpublished book has been chosen as Book-of-the-Month in the U.S.A., which will result in the printing of a much larger edition than originally planned and a considerable monetary reward for the author. 9 April: *Seven Gothic Tales* appears in New York and is enthusiastically received by critics and readers. 22 April: the publishers reveal the identity of Isak Dinesen. Constant Huntington of Putnam's buys the pseudonymous author's book unaware that it has previously been offered to him. 6 September: *Seven Gothic Tales* published in England, where it enjoys a great success.

1935 25 September: *Seven Gothic Tales* appears in Denmark, translated by the author. September-October: Karen Blixen goes to Geneva and with the aid of a press card obtained through Danish connections is enabled to be present at the meetings of the League of Nations when they discuss, among other things, Italy's invasion of Abyssinia. Her plans to write a book about her years in Africa are taking shape.

1936 Karen Blixen works on the English version of *Out of Africa*. Part of the book is written in the old fishing village of Skagen in Jutland, the northernmost town in Denmark.

1937 The English and Danish versions of the memoirs are completed. The book is published, with the title *The African Farm* in Denmark on 6 October and with the title *Out of Africa* on the English book market in November. *Out of Africa* makes Karen Blixen's name as a modern classical writer.

1938 *Out of Africa* is chosen as Book-of-the-Month for February in the U.S.A. and published by Random House, New York, in March. "The Caryatids", one of the unincluded *Gothic Tales*, is published in the Swedish periodical, *Bonniers litterära magasin* in March.

1939 27 January: Ingeborg Dinesen dies at the age of 82. Karen Blixen becomes mistress of Rungstedlund.

1940 Karen Blixen is commissioned by the Copenhagen daily newspaper *Politiken* to spend a month in London, a month in Paris and a month in Berlin and to write four articles about each city. She travels to Berlin first and stays there from 1 March until 2 April. The German occupation of Denmark takes place immediately after her return from Berlin, and the other visits have to be abandoned on account of the war. The articles on Hitler's Germany are published after the war, with the title *Letters from a Land at War*, in the Danish periodical *Heretica*, 1948. (Printed in English in *Daguerreotypes and Other Essays*, Chicago and London, 1979). During this period Karen Blixen works on a new collection of stories, but the completion of this is delayed owing to long spells of illness.

1942 *Winter's Tales* published in the U.S.A., England and Denmark. In America the book is chosen as Book-of-the-Month.

1943 Karen Blixen feels herself to be encaged in Denmark because of the war and that she lacks any incentive to start on a new piece of serious writing. To amuse herself she writes the historical crime story, *The Angelic Avengers*, which contains hidden references to the difficult political situation during the occupation of Denmark.

1944 *The Angelic Avengers* (originally written in Danish) appears in Copenhagen under the pseudonym Pierre Andrézel.

1945 Clara Svendsen, M.A., begins her work as secretary to Karen Blixen at Rungstedlund by writing the English version of *The Angelic Avengers* from Karen Blixen's dictation. Their collaboration is to continue until Karen Blixen's death, after which Clara Svendsen as literary executor in association with the Rungstedlund Foundation administers the artistic and financial rights of Karen Blixen's writings.

1946 *The Angelic Avengers* is published in England. During the last few years Karen Blixen's attacks of pain have increased in both severity and frequency, and in February she resolves to submit to a spine operation to remove the pains. The operation, which involves severing various nerves, is successful. In the years following, Karen Blixen, with indomitable youthful courage, gathers around her at Rungstedlund a small circle of younger friends and colleagues, several of them connected with the group attached to the literary journal *Heretica*, published between 1948 and 1953. Future leaders of Danish intellectual life, including Thorkild Bjørnvig, Jørgen Gustava Brandt, Aage Henriksen, Ole Wivel and Knud W. Jensen, who is to inaugurate the Danish Museum of Modern Art, Louisiana, in North Sealand, are among frequent guests at the house. Concurrently she maintains numerous contacts abroad; with her international reputation it is essential and natural to her to keep her door wide open to the whole world, as far as her limited strength will allow.

1949 Professor Hans Brix, the Danish literary historian, publishes his book, *The Tales of Karen Blixen*, the first complete and comprehensive interpretation of her writings.

1950 24 March: Karen Blixen introduces a series of talks for Danish radio with a description of her African Somali servant Farah, and her aptitude for broadcasting does much to make an otherwise exclusive writer known and loved throughout the whole country. With "Babette's Feast" begins her collaboration with the important American magazine *Ladies' Home Journal,* which publishes a number of the stories in *Anecdotes of Destiny* for the first time.

1951 3 to 26 May: journey to Greece and Rome with Knud W. Jensen and his wife.

1952 In the autumn Karen Blixen takes part in the controversy in Denmark over experiments on animals, which she opposes. "The Cardinal's Third Tale" is published in Danish in a bibliophile edition.

1955 17 April: Karen Blixen's seventieth birthday. She is universally feted. But this is the year that brings a decisive breakdown in health. In August a new, serious operation becomes necessary, in which several spinal nerves are severed, and after an extensive operation for a stomach ulcer six months later Karen Blixen is to be an invalid for the rest of her life. From now on she has difficulty in eating anything at all, and at times her weight falls to below 35 kilograms. But when her strength allows she works purposefully on the completion of the manuscripts of two collections of stories.

1957 Karen Blixen is repeatedly named as the leading candidate for the year's Nobel Prize for Literature, but is not awarded it. (In 1954 Ernest Hemingway had mentioned her as a suitable candidate). *Last Tales* published in November in the U.S.A., England, and Denmark. As usual, both the English and Danish versions of the stories are original works by Karen Blixen. Visits Rome, Paris, and London during November and December. Appointed an honorary member of the American Academy.

1958 The desire to secure the future of Rungstedlund results, after several years of consideration, in the establishment of the Rungstedlund Foundation, a private institution that from now on is to own the historic building, the 60 hectares of garden and woodland, to be preserved as a bird reserve, and the rights of Karen Blixen's works. 6 July: Karen Blixen gives a radio talk on the past and future of Rungstedlund (published in *Daguerreotypes and Other Essays,* 1979), in which she asks every listener to support the cause by sending just one Danish crown to the Foundation. Over 80,000 listeners comply with her request. In October *Anecdotes of Destiny* appears in the U.S.A., England, and Denmark. Short visit to Amsterdam. Despite her age and extremely frail state of health, Karen Blixen plans a comprehensive visit to America.

1959 3 January to 17 April: first and last visit to the United States, staying for three months in New York with a heavy work program. 28 January: Karen Blixen is guest of honor at the annual celebration of the American Academy and is guest speaker, talking "On Mottoes of My Life" (published in *Daguerreotypes and Other Essays*). 17 February: Ellen Dahl, her sister, dies in Copenhagen while Karen Blixen is visiting Cambridge, Massachusetts. At one point during the stay in America even the willpower of a Karen Blixen cannot prevent the extremely undernourished patient from breaking down, but a short stay in hospital in New York brings about so much improvement in her condition that Karen Blixen gathers enough strength for yet another month in New York, closely packed with appointments.

1960 Radical restoration work carried out to the eighteenth-century main building of Rungstedlund. The new book of African memoirs, *Shadows on the Grass*, appears in England and Denmark. 28 November: Karen Blixen is one of the founders of the Danish Academy. Another spell in hospital.

1961 25 June to 9 July: visit to Paris, Karen Blixen's last journey. Brief stay in hospital in the autumn. *Shadows on the Grass* published in America.

1962 In August, after a summer with many guests from home and abroad, Karen Blixen's general condition worsens. 7 September: she dies peacefully at home at Rungsted after having been unconscious for twenty-four hours, aged 77. 11 September: the nearest members of the family and closest friends bid farewell to Karen Blixen at a short ceremony in the drawing room at Rungstedlund. The coffin is then carried out to the courtyard and taken by horse-drawn waggon through the wood to the grave at the foot of "Ewald's Hill." The Danish edition of the *Memorial Anthology* on Karen Blixen published on 11 November.

1963 The posthumous tale, "Ehrengard" appears in America, England, and Denmark. (The Danish edition was translated by Clara Svendsen).

1964 Publication of the Danish memorial edition of Karen Blixen's *Works*, vols. 1–7. Robert Langbaum's book, *The Gayety of Vision: A Study of Isak Dinesen's Art*, appears in America, England, and Denmark.

1965 *Isak Dinesen: A Memorial* appears in America. Karen Blixen's *Essays* published in Denmark. Aage Henriksen's *The divine Child and other Essays on Karen Blixen* published in Denmark.

1970 *The Life and Destiny of Isak Dinesen*, by Frans Lasson and Clara Svendsen, published in America and England (new edition, Chicago, 1976).

1974 Three books of memoirs of Karen Blixen published in Denmark: *Tanne*, by Thomas Dinesen (English edition: *My Sister Isak Dinesen*, 1975), *Notes on Karen Blixen*, by Clara Svendsen, and *The Covenant: My Friendship with Karen Blixen*, by Thorkild Bjørnvig.

1975 Inaguration of the Karen Blixen Society in Copenhagen. 1 October: *Posthumous Tales* published in Denmark, edited by Frans Lasson. (Three of these tales were written by Karen Blixen in Danish, eight in English.)

1976 First volume of the Karen Blixen Society's series of yearbooks published in Danish. The Karen Blixen papers are deposited in the Royal Library, Copenhagen, which thus becomes the center for future Karen Blixen research. 30 August: death of Anders Dinesen, aged 82.

1977 *Carnival: Entertainments and Posthumous Tales* published in America and England.

1978 16 June: First large-scale Karen Blixen exhibition opens at the Royal Library, Copenhagen. 3 November: *Letters from Africa 1914–31*, vols. 1–2, published in Denmark, edited by Frans Lasson.

1979 10 March: death of Thomas Dinesen, aged 86. *Daguerreotypes and Other Essays* by Isak Dinesen published in America and England.

1981 *Letters from Africa 1914–31* published in America and England (translated by Anne Born).

Translator's Note

Karen Blixen's style and command of language in her letters are virtuosic, notwithstanding bilingual features and discrepancies in punctuation. These letters offer the student of literature a unique chance to watch the development of a writer's linguistic skills, as well as of her personality. In her Danish letters to home Karen Blixen deliberately set out to exercise and improve her powers of expression in her native language; the conscious employment of wide-ranging vocabulary, the zealous search for the exact term, the sure choice of idiom and the clear, uncluttered and precise style: all these features are perhaps most apparent in the long discursive letters to Aunt Bess.

It has been my aim in translating the letters to reproduce them as exactly as possible in meaning and to use the tone and expressions of the period. The English words used by Karen Blixen have been transcribed unchanged (they are denoted by an underscore in the text, while emphases in Danish are in italics). At the request of Frans Lasson and Clara Svendsen I have added a few extra notes where further explanation for English-language readership seemed necessary.

I should like to express my gratitude to Frans Lasson and Clara Svendsen for inviting me to undertake what has been an enthralling year of work in translating the letters. I owe a great debt to Clara Svendsen (now Clara Selborn) for her constant and watchful care in reading my work and for pointing out many instances where her immense knowledge of Karen Blixen's life and writings led to improvements. My thanks are due also to the Karen Blixen scholar, Else Cederborg, for advice and the initial introductions. Elisabeth Mills, M.A., advised on the translations of quotations from the sagas. Mr. R. S. Hetherington of the Midland Bank Trust Company, Oxford, kindly helped with some financial terminology. Not least, gratitude is due to my patient family.

Throughout the work I have been conscious of the presence of the writer of these letters, Karen Blixen the autotranslator.

Anne Born

On 23 December 1912, at the age of twenty-seven, Karen Dinesen announced her engagement to her Swedish second cousin, Baron Bror Blixen-Finecke, of Näsbyholm in Skaane. The enthusiastic accounts by their uncle, Count Mogens Frijs, of the extremely favorable future prospects in East Africa encouraged their decision to emigrate to what was to become the Crown Colony of Kenya, and in 1913 Bror Blixen went out to investigate conditions there. He took with him a considerable capital sum that had been placed at the disposal of the young couple by Fru Ingeborg Dinesen, Karen Dinesen's mother, and Fru Dinesen's brother, Aage Westenholz. Bror Blixen soon made contact with the Swedish colonists. Before many months had passed, he had bought the coffee farm "Swedo-African Coffee Co." from his compatriot, the engineer Åke Sjögren.

On 2 December 1913, Karen Dinesen left Denmark and, accompanied by her mother and her youngest sister, Ellen, traveled down through Europe to Naples, from where the German-East African Line ship "Admiral" *sailed a fortnight later. She parted from her family in Naples, and the first letter in the collection was written on board ship to her mother, five days before Karen Dinesen was met by her fiancé on the quay at Mombasa. On the same day, 14 January 1914, their wedding took place.*

1914

To Ingeborg Dinesen

9.1.[1914]

My own dearest Mother.—

I am going to get this letter sent off to you as soon as I reach Mombasa, because I am not sure that I will stay there long enough to be able to write, so that I will not be able to send you any news of your beloved Bror, and in general nothing of particular interest.— However, there have been some changes in regard to my servants that will probably interest you. First, I now have an Indian servant, who was waiting with a letter from Bror when I went ashore in Aden. The poor fellow had been sent to Tabora and had then been obliged to wait in Aden for a fortnight, and he was delighted to see me. He was really pleasant, smiling and greeting me with his hand to his forehead, extremely respectably dressed, but he spoke English badly and also had such a terrible stammer that he seemed about to die every time he tried to speak. Bror wrote that he was reliable and pleasant. Now he is here on board ship. His name is Fara; I hope he won't turn out to resemble Fara the Warrior.—

Now you must not be shocked when I tell you that I have engaged the stewardess on this ship to come and work for me after the voyage. The fact is that I came to realize after I had left that it was stupid not to have brought a maid with me. It would not have mattered if I had been fit and strong, but you know how pampered and unaccustomed I was to exertion when I came on board. I kept on thinking about the woman in "Dombey & Son" who is always saying that an effort must be done, for everything was an effort for me, getting up, dressing, the whole business of living, and time after time—now you must not mind if I write really honestly,—I was so tired and depressed that I felt that I would not survive until I arrived in Mombasa. . . .

If I can arrange things as I want—and if I cannot, I will not post this letter—she will leave the ship at Mombasa and come with me, and when six weeks later the ship returns to Mombasa after having called at Durban, she will go back on board, *if* I cannot manage to keep her by dismissing one of the boys,—not the agreeable Fara, but the other one,—and we are mutually satisfied. It is of course a great opportunity to be able to get her from the ship and actually a great favor on the part of the captain. Martha the girl is herself tremendously keen to come. . . . She can train Fara for me and put the house in order, and then I would probably regain my strength more quickly. But if I should not or should fall ill in some other way, you must not think it too dreadful if I keep her, because then I could not face being without her. . . .

A German officer, von Lettow, who belongs to a very old Mechlenburger family, has been such a friend to me; what he has to tell about his people is exactly like "Landmandsliv" [Country Life], and I am sure Aunt Lidda would find that it conformed to her ideal. I expect to write to you again before Mombasa. If only I could be with you for just one minute; I embrace you all and imagine I am looking into your beautiful, blessed eyes, Mother dear. . . .

To Ingeborg Dinesen

Hopcrafts Shooting Box 20.1.14

My own little Mother.—

I ought to have written long ago, but you have no idea how time has flown, and I wanted so much to write something sensible and worthwhile. But now I am sending this by runner, so you must take it as it is and despite the muddled style try to get an idea of this great new life and everything that has happened out here. I am in bed, not on account of illness but of night hunting, in a little log cabin, two rooms with wooden floors, with a fireplace in one of them, and all around on every side the most magnificent and wonderful scenery you can imagine, huge distant blue mountains and the vast grassy plains before them covered with zebra and gazelle, and at night I can hear lions roaring like the thunder of guns in the darkness.

But now I'll begin at the beginning.—Bror was in Mombasa to meet me and it was wonderful to be with someone one feels one belongs with again, but Mombasa is a fiery hothouse and the sun blazing down on your head almost makes you unconscious. We went up to look at a very attractive old fort, and at eleven o'clock we were married, with Sjøgren, Prince Vilhelm, Bostrøm and Lewenhaupt standing as witnesses; it was extremely easy and simple and only took ten minutes at most. Then we drove out by ricksha to have lunch with Hobley, who had married us; he had a really delightful villa right on the shore,—and from there to the train, a special train for Prince Vilhelm, with the Governor's private dining car and Macmillan's chef and kitchen, which was absolutely splendid. To begin with it was fearfully hot, but toward evening it grew cooler. There is no sleeping car, but Bror had brought sheets and blankets. By the following morning the landscape had completely changed and then it was the real Africa, vast grass plains and the mountains in the distance and then an incredible wealth of game, huge flocks of zebra and gnu and antelope right beside the train, and although when you hear about that you don't attach much importance to it, when you see it for yourself you find it really impressive.—

In Nairobi there was an official reception and luncheon with the Governor at his charming house,—I had the Governor on my right and the Vice-Governor on my left and everyone called me Baroness every other word; to start with I didn't realize they were addressing me. I must admit that it was a pretty exhausting experience after a 24-hour train journey, with crowds of people I had never seen before.—Immediately after lunch Bror and I drove out by car to our own farm. It is the most enchanting road you can imagine, like our own Deer Park, and the long blue range of the Ngong Hills stretching out beyond it. There are so many flowering trees and shrubs, and a scent rather like bog myrtle, or pine trees, pervades everything. Out here it is not too hot at all, the air is so soft and lovely, and one feels so light and free and happy.

There was a surprise in store for me when we arrived at the farm. All the thousand boys were drawn up in ranks and after a really earsplitting welcome they closed ranks and came up to the house with us, surrounded us when we got out of the car and insisted on touching us,—and all those black heads right in front of one's gaze were quite overwhelming. You have no idea how delightful the farm was and how beautifully everything had been done up. I have a bathroom next to my room which could not be nicer, and a lavatory which is the only one in B.E.A. I think the garden can be made delightful; for there are fine trees and it is so beautifully situated.—

Bror has six white men on the farm; they had prepared a magnificent tea for us and gave us wedding presents and a fine address; it was moving to see how these homeless people with no families, several of whom had probably been in a pretty desperate situation, took such pains to make much of me and seemed to enjoy joining in a kind of wedding.—

We left again in the car after I had promised our boys meat in gratitude for the fine reception they had given us—meat is the greatest treat they can have—and Bror and I had a quiet dinner in our room at the hotel, something I was in need of after these pretty tiring days.—I think it would give you great joy to hear how everyone I have met out here speaks about Bror. Everyone without exception comes up to me and says that he has put in an exceptional piece of work on the farm and is an example for the whole of Africa.—A runner is just leaving, so I must send this off. More next time. 10,000 greetings—

Tanne

To Mary Bess Westenholz

MBagathi Estate. 1. April [1914]

Dearest Aunt Bess.—

I want to write and thank you for your letters, but this letter will not be specially amusing or, in fact, private; but actually it is almost impossible to write private letters home. Also I am still kept prisoner in bed, as my temperature will not go down and everyone says you have to be careful the first time or it will come back again. It is a little tedious as Bror is naturally out a lot, but a great comfort when you begin to get better; malaria makes you feel so miserable that—to quote my own apt comment—the whole world disgusts you like an ill-fitting dress. Fara is my great comfort and support, better than a white lady's maid and so thoughtful and sensible, and then the Somalis have a bearing like Spanish grandees.—

The natives (among whom the Somalis cannot be included, they are immigrants from Somaliland, Muhammadans and of Arabic stock, who look down on the Negroes) are my greatest interest out here; but I think that I,—and Bror,—are about the only people here who really do have this interest. Where the natives are concerned the English are remarkably narrow-minded; it never occurs to them to regard them as human beings, and when I talk to English ladies on racial differences and such matters, they laugh patronizingly, touched by my eccentricity. Of course, the natives, who in many ways are more intelligent than they are, take advantage of this, but there will never be any understanding and cooperation. You have to laugh when you hear the English speaking their language; each tribe has its own language, but Swahili, the language of the coastal people, is a kind of universal tongue, which is spoken by the more cultivated in all the tribes. I think the reason why people often cannot get workers is that they will not show them any consideration, but, for instance, insist that they work when it is raining, which they hate.—And it never rains for more than a few hours,—and always disturb the Muhammadan time for prayer, which as you know is at precisely six o'clock at sundown.—(It is rather beautiful to see our old cook spreading out his little mat on the grass every evening and praying so devoutly with his face turned toward Mecca, and beating his brow on the ground.)

With a little understanding and interest this society is in many respects ideal: social problems don't exist here,—and they will not arise providing there is no mixing of the races; but I think the races differ too much for any intermixture to take place, I have never heard of half-castes here; on the other hand, there are a good many coming from South Africa. When I observe the various races here I feel that the superiority of the white race is an illusion. We are able to learn much more than they; even the Somalis have difficulty in handling a machine, and can only just manage a lamp (yesterday they let one smoke in my fine white bathroom so that it was black all over). But when it comes to character I think they surpass us. When I think that we have 1200 young men on the farm here, who live ten or twelve to a wretched little grass hut, and that I have never seen an angry face or heard quarreling, that everything is always done with a song and a smile, that from what I have heard, coarseness or impertinence are completely unknown concepts, that they are constantly seen with their arms about each other and pulling thorns out of each other's feet,—and think what trouble there would be with 1200 white workmen, I think they are better people than we are. They never drink, but are very addicted to every kind of tobacco, to smoke and to chew, and become intoxicated to the point of ecstasy with meat, which they love, and dancing.—

Then they have great dignity, and real taste in all color combination and draping, and really beautiful natural manners.—Recently I saw Sjøgren, who has enthusiastically adopted the English stupidity, greeting their big chief, Kinanjui,—who was on a visit here,—guffawing and blustering, playing up to all of us and emphasizing that he was condescending to talk to a native; and Kinanjui, who rules over a million Kikuyu, sat absolutely motionless with half-closed eyes (you can always pick out the chiefs by their dull, half-closed eyes) wrapped in his blanket—far wiser than Sjøgren and in a position to bring all his work to a halt by keeping his people away from it, which he does. I spoke to him a little; he promised that we would always have workers, this is an invaluable asset here. I go riding almost every day in the Masai Reserve and often try to talk to the tall, handsome Masai. They are always friendly, look one in the eyes, but never look at one's clothes or outfit; probably that is considered bad manners. . . .

With regard to "The Revenge of Truth," I don't want anything in it changed; but I imagine there is little chance of it ever being published. I don't think there is anything blasphemous in it, simply that it is written from an atheist's viewpoint. I believe that it would be impossible to write if one gave consideration to who is going to read one's work,—but for that matter I don't think I will be writing anything in the near future. On the whole, I don't think there is room for so many considerations in life, or the world. If one can't do without them, then one must withdraw, create one's own little world with that as a condition,—and perhaps it is best that one does that, or best for some. Life here is more brutal and would probably upset you more than the worst revelations from life at home; I, for one, prefer it like that, but still I well understand the happiness,—and charm,—of a quiet and peaceful spot that shuts its eyes and doors against all brutality. There is, naturally, only one choice possible, and the test of whether one has chosen rightly can never be made by considering what is best, only by whether one has rightly judged what made one happy. . . .

To Ingeborg Dinesen

MBagathi Estate [1 April 1914]

. . . In reply to your question, this is to tell you that for my wedding I wore my shantung suit and a helmet and one of the blouses we bought in Naples. For everyday wear here I use exactly the same clothes as at home, a blouse and short skirt, often a divided skirt, brown boots, always a double-layered felt hat or a helmet. . . .

This house is desperately in need of a veranda; it is so hot in the rooms that one almost expires, and on the veranda it is always sunny and always airless, because it is actually inside the house. I am planning to use some of your money to build an outside veranda and then make a sort of small sitting room out of the existing one; I really need that because the present one passes as a kind of smoking-room and office; it is always full of men wanting to talk to Bror. . . .

To Inger Dinesen

5.4. [1914]

My own Ea.—

A thousand thanks for all your letters. They have been such a comfort to me while I have been in bed. Fortunately I was up again yesterday and took a walk around the farm, and it was interesting to see how much everything had changed since I saw it last. When I recall how it looked when I arrived I can hardly recognize it; great areas of land that were then virgin forest are now like a stretch of garden with all the new little coffee plants in dead straight rows and the soil between them without a single weed.—Yesterday the Governor's wife paid a visit here, which appears to be something of a rare honor; her car got stuck along the road and had to be hauled out by our Kavirondo. I believe that our somewhat unapproachable attitude out here on this farm commands a certain respect, as after all we must be regarded as among the more distinguished settlers; Lady Belfield (the Governor's wife) talked despairingly of the social life in Nairobi that was so infinitely provincial and full of so much jealousy,—the Lord preserve me from that. I think you could count the decent women in this country on one hand. . . .

Most people out here are plagued by chiggers, a species of white maggot [more accurately, "flea"] that bores its way under the toe nails and lays its eggs, whereupon the whole toe becomes inflamed; the nail drops off and the whole leg may be infected with blood poisoning. The boys are adept at picking them out with a needle,—poor Bror had four in one foot and was quite ill. All our oxen have been vaccinated against rinderpest and so cannot work. Bror has gone to Nairobi today to sell the weakest ones that he did not have vaccinated as he thought they would not stand up to it.—up to 5% die from being vaccinated, but rinderpest, if once contracted, can wipe out the entire stock. . . .

To Ingeborg Dinesen

10.4. [1914]

. . .Time seems to pass so quickly here.—It is interesting to watch the plantation and quite remarkable when I think that the thick dark forest, with a narrow little green path through it, that I was walking along on 15 January when I came out here with Bror, has turned into the smooth peaceful coffee field, which is kept in exactly the same orderly way as the kitchen garden at home. . . .

—I am very busy with my building plans here. This house is so badly built, because the veranda faces west; from 12 until 6 it is quite impossible to stay in it because of the sun, and the sitting room (with the bow-window) is the same, and since those are the hours when one cannot be outside it is very trying. In this country you cannot have west-facing windows without a veranda outside, and it is essential to have one room with a veranda right round it. Now I intend to build a veranda on two sides and make a kind of little sitting-room out of the existing veranda. . . . It is still not as comfortable here as it might be, but I hope to improve things. Some Indian workmen have been to repair the damage caused in transit to our belongings, and have done it beautifully. All the inside walls of the house are wooden, but Bror had had them very well done up, covered with canvas part of the way up (to the upper lintel of the doors, as a sort of paneling); this is topped by a broad wooden list, and above that they are white, nice and fresh looking. In here in my bedroom it is pale gray which goes well with my pink rugs and the flowered cretonne. The dining room and corridor are green, the sitting-room brownish-gray. Bror has his big inlaid cupboard in there and it looks very nice; also some paintings sent by Uncle Frederik look really good. . . .

Every day between 50 and 100 boys come here asking for work, but we have to send them away. There are certainly vast resources of labor here; of course, we adjoin the Kikuyu Reserve with its millions of people. But as a rule they do not want to work and have no need to. I think they want to be here partly because they enjoy being with so many others. When they have finished work in the evening they go down and play in a large meadow. They stand in a long row with their long sticks (which are pointed and hardened in the fire, so they are as hard as iron), one, standing at the end of the row, throws a barrel hoop down along it, and they throw their spears, trying to send them through the hoop as it rolls past. It is probably a form of practice from their hunting life, for they are a hunting people. . . .

I often think the boys are very funny. When we were on safari they usually had to wake us at 4 o'clock when we were going lion hunting; one morning our kill was a long way away and we told them to wake us very early. So at 2 o'clock they came and knocked for us and said: "Now it is very early." That is the sort of thing that makes many people out here get so angry with them, but they do it only to please. . . .

To Thomas Dinesen

MBagathi 22. 4 [1914]

. . . As I have probably written time after time, one loses a good deal of racial superiority out here; it seems obvious to me that the natives surpass us in many ways. Admittedly they cannot learn as *much* as we can, but when it comes to acquiring the skills needed in order to live out here, they are far more adept than we are,—there are many English people who have been here for ten or fifteen years who are quite ignorant of the appearance of the various tribes, not to speak of their character, although it would be greatly to their advantage to get to know them; while the natives immediately recognize the character of each of us; and the English cannot even pick up the necessary rudiments of Swahili but speak a kind of English, while I think that the natives make themselves conversant with our habits incredibly quickly. For instance, I think it is really good that in only six months an old Somali can learn how to put a menu together so well that he can achieve variation in six or seven courses; I'm always expecting to get the soup after the sweet.

I often think that our life out here with all our thralls must resemble that of Erling Skjalgsøn or Haarek of Thjotta (except that we have not played that sort of part in the history of the country). You, with your interest in sociology, would find plenty of study material here. There are no real social problems here, there is conflict neither between rich and poor nor between men and women. Unfortunately this Golden Age is drawing to its close. White laws and regulations do not suit the blacks and even though as yet they are perfectly satisfied, I think one can see the end approaching—chiefly through the influence of Christianity, and because they are no longer allowed to fight, which in the past was their chief occupation. The Masai, the proudest of the tribes, are dying out from lack of space, and the others from intermarriage, since they can no longer seize women from neighboring tribes.—

Proof that the influence of the missionaries is very bad is the fact that no one will accept a worker from the mission schools; everyone says that they lie and steal. However did Christianity come to acquire so much power? - since it is, and is acknowledged to be, unworkable? Muhammadanism seems to be a religion that can really be lived by. Our house Somalis are Muhammadans. They are actually afraid of nothing; they will go straight for lions—which are generally considered to be afraid of Somalis. A few days ago when a man at Swedo fell ill and died, of plague it was thought, all except the Somalis ran away. I asked Fara if they were not afraid of infection; he shrugged his shoulders and replied that they knew better; if God decided they were to die, they would die—if they were to live, they would live. . . .

As I've probably written, the great beasts of prey give color to the country. I'm sending you a book, "The Man-eaters of Tsavo," so that you can see what conditions out here are like for engineers. Beasts and birds of prey are really the most magnificent fruits of the earth, and to have one's life truly affected by them, hear them, have one's stock devoured by them, see them at liberty—an extremely strange experience for a cultivated person—but they bring a breath of air from "Big Game" and the "Spirit of the Stone" into everything.—

As far as writing books out here is concerned, that will not amount to much. I am more of a tradesman. With a capital of 3,000 rupees I make between 400 and 500 rupees a month on my sheep. This may sound as if I am rich, but that is not so, I'm only quite well off. Everything is so damned costly out here. When I have my garden it should be better. . . .

I hope you can read this long letter. *Unfortunately* I am still in bed, where, except for a day or two, I have been since 17 March,—but don't tell Mother, she worries so about malaria, which certainly is a beastly disease. Bror sends his regards—he is a much more genuine anarchist than you are—(or at least just as much). If you read a good new book, do send it to me; you don't know how much one longs for that here, where you can only get asinine English stuff.—Goodbye now, my wise philosopher and burly sailor man. Kiss Mother. Don't quite forget me, remember that my arms are always ready to give you a welcoming hug. Good luck in everything you do; may the spirit of the eagles, the lions and the sea be with you.

Your Tanne

To Ellen Dinesen

MBagathi 13.5.1914.

. . . I have been commissioned to buy ten mares for the Kaiserliche Schutztruppen at Dar-es-Salam [sic]. It is a piece of business that will not yield any profit, but still is quite interesting. Perhaps von Lettow will send me a carpet for it if he is satisfied; they have such beautiful carpets at Dar-es-Salam. . . I like the Germans much better than the English. . . . The English ladies are particularly dreadful. Quite apart from the decidedly commercial flirting that all the English ladies indulge in—I doubt if there are ten decent women in this country,—they have such appalling taste, always appearing in khaki down to the knees, with cartridge cases, and below the knee sheer silk stockings and high-heeled suede shoes, they are over made-up, screech frightfully and laugh hysterically, scold their workmen like fishwives, are furious about everything in this country and all have to look like girls of 17. Englishmen are incapable of imagining any other kind of feminine grace and charm than a 17-year-old with a <u>mass of golden hair</u> and <u>slim girlish figure</u>, which doesn't quite match the pretty seedy type out here—and which, incidentally, makes all their novels so unbearably tedious.

In a day or two I am going to ride over to the French Mission and am looking forward to meeting some Latins.—How glad I am that you are better and I am sure that you and Ea have had a grand time together at Lugano. I have only gradually come to realize what a distressing business Ea's deportation must have been, I sympathize with her; and yet it must have been quite an experience. . . .

If you ever get married, which you really must, *then allow yourself plenty of time to learn housekeeping properly first*.—It's insupportable to be as stupid as I am. I don't think Nature has left me completely without talent; but when I think about it I feel that I have learned nothing whatsoever. If I knew anything about it I could teach the natives: gardening, carpentry or nursing,—in a way I could be a missionary, for I really love them, except that I have nothing to teach; they know my best philosophy better than I do. I read in "From the Eighth Brigade" that one "loves soldiers as one loves young women, without limit," and the natives inspire a similar love; but don't repeat this at home, for people might misunderstand me,—just like Bror, who threatens me with seven years in jail. It is a pity that one's houseboys have such a weakness for getting drunk,—not the Somalis, who are Muhammadans and never touch wine, but the Kavirondo. They take all the dregs from the glasses, whiskey, wine and lemon juice, and mix them together in a bottle, which must make a delicious drink for them. I'm obsessed with it now and when somebody comes to dinner I keep a strict watch over half-empty glasses.—

The other night when Bror was away in Nairobi and Fara was out on a sheep deal, a big Kavirondo boy we have, got drunk and tried to murder a little Somali; the victim came into my room in utter terror, all torn to pieces and covered with mud and blood from his nose, begging for protection, and I had to get out of bed and go into the corridor, where the murderer was standing with a great log in his hand, and talk to him in Swahili and turn him out of the house. All the same, one is never afraid of natives, or no more than one would be of —one's own—savage dogs. When Mother thinks I can train a Bibbi ["married woman"], it certainly shows that she has the wrong idea about them. The Kikuyu and the Kavirondo are from the Stone Age, the Masai from the Iron Age, only the Somalis reach historic times, but they will not—any of them—let their women out to others. . . .

To Ingeborg Dinesen

Swedo-African Coffee Co., Ltd.,
H'ruru Estate,
Ngong
MBagathi 28.5. [1914].

. . . It has been a very busy time with planting, it seems we have been unusually lucky with the weather and have had more than the normal amount of rain; in fact the rainy season is just about over now, but everything here has been planted. Bror, who needed a bit of a holiday, went to Naiwasha one weekend to decide the site for

Uncle Mogens' house; I didn't go as it was raining ceaselessly at that time, and then all the roads get quite impossible. . . .

All the white people out here are pressing the government to raise the "Hut Tax," the tax on natives, from 3 rupees to £1, in order to make them work; I think it is a sorry idea to force an entire nation that is now rich, into poverty in such a way, but on the other hand I don't think the natives can go on living in their present fashion; life has grown too easy for them, after the tribal wars; to a certain extent the wild animals, and especially the dangers of the Arabian slave traders, have disappeared; previously the men had enough to do as hunters and warriors, now they do absolutely nothing, let the women, as before, work the soil and the cattle, and degenerate. As a whole I don't think black and white can live together in one country; the black will be destroyed. . . .

To Ingeborg Dinesen

MBagathi 6.6[1914]

My beloved Mother.

Just a couple of words to say that you will probably not hear from us for three or four weeks, because tomorrow we are going down to Southern Guasha Nero. The doctor has strongly advised me to have a change of air, and as we don't feel like going and sitting in a hotel we prefer to have a little camping life, and it will be absolutely wonderful to get out into the great outdoors again. You can't imagine how splendidly Bror arranges everything for me, he is so practical and meticulous and thinks of everything; I have never known anyone so unselfish, and while you think that I am "roughing it" in the wilds of Africa, I am wrapped in cotton wool. I'm sure we will have a wonderful time. We are taking a mule wagon and will have a cook, Fara and Ferasi,—our kitchen boy, the nicest, sweetest boy I have seen, Ferasi, by the way means horse,—with us. I am much better, incidentally, but it is not so easy to regain one's strength after malaria, so I think it will do me a lot of good to go away. Bursell is going to lay out the garden while we are away. . . .

To Ingeborg Dinesen

Mountain Health Resort
"Kijabe Hill"
British East Africa.
14.7. [1914]

My own beloved Mother.

Just a few lines from Kijabe, where we arrived with our wagons and boys late last night after 13 hours of driving. Perhaps this may catch the German boat. We will stay here at the health resort for one day and enjoy all the conveniences of civilization. We have had an *absolutely marvelous* time, I have never in my life enjoyed myself more. I will give you a more detailed description, perhaps with some photographs, by the next post. It was a tremendously successful safari, six big lions, four leopards, one cheetah. As well as all the usual kinds of game, eland, impala, gnu, boar, jackal, marabou—I shot one lion and one big leopard.—Bror has taught me to shoot and says that I shoot well. . . .

To Ingeborg Dinesen

MBagathi 12. 8. 1914

. . . It is dreadful to be away for such a long time. But when we telegraphed home it was already then impossible to get back, Suez is still blocked. They think there will be disturbances on the frontier here, and Bror has joined the volunteers with the other Swedes; that is, not as a soldier, but among themselves, they have organized a kind of telegraph service with motorcycles and cars and cycles from the frontier to Kijabe. Bror, who is in command of it, went off yesterday. I am also leaving tomorrow to look after our station at Kijabe. There is nothing to do here on the farm; we have dismissed our boys and stopped the transport of wood, because no one knows when money will get through again and whether Swedo will ever get any.—And the repair work on the house is at a standstill. . . .

To Ingeborg Dinesen

Uasha Nyero 23. 8. 14.

. . . If you received my letter from the farm you will know that Bror joined up as a volunteer,—a kind of "unfighting," as he went for the purpose of passing information; Ture, Gethin, Fjæstad (from Swedo) and Kjellberg are serving under him, and they have various stations to man on the road between Kijabe and the frontier. They all went off on Tuesday the 11th. The idea was that I should stay at Kijabe with Kjellberg and help him look after the terminal station there, and I went up there with my boys, my lovely new horse Aimable, and Dusk [her dog]; but just as I arrived, our transport man who was to come down here with supplies—petrol for the cars and motorcycles, food for themselves and the boys—was put in jail as a German subject and as in these troubled times I dared not let the boys go alone with our valuable goods,—posho ["supplies"] are almost unobtainable, and natives must not be given sugar, flour etc., so I was afraid that they could not manage to explain themselves, and that everything would be confiscated,—I went with them. If you see Uncle Mogens you can tell him that I walked in four days from Kijabe to Narok Boma, the same road that they took, with two ox wagons (41 oxen) and eighteen boys, and ask him whether it is any sinecure to go that way on foot; I dared not take Aimable out here, it is bad horse country, and they cheated me of a mule so I had to take to my feet. However, I took a bicycle from an Indian on the road, but in most places the road is like Cheop's pyramid and is not fit for cycling. It is 73 miles. . . .

One evening, when we had been caught on a stone in a sunken road and were busy getting it— the wagon—up, a lion leaped out on one of our reserve oxen not two meters away from me. I was standing giving light from a lantern so that I did not see it, but heard the ox scream and rush away, and naturally all the oxen were terrified and upset. I ran up with Fara into a small hollow after the ox and shot, and all the boys raised a great alarm, so the lion let go of the ox; its back was badly torn by the lion's claws. Then we were obliged to camp where we were, though it was a very bad, narrow pass surrounded by steep cliffs; but it was too dark to go on, and we built a boma [''defensible enclosure''] of thorn and made a big fire, and Fara and I sat up all night with guns.

If the oxen run away in such terrain, you never see them again. The lion came back during the night and frightened us rather, but we kept our oxen together and got away in good order next morning. Our old cook, Esmail, armed with a large kitchen knife, did not once move from my side. Luckily a man along the road had presented me with a gun and 200 cartridges so that Fara could also be armed. I have fortunately acquired a reputation among my boys as a first-rate shot, so they are not as afraid as they have reason to be in a terrain completely lacking in game and as calmly as you please tell me to pica [''prepare''] this or that for them,—on the trip here I was lucky and managed to shoot something for them every day; I shot a Grant with *very* large horns in the Kedong Valley. I arrived at the boma on Wednesday night, dirtier than I had ever been in my life; I found none of our people, whom I had been expecting, there, but had dinner with the D.C. and pitched camp.

I had Dusk with me for the whole trip, it was somewhat difficult but very nice. On Thursday I went out and shot some big birds, which taste like turkey; when I got back Bror arrived, quite brown and very tired. He had been with Lord Delamere the whole time, who seems to have been very pleased with him and who said that he did not know what he would do without him. . . . The next day was absolutely frightful. We broke camp next morning and were just about to leave when among all the rubbish Bror found a bottle which he thought contained soda water, and started to drink from it, but it was concentrated Lysol! You can imagine the agony he was in and that he, and I as well, thought he would die. Luckily there was water nearby that he could rush down to, and I was able to rush up to the D.C. and get milk, but at first you don't realize what has happened. I don't think he could have swallowed much, although he vomited terribly; but the whole of his mouth and throat were severely burned and all afternoon he was in terrible pain and in the evening his temperature went right up and he could not sleep all night. But yesterday he was so much better that we were able to move camp ten miles to the south, and now this morning he left to rejoin Delamere—twenty miles on foot!. . .

This is the time when the Somalis keep their fast month, Ramadan, when they may not eat or drink a drop of water between midnight and six in the evening; you cannot imagine how moving it was, when we came to some water on the trip from Kijabe in suffocating heat, to see our old cook, instead of drinking, take out his prayer mat and lie down to beat his head against the earth. Today, thank God, it is over, and will be ended with a feast, although it's a riddle to me to know how Muhammadans celebrate, as they do not drink, live on dried veal and dried dates and something they call ghi which smells so foul that you cannot eat after you have been near it,—but perhaps they have other pleasures. . . .

To Ingeborg Dinesen

Webbs Store, 23. September [1914]

. . . I went out from Kijabe as a transport man with three ox wagons; later on I went much further south to fetch food supplies from a big safari camp that had been deserted in frantic haste when the people there heard about the war.—Bror meanwhile was staying at a camp at Guasio Nyero. I traveled alone with 17 boys, and it was enormously enjoyable, I can tell you. I am absolutely convinced that the natives are the "best class" out here; I find it quite impossible to take any interest at all in the English middle class, but the boys are absolute gentlemen; I think their excellent manners are to a great extent due to the fact that they come from so many different races. In Denmark the inhabitants of Funen find it hard to believe that there is anyone in existence other than Funen people, but here Kikuyu, Kavirondo, Swahili, Masai, Somalis, who all differ from each other as greatly in appearance, language, life and customs as Finns and Italians, live together all the time. . . .

A few days later, to my great surprise Bror came out to see me, he had been with Lord Delamere when he had contracted dysentery and taken a few days off and by some marvel had found my tracks in the wilderness; he had walked 86 miles in two days!—his legs were completely stiff and he could not sit down unless we bent him together; he had slept in a Masai Manyatta ["village"] and gone without food,—nonetheless he went out hunting with me in the afternoon and I shot a very big eland bull —we think a record. . . .

Now Bror and I have a camp together by a store out on the plains; although today I am going to move my camp three to four hours from here to a place where there are rhinoceros, but I will still be able to get messages from him quickly. I would have gone home to the farm but it is so tiresome because any news from here has to go through Nairobi so I will stay here at least until we get some idea of what is happening. Bror is quite well again now. The intention is to bring troops over here from India and go into German East from Dar-es-Salam, Voi, and the lake, and as the Germans don't have many troops out here and it is impossible for them to get more, it is thought that they will soon surrender; but it is incredible that the English have dawdled so much that the Germans have managed to get here first, and it has made the natives very uneasy. They have heard about airplanes and are always asking us if the Germans are going to come and fly off with their cows and women. All the Masai "Elmorans"—young warriors—are out in full warpaint; they are roaming the country by day and by night, at night with fearful howling—just next to us here we have a camp with 200–300. . . .

To her Mother. Private.

. . . I promise to write to you straight away. . . but you must promise me not to mention it because I always think it rather embarrassing when there is talk of an expected child so far in advance. But another thing is that I think it would be best if it did not come about for the time being. You may think it would be lovely to have a grandchild; but really Africa is most unsuitable for small children, at least until one has grown a little accustomed to conditions here and is acclimatized. The two other white women on the farm, Mrs. Gethin and Fru Holmberg, are expecting babies now and are in despair, ill and hysterical and always wailing about the awful nuisance it is to have a child. I think that is a pity, and that it is better to wait. It certainly would not be suitable on this safari life and that is really Africa's greatest charm. But I promise you to write at once when it happens. . . .

To Ingeborg Dinesen

MBagathi 6. 10. [1914]

. . . The house looks terrible. In the event of a native uprising it has been chosen as headquarters and assembly point for all the farmers in the district, and that I can well understand since it is almost impossible to get into. The Indians have built the outer veranda wall up to where the floor should be; it is quite high, as the house has a ventilated foundation; but as they have not laid the floor, and all the staircases have been removed, you have first to climb over a wall then struggle through a trench full of rubble and then try to get up into the house. In addition, none of the painting is more than half-finished and one window and door have been taken away. I am much afraid that it will be a long time before there is any improvement. The garden looks like the Sahara without a blade of grass. I began my housewifely activities by giving (not personally) each of my "totos" (small houseboys) 20 strokes of the kiboko [a whip cut from hippopotamus hide], because they had been stealing and getting drunk and had just about murdered three other boys! They had been so nice and it is always a pity when they start drinking; but I hope that this will have scared them off it. I have never punished my boys with the kiboko before.—At the same time, to counterbalance this severity I bandaged up a little boy who had been kicked in the bottom by an ostrich—they are quite fearfully spiteful and can kick people to death. He had a long wound several inches deep and I put a really good tight bandage on it, but afterward I realized that it had probably made it impossible for him to go to the bathroom. I strictly forbade him to touch the bandage and hope he doesn't die of it. . . .

Bror speaks and writes English so well, much better than I do, because I spend most of my time in Somali circles and have come to speak like Friday in "Robinson." The Somalis call me Arda Volaja,—which is supposed to mean everything good, the great, wise, etc.; the only other person to have been given the name was Queen Victoria! So I must feel myself honored and hope that it doesn't refer to outward appearances. . . .

To Thomas Dinesen

MBagathi Estate
Nairobi
(Received) 17. Oct. 1914? [Thomas Dinesen's note]

My own Tommy.

I'm sending this letter to you because you are the one person at home who will best understand the exhilaration that comes with the experiences that I am going to describe. I have spent four weeks in the happy hunting grounds and have just emerged from the depths of the great wide open spaces, from the life of prehistoric times, today just as it was a thousand years ago, from meeting with the great beasts of prey, which enthrall one, which obsess one so that one feels that lions are all that one lives for—strengthened by the air of the high mountain region, tanned by its sun, filled with its wild, free, magnificent beauty in heat-dazzling days, in great clear moonlit nights. I must humbly apologize to those hunters whose delight in the chase I failed to understand. There is nothing in the world to equal it.—

Just before I left Bror gave me a rifle, a 256, with a telescopic sight, a splendid gun that I was scared stiff to fire at first but that I gradually learned to handle. Bror is an excellent instructor. I lost a whole packet of cartridges the very first day and as I already had too few I had to watch my shots very carefully; out of 100 cartridges I shot 44 head of game. It is very tempting out here to shoot from too great a distance, but Bror was strict and stopped me doing that and was very good at getting one close up to the game. However, from over 400 meters I have put a bullet right in the heart of wildebeest and duiker. I shot 20 different kinds of game—all the ordinary species of deer, zebra, wildebeest, eland, dik-dik, marabou, jackal, wild boar, one lion, one leopard, a number of large birds; I cannot use a shotgun. It's still a thorn in the flesh to me that I missed a big leopard that I saw early one morning approaching over a rise and walking past not more than ten paces from me, calm, majestic; if I had not been an utter ass I would have got it, but I thought it was going to come up to a kill that was just in front of me and so did not shoot, and at some movement or sound it was gone in a flash. I also saw two lions in the moonlight only five m. away and heard them eating a zebra and making an unearthly din.—

We traveled in three mule wagons with nine boys. This was a new way of going on safari and was regarded with some skepticism, it is usual to take bearers and ox wagons, which takes at least twice as much time and creates a great deal of fuss. . . . Our safari went to Southern Guasha Nyero,—a river 90 miles from civilization,—and 40 miles on the other side. It is in the Masai Reserve and you see the Masai everywhere with their large herds of sheep and oxen. They cause one plague: the flies, which practically eat you up. The inside of one's tent is black with them; so immediately is any food that is put out. There is just no alternative but to accustom oneself to them, and in the end I could let them crawl over my face quite calmly. The Masai always have the corners of their eyes full of flies; it does not worry them a scrap.—The route down there crosses a range of hills and is very difficult because the road is indescribably bad; one drives over blocks of stone as if up and down a pyramid, with the left wheel six feet higher than the right. It takes four days. There is no game there. But then the dreary bush gives way and the plain widens out; before one lie the great tablelands, surrounded by a magnificent panorama of blue mountains, teeming with game. Now the animals here are not as beautiful as those at home. The zebra are sweet, but they look like horses of course, wildebeest (gnu) look dangerous but are not; a most wonderful sight is a herd of giraffe, and the first time you see them you can hardly believe your own eyes when you see their incredible height and slenderness, like a flock of great snakes with the most strange rocking movement.

I must say that in fact I suffered more from cold than heat on this safari. When you are traveling you always have to rise early, for it always takes a long time to break camp and load up; just as when you put out a kill for lions and hope to find one at it just before sunrise, so you often have to start off in pitch darkness, and in the thin air the cold is intense. Then by midday the sun is blazing, it is hard to shoot because the air is shimmering in the heat. Then comes a delightful time, especially toward evening, between 4.30 and 7, when all the colors are wonderful and the air delicious.—A thermos flask is an excellent thing to have if you fill it really cold in the morning, it is refreshing at midday.—There are many flowers on the plains, especially purple ones and almost everywhere masses of forget-me-nots.

We had the first news of lions from a man we met on the road and had dinner with; you are very hospitable and glad to meet people in the wilderness; you get to know who is out traveling or bringing "stores" to trade with the Masai, and you take an interest in each other's hunting. With another man he had been out stalking fifteen lions, had built a boma—a shelter made of piles of thorn branches with which you surround your camp near your kill—and during the night, in the moonlight, after having shot at one, they had been attacked by all fifteen and felt certain they were going to be devoured, but had seized on the idea of making a din by beating two tins together, which terrified the lions into running off. He had had enough of them, but he showed us to the place. On the road we met his friend, Wilkes, who had taken a very rich European, Ralli, out there and was then going home with five lions. After much trouble we got to their old camp in an unhealthy spot in a river bed and found a great many lion tracks. Bror sat up in the boma with his gunbearer Esman the first night but it was pitch dark and he missed a lion he shot at. On the same night I heard a noise outside my tent which was quite a distance away from the boys and was open, and when I went out to see what it was I was met by a deep growling right beside me; I went in again and shut up the tent, and in the morning we found the tracks of two big lions there, they had been down near the mules as well. After that Fara stayed in my tent when Bror was in the boma. While we listened for shots during the night he told me about horse breeding in Somaliland, which they do by letting their mares out to graze beside the rivers; there are magic stallions living in the river that visit them during the night and produce foals as swift as the wind. The Somali ponies that I have known cannot have been bred by that method. He and the gunbearer Esman belong to a tribe who are forbidden to do anything evil and are therefore greatly respected by the others, and that is very nice for us. He said that it was quite safe for us to shoot more than our licences permitted, because they could not report us.—Later on, when there was moonlight, I sat up in the boma as well.

Meanwhile, a ghastly American woman arrived, a Lady Mackenzie—whose safari had been financed by a magazine and given immense publicity, and who travels with seven white men and 200 bearers—at our camp, pitched camp here and shot all around us against all the rules, put a kill out herself and built a boma and chased all the lions away so that we were obliged to clear out and go eastward. The unreliable information about lions that you get from the Masai is confusing; they see them everywhere. However, we got hold of a good guide, an "Elmoran," a young warrior; all the Masai have to undergo some years of military service, and during this time they are extremely dashing, always armed; they live apart from the tribe, either a few of them in the mountains or in large "barracks" with huge parade grounds. This one however did not look like an Elmoran but exactly like a Danish dairymaid, so we called him Maren; but he was bright enough and killed an eight-foot-long snake with his spear. He led us to a place where the mountains and plains met, where I believe no white men have ever camped before. Anyhow the game there were quite tame and flocks of eland and zebra, very inquisitive, came close up to us. I tried to take photographs of them but unfortunately without success. Neither did we shoot much here, in order not to frighten away the lions, only for food and for kills to put out for lions. There were lions everywhere; we heard them at night very close to the camp and saw their tracks in all the riverbeds, but they would not go near our kill. Morning after morning we went out to look at it, but it had not been touched, and then you need luck to come across them in that difficult terrain, full of ravines and thick scrub.

One afternoon we went out to shoot food. The syce was to follow us with the horses. He came up with us tremendously aufgericht; a big Simba had been lying by a crossing place on the river and had not moved as he passed by, only stared terrifyingly at him. We did not entertain much hope of finding it at the same place, but we went along there with him and tramped about in a big crowd all around the ford—and then I suddenly caught sight of an enormous animal lying in the tall grass about 100 m. away from us and I touched Bror,-he put the telescope to his eye and said quickly: It's a lion, changed guns and shot—the lion was lying with its head on its paws looking right at us. The shot hit it full in the chest and it fell without a sound. It was a big male lion. I went right up to it and watched the life ebbing from its eyes; it was my first meeting with a lion and I shall never forget it. In their build, carriage and movements lions possess a greatness, a majesty, which positively instills terror in the human being and makes one feel later that everything else is so trivial —thousands of generations of unrestricted supreme authority, and one is oneself set back 6,000 generations—suddenly comes to feel the mighty power of nature, when one looks it right in the eyes.—The boys were in an ecstasy, ran to meet us yelling and laughing; to them lions really are natural enemies, they take their cattle, and Fara said there was not one Somali family in which someone had not been eaten by a lion. Among white lion hunters they calculate that 10% (one for every ten lions) is killed.—

There was a great feast and ngoma [''dance''] in the camp while they were skinning the lion, it was 11'8'' long. When you see them being skinned you can really see how every inch of their body represents power; there is no trace of superfluous fat on the colossal muscles and sinews. Next day at 3 in the afternoon we saw six lions on the plain, but we were riding carelessly and startled them away and did not get a shot at them; we stayed on a few days more in that camp but then moved further into the mountains. At this point I had been sitting up for two nights in the boma. When no game come to the boma that is the most hellish pastime one can imagine. One is locked in there at 6 o'clock; then it gets dark, and there is no possibility of getting out before 6 in the morning when the sun rises. You must not fall asleep for fear of spoiling your chances. Your stinking kill is just in front of your nose, placed so that the wind carries its scent right on to you; you sit extremely uncomfortably with a couple of Somalis right on top of you, and you must not move, nor make a sound. A night like that can seem like fifty years; on one night I had a couple of ghostly hyenas that came and ate the kill, the other nights nothing at all. So I stayed in my tent the first night at the new camp;

I heard Bror shoot four times, and he came riding back early next morning and in the course of the night had got four lions—we found three of them, the fourth had gone into such thick scrub that it was impossible to find it without dogs. They were magnificent skins; but unfortunately the hyenas had eaten part of the best one before we found it,—it was only 100 paces from the boma, but in thick bush. On the same day we went on a long excursion, found rhino and buffalo tracks and could certainly have got a rhino if we had wanted to and had not been concentrating solely on lions.—

The next night I experienced a real night of game in the boma,—the most wonderful thing you can imagine. There was bright moonlight, and as you are sitting in a boma with your kill not 8 feet away, you can watch the big animals as if you were actually sitting among them. The first to come are the shy, shadowy hyenas, they retreat a couple of times before finally daring to start eating; more and more of them come gliding out of the darkness, you can hear every sound from their teeth in the meat. Then the eager little jackals come, they resemble foxes and are tremendously lively and attractive; I saw mothers playing with their young ones many times in the mornings and it was really delightful. You can see everything quite clearly in the moonlight and could almost touch them with your hand while you sit there as quiet as a mouse with your cocked rifle resting on a branch, ready to shoot.—Then. . . . [one page of the letter is missing] those that Bror had lost, because they went too far, right in the neck, and it fell without a sound. Unfortunately it was only a very big old lioness, both Bror and I thought it was a lion, it was so big. On the same night Bror shot another lioness, a good deal smaller, but a beautiful skin. Black and blue, tired out and happy you wake up at sunrise after a brief sleep and make for home, to be congratulated by the boys, go and lie down and get eaten up by the flies.—The next night I was in the boma I shot a fine big leopard and in the morning I saw the one that I did not get but that was like a vision.— Then, alas, we had to come back, most regretfully. From the great wild plains you go north, leave the Masai, hear no more lions, come to the most outlying "Stores" again, meet white men, arrive at Kijabe Railway Station, take the train and are fetched by Rundgren in the motor car. . . .

All was well at the farm. But how drearily civilization lays its pall over life! The very security that it strives for with might and main, and its efforts to know and systematize everything, take away all its charms,—not until you get into the "jungle" of the really big cities do you find it again. . . .

Karen Dinesen, photographed by Juncker-Jensen, 1913.

Karen and Bror Blixen at a ngoma in honor of Prince Wilhelm of Sweden, 1914.

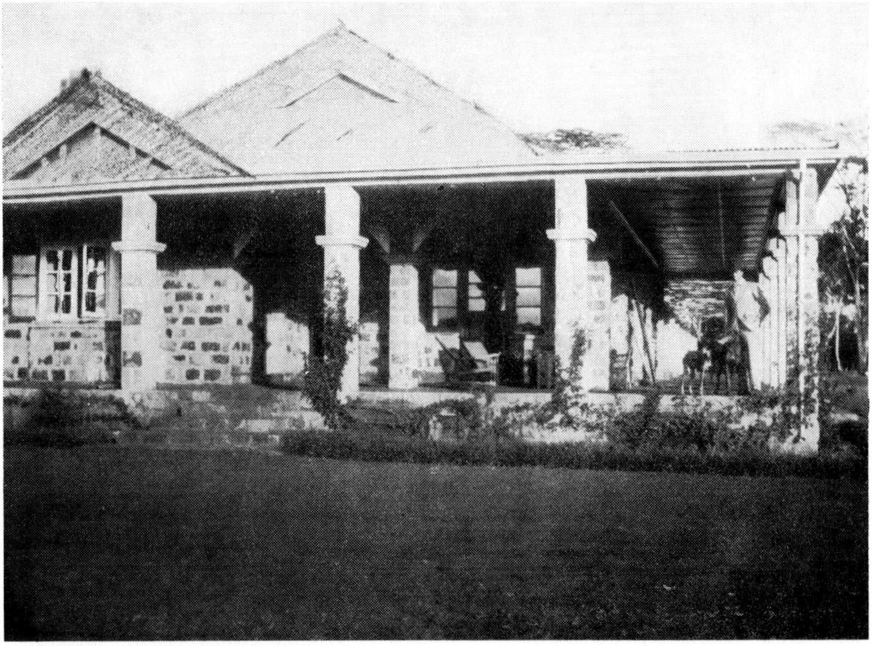

Bror Blixen in front of MBagathi, 1914.

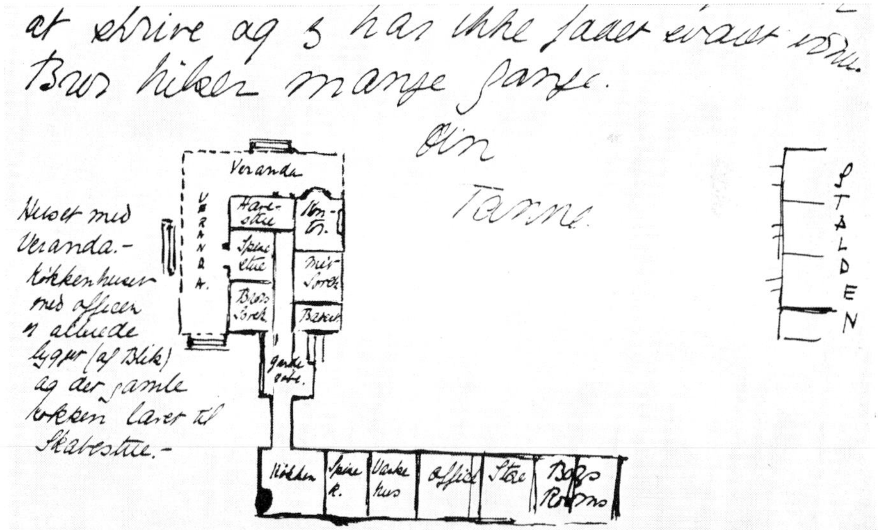

Plan of the first farm (mentioned in letter to Ingeborg Dinesen, 1914).

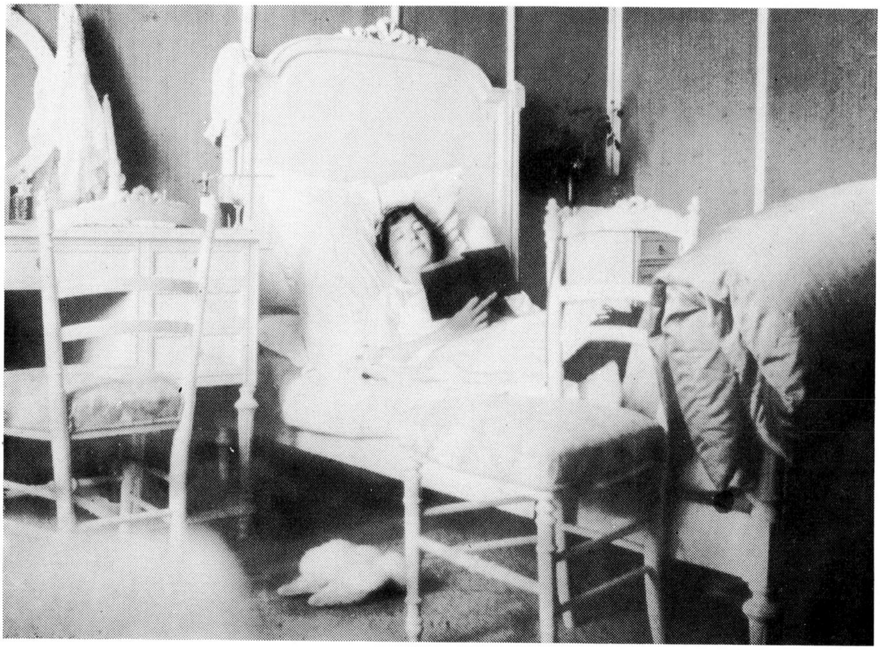

Karen Blixen in her bedroom at MBagathi, 1914.

Bror Blixen ready for safari.

Ox transport from Kijabe, 1914. Farah in the foreground, Karen Blixen seated on the slope.

Karen Blixen with shot buffalo, 1914.

Hunting lion, 1914.

Karen Blixen in hospital in Copenhagen, 1915.

The new, larger farm Bogani, purchased in 1916.

The study at Bogani, 1917.

Karen Blixen with her first dogs in Africa.

Karen Blixen in the livingroom at Bogani, 1917.

At the window, Bogani, 1917.

Bror Blixen in the office, 1917.

Eric von Otter and Karen Blixen.

Rouge, Karen Blixen, Kamau, Peter, and Poor Box with groom.

Karen Blixen with Dusk in the Ngong Hills, 1917.

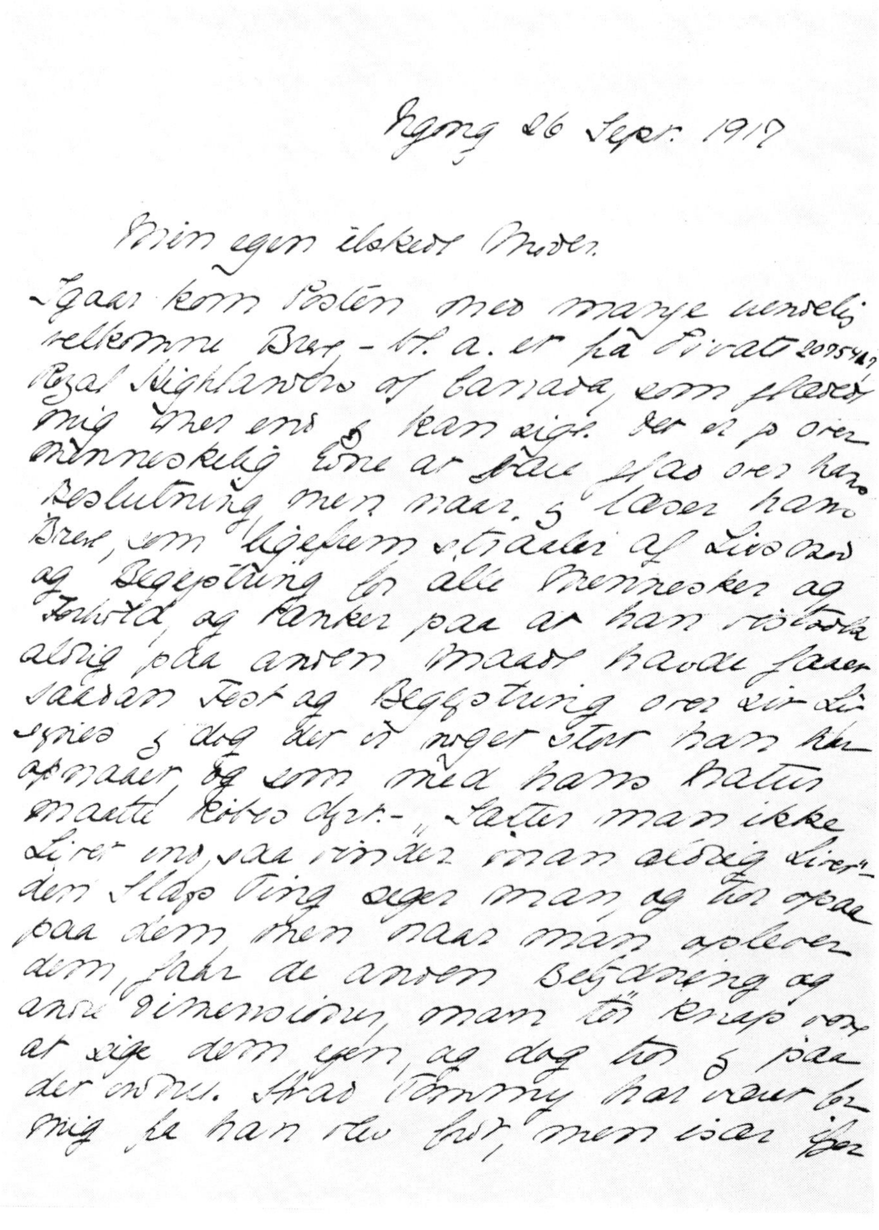

Ngong 26 Sept. 1917

Min egen elskede Moder.

Igaar kom Posten med mange uendelig velkomne Breve — bl. a. et fra Private 2075417 Royal Highlanders of Canada, som glæder mig mer end jeg kan sige. Det er jo over menneskelig Evne at blive glad over hans Beslutning, men naar jeg læser hans Breve, som ligefrem straaler af Livsglæde og Begejstring for alle Mennesker og Forhold, og tænker paa at han vistok aldrig paa anden Maade havde faaet saadan Fest og Begejstring over sit Liv, synes jeg dog der er noget stort han har opnaaet, og som med hans Natur maatte købes dyrt. — „Lader man ikke Livet ind, saa finder man aldrig Livet" — de store Ting siger man og tror ofte paa dem, men naar man oplever dem, faar de anden Betydning og andre Dimensioner, man tør knap nok at sige dem igen, og dog tror jeg paa det endnu. Hvad Tommy har været for mig før han rejste, men især før

First page of a letter to Ingeborg Dinesen (26 September 1917).

THE F

"A Great Success was
Residence, on' Oct. 5th,
managed to Indu

Baroness von Blixen takes Sir Northrup McMillan in hand to show him where he can best spend his money.

The first newspaper picture of Karen Blixen, photographed here with Sir Northrup McMillan (mentioned in letter to Ingeborg Dinesen dated 23 October 1918).

Thomas Dinesen 1919. Photographed by Juncker-Jensen.

To Ingeborg Dinesen

MBagathi Estate 22. 10. [1914]

. . . Fara has asked my permission to go out and trade for me for three months. The Somalis are a nomadic people and fall into deep depression if they have to stay in one place for long, so I feel it is a shame to force them to do that; even though they are actually content where they are, they have to have variety. At first he took it into his head that he wanted to go to school and learn to read; but I would not help him to do that because I think that leads to their becoming unhappy and useless. His restlessness has probably arisen because he has had a letter telling him that his wife in Somaliland has had a toto. We have long been looking forward to this event and counting on our fingers after my departure from Aden, as it was when he was there to meet me that he was married and the child was conceived, and now he is obliged to go out and earn some money for it. The Somalis are tremendously rich, I believe many of them are millionaires, but they put all their money into cattle, and live, dress and eat exactly as in the time of Abraham. It is a strange idea to a European: the striving for wealth, and great wealth at that, without any suggestion of luxury. I asked the Somalis if they would wear boots when they had earned enough money and were going home to Somaliland, but they repudiated that idea with hoots of derision. The Masai are the same. Many of their big chiefs have 50,000 head of cattle as well as great flocks of sheep; like the Somalis they are tremendous money-grubbers, but the chiefs live in identical houses, dress in the same sheepskin and live in exactly the same way as any other Masai. I don't know how they have succeeded in realizing this absolute equality. But anyway, Fara has promised that he will never leave my service. . .

One cannot help—despite ancient hatred of the Germans—reacting against the incredible boastfulness of the English; for instance, they are always saying that they are the "only people who have brains," and when they constantly say that the German guns are sheer rubbish, that not a single German soldier can shoot, and give lurid descriptions of the frightful atrocities committed by the Germans, while the English invariably behave like perfect gentlemen, one cannot go along with the colossal self-satisfaction. But that it would be the greatest disaster for Europe if the Germans won is without dispute, and it is frightful to think of them in France. As far as atrocities are concerned, I think all civilized people turn into savages in wartime. But it is probably the Germans who demonstrate their Hun tactics most shamelessly. . . .

I am so distressed to hear that Mama is unwell, and wonder if I will ever see her again. But it is probably a good thing that she is not aware of this war, which would have been so terrible for her. When you write about things at home I see it so clearly, and when I think of the shadow of war that hangs over all those peaceful places I can hardly grasp it. When I look towards the north I seem to see a huge conflagration in the sky, above where Denmark, Rungsted, the Sound must be. . . .

To Ellen Dinesen

MBagathi 26. 10. 1914

. . . A tragedy has just befallen my cat, which has had kittens out in the forest again; yesterday evening she came rushing in to the boys in the kitchen, bringing first one and then another kitten in her mouth, and they were covered with the horrible big black ants that literally devour one. We picked them off and put the kittens in a box, but last night she carried them out again, probably because she was afraid of Dusk, and this morning she came to me crying and wailing and made me follow her out into the forest to the place where she had kept them hidden, but by then there was nothing there but a swarm of ants and a little skin and bone. You have to be very careful with those ants as it is horrible if they get on you; they bore their whole heads into your flesh and find the most uncomfortable places.—

I have been reading some of Tolstoy's works and I can say that I have never come across such a brilliant person who seemed to me so utterly uncongenial. A great deal of what he writes is really repugnant to me, and I would prefer death a thousand times to a world in which his ideals were realized. On the other hand I have read an entertaining and excellent book, "La Revolte des Anges," by Anatole France, and two amusing Swedish books, "The Penholder," and a new one, "The Åbergson Firm," which would amuse Tommy, anyway. I am able to read a good deal out here, but the English books are too feeble for me, I find that nation quite, quite unbearable. What I think about so often, and will go and look at properly if I ever get home and they still exist, are the French Impressionists; altogether I feel a great longing for everything French and Italian, and how delightful it will be to get to see old and beautiful things again, if the Germans don't manage to destroy everything. . . .

To Ingeborg Dinesen

MBagathi Estate 18. 11. [1914]

. . . I have tried to put a little more order and cleanliness into the house, and I think it is going really well; I have also dismissed my old Somali cook and engaged another, who can't do much, but is otherwise honest and anxious to please, and I have tried to teach him some variety from the frightful English cuisine, so I have been spending most of my time in the kitchen and have really achieved quite a lot. It is very pleasant to be able to make one's friends happy, and the Swedes out here show a devout joy when presented with stuffed white cabbage and pancakes. . . . I think the boys out here are incredibly good; if one only shows patience, especially in explaining, and does not get irritated with them, they can learn everything and it pleases them no end to do something well. Our syces, for instance, keep the horses in prime condition, and my cook makes brown cabbage soup like the chief chef in the royal kitchens. If you could find a cookery book from 1830 to send me I should be overjoyed. The one that I have is too modern. . . .I have turned into a law breaker now because Fru Holmberg, who is always having words with her boys and beating them, had been hitting her boy and then insisting that he was about to hit her back. She and her bosom friend, Mrs. Gorringe, worked themselves up into a terrible state over this, sent a message to our District Commissioner at Dagoretti and tried to get the boy sentenced to 100 strokes of the kiboko and three years' imprisonment. The boy came and sought refuge here, shaking all over with terror, and I hid him in my boys' huts, and when I heard from Fru Holmberg that she was going to send some Askari to search the whole farm for him I let him go and hide himself in Kikuyu for a few days; after that he came back here to stay. Particularly now when so many men have gone away to the war there is complete hysteria among all these "lonely women" who go in terror of their boys; they are always getting into a panic, and the other evening Mrs. Gorringe came tearing up here in a state of complete frenzy because a cattle thief, possibly a murderer, had broken into her farm. Bror went over there and it turned out to be a harmless, extremely scared Kavirondo who had gone in there to ask directions.

A lot of this is due to their ignorance of the language, but also to the stupid way they behave. I know myself that I should never be afraid of a native. I kept this fugitive here for a time, but as Mesdames H. and G. were still doggedly pursuing him and this was really disturbing him and he was threatening to take a fearful revenge, I persuaded him today that it would be better to go and report himself, so he went with a letter from me to the District Commissioner, I hope he will be let off lightly. The kiboko does not do them much harm, but when they are put in prison they generally die.

It is always irritating to hear the white people here, especially the Englishwomen,—although some of the Swedes have learned it from them,—talking about having "laid the boys down and given them 25-50 and so on," as if it was something fine, although anybody can do that. They do not understand the language and beat them for a misunderstanding, so they are reduced to rags. The women are the worst. So the result is that they cannot get any boys, which is not surprising; I myself would certainly not go and work anywhere where there was a risk of being thrashed. None of our neighbors can get a boy and are furious with us; all the boys who were working here during the last rains are coming back now from as far away as Embu and Kisumu, we have hundreds more than we can use, and they work well here, but if we do not take them on they prefer to go back rather than work anywhere else. It is the same with houseboys.

It is remarkable how all the English agree that the biggest difficulty out here is the labor problem, and then do nothing about it except to shout at the government to tax the natives more heavily. My own experience has shown me that the labor problem is not difficult to solve. It never occurs to them that the natives out here do not *need* to work; they are more interested in entertainment: buying themselves a few luxuries, lamps, tobacco, etc. So the question is quite different from that at home. In contrast to the English, I think working conditions are ideal here, and unlike an English lady on the boat who said she would go anywhere and do anything if she could only be free of servants, I think one can put up with any sort of hardship if one has plenty of servants. . . .

To Ingeborg Dinesen

MBagathi 3. 12. 1914.

. . . I think the English are starting to look slightly askance at us, that is, at the Swedes, which is not so surprising actually, since every one of them sides with the Germans; often this is not very pleasant for me, since this house is a kind of meeting place for them, where they come to discuss the war and the future. But they have in fact behaved decently and volunteered for service, which is more than many of the English have done. Our neighbor Van de Weyer has made a collection to help the Belgians and the Danish and Swedish farmers are trying to improve their position with a generous donation to this fund from the Swedes and Danes at Ngong—but it is hard to raise money these days, God knows. It is unfortunate that Denmark and Sweden have no colonies; so one always feels a foreigner,—now, the English are particularly foreign to me, so it is lucky that I feel for the Somalis and natives like brothers. . . .

Poor Bror is in despair over his transport, as the Government has taken his wagons, and his oxen are dying. It would certainly have been a great advantage to this farm if they had laid a railroad to Nairobi. We have tried to solve the problem by making a contract with Swedo to make charcoal from the timber and now have 21 charcoal stacks burning; it is interesting to see it. We were thinking of going on a short safari at Christmas, but he thinks that if he goes away they will all (the oxen) die, like last time, so now I don't know what is going to happen.—

I am very busy training a completely ignorant cook. As I can't cook myself, and it has to be carried on in Swahili, it is hardly easy, but is actually not going at all badly. It is no worse getting one who knows nothing than one who has learned English cooking. I wonder whether the English ever eat any other sweets than sago pudding and roly-poly that's as heavy as lead?—My cook and I can now make perfect puff pastry of different types, custard flans, meringues, pancakes, layer cakes, various kinds of soufflé, cream horns, apple cake, chocolate pudding, cream puffs—and he is also good at all kinds of soup, bakes good bread and scones and roasts really well in our miserable little oven. I think it is very important to have attractive food and, especially, some variety. I have been thinking of making up a weekly menu, like those in prisons and workhouses; I really do arrange it out here so that we don't have the same thing every day.—You may find it hard to believe that my house is renowned for good food; the Swedes out here say that it is the most well run house according to Scandinavian taste in B.E.A., but then there aren't so many out here. (You must not repeat this bragging). . . .

Regarding lions—which Thomas ought to have kept to himself—I can only say that I do not believe that any normal person can live in lion country without trying to shoot them. Perhaps it is wrong from the moral point of view, but seen in relation to the lion itself I must say that if someone should come and shoot me in the full vigor of youth, so that I died in five minutes, without having any suspicion of it in advance, I would be *sincerely* grateful to them and not resent them standing looking at my last moments, with deep admiration for my greatness.—Nature's plan for human beings with a long decline and long, drawn-out suffering is so hard that it seems no disgrace to intervene with a brisk bullet (it is always disgraceful to wound, of course, but my little bullets don't do much harm when they don't hit the mark), and you have to be very unlucky in any kind of warfare to experience the same sufferings as, for instance, someone who dies of cancer.

Regarding mules, I have *no* sympathy for them, and neither would you have if you had suffered from their spitefulness. All our mules are fat and well cared for; but they would sooner be beaten and kicked and jabbed with sticks than get moving, and that is up to them. . . .

1915

The following letter is the only one in the collection originally written in English. Because of the war, censorship was imposed on all letters from British East Africa. These therefore had to be written in a language understood by the censor.

To Ingeborg Dinesen

MBagathi Estate 24.2.1915

My own dear darling Mother.

I have not heard from you for two months and had nearly given up the thought of writing as I thought all mail was stopped, but today I had one letter from Elle, with another from Cæcilie inlaid, and I will try my luck again and send off this. You must thank Elle a thousand times for her letter, you don't know what it means out here. They say there is a mail in Aden that has been lying there for months, and I hope it will come forward some day and bring good news from you all. All letters have now to be written in English. . . .

It has been fearfully dry and I dont know what the poor Natives shall do, as their shambas ["plots"] are absolutely black, the Masai and their cattle are dying by the Hundreds from Thirst and Heat. I have suffered a good deal from it too. Bror wrote a long letter to you—and in English too: but I tore it out because he was at that time very anxious about me and it was all too sad. But I am ever so much better now, though I have really been rather sick through empoisoning myself with Veronal.—I had not been able to sleep for some night and as you know that is not usual to me I grew very impatient with it—Elle will feel for me—and after I had tried one and two Powders of Veronal I took four the last night, and never thought I should wake up again. Bror came down by chance in the afternoon and tried to call me back to Life, but when he could wake me up I was vomiting(?) the whole time, and this went on for 2 days. After that he made me go to a Doctor in Nairobi who had a very careful look at me and ended by saying that he had never in his life met with such a healthy constitution. "You absolutely impress me," he said the whole time, "Your heart and lungs are the finest I have come over." But he thought the

Heat and dry weather had been a little too much for me and gave me several tonics that I dont believe much in. . . .

I am going out on Safari with Fagerskiöld on Monday, for about 2 months to Lakepea, Aberdaire and Kenia, it is cooler there than here and I am delighted to get out. There are Buffaloes there, and sometime Elephants, but at any rate it is good to come out and see new places. Bror has arranged everything so excellent, he is splendid at that, he makes everything so easy for me.—I hope to find my Garden a little less like Sahara when I come back, and that the Veranda will be quite finished, already now it is a lovely thing to have and we are nearly always staying there, but there are no stairs and it is high to climb. . . .

I have got 3 more dogs now, one I got as a present from a young Masai warrior, it is the ugliest dog I have seen. Fara is always bringing me presents too, old Somali Embroideries and weapons, spears, knives, and shield, with Silver Handles, Somalis are always very great in Gifts.—Now Bror has made a bath ready for me and is crying that I must not sit up so late, so now Goodbye to you all, excuse this stupid letter, you dont know how idiotic I feel when I shall express myself in English.- Goodbye and keep well and happy. I hope I shall hear from you soon.—Goodbye.

Yours Tanne

By this time Karen Blixen was already seriously afflicted with the syphilis that she had contracted in her marriage with Bror Blixen. In the third yearbook of the Karen Blixen Society, Blixeniana 1978, *Professor Mogens Fog, her doctor for many years, gave a detailed account of the course of her illness, based on documentary case history material and his own notes. Among other things he writes: "There was never the least sign, in Karen Blixen's case, of syphilis of the brain, only a painful but limited infection of the spine. She must quickly have recognized the symptoms, for as early as 1914 she consulted a doctor in Nairobi and was treated with mercury tablets. She did not improve. She wrote to her mother in May 1915 that she was ill with a high fever. The doctor advised her to return to Denmark and she arrived in Copenhagen in June.*

"She went immediately to see Dr. C. Rasch, professor of skin and venereal diseases, who took charge of her treatment when she was at home during the following 10–12 years.

"She was obliged to undergo several lengthy courses of treatment in the Copenhagen national hospital as well as receiving ambulatory treatment. In his case journal for the last stay in hospital in 1925, Rasch wrote a resume of the course of the disease and the investigations.

"From July to December 1915, five Wassermann blood tests were made, (a specific syphilis reaction) only the first showing positive results, the rest proving normal. In September 1915 the spinal fluid showed a greatly increased number of white blood corpuscles, slight increase in later tests, otherwise normal results, at no point was there a positive Wassermann reaction. The early normalization of the Wassermann reaction in the blood signifies that 'active' syphilis and thus the risk of transmitting infection had ceased at the second stage. . . .In 1915 Rasch gave two series of salvarsan injections, but this treatment was apparently not yet in use in Nairobi. . . ."

To Ingeborg Dinesen

Paris 28.5.1915

Do not be the slightest bit worried. *All is well.*
My own dear little Mother.—

I have just been having lunch with Baron Bech Frijs and he said that if I made haste I could send a letter with a Swede who is going home today. I think it is better than telegraphing and send this with him to say that I am here in Paris on my way to London to talk to a specialist in tropical diseases there. I have actually been rather ill again and the doctor in Nairobi prescribed a change of air at home for me. They thought that if I did not leave right away there was a risk that my fever would never go or that I might get "Black Water" which you can get from taking too much quinine (I think it is a kind of bladder disease) and especially when they said that after this disease you risk being unable to have children,—(but you don't need to talk about this)—so Bror and I decided there was no point in my staying out there any longer, so I sold all my trading shauri ["ventures"] and took ship a week later, and have had an excellent voyage and already I am no end better and have got quite fat.—

It seems that in London they give some kind of injections for malaria that cure you completely; a doctor in Nairobi gave me one but that merely caused severe blood poisoning in my arm,—but perhaps it won't be necessary, and in any case I will come home as soon as I can, but only for a short visit. You can imagine how upset I was at leaving Bror; please give my love to Aunt Clara and tell her that he is *very well,* and I will come and give her a big hug from him right away. I am staying with Henrik and you can send a wire here when you have received this letter. I had Fara with me as far as Marseilles, as I was rather ill when I left Mombasa, but sent him home from there. Here I am at the same boarding house where I stayed in 1910; the Swedish Attaché and Attaché Militaire live here as well. I heard the guns today when I was out looking at the roses in the Bagatelle; they were shooting at a zeppelin that flew right over us.—

Dearest Mother, how wonderful it will be to see you and everyone. You really must not be worried about me;—I *really* am much better and feeling strong, and it is absolutely delightful here. I am not in the least afraid of submarines, I will go via Bergen and will probably get home about 15 June. I embrace you all and am longing to see you.

Your Tanne.

After her return to Denmark in June 1915, Karen Blixen stayed for over a year with her mother at Rungstedlund, apart from the total period of three months she spent in the hospital for tests and treatment. In 1916 her two sisters were married. After having passed his final examinations at the College of Technology, her brother Thomas expressed his desire to volunteer for service with the French army. Both his father and grandfather had won the cross of the Legion of Honor as officers in the French army, and Thomas Dinesen felt that he too must take part in the struggle to halt Germany's threatening advance in Europe. As he himself wrote in Tanne, *"in the summer of 1916 I presented my decision to Mother, who immediately grew very distressed and seemed unable to understand me. I then asked Tanne if she would help me, and after she had talked to Mother alone for several hours, complete agreement was reached. Now I met with nothing but warm and affectionate support until I came home, unwounded, from the Canadian army in January 1919.*

"During the summer of 1916 Bror spent several months in Denmark and Tanne returned to Kenya with him in November full of confidence in the future of the farm. Because of the exigencies of the war, everything that Kenya produced was fetching high prices in Europe—it looked as though Tanne and Bror had found the right place for their future prospects. A large limited company, The Karen Coffee Co. Ltd. was now formed, various members of the family invested money in it, bought shares, and a bank loan of one million was obtained."

Now Karen and Bror Blixen were able to realize their wish for a larger and more elegant home. The company bought the house and land that Karen Blixen described in Out of Africa. *On 10 November 1916 Karen Blixen and her husband traveled via Gothenburg to London where they took rooms in the Carlton Hotel. They had originally planned to go to Marseilles via Paris, but as Bror Blixen's brother-in-law Gustaf Hamilton was to accompany them to Africa and they had been warned not to use the Marseilles-Africa route because of the danger of torpedo attacks in the Mediterranean, they thought it advisable to take a ship from London and managed to get reservations on the otherwise fully booked* "Balmoral Castle," *which was to sail around the Cape to Durban.*

Karen Blixen writes to her mother in November 1916, "I felt a really deep grief over not getting to Paris. But one cannot expect to travel during a great war in the same way as in peacetime. It is remarkable how much of a 'deep sea sailor' one becomes when one has once tried it; the great routes take hold of one with an irresistible power and it is a real joy to me to drive down Piccadilly. If I ever grow rich I will live in a great city; there is something inexpressibly delightful about them. And it is quite wonderful how the sight of the very first soldier completely alters one's view of life. It is painful, but mostly because one is confronted with the greatness, with the emotional force of vast events, with life and death in the ordinary, businesslike figure, with shame for one's own little sorrows and—strangely enough,—with a kind of bitter grieving over not participating in it oneself. Of course I thought of Tommy—of our own Tommy I should say, for they are all Tommies here—and I understand him so well. The terrible thing is that the war really is going on; it is almost unavoidable being caught up in it in one way or another, and here in London one feels what one has so often felt an indication of at home, that if one misses it, one perhaps misses life itself—("in flight from fate there is no happiness. The outward gain brings only inward sadness"). The great storms have risen, and one is in their power, and then one meets that feeling of fellowship that is lacking in everyday life; it gives strength, but how can one find strength enough?. . ."

The next day in a letter to her mother she writes, "Just a word or two to say that we are well and tomorrow are leaving delightful London, where I would have liked to stay longer. Every minute has been taken up with shopping, calls at police stations and legations, banks, steam ship offices, and so on. Today we visited Queen Alexandra, who was quite exceptionally gracious and kind, later we lunched with Henrik, then on to the Swedish Legation and several shops, and then the Reventlows dined with us here. . . ."

The ship finally sailed about 20 November.

1916

To Ingeborg Dinesen

Union Castle Line
R.M.S. "Balmoral Castle"
Monday 27 November [1916]

. . . We should get to the Cape on the 8th and stay there two days. Then it is five or six days' voyage to Durban, with short calls en route at East London and Chinde; we have to leave this ship at Durban and wait for another smaller one from the British India Line, and at most that will be a fortnight. . . .

This is a fine ship and not nearly full, but those people who are on board are nothing special, which is natural enough in wartime when no one travels who is not obliged to. There are a number of officers here, and most of them have been at the front, but the English are so strange, they are always absolutely the same whatever may have happened to them, yes, in fact from the time they are ten until they are ninety. They think of nothing at all except their deck games and if one did not know there was a war on, one could be with them for the entire voyage and never discover it. . . .

Bror is terribly kind and thoughtful about helping me and he himself is enjoying the restful time on board before he has to get going in Africa. He has so many plans for organizing Swedo and the coastal land that we are going to be busy. I am *much* looking forward to arranging my house. . . .

To Ingeborg Dinesen

Union Castle Line
[1916]

My dearest Mother.

We get to the Cape tomorrow and I will send off my letters,—and hope to find some telegrams there. It has really been a lovely trip, ideal during the last few days, but probably the worst is yet to come, especially the voyage from Durban in a small boat; but one must be glad of each day that goes well. Today there are signs that we are approaching land, there are numbers of albatross flying around the ship, and you cannot imagine anything more beautiful than the great birds with their sailing flight, and hundreds of dolphins are leaping around the ship. . . .

It is a strange thing in this war that all the English as one man stick to the futile and hollow slogan, Keep cheery. They certainly take it so literally that they yodel and sing negro spirituals every evening, get up to the most absurd pranks on deck every night, promenading in full dress and making fun of everything. I have the feeling that they do it because they don't dare to be serious; they cannot do it, and are afraid of the vacuity of their own character,—but perhaps that is wrong. At any rate it is strange to be among people who are at war and hard pressed for weeks and to find that the enthusiasm, the spirit, the inspiration, they might be expected to communicate, is absolutely lacking. Of course there is the exception among them who realizes the situation, but it is quite alarming to see the others carrying on with their jokes about poor old Kaiser Bill and The Clown Prince, when one thinks of their adversaries who certainly know what deadly earnest the war is. . . .

To Ingeborg Dinesen

Hotel Edward
Beach, Durban.
Christmas Eve 1916

We have bought a car here in Durban after hearing by telegraph from Nairobi that there were none to be had there. Gustaf has bought himself one, too; his is a four-seater but ours is only a two-seater as of course we don't need an omnibus up on the farm. It is great fun to have it here, and the day after tomorrow we are going on an expedition up-country, to see various farms that have been recommended to us through the Swedish Consulate, cattle farms, dairies, sugar farms, and so on. We are to spend the weekend with some people, the Hon. Joseph Baynes, who go in for large-scale breeding of Friesland cattle and horses; their place is called Nels [*sic*] Rust. We may get up as far as Ladysmith and Colenso, on the first day we are going from here to Pieter Maritzburg. I am very much looking forward to it. . . .

The other day we drove out to an absolutely delightful place, Amanzimtoti, with a splendid beach, like Fanø. I am learning to drive and it is tremendous fun to drive oneself.—

We have given up any idea of celebrating Christmas Eve; it is quite hopeless to do anything out here. It will just be a toast to Absent Friends and perhaps a few flowers and candles. . . .

1917

To Ingeborg Dinesen

Hotel Edward. Beach, Durban.
7 January [1917]

On the 27th we left here for Maritzburg. . . . We had received an invitation, through the Swedish Consul, from an old farmer, the Hon. Joseph Baynes, who has rationalized the agriculture of Natal, and the visit was really interesting and enjoyable, and they were some of the nicest people I have ever met. His property is called Nel's Rust,—Nel's Rest—and Nel was Botha's maternal grandfather; it is like a whole little kingdom on its own with hundreds of fine animals and of natives, who for the most part are second generation and born there, and who appear to love old Baynes. He was a great character, lives for his farm, but very well up in the Bible and Shakespeare; he knew everybody in England and had been a guest in the highest places, when he was at home, and had taken part in the coronation of both King Edward and King George, but he would not leave Nel's Rust for anything in the world.

A year or two ago he was ill and went back to Europe for a big operation, and all his natives came and implored him to have his body brought back to be buried at Nel's Rust; when he was recovering in England he went to a big gramophone company and got them to record a talk in Kaffir for all his people, saying that he was alive and coming back to them, and this was sent out and played to them on the veranda; their man out there said that he had never seen people as moved as his natives were. . . .

To Ingeborg Dinesen

Hotel Edward, Beach, Durban.
10 January 1917.

Dearest Mother.

The mail goes tomorrow so you will have a last greeting from Durban. Yesterday we went to Maritzburg again to see a brick works, and as far as we could tell it would be an ideal thing for Karen to start. The expenditure would not be very large and with a town that is growing at the rate that Nairobi is one would think there should be great possibilities. . . .

12th.—My letter did not go off yesterday, but as the mail is not going as advertised anyway, it does not much matter. Bror and the Belgian Rolin, who is a clever little chap, were in Maritzburg yesterday arranging a new enterprise, the establishment of a blanket factory—though luckily with Belgian millions. It's not at all a bad plan; as things are now, quantities of wool are transported from the Free State to Europe and brought back as blankets. The Belgian has a friend who has a big blanket factory back in Belgium, which only makes a small profit now; he met him here in Durban, on his way back to Belgium after fighting in East Africa, and they spoke of it to Bror, who then went up to Maritzburg to talk about it with old Baynes. It is really fortunate for us to have made his acquaintance, he is considered to be the leading man in all that concerns farming in South Africa, and he regards Bror as a son and predicts an enormously great future for him. He immediately wanted to have a part in their factory, set it up on his own land, put £10,000 into it himself and act as chairman of the board. . . .

To Ingeborg Dinesen

British India Steam Navn. Co. Ltd.
S.S. "Karoa" 18.1.1917.

Dearest Mother.

A mail boat is going ashore to Beira today so I am sending a few lines to tell you we are well and at last approaching Frydenlund, for which I have the most incredible longing. . . .

One tiresome thing is that the whole ship is crawling with ants that get everywhere, into suitcases, beds and food and are a perfect pest. I don't think anything can be done about it so it is a good thing that there is only one week more.—I have started painting a little on board; I bought some water colors in Durban and have painted Gustaf Hamilton and it has turned out reasonably well.—Bror has begun to write a book on Africa, I think it is going to be first class. . . .

To Ingeborg Dinesen

Brit. India Steam Navn. Co. Ltd.
S.S. "Karoa" 22.1.1917.

. . . Bror is very impatient to get home and get started on all his plans. He intends to have at Karen: cattle, pigs, chicken, bees, flowers, brick works, a coconut nursery on the coast.—And we think it will go really well. Also we think that we can profit in various ways through Gustaf's company; for instance, they intend to establish a big sugar plantation and factory and Bror thinks he can get the land cheaply for them, and thus Karen would get hold of 1,000 acres of sugar land, from which they could sell the sugar to the factory,— Gustaf is a very nice chap, but I am absolutely sure he is no business man, and as a whole I have no faith in soldiers in business, their ways of thinking differ too much. . . .

To Ingeborg Dinesen

Brit.India Steam Navn. Co. Ltd.
S.S. "Karoa"
23.1.17.

Dearest Mother.

We should get in to Mombasa early tomorrow, it seems almost incredible. The ship is going on to Aden so there is a chance that this letter may get through quickly.

We went ashore at Zanzibar yesterday, but as the hotel was very bad we came on board again for the night. It is a beautiful place and probably very interesting, if you get to know it, but they have built so many new corrugated iron houses and sheds in among the old Arab houses that one doesn't notice them until one gets right into the streets. . . . We took a long car trip around the island and saw a lot of plantations and nurseries and the Sultan's villas which are beautifully situated. When the English took over B.E.A. they made a contract with the Sultan of Zanzibar to stop all slave trading; he must have made huge profits from that, as the East African protectorate alone pays him £70,000 a year in compensation. The English Government also contracted with him to find labour to replace the slaves, as the Arabs will not work; so you see a great many Kikuyu who come down from our region to work on Zanzibar in settlements which are run and controlled by the English. The Sultan, for whom life out there has lost its excitement, was in Paris. We saw the old slave auction markets and numerous ruins of old Arabian fortresses and towers. Just outside the harbor the mast of the "Pegasus," which was sunk by the "Königsberg" at the very beginning of the war, is sticking up out of the water.—The whole of Zanzibar is a dazzling white town with many very picturesque corners and streets. . . .

Tomorrow I should be meeting Fara and hope to hear from him that all is well at home.—We should be in our own home on Friday, but then it will be eleven weeks since we left Rungsted: I hope I will not have to make this trip again. . . .

A telegram dispatched from MBagathi on 26 January 1917 and received on 29 January reported that Karen Blixen and her husband had arrived at the farm.

To Ingeborg Dinesen

MBagathi 1.2.1917.

My dearest Mother.

At last we are home again! It seems like a dream to be here, and like a dream to walk around and look at everything again. One of you at home must come out some day and link up the world at home with this one; now it seems far too much like two separate existences.—Everything is going well. The farm here looks excellent and at Swedo it is all much better than ever before. Strangely enough it has been raining and continues to rain every day, which is not normal at this time of year; we hope that this does not mean that we won't get any rain in April when we will be planting. The coffee is flourishing although it has been somewhat set back by frost.

The house here has been improved beyond all recognition since I left. The loggia and the veranda are completely covered with creepers and shaded; a large bow-window has been put into my bedroom which makes the room twice as big and very airy, the garden is green and filled with flowers and the park quite delightful with thick green grass under the trees. But all the same I am looking forward to moving over to Swedo; I have been over to see it, and the house there is so beautifully cool, the rooms so high and airy and there will be the most wonderful view when I have had some trees taken down around it. There is a good deal to be done, as the rain has got in and it is somewhat dilapidated, but I hope to be in after a month and then will send you many grateful thoughts.—

Fara came to meet me at Mombasa and it was really touching to see him again. Hassan and old Ismail have been out to see me, all our people are really happy that we are home again. It was such a pleasure to be driving up through the country again seeing all the game. . . .

Compared with all that I saw in Natal this is a model farm and the land here is better than anything I have seen elsewhere. Bror will be writing to Uncle Aage about everything here. It was a shame for Bror that Bursell gave notice the first evening we were back. He can no doubt get a better-paid post out here; the rates of pay have risen drastically and he is considered to be very efficient. However it is because we have helped him that he is in such a favorable position now; but you cannot rely on loyalty from that kind of person. Now Bror has agreed to his demands,—£60 a month plus 10%—until he gets a reply from Uncle Aage, meanwhile we must see about getting another man out from home, preferably a Dane. . . .

To Ingeborg Dinesen

Uncle Mogens's Farm
7.2.1917.

. . . Gustaf and I have been here for a couple of days. Bror came up here with us but went off again; he hasn't had a spare moment since we came back. In the two days that he was here we went around looking at cattle farms—he is really very keen on starting cattle and wants to get to know as much as possible about it. Today he has gone to a cattle auction at Naivasha; Bursell is joining him and they are going on from there to look at flax farms at Gil Gil. . . .

There is a lot of game here; yesterday after we had been over to Hopcraft's farm to look at his cattle, on the way home we shot from the car partridge, guinea fowl, dik-dik, waterbuck and serval cat. I have not heard any lions, probably because of this unusual raining season. Normally they come to the lake to drink, but now there is water everywhere. . . .

We go home the day after tomorrow. Up to now Gustaf has been staying with us but he is now moving to Rundgren's, which is very nice; partly because one is in need of a change when one has been together with someone for over three months, for all meals and every hour of the day, partly because I will have more time to concentrate on my removal to Swedo,—"Frydenlund" or "Ermitage," as of course the English cannot pronounce the former. I often go over there and am constantly discovering new things which I look forward to having in my possession—for instance, a really big library, with all the works of Kipling, Stevenson, Wilde, Bret Harte, Selma Lagerlöf, Bjørnson, Heidenstam, in very fine bindings and clearly never opened. It is always beautifully cool at Swedo, and there will be an absolutely glorious view. Recently I walked through the forest fronting the house with a white man, Anderson, and marked out the trees, and when one looks through them one can see right across the plain and the mountains on the other side. . . .

To Ingeborg Dinesen

Lumbwa 2.17.[February 1917]

Dearest Mother.

We are here at Lumbwa to study flax. According to what we have learned it seems to be the best enterprise of all out here and Bror is very keen for Karen to go in for it. . . . We spent two days at the East African Syndicate's farm at Gil Gil, also to study flax. An old farmer, Buchanan, is manager there; he and his wife are in the same position there as tenant farmers at home and are very congenial. From there we drove over to see another farm owned by a man called Cole, the nicest man I have met out here. The big cattle farmers live out there in the district around Gil Gil and they are likable people, and it is a pleasanter life than on the coffee farms around Nairobi, but I do not think so profitable. Cole has never shot on his farm, so he has game wandering about just as in the Deer Park [in Denmark] and an incredible number of birds on a large lake. We had lunch with him and enjoyed ourselves greatly. It is rather unusual to travel around like this but people are extraordinarily hospitable, and I have Fara with me which is an invaluable help and joy to me. . . .

I do so much want to start painting again and hope I will have time when I get everything in order at home. Some time when I get back to Denmark I will go to art college. I think that one must have a certain amount of experience before one can assimilate one's personality in some kind of art, but I think that later one can then transform it again into the art; I believe that I have much more feeling for color and line now than a few years ago. . . .

To Ingeborg Dinesen

MBagathi 13.3.1917.

My own dearest Mother.—

I don't think I have written for some time, but we have been out traveling again and did not get home until yesterday.

—I have only just received the news of Daisy's death; Else wrote to me about it, that was good of her,—and it was a terribly great grief to me. I feel that so much color and radiance has gone from life with her passing, and for me so much of my youth. Although I have seen so little of her in recent years there are few people I will miss more and now that she is dead I realize how much I have indeed thought about her and thought how, if we ever made any money, we could do something for her.—She was a wonderful person and one of the best I have known. I don't think that one can say that she was unhappy. She felt more joy in life than most people, she was always engaged in something and had so many interests and she was loved as few people are. I would gladly exchange my life for Daisy's.—

I find it impossible to comprehend that I will never see her again. I constantly think of her at Assisi and of how amazing it was that such a modern person could step right into that world and belong there, as she did.—Poor Henrik, I feel so sorry for him; it was good that Daisy was with him when she died; he is the only one who was really good to Daisy, and although one can say that he is the only person she wronged in her life, still I think she did him more good than harm. The time he spent with her is probably the only period when he was really alive, and he must realize that himself. There are so few people who can lift life up out of the mundane run and give it poetry and in spite of everything I believe that what one feels most for them is gratitude.—

We have just returned from a trip up to the farm at Uasin Gishu. It is a long and trying journey; I did not really want to go up there, but because Bror always wants me to go with him and see all the different branches of Karen Coffee Co., and also because I think it is wise, I agreed to go. . . .On the way home we went to the annual Government sale at Naivasha, it is an event here corresponding to the Derby; it was interesting to see it and to meet a few people. Lord Delamere and Galbraith Cole were there, the Buchanans, with whom I stayed at Gil Gil, Van de Weyer and various officers I had met in the Reserve during the war. I wish we had gone in for cattle instead of coffee at the beginning, it is a pleasanter life and one meets nicer people; but now we are going to start a model dairy here no doubt many cattle people will come to see it. . . .

I have made a contract with Fara, for him to supply me with eggs, butter, meat, poultry and vegetables for £2.10 a week. I think he will make a profit out of it, but it will save me always having to get supplies, which is quite troublesome. He will get the same amount no matter how many people are here, and it is an advantage to be able to budget and be *sure* of having enough money to go around. . . .

To Ingeborg Dinesen

Frydenlund 24.3.1917.

My dear beloved Mother.

This is my first letter from Frydenlund, we have now moved in and I am extremely glad to be here—despite living in a temporary state of chaos. The workmen have not done a thing since I gave them their orders two months ago, and the roof has been broken in and the floor up—but it is still lovely to be here. It is always cool, and wonderful to be in large rooms again; to me they feel like state apartments, although at home they would probably not appear very impressive. . . .

I have started to paint a little again but for the moment there is too much muddle here and not enough time.— I am just longing to get out shooting again. I have got hold of a gun from Sjögren,—with the house,—which is excellent. I have to restrict myself to pigeon shooting here, yesterday afternoon I shot 21. . . .

You should hear how they talk about von Lettow out here. As the greatest genius of the age. It is really interesting to have known him. They say that his tactics are based on the sole aim of keeping the war going out here until peace is made in Europe so that Germany can press demands for G.E.A.—and that he is maintaining this with incredible brilliance and perseverance.

Fara is standing here behind my chair engaging me in conversation whenever I put down my pen. When Bror is away we always have very pleasant evenings together; he tells me all the news from Somali circles. . . .

To Ingeborg Dinesen

Frydenlund 31.3.17

. . . They have brought in a complete state of conscription out here now and all the whites must carry out some kind of work, and all the blacks who are not absolutely essential to the farms. It makes life very difficult at times, but of course it is good if it leads to an end of the crazy war out here. It is good that the news from home is optimistic—but alas, there is so little. I have had three letters from you since I came back to Africa; the last mail boat brought mail from London but nothing at all from home, for some reason.—

We now have a really good mechanic on the farm and I am having driving lessons every day. I can drive quite well, but there are many things such as small repairs that it is a good thing to know something about. It is a really excellent car and indispensable to Bror, who has so many concerns to see to.—

The farm is flourishing, although in need of a good soaking of rain. It is not nearly as hot as when I was out here before and you can be sure that I rejoice each hour of the day over this lovely cool house. My household now consists of

1. *Fara,* who fills the post of butler and looks after all the shopping.
2. *Ali,* cook, a really decent Somali.
3. *Juma* and
4. *Esa,* houseboys, both very good.
5. *Abdullah,* Somali.—

6. *Kebrik*, Nandi— }
7. *Kamao*, Kikuyu— } totos, i.e., small boys between 8 and 12.

They should certainly be able to keep this reasonably small house in order. I have ordered a Danish flag from an old Dane in Nairobi. There is a Swedish one and an English one here, but I don't want to raise them before I have the Danish one to put on top. . . .

To Ingeborg Dinesen

Ngong, Nairobi, 19.4.1917

. . . You've no idea how delightful it is becoming out here as the work in the park and on the house progresses. One thing that gives me great joy is that there is the most lovely bird song all around the house, exactly like nightingales,—and I wonder whether they are in fact nightingales? We have most of the migratory birds from home here, swallows, which are just gathering now in big flocks ready to fly away, and which you perhaps may see on the telegraph wires along Strandvejen, and storks that stroll about the meadows on the farm here just as if they were in a Danish marsh. Bror thinks we should call the place Bird Song. I can't get the English to pronounce Frydenlund,—*Fuglsang* even less I am sure—but the natives call this house Bogani; it means The Forest, and that is a good name for it, too. . . .

Bror is very pleased with von Huth and thinks that he keeps his books very well, is very quick and clear and a great help. I don't think that it is easy to keep the books for Bror, as he is never very accurate about all the details; so it is a good thing that von Huth can manage it. . . .

Life here is very like it was in Denmark about the year 1700. We get mail at most only once a month, the roads are impassable as soon as the weather is bad; for instance, it is impossible for me to get into Nairobi at the moment. Bror rides in and out, but as you can only ride at a walk in the mud I find it too much bother. . . .

To Ingeborg Dinesen

Ngong, Nairobi, 26.4.1917

. . . I think it is very difficult to start off in a new country under new conditions without making mistakes and experiencing difficulties to begin with. It is probably easier for people like Kjellberg, who is extremely cautious and restricts himself to things that have been thoroughly tried out by others before him, and does not look around for new possibilities; but then nothing new will ever be achieved. The fact that communications are so bad because of the war makes it very difficult for both Bror and the management at home. Under normal conditions Uncle Aage would be able to come out here or to send a reliable man to get a clear idea of how things are going.—We must hope that it will not be too long before this is possible. . . .

It costs just as much to live out here as Bror gets in salary. Probably people at home would think this quite a lot, but everything is so costly here, and also we have to be prepared to receive guests at any time. Do you not think that it is a rather unfair arrangement that if the farm yields £10,000 net profit (and we get 10% of this) in the future, we are only to receive £50 in salary? For this would precisely show that we have done a good job here, and that should be an unmitigated joy and also reward for us. Do you think that when that situation arises you could get this changed for us? . . .

There are times, when I feel that there is so much lacking in the life here and that I am so far away from you all,—especially from you,—I could wish that I had a goal different from purely and simply earning money. I do not think it is going to be easy to get home. For after all, Bror and I have very different ideas about so many things. I hope that he does not get the idea of working out here in order to buy back Dallund, and then, if we do not have children, leave it to Carl's boy or Hans's, I sometimes think that getting Katholm back would be an aim worth enduring much for. But actually I am not so tremendously devoted to Katholm. . . .

To Ingeborg Dinesen

Ngong, Nairobi 1.6.1917

. . . I am sitting writing in Bror's smoking room or office,—at Frydenlund,—the only room that is in order so far. . . . We are *very* fond of this room; it has a ten-foot-wide window on to the veranda and is always beautifully cool and shaded; it is furnished with Sjögren's things and some of our own from MBagathi, and it is a great advantage for Bror to have a peaceful room where he can write and keep his papers. There is only one door, as in the office at home, so there is no through passage, and only people who have something to do come in here. It is also very nice for me to have a really comfortable room where I can be undisturbed when I am alone at home some evenings. . . .

My two little dogs, Askari (the policeman) and Banja (the rat), are here; Bror has taken Dusk with him,—he cannot be without him and takes him into hotels and in the car. These two were just born when

I arrived, and are so comical, they are the image of Dusk in both appearance and character. These deerhounds are very faithful, and intelligent, sweet dogs. Unfortunately, to my great sorrow I have lost Dawn, their mother,—she was taken by a leopard. She was a particularly sweet and intelligent dog and unlike Dusk was most attached to me, but she was far too daring. All the dogs were asleep on the veranda and in the middle of the night I suddenly heard a terrible noise, and when I went out no dogs were to be seen; after a long search I found the two puppies trembling in a corner, but there has been no sign of Dawn since. . . .

Out here the war is becoming a heavier and heavier burden for us, it makes everything difficult and some things impossible, and the worst thing of all is that they have to take so many natives down to G.E.A. as porters, so the labor problem casts a longer and longer grim shadow over all the plans. I am glad that I have such good boys, Fara, Juma, who was at MBagathi keeping that in order when we arrived, a quite elderly boy, Esa, who is truly a treasure,—he had been fourteen years in his last post,—a really good Somali cook, who, however, I strongly suspect of being a thief, and a little nine-year-old Somali boy, Abdullah, who causes me great amusement. He behaves toward me just like an old nanny; but at that age black people are far cleverer and more reliable than whites of the same age. . . .

The day before yesterday Bror shot a python fifteen feet long. . . . We were out walking around the farm not far away from here, but I had just said prophetically to Bror that I thought there were pythons here when we saw the grass being moved by a big snake. The grass is very tall now, so it was chiefly through luck that Bror hit it,—though more or less with a grazing shot, so it was enraged, raised itself up and struck out to every side. With their long, tremendously strong bodies they can hit out at two places twenty feet apart in one second, and I don't know of anything that looks more ferocious. I was quite beside myself with fright, because stupid Dusk kept jumping after it, and it bit him in the nose and drew blood, and I, who could only see its head and part of its body above the grass, thought it was one of the great black, poisonous mambas. Then Bror shot it in the head. It is beautiful skin and I have a mind to send it to Hellstern in Paris and have a pair of shoes made out of it.

We now have over a hundred acres of flax on the farm. It is so beautiful, it looks like a field at home, and the fresh bright green color is something unique out here where all the colors are so dried up. It smells lovely, like a forest floor with anemones in the spring. The grass that I planted under the trees around the house is beautifully green too; it has had an unusually good start with this heavy continuous rain. I brought a lot of palms and flowering shrubs back from the botanical gardens at Durban, which I have planted, and they are all flourishing. . . .

To Ingeborg Dinesen

Ngong 11.6.17

. . . You can imagine how the news about Ea moved and gladdened me more than I can say. I only hope that all goes well and she will not be too indisposed this summer; but she will be looked after as well as anyone in the world, and how lovely for her it must be to have you nearby, my beloved little Mother. I think it is most delightful to think of Ea as a mother, I think she will feel the greatest joy and happiness in her child and it is bound to love her. Just think how she will sing to it, all Lillebror's songs and everything that brought beauty and brightness to, and in a fashion enclosed, the whole of her youth. . . .

I do not think that you need worry because Viggo apparently does not appreciate Ea sufficiently; she has written to me time after time that he makes such a fuss over her and is so indescribably kind to her, and she is so happy with him. On the whole I do not think that one can judge the relationship between husband and wife in this way; I think that as a rule it is difficult for newlyweds to know how to behave toward each other when others are present, and the teasing manner they exhibit is one form of expression that they find, while the intimacy and sincerity they show each other when they are alone together is something others never see, but is infinitely more significant. . . .

Perhaps you may think, Mother dear, that this news is difficult for me to hear, but in fact it brings nothing but happiness; I rejoice so fervently with Ea in her felicity,—and strangely enough it has been hearing about children that are nothing at all to do with me that has been painful. But another thing is that I have certainly not given up hope of having a child,—on the contrary, I feel extraordinarily sure that it will happen, as if it had been promised me. I feel that everything we have been through has given meaning to both past and future, and although of course there might be some other meaning in it that I cannot see, yet I am bound to feel that this would be the greatest and most beautiful thing. Rasch did not want us to start a child for the first year, but when that is ended I will still not be so old that it should not be possible, and then I think that we are both getting better every day. Rasch is a *very* clever man, and I will be grateful to him for the rest of my life; I really think that it was a great miracle he procured for me. . . .

But just at present I am not very well; I think I have a touch of sunstroke and I am making use of the time while Bror is in Mombasa to stay in bed. My boys are so exceptionally good, and in this lovely cool clean house it is a real pleasure, almost like the National Hospital. I think it might be a very wise idea to spend a week like this every third or fourth month. Life out here in the strong light with so much of the time spent outside in the air, and that air so high and rare, makes extra measures necessary. I have a little Somali boy aged nine, a nephew of Fara, Abdulla, who is a great joy to me . . . the Somalis are not permitted to touch dogs, and never own them, so my dogs are his first experience in that respect and he is so preoccupied with them, especially the two little puppies, that he has not much time left over for anything else. It is most likely that when we are not looking there is an infringement of the Prophet's prohibition, for they love him in return and are always at his heels. They are really so sweet and are the very image of Dusk. . . .

To Ingeborg Dinesen

Ngong 14.6.17

My own beloved Mother.

Just now one single letter from you arrived—either delayed from the last mail or by a later one—written on my birthday. I must reply right away, even though briefly, because you write that Tommy is sailing to America via Bergen. Beloved Mother, how I wish I could be with you and hold you in my arms. I think we have exactly the same way of thinking about that dearly loved boy, that what counts most of all is his happiness, that he must be enabled to stop feeling useless and isolated, and join in the society of others, feel himself a part of life,—"and if one does not set life at risk, then life is never won." I believe that Tommy is so clearly aware of his own faults and failings, of his difficulty in getting started on anything and making a success of it, and probably he can only escape from this by being carried away, not merely by an idea but through "the baptism of action."—

But you, my own little Mother, have to suffer because you have these singular children who have to be redeemed by a revolution or by joining in a world war; for others it may suffice to attend Miss Zahle's School or to learn to drive a car, thus causing infinitely less worry. And yet there are not a few singular people in the world, explorers to the North Pole, artists and members of the Salvation

Army, whose mothers have been forced to fold their hands and reconcile themselves to the fact that it was their children's fate and fortune to take these winding roads,—and perhaps, when all is said and done, there is as much danger attached to an office in a ministry as among polar icebergs. If you recall the story of the stork,—about the two men who lived in a little triangular house, and the water that came pouring out of the fish pond etc.,—I often still find the answers to life's problems in it, and I believe in it implicitly, like Queen Draga in her time. Just when one feels one is floundering in the deepest despair,—"fall into a ditch, get out again,"—is when one is perfecting the work of art of one's life, as microcosm. I have experienced this in my own life, and the greatest moments have been those when I have been able to glimpse the stork—(don't misunderstand me).

Even if Tommy should not come to join in at all, or even if he does join in and comes to experience what he visualized as great visions as ugly and drab, yet perhaps he will be fulfilling the destiny of his talents and abilities and will make something complete of his life.—

Bror is in Mombasa, but I have been talking to Fara about Tommy this evening, and there is something truly impressive in the Muhammadan's unwavering submission to fate; what is striking is not anything that they say but the wisdom about life that gives a completely uneducated person like Fara peace and superiority. Even apart from the natives one does meet out here,—in the midst of the fearful living death of the English middle class mediocrity,—some people who in a completely simple and straightforward way are looking for the primordial values of life. Such for example are Lord Delamere, Galbraith Cole and some of The Dutchmen like Posma and old Kolbe, whom I wrote about. And something that one has to admire in the English is their clear, almost inspired and simple understanding of their own nature and the completely unperturbed way they live in accordance with it. I believe that Tommy resembles them, but that he lacks the aplomb or faith in the rights of his own nature that leads Lord Delamere, for instance, to turn his back on everything in England and live among the Masai. Inexplicable as they are to conventional people like Gustaf Hamilton, who is quite unable to understand why Cole prefers to stay on his farm at Elmenteita than at the Carlton Hotel,—and no doubt successors to the check-suited Englishman in "Pontemolle" and like-minded others,—I believe that they are some of the happiest people in the world. I think Tommy is like them, and also that he would be very happy out here; I also think that he could find happiness among comrades in a trench, but I feel that recently he has not been happy in the easy situation he was living in, and felt himself depressed by his own ingratitude and unreasonableness. But

I think this is so with by far the majority of young people who go on living in their childhood home. No idyll in the world can make them happy, because they aspire to great achievements,—"He loved the legend slumbering beneath the great stars; he craved to become the echo of a sung legend,"—and in losing them their home gains them, for from far away they see it more clearly and feel its power more strongly than when it is close, and it draws them back irresistibly, especially through the remembrance of play and tenderness.—

Dearest Mother, I sit here writing and perhaps I am expressing what I want to say badly, but what is one to do? Such great distance is between us, and everything I feel I would say through an embrace I have to put down laboriously on a piece of paper. When I think that you and Tommy are to be parted my whole heart beats so heavily, because you two are so alike and to me are the most beautiful thing I have ever seen, you love each other so deeply. But then you will see how wonderful it will be when you meet again.—

Every time I think I am going to write to you about my everyday life here something comes along that makes it seem utterly meaningless, first Ea, then Tommy. But dearest Mother, you will see that out of the anxiety and turbulence of the great happenings that you feel are wearing you out and tearing you apart there will appear a really marvelous stork,—"Life itself," so glorious that no idea or dream could ever create anything so beautiful and rich.

I embrace you, my beloved Mother.

Your Tanne

To Ingeborg Dinesen

Naivasha, British East Africa
1.7.1917

Dearest Mother.

Only a short letter from Naivasha, where I am alone this evening, because Bror has gone back to Ngong and I am surrounded by only boys and dogs. Bror and I came up here for a weekend, Gustaf has left now and the planting season is more or less over. It is absolutely delightful here,—I think that Naivasha is a paradise on earth, very like Scotland, with the water and the mountains around the lake, and the air is so lovely here and it is so peaceful without any people and so much game. The country up here resembles the Deer Park or some other big park, with great spreading trees,—although only down by the lake, to be sure,—with thick, short grass beneath them. All the sheep brought from the Masai Reserve pass here on their way to

Naivasha, so there is a constant stream of Somalis with hundreds of sheep on the road alongside the lake; in the nighttime their camp fires shine from far away. . . .

I have brought my painting things with me and am delighted to have a chance to paint in peace here,—it happens rarely at Ngong. One has to get accustomed to the colors out here, especially to the lightness of everything; and then the colors are so dry, never anything fresh and green and the sky for the most part white-violet. . . .

To Ingeborg Dinesen

Ngong 29.7.17.

. . . Our time recently has been completely taken up with a very unpleasant affair, which now seems to be drawing to a satisfactory conclusion, I am glad to say,—a series of articles in The Leader, seeking to cast suspicion on the Scandinavians here, in particular on Bror, and which ended by directly accusing them of harboring German interests and receiving money from apparently tainted sources. They aroused much attention; even Fara came and asked me about them, as all the Somalis were talking about them, and one could feel that they were believed in many circles. It is difficult to defend oneself against that kind of thing in a foreign country and in a foreign language, and none of the other Swedes would do anything or seemed to know what could be done; but in that sort of situation it is an advantage that Bror takes everything so calmly and never gets angry. I think that a public dispute in the newspaper would have caused us great harm, and Bror acted quite rightly in writing to the author of the articles and getting an interview with him that resulted in their getting on very friendly terms, and Mr. Bromhead promised to retract it all in the same newspaper in which his articles had appeared.

After that Bror went to speak to the "acting Governor" (the old one has returned to England and no new one has yet been appointed), who also was very kind and spoke very decently about the Scandinavians here. He thought that we should arrange to get a Consul, and if that is not feasible before the war is over, a kind of spokesman or representative for the Scandinavians, whom he could negotiate with in such cases; it would most probably be Bror, and even though it would involve quite a lot to do, it would no doubt be an advantage in many cases and would give him a sort of position among the Scandinavians, at any rate. . . .

I can't remember whether it is you or Aunt Clara who sends us "Politiken," but in any case we don't want it any more,—but we should like "Berlingske Tidende" and "Verden og Vi" instead. "Politiken" is a disgusting paper, and when one reads it out here, so incredibly provincial. It gives a bad impression of the Danish nation, petty, frivolous and vulgar. . . .

To Ingeborg Dinesen

Ngong 5.8.1917

. . . I hasten to write a few lines to tell you about Tommy's letter. It was so sweet of him to write, and such a happy, jolly letter; he has really leaped into life . . . and were it not for the horrible anxiety about him, I really think that life among his comrades, even in the trenches, is what does suit him best. He does not bother about hardship and rigors, there is even a kind of craving for them in his nature, as I remember him at his jolliest at Finse, nose and fingers practically dropping off from the cold as one battled blindly on through the blizzard, or at sea in a real gale and cold. I think that is a markedly Scandinavian characteristic, in contrast to the Southerners whose chief aim is enjoyment,—albeit in the highest and most beautiful sense,—and that it can be traced right back to Viking times; I never read the sagas without being reminded of Tommy, and he and I always quote them to each other in our letters; when he wrote to me from the boat to America he started by citing the saga of Olaf the Holy:

"Erling had the longboats
launched against the King—"

I think the old sagas have been to us what Ingemann's romances were to your generation; they still thrill me more than almost anything else,—and when Tommy directs his actions in their spirit I think that the greatest experiences he has had light him along his way. . . .

To Ingeborg Dinesen

Ngong 11.8.17

. . . Since Tommy left you two have never been out of my thoughts for one minute , and I have to hold you fast each moment of the day. You can imagine how glad I was to get his sweet letters, first from the steamer and then from New York. All through them you could feel how the world had opened out for him and how he was enjoying everything, his youth and freedom and independence; but with his nature I think he could never do it unless something greater, something that demanded far more and was more decisive, was illuminating him from behind, and that is to a great extent what one loves him for. I keep thinking about Father and Grandmother when he went to fight in the French war; it must have been almost harder for her than for you, although there is no question of degree when it comes to the grief of the heart,—when she had undergone the anxiety once and had him come back again, and I can't help thinking that Grandmother is sometimes sitting in the room with you, drawn from the far beyond by that fellow feeling that must bind all mothers to each other, and by that wonderful understanding that you both have for all incomprehensible children, that you blessed, miraculous mothers have and that without any words makes absolutely clear to you the strange ways of little Wilhelm and Thomas, that it is completely necessary for them to follow.

Believe me, Mother dear, I do understand that a mother is a martyr, but then you are also loved above all that is human. I will never, never forget what it meant to bring all the pain and trouble that was hunting one to you,—and suddenly it seemed no more than when one had broken a cup as a little girl. Nobody but you could have worked that miracle; no being, even the cleverest and wisest in the world, could shine upon me with such a face and bring me peace, except you, and I know that when I am with you once again there will be the same unending joy. To return to one's mother and feel her arms around one is the same eternal, natural miracle as when the trees break into leaf every year; the bleak and open fields where one is buffeted by all the winds of the world suddenly arch over into a shelter, a hiding place, yet so free and alive and fresh, everything bows down over one as if to bless one, and when one goes on again that blessing remains with one always. . . .

To Ellen Dahl

Bogani 13.Sept.1917

. . . I was happier than I can say to get your letter from Paris, and it is marvelous to think of you and Knud in Paris, and that you are experiencing the delights of Paris and France. . . . Even when I was there in war time in 1915 I felt that Paris was illuminated with a splendor possessed by no other places, and the solemnity of the war seemed not at all in contrast to the beauty and life of Paris, and that indeed I think is the greatest charm of Paris and of France as a whole—and the great gift of the south, where everything is in harmony; they can assimilate all the various elements of life into one beauty. Everything that in less perfect natures exists in a state of contradiction: body and spirit, nature and ideal, theory and practice, art and life, life and death,—there becomes the most delightful harmony. I would like you and Knud to meet us in Paris in April 1919, when I go home.

To me France always represents the Holy Land; from there arise beauty and liberty, the most divine forces of life. . . .

It has been so lovely here recently,—unfortunately now it is raining heavily, to the great despair of Bror, who is presently pulling flax,—but in between the rainy days there are some absolutely perfect ones, like May at home, with everything so green and fresh and the air like that of Fontainebleau, I think. I have a large lawn in front of the house,—actually, on every side of it, as Njovana Bogani,—the Forest House,—is situated in the middle of a large forest, but I have not yet managed to get it mown by machine except in front of the house,—which is very popular with the totos who mind the goats; sometimes I have a hundred Kikuyu goats and sheep and a swarm of little brown youngsters in charge of them here, and with the delicate shadows of the trees on the grass I don't think there can have been anything lovelier to look at in Arcadia. Now and again they play the flute and dance; last Sunday they held a big dance for over a thousand people in front of my house. . . .

I have Fara, who is truly an angel, and all my boys are exceptionally good. I am particularly fond of a little Somali boy called Abdulla, I think I love him as much as if he were my own son. I went to visit his mother in the Somali town in Nairobi the other day; it is interesting to see how they live, and incidentally the Somalis have many beautiful things, especially woven and embroidered colored straws; I find Johannes Poulsen's book extremely irritating, because he says that Muhammadanism is devoid of spirit. I do not think there are any people with more self-esteem and calmness and courage and dignity than the Muhammadans; my best friends are Muhammadans and they are vastly superior to the English people here. Since Johannes Poulsen bases his opinions on a visit to Port Said only, it is as if someone who had merely seen Nyhavn and Lille Kongensgade should condemn Christianity,—and indeed, it is Johannes Poulsen who is devoid of spirit; it amazes me that such a thoroughly feeble and vulgar book has had such a success at home. . . .

To Ingeborg Dinesen

Ngong 26 Sept. 1917

My own beloved Mother.

The mail arrived yesterday with many infinitely welcome letters,—among them one from Private 2075467, Royal Highlanders of Canada, with which I was overjoyed. Of course it is not humanly possible to rejoice over his decision; but when I read his letters, which absolutely glow with high spirits and enthusiasm for everyone and everything he is experiencing, I realize that this is probably the only way for him to have gained such an enrichment of his life, and I feel that he has achieved something important, which with his nature had to be bought at great cost. . . .

Bror says that he is quite as devoted to you and to Thomas as I am, and is looking forward just as much to seeing you. I am happy that, in these days, when Sweden and Denmark hold divided sympathies, we have quite made up our minds to be Danish and live in Denmark. I think that what most appeals to Bror is the possibility of buying back Dallund. Although I cannot say that I am particularly drawn to the idea of settling down in Funen far from the sea, I would still be very glad to go along with the idea if it would make Bror feel really happy to be Danish,—for to leave the country where one has grown up and which one has always felt to be one's fatherland is no small matter, and although I believe that I could always have persuaded Bror, I don't think that I would have dared to do it, because I think it is something one might come to regret deeply, and Bror does have a strong feeling for the old ways. . . . You must not talk about this because Bror anticipates a Rama shriek from Sweden, and especially that his father will be very angry and upset and possibly feel it a reprimand; but Bror is right in saying that they have never given him much consideration in Sweden because he is not an officer. Besides, everyone would naturally find us laughable or big humbugs if we talked about buying Dallund now. . . .

Of course it is stupid in a way to work for that sort of future when one has no children, and we may change this plan after a time, but for the time being it gives me pleasure, and then I do still nourish the hope that I may one day have my little Wilhelm to bring up,—not so much to run Dallund as to take over our concern out here and develop it further. . . .

To Ingeborg Dinesen

Ngong 2.12.1917

My beloved Mother.

First of all congratulations on the birth of your grandchild; may she bring you joy and happiness for many many years and come to resemble you. It is so delightful to think of you two, you and little Karen, how much you will mean to each other, how you will love each other,—how many happy hours you will spend together, and how young and lovely you will grow with her. It is so charming to have a child in the family, just like a new springtime and so filled with promises and possibilities. . . .

56 I have spent some really enjoyable days, first a weekend with Greswolde Williams in the Kedong Valley, then with the McMillans at Juja. Uncle Mogens will tell you that Greswolde Williams belongs among the dregs of society; but you know that you cannot always rely on Uncle Mogens's opinion. He is quite an extraordinary person, possesses many millions and lovely places in England; but as his father would not have anything to do with his children, he was brought up by grooms and in appearance and manners is exactly like a groom himself, but I find him an unusually kind and nice person. His only son fell last summer in G.E. at the age of 17, and since then he has lost an eye in an accident with a rifle which exploded. He took me out on an excellently organized buffalo hunt, they beat the bushes and sent a big buffalo bull straight out toward us; unfortunately I sent two shots wide of it, partly because G.-W. had lent me his 450 rifle, which I did not know and which was too heavy for me.

After that we went out to the McMillans, and it was lovely to be out on a real shooting farm again and to see the masses of game there; it is always a joy to see giraffe, there are many of them there. I went out shooting early one morning with Mr. Bulpett in McMillan's car; it was really beautiful with the snow on Kenya glittering in the air. . . .

I like McMillan very much, but his wife rather less; but as she loves Bror that is quite all right. The nicest person there is old Mr. Bulpett, he is unusually nice and amusing; he reminds me so much of Uncle Laurentzius in his younger days, but is more brainy and has had such an interesting life; it was he, you know, who used up a great fortune on la belle Otero. In his early youth he was one of the first to climb the Matterhorn, and here my intimate acquaintance with Whymper, Michael Croz and Lord Douglas came in useful and greatly impressed him.—McMillan is going to Egypt this month as he is suffering from fever; the poor man weighs over 400 pounds and probably has not much longer to live; it is most likely the same disease as that of Prince Gustaf, but worse. . . .

1918

To Thomas Dinesen

Ngong 12.1.1918

My dear Tommy.

Many, many thanks for your two letters from England, which arrived just in time for Christmas Eve and were the nicest Christmas present I could have had. We sent you a telegram but I fear you have not received it; but you would know without a telegram that we were thinking of you and wishing you everything good in the world, and that next New Year we must be together here celebrating Christmas by our camp fire—in the "Masai Reserve."

Every single day I think of you, my old Tommy, and wish that I might see you soon,—and hear about all you have seen, and we must talk too about the old days at home, about the wild ducks' flight and Finse blizzards, and about the Saga of Olav the Holy and d'Artagnan and Porthos. The little photograph that you sent me of yourself in uniform is on my mantelpiece and I show it proudly to everyone who comes, and tell them that it is my soldier brother. . . .

I went to the moving pictures the day before yesterday and saw pictures from the front and the Battle of Arras, and although one does not get a real impression when one does not hear the terrible noise, it is still extremely impressive. Unfortunately there were only English soldiers ,—for though I am of course more closely related to the English, yet it is always France that holds my heart; and if it were not France's struggle that you have joined it would be so hard to be resigned to your going,—and it is hard enough! I think that everything has been destroyed by this terrible war: Christianity, culture, human ideals,—only one thing still illuminates the ruins: the sacred name of France, as so many times before. Oh, God, let it not be for the last time! . . .

Out here they are saying now that the war is over, although they have still not caught von Lettow, and they will probably never do that. It is a fine quality in the English that they will admit to and admire the abilities and greatness of their enemies; they all speak of von Lettow with the greatest appreciation and consider him to be one of Germany's top men in this war. I think it is interesting to have known him; one does not meet so many outstanding men in one's life. How much the world has been changed by the war! When I think of how von Lettow and I would sit and gossip on the deck of the "Admiral," and how he was traveling straight into such a fearful great adventure, I can hardly comprehend that it is the same existence,—but it is hard to see which is the most natural form for human beings.

I have just recently met someone who lives solely for war, and thinks that it is the only way to happiness, and I have been wondering whether it may prove the same for you,—Eric von Otter, who is back on leave from G.E.A., and whom I have been really glad to meet again; I would think that his character resembles Father's, he is so interested in all nature, hunting and war, and particularly in the natives, their customes and ideas,—so you will understand that it interests me to talk to him about things. He is a complete Muhammadan, knows the Koran by heart and is the only European who is permitted by the Muhammadans themselves to touch it, when, for instance, they are sworn in at the military tribunal,—and he carries "The Three Musketeers" with him and speaks about it with the same reverence as Elle and you. . . .

Heaven knows where you will be, my own dear Tommy, when you read this, perhaps already in France and experiencing so many things that are quite unimaginable out here. When I look up at the stars at night here shining among the great trees, I always try to remember their names, that you taught me, and wonder whether you are looking at them from a trench,—in one way so far, far away from me, and in another close, for we will always be close to each other; our thoughts have traversed the same paths so very many times and surely will continue to meet in many great countries where they will find their way,—in Almannagjaa, and on board ship forging grandly ahead urged by the boys past the coast of the Seal Islands. I have a record of "Wide sails over the North Sea" here,—a strange combination, but such is life,—and I can never listen to it without weeping, because it makes me think of you; I feel that we have stood together "high on the quarterdeck in the morning." I will never be able to thank you enough for what you have been to me, from the time when you were a little boy until as my big brother you comforted and helped me in my time of need when I was last at home; you are the only person in the whole world to whom I can say everything,—if only you were here now!

I was so very glad to get your letters from Canada,—I sent replies to them there, but perhaps you never received them. It was a great joy to me to hear that you were enjoying life like a vigorous young man after having been a wise astronomer for so long. I sent you a New Year poem to England, which I thought had a certain beauty, and expressed a little of what I hope life may have in store for you in the new year. I wish for you the strength to bear what you may see and experience, and that it may enable you to love it all the more.

You probably get news from home now more quickly than I do; the last letters that I received took almost three months to arrive. I think it is such a pity for Elle that she is still ill.—Thank heavens she has Knud and that my wishes did not come to fulfilment there; Mopsus was certainly right in saying that God is infinitely more ingenious than we are. Now if only, if only, if only He will bring about a lasting peace, and a meeting between Mother and you, which one can barely begin to visualize. I wish you every blessing now and always, my own beloved Tommy.

Your devoted sister and friend, as long as I live,

Tanne.

To Ingeborg Dinesen

Bogani 14/2.1918

. . . I have been down to shoot for a fortnight with Eric Otter on the Tana plains to get buffalo and rhino, which I had not hunted before, and we shot some of both and had a fine safari. It is so beautiful, an absolutely enchanting "romantic" landscape, like Claude Lorrain's, with domed blue mountains, vast brown plains and wide flowing rivers bordered with a wealth of palms and great green trees. But it is fearfully hot there, it is only 3,000 feet—and there is a really hellish plague peculiar to Tana Plains, the small ticks that attack you by the million and completely ruin life for you. They are almost invisible, but when you have been out walking in the high grass you look down and see that you are gray with them, worse than the soldiers in the trenches with lice, I think, and it is remarkable that such small creatures can pump you so full of poison and misery; you look as if you had measles all over you and feel as if you are bathed in flame. But there is something about safari life that makes you forget all your sorrows and feel the whole time as if you had drunk half a bottle of champagne,—bubbling over with heartfelt gratitude for being alive. It seems right that human beings should live in the nomad fashion and unnatural to have one's home always in the same place; one only feels really free when one can go in whatever direction one pleases over the plains, get to the river at sundown and pitch one's camp, with the knowledge that one can fall asleep beneath other trees, with another view before one, the next night. I had not sat by a camp fire for three years, and so sitting there again listening to the lions far out in the darkness was like returning to the really true world again,—where I probably once lived 10,000 years ago. . . .

We came back last Wednesday. . . . I found all well here, but fearfully dry, and I think Bror is thin. There had been a great commotion at the house here, as there had been a break-in at the boys' houses and all their belongings stolen; 500 rupees from poor Fara, his gold watch and chain that I gave him, and five gold rings. Since then we have had black detectives in the house and they think they have found the worst thief in my syce, Jogona, who is at present locked in my meat-safe waiting for the police to take him to Dagoretti. He is not to be envied for I think they use torture without much scruple; but he could have kept his hands off his best friends' possessions. I do not think that the natives think anything of stealing and so probably can never be trusted in that direction. They nearly always give themselves away because when they start drinking at their big gatherings, singing and beating the drums, they can't resist boasting of their exploits; that is how they caught Jogona, and the other day four murderers at Lumbwa, who declared in their jubilation that they had killed a mesunga [''white man''] with nine spear thrusts; they were hanged. . . .

To Thomas Dinesen

Ngong 26/2 1918

. . . People out here have begun to show us such kindness and friendliness, which makes me very happy; I think that by being reserved and not pushing ourselves on anyone we have gained a good position here,—and only those who have been under suspicion of being pro-German can understand how truly loathsome that is, so it is really a great relief. In time I think we will take our place among the leading people here; I have a feeling that this country belongs to us. It has a kind of charm that not everyone can understand and strangely enough some of its worst qualities contribute to that charm: its dryness, colorlessness, monotony,—but one comes to love it in a way I had never thought one could love other countries besides one's own, one's childhood country. The fact that most white people here hate it and have nothing good to say of it brings it in a way still closer to the hearts of those who feel that they can understand its voice and that it has spoken to them. . . .

I have written a whole lot of letters to you, sent both to Canada and to Shoreham; I do hope you have received them. I enjoy writing to you more than to anyone else, and of course I can say anything to you,—but of course at times there isn't so much to write about.

But I have the feeling that you take more interest than anyone else in everything out here, and the country,—and I,—are always waiting to embrace you in welcome. . . .

Poor Aunt Bess, I agree with you that it is sad to think about her, and I always have a feeling of ingratitude where she is concerned,—for in a way she has given us her all, and we cannot repay her with what she desires from us. She wanted to teach us all her ideas and thoughts about life, and most of what she taught us was negative: in order that we should avoid a destiny like hers. And yet in a way she is one of the warmest hearted people I have ever known and a highly talented person,—how can that be? I believe that life demands of us that we love it, not merely certain sides of it and not only one's own ideas and ideals, but life itself in all its forms, before it will give us anything in return, and when you mention my philosophy of life, I have no other than that; I feel that the people, despite lack of talent and ability, who have this love, get so much more out of their existence than the most talented who are rendered the poorer by their lack of it.

I heard from home that old Miss Merwede has died,—I think that she was one of those people who loved everything in life wholeheartedly, and was in a way richly repaid. That is what I most wish for you: that you may love everything that life brings you. I do not know how it can have happened that all the ideas and ideals from the nursery at Matrup should have gained such an irrefutable and incorruptible place in Aunt Bess's and Uncle Aage's consciousness and thus gradually through the years changed from a blessing to a curse. . . .

If I have a child, which I so fervently hope for, and reasonably soon, I will not presume to think that I have a complete knowledge of all the truths in the world, but will allow it to be educated by other people and conditions just as much as by my own ideas; for there are surely many occasions when outside influences unconsciously teach one far more than the most carefully considered and imposed principles. I wish so much that I could be something to Aunt Bess and repay her a little for her great love; but she would have to reconcile herself to so much in my life and my ideas before she could get any joy from me, and that she cannot or will not do, I can feel, even in letters. . . .

Eric and I took "Deerslayer" and "The Three Musketeers" on safari with us, and they reminded me so very much of you. You may laugh when I wish you the spirit of both deerslayers and musketeers, but probably you'll understand that what I wish for you is something bright and living and strong.

 Well then, goodbye for now, little Tommy.

Your Tanne.

To Ingeborg Dinesen

Ngong 27/2 1918

. . . I have recently been reading so much about Muhammad and Muhammadanism, books I have borrowed from Eric; once one starts on it it becomes so fascinating. Poor Bror has refused to hear anything about Muhammad between twelve and four. I think these times suit Muhammadanism, so for a follower of that creed there might perhaps be some meaning in it all. Eric says, too, that their Christian "Askaris" ["soldiers"],—invariably become Muhammadans after a few weeks in the field, and it is only then that they are of any use. Johannes Poulsen is not right in saying that Muhammadanism is devoid of spirit: but I do think that to understand Christianity requires a higher spiritual level, which does not suit these people here, but Muhammadanism brings them much benefit. It is actually more of an extremely firmly defined code of ethics than a religion—I do not think they have any religious dogma,—but it rests upon complete submission to fate and a belief that God is with them, and primarily it gives them self-esteem, a feeling that they are above other people. Their morals are very charitable because unlike Christians they have no concept of *sin*, and their moral code consists of hygiene and ideas of honor—for instance, they put discretion among their first commandments, which must be very agreeable in Muhammadan social life, and one could wish it to be adopted by Christians. I also think that the Muhammadans have realized the idea of fellowship to a far greater extent than we have; there seem to be hardly any,—anyhow not here,—poor Muhammadans, and they stick together and help each other in a way quite unknown to Christians, but whether out of love exactly I do not know, probably rather as a family whose members can quarrel violently but which bands together against the rest of the world.

From what I have observed there is on the whole something remarkably dry about the Muhammadans I know despite their passionate nature; but I don't know whether this is due to the religion or the race, or perhaps due to the fact that they never drink wine. I wonder whether a nation which is never intoxicated comes to be lacking in the "lyrical" element in their emotions, and also for instance that corresponding in their sense of humour to what we call conviviality? Although they are easily moved to laughter they generally laugh at completely different things from those that amuse good-natured people at home; it is more like scorn or malice. They are more liberal in their religion than we are; a Muhammadan always finds it good to go into a Christian church, if there is no other available, and they greatly respect the Christian Bible, although I think the Christians themselves less because they say that they do not themselves keep the commandments of their religion; it is true that they probably do not keep them nearly as thoroughly as the Muhammadans do theirs. Whenever one quarrels with a Muhammadan it almost always ends with him holding up three fingers and saying: we say that God is THREE, then closing his hand: they say that God is ONE,—"but only God himself knows who is right,—and therefore one can have different opinions about everything in the world." Then apart from his teaching, which has no doubt been adulterated with a considerable quantity of foreign elements in the course of the years, I think that Muhammad is one of the most interesting people that I have read about. Do you remember "The Hero as Prophet" in Carlyle's "Hero-Worship"? Good though it is, I think it lacks something; there is something impressive in the capacity to hold ignorant, undeveloped people, who cannot even read, in such complete obedience to the smallest trifles for many centuries, and with such fervor. Forgive me if I have written about this before, and if it is as boring for you as it is for Bror.

A thousand thanks for a letter to me dated 1st November, which arrived yesterday, so almost four months old. . . . Thank you too for your affectionate letter to Bror. It helps so much to hear that someone really believes in one,—and Bror was so happy about that. He has been writing to you this evening, but whether it will be sent off remains to be seen. . . . I want to earnestly beg all of you who are fond of and believe in Bror to have so much faith in him that you do not judge him quite as you would other people; he is not like others, and he must have freedom to be as he is if he is to achieve the best he is capable of. . . . Everyone must have someone who believes in them in this life or they will never achieve anything and I beseech you, as my first and last wish, to turn a blind eye on Bror for two or three years more, so that: "If he steals twopence from a blind beggar and buys poison for his mother with it, you will say it was only his high spirits,"—and then I shall be so infinitely grateful to you, and you will see what good results it will bring. . . .

64 To Ingeborg Dinesen

Ngong 25. March. 1918

. . . Bror is at present at Uasin-Gishu on a long trip,—he left on 18 March and probably will not be back before the end of April . . . of course I am rather lonely, but otherwise quite all right, except for a tiresome inability to sleep. I think it is because of the drought. I get frequent visits from Somalis and from officers from the K.A.R. camp, which is not far from here. . . .

I have had my fortune told by an old Arab priest who is very renowned for his art and will only consent to prophesy for a chosen few, who predicted that a "young man of my blood and heart" (Fara translates this as meaning either my brother, husband, or son) will be greater than kings and known for all time like those in the scriptures (the Bible or the Koran). So now it is up to Bror and Tommy. Furthermore that I myself will come to exert a tremendous power over people and be able to do with them as I wish; for I was "fearsome as a lion about to spring, yea, as an army with many banners." Great good fortune will follow my friends, but my enemies will die without sons. So now you know. . . .

Your books have just arrived,—many thousand thanks. This is about the greatest joy one can have out here. I have not yet had time to read any but have looked through them and am looking forward enormously to reading them, especially Seedorff and "Mos og Muld" ["Moss and Soil"]. I cannot tell you how much one longs for books and music and all the arts,—the English are so utterly lacking in talent. I am often afraid of becoming a complete idiot; I have just been trying to read one of Bergson's books in English, and if it is not badly translated I must be witless already. Tommy did send me two books: "Eegholms Gud" ["The God of Eegholm"] and "Clara van Haags Mirakler" ["The Miracles of Clara van Haag"]; they never got through, but if it is not too much trouble would you please send them to me, as he wrote to me about them? I think that the Muhammadans have much the finest cast of mind out here. . . .at present they are teaching me some of their sorcery; but it is strictly secret so I cannot tell you about it. A special spell was made for "my sister's toto," and I hope it may bring the little puss good luck. They have such a remarkable philosophy of life,—incidentally, I think it greatly resembles that of many modern people who have rejected Christianity,—that fate, life, God, is so enormously great and they are so small that nothing that they themselves can do is of any importance whatsoever; I do not think they have any notion of the concept of "sin," presumably it cannot exist in such complete fatalists, and I do not think they could have any understanding at all of the worry and despair that it brings to the best of Christians. . . .

To Ea Neergaard

Bogani 27.3.1918

. . . It made a tremendously deep impression on me to hear that you had met Ellen Wanscher in Vimmelskaftet [a street in Copenhagen]; but how in the world can it interest you to hear that I have been to Blue Post with Lieutenant Cartright? But I suppose that something of my life here,—coffee and flax, Fara, Dusk, Lord Delamere, safaris, and trading, is gradually making itself felt in your consciousnesses, and for me at least it is lovely that you know something about my experiences. How much more interesting it will all be when you have been to see it. I look forward to your and Viggo's visit more than I can say.—

Unfortunately at present we are experiencing a drought here that exceeds anything one can imagine at home. The whole country will perish if it goes on much longer, and as it is, it is bad enough. Now we are beginning to notice the privations you have suffered so long in Europe; butter, milk, cream, vegetables, eggs exist more or less only in memory. All the plants are withering, the plains are on fire every day and are completely black and charred, and when one drives into Nairobi the town as you approach it seems to be enveloped in a vast conflagration,—an impression caused by the dust that hangs over it day and night, in thick yellow clouds,—with the wind blowing from the Somali town and the bazaar,—you feel that plague and cholera germs are whirling merrily around. Then there is a hitherto unknown mortality rate among small white children in Nairobi, and this scorching hot, perpetually drying wind gets on the adults' nerves so much that we have to be extremely cautious in our dealings with each other.—But I suppose that one must regard the drought like so many other things this year with the thought that it must come to an end some day, and meanwhile one must endure it as best one can,—aber frage nur nicht wie. . . .

You can't imagine how much I miss music, and for that matter all the arts; the English are such philistines,—and my gramophone is rapidly becoming only a hoarse echo of distant melodies. I have been playing two duets from "The Magic Flute," and one in particular: "It sounds so delightful that I have to dance" has sometimes been a real source of rejuvenation. You at home are lucky in that even in the midst of worries and miseries, and even in the Slagelse Music Society you can have recourse to the wonderful old wise masters' world of beauty. I am often filled with such longing out here to see the new things that have been purchased for Thorvaldsen's Museum, or to see "Jeppe paa Bjærget" [Holberg's play, "Jeppe on the Mountain"], and of course if one were at home one would not go anyway. But there are so many riches at home; here there is really less than a war ration of intellectual food.

Fara is enormously interested in your little girl; he and Abdullah have given me a necklace of amber exactly like mine,—it is supposed to bring much luck,—and a sash made of multicoloured silk for "my sister's toto." I don't know whether the little puss will appreciate them; anyway the sash will go round her at least twenty times. . . .

To Ingeborg Dinesen

Bogani 6. April 1918

. . . I have not been very well recently, I really think because of the drought; I have had so much rheumatism and then such trouble in sleeping and that does not help one's nerves. . . . Now today for the first time it looks like rain, and hope springs again,—pray for us, please: Everyone is saying that "the long rains" will fail this year just like "the short," but I don't know what they base this on. Many people out here seem to acquire a very bad habit of looking on the black side of everything and going around depressing others with their view of life. . . . On the whole I must say that I hate this kind of little community, that cuts itself off from everything else and lives on itself; I think that through a kind of self-poisoning they always end up as pure venom, and am glad to be completely outside their little shauris [here "troubles," "disputes"] and scandal mongering.

I went to a very enjoyable dinner yesterday at Muthaiga in Nairobi; Cartright is going to fight in Mesopotamia and I had promised to have a meal with him before he left. We were just four, the previous Governor's daughter and an unusually charming person, Dennis Finch-Hattan [*sic*], whom I have always heard so much about but never met before. He is one of the old settlers, like Delamere, Galbraith Cole, and van de Weyer; they are a much better type than the later ones. He would like to buy some land here so as to have a house near Nairobi; his farms are further up-country at Movoroni and Uasin Gishu. I think that many people will do this in future,—now the road is good one can get in by motor-car in half an hour, and Ngong is the best place in the whole of B.E.A. for air and climate and beauty; Eric Otter is also talking of buying land from van de Weyer and living here. This would increase the value of land here, but I must say that I feel that it would be highly undesirable if the area were transformed into a residential district with building plots. One always grows so attached to the place where one lives and all the places and their names make me feel so much at home here now: Dagoretti, Ngong, Donja Sabuk, Kabiti, just like Humlebæk and Helleholm. For it is beautiful here,—if only, only the rains would come soon. . . .

To Ingeborg Dinesen

Ngong 17/5 1918

. . . Last Sunday we had a very good hunt for General Llewellyn. We were only the General, Major Davis and his wife, Eric, Captain Gorringe, van de Weyer, Finch-Hatton, Bror, and myself; we got more than 30 buck, two jackals and a leopard. It was raining a little so it was pleasant to have a fire in the dining-room, and I had taken some pains to put on a cold lunch. Naturally Finch-Hatton and van de Weyer stayed to dinner,—it is the custom in this country that people decide to stay on from one hour to the next,—and for the night as well; then I went into Nairobi next day with F.-H. for lunch . . . I am really sad that he has gone; it is seldom that one meets someone one is immediately in sympathy with and gets along so well with, and what a marvelous thing talent and intelligence is. Then a certain class of Englishmen have an extrordinarily pleasant nature; Alan Thompson, my traveling companion on the voyage home in 1915, was rather similar, but still far less charming than Denys. He has now gone to Egypt to get flying instruction, probably in Cairo, and will go on to Mesopotamia; I sincerely hope that I shall see him again. I think it is great good fortune for a country to have a class of people who have nothing other to do than follow their own bent, and who have been brought up to observe the phenomena of life from above,—and if I had a son I would send him to Eton. In Denmark where everyone has grown up in the same restricted conditions I think it would be a good thing to have a little injection of different ways of thinking now and again; out here one sometimes feels that most people's horizon at home is restricted to an unfortunate extent.

Bror is a marvelous nurse, far and away better than the heartless Motherwell, and my boys are true angels to me. It's true that Miss Motherwell was shocked to see how little control I had over them and thought that I am far too liberal; but at least I have achieved the two things that I chiefly aim at as a housewife: to keep the house clean and to have no shauries (which everyone else has with their boys). Besides, it is impossible to have good boys if one keeps running after them to see they don't eat the sugar. I have inherited a Somali from Denys Finch-Hatton; he would not change to any other house but mine. But naturally economy is unfortunately not my strong point. I would rather die than hide myself away in order to save; and it is really a far more thorough system of economy. If I could only make a great deal of money I would give a lot of fun to many people,—but no doubt we will. . . .

When one is so far away the past and the present blend together so strangely, and one often feels too that the difference between life and death is an illusion. I get the feeling here that Mama's Folehave is just as real and existing as the later one. And in just the same way when I think of you I feel that you are the young Mother I can remember wearing a blue and white striped dress from the time before Father's death, and Tommy and Anders the small boys sailing their boats on the shore just as much as the young men they now are. No doubt many things are seen best from a distance, like impressionistic art. For there is always,—almost every single day,—something of life that comes to an end; thus one can say that one daily experiences death, but I do not at all think that that is of any account, and out here one feels that the House on the Marshes with old Madame Frederiksen, and the Pine Hills when we went for picnics are still as they are, and that the path through the glade can never die. If I were to die here I am certain that I would be much closer to you than I am now, and just as alive, even if you do not get this little bit of paper with ink marks as proof of it. Do you remember Musset's poem for Victor Hugo? I think about it almost every day here:

> "—et nous nous souvenons, que nous marchions ensemble
> que l'âme est immortelle—
> *et qu'hier, c'est demain.*"

Remember, my beloved Mother, that hier c'est demain.

Many thousand greetings, your Tanne.

To Ingeborg Dinesen

Ngong 20/5.1918

. . .You write that I must be absolutely honest about my state of health; but it is not always so easy to judge that myself. Bror is in despair over my getting so thin and says that he doesn't want to be married to a skeleton, and I must say that I think that I have lost the 35 pounds I gained when I was last at home; the Drecoll dresses I bought in Paris in 1915—and which later I could not squeeze myself into even with a great effort,—are now almost too big, and that is pretty annoying. But otherwise I am perfectly well and feeling very fit, except that I have difficulty in sleeping. . . .

I think this country has a quite distinctive fascination of its own, which perhaps exists in every new country that one feels is there waiting for one, and where one is going to be able to do so much; you must read Kipling's poem on South Africa ("Lived a woman wonderful")—about the people who have been captivated by this charm, from which they can never tear themselves away:

> "They esteemed her favour more
> than a thrones foundation
> for the glory of her face
> bid Farewell to breed and race
> yea and made their burial place
> altar of a nation."

I think that Bror has this feeling even more strongly than I; we have been talking about it today and wondering whether, if for example we could have made a couple of thousand pounds a year, we would go home and settle down, and he said that what counted for him was not the money, it was achieving something here and helping to shape the future of this country; and I am sure that he is going to do this; you may laugh at me if you like, but in these hard times I feel like Khadijah, the Prophet's wife,—and am certain that I have married a great man. . . .

I had a lovely letter from Tommy too by this mail. . . . I am so happy that he writes in every letter of his plans to come out here. I really think that it would be an ideal country for him. I would so dearly love to go on safari through Somaliland and down the Nile with him one day. I must go to Somaliland; the whole of that tribe has such great charm for me,—particularly now that I have heard Denys Finch-Hatton talking about his expeditions there. As a matter of fact he had a lot of troubles especially with thirst, but then it is a vile tribe, and of course Abdullah Hassan, "the mad Mullah," is rampaging about up there; but don't you think that would be something to appeal to Tommy? I have learned a bit of Somali, but it is a pretty hard language. . . .

Society here is divided up by a strictly defined order of precedence which rests almost solely on the length of time one has been out here. All the "old" Settlers club together and look down on the new arrivals with the greatest superiority. People like Delamere and Cole and van de Weyer, who were here before the railroad came, are quite unbeatable, and those who arrived last year or this are of absolutely no consequence. Incidentally, Galbraith Cole was once deported because he shot a native who had stolen his sheep; but he came back again when war broke out.

Bror is very keen for me to take a trip to Cairo. Mary Goschen wrote a very friendly letter recently. Of course it would be most enjoyable; but traveling is very difficult these days and I don't know whether one would be permitted to go ashore. Bror is convinced at present that the only thing in the world I care about is to see Finch-Hatton again, and he is now in Cairo. Even if that is something of an exaggeration, I am really glad that this time I have met so many people here that I genuinely care about and count as real friends. . . .

—I have sent Tommy some poems as he is always so kind and enthusiastic about my writing. And by the way would you please, if you have it, get "The Spring" typed out for me and send it? I would like to include it in a real collection for Tommy. But there is only the one copy of it, which I am sure you will take care of; it would be useful to have several copies. . . .

To Thomas Dinesen

Ngong 1/6.1918

My own dear beloved old Tommy.

Thank you for your letter of 19/3. I just can't tell you how much it enthralls and moves me to know that you are in France; one's everyday language has no words for what one is feeling these days,—and yet it's probably only the old old human feelings,—Bergtora and Bergliot felt the same way. May God protect you, may you find the glory that you seek, and Oh, may we be together here next year, or at home beside the Øresund: "The same beeches and light nights—the same joy." . . . So many, many times do I wish I could sit and chat with you as in the old days, and perhaps my letters may be something of a substitute. And if I can't think of anything else to write I can send you a poem, as I have in fact done a couple of times,—I sent you one the other week: "The boat is gliding with the stream."—remember to tell me some time if you received it, if not I'll send it to you again,—to tell you how much I think of you every hour of the day.

I should think that by now you have received both my telegram,—I can't remember when it was sent,—and my letter about our plan to buy out the other shareholders of K.C.C., so that you will know that it has been abandoned. I admit that you are absolutely right in everything that you say in your letter, but you must understand that we were urged to it by unusual circumstances and particularly by the feeling that there was no trust in us at home, and by the uncertainty about everything that this produced. . . . Well, that plan no longer exists and our shareholders must take the rough with the smooth over us; I hope it will soon be mostly the latter.

But what is very much alive still is the plan for a "Soldier-settlement" that Bror submitted to the Land Commission and that I wrote to you about in my last letter. It is in fact so much alive that for the time being the newspapers are not interested in anything else, and I cannot open them without finding long attacks or defenses, right down to details such as "The Dinesens are the Baroness Blixen's family and known to be anti-German." I will try to send you some clippings. On the 16th there is to be a meeting to discuss it at Nakuru, Bror has to attend it, and I am glad that he is to stay with Lord Delamere and go to the meeting with him; it is always better if some of the country's own people support one, and on the whole I must say that the people who really mean something here, like Lord Delamere, Hunter and the real old Settlers, have all shown great enthusiasm for Bror's scheme and have been tremendously friendly and helpful lately.

I am glad—especially now that our relationship with most of the Scandinavians here has grown more cool ,—that I have met so many congenial English people recently. I always believed that traditional idea of the English, that they themselves are always expressing, of their calmness and indifference being due to reserve that hid their real feelings, in fact meant that they didn't have any feelings at all; but now that I have come to know several of them better, I can see that many of them , even if emotion is not perhaps their strong point, have beneath their imperturbable calm at any rate a great deal of intelligence and a completely individual view of everything in life, much helpfulness and faithfulness in friendship,—but not, I think, in love,—and an absolute fearlessness that amounts to a contempt for death, and then a pleasant if not particularly interesting cleanliness of both body and soul, a straight-ness of thought and action, which I think is seldom found on average in other nations. . . .

Fara has gone to Mombasa to be married; he was in a rush to get it done before Ramadan, which is about to start with the new moon, and during which one must renounce all the joys of life, including doubtless those of love. I am having a house built for him, and my other Somalis are delighted at the prospect of having a young woman of their own race here. The Orientals are very chivalrous toward their women, whom they probably regard as the highest, possibly the only true benefit in life; the other Somalis are very busy making everything as fine as possible for Fara's house, for "when Fatima comes." There are very strict rules governing who may enter the house of a married man, and the various tribes have different rules; the woman's tribe is free to go into all the rooms in the house even when the husband is out; his own tribe may enter the living rooms and people from any other tribe may only cross the threshold on invitation. . . .

To Ingeborg Dinesen

Ngong 1/6.1918

. . . We are in despair because the rain has stopped again before we had had anything like enough. What an abnormal and trying year this has been. . . . Even before the rain the natives were on the brink,—indeed, come to that, over the brink,—of famine, and their maize and beans are not nearly ready; during the past few months they have kept alive partly on maize brought in from South Africa. Most of the farmers have been forced to cut down their labor force to a very great extent because they cannot get posho for their workers, some have even brought all work on their farms to a halt. . . .

To Ingeborg Dinesen

Ngong 11/6.1918

. . . I have written my first letter to Tommy in France. I feel that when one reads his joyful, happy letters that show how much good it has done him already, one cannot say that he has done the wrong thing in going off; it is only for you that I think it is much too hard. But then I recall that he has never brought you sorrow during the whole of his life, and has been such a model boy in every respect that we almost owed it to him to allow him to think of himself more than others for once. I think you might perhaps have been able to persuade him not to go, but then something of what is between you might have been lost,—and now I think that there has been nothing but love and understanding from the very first day that you had him; and now you are showing your greatness, my little Mother, in not nurturing the least scrap of bitterness toward Tommy for getting his own way. . . .

Here all our thoughts are directed almost exclusively toward one thing,—the rain that does not come. It is heartbreaking to see, think about, and write of. I dread to think what will become of this country if the rains fail completely. The natives will die in tens of thousands. At present it is impossible to get ships to carry sufficient supplies from Australia or America; moreover these natives are accustomed to their own food and will not eat anything else, probably they cannot. Many have died already, especially small children. Among white children as well the mortality rate is higher than ever before; they are dying of dysentery brought on through lack of milk because of the want of grass. . . .

I was the first to see the new moon of Ramadan yesterday, which gained me much esteem among the Muhammadans, who think that this should bring great good fortune,—if only it would bring the rain. . . .

To Ingeborg Dinesen

Ngong 29/6.1918

. . . Yesterday there was a prayer meeting for ancient Kikuyu women here; some of them looked like disintegrating relics of antiquity summoned out of the grave to invoke rain, and it was tragic to listen to them crying out to heaven that their children were dying, their sheep were dying, their shambas were dying. I am trying to get a "Children's Samaritan" started; it is unbearable to see the poor little mites,—one has just been brought up to me who must be on the point of dying of starvation; I have never seen anything like it, he is nothing but skin and bone with appallingly swollen glands; I thought he was dreadfully ill but his parents said that it was nothing but hunger because he had been having only grass to eat. It would be something if one could keep some of them alive...I have been speaking to Lord Delamere, because he is trying to shoot down all the zebra on his farm just now,—for fear of epidemics,—and sending them down to Nairobi; he charges 5 rupees a carcass, and with transport costs they will probably cost about 10 rupees here in Nairobi, and they are about as big as a small horse and almost always plump and fat, but I do not know whether the children here will be able to eat them; in normal times no native will eat zebra, and on the whole Kikuyu and Masai will eat game only out of sheer necessity. White people cannot eat zebra; I once tried some soup made of it but it tasted too awful. I am going in to talk to Dr. Burkitt today,—he is a great character, a half-crazy Irishman, but a genius, unlike the English, and a scientist,—who is a great friend of mine, and we will try to do something about it. We must take some action because our first attempt appeared in the paper as a leading article. Most of the whites take very little interest in their natives, regarding them partly as their natural enemies; and even if one does not take a humanitarian view it must be remembered that the future of this country does depend on <u>native labour</u>, and it is in one's own interest to take care of their children just as much as calves and foals. . . .

Ngong 9/7.1918

. . . Everything goes on in its usual pretty disastrous way here. I have never known the like of this weather,—such a damp and icy drought! Everything is enveloped in a deathly chill, clammy fog the whole morning, and the nights are really unpleasantly cold,—and at the same time everything in the ground is withering and dying from lack of water. This is what an abortive "long rainy season" is like; I have not seen it before, of course, and hope I shall never see it again. . . .

Olga Holmberg and Fru Windinge are still living at MBagathi and are delighted to be there, and it is really pleasant to have them, just as in the country at home; there is always somewhere to visit or ride over to, and it is good to have some women to talk to sometimes. They are so eager to help me and compete with each other to do my mending and washing and all kinds of things. Fru Windinge sings really beautifully,—so one thinks out here, where there is so little to hear,—even though she has a small voice. She can sing all of Ea's old repertoire, Schubert, Schumann, Grieg, Heise; you can't imagine how touching and moving I find it. Incidentally she reminds me a little of Ea. Johnny van de Weyer is in love with her and I think this is a help to her in her loneliness. She has an incredibly sweet little boy of 16 months and is expecting another child at Christmas. . . .

I was interrupted just now by some Kikuyu who came and asked me to shoot the big baboons that are eating their shambas [cultivated plots]. Shortage of food has made them really bold now; the natives are afraid of them, and they are really loathsome. I went down and saw a whole lot of them, but shot wide, but then I shot an egret, the big white bird with such beautiful feathers, like "Esprits." Now I almost regret shooting it; it was much too beautiful as it was sailing along high in the air. I shot it with my little rifle.

I had Hassan's and Fara's wives here to tea yesterday. It is remarkable that although the Somalis are so completely civilized their women are not so at all,—they are oriental, straight out of "A Thousand and One Nights." They are very beautifully dressed in silks and embroideries but creep about soundlessly like cats on their little bare feet, and they have such big flaming black eyes and white teeth; there is something of the big cat, lioness or leopard about them. I showed them all around the house, all my clothes (!), china, glass, etc., they were intensely interested and so tremendously lively, like children. Hassan's wife is a real beauty. . . .

Ngong 17/7 1918

Dearest Tommy.

Many thousand thanks for your English and Danish poems, which have just recently come by a mail that brought nothing else. I have read them all many many times; the little English book with your markings and underlinings is just about the greatest treasure I own. It is probably easier for those who are taking part in the war or about to do so to read that sort of war song; to us others the glory of it all,—the horrors, the courage, the will, all those destinies that are shaped and played out in the course of one moment on a very much larger scale than we are accustomed to,—is almost too overwhelming; one reads and is moved by the work of art. If the songs were about the wars of Alexander or Napoleon one could let oneself be quite carried away by them,—but this is real; while we are reading about it, it is actually happening, it possesses a far too overwhelming power. But as it gradually sinks in, it grows clear, and the great impression that remains is—equally overwhelming—: the victory of spirit over material, the great glory of the human spirit, not in its great ones but in every human being,—particularly in the fact that the most ordinary, least gifted can rise so completely above circumstances that the most fearsome things that life can offer become meaningless. For me the sagas have had something of the same effect. This is where it becomes truth: "Death, where is thy sting, hell, where is thy victory!" [*sic*]—but then humanity returns and pleads for its rights,—as in"Milking Time," so infinitely sadly. I can so well understand how, when this great glory was really taking place you, and all those who have felt like you, knew that you could not go on living outside it,—but what terrible agony that it should be taking place. For whether or not this can be followed by a new Heaven and a new Earth it is nevertheless Ragnarok,—perhaps we who are outside it are able to feel that best.

I have probably written about this to you before,—that the greatness of the sagas, which to me represent one of the highest worlds that I have known, is always linked together with you,—indeed, so much so that,—when I play "Wide sails sweeping over the North Sea,"—I feel that it recalls not only a song but an experience; I have been standing on the quarter deck with you,—and Erling Skjalgsøn,—and all those young heroes,—Erling, Olav Trygveson himself, Einar Tambeskjælver,—have your features or resemble you as brothers. "Face to face should eagles do battle"—I read it in your dearly beloved face that I have before me here, enlarged from the little photograph of you in uniform that you sent me from New York. I don't think I have ever read greater, clearer, more powerful words than this short sentence. I am so proud of my brother; so much of what I myself have dreamed but never achieved has been realized through you,—but all of this makes the anxiety that is always with us now so infinitely much greater, that we might lose this glory, all that is most glorious and strong could go out of our life and we would remain and continue our flat existence,—as if we had broken faith with what is greatest. I cannot talk to anyone about this fear, but I can say it to you, and can also say that if it should come about that we are parted, then I have loved you infinitely,—and that for us you are Olav Trygveson,—and much, much more. . . .

I have written some stanzas which I am sending you; unfortunately this time they are rather sad ones, but you'll get some jolly ones next time. For it is ,—quand même,—my firm belief that life is very beautiful and rich and great; indeed, should I die of plague on a dung heap I would still believe it. And it is this that I will always, always wish for you, beloved brother, that you may see life's gloriously beautiful face through all the misery you come to see, and may preserve that faith. I have probably become something of a Muhammadan through having been with Somalis so much; if Fara comes to Paris—I will take him with me if I go,—you will see what strength there is in their simple, unperturbable belief in fate.

If there is ever anything that you do not want to write to Mother about, do write it to me, just as I will write everything to you, my dear best friend. And every day I think about how delightful and pleasant it will be for us when you come out here after the war,—how much there will be to talk about, and how wonderful, wonderful it will be to see your face again.

Always always your

Tanne.

To Ingeborg Dinesen

Ngong 30/7.1918

. . . I have had to give up my "Children's Samaritan" as I could not get any maize; they are issuing rice to the natives in various parts of the country as a substitute, but I dare not try it here as they get "Beri-beri" very easily from it if it is not cooked properly; it is a "famine disease" that they suffer from particularly on the West Coast, and is actually worse than hunger itself. Apart from that it was lovely to see all the little black children absolutely delighted with their food; the smallest ones were in a hurry to take their portion safely out of the way of the big ones, so I had a little colony of two-year-olds,—three dozen or so,—sitting in a corner of the lawn with their little bowls of posho in silent rapture. The big ones were twittering like sparrows, beside themselves with joy. But then I had to stop; too many children were coming, and the man we had the maize contract with was obliged to break it. . . .

A topical question here at the moment interests me a great deal; it is the introduction of the "Native Pass," which has caused a great stir especially among the Somalis, who are to be registered under the terms of this regulation together with the Kikuyu and the other local natives, whom they call "Ushesis," i.e. slaves, and for whom they have a deep contempt. I take the side of the Somalis, of course, and consider that they are being unfairly treated,—according to this ruling they will not be able to take their cases to appeal but are in the hands of the small local officials; they are not allowed to reside in Nairobi unless they are in the service of a white man, etc. I think there has been an utter lack of tact in bringing in this whole business; what sense can there be in bringing a whole nation up in arms against one for the sake of an almost nominal regulation? It would have been easy to arrange differently by giving the Somalis a special pass. I talked to Lord Delamere about it when I went to dinner with him the other week; he is of the same mind as I am, and he probably knows the Somalis better than anyone else in this country.

It is a pity that this war has forced the English to adopt a system that is against their true nature; before it they really were "a free people," but now they have had to resort to a great deal of new organization, which is unsuited to them. The best of them will have nothing to do with it; both Delamere and Finch-Hatton said: "People in uniform are not human beings." Also it is difficult to introduce it so suddenly,—for the people who are now forced by circumstances to rule with an iron rod have not themselves been brought up to discipline and are only conversant with the system from one side: from above; in the less gifted this can lead to much despotism. In my opinion it is completely un-English to attempt to crush the self-esteem of others,—it is because they did not do this that they have hitherto kept their natives in the various colonies in hand; but it is not surprising that this war, that turns everything upside down, also causes confusion of ideas among the average classes in the warring nations. . . .

Ngong 12/8.1918

Dear Erling, Kaare, Pan Michael, d'Artagnan—my own beloved, wonderful Tommy!

Many many thousand thanks for two marvelous letters, of 25 March and 22 April, which I found when I returned yesterday from safari, and which I am absolutely delighted with, enchanted by, infinitely grateful for; I have already read them many times, you may be sure, and will keep them,—like all your letters,—as my most precious treasures, and I have read them to Bror, who is just as interested in them as I am. How proud of you I am, my beloved brother, even though it is no more than I had expected of you: that in the hour of peril you would be worthy of all that we have loved and dreamed of, and have stood no less fast in the trenches than they stood at Svoldr and Stiklestad,—and at Dybbøl. . . I imagine that for all of you out there there must come hours of terrible fatigue or when your nerve fails you and you think that you can endure it no longer; but when you write that you have "seen the god, your father's god,"—then it must be worth being dearly bought; these are life's highest moments and whatever may follow: "Blessed the head over which the eagle of exaltation has rushed with wide wings. . . ."

I always imagine you taking part in every action that I read about; when it is stated that they have advanced 4,000 yards, I think of you taking each step of them; when we hear that it is raining I see you in the rain; if there is news of a heavy bombardment I see your dear head as you listen to its thunder. Vive l'Armee! Long live the brave English army: And God keep you through it all, my beloved courageous Tommy.

As you know,—if you have received my letters,—I suggested to Mother that she should meet me,—and you,—in Paris, if there was a chance of you getting leave and going there. I believe that in a way it would be much better for Mother to take part in France's "gloire" and in its agony, where every single mother has her heart in the trenches, rather than be swimming around in all that goulash at home. And I thought that the idea of seeing you would enable her to overcome any misgivings, even the best and most sensible. But apparently it seems impossible to her, since she has written that she will not go. I have telegraphed to you today to say that if there is any chance of seeing you I will come at once . . . I will gladly defy both the submarines and, what is worse, the pangs of seasickness, to experience it. But now I await your answer. . . .

I saw a farm for sale up in Naivasha that I think would be ideal for you. I sent for the details of it but have not yet received them; if I think the terms are reasonable I will send you a telegram. It is situated beside beautiful Lake Naivasha, a big lake with clear blue water and mountains and plains around it,—with a long frontage to the lake and land behind with plains among the mountains; it is 5,000 acres. It is simply overflowing with game, including lions, and as the Masai Reserve adjoins the rear part of it, it is easy to go down there on long safaris. There is a house on the farm, on a high-lying site with a view over the lake; there is a lovely long grassy shore beside the lake. You could have a small car and a motorboat on the lake; when I was there there were millions of duck and geese that came on shore to graze in the afternoon. I have never seen a more beautiful or free place than Lake Naivasha in the whole world, and I think the life out there, especially there where it is cooler and more open than here, would appeal more to you than anywhere on earth,—your trench excepted, that is. . . .

To Ingeborg Dinesen

Ngong 12/8 1918

. . . First and foremost I must thank you and embrace you, beloved Mother, for your lovely, loving, brave letters, which came after this long silence as rain would come now on our dry shamba. I have been so anxious and worried about you, and when I myself was unable to sleep I thought and thought about you, lying all alone in the house at home,—but I hope no longer in the little narrow iron bed,—with no one to interpret the night's text,—and the Lord help us, there can hardly be anyone who is able to interpret that text,—and I think I have been sitting on the edge of your bed every night, little Mother. . . .

You can imagine how much Tommy's letters moved me; no doubt he has written in the same way to you, and I feel that when he views it like that and has experienced something so glorious and infinitely happy one must say that he was right to go, and that if we had made him give it up we would have deprived him of something that could never have been replaced. . . . Tommy has experienced "the wonderful" in a manner that has not separated him from his contemporaries, but that must almost be said to be the norm for the youth of Europe now; if he had gone on a North or South Pole expedition he would have been just as exposed and would have been so isolated, different from all the others; now he feels himself at one with them all, which I think is a great joy, especially for one with a nature like his. . . . Of course one does not dare to hope for too much, but neither must one be such a coward that merely out of anxiety for disappointments one crushes all faith and hope completely, and when just by reading about it one can see the whole world changed; what must it be like for those who are in it and who are turning the whole course of world history with their own hands? But I am even more proud of you than I am of Tommy, and he feels the same himself; he wrote so infinitely lovingly about you. You may be sure that there are not many minutes of the day when he and I are not very close to you.

I am writing today with a heavy heart, I have had a great sorrow, almost the greatest that could strike me here: I have lost Dusk. And it was all so distressing; it is hard to realize that a dog who was such a good friend to me all his life, and of whom I was so proud, could die in such a way,—and through my own fault.

At the beginning of August Bror and I and von Huth went up to Nakuru and Naivasha, where Bror had some bussiness [*sic*]. Bror and Huth left on Wednesday, I on Friday; we were to meet at Nakuru. I took Dusk with me, he always hated being left alone with the boys and loved driving, and we took our car with us. Strangely enough, on the way up he was nearly run over by the train, at Kikuyu Station, where the two trains met;—I was standing in the door of the carriage while Dusk was getting an airing on the tracks, and I did not see the other train approaching until it was only a few yards away from him,—I had just time to rush out and get hold of him and tear him away; the engine hit both him and me,—it struck him with a big crash,—but as I was pulling him at the same time it rather helped me to throw him away from the rails; he howled frightfully but was not hurt in the least. At that moment I did not give a thought to whether I was in danger, but afterward Lord Delamere, who was in the carriage, said: "It was the pluckiest thing I have seen in my life"—and everyone came rushing up because they thought that someone had thrown himself in front of the train; then I was so happy and proud that I had saved him,—and really it would have been much better for him if he had died there.

On Saturday we were going to drive thirty miles out from Nakuru to the camp of a man called Collier; Bror, Dusk, and I in the car, Huth on a motorcycle. When we were three or four miles from the camp the car broke down, and Bror wanted to drive back to Nakuru with me on the motorcycle while Huth and Dusk went on to the camp to stay there until we could get a man to fetch the car and them on Monday morning. I was so upset to have to leave Dusk,—I have hardly ever done that except when I went home, and I asked Huth again and again to take great care of him, keep him on the leash and not let him out of his sight; after they had started to walk away I went up to them and said: "You *must* take great care of him, I risked my life for him yesterday and would do so again today; I prize him more than anything in the world." Bror and Huth laughed and said: "Don't take such a touching farewell."—Dusk was standing looking at me so solemnly.

On Sunday Bror and I were going out to lunch with Lord Delamere, who has a farm twenty miles the other side of Nakuru, and we arranged that a man should fetch them on Monday morning, and we stayed the night with Delamere, and he drove us to Naivasha on Monday, it is on the road between Nakuru and Kikuyu and we were to make a camp there, as Bror has a contract to plow land there. We were going home from Naivasha on Wednesday morning and I was expecting to meet Dusk at Naivasha Station, but he was not there, and not until we were almost home did Collier, who was on the train, come and tell me that on the Sunday evening he and Huth had taken Dusk out shooting with them and he had run away from them in the half-darkness and they had not seen anything of him since. So I went back again with the train,—I spent fifteen hours in the train that day,—and arrived at Nakuru in the evening at seven o'clock, and then two Somalis came up and told me that on that same morning they had seen a dog like Dusk at Njoro Station; he had gone to their camp and stayed all night there, although they had chased him away, and in the morning when they were striking camp, he had been sitting there howling. By a lucky chance I got hold of a car and drove out there the same night and drove all around asking everyone I met if they had seen him, but no one had. Huth was staying at the Nakuru Hotel, he had not made the least effort to find him; after he had disappeared on Sunday evening they had quite calmly struck camp on Monday morning, so that he did not have the slightest chance of finding them, and it is thick bush there with not a single human being anywhere near. He said: "I really regret that it happened."

I stayed at Nakuru,—cursed place,—for three days searching everywhere, but no one had seen him, and I promised 300 rupees to anyone who should find him; but finally I came to believe what Bror had been saying the whole time, that he had been caught by a leopard the night he had run away, so I returned home on Saturday, but left Fara there to go on searching, and he got a mule and rode into the mountains. He found him [Dusk] there on Sunday morning, he was terribly thin and ill; he was lying beside a zebra foal that he had bitten to death, but he himself had been wounded in the chest by a kick and was coughing blood; he recognized Fara and whined when he saw him, but he was very ill, could not walk or even drink milk, and he died the same afternoon. Fara was not even able to bring him back here but only laid him in the bushes, so now I will never see him again.

You will understand what a great grief this is, not so much because I will miss him, but because he suffered so much and through my fault, for I should never have left him with such a careless and unreliable person as Huth, he who in every way was so much better than most human beings. He was so faithful to me; when I was alone at home he never left my side, and then I had always had him here, and he was so beautiful and intelligent, I was so proud of him. I believe that when I die, I will see him again, and then I will most fervently beg his forgiveness for leaving him. My wonderful faithful Dusk. I miss him so much, and if I live to be seventy I believe I will never think of him without weeping. . . .

I have thought many times of writing to you about Anders, but it is always difficult to write from such a distance; one can so easily get completely false ideas of things. But partly because of what Tommy writes of in his last letter, and in fact several times, I will express my opinion that it would be foolish not to let Anders come out here before he has settled down at home. I think that this country would suit him excellently in every way and even if he did not stay out here it would interest him immensely just to see it. . . .

Of course the question with regard to Leerbæk is whether he will be happy there; if not there would be no happiness in it either for him or the Sasses. I feel that Anders's greatest (almost only!) fault is his lack of self-confidence, and I think that it is unfortunate that Aunt Lidda has an almost unique capacity for depriving most people of this even if they do possess it. I fear that Anders could never carry through anything, could hardly suggest anything, unless they thoroughly approved of it, and that his own talents could never flourish there,—and here I think that they could. I also feel that the great defect in Aunt Lidda's moral code is that it does not distinguish between important and unimportant matters, so that it is one and the same thing whether one gets drunk or commits murder; this might well lead enterprising people to take to murder, but in more reticent natures I think it puts a stop to all initiative. I always feel that Anders was so much nicer, more interesting and on the whole more at his best at Katholm than at Folehave, where he was criticized so much; like me, he was most happy with Father's family and it would have been better for him to have settled down by the avuncular arm chair than with Aunt Lidda. . . .

Galbraith Cole has just married an extremely nice, sweet girl, a niece of Balfour. She looks like a high school girl at home—she said that she had written to her uncle about Bror's soldier-settlement scheme. They had had a large and beautiful house built at the top of a hill with a view over lovely Lake Elmenteita,—which is all owned jointly by Cole and Delamere,—and were exceptionally happy there—we went there with Delamere for tea. It is fine land everywhere there and I wish we had a cattle farm, but perhaps we will get one some day and avoid making such foolish mistakes as we would if we were newly-arrived settlers. . . .

To Ingeborg Dinesen

Naivasha, British East Africa
26.8.1918

Dearest Mother.

I am writing this from beautiful Naivasha; we have moved up here, as you will know from Bror's telegram, because he has a contract with Longenot Ltd. to plow 2,000 acres in eleven months. We are living in a little tin house built by our boys, with an absolutely wonderful and enchanting view over Lake Naivasha and the mountains on the other side. I can't tell you how lovely it is to be out on the march again. And to me Naivasha is one of the most heavenly places in the world; the delicate browns of the grass and the plains,—ochre, terracotta, sepia, terra de Siena,—and then the clear blue ever-changing lake and the airy blue—bleu horizon—mountains and hills beyond,—it is like a beautiful, delicate old painting. Then it is so lovely to be near water again; we have a little sailing boat which bears the proud name of "The Flame," in which we go sailing on the lake when we have time. There are millions of duck and geese and moorhens, grebe and flamingos and herons, and the chalk white egrets, but it is forbidden to shoot at present, so we content ourselves with looking at them. . . .

I have two Somali boys here,—Abdullah and a friend of his, Said, who are 12–14 years old, and Bror thinks that our entire time is spent amusing them. Said is a sailor and comes out with me in the boat. Abdullah is a gun-bearer and yesterday himself shot a kongoni ["hartebeest"] with my Paradox; I think both of them are in absolute paradise. I left Farah at the house so that he could have a honeymoon with Fathima, and Esa, who is to do the garden. I cannot remember whether I told you that I have signed a contract with Hindoo, who is going to clear my park,—the jungle, that is, and leave the big trees standing,—for firewood. It is really nice—the house has now completely lost the enclosed appearance it had before, and you can see the beautiful Ngong Hills through the tree trunks, they never look the same, sometimes appearing to be quite near and at others far away.—When I look at them I invariably think of the psalm: "I will lift up mine eyes unto the hills, from whence cometh my help." . . .

This house looks very shabby as it is put together with sheet iron of all possible shapes, age and color, but inside it is lined with papyrus and very neat and quite cool even at the hottest time of the day; but the floor is just several feet of sand. We have two rooms and a little bathroom, no windowpanes but shutters for the windows so we can make it completely dark. There is always a strong wind blowing here, like the real easterly equinoctial gales at home; it makes a frightful row especially at night, in the old iron sheets and the papyrus. We have a view on every side, and in the morning the dogs sit outside watching the game coming down to the lake to drink from several square miles around; my little dog Banja gets so excited that he can't keep quiet, but sits there howling and whining all the time, —all in all it is quite lovely here. . . .

To Ingeborg Dinesen

Naivasha 5.9.1918

. . . We are still here at Naivasha, where it is lovely. We hear lions every night. My little dog Banja had a fight with a big boar that tore his chest badly, but I think he is recovering. I am laid up myself with a bad leg; I was riding peacefully along on my mule when it was suddenly frightened by a jackal in the bush and threw me off against a stone; I am as black as ink and badly grazed, but Bror can bandage like an angel and wraps me and Banja up like two mummies.—He is very busy, of course, but that is what suits him best, and then we are so pleasantly free from "shauries" up here, particularly because there are no white people; a fat boy called George drives the motor-plow and eats with us, it is true, but as he has turned out to be extraordinarily stupid, he will probably have to leave,—but he is harmless enough as he only opens his mouth in order to eat. . . .

What you and Viggo write about the harbor at home makes one's hair turn gray. The papers give me the impression that people are becoming more and more revolting at home; the class that is in government now—like the Apothecary,—are almost the worst kind! I often wonder whether, if Sønderjylland comes back to us after the war, they will not be frightfully disappointed at coming into the goulash atmosphere and futile regime. I think that it is wonderful that we have a fair amount of land to fall back upon, the rear garden and the copse, and further up the forest and the marsh,—we must make sure that that stays unchanged. How much I long to be walking there again with you,—in the *shade,* for we never have that out here,—no words can express. . . .

I'm always thinking of what season it is at home,—for here, after the rainy seasons seem to have ceased, we live in a completely seasonless year,—and now I expect you will soon be getting grapes and nuts and apples. There is nothing in the world as beautiful as a September day at home. Now the day after tomorrow it is three years since Mama died, and I am recalling those wonderfully calm, quiet days we had then, especially the day when Mama was taken away, and the coffin was standing out on the lawn. There was such infinite harmony there, like Mama herself.—

I would very much like to hear from Aunt Clara whether the injections she is having can possibly be sent or obtained here. I do not know what they are called. I was talking to Galbraith Cole about them the other day. He is only 40, poor man, but completely stiff and bent, suffers terribly and thinks that he will not be able to move at all in a few years' time. He says he has tried everything possible but nothing has helped him. He is a brother-in-law of Delamere, in whose house I saw a picture of Galbraith Cole taken fifteen years ago, the nicest and most handsome officer one could imagine, so it is a frightful shame for him. . . .

To Ingeborg Dinesen

Naivasha, British East Africa
11.9.1918

My beloved Mother.—

I am writing more to send you and everyone else a greeting than because anything is actually happening here. We are still up here and it is lovely, but very dry. My leg is no better and is really a great nuisance. Wounds develop in a disgusting manner out here, they heal on the outside, but ooze and spread underneath; that is what they call "Veldtsores," and it is almost impossible to get rid of them.—We have nearly 200 oxen here now and should be plowing 30 to 40 acres a day, it is a fine sight when they are all working; huge clouds of dust follow each plow and shine in the sun, it looks beautiful, as you can imagine it did when Gefion was plowing Sealand out of Sweden. I think Bror enjoys being up here dealing with oxen and plows.

The day before yesterday we sailed across the lake in our little boat to visit some people, the Mortimers, who have a lovely house on the other side of the lake. Our sailor boy, a marvelously beautiful fourteen-year-old Somali who exactly resembles Johannes Poulsen at that age, was previously a diver in Aden and loves to show off his tricks and disappear like a stone sinking to the bottom and then pop up 300 yards away. . . .

To Ingeborg Dinesen

Ngong 23/10 1918

My own beloved Mother.

I am sorry not to have written for so long, but actually I have been ill most of the time. As you will know from my telegram, I developed blood poisoning after my fall from a mule (I wired "horse" as I thought you perhaps might not understand mule!). Just after I wrote my last letter,—of 11 September,—to you, I got a high fever, and in the evening of the 12th Bror put me in an ox cart in which he had made a bed, and took me to Naivasha, and luckily a train was going to Nairobi early next day. I drove straight from the station at Nairobi to Dr. Burkitt,—a mad Irishman, but the best doctor here and such a nice man,—and he gave me chloroform right away, in safari clothes and riding boots, despite my loud protests, and cut open my leg from the knee right up to the hip, and took out a lot of "dead flesh," which made a very large wound. Then I had to stay at the Kenya nursing home in Nairobi for a fortnight, which was anything but fun, and after that I stayed with the McMillans at their house in Nairobi. Burkitt sewed me up twice and gave me chloroform twice, and you know how terribly sick that always makes me; I have had to stay in bed here until now, and it is still far from healed, but much better now and not much trouble, except that unfortunately it is going to leave a big scar, which I am very upset about. Bror has been wonderful in looking after me and is an expert at bandaging. It is much nicer to be here again with my good boys who are so extremely kind and helpful. Thanks for your telegram which was a great comfort. I think I have got over this misfortune now but it has taken a long time. I don't think that a doctor at home would have cut such a large hole; but Burkitt assures me that I came to him at the last moment and that he could not avoid it.

The good news from home,—from France, I mean,—has been an immeasurable help to me; it is sheer joy to think of the Germans retreating through Belgium and France, where they were advancing so confidently and sure of victory in 1914! If only, if only peace is not too far away. Surely the whole world without exception would give an endless sigh of relief and joy on the day that peace was signed, —and surely no one, not even the Kaiser himself, would have started on it if one had known what it would be like; and yet it cannot be peace yet. It is as if they had set such mighty forces in movement that they can no longer control them, and it is as in Goethe's poem about the sorcerer's half-educated apprentice, who calls up the spirits and commands them to carry water, and then does not know the magic word to stop them, and is about to perish when the sorcerer comes and stops them with one word. But when will the sorcerer come and utter the word!

While I was staying with the McMillans I borrowed so many books about the war from Bulpett, especially French books; it is marvelous to read them as a change from English; there is so much that is beautiful in them, although one ought not to read them. In particular I read one called "Lettres d'un Soldat," with a foreword by [name missing]. It consists of letters from a young French artist, and what especially impresses one is the view of the war given by an extremely refined individual, who before the war lived exclusively for art and beauty, and was then hurled as a foot soldier into the thick of it totally against all his inclinations. It affects one so strongly and painfully because it is not only one single person's experience; but behind this soldier one sees the young generation of artists and scholars, not only of France but of the whole world, who have been torn away from their work and their future and sent out into the lice and mud and blood of the trenches, —and yet have been gripped there by the immense glory of this battle. I also read "Anna Karenina" again there; I think that the whole of Kitty and Levine's love story and their marriage and their life in the country is one of the most delightful tales one can imagine. . . .

I'm enclosing a clipping from the newspaper with a picture of McMillan and me so that you can see him in all his immensity. [See illus.]. It was taken at a garden party for the "Star and Garter" Fund, that the McMillans held in Nairobi. They made 20,000 rupees, which was pretty good.—

Spanish flu is raging out here to a most worrying extent; last week 22 people died of it. Major Elkington is at the point of death today. There is also a lot of small pox so I have sent for the doctor from the Scotch Mission down here to come and vaccinate Bror and me today. All our boys are to be vaccinated; we have had one or two cases on the farm. . . .

To Thomas Dinesen

Ngong 7/11 1918

My beloved Tommy.

Thank you for a short letter of 17/8 telling me that you had taken part in the great offensive and promising to tell me more about it. I have not received any more yet, but you can imagine how those few lines set one's mind working! You write that you went over the top ten minutes after the drum fire started, and not only do I see you standing and waiting and then going forward, but feel I was there myself hearing the firing and seeing the trenches and the battle. Beloved Tommy, you bring a breath of the glory you are experiencing to us all. May God continue to preserve you. "Victory in your hand and victory in your foot, victory in all your limbs, with victory may you return!" How I wish I were a young soldier helping to put the Bosch [*sic*] to flight; but so much of the glory descends on me from you. How much I long to hear you talk of it.

If, in spite of the joy with which the good news from France fills us, this letter should sound somewhat depressed, it is because of the Spanish flu, which is raging out here to an alarming extent . . . Bror and I and every one of our boys are laid up with it, so things are pretty difficult. There is a great deal of small pox about too, on our farm as well at present, so we have all been vaccinated, and it will takes its toll of one's strength. However, we must hope that it will soon be over. And we have had one stroke of great good fortune,—at long last we have had rain, so everything is blooming and promising the best for this season. The farm looks in excellent trim, and I hope and really believe that soon you will be getting good dividends on your money; but I could not go through another year like this one. Being responsible for other people's money is no joke especially when one has been entrusted with it out of kindness; I hope you will never have to experience that. But I do not think it will be very long before Mother can have 50,000 kroner a year from here, and that will certainly make up for these hard times. . . .

There has been some trouble in the Masai Reserve, which I think may be over now. It broke out because they wanted to recruit some of the Masai, who opposed this and worked themselves up into a great state of exitement [*sic*], offered resistance, stole cattle and burned all the stores in the Reserve. I think that the military authorities could have gone about it with more tact, but that is never their strong point,—forgive me for saying so,—and when they had made a mess of it they were obliged to ask Lord Delamere, who is the "Little Father" of the Masai, to go down and sort it out for them. Lord Delamere then disappeared without a trace into the Reserve and as far as I know has not yet turned up again, but no doubt he has thrown oil on the troubled waters by his sheer presence. I can imagine that it is a relief to him to go down and sit and talk with his old Masai chiefs, so they won't get him back too quickly; he has to tear about up here between his farm and a whole lot of committees and counsils [*sic*] for which he most probably has a hearty distaste. . . .

My leg has still not healed up and it will soon be three months since I hurt it; but wounds are a great nuisance here. I have been through so much with it, chloroformed twice, stitched and opened up again twice,—so that I feel rather like an old soldier. I have a disgusting scar from the knee to the thigh, which I'm very upset about; Bror hopes that not many people will see it. . . .

Mother writes that you are intending to become a pilot, but I cannot work out whether the training school you are in now is a flying school or not? I can understand your wish to fly and will look forward to going for a trip in your plane after the war. If you should get to France as a pilot it is just possible that you will meet someone called Denys Finch-Hatton, who is also a pilot on the French front, and that would make me very happy. For I have been so fortunate in my old age to meet my ideal realized in him, and it would be good if you two could meet. . . .

"Eegholms Gud" and "Clara von Haags Mirakler" have finally arrived; I have been reading them with great pleasure and Bror is reading them in bed now, protesting loudly that the author is crazy!

Well, goodbye, my dearest Tommy, and let us hope that it will not be so long before we meet again that I am gray haired. I think it would be fine if you were to become another Captain Dinesen!

Many many thousand greetings

Always always your faithful sister Tanne.

To Ingeborg Dinesen

Ngong 15/11 1918

Dearest Mother.

I am writing for the first time since the signing of the armistice and the end of the war!

Probably no one knows yet what is going to happen and what will become of the world; all that I can really comprehend is that the shooting has stopped and that no more dead and wounded will be brought in.

If only I were at home or in France or England, but particularly at home, and could be with you all at this time. Now you will reap the reward of your heroism. Now one can hardly understand how one stood it. Nor can I understand how those who had the power to make the decision could keep on and not make peace long ago, but held firm to their first demands; but it was right, of course, only one did not think so five months ago. Now when one thinks back on the war, on the first months, Verdun and then the last German push against Paris, it seems inexplicable to me that France and the whole world were saved. . . .

Tonight there is to be a great torchlight procession with music in Nairobi to celebrate the peace. We have been invited to it by Otter, who is in charge of some of the arrangements. 5,000 black soldiers will march through the town with torches. They have good reason to rejoice, poor things; the war has taken a terrible toll on the native population.

Out here the crazy Gorringe has got all the settlers to agree to celebrate it with a "Bonfire" up on the Ngong Hills, which is also to take place tonight. As it is a very awkward journey up there even in the daytime I don't know how they will manage, especially as most of them are very old women. But the English have enough enthusiasm to overcome all obstacles where picnics are concerned. . . .

To Ellen Dahl

Ngong 10/12 1918

. . . You cannot believe how proud we are of Tommy and delighted about his V.C. Of course I always knew that he would be brave and brilliant; but there has to be luck as well, and most of those who deserved the Victoria Cross no doubt fell on French and Belgian soil. I think that Mother must be boundlessly proud and happy both over his having come through it,—when one thinks that he is out of danger it's as if seven tons were lifted off one's shoulders,—and then over his having done so well,—how proud Father would have been of him; and I think too that everyone at home who felt bitter toward him because he did not take Katholm must now be thinking that after all he has kept up the family traditions in a far better way. . . .

All in all, despite the fact that this year has been very troublesome with the frightful drought and abnormal conditions generally, it has brought me a great deal of enjoyment. When I was out here before I knew very few people, but now we are on the friendliest terms with everyone of account here in B.E.A., and I have so many really good friends. This is partly due to the fact that we have a much better house now; in the old one there was no room to invite anyone, but people come out here now all the time and they are all most enthusiastic over this place. You would probably laugh if you saw this house after hearing so much about it; for at home it would be an extremely small house, but here it almost counts as a palace! . . .

I long so much to see your beautiful house; it must be a delightful place, and how much you must be enjoying being settled in your own house without the fear of having to move. I would actually very much like to live in Copenhagen myself when we eventually get home, but think that Bror would get tired of it. Anyway I think it will be a long time before I can get Bror to leave this country, however things go; I think it suits him much too well. Probably what is most necessary if one is to succeed out here is a passion for farming, and then original ideas, not being content to follow the old traditional lines but having a high regard for liberty. Even I, who at heart hate the soil in its primitive state, have come to feel that there is something totally fascinating about clearing and plowing and cultivating it. But all the same: "Plus je vis dans la Nature, plus j'aime l'art!"

To Thomas Dinesen

Ngong 13/12 1918

My own beloved, wonderful Tommy.

I don't know how to congratulate you enough on your V.C.—Living among the English I do know how immeasurably much it means, "the only order in the world"; perhaps that is not really properly understood at home. I have heard that yours was about the thousandth to be awarded, so that means that you are among the thousand bravest men in the world,—which of course I have never doubted, but it is good to have it in black and white! I am so proud of you and so *overjoyed* at how it has gone that every single day I wake up in the morning as one did on one's birthday when one was small! Some of the hero's glory does indeed descend on his sister, and people out here have been so kind as to say that courage is a feature of the family. Apart from the honor,—which is le superflu, that is, le necessaire,—you have benefited us greatly with your cross. It has been announced in the local papers and really put a stop to the continuous gossip that some people were spreading with incredible persistence about our being pro-German. . . .

If only you would come out here. You are probably being well feted where you are, but we would prepare a grand reception for you, I can tell you. But in any case I am more grateful to you than I can say; for your V.C. came at a time when I had been suffering much adversity and was beginning to lose faith in the eternal gods, and there is no greater misfortune than that. Now I have regained my belief in both gods and heroes, indeed, even in their very close presence.

Now I am going to tell you something remarkable. When you first went to war I was terribly worried about you, and I used to talk to Fara about it, and he suggested that we should get the old Somali or rather, Arab sheik, i.e., priest, to cast a spell to keep you safe in all the danger. This was done on three successive Fridays, and consisted of a small piece of paper covered with passages from the Koran, which Fara and I had to bury, and not tell anyone where we had buried it or anything about it; we obeyed this command. Probably you will laugh when I say that it was often a great comfort to me, and still more when you hear that, despite the fact that it was a period of straitened finances for me, I paid the old sheik 1,000 rupees to make it up. But now listen and stop your mocking. The sheik's sorcery called not only for you to come safely through the war unharmed by enemy fire but for you to SLAY TWELVE OF THE ENEMY, BE AN EXAMPLE TO ALL AND GAIN GREAT HONOR!—And yesterday I received a clipping from the "Times" that said the same thing in identical words! Don't ever let me hear you deny that we are in league with the higher powers! It has made a profound impression on me, I think it is absolutely uncanny, and you must think of me and Fara with gratitude. The old sheik is going to come out here one of these days, when Bror is away. He had to write your name and your mother's maiden name on the paper, in translation, and it was very strange to see Ingeborg Westenholz in Arabic. I am not sure that I am allowed to be telling you all this, but I simply must tell it to someone!

You write about the farm at Naivasha. It has not yet been sold, but as a foreigner you cannot get a transfer on it,—the generosity of the English!—and as the war is over now and you can come out here yourself, there is no point in my buying something that you have not seen for yourself. . . .

Huge fortunes are being made out of sisal at the moment, it is a kind of fiber. Of course it is possible that the prices will fall again when everyone is planting it; but if one is speedy enough to be among the first to plant there is still a good chance. If you felt like putting up £2,000 now, and £500 a year,—a good part of which you can borrow on the land from the banks here after you have got something planted,—for the next three years, you could have a large plantation going by 1923, which, with the current prices, should give you £50,000 a year,—and even if prices are reduced by half, £25,000. Then if you did not touch this but put it on one side or invested it, by 1928, in ten years' time, with your plantation still going, you would be in a position to make the Colletts an offer.—The best thing would be for you to come out here as soon as possible bringing with you the money you might intend to put into it; then you could look at the land yourself and talk to people, and strike while the iron is hot, for that is what counts.

To convince you of the truth of all this I am enclosing some figures. (The people who planted sisal in 1915–16 and started with a capital of £1,000, made £30,000 net profit last year.)

Naturally we should be only too pleased to help you and look after it for you. We have the opportunity to offer this because we are at the moment trying to arrange our affairs here so as to obtain our freedom. We ourselves and our neighbor Johnnie, who wanted to put up the guarantee, have suggested to our shareholders at home that they should lease the farm to us for five years at a rent of 7½% on the capital this year, 10% next year and in the following years 12½%, 15, and 17½%—that is, as was envisaged when we were at home in 1916; only that everything is delayed by two years, and they will have lost the interest on their money for these two years, but that is due partly to the war, partly to the terrible conditions last year, and a new venture is always exposed to that kind of disappointment at the start. In addition we are also to plant 200 acres on the company's land, partly at Ngong, partly at Uasin-Gishu, every year, which would also bring them a reserve capital and an increased income two or three years after planting .

Do you think this is a good proposal to make them? My own point of view is this: I have absolute faith in this country, actually more and more the more I see of it; but so little is known about it that it is difficult to make calculations, and the last year's experience has shown that the climate is so unreliable that one has to be prepared for surprises. An enterprise such as ours, therefore, needs a stronger capital outlay than we have had. I am sure that anyone taking out this lease for five years would earn by it; but it is, of course, possible that 1919 will turn out to be like 1918, and then we cannot manage without more capital from home, and how will they react to that, and what will our position be like then? . . .

Johnnie van de Weyer, who is to be a half-partner in the enterprise, is our neighbor, a former officer in the Scotch Guards and an exceptionally nice person, quite a character. We are now awaiting a reply from the management at home and hope so much that they will agree to the proposal. We would manage the farm as before and naturally continue to live here, although I think that Bror would come to lead something of a roving life. It is possible that if the plan is going to be realized, I might come home as soon as possible. If so, would you meet me in London,—then we could travel home together via Scotland? Oh, my dearly beloved Tommy, is it really true that I am going to see your face again, as I have dreamed a hundred times!

Indeed, love is the most divine of all the world's forces. It has created everything beautiful in the world,—the song of the nightingale, the flowering trees, every work of art and then of course most V.C.s. I wonder if you know enough French to understand Musset's sonnet about Beatrice Donato in "Le fils de Titien," "Vois donc combien c'est peu que la gloire ici-bas-puisque tout beau qu'il soit ce portrait ne vaut pas-crois m'en sur ma parole! un baiser du modele!"

And what could surpass a walk beside the sea on an autumn day with a newly acquired Victoria Cross and a lovely girl whom one loves. Then one has come into a heritage of pure gold and can laugh at all eventualities, even those that can bring great pain—"Alles geben die Götter, die unendlichen ihren Lieblingen ganz: Alle Freuden—die unendlichen,—alle Schmerzen, die unendlichen, ganz." (Apologies, censor.)

My heart rejoices when I think of you. How proud Father would have been of you; how much I feel myself that you have lent us luster, and how happy I am that I have won the famous bottle of champagne from you and that you have followed old Absalon's theory with such success: that there are many great and beautiful arts in the world, but the greatest of all is the art of living. Go on living beautifully!!

Your Tanne.

1919

To Thomas Dinesen

Ngong 8/1 1919

My dearest Tommy.

Happy New Year! I wish that all the best things on earth may be yours in 1919, and that we may meet, either here or at home,—the very best thing would be if we met in Europe and you came back with me. I may tell you that you are very popular here already; all the Somalis ask after "my brother," and know about your Crosses, and I have several boys who are eager to enter your service when you get your farm here. They usually ask whether you "shinder" me,—outshine, put to shame,—and when they hear that you *shindar* me *sana* (thoroughly), they beg me fervently to recommend them to you.

Thank you for your letter telling me about your Croix de Guerre. I am absolutely *delighted*; the V.C. may be even finer but the other one comes from France, which to me is for all time the holy land where liberty and beauty originate. How proud Father would have been of you. There cannot be many to hold both the French and the Victoria Crosses. I am sending you a clipping from one of our newspapers from which you can see how much good you have done for us. I have read the accounts of the fighting in the trenches hundreds of times and gained a real impression of what it was all like, and of what one must feel. There was valor indeed.

I have bought an island in Lake Naivasha for you and am negotiating for the farm of 5,000 acres that I wrote about earlier. I believe the island can be made into something unique, out here if not in the whole world. It is true that it is not large, in fact *very* small,—about the same size as the piece of garden between the canal and the shore road at home!!!—but high, formed of rocks descending steeply to the clear blue water, with big trees everywhere. One could have a windmill for pumping water, and plant roses and rhododendrons everywhere. Then one could have a swimming place and a little harbor for one's motor boat, and go out in it in the mornings before it gets too hot, and shoot duck and geese, there are millions and millions of them, and sometimes an old hippo. There are no fish, but they are going to try putting some trout in it; you could join in with that. I think can get the island itself for £100, but of course there will be the expense of building a house and making other improvements; but that surely could not amount to a great deal.

Then there is the farm on the shore. . . . I was at a dance in Nairobi the day before yesterday,—very enjoyable, incidentally,—and met there a very nice and charming person, Colonel—or Major!—Buxton, who was leaving for England the following day. He has bought 300 acres of building land adjoining, or actually part of the farm that I am thinking of for you, and wants to buy 5,000 acres adjoining it. . . . You might perhaps be able to buy the farm in his name, if being a foreigner causes more difficulty; he will certainly do what he can for you,—partly because he and I are such good friends, and partly because he has a great admiration for you and thought he would be able to find you in England without an address, as you must be very famous. Remember whatever you do not to tell him how old I am, as he suggested that I was twenty-seven, and I said yes,—you must *never* tell any of my friends here about it; on pain of everything being over between us!!!

I have just returned from a splendid safari during Christmas and New Year at Greswolde-Williams's at Kedong. . . . I shot a lion that we were tracking and following all day. It was very exiting, [*sic*], for I had taken a shot at it, and it ran over a hill and we lost sight of it, and we ,—Frank G.-W. and I,—went galloping after it, but could not see it, and it is very difficult terrain with little hills and thick bush,—when our horses suddenly bolted, and there he was in a thornbush in a small crevice, not five yards away! I practically fell on top of him, for that was where I had least expected to see him and the horse was quite beside itself with fright. We hastily dismounted and could see him moving about in the bushes where he was raging and growling, but could not really see him clearly and one does not want to risk shooting at random; but at length, when I thought I saw his silhouette with swinging tail in the thorn, I shot and hit him in the shoulder,—but it was only a small bullet for such a large animal, and out he came right at us, straight as a cannonball, and believe me, a charging lion has an expressive face. I managed to give him a bullet right in the chest; he fell almost at our feet. The skin is not particularly good; I was going to ask if you would like the head , but perhaps you want only your own lions.

The "Swedish Soldier-Settlement Scheme," that I wrote to you about earlier, has been approved by the Land Commission here; now we must see whether we can get anything to do with it. Perhaps as an ex-soldier you could apply for a farm; I would think that would be a good transaction.

The law regarding native passes for Somalis has not yet been enforced; it is possible they are waiting until the new governor arrives. That will probably be during the first week in February and he is to be welcomed with a week of racing and other sport, which should be enjoyable, as all the organizers are people I know well; I wish I had something other than rags to wear, but I haven't, partly because of being poverty stricken, partly because you can't get anything out here that is at all fashionable. If only your Lilian could buy me something. It is amazing how much clothes mean; perhaps I value them too highly, but nothing,—be it illness, poverty or loneliness or other misfortunes, distresses me more than having nothing to wear; and I have never been brought so low that I have not been cheered at the prospect of a new hat!!—which is probably utterly idiotic. . . .

To Ingeborg Dinesen

Ngong 14/1.1919

. . . Demobilization is now under way and they are sending a lot of troops home. The first contingent left after the dance last Saturday; there were a great many people at the station, including the Governor, the General, and most of those with influence in Nairobi, and there was music playing. Also on that train were Geoffrey Buxton and Algy Cartwright; I had lunch with them beforehand, but unfortunately I was attacked by sunstroke during the departure ceremony, so badly that I thought I was going mad. It is amazing that one can continue to be so easily affected by the sun; it seems to get worse, and you get such frightful pains in the head and cannot see; the only thing that helps is darkness.

It is strange, too, that the sun prevents wounds from healing here; my leg is not nearly healed up yet after almost five months. and it has not been exposed to the sun ; it must be something to do with the climate, for any wound I got at home healed immediately. There is still an open wound about the size of a matchbox and quite deep; I don't think it will ever heal until I get home. Otherwise I have been very well recently and have grown plump again; I am taking some arsenic, which does wonders for me. . . .

To Ingeborg Dinesen

Ngong 26/2.1919

. . . We have had rain!! More than 4″ in three days, and no one could imagine what a difference it makes to the shamba,—and so to the whole of life! I keep thinking of the song: "Nun, armes Herz, vergiss der Qual! Nun muss sich alles, alles, wenden." Perhaps now our time of tribulation is really over and better times are on the way. Now even the furthest, deepest valley is turning green,—it is something of a miracle how quickly everything here is transformed by the rain; the Ngong Hills and the Reserve, that were burned to the likeness of a doormat, are now brilliant with the finest, most glorious green, and the whole shamba is flowering. If only it will go on. . . .It is so beautiful here, a paradise on earth, when there is enough rain. And in a way, during the times of tribulation one comes to love this intractable country still more; I have a feeling that wherever I may be in the future, I will be wondering whether there is rain at Ngong.

The race week was a great success, and I really enjoyed myself tremendously, although a lot of it had to be regarded in a humorous light. There were two race-days and numerous lunch-parties and dances. Of course it was all in honor of the new governor, Sir Edward Northey, who seems to me to be extremely pleasant and most intelligent. I do not envy him his post. I saw a good deal of him, as I met him at a dance and sat beside him at a lunch given by Delamere on the race course. . . .

We had a shoot here on the Sunday after the races; it is a nice, easy trip out here from Nairobi and people are always glad to come. Among the twenty people who came were Delamere, the General and his very charming brother, Colonel Llewellyn, Denis [*sic*] Finch-Hatton and Johnnie van de Weyer; it went very well. Finch-Hatton was ill with fever and stayed out here, he is still here now, and I am delighted to have him; I don't think I have ever met such an intelligent person before, and one does appreciate that here. . . . I must stop now as I am going out with Denis. There are big clouds promising more rain—"nun muss sich alles, alles, wenden." I hope that with you too everything is filled with promise after this terrible year.

Your Tanne.

To Ingeborg Dinesen

Ngong 12/7.1919

Dearest Mother.

. . .The reason for my enormously long silence is that literally every day since the beginning of April we have been thinking that we were on the point of leaving for Europe. The arrangements over boats for the military and civilians wanting passage home are so appallingly chaotic that most people have been kept in uncertainty for the last three months, and naturally everything else in the country is affected by this. . . . Not a soul here knows when the various ships are due to arrive or to whom places will be allotted; many have been waiting in Mombasa for weeks and months waiting for a chance,—this may perhaps be our last resort. . . . It is still worse for the military personnel waiting to be de mobilized, for they can only go by specific ships. Denys Finch-Hatton, for instance, had been waiting for eight months and had orders to get demobilized in Egypt; we wanted to go down the Nile together, but it was closed because of the disturbances there. . . .

All business here is naturally suffering because of the rate of exchange which means that at present one loses 25% on any money transferred from England. In my opinion, sooner or later the Government must take a radical step to remedy this, if this country is not to go bankrupt,—for instance, to adopt the same currency system here. But it looks as if they are not concerned about it. . . . Remarkably enough, land here is still going up in price. The farm at Naivasha that Uncle Mogens had an option to purchase for £8,000 up to three months after peace was concluded,—that he declined in 1917,—was sold the other day for £12,000,—out here, that is, £15,000 in London. . . .

We have been invited to stay at Government House during Race-week. The House-party consists only of ourselves, the Polowtzoffs, and Delamere. I am very reluctant to go as I have absolutely nothing to wear; but the General is begging me to come and help to get some sort of a permit to go home, either by sea or the Nile.

I have been able to follow Uncle Aage's activities in a batch of "Politiken" that came by the last mail. I think it must be a dangerous venture since actually one has so little knowledge as to who really is right. I read an article in "The English Magasin" [*sic*] for February by a man called Hamilton Fyfe, who has lived in Russia for many years and gave the impression of being sensible, and he expressed what I have felt myself, that Bolshevism is the first attempt at realizing democracy and may very well end in something good. It is true that there are excesses, but no worse than during the French Revolution, by whose ideas even the most arrant opponents live now. It is doubtful whether anyone knows whether it is so much worse than what was perpetrated by the Czarist regime. . . .

The Government here has arranged a kind of lottery of farms for ex-soldiers, entailing the giving out of a great deal of land. I think that they are making a sorry hash of it and that not a single soul will be satisfied, but probably that sort of thing is impossible to arrange satisfactorily. I applied for a farm for Tommy and had the satisfaction of hearing that he was the only foreigner who had been accepted.

However, he'll have to wait for the lots to be drawn at home in England. I applied for a North Kenia farm; it is so beautiful—and I think it would be pleasant for him to have had a farm in return for his war service.

Yesterday we returned from a fourteen-day safari to the Kedong Valley and Naivasha with General and Madame Polowtzoff. . . . As I have written, she is Madame Ignatieff from the Russian Legation at home; Uncle Mogens and Sofie met him out here in 1911, when they were camping at the foot of The Mau, if they remember; he says that Aunt Fritze and Sofie sat with the parasols over their knees to hide their trouser legs. He was Governor of Petrograd, and they fled during the Revolution; he is an exceptionally charming and talented person. They are eager to leave now, as they have had a telegram from his brother in Paris saying there is much to be done; it seems that most of the Russians of the old regime who escaped are gathering there. They have lost all their money, but say all of them have, and they are selling their jewels in order to live. They want me to travel home with them and have invited me to stay with them in Paris or at their house in Monte Carlo; I would like to very much, they would be interesting people to meet and an almost historic circle to get to know. . . .

On 14 August 1919 Karen Blixen and her husband sailed on the S.S. "Pundua" *from Mombasa Harbor, Kilindini, East Africa, to England via Bombay. After a stay in London, part of which they spent with Denys Finch Hatton, who was at that time visiting his family, and part with other people, they arrived in Denmark in November. During the following year Karen Blixen lived with her mother at Rungstedlund while receiving treatment for her illness from Professor Rasch at the National Hospital. According to Mogens Fog's account in* Blixeniana 1978, *in 1919 Karen Blixen suffered from both Spanish flu and blood poisoning and was ill for five months.*

After a fairly long visit to Sweden, Bror Blixen returned to Kenya in March 1920; almost nine months later Karen Blixen went to England with her brother Anders and took rooms in London, where Thomas Dinesen had been staying for some time. After a few days she and Thomas Dinesen were to continue the journey from here via Paris to Marseilles to embark for Africa on the "Garth Castle". *For the whole of the voyage Karen Blixen was in a state of acute despair. The uncertainty regarding the future of the farm was greater than ever before; various ominous telegrams from both Africa and Denmark concerning a finally decisive loan crossed each other at her London address, causing her to swing between hope and dread.*

1920

To Ingeborg Dinesen

Hotel Washington,
Curzon Street, Mayfair, W.
[November 1920]

. . . I am still suffering somewhat from the effects of the truly horrific thirty-six hours on the North Sea, but otherwise am well and am indescribably happy to be here with the boys. It is cold here,—apparently even worse in Paris,—but we have had clear, still weather. I love London and at this time of year there is something so poetic about great cities; this evening I saw against the new moon an old owl sitting in a tree in Piccadilly with all the cars and their lights rushing by.—

I have a number of things to do, of course, but then the boys go off together and are really enjoying themselves. One thing causes me great chagrin: Prince Vilhelm and Sjögren are to be on the "Garth Castle." It is such a miserable position to be in, with Sjögren's 25,000 exchange and everything, and naturally there will be festivities on their arrival in Africa,—they are to stay at Government House,—where we too are probably expected to give a dinner, which is rotten for me. . . .

To Ingeborg Dinesen

Hotel Washington,
Curzon Street, Mayfair, W.
24.11.1920

My own beloved Mother.—

I want to write you a couple of lines before we leave London. We have had a really delightful time together here. I think Anders has enjoyed it immensely, and Thomas and I having him with us. Yesterday we went for a really lovely trip to Tommy's old camp at Hazlemere [*sic:* Haslemere], it was so moving to see all the places one has visualized him in, the cross on Gallows Hill and the little Tea-rooms, and it was the most wonderful quiet weather with sunshine and a light hoar frost. The countryside there is very beautiful with big hills and fine trees, particularly oak. I envy them their fences of oak palings, that would be something for "Blokken,"—Thomas so much enjoyed showing us everything, he had a very happy time there. But Anders is never as interested in what others are telling him as in finding analogous things to relate.—

In the evening we went to hear "Faust" at Covent Garden; it was a bad production, I thought, with a terrible Faust, but Anders was delighted with it. Thomas and Anders had a rather difficult parting this morning but we must hope that the future will be smooth for them and that they will meet again with joy. I think they have both developed a good deal this summer; they are much more mature.—

As you know, my plans are uncertain, it is very trying, and it is frightfully unlucky that Buxton is just coming home so that we will cross each other; if only he had been here, or in Africa, for a week at the same time as I, I am sure we should have been able to arrange something. I am very, very reluctant to remain in Paris, particularly because I am staking everything on one card,—Buxton,—and I have no time, or knowledge of how things are, or any means of communicating with them in case, for instance, Buxton's terms should be unacceptable to me. I am even afraid of being alone so long in Paris with nothing to do; that is to say, of course I could find something to do, but I cannot concentrate on anything except Ngong for the time being. For the sake of all eventualities I have telegraphed for power of attorney for Thomas; for if Milligan definitely advises me to stay—if the arrangement with Buxton proves workable,—Thomas will have to go out and see what he can do about things out there. But I am setting my hopes on finding a telegram in Paris which will enable us to travel out together, we had both been looking forward to that so much. . . .

It is so lovely to know that Rungsted and you, and Folehave and all of you are there.—But Ngong, Ngong, it is written in my heart. . . .

To Ingeborg Dinesen

G[d] Hotel Louvre & Paix
Marseille 1.12.1920.

My dearest Mother.—

I have had some terrible days since I received Bror's telegram asking me to stay here and wait for Buxton. When one knows what is the right thing to do one can always manage to do it, but in this case I really did not know what was most sensible. Of course staying here was staking everything on one card: Buxton.—And then naturally all depended on how good that card was. I was really prepared to do what I believed was best,—but some risks must be taken,—and now I am going, hoping and hoping that this will not lose me my best chance.—

If only Bror had kept me informed of developments I am sure that I could still have reached an agreement with Buxton here, but now I feel that I know far too little,—as, for instance, *what* interest the farm can pay on a loan, or whether I can sell Uasin Gishu and for how much. Then Bror keeps assuming that we are going to *sell,* while I feel sure that it must be just as advantageous to keep hold of the property,—and I would so much rather do that. No, I feel that I must go out there, and hope to Heaven that is the right thing to do. When I telegraphed to you about a power of attorney for Tommy it was my intention to let him go out and I myself remain here,—of course, I know he would do his best, but he knows nothing of the people and conditions out there and would almost be obliged to do what Bror told him. . . .

Dearest Mother, I have longed so much for your presence at this time. But there is no help for it. If only I can arrange things so that you get your money, and I myself some kind of occupation and the possibility of making something of my life,—then it is not too dearly bought. I will probably come home again soon, I think. . . .

To Ingeborg Dinesen

Marseilles 4.12.1920

. . . I am writing in pencil because I am confined to bed with an unknown complaint. I have just read that there is a new plague in Paris, and hope I have not caught that. My disease consists of constant vomiting and dizziness, but I do not know whether it is a kind of poisoning or the effects of strain after my difficult decisions in London and Paris,—I don't think that one can usually tell what is mind and what is stomach. I hope I will be well enough to travel the day after tomorrow, but if not it is a good thing that Tommy has power of attorney.

About business, I will merely mention that I have had another telegram from Bror saying that he thinks my house and park should be put in commission to whoever gets the loan for me. This is a truly fiendish idea,—undoubtedly hit upon by Bror himself, Buxton or Denys would never have suggested it—but Bror has never been able to appreciate the fact that I cared for my home out there. I hope with all my heart that it can be settled in another way. . . .

You really must let me know whether Anders did enjoy his stay in London,—it doesn't seem possible to make him say anything himself. Otherwise he is touchingly honest and said, when Thomas and I asked him if he ever thought about us when we were not there: "Good Lord, no, I never can. There must be something wrong with me, but I can only think of what is just in front of me." But he is so sensible and intelligent, and is sure to succeed, and I really think that one should not try to make him take an interest in anything that does not come naturally to him. I have also come to the conclusion, having seen so much of him when we were in London, that it would be wrong to try to make him get married. He is actually very gentle and could probably quite easily be induced to embark on something that he was completely unprepared for, which could lead to unhappiness for him. I think that in some ways he is late in developing, and that perhaps it may be ten years before he can venture on what is normal for his contemporaries now, but I think it could lead to real unhappiness if we were to force him. . . .

To Ingeborg Dinesen

Garth Castle 13.12.20

. . . Now we have caught sight of Africa on the horizon, and I hope that the dearly beloved country will greet me with the same friendliness that I feel for it.—I do feel that it is there that my life lies; the nearer I get to it, the closer seem the bonds that bind me to it. . . .

To Ingeborg Dinesen

Mombasa Club,
British East Africa.
30.12.1920

Dearest Mother.—

We arrived here all right, and Bror, Fara, and Abdullah were here to meet us.— Thomas is thrilled with Mombasa and everything else here, and it is so lovely to have him with me.—According to what I understand from Olga everything is in an appalling mess at my farm; apparently Bror has taken out a new "Bill of sale" on all my furniture, which will probably fall due soon; so I do not know what is going to happen. I think there have been people living in the house the whole time, and Olga says that a lot of things have been ruined,—including all my glass and china, which were used for targets to shoot at! Bror thinks that there is absolutely no possibility of a loan and thinks there is an agreement between Ekman, Bursell, and—Aunt

Fritze to put a stop to everything for us and then send an offer to purchase on 1 February.—Well, God knows how it will turn out! All along I have been so afraid of fresh surprises, and doubtless this is not the last. . . .

During the next few months the economic position of the farm deteriorated still further. Finally, the chairman of the company, Aage Westenholz, went to Kenya with the definite purpose of selling the plantation. However, Karen Blixen's heartfelt desire to carry on the enterprise resulted in an agreement, signed on 19 June 1921, whereby she was appointed managing director, on condition that Bror Blixen, who had proved to be completely unfit for the post of responsible director, should have nothing further to do with the plantation or the Karen Coffee Co. Karen Blixen, despite some bitterness, accepted this agreement rather than relinquish the farm.

1921

To Ingeborg Dinesen

Ngong 19.5.21

My dearest beloved Mother.—

I will not make excuses for not writing; I know that in a way it is inexcusable, but I have somehow felt that I just *could* not. Everything has been so uncertain; not only could what I wrote one day be completely reversed the next, but I myself did not know what to think or believe, let alone write. . . .

I would rather not write about my plans yet; for I do not know what the outcome will be. But we have had some rain, which was the most important thing, a really good rainfall of four inches in the last six days. Now everything looks fine, and that was a great joy after the worrying drought.—

It has been marvelous to have Uncle Aage here, and he is wonderfully kind to me. He and I are so unlike that we do not always understand one another, but even so he has been of enormous help to me. Thomas and he get on very well together and have excellent discussions. Thomas is well, I think. I cannot tell you how good it has been to have him with me, and how immensely kind and sweet and helpful he has been. . . .

Wasn't it a tragedy that Denys was sailing out of Aden just as I was sailing in? Now I have no idea when he will be coming out here again. A lot of my old friends have now left this country, but I have got to know several nice people whom I had not met before. In any case we have been leading a very quiet life; Uncle Aage, as you know, does not care about meeting people, and we have had plenty to do with our shauries. . . .

To Ingeborg Dinesen

Ngong 29.5.[1921]

. . . It is very difficult to write when one really does not know whether one has been bought or sold, or how one is actually to view life at this particular time. But I hope,—and believe as well, now,—

that this state of uncertainty will soon be over, and everything will "blossom like a rose garden.". . .

I think Uncle Aage is much better now than when he arrived,—very well, in fact; he can go for very long trips on foot or bicycle, and only gets tired if he misses his afternoon rest, and that has happened only twice since he came, and will not happen again. He and Thomas have endless discussions that I think they both enjoy. The boys here are impressed by Uncle Aage's youthfulness and strength; when he arrived they called him Bwana Mesei,—the old gentleman,—but now they call him Bwana Ngufo, the Strong One. Also because he takes cold baths, which they are used to my avoiding like the plague. I think even that Uncle Aage has put on a little weight here and he has a very good color. Today we are holding a big ngoma in his honor; the Kikuyu chief Kinanjui is coming and we are expecting thousands of dancers. It is really interesting when you see it for the first time.

But now and again I do feel rather worried about Tommy. He is so immensely good and kind and so gifted in so many ways; but he seems to find it hard to be happy or find a place in life for himself. It is difficult to help him or do anything for him because he seems instinctively to have the ambition to do everything himself. I think, for instance, that a safari which I arrange for him or merely plan, immediately becomes distasteful to him. I thought that, having been out here for so many years and knowing the country and the people, that would be a help to him, but now I believe that it has the opposite effect, and makes it difficult for him really to take an interest in it. . . .

To Ingeborg Dinesen

Ngong 4.7.21

My own beloved Mother.—

It is strange to think that Uncle Aage must be almost home now, and that you will be able to hear everything about things out here from him. I do not know what his impression of the country was really like, I almost think that he did not take any special interest in it. But you will certainly hear all about this farm, house and so on, from him, and he will be the first person to give you a really accurate description of it. . . .

Yesterday Thomas and I went for a very exciting hunt in the Ngong Hills,—the first time I have been out shooting since I came back here,—no doubt he will send you a description of it himself. Thomas shot a buffalo,—his first,—with a very fine shot straight in the heart at a range of 500 yards; it fell so that it was hidden in the tall grass and bushes, and we had to search a long time for it with rifles cocked and our hearts in our mouths, as it is considered the most dangerous game to deal with,—then we found it, stone dead, right at our feet. Thomas loves this countryside; the Ngong Hills were particularly beautiful yesterday in mist and light rain. We were soaking wet right up to the armpits from the long grass and thick bush. . . .

To Ingeborg Dinesen

Ngong 26.7.21

. . . We have spent a lot of time this month traveling around looking at factories, as we are going to start our own. I think we have the best machinery in B.E.A., but very bad buildings and no system in anything. Now Thomas has taken over the building of the factory and setting up of the machinery, and besides its being a very good thing for the farm, I am glad he has some real work for his own sake. . . .

I had a long dream about you all last night; Elle was telling me about her trip to Italy, and Mitten was there too, and I was thinking in the dream and when I woke up as well: No, now I *will* go home.—I have come to believe now that it would have been far happier for me to have stayed at home from the start, instead of coming out here. But now I had better stay for another few years; for there is far, far too much that holds me here. At the moment I have the most terrible longing to be with you all, but perhaps it is not impossible that some of you may come out here.—

I have been up at Njoro for a few days to negotiate for oxen. . . I stayed with some Swedes called Lindström; they are really nice people, in particular she is unusually sweet, and it is pleasant to meet a woman sometimes out here, otherwise I am nearly always in male company.

Dearest Mother, I find it so hard to write about my private affairs, but I must just send you a couple of lines. During these six months I have come to realize that I am very, very reluctant to separate from Bror. There is so much here that binds us together, and it is impossible for me to stop believing in the good in him, and to think that his various inexplicably thoughtless and heartless outbursts are other than a kind of frenzy, that should surely subside. Perhaps it is simply that I care too much for him; I feel that I cannot abandon him now, when things are so difficult for him. . . .

Karen Estates
P. O. Box 223, Nairobi
Kenya Colony
Ngong [Autumn 1921]

My own beloved beloved wonderful little Mother.

I have not been able to write to you for so long, and I know very well that that is not right. But everything has been so uncertain, and there have been so many trying things. But that is going to be changed now.

Now I want to beg you earnestly that in future—perhaps for a year, but perhaps not for so long,—I may feel that I am able to write to *you only,* without any one else reading my letters. I am quite aware that the others take such a part in how my affairs are going, and in my joys and sorrows, that they will be hurt by this; but it must be like this for a time; for otherwise I have come to realize that as God is my witness it is utterly impossible for me to write. It is not that I am not just as much attached to them, but in these times, with a fearful drought here, worse than in 1918, and with all my shauries with Bror and so on and so on and so on,—I just cannot have the feeling that my marriage and my money affairs and my future and my state of mind and my bills are being discussed at Matrup and Leerbæk and Holbæk Ladegaard,—or anyway not every single word that I might write *to you* in a momentary loss of self-control.

Also it is impossible for me to reply to their letters in the way they would like. I am having a terrible time out here; I am involved in so many things,—both purely practical and also where my feelings, my life itself are concerned,—possibly by my own fault or perhaps quite by chance, that it is going to take all my strength if I am to get through them or over them; you are all well aware of this. I believe that I am going to get through; there may well come a time when I feel that I am the happiest of us all and that it will have been worth all the trouble. But as the situation is now, and as every day I have need of all the strength I can muster in order to manage things, I cannot enter into discussion about it with a whole crowd of young and older women and uncles and brothers-in-law and friends.

If I know that I can write to you alone, I will tell you everything I am thinking about; all my plans, when I have any, will be for you to hear, but I must be absolutely sure that you will not show my letters to anyone, without one single exception.

I love you all,—indeed, I am certain that I am fonder of, for instance, Aunt Bess than Ea or Elle is; when I have cleared up some of the problems then of course I should be able to "come back" to the whole circle, and I really like to hear about their daily lives and doings and interests, about Folehave and Rungsted, Elisabeth, Malla,—and especially, of course, about Mitten; but they are not to write about my intimate circumstances, for they do not understand them in the least, and it is merely upsetting to read and completely impossible to reply to.

I see now that I ought not to have gone home last time; it was unnatural and in fact separated me more from you all rather than bringing me closer. It may well be that I will not go home again for a considerable time. I have been wondering, if I can get away from here for a while, whether you and I could not spend a few months in France, for instance, in Paris and the south? For after all it is *you* who represent "home" to me and all that I love best in Denmark.

I think my greatest misfortune was Father's death. Father understood me as I was, although I was so young, and loved me for myself. It would have been better, too, if I had spent more time with his family; I felt more free and at ease with them. I feel that Mama and Aunt Bess and the whole of your family,—and Uncle Aage when he was out here,—if they care for me at all, do so in a way in spite of my being as I am. They are always trying to change me into something quite different; they do not like the parts of me that I believe to be good.

You must not think that I am saying this as a reproach, the only person to reproach is myself, because I did not tear myself away before, and then because when I did tear myself away after a fashion, or anyway took myself away from it all,—I accepted help from you in order to do it. That is the one great mistake I have made in my life, and suffer and have suffered all the pains of hell for it. For otherwise what would it matter whether it rained or not out here, and whether land went up or down, in fact, what would anything at all matter? I should surely be able to manage somehow or other.

But it must be possible to manage it somehow, I think the best way would be by purchase, and I shall surely be able to get through these difficulties I have brought upon myself.

But,—if I can do it and make something of myself again, and can look at life calmly and clearly one day,—then it is Father who has done it for me. It is his blood and his mind that will bring me through it. Often I get the feeling that he is beside me, helping me, many times by saying: "Don't give a damn about it,"—about many of my shauries.

No doubt each one of your children thinks that he or she loves you most, and so do I. It is probably not true. But each one cares for you in his or her own way, and I think that there is something in the way that I love you that resembles the way Father loved you. For me you are the most beautiful and wonderful person in the world; merely the fact that you are alive makes the whole world different; where you are there is peace and harmony, shade and flowing springs, birds singing; to come to where you are is like entering "heaven."

And so you must allow me to write to you as you would have allowed Father to write. Without showing it to anyone and without confronting me in your mind with the judgments of others.

If Father had ever written and told you that he had committed a crime, or had come and told you of it, surely then you would not have given a thought to what Aunt Bess would have said to it if she had known of it, or that perhaps it was wrong of you to hide it from her. It would have been something entirely, eternally, between you and him. Now I am asking you to treat my affairs and letters in the same way.

These *are* difficult times for me, far, far more difficult than, for instance, when I was ill here. Your love and understanding are lights and stars shining and sparkling through them. And I have to take them in my own way; otherwise I will die of them, you must understand that. And I am sure you have the strength, little Mother, to keep this understanding in spite of others' condemnation. Uncle Aage's grass-house and office-work, and Aunt Bess's comparisons between me and the Major's wife, etc.—for heaven's sake, in these times that is sheer rubbish, for this is deadly earnest.

When they talk like this, then listen to them and say yes and amen, but smile in your heart of hearts. Don't let them make you see it in their way; understand me, as only *you* can. And imagine that Father is sitting beside you perhaps talking anxiously too about this child of yours out here and saying that she has used up too much money and been improvident in many ways, but perhaps he might see some sense in it as well and would say: "But she is brave, and she loves you and me more, perhaps, than any of our other children; give her a little more time, then you'll see that she will manage."—Yes, talk about me to Father. It is really he who is responsible, for he deserted me and must have seen that things were not going to be easy for me.

But do not discuss me with the others; just let them say what they like, and let me write to you alone. For I love you so very deeply.

A thousand, thousand thanks for paying Borre. That was far too good and kind. But you really must not pay anything else. Of course it is frightful that I have so many debts. But it will all work out.

Will you thank Aunt Bess very much for me for her letter, it was sweet of her to write. But I do not really know how to reply. I do not feel that one can consider one's own circumstances in the light of

"Gösta Berling's Saga." Quite apart from the fact that I do not think anything can be proved through a comparison with Selma Lagerlöf, because she lives in a world entirely her own, and you really get the feeling that it could just as well have turned out quite differently, I do not think that I am in the very least like the Major's wife. I may have said as a joke that from now on I was going to imitate her, but even Aunt Bess surely does not think that there is any resemblence. But if she persists with it you can ask her what she thinks would have happened if the Major's wife had been married,—when she was younger,—to Gösta Berling? Then, anyway, the whole book would have had to be rewritten.

I really wanted to write something about Thomas, since that is what you most want to hear about. In some ways all is well with him, he is busy building the factory, which is a great service to me and the company. But the better I get to know him through living so close to him, the more I realize how hard it is for someone like him to find something that he feels is really worthwhile. For it is only the truly great things that exist for Thomas; he cannot, as I can, find pleasure or consolation in difficulties through little things,—and one does not come upon great things every day. Indeed, these times are not improved for that very reason, I feel. "Blessed the head over which the eagle of exaltation has rushed with wide wings,"—but no doubt it is hard to realize that one will never hear them rushing over one again, but must be resigned at best to sparrow twitters and duck quackings which tinkle doubly, indeed, ten times as intolerably. It may well be that this country is not right for him. You may laugh at my main reason for thinking this,—that there are so few young women here that I do not see how he could find a young bride here, and for Thomas's sake all my hopes are set on his finding her. But for that very reason I would be equally reluctant to see him go to America, a possibility that he may be entertaining.

I have just had a young man called Lord Doune staying here for a week, and much in his state of mind seemed to me to resemble Thomas's. He was the same age and is said to have done well as a pilot during the war, was good-looking and seemed to have plenty of money, had been six months on safari here and was going on to India and Persia,—and he said to me, with absolute honesty, I'm sure, that every time he saw a shooting star he wished that he might not live out the year. He said that his mother was very eager for him to get married, and I feel for her. I think it is a condition that to a certain extent is common among, not all the young men who fought in the war, but the élite. They are no longer able to be satisfied with ordinary life, and the glory that for a brief time was reality has not only disappeared but has been vulgarized, turned into humbug and triviality.

But all the same, I believe that the great and glorious do exist, and they should be the first to realize it when it reveals itself again. For it is surely not only righteousness about which it can be said that those who hunger and thirst after it are blessed, for they shall be filled; but it is true also of the truth, as Thomas says, and about everything glorious in the world.

Now I must end for today. Next time I will write about my "plans," both present and future.

Goodbye, my dearest dear Mother. I feel you taking me into your arms now. And so I will write to you alone.

Your Tanne.

To Ingeborg Dinesen

Ngong 25/10.192[1]

My own beloved Mother.

This time I am writing, as I said to you in my last letter, with the thought that only you will read this. It is so necessary for me to know this that I don't think that I could write at all if I did not feel assured of it. You must not make any exception of any of my letters, even if they should not contain anything secret or confidential. I need so much to have the feeling *always* that I can write about everything to you.

I am going to beg you, dearest Mother, not to write to me any more concerning my marriage or Bror. Of course I know you do it with the best intentions; but sometimes even things done in this spirit can fail, and what costs you effort and pain to write, costs me effort and pain to read, and I do not think anything is gained by it other than my realization of how little you understand me. Or I believe that in this matter,—which in no way should ever have been the subject for general family discussion,—you have talked yourselves into such a state that you have lost sight of any impartial or objective view of it and are judging it completely out of context. My little Mother, you must not think that I am writing in anger or bitterness; but I think that this is the reason for even *you* writing as you do, and I do so deeply wish that it would stop.

How can I explain otherwise why, for instance, you can write that I must choose between Thomas and Bror? If you could apply this in your thought to one of the others you would see that it is unreasonable. Let us imagine that Knud and Thomas,—or Viggo and Thomas,—had a really terrible quarrel, to the point even of a real break, indeed, literally to blows. Say that you all sided with Thomas, that even Elle,—or Ea,—felt that he was right. Yet none of you because of that would think it necessary for Elle to divorce Knud,—or Ea, Viggo. But it would be quite appallingly hurtful for Elle or Ea to have the subject discussed, the more so the more it was motivated by Thomas's love and kindness. I really think it is a unique situation when a whole family tries with all its might to persuade, almost force one of its members into divorcing. Have you ever heard of this before? Even in the unhappiest marriage, you know, you yourself must realize that this is an unreasonable interference in private affairs, which *cannot be judged by others.* Or imagine it even where Uncle Mogens and Aunt Fritze are concerned; even in that case his family would have to stop agitating if he declared that he had made up his mind not to get a divorce. Yes, even where a criminal was concerned, such as Alberti, they could not go on with it.

There are two things that none of you understand: how different from you I am and always have been. What makes me happy or unhappy is completely different from what makes you happy or unhappy. I could live in conditions that you would think frightful and be happy, and in conditions which you would think perfect I would be miserable. And you cannot make judgments in advance regarding these conditions; you do not know and can never know what effect they will have on my state of satisfaction, and thus you ought to be careful about the advice you give; you might come to regret it most deeply. For instance, to me my illness was not such an enormous disaster, indeed, if I had not still been under your influence I would have thought it even less of one; but I was constantly aware of the sorrow it would cause you. I actually enjoyed being in the hospital, although it was a hellish cure. No doubt it would have been quite a different matter for one of the others. But not for anything in the world would I go back to the time when I had to go to Folehave for dinner every Sunday. You must not think this is written out of hard-heartedness. I would really rather leave it alone; but it *cannot* be avoided when you write as you do, and I think that you have written things to me now that have hurt me still more, and this is the only way that I can think of to put a stop to it from both sides.

And the other thing that you do not understand is that every letter of this kind that you write to me separates me still more from all of you. To enable yourself to understand this, imagine that Aunt Ellen, Uncle Edmund, even Aunt Bess and Aunt Lidda were to write to you about your relationship with Father with the intention of getting you divorced at any price. Well, even if Father had wronged you most terribly, had squandered all your money, sold your home, behaved scandalously, *you would not have accepted it.* Think if it were another kind of problem concerning one of your children, for instance, if they all wrote to you about Anders,—say he had been guilty of some great fault or other,—and tried to force you to wash your hands of him. It would separate you from all of them; if they did not listen to you in time when you asked them to stop it, it would lead to a break. I beg you all earnestly not to write any more, give thought to it before it is too late.

I cannot help thinking that when all is said and done, it is the matter of finance that is at the bottom of it all. I sometimes think that Aunt Emy is right, and that money is the thing of first importance to all your family, and my two brothers-in-law consider it the only measuring rod there is. If Bror were able to support me and did not cause you financial difficulties it would never have come to this; you would never have demanded that we should be divorced. This must not lead you to think that I do not understand how enormously much I owe you for putting so much money into our projects, which is still at risk. I will do everything I can to see that it works out well for you. I have also agreed, and I agreed at once, that Bror should not have anything more to do with it. *Indeed, I gave my word of honor.* But I do not think that you can make demands except in business matters. If someone demanded that I become a member of the established Church, even if, to put it bluntly, he lent me £20,000, I would reject that in the same way and think that he was unjust. And what would he gain by it? Say that I joined the Church and promised to go to communion every Sunday,—it would only be purely outward appearances he had gained. And I cannot comprehend how a divorce that is forced upon people can be anything else.

Perhaps I have written too much; and I have had to bring force to bear on myself to do it. Therefore I will never write about it again. If you continue to write of it you will get no answer, and you can tell the others this as well. It is impossible for us to discuss it without bitterness, and I would not have that for anything in the world.

I love you far, far too much. . . .

Fru Lindström from Njoro and her two small children are staying here at the moment while her husband and Bror are on a film safari, and this is a great pleasure for me. She is extremely nice, sweet and natural, the perfect type of Scandinavian lady, and after all they do surpass the English so much. Her little girls are Nina, who is six, and Ulla, four. Thomas and Fru L. are considering driving around Kenya in a sidecar; it would be really good for Thomas to get away for a while, poor thing, he has been stuck here for so long and I always like him to have somebody with him. Of course it is always his ambition to do everything alone, but that is a barren joy. I think it is so empty if one does not have anybody to discuss one's experiences with afterward. I think, incidentally, that Thomas has developed so enormously much in the time he has been here, or that somehow he can express himself more easily, is not so stiff,—mentally,—as before. I think that he has enjoyed building the factory, and he has done it so well. Everyone is impressed with it. I think that Thomas is much more clever than he gave the impression of being at home, or, rather, that he is more practically gifted, and I wish that he could have Uasin-Gishu, which he would very much like, and get a real job, and not just sit reading Einstein,—which he is very good at, too, but he has had enough of that kind of thing, indeed, perhaps more than enough. Incidentally, he found a kindred spirit in Doune, who was mad about Einstein as well, and they spent hours discussing him, which exceeded all ordinary human understanding.

Now it is my fervent hope and constant thought that all of you at home will approve my plan for dividing up the farm and reorganizing the management. I have been thinking about it day and night during the last few months, and I believe it is good. I really do think,—don't say that I have folie de grandeur,—that if you will allow me to be in charge of this farm and give me a free hand there will not be another farm in B.E.A. to match up with it. It is because I take such a passionate interest in it. Hunter laughs at me,—but I love it, every acre, every native, every coffee bush. . . .

Dearest Mother, please understand this letter, which is written in the greatest, greatest, greatest most fervently deep love . . . then you will truly understand how I tremble at the possibility of these misunderstandings becoming real. Understand, that I do *not* want that to happen, not for anything in this world or the next; I would rather never see any of you again than that. And as Doune said: Remember that when you ride you are holding *on to a mouth,*—I say to you, remember, when you write, that you are striking a heart. And then remember how far away from you all that I am; the effect is so different at such a distance. As Cyrano says: "Je mourai si de cette hauteur Vous me laissez tomber un mot dur sur le coeur." . . .

Goodnight, my above all else beloved Mother.

Your Tanne.

To Ingeborg Dinesen

Ngong 30/10 192[1]

. . . I think you have allowed yourself to be influenced by the others and by their view of me, so that you no longer understand me, and you must know how sad that makes me; but I am quite sure that it will all be clarified one day and that it is only a misunderstanding brought about by these difficult times and conditions. But as long as it continues I think it best that I do not write home. As I wrote to you before, I thought that I could go on writing to you even if I broke away from the others for a time; but after these last letters I can see that it will not do. When you cannot prevent the question of whether I am to be divorced or not from being discussed at a management meeting,—in connection with the question regarding the dismissal of a functionary on the farm, which has nothing whatsoever to do with it,—our ideas have diverged to such an extent that I am really afraid to write and to receive letters and would rather put an end to the correspondence. After this I do not see how I can ever return to Denmark. I think you have all talked so much that your ideas have become completely confused where I am concerned, this is the only conclusion I can arrive at.

You talk about the humiliation to which Bror has exposed me. But just once endeavor to compare seriously in your mind some humiliation that Father might have imposed on you in your private relationship with the humiliation it would have been, for instance, if Uncle Gex and Aunt Ulla, Ulf and Uncle Alfred had been called to a meeting to discuss whether you should get divorced or not. I cannot understand how you can believe that I could ever forget it. But when we have grown so far away from each other and I can see that each letter makes the distance even greater, I have decided that I will not write home to any one, and to ask you all not to write. Or, rather, I had better say that any letters that arrive from home will be returned without my having read them, including yours, beloved Mother, for you must understand that I do really consider that it is best to break off communication for a time. You must not think, my own dearest Mother, that I am doing this in anger, but only because I believe that it is the best thing, and that it is more dangerous to go on writing, and because I have been thinking that it would have been better if I had done this with the last few letters I have received from home.

You write that home is where I belong—but recently I have come to see that your way of thinking is completely foreign to me; I will never belong to it. The spirit you write about seems to me, now that I have seen it from the reverse side, like quite shattering pharisaism; I could never possibly feel in tune with it. I also think that I must accept the fact that my relationship with many people to whom I have been very close at home is over and done with. But our relationship, beloved Mother, can never be broken, and has nothing whatever to do with distance and divergences. Even if I never go home again and even if perhaps we do not see each other for many years it would not matter in the least. Indeed, even if we were never to meet again I do not think it would really affect the great love there is between us, little Mohder.

But then it is probably best to stop writing for a year, for instance, rather than let the influence of others cast the slightest shadow over it.

But of course you will hear my business letters to Uncle Aage each month. I have given thought to the idea of leaving this farm; and perhaps it is a weakness in me not to do so . But I am staying because I am convinced that if I left it would fail. And it is not merely the thought of your money that makes me wish to prevent this happening because of some step on my part, but because it is my life's work and I cannot relinquish it. The natives here, who rely on me, everything, even our oxen and our coffee trees,—I could never think about them with the knowledge that I had deserted them. If you do not wish me to stay, whether you say so directly, or, by some demand or other that my pride and my self-esteem will not allow me to comply with, drive me away, then it will be your responsibility. I know now that I cannot take it, and I am writing this to you in explanation of what may seem incomprehensible to you all, my staying on here.

And now goodbye, my dearest, dearest, dearest Mother. I cannot tell you how deeply I love you, how much I will always bless you.

Your Tanne.

To Ingeborg Dinesen

Ngong 24/11. [1921]

. . . There is no one at all at home that I would not wish you to greet from me when you see them. It is so pleasant out here to think of the Misses Lutzen and their sitting room and their cosy teas, and of Annette Tegner and Aunt Ada Grøn, and of Gerda and her awful child and Else Reventlow,—I have thought a lot about her; please write and tell me how she is getting on. From out here one can see how many, many generations of Danish people it has taken to produce them, not only the individual great-grandparents and great-great-grandparents, but the whole of old Denmark, Copenhagen or the provinces or the country, the climate and the agriculture and shipping, Frederik VI and Fru Heiberg,—it is like a work of art that has slowly, slowly been completed and that cannot be imitated . And then now and again I wish so strongly that I really belonged to it, that I was like Fru Tegner and Ada Grøn; I get really homesick, you know, not merely for one particular home, but for the idea of home, in every

Ea de Neergaard with her daughter Karen, 1918.

Anders Dinesen, 1919, photographed by Juncker-Jensen.

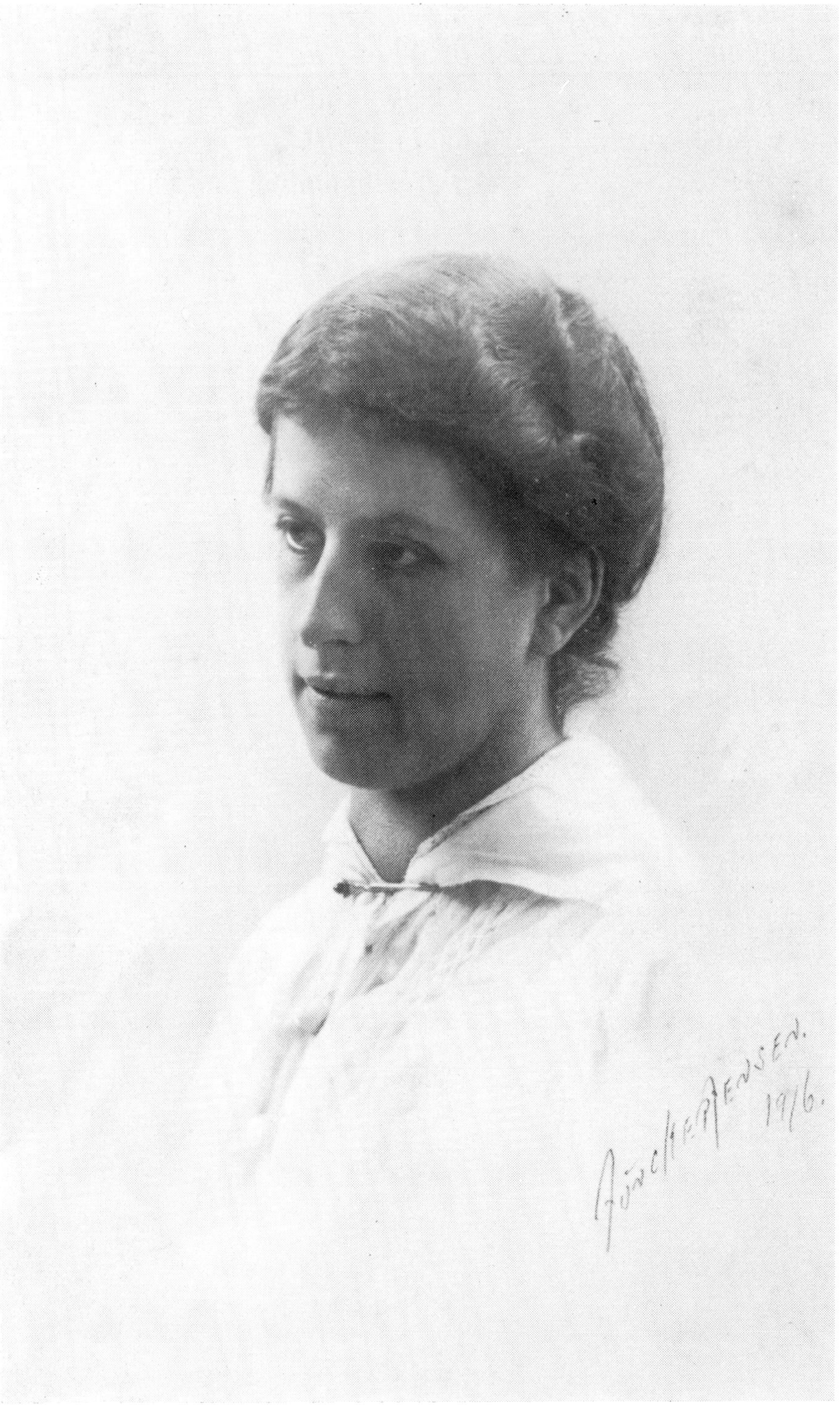

Ellen Dahl, Karen Blixen's younger sister, 1916.

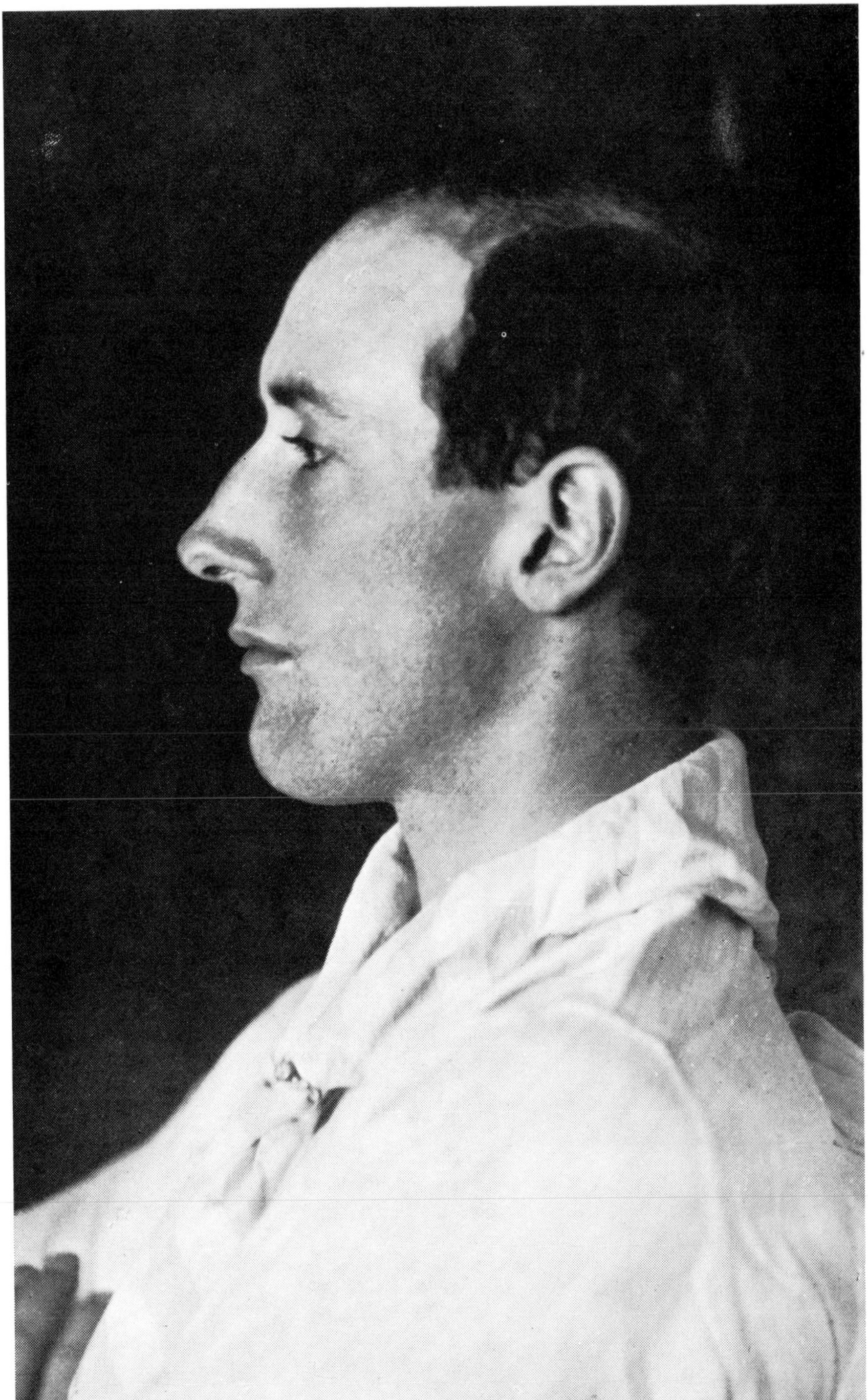

Denys Finch Hatton (1887–1931).

The oxen beside the farm dam, 1922 (photograph by Thomas Dinesen).

The Ngong Hills, where Karen Blixen went several times to find subjects for paintings (photograph by Thomas Dinesen).

Ingeborg Dinesen and Ea de Neergaard at Valdemarskilde, about 1921.

Karen Blixen with her dogs, about 1922 (photograph by Thomas Dinesen).

Thomas Dinesen about to go on an expedition. Karen Blixen sitting on the steps in front of the farm, 1923.

Thomas Dinesen on Mount Kenya, 1923 (photograph by Gustav Mohr).

Thomas Dinesen and Karen Blixen in front of his house on the farm, about 1922.

On a picnic with Uncle Aage Westenholz, 1921 (photograph by Thomas Dinesen).

Kikuyu Morans in front of the farm, 1922 (photograph by Thomas Dinesen).

Nairobi in the 1920s (photograph by Thomas Dinesen).

Abdullai, Lullu, Siegfried, Farah, and little Mahau (photograph by Thomas Dinesen).

The manager Dickens's house on the farm (photograph by Thomas Dinesen).

Aunt Bess, Ingeborg Dinesen's sister Mary Bess Westenholz (1857–1947).

Karen Blixen and Thomas Dinesen in the garden of the farm, 1922.

Karen Blixen with long-stemmed lilies, 1922 (photograph by Thomas Dinesen).

In the garden on her favorite horse, Rouge (photograph by Thomas Dinesen).

Farah's half-brother Abdullai with Pania (photograph by Thomas Dinesen).

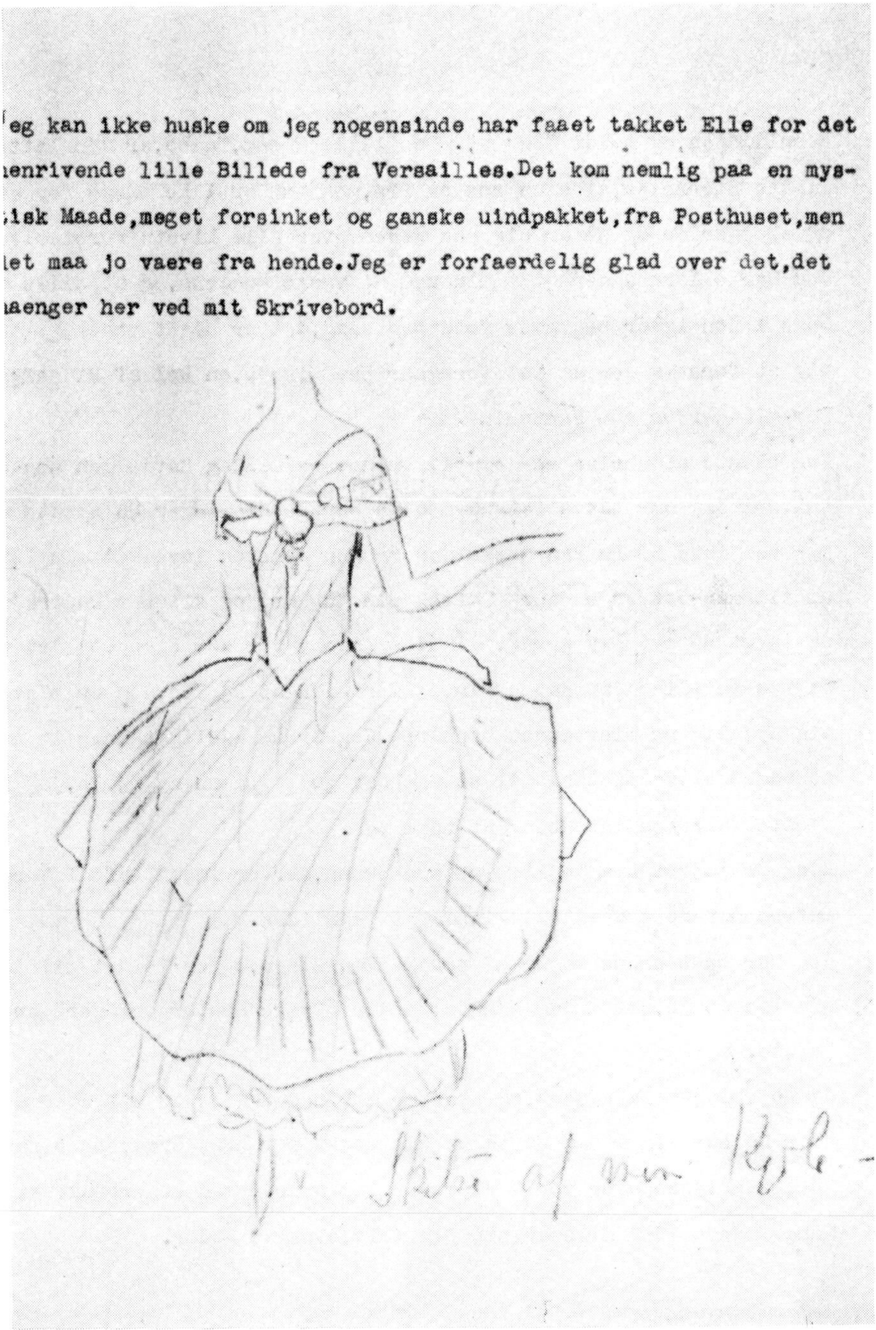

'eg kan ikke huske om jeg nogensinde har faaet takket Elle for det
ienrivende lille Billede fra Versailles.Det kom nemlig paa en mys-
;isk Maade,meget forsinket og ganske uindpakket,fra Posthuset,men
iet maa jo vaere fra hende.Jeg er forfaerdelig glad over det,det
iaenger her ved mit Skrivebord.

"Sketch of my dress," from letter to Ingeborg Dinesen, 11 November 1923.

Karen Blixen in the coffee plantation with Carl Søgaard, who for a short time succeeded W. H. Dickens as farm manager, about 1929.

way: as a society, a circle, where one does really belong. The other day I was sitting thinking of Mourier Petersen at Ruggaard with such longing, and thinking how much I would like to be he and be so thoroughly rooted in a definite social class, in the country, at Randers. I wonder if it would ever be possible to put on my tombstone, as on Stevenson's: "Here he is, where he longed to be, home is the sailor, home from the sea, and the hunter home from the hill"? . . .

Tell Aunt Bess that she must read a book called "Eminent Victorians"; I have forgotten the author's name, but it is really interesting.

Dearest Mother, you must feel that Thomas and I are with you everywhere you go this Christmas. We will be sitting beside you on 23 December talking about the old days, and we will go with you up to the churchyard and on to Rungsted church if you are there. On Christmas Eve we will sit with our arms about you listening to the old carols. As you can imagine, we will be talking about you and everyone at home; it is only that it is rather too far away for you to be able to hear us.

It is such a calm, clear, starry night here. The world is so great and strange,—and yet one holds it all in one's own heart.

Give my greetings to everyone, everyone, everyone. Give Blackie a pat for me. My beloved Mother, did you feel this kiss?

Your Tanne.

To Ingeborg Dinesen

Ngong Christmas morning 1921

. . . I am writing this in bed, having only just managed to get home yesterday; but it would have been too dreary for words for Tommy to have been all on his own here and for me to have been in the hospital on Christmas Eve. I was taken ill last Sunday,—a week ago,—and the doctor took me in there right away. I was quite sure I was going to die, but then I always think that when I am ill; but everyone in there thought I was dying too. Three doctors who were summoned could not say what was wrong. . . .

Please thank Aunt Bess very much for me for her interesting letter. Would you tell her:

1. That she is utterly mistaken if she believes that those who put money into a horse, even if it comprises their entire fortune, have the right, or ever have occasion, to use whip and spurs.

2. That on the whole, whip and spurs should be used with the utmost caution even in the run up to the finish, or at a fence or bend, but never without a particular reason, and certainly not in connection with what money one has settled on the horse.—

3. That I find it altogether degrading to be compared to a horse, especially one that needs whip and spurs, because that is a worthless horse,—(unless for instance, some special circumstance is involved, such as getting a message through, when the horse must be sacrificed).

4. That she must not imagine that the Major's wife was forced to marry Gösta Berling. She liked him and did not at all despise him; she could see his great qualities.

5. What kind of down-at-heel cavaliers in the K.C.C. does she think I help, protect and live for? Does she think the white employees of the company are engaged on this account? That would certainly not meet with approval at home. . . .

1922

To Ingeborg Dinesen

Ngong 13/1.22

. . . You can imagine how much Thomas and I are thinking of Ea at this time and how happy we are to have letters with good news about her. I should think she must have felt the first sign of life shortly after your last letter and that we shall hear about that in your next letter. God grant that all may go well with her and she may get her great reward for this difficult time. You must promise me that when the child is born and you telegraph to us, to put the *date* and not just "to-day," as you did with Mitten, so right up to the day I arrived home I had a wrong idea of her birthday. . . .

Thomas came back in great form from a visit to the Lindströms at Njoro, where he had gone on behalf of the company in order to try to get contracts for maize and oxen . . . I had him staying here again,—otherwise he has been living down at his bungalow near the factory,—but now he has gone back there again; he is very fond of having his own house, and it is in a beautiful situation. It is nice to be able to go down there for tea, it makes a pleasant change. Particularly now that I am going to move into the grass house, as I must in order to save, he would not be able to live with me, and his household expenses are very low,—one toto at five rupees a month,—and I think he feels more free and independent with his own ménage. . . .

The Governor's wife has invited herself to tea here tomorrow, this of course, is an "honor"; I think they wish to demonstrate clearly that they understand my present extremely difficult position. The Governor rode out here recently and was extraordinarily kind. Otherwise I don't see a lot of people,—everyone is so hard up, you know, and they are not in the mood for visiting, and it is really irritating how they all get together and talk of nothing but prices and shauries. It is something one must take pains to resist; otherwise one will be quite unbearable when one comes to meet decent people again.

My horse is still a great joy to me, but now the doctor has forbidden me to ride for a time. I have had a recurrence of the same, really terrible pains that sent me to the hospital; they maintain that the cause is an inflamed appendix, but surely it *can't* be that? . . .

To Ingeborg Dinesen

Ngong 23/1.22

My own beloved Mother.

I want to write and give you some sort of explanation of my relationship with Bror since I came back. For I think now that we are in fact going to be divorced, and there is no need for this to be kept secret, although I am reluctant to have it mentioned to outsiders. This development has come about because Bror wishes it, and because he seems to think that he can manage better in the future if we are divorced, and probably believes he will be happier then.

I have said all along, which I am sure you can understand if you really put yourself in my place, that I would never demand a divorce or try to push it through against Bror's will. I do not know how anyone can do that unless one is quite frenzied; and even though I have occasionally been angry with Bror or, rather, perhaps, in despair over his behavior, there is far, far too much binding us together from all the years and difficulties we have shared here, for me to be able to take the initiative in putting an end to what, if nothing else, was a most intimate companionship.

When I see how close Thomas and I have grown during this past year, which after all is only a fraction of the time that Bror and I have spent together here, I am quite unable to comprehend the state of mind of anyone who can cancel such a relationship. Of course I can perfectly well imagine that it can change a great deal, and in theory, as you know from when I was at home, I could talk of divorce; but as soon as I came back here and saw Bror again I realized that it would never be possible for me to desert him and our marriage. But where this is concerned Bror's temperament is completely different from mine; I think that in some way he can wipe out an entire period of time and an entire emotion from his consciousness and direct all his concentration on the present moment and on what is to come. I don't know whether he will always feel like this or whether for him too there will be many memories of a past time.

In any case, it is my heartfelt hope that he will be happy.

You must know how hard this is for me. In many ways my relationship with Bror was a problematic task,—one that I believed to be the most important of my life,—and that I have been quite unable to fulfill. As you know, I have put into it a great deal of both time and effort. It could no doubt be said that I ought to have given it up earlier; but I do not think that would have been possible for me, and things had to take the course that they have. But much of my youth and my strength has gone into it, and I think something of my soul. And yet this is far from what I feel most strongly about; but I have cared indescribably much for Bror in spite of everything, and for many years he has been the person I was closest to in the world. There is something terribly bitter in the realization that now there is, if one is to face it, nothing left at all of our relationship. And yet you must not think that I am bitter; I think that I feel much more as one does if one has a child who dies.

I feel for Bror now, and will until I die, the greatest friendship or the deepest tenderness that I am capable of feeling. I would also sincerely beg of you never to think of him with anger. I think you will find it easier to do this when he has gone away and you are no longer afraid of his influence. I do not think that Bror is responsible for his actions in the same way as other people,—due partly to his character and partly to upbringing, I think; if one really understands him I don't think one can feel any kind of anger or bitterness toward him, although I quite understand that one would not wish those one cares for to be, for the sake of their interests or happiness, in any way dependent on him.

But I believe that if I can stay and achieve success with the task I have taken upon myself here, I will eventually regain all my strength and in spite of everything feel that my life has in some way been glorious and rich and happy. But in these times it is impossible to see how things will turn out. And if I have to leave my home here and this farm I have no idea what will become of me. I am not writing this to try to influence your business decisions, you must look at them from a different angle. But I feel that you may as well realize now that if this has to be relinquished and come to nothing, no one must expect anything more from me in this life. You might come to think later that it was wrong of me not to tell you all this now. I know that when one discusses things with others, mutual belief in a view that has nothing to do with the reality is often consolidated. So you must not make plans to arrange something or other for me even though you all believe that it would be better for me, much better than my life here. For there are some things that simply *cannot be done*. I cannot come home, if I have to give this up I *cannot* see you all again. Of course I know that you would take me to you with the greatest love and sympathy. But it would not be enough. And you would never have any happiness from it.

I am only writing this because I so much wanted to *write* it to you. Dearest Mother, you must know that of all people in the world I want you really to understand me.

But of course it is far from certain that it will be like this; I hope that I will be able to bring Karen Coffee safely through these difficult times, and I do believe I will. And then there would be so tremendously much in my life here that would give me more joy and a greater feeling of wealth than you could possibly understand. The fact that there are so many people here,—from Farah, whom I care for almost as much as anyone in the world, to my poor little totos,—dependent on me, who have put all their trust in me, calls for all my strength, and this steadies me in difficulties and brings out the best in me to a greater extent than I can explain. And my situation here, when things are more clearly settled,—as you can imagine, it is not too easy at the moment,—is precisely what I could wish for.

I meet many people here to whom I become very attached,—like Denys, who is about to arrive now, and Doone [*sic*]—I would probably never have met in Denmark. And I am so very fond of my house and garden and the whole farm; I have the feeling, which one seldom gets at home, that I have created this myself and that it is a part of me. If you ever come out here, which would give me more joy than I can conceive of, I am sure you will like it too and will understand that I have become what I was meant to be here, which is perhaps something better than you at home can believe. And if I could bring you, and everyone else, a little happiness and credit,—and there has been precious little of that up to now,—that would be the greatest happiness that I could achieve. . . .

[Addendum to letter of 23 January]
Beloved Mother.

I am adding a couple of lines to my letter to tell you that I am probably going to take the step you so much wish for; Bror and I are going to be divorced. I would ask you not to talk about it, but I wanted to tell you. Please understand that the decision has not been made before because Bror has been in such a terrible situation here. He has been without work and money, wanted by the police; he has been hiding out in the Masai Reserve without a tent or shoes. It was impossible for me, in consideration of other people here and of myself, to start to talk of divorce. But I think that things will go better with him now; he is probably going to get married as soon as it can be arranged, to an English lady who wants to help him.

I am bound to say that it is very hard to look back at a whole period of one's life and have to admit: it came to nothing. But apart from this, and the actual pain of parting from someone I have loved so much, I think I will come to feel it as a relief from many impossible situations.

I would like to ask you, when people get to know about it, to help me to preserve a good position. Bror is not a martyr, not someone I have got rid of when I myself was in a secure situation. It is possible that Bror will present it like this and that his family will believe it. It means a lot to me not to have it understood so. I was most reluctant to be divorced; I was willing to give Bror complete freedom provided there was no scandal, and to help him as much as I could; but I was most loath to have our marriage annulled. It is Bror who thinks now that the best chance in life for him is to get a divorce, and who wants it. Even now I would rather, if he does not continue to insist on it, give up the idea of divorce.

But if it does come about, as I believe it will, I will try to make the best of things nevertheless. So I beg you all, and especially you, to help me by speaking well of me, and also thinking kindly about me; it is harder for me than you perhaps understand. . . .

To Ingeborg Dinesen

Ngong 25/3 22

. . . I have thought of writing to you several times to say that I do not think you should assume that Thomas's future lies here, or that you should plan for this; but somehow it always seems disloyal to write about the people one is with behind their backs,—even if it is with the best of intentions. But I think I ought to write now. You might think, of course, that enthusiasm for safari life, for instance, or something similar, or because he has no other plans, might encourage Thomas to settle down here in Africa, but I think definitely that this would not bring him happiness. Thomas is not suited to being out here; this is absolutely clear to me, although I would find it difficult to define why. And I think he would be going right against his nature if he tried to get up an interest in farming of any kind. Thomas is not practical and has no interest in practical matters; I think that his talents lie much more in the direction of theoretical science, of almost any and every kind.

This has been something of a disappointment to me as well, partly, of course, because I would so much have loved to have him here, partly because I thought that I, or Africa through me, could have helped him over a time in his life when he was without purpose, and given him interest and occupation. But after seeing him out here I think it is quite clear that he could very easily find something that suited him far better and would interest him much more. It is these long discussions that I hate with all my heart that actually interest him more than anything else, and I feel that I am a bore for him when I keep returning to oxen and plowing and the most prosaic kind of calculations. He has been studying the New Testament recently and been completely absorbed in it, and constantly returns to the subject; and not only do I feel unable to make an adequate contribution to a discussion of it, but I cannot think of a single person in the whole of this country who would satisfy Thomas in a debate.

The things which really interest him most are social science, and philosophy or science such as that of Einstein. I think it would surely be easy for him to get into this kind of work, particularly since he is financially independent and obviously possessed of far more than average gifts. I feel that Einstein or Wells, or another of his idols, would be able to use him, if he went to them and placed himself heart and soul at their disposal; and I have talked to him so many times about writing to them, but I don't think he has done so. Of course, I will miss him dreadfully when he goes away; but it would be much worse if I persuaded him to start on something that did not suit him. . . .

I have had Spanish flu which confined me to bed for three weeks of this month apart from short intervals. It is all over the country now so no doubt one has to go through it. . . .

The most extraordinary accidents have afflicted me in Africa,—did I write about the rooster? That brass rooster, you know, that I brought back with me. It was on top of a cupboard, and as I was trying to shut a drawer that had got stuck, underneath the cupboard, it fell down on my head. I collapsed completely and woke up in a pool of blood; Farah came in and raised his arms to the skies at the sight of me. If I had died it would have been romantic; because it was, of course, an old West African idol, and I think it would have looked rather grand, if anyone had been there to see when it fell and hit me with its beak. . . .

I have had a letter from Denys Finch Hatton; he is coming out at the beginning of April. I will get him to give me some good advice about the sale of the farm; I am sure he could help me with that better than anyone else. . . .

Early in 1922 Karen Blixen's eldest sister Ea de Neergaard fell seriously ill after giving birth to a stillborn child. Her condition gradually worsened, and she died on 17 June, at the early age of thirty-nine.

To Ingeborg Dinesen

Ngong 7/4.22

Dearest Mother.

Thank you for your letter of 4 and 5/3. It is always a great comfort when such letters arrive that it is anyway a month or more since they were posted; if you only mention a sign of progress one has the hope that when one comes to read the letter, things are much better than the letter itself reports. But you may be sure I understand what a terrible time it has been. Naturally I am thinking of you all the time; I seem to see everything at home so clearly: Aunt Bess coming down from Folehave and in at the garden door, all of you sitting and talking, perhaps in the playroom, as it has been so cold, and Mitten coming in, and then you going softly, softly in to Ea in her old room. And then I see you sitting waiting for the doctor when he is coming out in the car with Knud. The whole time I can do nothing but wish and hope for her and for all of you. When I think of that frightful day at Valdemarskilde, and how hope seemed to be fading further and further away, and yet then, before I left, I saw her looking so well and radiant, surrounded by young people at Kilden, when Thomas and I were down there before he left, then surely I may believe that it can be so again, and so one can come through,—or in a manner forget,—all the terrible anxious hours one has endured.

When I was in Paris on my way home from Africa in 1915 I talked to a French doctor; I asked him if he thought I would recover, and he said that he would be honest with me and told me plainly that he doubted it very much; and I remember so clearly lying in bed in the hotel in Zurich looking out over the square and the Town Hall clock, thinking that I was quite certainly going to lay my bones to rest there in Zurich, and that it was only a question of how many hours I had left to look at that clock in.—And look! Now I'm as fit as anyone in the world, and all that agony is utterly vanished and forgotten and seems to have existed only in dream. There is something so wonderfully and indescribably touching in the thought of Mitten, who has been in such danger of suffering the greatest misfortune possible for such a little person, without the least suspicion of it. It is almost impossible to comprehend that there might be forces in the world strong enough to separate mother and child, and certainly nothing so external and unmotivated as an illness. . . .

Ngong 19/6 22

My own beloved Mother.

Your telegram came today. It is almost impossible to write,—one is far too overwhelmed, but I do so want to feel as close to you all as possible; the distance that separates us seems so abysmal.

Dearest Mother, we have all lost so indescribably much; I cannot understand that we have been bereft of so much richness and beauty, so much warmth and love, and it is such infinite loss, such great emptiness that I am quite unable to comprehend it now; but above everything else I feel gratitude toward her. I feel that every single thing I come to think of is so sweet and like a blessing, and I think that everyone who came into contact with her felt that, no matter how slightly. I can't imagine anyone more deeply loved; I think everyone who knew her came to love her. . . .

Tommy is such a dear, I am so thankful that he is here, but when are we going to see all of you? Give our love to everyone, to poor Viggo, and to Elle. I am quite unable to write about what I am thinking; every moment more and more comes rushing into my mind. I think of Ea's singing, and I feel that there is something, something so glorious, so sweet and rich and loving shining over us all, that will always continue. Goodbye, dearest Mother, all, all my thoughts are with you.

Goodbye, dearest Mother. Your Tanne.

To Ingeborg Dinesen

Ngong 25/6 22

My own beloved Mother.

The long distance between us is so terrible and I don't know how to come closer to you all. I don't seem able to realize it, life here goes on in its usual way, of course; there is no one here we can talk to who knows anything at all about any of you at home, and that little piece of paper, your telegram, is the only visible sign we have of the tremendously great change. So that in some ways it seems to go on feeling like a dream, and I constantly imagine that I am going to wake up and find everything as it was before. It was strange that for two nights running before the telegram came I dreamed that Elle was dead; I saw you all so clearly and woke up all bathed in tears; I told Tommy in the morning how worried I felt about Elle. So now I can't stop thinking that it is a dream. I think of you all one by one and see your faces so plainly: Aunt Bess, Elle, Malla, and wish so inexpressibly that I were with you, but it is almost impossible to write.

Tommy and I have been talking so much about the old days and going over so many memories; I do not think there is a single one that is not peaceful and beautiful. When we were little children it is true that Ea and I could sometimes squabble, but after that, and more and more in recent years, there was nothing but love and understanding and true warmth and kindness that always came flowing over one when we were together. We talked about all the sailing trips and how much she enjoyed them, and then about these last few years when there was always such a warm welcome waiting for one at Kilden. I thought so much about that on Christmas Eve in 1915, when I was at home, just before she became engaged; we were decorating the Christmas tree, and at the last moment we put on our coats and ran over to church, and on the way home Ea talked so much about her future life. I think of her too on her wedding day, when she was looking so lovely, and then of the day when I went down to Kilden with you to see Mitten for the first time; and that was just before she fell ill, in October. . . .

Dearest Mother, could you consider now coming out here for the winter? I haven't anything special to offer you, of course; in some ways it is not worth traveling so far for, but at least it is warm here and you would get away from the cold winter at home. Then I think it would be a great joy for you to see the boys out here together, see them going out on a safari together and hear about everything when they came back. I think safari life would be paradise for Anders. For me it would be a quite indescribable joy, but you know that very well.

Thomas is thinking of taking a trip to Uganda for a couple of months; he also wants to get to the Congo, he is hoping to start next week. I hope Denys Finch-Hatton will come and stay here while he is away. Thomas has probably written to tell you that I have been ill for three weeks in the "Kenya Nursing Home"; it was anything but pleasant. I am quite well again now. . . .

To Ellen Dahl

Ngong 4/8 22

. . . I had always thought that when we grew old it would be Ea who would gather us all together, and it would be at her home that we would talk about the old memories; it was probably because she was the only one of us to have a child that I thought that she and her home would be the center for our generation, but above all because she was so radiant, glowingly loving and sharing. But now I feel that in a way, now she is gone, she is binding us all even more closely together. I do not know whether Ea was as kind to anyone else as she was to me. I think constantly of those last days when I was at home, when I was at Valdemarskilde, and when you and she went with me across the Great Belt,—what was the name of that little station you had to take tickets for?—I seem still to feel her warm loving arms around me and see her gaze following me. She was so well and happy then, she herself felt she was at the height of happiness; and I have only heard about her long illness in letters, so it will never seem really real to me, you know. . . .

It is strange not to know anything about the plans for Mitten. If I had been at home now and in more normal circumstances I might perhaps have had the beloved little one with me, at least for a time. It is so unspeakably sad to think of the tremendous change in her life, that she is quite unaware of. But I cannot help thinking mostly about the necessity of arranging things so that Mother is not too terribly harrowed; in the end Mitten will no doubt be all right; for after all she is surrounded by people who love her. I think it will be difficult for Mother to realize that she is actually half a Neergaard, not merely in appearance, but that she will be able to understand much in their strange nature without the least difficulty. If, as she is growing up, she and Viggo engage in power disputes, it may well not affect her in the least, but seem quite natural to her.

I am thinking of myself in connection with Father's family; I think it would have cut Mother to the heart to have had to leave me in their charge,—if she herself could not have kept me,—and yet I believe that I would have thrived on their care, despite their somewhat halfhearted or superficial manner. . . .

To Ingeborg Dinesen

Ngong 10/8 22

. . . I don't want to bother you, but if you are coming out here there are some things I would like to ask you to bring with you . . . I have painted three pictures here that I am sending to Aunt Bess, and I am wondering whether she will help me with some paints again. . . .

I would very much like to have the books in bound copies; one cannot get binding done out here and it is a pity not to be able to protect such treasures as books are here. Aunt Bess has sent Tommy a book called "Kristin Lavrandsdatter," which he and I have been completely absorbed in for the last fortnight; we have discussed it endlessly and kept returning to it. I think it is the most beautiful book I have read for many years.

People here are saying that the Governor is to leave, and that we are to have the Governor of Tanganyika in his place. He is said to be pro-Indian and distinctly pro-native, which will suit me very well. I have grown most interested in politics here, far more than I ever was in Danish politics, and felt like writing to Winstone [*sic*] Churchill and the Archbishop of Canterbury, you may have read that they have been making speeches about this country in the House of Commons; but I have not managed to do so yet. . . .

To Ingeborg Dinesen

Ngong 11/8 [1922]

Dearest Mother.

I am opening my letter again because I received one from you and Elle yesterday evening,—that is, they were for Tommy on his birthday, but he showed them to me,—and from what you say it seems as if you are going to give up the idea of a trip out here. . . . Of course I do understand that you feel your duty lies chiefly with Mitten, and heaven knows I do not grudge the beloved little one your love and tenderness; but she does have so many years ahead to look forward to with you,—and I feel that if you do not come and stay with me here this year you will probably never come. Of course I know that we can meet at home; but you must try to realize that this place is a kind of child for me,—the only one I have in this life,—and I wish so much for you to see it. . . .

To Ingeborg Dinesen

Ngong 26/8 22

. . . Thomas left a week ago to go up to the Lindstrøms and from there was going to tour round Kenya. I have not heard a word from him since then and hope that he is all right. Denys Finch-Hatton was staying here for a few days after which he and I went out to the McMillans' at "Donya Sabuk,"—(The Buffalo Mountain),—60 miles the other side of Nairobi, for the weekend. It is a lovely trip, and we went for some fine drives from there as well. They are building themselves a kind of Escurial out there, an enormous house, and are moving great mountains about in order to make terraces and so on. It will be rather fine, though. It was as dry as the desert there, and you can imagine my joy, on returning to the farm, to find that we had had over 2″ of rain, and it is still raining. There will be plenty of coffee blossom, and it has done my maize no end of good. And Dickens had put the road in order while I was away, which is a blessing. . . .

Ngong 3/9 22

. . . I do not know how to put it,—but I know that this shaurie with Bror has been worse for me than Ea's death. When Thomas and I sit and talk now about her and about all the happy hours in the old days, it is so intensely painful; but all the same it *is* a great joy that can never be lost. I am quite aware that we, who were not at home last winter and therefore did not experience Ea's illness with her, cannot feel in the same way as you now; but yet in her illness she was the same, and the love and understanding among you all, the same. I have in mind Mama's last years; in one way it was such a terrible grief that she should suffer so much,—and yet I feel that the memory of poor, weak, suffering Mama shines with an almost brighter luster than all the memories of her from the time when she was strong and happy. I cannot express it properly, but feel there is something in life,—the very most central, eternal thing in it,—that is made easier to understand through this great sorrow; it is as if everything has been more unified. . . .

What you write about Viggo and Mitten is so touching. What sort of imaginary stories does she read from the newspapers?—we have never heard about them. I thought that Viggo might perhaps become completely withdrawn, and think that it is a great and unexpectedly good thing that he can accept it like this, and that he and Mitten are growing closer to each other. . . .

To Ingeborg Dinesen

Ngong 10/9 22

. . . We are having such lovely weather at the moment, after over 3″ of rain,—when it is like this I do not think there is anywhere else in the world with such fresh and beautiful air as here; as they say in "Familien paa Gilje" ["The Family at Gilje"]: "Every breath a drink of the purest life." I have had to go to Nairobi many times during the last week about shauries, but have also had a most enjoyable time there. The day before yesterday I went with Denys to have tea with Lord Delamere; I do like Delamere, he is a really great man. On the way home we drove through such rain as I have seldom seen. I had Juma's little girl with me,—Uncle Aage has seen her,—she has come to seem more and more like my adopted child and is quite mad about driving in the car. I think that at this age,—she was born on Armistice Day,—black children are actually more intelligent than white,—with the exception of Mitten, of course,—she is really a great help to me, sets the table and makes toast and is full of her own importance as a houseboy. She is so deft and graceful and quite mad about clothes. I have presented her to Denys and he has bought her shoes and scarves, which has made her speechless with ecstasy. If only other people do not spoil her for me, but she is so comically serious and so completely unaware of it that no one can really help it.

Lady Northey held a fete yesterday; I had not planned to go, but by the evening I was so depressed over all my shauries that I felt I had to do something, and suggested to my two Somali children that we drive in. One advantage of running the house with just totos is that one can always get the whole household to join in such undertakings. They had all my things fixed up in a trice and draped the car with a red lantern, as I have no rear light, and we drove in at about 11 o'clock,—and then I was very glad I had gone. Everyone was so friendly and kind, and Denys and Delamere took me up to the new Governor,—I had already met him previously, by the way,—and he was extremely friendly and I thought was making a very good impression. It is probably quite difficult for him to start here in these difficult times. Delamere says that he has been everything imaginable here, white hunter and policeman,—he is South African,—it may well be better in some ways to have a gentleman like Northey, but Coryndon will probably come really to grips with things here, and he does know Africa,—its nature, natives, game,—through and through. . . .

I am very upset because I am losing all my hair, this started to happen after I was last ill. I only have to touch it for whole handfuls to fall out, lovely long hair, which will take years to grow again,—if it ever does grow again. I haven't enough hair now to hold a hat pin. But otherwise I am better now than I have been for a long time, and so well that it is a joy to be alive. . . .

It is strange how accustomed one grows here to living in memories, or in the thought of things that are far away, so that one loses the sense of distance, not merely in space, but in time. I can't explain it exactly,—but I can no longer feel any difference between past and present. Thomas says that Einstein says the same thing: that the same laws govern time as well as space; it is true that we are conscious of being in one particular place, but it is only a prejudice to suppose that other places in space and time do not exist in exactly the same way. With the support of such a great authority I am surely entitled to believe in the truth of something I cannot express but sense or feel so strongly. If I never went home again, the old road through the grove, for instance, would be just as real to me and as true as Laura's alteration of it. And in the same way I see you many times as our very young mother, as I remember you so well in a blue and white striped cotton frock. It is the same with the Sound and the woods at

Folehave, *they are not here where I am;* but still I am not so shortsighted as to believe that they no longer exist because of that. . . .

To Ingeborg Dinesen

Ngong Sunday 17/9 22

My own beloved Mother.

Thank you for the newspapers about Ea, and for the photographs of the drawing room at home and the church, which arrived yesterday. I think it is hardly possible for you to imagine what it is like to get them out here; it makes it seem so real suddenly,—for a moment I seemed to be actually with you in the house at Rungsted. I have been sitting looking at them for so long; there are memories of so many years in that room,—where the Christmas tree has stood so many times, and where we have sat in front of the fire on so many evenings,—and it has been filled with Ea's songs and her wonderful voice. . . I think the obituary notices say beautiful things about Ea; but nevertheless it is those who knew her best who will provide her truest memorial. I have been thinking of the inscription her young friends wanted to have engraved on a stone at Kilden; I cannot properly remember the verses that Father wrote for Grandfather and Grandmother, but would it not be possible to adapt some of them suitably for Ea? I think that both Grandfather's "Quick eye and quick wit," and Grandmother's "Thought of others' good alone" and "Noble, faithful good woman and true" would suit; but, as I say, I cannot really remember them and perhaps it would not be possible to coordinate them. . . .

Monday 18/9. [1922]

. . . I am now a first-class driver, and I think one of the greatest pleasures in the world is driving an automobile. I can't understand why Elle does not drive herself; it is not tiring and I am sure she would love it. . . .

I am about to see a long-held wish fulfilled by having the factory painted, and I hope it will be finished by the time Thomas gets back. Most utility buildings here are built of corrugated iron, which is certainly not attractive material, but which is much improved in appearance when it is a uniform color all over. Our factory is built of all kinds of bits of old iron,—now we are painting the roof red and putting tar on the walls, it will be really fine. . . .

We have had the loveliest weather recently, fresh and clear like a spring day at home. This country has the most beautiful air I know.

Then in the evening I can see Venus shining so indescribably clearly in the western sky; every evening I wonder whether you are looking at it too. I think you can see out here that it is not placed in the firmament but is floating in a space, one can see the depth behind it. What a wonderfully clear, dazzling star it is. Can you remember the little poem I sent to Thomas during the war, about the star above the trench? I still think always that your heart, your love is shining over and toward us, exactly like a star, so clearly and ineffably beautiful, and so calm and always the same . . . .

To Ingeborg Dinesen

Ngong Sunday 8/10 22

. . . The weather is changing, I think the short rains are not far off; in a way it is disappointing as after the chilly summer months we have been enjoying the heat and the lovely clear weather, but of course it is good if we get normal rainfall again, and it is about time that we do, the whole countryside has been burning hereabouts. It is rather splendid to watch the fires on the Ngong Hills, especially just after sunset, but it looks dreary when one goes out there. Tommy and I drove out there the day before yesterday,—on faithful old Harley for once, it has been given a thorough course of repairs—as the car is in being fitted with new batteries,—and all the "foothills" are completely black and brown after the grass fires. It is quite a special color scheme, and as typical for this time of year here as the autumn colors at home. . . .

To Ingeborg Dinesen

Ngong Sunday 15/10. 22

. . . The Governor came out here last Thursday,—the new Governor, Coryndon,—I had met him at dinner at the McMillans' a few days earlier, and he is always enormously friendly and had said that he would like to come out here for tea. I thought he would want to see the farm, but he had not thought of that at all, but we had a very pleasant tea. . . . We talked a lot about the natives and discovered we had very similar ideas, in that we consider that the future of the country must depend far more than is now the case on native production. In Uganda the natives produce,—and export,—very great quantities of cotton, sim-sim [sesame] and also coffee, and in all probability these tribes could be taught to do many things. . . .

I think the rains are coming. I would so much like to go out painting in the Ngong Hills before they really get started, and we are thinking of driving out there tomorrow, on Harley, and perhaps camping for a couple of days, Thomas in order to shoot,—there are incredible quantities of birds there at present, particularly quail and guinea fowl,—and I to paint. I am terribly glad you are sending me paints with Viggo. Unfortunately I have to confess that I have given my best picture to Finch-Hatton, as, although he usually does not admire anything, he likes that one. But I will certainly send Aunt Bess something better when I really get going.

I so much regret that I did not manage to ask you to send me Sophus Claussen's "Djævlerier" ["Diableries"] via Viggo. I had a copy, which I had got from Elisabeth, but unfortunately it was lost, and I find it hard to live without it. "Aphrodite's Vapors" and "Man" are a kind of gospel for me. So I would be very grateful if you would send it to me. It should be possible even if there is no one coming out here who can bring it. . . .

I have been tidying up my books and have found an old "Buch der Lieder." They are all Ea's songs, as you know, that she sang as a young girl at Rungsted. When I go through it here I feel that I can hear her voice and see the lilacs and the new beech leaves on some light evening—"im wunderschönen Monat Mai.". . .

To Ingeborg Dinesen

Ngong 27/10 22

. . . I do so sincerely wish that Thomas could be really happy, but it is so difficult always to know how to advise. I think he should try to spend a year in Germany; he might be able to study under Einstein himself, and I think the German way of thinking would appeal to him on the whole, and that he could learn a lot there. I cannot help thinking that Germany is being unfairly treated at present, and this makes one more aware of their good qualities; for as a whole all hatred even of one's bitterest enemies must disappear when one sees them reduced to such depths. But also when one compares them with the English, whom I have in fact come to appreciate more and more, the Germans can in many instances hold their own; for instance, how much one longs for German music!—and for all the poetry and richness of life that it represents, and which the English, with their "long legs and cold faces" have so little of. . . .

To Ingeborg Dinesen

Ngong Sunday 29/10 22

. . . I think so often of those words in the Bible: "I will not let thee go before thou blessest me." I think there is such deep meaning, something so glorious in them; I almost take it to be my "motto" in this life. I feel that it applies so profoundly to all circumstances, to everything that one experiences; even where this farm and this land are concerned, although no doubt you may find it laughable, come back to it. The hardest thing for me has been that I have been unable to carry it through in my marriage,—although it really was as good friends that Bror and I parted.

But I do consider also that when one says these words, then one must agree and consent to let go of that which really has given one its blessing. For it happens almost every day of one's life that a time, a circumstance is past; one cannot struggle against that. But when one has received a blessing, one has that to keep that can never be lost. And when I think of how intensely and constantly Ea blessed you, when there has certainly never been one single moment in which her heart was not full of blessing toward you, then I am bound to feel there is so much light in the darkness around you. . . .

In 1922 Karen Blixen believed herself to be pregnant. In a letter to the editor of these letters, Thomas Dinesen recounts that one night his sister sent her watchman to his house with a message that he should come to her. She had been disappointed in her hope and belief that she was going to have Denys Finch Hatton's child, and she was beside herself with despair. Her brother tried to comfort her as well as he could, and after three hours had passed she became comparatively calm again.

To Ingeborg Dinesen

Ngong Sunday 12.11.22

My dearest Mother.

I did not manage to write last Sunday because Crighton and Milligan came out here in the morning and stayed for most of the day in order to go right around the farm and discuss the situation generally and the possibility of telegraphing home about an arrangement both to their firm and the management of Karen Coffee Co. . . .Then we arranged a meeting with Hunter early on Monday morning, and it was almost impossible for Thomas and me to get in on the Harley,—(the car is in having the batteries charged),—because there had been very heavy rain overnight. In some places the road resembled a roaring torrent. For safety's sake we had our oldest clothes on,—and that's quite something just now!—it would be quite impossible to go to a business meeting in Hørsholm, let alone Copenhagen, in such a get up. But we have become absolutely superior where clothes are concerned here. It is utterly unimportant whether one's elbows are sticking out of one's shirt and one's knees out of one's trousers—where the men are concerned, that is,—as long as the clothes stay in one piece sufficiently to stay on one. . . .

It is amazing how much interest Thomas takes in books, and how important they are to him; I feel more or less an idiot because as time has gone by I have become so bad at reading and find so little to satisfy me in books. Thomas has been very much absorbed in replying to Aunt Bess's letter about "the morals" of his journal, and we have had a lot of discussion on this interesting theme; Thomas is very indignant with me and thinks me a complete reactionary,—he will probably write and tell you that I am about to be converted to Rome, but that is not at all so certain. . . .

I have such beautiful white lilies just now, bigger and whiter, I think, than those at home. It does not seem to me at all strange that they should be considered holy flowers and that they are always portrayed in the hands of angels; they are almost supernaturally white. There is a species of bird here, called egrets, they are equally white and look quite unnatural in the setting of the landscape. Some time ago I had a dam built beside the road; a big lake has now formed, and crowds of birds come there, duck, snipe, moorhen, and egret. There is so little water here that there is great pleasure to be had in even a small dam; Thomas and I were sitting out there for a long time last night smoking our evening cigarettes and watching the reflection of the sun in the water and later on, Venus, shining so very clear and beautiful. . . .

Mannehawa, Juma's little girl, was just four years old yesterday; she was born on Armistice Day, so I remember the date. She is a funny sweet little thing who runs about behind me all day long. I have been thinking that she might be married to Abdullah, although that would be a mésalliance for him; but I cannot see that Abdullah will ever be able to afford a Somali girl; they have to pay £200 for them. Abdullah has a wretched family situation, a rotten father who never gives his wife anything; the whole family lives on Abdullah's wages from here. . . .

I have been reading a book by Wells about the Washington Conference, it is not very encouraging; he considers it well within the limits of possibility that our civilization is on the brink of disintegration, comparable to the Greek and Roman cultures in their time. I feel it is so strange, that when one can read about all the horrors in Russia and Central Europe, the English go on thinking that everything is continuing as before, as if a house were on fire at one end and there was no hope of putting it out, and people were having a dinner party at the other end of it. Thomas, who of course is more or less a Bolshevik, does not think that it would be so terrible if it really did happen; nor can I say whether it would be such a great misfortune for the world, although I certainly hope that I may disappear with the old civilization!. . . .

To Ingeborg Dinesen

Ngong Sunday 19/11 [1922]

. . . We have completely run out of money, I do not know how the management at home can imagine that we can manage on £200 a month when our normal expenditure is £500. But for the time being we are surviving. I have sold my dresses to a Jewish lady in Nairobi,—it is comical to see her in them,—and Thomas did have some money in the bank; he was trying to pawn his guns. Fortunately, anyone in the way of Indians and natives has great faith in me. I pray God they will never be disappointed. . . .

I am hoping very much to get some paints, and particularly canvas, from Viggo when he comes; I have run out and am longing to have my brush in my hand again. By the way, would you or Elle ask Stelling or Wieth if it is possible to make painting canvas oneself, it probably only needs covering with some mixture or other. Denys Finch-Hatton has encouraged me really to start painting again; he has a great talent himself but cannot be bothered to do anything about it. . . .

To Ingeborg Dinesen

Ngong 19.12.22

My own dearest Mother.

I have not managed to write for the last few Sundays, partly because Tommy wrote and there is not so much news for us both to write, and partly because I have been so busy painting again; when there are as many shauries as there have been lately I find it my greatest joy and recreation. Sadly, it is clear to me how difficult it is to do one's best when there is no one to assess it, and often one gets most appreciation,—from the fools to whom I sometimes show my work,—for one's second best, or even inferior, things. When I had Fru Dorph to criticize me I did not dare to be slovenly. But still, I think it is going quite well, and it is always a pleasure. . . .

I have lost one of my old boys, Isa, to my sorrow. He had been with me for more than five years and I was so fond of him. He took only three days to die; actually, I think his wife poisoned him; they tend to do that here. Thomas and I attended his funeral in the evening; he was a Muhammadan and it was interesting to see the ceremony.

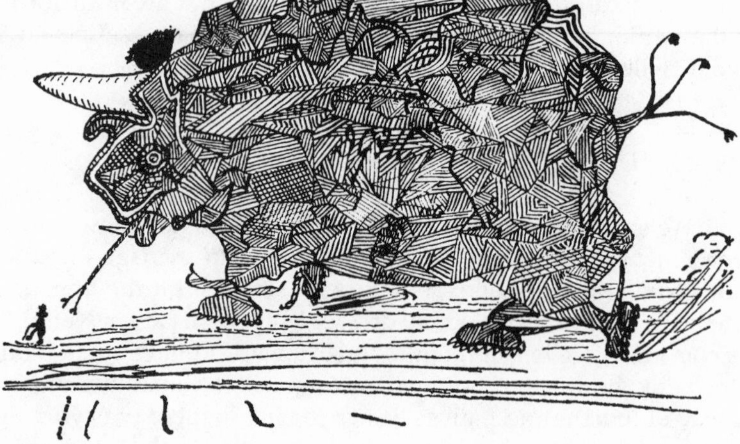

A rhinoceros, drawn by Denys Finch Hatton in a copy of Coleridge's *The Rime of the Ancient Mariner* (now at Rungstedlund).

The Kikuyu, on the other hand, will not bury their dead, but put them out for the hyenas, a custom which with the progress of civilization will seem increasingly weird and difficult to practice. This week a young Kikuyu girl was killed, she fell off an ox cart just outside my house and was run over. None of the Kikuyu would carry her away, and our District Commissioner sent a message telling us not to touch her as they wished to investigate the matter; but they did not send anyone for three days. The Kikuyu are frightfully superstitious and did not dare to go past there after sunset for three days; only a little, semi-idiot toto, who I keep to look after my dogs, and who was at the Scottish Mission and converted to Christianity there,—something I have previously been skeptical about,—showed the strength of his religion by fearlessly making himself useful in taking messages along that road, which goes between my house and Dickens's! In the end Dickens and I had to bury her ourselves, carry her to the grave and fill it in,—Thomas was away on a trip with Mohr. The beastly, heartless parents would have nothing to do with the accident but only tried to get money out of me by saying that it had been my oxen who ran over her. Now and then one gets so furious with the natives; the Kikuyu really are a base race,—and yet there is something touching about them and about the amazing faith they have in me and in my ability to see them through all the circumstances of life, which disarms one's anger. . . .

Ngong 31.12.22

. . . Viggo and his cousin have been here now for over a fortnight; they are staying down at Thomas's house, which seems to suit them well, I think, as it gives them more peace and independence; they are tremendously pleasant, easy guests and I think they like the country. Of course we have had to go to Nairobi on numerous occasions and also spent a lot of time going over the farm, and it will probably be quite a while yet before they get out on safari, if they ever do get started. . . .

We spent an extremely quiet Christmas Eve, but it was a pleasant time, I think. Thomas and I had tried to decorate with spruce and candles, and we had rice porridge, turkey and a kind of almond cake. There is something so homely and genuinely Danish about Viggo,—and his cousin as well; Thomas and I often laugh behind their backs at their dress and appearance, which they refuse to alter to conform to conditions out here, but there is something almost touching about it. We thought such a lot about you all and wondered who was at Rungstedlund—one always feels that one has grown so old that Christmas has almost lost its meaning, and then when it comes one realizes how much it still means. After the others had gone to bed I drove in, first to an evening party at Lady Northey's, she had kept asking me to go, and where most of my friends out here were gathered, and after that to Midnight Mass at the French Mission. Now you must not think, as Thomas says, that I am about to become a Catholic, but the French priests are always so friendly and kind, and their church is really beautiful. The Northeys took me back to *souper* with them afterwards, so I was home late. It was the most lovely starry night; since then we have had more rain, over one inch in a week.

I took with me a little Kikuyu boy, Kamante; perhaps Uncle Aage will remember him. He was very ill with big sores when Uncle Aage was here; later on I sent him up to the Scottish Mission, where they cured him and converted him to Christianity, so he insisted on going to church, and I hope that the difference between the Catholic and Presbyterian,—or whatever it is,— service will not cause a conflict in his soul. He is the funniest little chap, not quite all there, but with a wonderfully sharp intelligence in some respects, I think he is the sort of material they made use of in the old days for court fools. . . .

Please thank Aunt Bess very much for the books; I have not read the third part of "Kristin," and that kind of supplement always makes you worried in case it does not match up with the beginning, but Thomas, of course, has buried himself in it with great enthusiasm.

I have read "Jyder" ["Jutlanders"] and "Den Fremsynte" ["The Clairvoyant"] again, after many years, with great pleasure; I think the latter is quite the best of Lie's works and a really delightful book. . . .

2.1.23

[Continuation of letter of 31 December 1922]
I didn't get this finished the day before yesterday and I have had a lot on since then. For on New Year's Eve,—after I had gone to bed and been asleep for a couple of hours—Finch-Hatton and a man called Lord Francis Scott with his niece, Lady Margaret Scott, came out here by car to fetch me for a midnight supper, and then some of them came back here next morning and stayed to lunch and drove me in again to Muthaiga yesterday evening, and I left there only this morning early. . . .

1923

To Ingeborg Dinesen

Ngong Monday 8.1.23

. . . À propos of nationality, you must not discourage Thomas from being "pro-German" when he comes home. After all he proved himself ready to give his life for the Allied cause, and there is something great about the fact that now he is ready to forget enmity. I know that I myself have very few opinions regarding politics and have probably allowed Thomas to influence me; but I think he takes great pains to be impartial. You write that Germany is thinking only of revenge; but that is understandable, and France certainly lived for that during all those years before the war. I think Germany would probably have been even more cruel to those they had conquered if they had won the war, but I do think the others are bad enough; I think that when you say that Germany would only have allowed France to keep "her eyes to weep with," it is not so far from what France,—if she could,—would perpetrate upon Germany; and can one sympathize with a nation that would subjugate another as a slave state? Now that I have spent so much time together with Thomas and talked so much to him about everything, I think one is bound to have the greatest admiration for the invincible love and desire for truth that constantly spurs him on. . . .

I have been wondering whether all Ea's compositions have been kept and collected; I remember there were so many beautiful things,—I expect almost all of them are at Rungsted. If it has not already been done, could not Elle collect and arrange them properly and perhaps copy them? I do not mean with a view to publishing them, but for us to have. . . .

To Ingeborg Dinesen

[January 1923]

. . . It is always interesting to hear what people are talking about at home. Also about Georg Brandes's little jaunt; it is really admirable that the old fellow still has so much energy. . . . When people retreat to Lucerne on their little romantic adventures, those who happen to come across them ought to keep quiet about it. From this distance Brandes can clearly be seen as one of those who have made the name of Denmark shine most brightly during the last quarter of a century.

Yes, you must really look forward to having Thomas home again. . . .though for me it will be very hard to lose him. But of course I can see that it will be good for him to get away from here; in many ways he has had an awful time,—although I think that both of us will always be grateful for the time we have spent together here, it has been so good and enjoyable. But I think it has helped him to develop a great deal, and that he has formed a clear picture of himself here and of what he really wants from life, and that is the most important thing. Perhaps Africa, as well as being a terrible place for shauries, will come to represent the mountain of revelation for him, and when he sees the Ngong Hills fading into the distance he will come to think, in spite of everything: Farewell, Mount Alverna, farewell, beloved, beloved mountain.

What you predicted about my hair growing again has fortunately come to pass in abundance. Since I cut it off and find it easier to manage, you can't imagine what a lion's mane I have acquired, more than I have ever had before. I should like to give all young women two pieces of advice: to have their hair cut short and to learn to drive a car. These two things completely transform one's life. For centuries long hair has been a sort of slavery; suddenly one feels freer than words can express, with a short mane that can be tidied in a moment and that the wind can blow through. And as nobody wears corsets out here you can really move as a man's equal. If it suited me I would wear trousers here, "shorts" as so many ladies do; but alas, alas, I do not have the legs,—or the moral courage,—for that. . . .

To Ingeborg Dinesen

Ngong. Sunday 28.1.23

Dearest Mother.

I didn't manage to write last Sunday, and in general there is not much to write about at the moment, the whole time is taken up with business matters, which you will no doubt hear from Uncle Aage. This time I have to report the sad news that our factory has been burned down. It happened last Wednesday night at about 11 o'clock, but I cannot think how it can have caught fire, as they stopped and cleaned the machine at 7 o'clock in the evening; presumably some sparks must have fallen on to a couple of old sacks and were smoldering there, then when it started to blow in the middle of the night they burst into flame. Thomas was the first to be woken up by the boys shouting, and he was down there working to extinguish it until 2 or 3 a.m. He was the one to be most upset because he did build it, and there is hardly a single bolt that he did not see put in himself; I have spent much time there, too, and most of Thomas's and my time together has been passed up on the scaffolding and in discussing how the next section should be built. So it is tragic to see the black ruins with the skeletons of our machines. However, I do not think we will suffer any pecuniary loss as it was well insured; and Viggo thinks that we can get hold of a little ready money from the insurance and by not having to renew all the machines at once. It is really good to have Viggo here in all the negotiations resulting from this; he is experienced in this sort of thing and is very practical and methodical. . . .

Now Thomas is thinking of going on a mountain-climbing trip to Kenya with the two young Norwegians, Mohr and Anker, the day after tomorrow. I can't deny that I am very anxious about this, but they have promised me to be careful. I have come to the conclusion that it is *deeds* that keep a nation, and individuals, alive; without action everything stagnates,—and so it is best to give one's blessing to those who seek achievement actively. I think that if Thomas were lucky enough to climb Kenya's hitherto unscaled peaks it would make him happier than anything else could. Mohr and Anker are very pleasant young fellows; there is usually a lot of "go" in Norwegians.

I have had Spanish flu and am up again, but very tired. There has been a lot of it on the farm, and whooping cough too; Juma's little girl was very ill and has grown so thin, but I think she is over the worst now.

Dickens went to a fancy-dress party at Limoru yesterday, as a Dutchman,—he looks just like one, small and stocky with a round, ruddy face. I helped him to make his costume, with clogs and a fur cap, to which I sewed my false curls, and was rewarded by his getting first prize, he was so proud and delighted. He needed some cheering up after all his efforts over the fire and the shauries that ensued; he was quite as upset as I was when our factory, that we were so proud of, went up in flames.

I have to go to Nairobi over some shauries, so I can't write any more today. A thousand greetings to you all. The weather is lovely here; we have had a little rain, and it is deliciously warm again now. There are so many hyenas about, they come right up to the house at night; I have become really fond of their long howls and screams, that are a part of Africa. . . .

Ngong. Sunday 4.2.23

. . . Everyone is obsessed with "the indien question" [*sic*],—which it is thought may develop into a revolution. What they are all saying is that they will not be a "pawn in the political game of chess," that is, in the British Government's dealings with India, although I think they will have to be if they are really enthusiastic about and faithful to "the Empire." I personally have so little racial feeling that I find it hard to understand them. I feel class differences so much more than racial, and would rather spend my time with an Arabian chief or an Indian priest than with a waiter from home. . . .

It is really distressing to hear how difficult things are for everyone. It is only gradually that one comes to realize the terrible results of that accursed war. It is almost more deplorable than the personal sufferings that this whole period has been reduced so low that anxiety for daily bread is its sole interest. I grieve more personally over the fact that no beautiful hats are being made than over being unable to get any. And how much more over other things! The goulash period was bad enough, especially in the heartlessness with which they made their gold out of blood; but I think it also brought out some good in people, and in these hard times so much goodness seems to be lost. . . .

On 2 March 1923 Thomas Dinesen parted from Karen Blixen and the farm to start his long-delayed journey home to Denmark.

To Thomas Dinesen

23/3 1923 [Thomas Dinesen's dating]

. . . As you will see from my telegram, what I am most concerned about is that they might not send me any money for 1 April. I do not know to what extent they had committed themselves to spending the £500 in question, and if they think there is no point they will probably not send it under any circumstances. It is really most unfortunate that none of the sales of which we had held out the prospects to them materialized. I have also had a letter from that agent we wrote to at Eldoret, saying no sales will be possible before the Indian question has been settled. A forced sale of the whole property under these conditions would naturally be completely disadvantageous, but if they quite lose patience at home they will probably pay no regard to that. . . .

The farm itself is looking first class,—much improved since you left, and we have finished plowing. On the 17th we had ¼" of rain, and I thought that meant the long rains were beginning in earnest; but we have not had any more since. However, it is so hot and thunderously oppressive that I think we can expect it at any moment. The inch that we had did us a lot of good and the whole shamba is full of buds ready to burst when the next shower comes. I think there will be more blossom this time than when you were here. Particularly in the piece that Holmberg pruned, and in the shamba to the east of the Kilimanjaro road, around Thaxton's house, there is a lot.

I am sure you know, even without further emphasis from me, how heartbroken I would be if we gave it up now, after so much work and when we are so close to harbor,—as I believe we are now. If you are convinced that it *is* the right thing to sell you will have to act on that conviction; but you must know that I will fight to carry it through as long as I have life and breath.

The future of the farm is bound to be: either that the company keeps it,—or that I borrow money and buy it,—or that it is sold by a forced sale and passes into strange hands. Now I will tell you how I think that the two first cases could be arranged; I will not concern myself with the last, that would have to take care of itself and probably I would have nothing to do with it.

To run the farm from now until 1 September,—what I think we must reckon on to be just about on the safe side,—£1,600 will be needed. The actual expenses will probably not amount to quite so much, but the insurance on the farm buildings falls due in the middle of April, and we have had a tiresome shaurie over coffee on the Uasin-Gishu farm, which was not tended in accordance with the instructions from the Department of Agriculture, and for which they are imposing large fines on us. Now I hold £150 of that £1,600. If they can be persuaded to send £500 of what was previously promised from home, we then lack £950. I think can find about £100 of this out of what I can save from the insurance money . . . so that therefore we would be short of £800 to £850 to keep the farm going until the harvest comes in. Now I wonder whether you could go to London and put the facts clearly to Gilliat's, and try to persuade them, in order to salvage their capital already invested, to offer a further sum, to be paid monthly, as long as we keep the farm going in a satisfactory manner, which they can ascertain through Milligan, who can also if necessary give them telegraphic information regarding the present state of the farm and the prospects for the harvest. If they could be urged to let us have as much as £250 a month for four months,—1 May, 1 June, 1 July, and 1 August,—we would then be on top of things; but they may well not agree. You will have to make your own judgment about this and according to what transpires agree to £200 a month or £150, or,—if all else fails,—£100, which would after all be a help. You would then have to raise the rest in some other way. I do not know whether you can or would wish to raise it privately, possibly you and Viggo together; of course it would entail difficulties and trouble, but surely success or failure cannot depend entirely on *this* sum. . . .

One possibility has occurred to me,—which I may as well write as there is no harm in discussing everything,—that you might get a loan of £1,000 and might *want* to put it into the farm. In which case you should (if the family will help us over the 1st of April, because before then nothing can be done) telegraph out and ask for instance Hunter, Taylor, Harrison, or someone else what he thinks the farm would realize from a forced sale now. If he says £20,000, for instance, you should then make an offer to the management to run the farm for four months in return for the option to buy it for £20,000 during those months! Surely it would be possible to come to some sort of terms with the company by which, if they saw at the end of that period that the farm was paying and wished to keep it they would in some way or other refund your £1,000. . . .

I do not feel that there would be anything unfair on my part in trying to buy under present conditions,—although this would no doubt be said. It would be better for Mother, surely, than if anyone else were to buy. My plan would be to sell Uasin-Gishu,—in the course of a year or two,—and pay off the loan, because it should be possible here at Ngong to get a smaller loan with less premium; perhaps one could arrange from the start that the percentage should be reduced if the security for the loan was improved through part payment.

I want to be in constant communication with you and hope you will write and telegraph frequently. If my idea of a loan is realized somehow or other I would prefer that the negotiations with Denmark go through you. In that case I will telegraph that *Denys Finch Hatton and I* can borrow money and buy. Of course I would not demand any privileges in the event of purchase, but neither do I want to be in a worse position than any other purchaser, for instance, that a part of the share capital would remain on a second mortgage.

Well, this is a great deal about my own shauries,—and is still, as when you were out here, relying far too much on your support in every way. But don't you think that, if we can get this put through now, there would come a time when I can repay you and all the others everything you have given to help me?—and if I cannot manage it now, then *in any case* all that will have been lost. That is why I am writing this to you. I have missed you so terribly since you left; I think that being left alone suddenly sent me slightly mad. And everything still seems so much out of balance, the whole of life, so much is at risk; I think there are two ways, two possibilities, for me now. Either this will really work and bring with it,—oh, every conceivable good for me: the preservation of my life here, harmony with everyone at home, if I can some day come home wealthy and succesfull [*sic*]; yes, I can't help visualizing it all right up to our safari sometime in the future when we will recall all the shauries like shadows and laugh at them,—or else: Failure, Failure, Failure, and in a way undeserved, I feel,—or how?

So now as before I rely on your understanding and your friendship,—let me hear from you soon.

Your Tanne.

To Ingeborg Dinesen

Ngong. Sunday 1/4 23

. . . There is absolutely no reason for you to be sorry for me because I am alone. To begin with I'm *not* alone; I see much more of other people now than when Thomas was here because as a rule he did not want to be bothered with them. And then anyway I do not in the least mind being alone sometimes. My situation here, with my boys and dogs and white people, has grown up around me naturally and been created by myself; it suits me and I am happy in it. . . .

Nor should you think that I am in need of "peace and quiet," as you say; I don't really know what you have in mind, but there is no peace and quiet for a mill that has nothing to grind,—on the contrary,—because it is not able to stand still. I dread being in a situation where one's life consists of "chatting" about everything and where one is obliged to make little shauries out of everything for oneself. You must never feel sorry for me about such things as loneliness or illness; I consider them of no account.

What I do fear, and what would really be a misfortune for me, is not to have continuity in my life; that, to me, would be the worst horror, would become a kind of insanity. Naturally it is tiresome to have so many shauries and worries as there have been these past few years, but that is how things are nowadays in most parts of the world, and as long as there is meaning and coherence in them it is worth the struggle, and is after all quite interesting; but it is quite a different matter when misfortunes are of the kind that reduce life to nothingness, meaningless, completely under the sway of chance. If my marriage had turned out differently, or if I had had children, I probably would not have felt this sort of terror hanging over me. . . .

Ngong. Monday 9.4.23.

. . . I think there are many delightful children who somehow cannot stand growing up; they come to nothing, and in the same way later on in life there are many people who cannot endure age,—the good qualities they had in their youth disappear and nothing comes to replace them. It is as if they merely fade,—without maturing. I have actually often thought about this: how age is the greatest test for everyone,—just as with wine; it takes a really good vintage to stand up to long keeping. And that does not only apply to human beings, but to art as well. The lesser harvest is best drunk right away, without illusions, it goes down well enough. But the really good one,—what charm and worth it acquires through being matured. As long as it is quite fresh no one can tell what it is worth; but after fifty or only twenty years! When, for instance, I read Oscar Wilde again, I feel that it is all so thin and feeble that one feels like spitting it out again; but Oehlenschlæger,—at his best,—and Aarestrup seem to me over the years to have gained such profundity and nobility, such a "bouquet" that I do not think their contemporaries can have felt when they read them. . . .

I am doing a painting of a young Kikuyu girl and hope it will turn out well. When I am able to paint here,—and it is going reasonably well,—and there is rain, and the air so fresh and fine, as it is in the rainy season, I find it a pleasure to be alive. I hope Thomas has remembered to get my paints in France; I have no more red and that is a fearful handicap. There is nothing but rubbish to be had in Nairobi. . . .

I have to go in to Nairobi several times this week about our insurance shaurie. . . . When I was there on Wednesday I met Finch-Hatton, and had lunch at Muthaiga with him. It was most enjoyable. I think Finch-Hatton,—in contrast to Geoffrey Buxton,—is the kind of person who will improve with the years, so that, as Stevenson says about d'Artagnan, he will ". . . mellow into a man so witty, kind and upright . . . that the whole man rings true like a good sovereign."

"Tilskueren" magazine is still being sent to me, it is probably actually Thomas's. Although I find it shamefully tedious there is in fact usually *something* interesting in it. In the last issue I found a piece about Frederik Frijs in Zahrtmann's letters,—presented as an example of a really distinguished noble youth, which I could not help laughing at. Incidentally they wrote in glowing terms about those one-acters by Otto Benzon that you thought were a complete fiasco.

I must tell you something that an old Scottish nurse said to me, that I think will please you; I was paying her a visit and we happened to be talking about how I had not visited my various neighbors who probably found me impolite. No need to worry about that, she said, when "everybody knows you are a true Christian woman"!—certainly that's something I can never be; but perhaps she might sympathize with a humanitarian heathen. Probably the natives have given me this good testimonial, and there is some justification for it because I really wish to do everything I can for them in this life. I do not actually know what it is that gives these primitive people their great attraction, but they certainly do possess it. The other day I read an article about Hans Egede and I think he must have had a wonderful career. If I were really a "believer" I would probably end up as a missionary, but perhaps one can be a sort of missionary even without faith. . . .

I do hope so much that we will be able to meet in the new year. At present it is hard to see how things are going to turn out for me. I would like to get to Europe next year, partly because I want to see Professor Rasch. In general I am very well, but I have been ill a couple of times without really knowing what was wrong; and it is a long time now since I last talked to him. I do not feel like going to Denmark next time I go back,—I would prefer to let a few years go by after this divorce shaurie; but I have been thinking that I might stay in Paris for a few months and do some painting, and then Rasch might recommend a doctor there for me. Now you really must not start worrying because I am writing this; there is probably nothing to worry about, one can't always be in perfect health, and actually I think it is one of the easiest diseases to deal with if one keeps a watch on it. . . .

To Thomas Dinesen

Ngong. 22.4.1923

. . . I had a pretty unpleasant time after you left here, so terribly many shauries all coming at once, and then I did not hear a word from home as to whether they intended to send money before 4 April, until I had a most welcome telegram from Uncle Aage. This was partly Hunter's fault, that I did not hear sooner that the money had arrived. The 4th of April was a particularly happy day; after I had been dreading every day that new shauries would turn up, a whole series of happy events came together on that day, and then I met Denys and had a pleasant meal at Muthaiga with him; but more of that later.

What I want first and foremost to write about now is what is occupying my mind most, that is, my possible loan and purchase of the farm. . . . After having, as you can imagine, thought at great length and depth about the whole business, I have really become convinced that as things are and with the money and people, etc. available, the best thing would be for me to be able to carry through with the purchase of this farm. . . .

In addition to this there is another shaurie, that I can write quite sincerely about anyway to you, although you will not mention it to anyone at the moment, and this is that I do not think, —if this purchase does not materialize, either now or in a fairly foreseeable future,—that I can stay here. I think there is little meaning in it for me. . . . You know that I have talked to you about it several times, but that anyway you would not advise me to give up my position here. I don't know how you now look at this from a distance; but I myself have more or less come to the conclusion that as things are now it is not worth putting all my efforts into. So I must ask you to be aware in your own mind,—for as I say, I think it best not to mention it to others,—not as certain, but as possible and probable, that if I do not succeed in gaining control of this enterprise myself I will give it up. . . .

To Ingeborg Dinesen

Ngong 29/4 [1923]

. . . Now Farah and I have sent little Abdullah, Farah's brother, to school in Mombasa,—I am contributing a certain sum monthly to keep him there. He is a joy to us; his teachers praise him and say that he is industrious and eager to learn. I would so much like to run a school on the farm some day; although I don't really know whether it would not be better to let the natives keep their primitive life-style. But I consider that is <u>out of the question</u>. In some form or other civilization will take possession of them, and so I think that one should see that it is in the best way possible. I would enjoy it so much, particularly to teach them some handcrafts as well, and better hygiene; they are eager to learn as a rule, but *frightfully* unstable; I think a native finds it a torture to stick at a job of work for a long time, except for the wretched sort of agriculture they have practiced for 10,000 years.

I can see this with my models; they groan and wriggle when they have to sit still and look at the same thing for long at a time, which you might otherwise think was in their <u>line</u>. I have just finished the portrait of a young Kikuyu girl; I'm quite pleased with it. . . .

I have just been reading Benvenuto Cellini again, I wish I could take a really good trip to northern Italy next time I go home; perhaps Thomas and I could go together, no other country in the world has so much charm for me; and then I think that its nature resembles this country, especially the colors, it is probably the olive groves that make it so.

Viggo said . . . that Aunt Bess has now completed the writing of Mama's biography. Has it been printed? And do you think Aunt Bess would let me have it? I think of Mama so often here; I think she would have enjoyed seeing Africa,—and then I so often think of the old days in Denmark and would really like to hear something about it, I mean about Mama's childhood and youth and even earlier times. Troels Lund's book about Bakkehuset sounds very interesting; I would like to have that some time. . . .

To Thomas Dinesen

Ngong 29/4.1923

Dearest Tommy.

Just a few words.

Yesterday I had a letter from Bror from the Congo. When he was at Government House he had heard from the Governor about my envisaged loan and writes that he thinks he can get it for me "from home,"—I do not know whether he means Sweden or England. He goes on to make various conditions regarding it. I am not saying that he is not doing this for my sake or in order to help me,—but he is doing it on his own hook and you will understand that I am a little anxious about what he may write and say about it, which may do harm to me at home. So you must realize that this is nothing to do with me; I have not arranged it,—if you should come to hear about it in any way. He also sent the woman he had been on safari with out here, he thought she would be able to arrange something through her father, who is very rich, but I said right away that I would not hear of that.

Everyone sends greetings to you, my boys are in despair because nobody goes out to shoot meat for them any more.

It is beautifully green here,—the whole reserve is shining when you look over to it from your old house.

You must promise to write to me about everything.

Your Tanne

To Ingeborg Dinesen

Ngong. Sunday 6/5 23

. . . It was most interesting to have the clipping from "København" about Skat Rørdam's lectures, and I would very much have liked to hear those lectures. One is so far away from that sort of thing out here. When Thomas was here we had long discussions on Christianity and the various other religions. I must say that I have up to now found no answer to what I gather was the theme of Rørdam's lectures: Who was Jesus of Nazareth? If one refuses completely to regard Christ's birth, life, and death as events in world history of enormous gravity, the decisive incidents in the history of man,—what are the Gospels, what is Christianity and what Jesus of Nazareth?—Certainly, one can get a good idea of what Jesus himself was as a person and a personality, even though there can be very varying views on this; but however great an impression may be made by a noble personality I do not think that in itself it is something that can continue to have the same influence for thousands of years.

And the teaching of Jesus,—what is it? Taken literally through the Gospels I think partly that many times it is inconsistent, partly that it contains many things that no,—or very, very few,—Christians really adhere to, that they cannot measure up to even in theory. And I think that if the question were posed,—as in "A Soul after Death,"—"Say then, what is the *spirit* of Jesus's teaching"—then among people who all considered themselves to be sincere Christians could be heard very varying answers, if they answered really truthfully and not according to tradition. Moreover I think that even the ideas of Christianity differ radically among serious Russian, Scandinavian, Italian, and English Christians.

At the same time I believe that the idea of an ideal life or merely of decent conduct is more or less general to the whole of humanity. I think, for example, that the thought of forgiving one's enemies in the simple instance will everywhere be deeply admired; I know that this is so among Muhammadans, who are otherwise pretty fierce in that direction,—and I think that it is in no way infrequent among orthodox Jews, even though they have been advocates of a severer principle; and even the Christians have now generally acknowledged it as a law or rule of conduct for life in general. Now I think there are very few of my own generation who on the whole have any belief in God; they are not interested in religious questions. But their overall view of how to live a good life coincides, where the best of them are concerned, with that of a good Christian or a noble-minded Muhammadan. . . .

I have not been feeling well for some time; recently I consulted a new young Doctor Anderson in Nairobi, he thought that I was suffering from malaria and had been for some time; he gave me some revolting stuff to take for it. I am not ill, but so tired,—I don't feel like doing anything. I simply don't dare go to Burkitt, although I like him very much in a way.

I am very glad to hear you have got Anna Bartels's daughter as a parlor maid; I remember Anna Bartels well, she was a nice girl. It is always a good thing to get people you know, and I am more and more convinced that everything depends on character, it is the key to everything. Zahrtmann, whose letters have made me like him immensely and agree with him in many ways, writes that during his long life he has come to the realization that all great artistic talent rests in or depends on moral stamina; He says also that all genius, in art as well, is "a greater degree of kindness." In order not to be misunderstood I have to say that I do not understand the concept of "moral stamina" in quite the usual sense. Nothing in my—rather long now—life has caused so much hatred and contempt in me as what is generally termed "morals." I think that among all the principles one can "adopt" in life that especially is the most miserable and misleading.

I would so much like to have Herman Wildenvey's "Love Poems," probably in the little edition from Gyldendal. There is also a little anthology, "Danish Love Poems," taken from every period, that Aunt Valborg gave me when I was at home, but which unfortunately has disappeared, that I would like to have some time. And tell Thomas that he must remember to send me "Diableries"; he knows best how many times I have thought about and been comforted by the poem about the divine serpent. . . .

To Thomas Dinesen

Ngong 17/5 23

. . . Regarding business matters, your letter was certainly very encouraging and I know you realize how much it means to have an approximation of security for anyway the immediate future after the terrible uncertainty I was in after you left. And I think your plan of going to London later on is a sensible one. We have really had a lot of rain,—9″ in March, 16 in April and 10 up to now in May,—it must be a record. As far as it goes this is very encouraging,—if only we get a good harvest as a result. But I think I must have developed a tendency to make worries for myself; it seems to me now that we will not get so much as we should expect after the really fine blossom we had. I had Trench out, and you have probably seen the report he sent to Uncle Aage; he thinks that it takes longer for a neglected farm to pick up than we had anticipated. He thought that *great* progress had been made, said several times that the trees were in "topping condition," but did not think we should count on getting the full crop that we should be able to get, this year. Now I do not know either how much one can rely on that sort of estimate at this stage, or what effect it will have on your plans at home, but feel it is anyway best to write about it.

As you can guess I am thinking about these shauries all the time and my own view is: that it is anyway better to keep the farm going through this harvest, both because then the Indian question will be settled,—in the event of a sale,—and because a good harvest will make a great difference to the value of this farm. In any case there is no doubt that this year it will be more than "self-supporting." . . .

To Ingeborg Dinesen

Ngong. Monday 28/5 23

My dearest Mother.

I did not manage to write yesterday, as I have a model at present,—an old Kikuyu,—and Sunday is my best day for painting; I get constantly disturbed on the other days, which makes me so kali ["snappy, irritable"]. When I was painting my last picture, of a young Kikuyu girl, I finished up in such despair that I flung brush and paints on the floor and said to Farah: "Take it away and burn it, I will never look at it again," and that sensible Farah quietly took it away but came up to me a day or two later and said: "Try one more day, then I think that God shall help you and it shall be very good"; everything in the conversations I hold with Farah turns on God and how much he will help us with the maize, the dogs, the car, etc.—and he did help me this time, to the extent that I got the picture finished, even if it was not very good. But I also like to have peace in which to write to you, and I do not get that on a week day, so you must forgive me if this letter is somewhat confused. . . .

You would all laugh at me if you saw me in my wet weather outfit,—at present I nearly always wear long khaki trousers and a kind of blouse reaching to the knee, and bare legs and clogs; now my hair is short I fancy myself as Tolstoy, without the beard. I have also taught myself to plow, so that I did not need to feel inferior to Tolstoy in a photograph. . . .

I would so much like to have some books on the Renaissance; I wonder if Knud knows of any? I seem to remember a German book on the Renaissance in Italy and its people being published a couple of years ago which was highly acclaimed and has probably been translated, but I cannot remember the name of the author. . . .

Ngong 12/6 23 [noted by Thomas Dinesen]

. . . The farm is in brilliant condition; every single tree looks so much better than last year, the work is going steadily and we have done many things that will not need to be repeated,—planting shade-trees, thorough plowing between the coffee trees, thorough repairs to the roads, etc. Expenditure is still decreasing, we have a large area of maize,—and much else. But when we have a situation of everything depending on 50 tons more or less, it is probably best not to count on things as they are just at the moment. . . .

It is not my intention to suggest something to Uncle Aage or the Company that the present situation does not justify. It has certainly not been my intention to suggest "bankruptcy" to them, as you write . . . I certainly do not want them to sell to me at a moment when they would prefer not to sell at all. But when it so happens that there is a possibility for this moment to occur at any time, surely it is reasonable that I for my part may prepare my position—insofar as it can be prepared.

You write that you have made use of all the trust they have in you at home to get them to believe in this farm. I take it that in this you have acted on your own conviction, even though at the same time I am most grateful to you. But with the strongest conviction, with *certainty* that an enterprise is of great worth, surely it must be taken into account that conditions may give rise to a time when resources are needed. But where, as in this case, there are no resources,—where things are runned [*sic*] so close that, as we know, 50 tons more or less can mean, not a more or less good harvest, not a greater or lesser profit, but the fate of the whole enterprise depending on it,—surely then it is always reasonable, even at the times when things look brightest, to work at thinking of other solutions in case such a moment does occur. Let us suppose that we get a really good crop, as good as could be envisaged, but that it is late, so that the trees have not sufficient time to develop blossom the next year. Then there would be again a point when we need a subsidy, either from home or from somewhere else.

My own standpoint is,—as you well know: that I believe in this farm; I am convinced that it is going to succeed. But the longer I stay here, and the more it comes to mean to me,—in 1915 I could quite easily have stayed at home without regrets, and even in 1920, it would not have meant my whole life to me,—it is rather a sensation of intolerable pressure to live as I have done and do, from day to day with this sword hanging over my head: that some little misfortune or other, or, as you know, possibly even a mood at home can be decisive for its and my fate. As long as I stay here I will always be seeking in some way or other to procure myself some kind of security. You may think that I think too much about myself and too little of them at home who have put so much into this place, and that may be so. But I have never tried, and will not do so now, to persuade them to sell against their will. The question of my purchase of this farm was never mentioned before they themselves had expressed their disappointment over it and their wish to be free of the whole enterprise. I know that to them it is a question of a large amount of money; to me it means my whole life.

Well, that was about business,—and most probably completely superfluous since the chances for this loan materializing are so remote.

Otherwise I will only say that I miss you quite terribly. In spite of the worries of the Wakamba totos I have not been able to prevail upon myself to go shooting at Orungi one single time. Even trips in to Nairobi in the dearly beloved automobile, now that the plains beside the road are just like "the sea in a headwind" with thousands of white flowers, have become so sad. When "Tilskueren" magazine, that paltry rag, came the other day, it seemed quite unnatural to have no one to read and discuss it with. It is so strange to have had first Bror as a partner in all my experiences here, and then you, and now both of you have gone and will probably never come back again. It is good that I still have Farah. He has been insufferable for a time, you know this can happen with Somalis, but has now turned into an angel, which makes a great difference to my life. He drives the car really well and is becoming more and more of a chauffeur; I think on the whole that colored people, when they have anything to do with cars find it hard to think about anything else. He keeps mine in an exemplary condition and that is always something.

Incidentally, the roads have been in a deplorable state and the government road was worse than ours. There were such deep holes along the stretch between Dagoretti Junction and Nairobi that the unfortunate people who were unaware of them and went along there when they were full of water had their springs and axles broken by the hundred. I was in Nairobi the other day as I had to talk to Hunter, and on the way back there were nine Indian carts stuck in a hole in the Forest Reserve. We had to help unloading them all and then loading them up again, and by then it was oziko [*usiku;* "evening"], so that on our way home we ourselves got stuck by Charlie's house; by then I was so tired with all that changing of gears, worry about the car and everything else that I just stood with my head against the car and wept as if I had been whipped, much to Farah's horror. . .

You can't imagine what a plague of fleas we have in the house; Farah says "only cats and dog, these two people bring them in," I don't know who is going to get them out. . . .

To Ingeborg Dinesen

Ngong. Sunday 17/6 23

. . . I must say, by the way, that in general I *hate* principles; they are hardly ever good—and how often does not pure and simple prejudice masquerade under the name of principle! I think Mario Krohn said something good and telling when he wrote to me: "Goodness,—not in the sense of a sermon, but defined as 'mobility of the soul.'" And this I think a child more than anything else can give. I have thought so often that no one can really judge of the relationship between marriage partners, because the outward appearance is so meaningless and can be so utterly at variance with what is within, and encircle something completely concealed from those outside except when they get a chance glimpse of it. I can remember feeling once that Viggo spoke to Ea so drily and without understanding, and that just after that she happened to tell me quite by chance that once, when she was tired and had gone to lie down, Viggo had sat beside her bed and had said to her: "I am not going to disturb you by talking; I just want to sit and look at you,"—and that was probably much more real and a more truthful expression of the whole relationship than all the things that other people listen to. Something similar exists between a mother or father and a child,—one has to guess one's way to the real, innermost core of the relationship. I think that Mitten is more to Viggo than he shows, perhaps more than he knows himself. . . .

To Ingeborg Dinesen

Ngong. Sunday 8/7.[1923]

. . . I did not get a letter written to you last Sunday as we had a big ngoma here from early morning onward. I must say I really hate ngomas; there is so much noise and it is so horribly monotonous, but this one was held especially in my honor on the plain in front of my house. Then a lot of old people always come, who have to be entertained and talked to, and that takes up a great deal of time, which in fact is the case with everything one has to do with natives; conversation with them goes at the same pace as with two-year-old children at home and with just as many repetitions. Maria Montessori constantly warns that children should never be "hustled" and I think this is so right; adults must adjust their minds to a different speed when they talk to them, and in general children only really understand a story and enjoy it when they hear it for the second time,—or third or fourth,—it is told, and the natives are the same and always take particular pleasure in hearing something repeated, as many times as possible.—

I can't really define what it is that makes the natives so likable; in reality they have more bad qualities than good ones and they are all stupid and unreliable. I think it is the remarkable,—and brazen,—trust they have in one, which ends up by working like a "spell." The longer I live the more I seem to realize the enormous power there is in "faith"; I really believe that it can move mountains if the occasion should arise.

I do not think one can ever really feel anything for people who have no faith in one, while conversely I believe that one could die with the greatest pleasure for those who do have it. . . .

The news of Uncle Mogens's death made a greater impression on me than I would have expected. I feel a really great sorrow in knowing that I will not see him again and it seems as if a whole age has disappeared with his passing. Despite all his short-comings there was much that was great and admirable about him; I think that as I grow older I shall come to share more of his view of the world,—and that if I had done so earlier I could have saved myself many difficulties. When I think about Frijsenborg now it is always so beautiful, so closely bound up with the Danish summer—indeed, with the loveliest impressions of Danish nature as a whole, summer, autumn and winter,—and youth. One grieves that it is all past. . . .

To Ingeborg Dinesen

Ngong. Sunday 22/7 23

. . . I am writing with a little tame bushbuck, "Lulu," lying under my desk; I have had her for a fortnight and hope she is going to live.

Just as Aunt Bess says that one suffers a lot if one loves animals, so I must say that my love for the natives causes me much suffering. For one cannot always help them,—just as little as animals. I expect Thomas can remember my boy, Esa, who was poisoned by his beastly wife. His wife Marjama,—not the poisoness but another one who is a nice young girl,—has taken refuge with me with her two little girls from Esa's family, who want her for his brother. This passes for law and justice among the natives and a young widow with two daughters is sought after because when the daughters come to be married they bring a lot of money into the family; but while she has been with me

Marjama has embraced Muhammadanism and has also accustomed herself to a higher level of culture, and has no desire at all to return to her husband's family, who are pretty primitive. This is giving me a lot of shauries and I am probably acting in conflict with the law. She feels safe here on the farm, but does not dare to go outside it, as she is afraid of being carried off and disappearing into the Machakos. . . .

Now you are having a lovely time at home with fruit and roses and bathing in the Sound; I miss all that very much. It will soon be Mama's birthday; that must always be the *clou* of the summer to all her grandchildren. When I think of Mama now I think the picture I have of her is chiefly from when I was growing up, before she became ill or began to look so poorly; I see her coming out of the garden door at Folehave and coming to meet us across the courtyard,—and the table was laid under the elm tree, with Fernanda in all her glory to wait on us. I seem to think we always had chicken and those white strawberries. Isn't it strange, too, that when my thoughts come to rest briefly on the house at home I always think of it as it was before the restoration in 99, with the steps to the kitchen along the north wall, and the door into the playroom from that corridor, and the steep staircase to the attic with the cloakroom under it. . . .

It is the Muhammadan Christmas,—or what corresponds to it,—a costly and troublesome festival for me. All Juma's family have gone to Nairobi for several days, as his little boy is to be presented to the congregation, or whatever it is; fortunately they are using the occasion to get his hair cut, up to now he has had long pieces of string plaited into it and looked like a German poodle. Mahu, his elder sister,—was so distressed over having only her old clothes to wear at the festival that I thought I had better get her something new; she was so enchanted when I brought the clothes home for her that she could not say a word and just stood looking at them for hours. She started off for the festivities in high spirits sitting in front of Farah on his bicycle, veiled like a Turkish woman.

Unfortunately there are a great many leopards around the house at the moment, I ought to have a trap made for them; they will probably get some of my dogs in the end. It is strange to hear them roaring around the house at night just as they did thousands of years ago. The other evening when I was coming home from Dickens's office one went across the road just in front of me; these big cats move in a special way,—if one merely sees the shadow of one in the darkness one can see that it is no other kind of animal. . . .

Ngong 2.8.23

Dearest Elle.

It was really a delightful surprise to get your letter from Tours. It was tremendously interesting to hear about your travels and you must have enjoyed it all greatly. . . . I felt an indescribable longing for France and the south when I was reading your letter.

All the same I can say, although this may surprise you, that I quite agree with you in what you write about France and England. I have been living among the English for ten years now and think I have come to understand them, and that I would understand England through them. I do not think now that there is any other nation to match up with them. In my opinion they have such great calm features in their temperament; when one has grown accustomed to living with them one feels that other nations make so much unnecessary fuss. I think that living with the best of them is like getting up into clearer air; they are "clean" in the same way as one speaks of clean air, and without being very "gifted" they have a wider outlook and more real absence of prejudice than I have come across in any other nation I have met with,—and I think an impressive natural unselfishness. The particularly English sense of beauty is most striking as well; they make everything so beautiful and harmonious without any "fuss." This is true, of course, of the best of them, but surely a nation must always be judged by its best examples, for I think some of the English "middle class" are fearfully deadly.—

In our talks here Thomas and I discussed several times how in our opinion a great many people at home (among them yourself) put too high a value on France, particularly in ascribing so much that is poetical to them, for I think this is not true; they are drier and clearer and harder than the people of the north. I had this in mind when I saw the big Spanish exhibition in London, and then immediately afterward Turner's pictures at the National Gallery; one sees the difference in the air of the two countries, the dry, burning, almost sinister clarity in the Spanish air, and in the—incidentally really magnificent,—Spanish art, in contrast to the semitransparent works of the English painter, so strangely full of promise. There is no softness in the southern nature, and one can certainly say, as you,—and Meta Hauch do,—that the south is cruel. But how brilliant, splendid, beautiful they are in every way,—and then I always feel in the south that one is on holy ground; it is as if the very soil has been ennobled through the life of thousands of generations; the nobility of the ancient culture shines through everything, and the life itself is like fine old matured wine, that "is offered in a crystal goblet"; I believe that when once one has been captured by the spirit of the south one never ceases to love it and long for it.

Incidentally, I think that there is a really fine time ahead for women and that the next hundred years will bring many glorious revelations to them. For there is hardly any other sphere in which prejudice and superstition of the most horrific kind have been retained so long as in that of women, and just as it must have been an inexpressible relief for humanity when it shook off the burden of religious prejudice and superstition, I think it will be truly glorious when women become real people and have the whole world open before them. Each year brings so many small advances, automobiles, for instance, which after all we can drive every bit as well as men! And can you remember that when we were young girls we really could not walk in the street alone after dark? All that has quite changed now. And it is reasonable enough for the woman's movement to vacillate a good deal before finding its,—more or less,—real answers; but I will never cease to be grateful to the old warriors,—from Camilla Collett to Aunt Ellen, because they worked with might and main for it, although they would probably not acknowledge the '"cause" in its present-day guise as their legitimate child!

You must know how much I too would like you to see my house here some day; I love it so dearly. I do not think this country has such a tremendous attraction for everyone,—to me it is endless beauty and delight. But there are very few people who really care about the natives as I do, and I myself think that I am slightly ridiculous over it. I think these highland natives have such great possibilities for development; I cannot see that there is anything to stop them from achieving a really high standard of culture, but it requires enormous effort and there is so much in civilization that is dangerous, and I think that it is especially "le premier pas qui coute." Last time I was at home I was greatly interested in reading about Maria Montessori and her system of education for very small children, and I think that most of her ideas about them apply to the natives here, and that they should be treated in the same way. I wish that I might some day be in the position to get a Montessori-trained teacher out here and start a school. I expect I should be fierce with her, like Bishop Absalon with the poor French monks he imported from Paris to Roskilde Monastery,—or even further out in the country; Aunt Bess knows all about that,—but I feel just like Bishop Absalon,—sans comparaison, by the way,—like a bearer of culture, and that is a great thing! . . .

Ngong. Sunday 12/8 23

Dearest Mother.

I do not have time to write much today as I have guests here, Mr. Martin and his wife,—the daughter of the previous Governor, Northey,—and their small five-year-old daughter, staying. They have been here for a week to get out of Nairobi for a while and it has been pleasant to have them. But actually I had an ulterior motive in asking them, because Martin is the director of the Land Department, and the week before I had had a letter from Harrison and Creswell saying that the Land Office would not wait a minute longer for payment of the 5,000 shillings the company owes them, and I did not know how we were going to pay them. In the meantime I have discussed the matter with Martin and arranged for it to be deferred. . . .

The other week I had a visit from Thomas's friend Mohr, who is eager to hear from him and sent his regards. He is a very nice young man; but it is strange that when one is accustomed to being with English people I think that when one comes to talk to Norwegians it so often seems like coming inside from outdoors,—not that Mohr is in any way bookish or sedentary, on the contrary, but their view of life is so much more limited. As long as they are being critical, for example about the English and their literature and customs, they give a very intelligent impression; but when it is a matter of more positive things, what they themselves admire and prize, then it is always so stamped with Christiania, and the most interesting thing is what Gunnar Heiberg has been saying about Winsnes and Winsnes about Sigrid Undset.

Mohr was immensely supercilious about Ibanez's books and thought they were utterly superficial, but gave me in return a book by Sven Elvestad [Stein Riverton], "Professor Umbrosius," which he was in ecstasies over, and which I think is merely tolerable. It is on the same theme that Thomas may remember from a little article in "Extrabladet," on the subject of Einstein's idea of looking at the whole of history backward, but the "Extrabladet" piece was more interesting, it is too much in a whole book. Thomas must read it and let me have his opinion of it. In fact it did interest me quite a lot, because I myself was very interested just then in an American, Branch Cabell's books, which are also full of fantasy, and all this has made me wonder whether a new direction in literature is about to develop, making use of fantasy. I don't think you would much care for "Jurgen," which I recommended to Thomas, because it is rather shocking; but I have read another of his books, "The Cream of the Jest," which I think is excellent, and in which I have found,—sans comparaison,—many of my ideas, for instance those in "The Revenge of Truth," about life and death and art, and so on. . . .

To Thomas Dinesen

Ngong. 13/8 23

. . . Otherwise I want to say that since I took on this shaurie I have given all my time, all my interest, all my thought to it. Dickens and Thaxton are free when the day's work is done and they probably do not waste much thought on the farm over the weekend; for me it is a matter of constant thought during sleepless nights and personal effort in interviews and discussions. It seems to me that it would be reasonable to expect a couple of months' holiday now, in fact it would have been so before this,—but for thirty months I have not been away from this farm for one week, in the last two years not for two days. I came straight from a spell in the hospital when I really believed that I was about to die, and resumed work on the farm without a week's convalescence somewhere where I could have become rested. I have a letter here from Dr. Burkitt, written in May, in which he says that I must and should go home, otherwise I run the risk of being an invalid for life; but they know as well as I do at home that I am not going to leave here. . . .

To Thomas Dinesen

Ngong. 19/8 23

My own dearest Tommy.

I don't know how to thank you for such a royal gift of £19, which arrived here the other day. . . .I must tell you that it could not have come at a better moment,—if an angel had come down from heaven with it it would not have been more appropriate. It was amazing, and I must tell you about it. I don't know if I wrote about a shaurie over a little Somali boy of 11, who was, in my opinion, wrongly accused of theft and sentenced to four years in prison. His family is very poor and the wretched Somalis would only help with paying half the costs of the case, and I had promised them 150 shillings; but when I looked at my balance sheet I realized that it did not look as if I would be able to do it, and Farah and I were in some despair over the case—"If Allah does not send us something special," said Farah. And then your money arrived almost immediately afterward. Perhaps you had better not mention this to others, they would probably think it was foolish. . . .

I am very grieved over the news of Eric Otter's death. It was brought to me the other evening by a runner who had been sent from the K.A.R. in order to try to get the address of his wife or mother through me; unfortunately I did not have either. He died of black-water in Turkana. He was one of my best friends here from the old days and it is so strange that everything from that time seems to be disappearing now.

Please thank Aunt Bess very much for a letter that I was terribly happy to have, but do not know how to reply to,—mostly because I have the impression from Aunt Bess's letter that my letter to her must have been completely idiotic, so I don't want to write any more of that kind. The worst of such discussions in letters out here is that when one gets a reply one cannot remember what one originally wrote. And yet I value that sort of letter from you at home so much, and especially from Aunt Bess. I *will* write nevertheless,—hoping it is fairly appropriate,—that I do believe that "freedom" and "happiness" are inner states, and that it is impossible to lay down rules for what produces them,—I do not even think that the simple rules Aunt Bess suggests are in the least necessary; I think that people can be pursued by the police and still feel free and happy,—and yet I think that for each separate individual there are outward conditions that more or less determine these feelings for them. Just as, for instance, coffee can grow,—and presumably feel free and happy,—under 7,000 and cedar over 7,000 [feet], I think that every human being requires a certain type of soil, temperature and altitude, very narrowly defined for some, almost universal for others,—in order to feel free and happy, that is to say, free to develop his nature to the utmost of which it is capable. I believe that one can feel completely free both in a Trappist monastery or at the court in Berlin; but I think it would have to be an unusual and an unusually gracious personality that would feel free in *both* places (and *also* in a bar, among Bolsheviks, and in Nøddebo Vicarage).

I myself would rather say that one is free when one is able to love the laws to which one's existence is subject. When, for instance, I hear people talk about the infinite freedom one feels on board ship, I feel a sensation of outrage because I feel that the laws of movement to which sea voyaging subjects one are against nature. I think that Aunt Bess feels free, as she writes, not because she is in a position to "give everyone his due, pay her taxes etc.",—except because order and honesty are necessary to her, and she loves them,—but because the people that she likes and who are of importance in her life, do not demand of her anything that she cannot give in accordance with her nature. Finally, I must disagree that talk of freedom is hot air in

Drachmann's mouth. I know of no one who has loved it more, no other poet whose works, when one reads them, leave more feeling of having been in "free air,"—in a fresher, freer atmosphere. . . .

I am expecting Denys, perhaps today, anyway this week, and so you will know that:

Death is nothing, winter is nothing. . . .

To Ingeborg Dinesen

Ngong. Sunday 19/8 23

. . . Last Sunday we had a big night ngoma here, around my boys' houses, in honor of little Betty Martin, who enjoyed it tremendously. Ngomas at night make a much better show than those they hold in the daytime and many hundreds of young men and girls attended this one; the old people do not join in these night dances. It was very well arranged and we were comfortably seated in arm chairs by some big bonfires to watch it. . . . You must tell Thomas that the steward with his burning twigs was even more "kali" than at the ngoma he saw; Betty was completely thrilled each time he "chastised" a frivolous dancer. . . .

There has been one joyful event on the farm. Dr. Hemsted killed one of the much-feared leopards in a gun-trap. It had taken his tame bushbuck, and he put this trap over it and caught the leopard at five in the afternoon. However, it was only a young leopard and there are several more on the farm, one came quite close to my house last night. Dickens and I have now decided to set a trap with a live goat in it; it is cruel but better than having all the dogs and goats on the farm eaten,—and the goat escapes with a fright, as the gun is placed over the entrance and the leopard is shot before it can get in. This cunning leopard will not go into any of the traps we have set over "kills."

This morning I went to visit our D.C. in the car with Farah. I had promised my squatters, that I would try to arrange permission for them to hold a private kiama,—native court,—here to decide their own affairs, mostly quarrels over women, which the government will have nothing to do with; but it has to be recognized by the government. For the time being they are under the jurisdiction of Kinanjui, but they want to appoint eight old men who will judge such cases on the farm. . . .

Ngong. 10/9 192[3]

. . . Since I received Uncle Aage's letter the scent has gone from the roses and the radiance from the full moon in my life here and I have been feeling much as I imagine Samson felt when they had cut off his hair: my strength has gone. I am no good any more at shauries with Hunter, Harrison, and Milligan; I cannot even hold back the impatience of my white people at having to wait for money,—and God knows I would not have found that hard ever before. No one knows how I slaved to get the Mbagathi house sold so that we could manage this 1st of September, and that was easy for me; now after this shaurie, and although I have been in to Nairobi about it ten times, I can't get to the point of getting the conveyance signed, which I know very well is my own fault; I feel that I cannot cope any more with Hunter's hesitations and Harrison's chicaneries. I can probably still be of use, like Samson, in the treadmill; but you can use a mule for that. . . .

As far as I myself am concerned, I have set my heart so much on this that there have been many times when I have felt absolutely certain that I would not want to go on living if I had to leave this place. I cannot say with certainty now that I would really be able to survive it. But then there are other times when I think that it is mad to set all one's hopes on one thing in life and that I ought to have enough strength left to be able to go on living even after so much had collapsed around me. But then one must start thinking a little about *how* this could be done. Up to now I have looked upon my parting with this place as an Armageddon,—after it there would be nothing left. But now I am writing to you to ask you to help me to realize *what* possibilities there might be on the other side of it.

First I would like to ask you whether, in the event of my leaving here, you would come out and put affairs in order according to my plans, so that I would not have to do this myself and would not, for instance, have to have Uncle Aage here during my last months on the farm?

And next: will you help me to make a new start in life, and if so, with how much?

I am not writing this in order to beg, but to know where I stand. If, for instance, you say that you are not in a position to help me,—which I imagine might well be the case if you should be thinking of getting married or taking on some business or other,—then you must not think that I would not understand perfectly well. I would just have to make different plans.

I could make a very good marriage as things are at present; but I have become absolutely convinced that I would not marry except for love or in order to achieve a position that I was really suited to fill. I will not entertain the thought of marrying in order to be taken care of. On the other hand, I might well consider going away with someone for a few years, someone I got on well with and who would help me to be able to manage for myself.

The way in which girls are brought up is really shameful. I am quite certain that if I had been born a boy I would now, with exactly the same intelligence and other abilities that I have, have been able to look after myself really well. But even now I would surely be capable of it if only I had some help to start with.

I do not myself think,—as perhaps all of you may,—that I am so very particular about what kind of life I want to live, but that I have been unfortunate in not being suited to the conditions into which I was born and which were thus available. There is *one thing* that I am completely determined upon: I will not live among the middle class. But I really believe that I could be very happy, when I had once got it going, in running a small hotel for colored people in Djibouti or Marseilles. (This is not something I have been seriously considering, just the first example that occurs to me.)

But of course I have not reached any decision and do not know whether the company has done so. I want you to read this and let me know what you think before making a decision, and you do know that I have always listened to your advice. I would therefore be very grateful to you if you will write and tell me in great detail what you really think.

I had not intended to write so much when I began this letter. But when I start writing to you it always grows longer than I had planned.

Denys Finch-Hatton has been staying here for some time, and is probably staying on another week, and I have been really completely happy, indeed, so happy that it is worth having lived and suffered, been ill, and had all the shauries, to have lived for this week.

Goodbye dear Brother.

Always always your Tanne.

To Thomas Dinesen

Ngong. 25/9 1923

. . . The first thing I have to say in this affair is that from what the company has said and written and telegraphed it is clear to me that they have not the slightest wish to continue to employ me as manager.

If that had been so they could not possibly have treated me in this fashion.

. . . Regarding my position here I can say that I have loved it and that I love this country and people and this place, if not above everything else in the world, then at least so deeply that I have been happy to give all my time and all my abilities,—what is generally known as "one's life,"—to its service. But that does not make it impossible to bring about such changes that my feelings would be altered. I can remember that Fru Casse had a theory, or I should rather say, an experiment in thinking, about her feelings for her husband, which took this form: if Peter had an arm or a leg chopped off, would I love him any less?—no. If Peter had his eyes put out, would I love him any less?—no. If Peter lost his hearing, speech, health, would I care less for him?—no. Etc. Even leaving out of consideration the fact that with one blow so much of Peter could be chopped off that the relationship would at least be completely altered, I think even the possibility that Peter could be so changed would be so ghastly for most people that if they had any chance at all of escaping from the relationship they would take it. But in any case it merely shows that for Fru Casse arms and legs, etc. were not the most important thing about Peter and she would presumably feel quite different if it were a question of Peter losing his intelligence, his principles, integrity, tactfulness, his love for her. We are then only concerned with what is essential in a relationship. For each person can probably bring about a change in his feelings and views according to circumstances. Perhaps there is an exception in the relationship between mother and child; but even there the point could be reached where an impartial observer would consider it a benefit when death, for instance, put an end to the relationship. In my case, my position here could be changed so much, where the spirit of it is concerned, that the outward circumstances: that I am still living in this house and being addressed as Managing Director, could not compensate for it. . .

I am well aware that it would be a terrible grief and misfortune for me to have to give it up and go away. But if it seems to me that I have distanced myself so far in regard to every concept of fairness and decency and justice from the people on whom I am dependent, and if I believe I have come to the realization that in their opinion I am accepting far more from them than I can ever give back, and in fact more than it has ever been right and decent of me to receive,—then, seen from whatever point of view, moral, or dictated by common sense, can it be right for me to go on living here? . . .

Otherwise I am well and have been happier than anyone else on earth because I have had Denys staying here for a month. I hope he will be coming back and will perhaps stay for Christmas,—he has gone on safari for a few months now,—as he is leaving the country in January. That such a person as Denys does exist,—something I have indeed guessed at before, but hardly dared to believe,—and that I have been lucky enough to meet him in this life and been so close to him,—even though there have been long periods of missing him in between,—compensates for everything else in the world, and other things cease to have any significance.

But by the way, if I should die and you should happen to meet him afterward, you must never let him know that I have written to you like this about him. . . .

To Ingeborg Dinesen

Ngong. Sunday 7/10 23

. . . I had a letter from Thomas yesterday that I would have replied to today if it were not that it is so long since I wrote to you. Please thank him very much for it and tell him that I will write very soon. Will you ask him too if he has read Bernard Shaw; if not he must really do so. I have been reading such a lot by him recently with enormous enjoyment, especially two of his most recent books, "Heartbreak House" and "Back to Methuselah." The prefaces to both of them are some of the most interesting things I have read. And then it pleases me a lot that Shaw hates Darwin, something I have always done, and thinks that it is amazing that the advocate of such a depressing view of life was not burned but on the contrary proclaimed as a prophet!—Incidentally, as far as I understand, science as a whole is turning more and more away from Darwin nowadays. . . .

To Thomas Dinesen

Ngong. 18/10 1923

. . . I look at it now in this way: that it is a question of the loss or recovery of Mother's essential income. And also considerable sums for Aunt Bess, Anders, and you yourself. It can also be said that it is a matter of the million in share capital that has been put into it,—and that it is to a great extent a matter of honor.

Among the possibilities that exist for recovery, I do not reckon on more money being sent from home. I am assuming that any further subsidy is out of the question.

But there are other factors than money, that in my opinion may be decisive, and I want to write to you about those today. I am not prepared to put my whole life into this, but I am willing to put *all* my strength and the *whole* of my time for some years into it. Now I want to ask you if you might also consider, if you think it might be decisive, making this enterprise the chief interest of your life for, for instance, one year?

I cannot at this point give you any definite plan or estimate. As I have written, I do not think we will get as big a harvest as we have calculated, and which is necessary in order to clear up all the business matters at once; I think we have been too optimistic in believing that a neglected farm like this could be worked up to full capacity in a short time. But I think that we have made great progress, and that everything on the farm will be in order if we have a little more time, and that things on the whole out here are improving. So that in my opinion it would be wrong to abandon it all now, if only it *can* be pulled through. . . .

I assume that if I telegraph for you you will be able to arrange to come out here. But I really think you should *come out in any case in February or March,* unless, for instance, a sale has settled everything. Can you manage to do this? I do not think you should think of letting it go before one of you from home has seen it, even at the last moment. You really should not let the fact that we have perhaps been too optimistic this year convince you that this is a hopeless undertaking. . . . It is my firm conviction that you and I, if we put everything into it during the coming year, can save it and make a real success of it. Do you feel that it would be worthwhile, and will you join me in this?. . . .

To Ingeborg Dinesen

Ngong. Sunday 21/10 23

. . . It has been a remarkable year with wild animals and lions,—they have been going right into Nairobi; for nights in succession a young lion visited the "zoological gardens" around Government House, in the end the Adjutant shot it just outside the house early one morning. We have heard them around here as well. I had some misgivings about them the other day when I was out riding many miles away in the Game Reserve—the grass was so high that it went right up above my boots as I rode, and suddenly Rouge and I fell into a huge hole that I had not been able to see; I felt as if I was lying at the bottom of a grave, and saw Rouge's back balanced over me, and he got up and the rein broke, and I crawled up and saw him standing with a scornful expression yards away from me. I was in such despair that I wept; it was late into the morning and baking hot, and Thomas knows what it is like walking in that long grass; you feel as if you are drowning, especially in riding habit and long boots it is almost impossible. I thought it would take me seven hours to walk home and that Rouge would disappear and get eaten by lions, but by a great miracle managed to get hold of him again and rode proudly home. . . .

There is one thing I want to ask you not to take so much to heart,—because I think it is completely unreasonable,—and that is his [Thomas's] love affairs or flirtations. . . . I do not think that the relationship between mother and son who live together,—which is after all always somewhat unnatural when the son has reached Thomas's age, it would be better if he had his own home soon, then all that sort of thing would be much easier,—is possible at all unless she allows part of his life, which will always seem to her to be dallying, to remain outside her sphere. Love affairs of this kind are natural to a young man, but cannot be understood by an elderly lady; I do not think any mother can have existed, from Mrs. Montague and Queen Bera up to Grandmother, who would not have been both anxious and shocked if she had taken the trouble to find out about everything her young sons got up to in that direction. And where the manners and customs of the age are concerned as well, I think you can leave everything to Thomas. I do not at all think that his respect for women or love have been affected by all his flirtation,—even if it takes a slightly different form from the courting habits of your young days. . . .

I think that sometimes you feel far too much *responsibility* for our behavior, which after all at our age cannot be anything for anyone to call you to account for. Perhaps it is rather that you take it too much to heart when people, and especially the family, criticize us. I think you ought to ignore it; we are not perfect, unfortunately, and so it is inevitable that when one is as surrounded with family as you unfortunately have become there are divergences of opinion regarding the children between a mother and the more distant relatives. But we ourselves are old enough to be able to take what brickbats we get from those directions with equanimity, if only you would stop worrying about it.

I think that in reality "what concerns respectability" does not mean so much to you, and that you would really rather have had Don Juan as a son than Ottavio, and that you could well have taken part in supper with the Commandant if you could have avoided being attacked by the criticism that was leveled at Don Juan. If you said to yourself: "Thomas is much more irresponsible than I had thought, and is up to all sorts of silliness, but I know that there is no real wickedness in it, and it is absolutely nobody's business"—then I am sure that your peace of mind and your happiness in him would still be unassailable. . . .

To Ingeborg Dinesen

Ngong. Sunday 28/10. 23

. . . I am painting a young Kikuyu,—I think it is the best thing I have yet done; but I always think that when I start on something. He is an appallingly bad model, and I find it hard not to lose patience with him; last time I went and fetched Thomas's pistol and threatened him with it all through the sitting,—but actually threats of death do not affect natives much; I think it is partly that they are not afraid to die, partly their natural antipathy for the sort of work they are unaccustomed to, and particularly something they have to keep on at, which seems to be insurmountable. I am hoping to get Finch Hatton out here when he returns from safari and get his advice, for he knows so much about all kinds of art, and there are so few people here who are interested in it. . . .

Berkeley Cole came to fetch me to attend a big dinner given by Lord Delamere at Muthaiga for the Governor and the Governor of Uganda, Sir Geoffrey Archer. He was previously Governor of British Somaliland and had Farah in his service while I was in Europe, and values him just as highly as I do. He said that he offered Farah everything he wanted to stay with him, but as soon as Farah received my telegram saying that I was coming out to Africa again it was out of the question to get him to stay under any circumstances. He told me about several of their campaigns against the Mullah, when he took Farah with him. It must be very interesting to be Governor there, and I think Uganda seems rather tame to him after that.

It was a big dinner, we must have been 50; I had the Governor here, Coryndon, on my left and Berkeley on the other side, and it was an exceedingly enjoyable evening. . . .

To Ingeborg Dinesen

Ngong. Sunday 4/11 23.

. . . I haven't time to write for long today, partly because I have a model and partly as Berkeley Cole is here for the weekend. . . . We thought of driving into the Reserve today but he is not yet up; usually my guests come out here to get some rest after the shauries of Nairobi, so that makes entertaining easy. Berkeley is an exceptionally pleasant person, very lively and original,—I think completely without any kind of moral scruples. He is interesting to talk to because, being on the legislative counsil [*sic*] he is very interested in the politics of this country; he is one of the old friends of the Masai and a great protector of the Somalis and a natural enemy of the Hemsted type, so we get on very well together.

I have had a fearful shaurie with a Somali who called Farah a pig,—it has ruined my life for several weeks; fortunately it has now been settled without any bloodshed, by having the slanderer pay Farah 500 shillings.

I have such a lot of white lilies, just as when Thomas was here and took photographs of me with them,—for the first time with my hair short. I hear that nobody has short hair at home any longer and feel that I ought to let mine grow, but it is so tempting to keep it short out here. You would be amazed to see how much hair I have now; I have never had such masses before, even as a child. It is so much easier to look after when it is short. . . .

To Ingeborg Dinesen

Ngong. Sunday 11.11.23

. . . It is three years now since I left home; so many things have happened since then and it is no exaggeration to say that they have been three terrible years for the greater part of humanity. I myself would not have missed these years for any price; it is true that I never really knew what shauries were before, but neither did I know what it was to be completely happy, indeed, to live. I have been sitting and thinking about it and have such a desire to look up "Adam Homo" to see how old Pastor,—or Madame?—Homo tells Adam what it means: "to be." In fact I really would like to have "Adam Homo" here, and also I so much want Anatole France's "Isle [*sic*] des Pingouins" and "La Rôtisserie de la Reine Pédauque," if some kind person feels like sending me some books one day,—the last two in French, of course. . . .

It is Mahu's birthday today; she is five and is very excited about it. I have given her a necklace and a calf. She and her little brother, who is two, have been romping around in here the whole morning while I have been writing, and holding a "Ngoma." The little boy, Tumbo, is the quaintest object, exactly like a frog, but he is afraid of nothing and roars with laughter and hits himself in the middle over all the eventualities of life. . . .

Thomas will probably be glad to hear that I am writing a little piece on sexual morality, if only I can get it finished. Actually Thomas and I could never agree over that question,—I imagine that he has some serious discussions on the subject with Aunt Bess as well. . . .

Ngong. Sunday 24.11.23

. . . Just a few words today, as I am still very dizzy and wretched after a particularly severe attack of sunstroke. I don't know,—or anyhow have not experienced,—any other complaint that "knocks you down" as completely as sunstroke. Besides being violently seasick for days and days, like being in a real storm in the Red Sea, head-, tooth-, and earache combine with the most horrific pains in every limb; it is as if the Sun God had hurled the rays of his anger straight on to one's topknot. Ask Thomas if this isn't right. I must have got it when I was out picking coffee on Thursday morning,—when you are bending over the sun hits you right on the back,—but felt nothing until the evening. . . . Friday and yesterday passed like a frightful dream, and I am still rather hazy, although recovered. . . .

To Ingeborg Dinesen

Ngong. 15/12 23

. . . I notice in the same paper that Thit Jensen is advocating "Birth Control" at home. It is surprising that it seems something quite new at home; in England and America I think it is completely established as the only responsible thing. I see nothing at all against it from the moral point of view,—except from the standpoint of really religious persons, but how, for instance, can they defend the use of lightning conductors or vaccination?—but aesthetically it is still somewhat distasteful and I think many people are confused in their judgment of it, as so often happens with matters concerning marriage and moral conduct etc. I think it is remarkable how often it is science that solves,—or rather cuts the Gordian knot in,—moral questions. I think too that the woman's movement will take quite a different turn when,—as will surely soon be possible,—parents can decide the sex of their expected children.

I am expecting Berkeley Cole here for a couple of days, and perhaps Denys Finch Hatton as well. It is worth coming out here now; everything is so fresh and green and the air quite wonderful. . . .

To Ingeborg Dinesen

Ngong. 23 December 23

. . . As one grows older I think distance comes to mean so little, both in time and space; I really feel that things long since past and everything that is happening now far away from me are just as much "present" as those I happen to be dealing with at the moment.

It is amazing how old one is getting; for I am the same age now as you were when Father died, and I can still remember you long before that, so clearly, in a blue and white striped cotton dress, with your lovely hair,—so now I almost feel that we are the same age. And I can remember Aunt Bess as a young girl; where Malla is concerned I think she has never been any younger or more beautiful than she is now, and I hope she will stay eternally young, or anyway until I get home again. I wish that I could smell the Christmas tree and the indescribably delicious aroma of roast goose out here; it is quite right, as in "Garman & Worse," that "le nez c'est la memoire,"—but I am sure that you will all be thinking about me when you eat the goose and light the candles, and when you sing "Now it is chiming for the Christmas feast," which I think is the most beautiful of all the carols and the one which most reminds me of Christmas at home. So "Happy Christmas" to you all, beloved people at home. . . .

In the hope of attracting workers to the farm I am going to start a school here in the new year; I have wanted to do this for a very long time, but Dickens was very opposed to it, but now has come to think better of it. We will use rooms in "Charlie's House," Thomas knows where that is, and I think it will be a great pleasure. It will only be in the evening so as not to interfere with work on the farm. Unfortunately the Wakambas in particular are very much against the Catholics,—I don't know why; they have a theory that they do not teach them enough,—so that I shall have to upset my friends at the French Mission against my will, but it is no good opposing the wishes of the natives in such matters when one particularly wants to attract them to come here. I think that every large farm ought to have a school; there is no point in saying that natives are more happy in their primitive state; besides that being very questionable in itself, it is impossible to keep them there and by making no attempt to educate them all that results is that they get hold of all the worst aspects of civilization, like the frightful type of "Nairobi boys" that has developed since I first came out here, which is on a par with those at home, with "their hair over their eyes," that Uncle Rentz thought should be taken out to Nørrefælled and shot. After all, it is an honest ambition in the natives to be eager to learn. As I say, I am very glad to be getting this going.

Major Taylor came out this week to look at the farm, and it was really a great joy to hear his opinion of it. He has not been out since February and so can see the changes in it better than I and Dickens, who go around staring at it every day. I expect he will be sending a report home. On the same day that he had been here something terrible and sad happened. I was in my bath before dinner when I heard a shot,—which I always hate to hear, especially at night, but I thought it was one of the white people shooting at a hyena. A little later Thaxton came tearing up here on his motorcycle and said there had been an accident; while his cook was out, his kitchen toto had got some other small boys together in his hut, and one of them had got hold of a shotgun that Thaxton was keeping on his verandah with which to frighten birds of prey away from his poultry, and had fired it into the midst of them. Thaxton was completely beside himself and did not know how many had been wounded, and asked me to go down with him. I put on some clothes and ran down to his house,—the one Thomas had during the last part of his stay here,— with him. I heard later that three other children had been slightly wounded, they had run off—when we got there there were only two. One of them, Maturri, whom Thomas may perhaps remember, such a sweet happy little toto, had been shot in the neck and chest,—he was lying unconscious in a great pool of blood; the other was sitting up with blood streaming out of his mouth, or what was left of his mouth,—the lower part of his jaw was completely shot away.

I bandaged him up as well as I could, but it was difficult with only the light of a wretched lantern, and then fetched my car to drive them in to the hospital. My lights were not working, that is to say, I have no lights, and the car would not start; it seemed an eternity before we got started,—it was not at all easy to get them settled in the car, and then you feel every bump in the road so frightfully in such a situation,—but we got there. Thaxton, and Kamante, whom Thomas knows, were with me; Farah happened to be away that night. When we lifted Maturri out of the car the poor child died. The other one had lost a great deal of blood, the whole car was covered with it, and was in a pitiable state, but is still alive. I went in to see him next day. I think it would have been better for him if he had died, and he would certainly have died if we had not taken him in, but one *cannot* think like that. I do not think he suffered, the shock had no doubt been too great; when I was running down through the wood I could hear him screaming and sobbing, but when I got down there and took his head in my hands and said to him: calm down, I have come to help you,—he did not make another sound, not once all the way in, when he was jolted about a lot. Maturri cannot have felt anything at all; he had the whole charge, with No. 4 shot, in the chest,—he was moaning but was unconscious.

We drove down to the police station at once to report it, and they kept us there for hours; we did not get back until three in the morning,—the accident had probably happened about half past seven. Of course the police cannot say anything; it was obviously an accident, or caused by children playing. But Thaxton will probably get a fine for leaving his gun out loaded. The poor child who shot it off has disappeared; naturally he must be absolutely terrified. It happened last Wednesday and we have been searching for him ever since, and of course so have his family, he is Kanino's son. I think he may perhaps have run over to the Masai and is hiding there; Farah has a theory that he will stay there until "he has married six or five wife," and as he is only eight it will no doubt be some time before I get to see him again. If only I knew that he was being safely looked after somewhere. One can never rely on natives' nerves. Three other children were slightly wounded, but nothing to worry about.

I had to go into Nairobi again the next morning as I had an appointment with Hunter in order to get some money for my white people before Christmas, which they naturally wanted and deserved, as they have waited for their money so patiently. I had lunch with the McMillans and then went to the hospital to see Wanjangiri. It is a really excellent native hospital and a good doctor. He had drunk some milk, and he knew me and understood what I said to him, and now they are going to try to sew him up; but they would not be able to see how things would go with him until later on, and I do not know what they can do, as his teeth and jawbone have been shot away. They said he had been well bandaged up and that had stopped the bleeding; that was pure luck, as I could hardly see anything. Since then his brother has been in to see him, and he was about the same. I caught such a cold from being out driving at night; I had hardly any clothes on, only a skirt and a coat and shoes, and next day I completely lost my voice, perhaps that was something to do with nerves; I was so tired when I got back that night from the expedition, as if I had walked for five miles, so I have been in bed for a day or two. Old Mr. Bulpett drove out to see me, that was nice of him.

Little Maturri who died was such a fine little toto; he was with me for a time but then went to work at sorting coffee at the factory, and he always waved and laughed when I went down there; I had seen him there the same afternoon, when I was there with Charles Taylor, and it seems so strange that he should have died in my arms a few hours later. . . .

I think I will be alone over Christmas; I have been invited to several dinner parties in Nairobi but I don't know whether I will go. It is possible that Berkeley Cole and Finch Hatton will be coming a few days afterward. Berkeley has wired to me that he is sending me a cat as a Christmas present,—when he was staying here there were so many rats about,—and I cannot find it anywhere and am afraid that the unfortunate cat is sitting at some station or other. Farah and I are going to drive in tomorrow to try to find it and to buy sugar, cigarettes, and snuff for everyone on the farm to distribute on Christmas Day, for 200 shillings, which we have been saving for the purpose. There will probably be about a thousand people, so the quality cannot be awfully good. . . .

I agree with you over what you write about "Kristin Lavransdatter." It is strange that while Thomas was here and we were reading it together I liked the book so much, and now it does not attract me in the least, in fact the whole book and particularly the author are distasteful to me. I think that it is in a way a monumental work, but expresses an awful philosophy of life that mars the book aesthetically, or makes it so strangely oppressive, without any artistic horizon, like a painting of which one says that "there is no air in it." I have seldom read about such a collection of miserable people and it seems to me that it is all the result of the fact that their view of life and they themselves mutually torment each other to death. The only time there is a slight touch of happiness is when Kristin and Erlend, in the first rush of their love for each other allow themselves to be carried away by their feelings, or lose their heads to such an extent that they forget to take other people into account, and the others can never forget this and grudge it them so much that they make them pay for it for the rest of their lives. With all the other characters it is one long tale of woe: Ragnfrid, Simon, Ramborg, Gunnulf, Audhild and Bjørn, Erling and Halfrid, Ulf. That some of them, such as Ragnfrid and perhaps Gunnulf, after having lived through their whole lives as slaves to their unreasonable consciences, should toward the end, by sacrificing *everything,* achieve some kind of peace,—well, that is the least they deserve. Now if the author raged at people destroying life for each other like this, as Strindberg does, or rose above them smiling in wisdom and pity, as for instance Anatole France does, the book would be lifted up on to a higher plane and one could be somewhat reconciled to it all; but she treats it in deadly earnest as the natural course of life, and I end up saying with Ronald Fangen (about Sigrid Undset): One reads this book and says to oneself, yes, this is right, lucid, beautiful,—but with a constant feeling of protest and distaste. And when one has put the book down for no more than an hour one suddenly realizes that it is asserting a ridiculous and hideous point of view." . . . And her whole philosophy,—does she really see things like this? "Everything one has experienced, teeming life, the wild exuberance of particularity. . .God above: Life! . . . a gigantic nursery tale!" And yet I don't deny that it is a magnificent work. Although I do not consider it great art; I think with Levertin that what I am looking for in imaginative writing is an illumination of what Goldschmidt calls: the magic of life,—and that is not to be found in Sigrid Undset, where there is really no illumination; it is like a great landscape that is constantly overcast and colorless; the magic wand is missing, it is "kein Hexerei," and I say with Otto Benzon (I think), that real art must always involve some witchcraft.

I am certainly in accord with you regarding "The Forsyte Saga" as well. It is an atrocious book and gives one the same feeling as when one hears a priest uttering the most terrible nonsense, that it is unfair not to be able to put in a word of protest against him. It is quite *impossible* for it to have happened like that; the characters could not have reacted to events in the way he would have us believe; from start to finish it is an insult to the reader's common sense—and decency. For instance it *just could not happen* that young Jocelyn, who is supposed to be both intelligent and sensitive, should undertake to analyze every member of his family to a man about whom the most he knew was that he had treated his own daughter, to whom he was engaged, disgracefully, to put it mildly, and who was now engaged in seducing the wife of his own cousin. But I do not think that this is in fact something unique in English fiction; except for the very best examples they have somehow completely separated "novels" from human life and humanity (and common sense), and in that sphere they have evolved their own absolutely crazy rules for probability, morals etc. . . .

To Ingeborg Dinesen

Ngong. Saturday 29/12 [1923]

. . . During the Christmas period I tried to make use of the time to work on my paper about "sexuality morality" for Tommy; but I find that I am having to restrict the subject somewhat and it will rather be about marriage, and I am writing with some trepidation as Tommy has always accused me of being reactionary. It is actually very difficult to write about this kind of thing when one is quite alone and also without access to the books from which one would like to quote, so I will probably never get very far with it. I grew so cross over not getting on better with it that I stopped working at literature in order to teach Hassan to make croustades, with more success. . . .

I went into Nairobi again yesterday. . . . I had the joy of finding my child in hospital much better; they were tidying up the wards, and he was lying on a strecher outside and waved to me when I arrived. I took Kamante, whom Thomas knew, with me, so that he could comfort him by telling him how ill he had once been, and now is so big and strong and plays football; so he sat on his bed and gave him a lecture, but as the conversation was in Kikuyu I could not take much part in it. . . .

I feel so sorry for the little toto who shot the other two; he has completely vanished. His family have been out searching for him all over the area; we have had people from Nairobi hunting too, but we cannot find the slightest trace of him. His own people think that he was so terrified that he has taken his own life; natives are so inclined to do this as soon as life becomes difficult, even about things one can see would be overcome in the course of a few days, but they find it impossible to look ahead. And then a little child like that, if he runs into the jungle to hide, can easily be caught by leopards or lions. But another possibility is that he has run away to the Masai,—that strange dying race is eager to grasp any of the children of other tribes that they can lay hands on, and they will not give them back; they accept them into the tribe and bequeath all their earthly goods to them, and they can be of great value, so that would be a kind of promotion for Kabiro; but of course they are lost to their own tribe. Something of this kind happened just recently to one of Kamante's brothers, who ran away from his family fifteen years ago because he had lost a sheep and was frightened of his father, and who recently, when he saw Kamante and his other brothers walking on the other side of the river, came down and called across to them and told them like another Joseph that he had been adopted by a chief's family, owned great herds and was married to two Masai wives, but that he had promised never to go back to the Kikuyu. This is a comedown for the Masai who used to despise the Kikuyu in the old days, but now no children are born to them. I hope this is what has happened to Kanino's son, but it is not possible to find out. . . .

PRIVATE

If Thomas has come home you can give this to him so that you need not be troubled with it. I am sorry to have to worry you with it, but if he is not at home I shall be forced to.

My divorce seems to be well under way and the decree will probably be made absolute soon. Now I want to ask you, if it is not too late, to try to arrange through Repsdorph, if possible to get some maintenance awarded me from Bror.

Of course this sounds anything but pleasant; but I *promise* you that I will never demand it. I want it to be legally arranged in this way because I think that it would improve my situation in the future considerably. For there is always some conflict as long as Bror is in this country, and as long as his friends and he himself feel that he has been unjustly treated and thrown out by the company and the whole of my family; if the *law,* which they know is impartial, would award this to me, which I could then refuse to accept from Bror each year, I think my position would be improved,—in actual fact it would make no difference. I am sure that Thomas, who is aware of the situation, will understand.

Then there is also the fact that according to English law the woman is always branded as the "guilty" party in a divorce case if she is not granted any maintenance by the husband. In this way it would look better for me; I think it would make no difference to Bror.

If you should think that this would appear as too ungenerous, I will merely state as my opinion that in the future it might prevent me from being accused of ungenerosity time after time.

I am really still very attached to Bror; I met him again recently and now, when we are no longer dependent on one another, I think we can be friends, but he looks at things so differently from me; the more I can safeguard myself against the influence on my life of his point of view the easier it will be for us both to be able to live in this colony and to meet, which is unavoidable. . . .

1924

To Ellen Dahl

Ngong. Sunday. 13.1.24

Dearest Elle.

Today I must write and thank you many thousands of times for Fru Slott-Møller's book and your Christmas letter. It is so moving to see Fru Slott-Møller's pictures out here and to read her book that it almost hurts; and it makes one long indescribably for Denmark,—and of course I know that there is absolutely no possibility of my getting home, anyway this year, and I think that the yearning is almost strong enough to make me a suit of feathers so that I could go flying home like the maiden Blidelil. Looking through her book is like rediscovering so many things that one has seen oneself. I don't think, of course, that she is a great artist, because she allows her subject to take precedence over her personality, which denotes a lack of honesty in the artist and in the long run takes a hard-hitting revenge, partly on the pictures themselves, which lack reality and thus are easily reduced to theatricality,—which I think is sadly the case with many of her paintings, for example Ebbe Skammelsøn at the wedding,—partly on the subjects themselves, since the viewer, particularly if he himself has previously known and loved them—(as I can say I have loved the folk ballads)—feels in his heart that they seem more beautiful to him than the representations he is looking at now. I can remember seeing many of her pictures at Charlottenborg as a young girl, and now seeing them again brings back the whole of that "Spring Exhibition atmosphere" to me,—at that time it seemed to me like a glimpse into a special world of beauty and intellectuality,—and it really makes me long for Copenhagen and the King's New Square on a spring day. Perhaps we will be able to go to the Private View together next spring! . . .

I have painted some pictures out here that I have been considering sending home, in particular in order to hear what Fru Dorph thinks of them. I do not have a great deal of time or peace in which to paint properly and neither have I learned enough, anyway not about portrait painting,—I really much prefer doing "Still Leben,"—but that is not at all easy here either because there are no really attractive things to paint here. I would be interested to find out whether there would be a possibility of getting them accepted for an exhibition; it would be a very useful way of getting an opinion on them. They would probably be of most interest as pictures of natives; I think that I understand them, or anyway "love them," more than most people.

I am not really clear about Thomas's plans, but imagine that he is in England now. . . . It would give me more pleasure to hear that Tommy was sitting listening with rapt attention at the feet of a beloved teacher or living in admiration for an eminent friend than to hear of some "achievement" he had carried out in majestic isolation. What does Thomas mean, for instance, when he says he will only get married if he finds a perfect woman? What is a perfect woman and what does one want of her?. . . If he said,—and really meant,—that he would not marry until he found a red-haired girl with black eyes who could swim underwater and play the cello, there would be some possibility of satisfaction and happiness; but I do not see any meaning in winning even Helen herself out of pure ambition, and if one does not really *love* this special form of beauty. What satisfaction could there be in being, like Ilsebil—like Our Lord himself, if one's creation was not of burning interest? If only Tommy,—in England or elsewhere,—could find something that was of really unlimited value for him in itself, so that when he held it in his arms,—spiritually or physically,—he would know and understand everything! There are so many people who want every happiness and good for him, but none more than I, to whom he has been more than I can say. . . .

Denys Finch Hatton has been staying here for a week, and we have been out every morning to shoot pigeon, which fly over at about five a.m. It is wonderfully beautiful here in the early morning when the sun is shining on the Ngong Hills and making them quite copper colored, while the woods as you wade through the soaking grass are still shadowy. He left yesterday; Colonel Llewellyn is staying here this weekend, so I am having a big tea-party this afternoon, and must go and make some puff pastry pretzels. I could wish that I could really afford to entertain some day,—I think that the best kind of social life has a real mission; I have always believed implicitly in reciprocity. . . .

To Ingeborg Dinesen

Ngong. Sunday 20/1.24

. . . I am finding "De Vises Sten," ["The Philosopher's Stone"] difficult to understand, but it is a most interesting book. The book that I think it most resembles is Goldschmidt's "Hjemløs" ["Homeless"], but I think that "Homeless" is far superior. Actually I no longer have the capacity for reading, that is, living in and being carried away by a book, that I had in my young days, when I read "Homeless." But I think that there is absolutely no doubt that Goldschmidt is far weightier both as regards talent and personality than this author, who constantly floats about on the top of the seesaw where his subjects are concerned; and how differently those old intellectuals were educated, so well and thoroughly, from the moderns, despite the fact that they have easier access to, and have probably explored a good deal, all kinds of knowledge.

I have also had much pleasure in reading "Herredet" ["The District"] particularly because it is so Danish, or Sealandish. I think the beginning is quite excellent; all the politics and religiosity that come later are really not in my line. From the start it made me think of Anders and Beendt, and hope things will go as well for him. . . .

A book that I would *very* much like to have some day is Fru Heiberg's "Et Liv genoplevet i Erindringen" ["A Life Recalled through Recollection"]. I will probably end up with a craze for Denmark in the earlier part of the nineteenth century, like that we always used to accuse Ellen Wanscher of. But in fact I have always loved Heiberg himself and greatly miss "Julespøg og Nytaarsløjer" ["Christmas Fun and New Year Jests"] and "Pottemager Walter" ["Walter the Potter"] for my daily edification. . . .

I rode all over the farm yesterday,—I haven't been out riding for some time, chiefly because I have spent so much time in the factory, a place where I like more and more to be; it is really extraordinarily pleasant to sit on one's coffee sacks and watch all the machinery working and the coffee pouring out of the turner and being sorted and packed and so on. One of Farah's Somali acquaintances has left a mule with a sore back here while he is on safari, and it runs with me like a dog, and is altogether a highly intelligent animal, occasionally it trots off to the Somali town in Nairobi and comes back here in the evening. The coffee is beginning to suffer from the dry windy weather; it looks like rain the whole time but nothing comes to anything. If only we get some soon, we can usually count on thunderstorms in January. . . .

To Thomas Dinesen

Ngong. Jan. 24th 24

. . . As I do not think anyone else on the Board would be willing to come out here I asked you to come, as far as possible with authority from the Company to make decisions, and also if possible from the bank auditors to postpone payment of the installments if the state of things is found to be otherwise satisfactory.

I can quite understand that in many ways you do not feel like coming out here; but you would not be making the trip for pleasure, but for necessity. If you think I enjoy being here enduring the same shauries every day you have got entirely the wrong idea. After all, you have been able to refresh yourself with new countries and new people since we last saw each other, but I have not left the farm for a year and through all that time have been staring at the same coffee trees,—and the same Nairobi offices. . . .

I am thinking so much about you just now; it is almost a year since you left, last January you were here with me. I wish you the best of luck in every every way. Often I have such a terrible longing for you; in spite of all the problems we did enjoy ourselves together so much. Everyone here sends you many greetings.

As you know, at times I myself am one of the happiest people in the world. In spite of everything I think that life is wonderful, wonderful, and the world a glorious place to be.

Always your faithful sister Tania.

To Ingeborg Dinesen

Ngong. Sunday 27.1.24

. . . As Thomas's flirtations still seem to be worrying you I thought that for once I might write a few words on my own views of the usual social conventions between young men and girls, as these have developed in the years since the outbreak of war; not in the sense that I have any wish to express my own opinion of what is right or wrong, commendable or otherwise, but according to what I have heard and seen believe to be normal and natural at the present time.

To what extent it was first the *idea* of equality between the sexes that has led to such *practical* measures as the independence of young girls and, for instance,—to my belief,—the universal practice of "birth-control," or whether it is, conversely, financial considerations: that during the war, for instance, girls were obliged to fend for themselves and manage their lives in the same way as young men, which in the general way of thinking has placed young men and girls on an equal footing,—I am unable to say; but in my opinion it is quite certain that the young men and girls of the present generation see themselves as completely equal in all situations of importance. This is particularly true where erotic relationships are concerned, which has of necessity brought about changes in these, and views on them, to a considerable extent. In practical terms this has meant that while formerly, that is, a couple of generations ago, social relations between young men and girls consisted of meetings on the more festive occasions,—balls, summer holiday visits etc.,—that were, so to speak, outside the sphere of the normal occupations of both parties and were expressed through flirtation, paying respects, a kind of wooing on one part with much reticence on the other and with a great deal of secrecy on both sides, there is now a state of continual togetherness in all forms of daily life; and I think that the normal and natural relationship between two young people who care for each other and are engrossed in each other nowadays most usually takes the form of what in earlier times was known as a "love affair" and which was then an exception and was viewed and treated as such. Even this situation must be completely altered when both partners consider that one should not take or give, risk or enjoy, or as a whole put more into it,—than the other.

In previous times there were such concepts as "to seduce," "seduction," etc., but I do not think that these exist at all any more in the way of thinking of modern young people, who have difficulty in uttering these words at all without "a shade of irony in the voice." If one looks more closely at these concepts, they must surely be understood to mean that a "seducer" in a relationship persuaded the other partner to, or led her into doing, something for his own purposes, that in some way or other would injure, destroy, or degrade her, which "the seducer" knew that "the seduced" would regret having done and which also demeaned "the seduced" in *the seducer's own eyes*"; for a man was not deemed a seducer for persuading or pestering a girl to marry him. In the cruder instances there could be cases where the seducer went as far as to promise something,—marriage, for instance,—which he had no intention of fulfilling; but this probably lies outside the main concept. Nowadays a love affair does not lead to any of these consequences and thus the whole concept (as far as this sphere is concerned, for it is still to be found in politics, for instance) has quite naturally disappeared from current usage.

I think the general opinion is without exception that both the young man and the girl take the same happiness in the love affair and can put an end to it with the same good conscience,—if they have in other ways adhered to the rules current for honest conduct. There are no particular risks for the modern girl who is independent, who is not lowered in the opinion of others, and who knows that she does not run the risk of conceiving an unwanted child. Of course there will always be a certain danger that one of the partners may grow more involved in and more dependent on the relationship than the other, but this is the same for both and in some cases is difficult to avoid;

for instance it can be found to a much greater degree in a marriage, where one partner may have the misfortune to love more passionately or for longer than the other and thereby come to suffer far more than in a free relationship; but each should feel able to take this risk without being injured by the other partner. In former times it was probably assumed that a woman put more feeling into a love affair than a man generally did; but heaven knows whether there is still anything in that when women have just as many resources in their lives apart from love affairs.

The most significant thing of all is probably this: that a girl is no longer disparaged in her own or in a young man's eyes through a love affair. I really cannot say whether it is the preponderance of free love affairs that has led to them being regarded in this way, or whether it is this opinion of them that has promoted the existence of more free affairs. Of course it is natural to find it difficult, even with the best conscience in the world, to be one of the exceptions. It was this, and not the nature of their relationship, that made Kristin Lavrandsdatter and Erlend unhappy, and it would certainly have been worse for them if, for instance, one of them had lost their faith in the Virgin Mary; that would really have been disastrous. Perhaps it is a change in taste, in the concept of "the ideal,"—but this again depends on practical conditions, because one and the same thing does not always mean the same. For instance, a couple of centuries ago a man would have had no hesitation in marrying a girl, even from the highest class, who was unable to write; today, of course, she would be branded as stupid. The Somalis in French Somaliland may not marry until they have killed a man; this does not necessarily mean that they are particularly bloodthirsty but can as well be because conditions there are so warlike that a young man who has not been in a life and death battle by the time he has reached marriageable age is probably a coward. A young girl in former times, when they were married at seventeen, who could find a way before that age through the barriers of convention and prejudice that surrounded her to embark on a love affair, must have had *"le diable au corps,"* and it would have been reasonable for a sober-minded man to have had doubts about marrying her; but the same way of thinking must make a modern young man consider a girl who has lived five or ten years in the atmosphere of freedom and eroticism that girls nowadays grow up in, without at least *believing* she has been in love, to be either particularly lacking in life or particularly calculating,—and have *his* doubts.

I have been away from home so long now that I don't know how things are in the Danish upper classes; but I think it would be exceptional in a circle of twenty-year-old English girls to find any who had not experienced a love affair,—in exactly the same way as in a group of young men. And this is no family secret among the female sex; to the young men who are friends with, work with, dance, talk, drive cars, fly with, and marry these girls, it is a natural matter in the same way as this same matter, when it concerns their young men, is for them.

I have heard so many men talk with the greatest horror about marrying a "jeune fille," Charles Gordon, Polowtzoff, Eric Otter, for instance; Polowtzoff, who in fact belonged to a somewhat older generation, once said that in his experience an inexperienced bride was the greatest hindrance to the success of a marriage; and when one reads books from a certain period back one cannot help feeling there is much in what he said. I can remember that when we were once discussing the freedom of modern girls, Eric Otter said that he hoped it would seem the natural and reasonable thing before his own daughters grew up, because he thought that so much of the difficulty and lack of understanding in his own marriage had been caused by the lack of proportion in this matter. That it was not so in former times and that neither partner wished it so was no doubt because the lives and spheres of men and women as a whole differed so much,—they had such totally differing assumptions. Now a young man who marries lives in the same conditions as his wife, partakes of the same life among the same people and encounters the same phenomena, and the young men would feel their wives' mental exclusivity unreasonable in the same way they would feel about many of the things belonging to women's dress of a bygone age.

Perhaps you are not at all interested in all this, and if so you must forgive me. I have not written it to put forward my own "ideals," only the view of modern conditions and ideals that experience has shown me. You may not have met many young people of this generation, influenced by the war, and I think that very often you worry needlessly by judging their manners and customs with a yardstick from,—perhaps even a long time back; because your own contemporaries were probably fairly old-fashioned in this respect, and when all is said and done you are probably going by the standards of Mama's time. . . . I don't really understand why Tommy parades his flirtations in front of you when you object to them, although I don't think I was much better when I carried on my friendships, etc. out of your sight because I thought you would object to them! It is rather like cigar smoke—if one wants one's menfolk to come and sit in one's own drawing room and wishes them to feel at home, one must grow accustomed to it.

If you yourself don't want to be bothered with all these considerations, will you please pass them on to Aunt Bess, with whom I have discussed matters so often. I feel that now and again I must exercise my mind a little on such things and also see whether I can still write in Danish; for I have not spoken a single Danish word since Tommy left. . . .

This letter has been interrupted by a very troublesome visitor, an old, blind, and drunk Danish fellow, who came to ask if I could let him have a house where he could make the kibokos that he lives on. I felt it impossible to refuse and have promised him the two rooms in Charlie's house where Palme lived; but I know that Dickens and Thaxton, who know him, will be dismayed. He came very grandly in a car with a kind coffee farmer from Kiambu, who had no doubt been similarly pestered to drive him out here! . . .

To Ingeborg Dinesen

Ngong. Sunday. Febr. 3rd 24

. . . I have had such trouble with the old Dane, Aarup, I promised could have a house on the farm for a while; that is the sort of good deed one really should not go in for, particularly when others come to suffer for it, in this case Dickens and Thaxton. He is almost completely blind and cannot do anything for himself, and then he is such a frightful chatterbox and sits by the hour telling the dullest stories at great length, à la Uncle Gerhardt:—"It was in 1889,—no, wait a minute, that's not true, it must have been in 1888 or 1887,—now, let me see, it was—," and for me it is always of *some* interest, of course, as it usually turns out to be about a brick dropped by the mayor of Kolding or some such tale; but the others can really not be expected to listen to it, and then he gets into a huff and comes up here to complain to me about them. I can't have him living in the house because he is almost always slightly drunk and is always getting involved in frightful quarrels with the natives. In spite of all this I like him very much, although I could wish him away again. I presented him with a big box of cigars that Finch-Hatton had left behind, which has made me "his friend for life," in his own words.—"Tobacco is both motherland and wife to me; if you should ever become blind you'll discover that," he said. . . .

I have been thinking such a lot about poor Aunt Clara. . . I myself am extremely fond of Aunt Clara and think she is an unusually good and marvelous person; but she is so terribly *biased* that I do not think I could live with her, in fact I can hardly read her letters without my blood starting to boil. . . . In particular she has such an infuriating partiality for men in every situation in life; the earth and all its riches always belong exclusively to them, and if they ever make a mistake it is always because women have beguiled them into it. If one expects to see some of the wonderful feats that men have achieved as proof of her belief one is disappointed, and no demands are made for this. This entire system of belief really cannot be adhered to nowadays any more than the privileges of the higher classes, absolute monarchy or the infallibility of the pope; I do not think there is any alternative to equality, including moral equality, for men and women, in the present stage of development. Neither can men's insistence on their great temptations,—Aunt Clara is biased towards this as well,—"hold water" any more, now that the circumstances of life are the same for men and women,—or can women really protest in every case that they are subject to great temptations, for instance to enjoy themselves, spend money and so on? Perhaps Aunt Clara has never had any of these "temptations," and I think that women like this do their own sex much harm by positing their own case as the norm, which is naturally gladly accepted by many men. I can imagine Aunt Clara as a sixteen-year-old newlywed was deeply impressed by Uncle Frederik's abilities, in everyday life for instance, for booking seats at the theater, arranging a journey, buying horses, understanding accounts and politics,—all of which lay completely outside the sphere of her understanding,—and on the basis of this she erected her whole edifice of admiration for the superiority of men; but now she must surely admit that the foundations have crumbled when she sees her own granddaughters battling with all these kinds of problems; how then can she demand that the building itself remain standing?

When I recollect how everything that concerned men's affairs at Näsbyholm, for example, hunting with beaters, cigars, wine,—were regarded as sacred rites (?), while ladies' hats and sewing circles were treated with ridicule, my whole being cries out for that exploit, that moral and spiritual greatness, or at least that intelligence on the part of the men, that would explain this. I do not dare let Aunt Clara see all this; she would reject it immediately as a disgustingly frivolous female urge to rebellion and lust for power. . . . I myself feel completely unmoved by all that sort of thing; I should only be too glad to subordinate myself to a man whom I admire, but I do not hold sacred a pair of trousers in itself, and I think it is a good thing that, like Geizler's (?) hat, they have been forcibly ejected from their lofty seats. Perhaps at one time they were a sacred symbol, and that may have been a happier and better time than now, but as it is, nobody any longer knows what they actually did symbolize. I suppose Aunt Clara must be allowed to act as their last venerable priestess, and as such one must respect her, but I wholeheartedly renounce the character of her ancient cult and all its works, and her own part in it. . . .

To Ingeborg Dinesen

Ngong Sunday Febr. 10th 24

. . . Old Mr. Bulpett came out here in his little car yesterday. . . . He is always so nice and charming, and I hope that I will be as lively and happy as he is when I am 73. We sat and chatted for a while, among other things about whether one would wish to live one 's life over again, and he exclaimed with the greatest enthusiasm: "Oh, every moment of it!" I really do think that he has enjoyed every moment to the full. Englishmen of that type have a kind of virtuosity for enjoyment, in a healthy, spontaneous manner,—of sport, travel, wine, gambling, and love. . . .

Old Aarup is still here and is a frightful nuisance, especially to my white people. I am very glad to have been able to arrange for him to get a kind of pension from the Government of two shillings a day! It is not much, of course, but it does make a difference for him, for otherwise he has nothing. He is so very Danish that I can't help liking him in spite of all his faults, but I must say that I do think Danish conviviality is frightful! For the moment he has only one plan in mind, which consists of enlarging the "dam" that Thomas helped to construct, and with the addition of some rowing boats, a swimming place and a small "restaurant" to make it into a "very popular Sunday resort" for Nairobi. He is completely unable to understand that I am not keen on this plan and assures me that it should make money, and would in any case bring "a little life to the farm.". . . .

This week for once the post did not bring a letter from you; but I had one from Aunt Clara from which I see that little Hans is getting better, which is a great joy to Aunt Clara and of course for poor Brita too. I can't help laughing over Aunt Clara's naive partiality; when she thought that it was I who wanted a divorce she wrote me long letters saying how reprehensible and destructive it was; now that she has come to realize that it was Bror who wished for it she has "become firmly convinced that it is far the best thing as long as it is done without bitterness from either partner." But all the same I am very fond of Aunt Clara, and she is of me, I think, but am sure that it would be quite impossible for her ever to take sides in any way against one of her sons. That she did in fact have to do this,—and was obliged to do so because a still higher idol, Uncle Frederik, was involved,—produced really a more horrible conflict than any writer of tragedy could ever have thought up, and I think that it has paralyzed her mentally in some way,—as rheumatism has physically,—or somehow cut her off from her spiritual and moral roots so that her development has been completely brought to a halt and she has been obliged to resort to the surface, where she seems quite happy to be floating. . . .

Ngong. Febr. 24th 24.

. . . I don't feel that in general I take much pleasure in complaining, but I do think that there is something in my whole relationship with my relations,—perhaps it is that we are so very different from each other,—that makes it very difficult for them to understand what I find hard, or that anything can be hard for me at all, and I so often think of Ragnhild's words, that:

> "—I have relatives in abundance—
> they see my cheek grow pale with affliction,
> but never realize that I am suffering,
> unless the dead look with pity from the grave."

—Now of course they cannot see my cheek grow pale with affliction; but really I would have thought that it did not need pointing out to them that these years have been very hard for me. . . .

I believe that I have done a good piece of work here and in many ways a unique piece of work. I am quite convinced that no one else could or would have done it, and there has been so much difficulty that anyone else would have given it up; in fact I really do believe that I have deserved to be given the V.C. for my work here just as much as you did during the war. But at home they would never think of discussing or thinking about all these things. The proof of what I am saying,—that the farm is now in a completely different state from when I took it over, that everything is prospering, that our bad name is beginning to be a thing of the past, and that the future prospects are absolutely different, that we have reduced expenses far more than was ever considered to be possible at home,—is never directly apparent to them at home; they can calmly ignore it and even if I send them the most reliable statements they choose to regard them as highly dubious; I even think that the very fact that I mention or point them out is a point in my disfavor and if I am not very careful will cause them to drown me in a flood of reprimand.

Then they choose to ignore the difficulties we endure out here, and if they become too acute it is bound to be my fault and there is nothing they can do about it. . . .

There is another problem which I probably ought to have written about before, the question of Mother's visit here. I must say at once that I would like to have Mother out here tremendously, but if I am going to have so many shauries and the position does not become more satisfactory I don't think it would be a very good plan. . . . One cannot live this way for too long without a break; no one else seems able to realize this, but I do. In addition to this, I am not well. And the happiness that I do have here is constantly being disrupted by shauries and the generally insecure feeling I have with regard to the future; indeed, in a way the more happy and satisfied one feels at the moment the more nerve-racking it is. With things as they are this year I do not think it would be a good thing for Mother to come. If everything gets straightened out Mother could perhaps come out with me next autumn, for I must go home next year; I seriously think that I will die if I do not.

I am sorry to write to you so often about my woes. But on the other hand I think that if I should die now,—for I believe I am like Monica: I do not bend, I break,—you might perhaps wish that I had written in time. Of course it is not certain that I am going to die; but it is a good deal more likely than anyone at home believes.

Many thousands of greetings.

Your Tanne.

To Ingeborg Dinesen

Ngong. March 3rd 24.

. . . When I think that you might really be walking through my rooms here, strolling in the woods with me and driving in my car I almost think it would be the greatest joy I could experience in this world, and I often think that we cannot die before you really have been here. But this too is very dependent on conditions. If this is to be my future and my "life's work" it is almost necessary for you to come out here; but if for one reason or another it has to be relinquished I do not think there would be any advantage in your having been here; it would be better for me if the whole thing could vanish, so to speak, with me. . . .

I am thinking of coming home next spring, that is, to leave from here in a year's time. I think it is necessary for me; the longest time that, for instance, any official is supposed to stay out here is three years, and I have had an exceptionally taxing time during these years. But I do not really want to go to Denmark; it would be so difficult because of all the shauries, I feel it would be better to go to Paris and stay there until it gets too hot, and then have a spell by the sea in France or England. I am not *really* well and think it would do me good to have some treatment or other; but Rasch can no doubt send me to a French doctor.

Then my mind is in great need of refreshment, which you will easily understand when you come to think that I have seen literally nothing but the farm and Nairobi these last few years. It may seem as if Anders has a pretty monotonous grind on his estate, but he does get off to Norway, on sailing trips and holidays now and again, and I think it is very wearing always to have the same worries,—and then really have no one at all to advise me about anything; on the whole this suits me very well. But sometimes I long terribly to travel, go to the theater and art exhibitions, hear music, see ancient or historic places, and think to spend all my time when I next get home, in these pursuits. . . .

To Thomas Dinesen

Ngong. March 15th 24.

My own dearest Tommy.

I have so many things to thank you for this time,—first a check for £40, which I am absolutely delighted with, and which could not come at a better time,—then a quite delightful little faun in Copenhagen china, which is standing on my mantelpiece and being universally admired,—and then I cannot remember if I have thanked you for "Hassan" which was a very great pleasure. A thousand, thousand thanks for everything!

I will not write any more now; I can't collect my thoughts. Denys is staying here at present and I have never been as happy, nor half as happy, in my life as I am now. You, who have known what it means really to care for someone,—and not because of reasons of circumstance and habit and so on, as seems to be the case in most marriages and love affairs that I have known, but solely because one has met with the most wonderful being on earth,—you can understand what it means to be happy in this way, and how it occupies all one's thought and all one's being, so you will excuse a short letter.

Don't mention this to the others. Nor if, for instance, I should die and you should later meet Denys, must you ever let him know that I have written or spoken of him to you; you are in fact the only person I have mentioned it to and it is actually a joy to have someone to talk to and who understands one. I know you can understand that there is a good deal of anxiety bound up in this shaurie; for me it has come to be more and more the only thing that matters in my life, and how will it end?,—well, that is not exactly what I mean, but the very fact of possessing something or having possessed something that is of such immense value to one, brings its own terror with it, and all my circumstances are so uncertain.

But there is no point in thinking like this at the moment when one is really aware of what it is to live and be happy, happy, happy— "Death is nothing, winter nothing—"

Many thousands of greetings, dearest Tommy.

Your Tanne.

To Ingeborg Dinesen

Ngong. 1/4 24

Dearest Mother.

I am very sorry not to have written for such a long time, but I have been ill in bed for a fortnight. I will not get a lot written today, either, and this is chiefly to give you some instructions regarding some paintings that I have sent home with the Bursells.

I am quite aware that they are no masterpieces, but they have come to mean a lot to me because I painted them here and the models are old friends and acquaintances of mine, and also they are the only things I have painted in the last few years. So you must not think it absurd of me to write at some length about them and beg you to take good care of them. . . .

I will enclose a list of the contents of the roll.

I would naturally be very glad if you could manage to let Fru Dorph see these pictures and ask her to give me her opinion on them. It is very difficult,—when one has learned no more than I have,—to go on painting on one's own and without any advice, and I should be enormously grateful for criticism. Not only from Fru Dorph but from any other connoisseur of art you could get to look at them. I don't know whether there might be a possibility of getting them into some exhibition or other; that would be interesting, naturally, because then I would get more criticism on them.

Geoffrey and Denys Finch-Hatton have promised me that if I sent them to London they would show them to some friends of theirs who are interested in art, and thought they could get them accepted for an exhibition there. I will be hearing more about that and if anything comes of it I will let you know and would be extremely grateful if you, or Elle if she would be kind enough to take the trouble, would arrange to have them sent and so on. In that case I would be really exceedingly grateful to Aunt Bess if she would lend out my old "Owl" to be sent together with these pictures, and of course it would be returned to her all right. If they were framed by that time they would of course look better but would be more trouble to send; but then it would be possible to put them in a crate. Otherwise I would have to ask Aunt Bess to have the owl taken out of its frame temporarily.

I am sorry to give you all this trouble, but it means more to me than is strictly reasonable and I will be *very* grateful if you will follow all these directions exactly. Many thousand thanks to you in advance for all this.

If they should be selected for an exhibition in this country,—that is, in Denmark, I mean,—I would ask you particularly to see that they are not given any fantastic titles, but those I have given them in the enclosed list. If Aunt Bess's owl should come to join them,—it is the same size and corresponds so to speak to the other still life,—it should be labeled: Still life with stuffed owl.

The rhino bird and the young girl,—with sticks in her ears,—are painted on "Americani," a material the natives use for clothes, and that I prepared for painting on myself as I had no canvas at that time. It produces something of a "flat" effect, and if Fru Dorph complains about that you must tell her the reason. I quite like it myself, but as it varies a lot the method causes uncertainty.

They are all very badly varnished; I do not think the varnish keeps well in this country, it gets so peculiarly thick and lumpy, and it probably needs to be done again. I hope they do not dissolve or stick together going through the Red Sea!! I could not very well inconvenience the Bursells with a large package.

That's all I have to say about my pictures.

. . . I don't know how your plans for coming out here are progressing, and as you know I am here all the time!—and if you will just telegraph from Marseilles I can get started on all the preparations that we are able to make! Today, with your arrival in mind, Farah has given Hassan and Juma three months' holiday and is now maid-of-all-work,—and chauffeur,—partly to ensure that they do not demand any holiday later on, partly in order to economize, so that we can present you with more dazzling splendor. . . .

Finch-Hatton had been staying here since the beginning of March, but in the middle of the month he had a letter saying that his mother was very ill, and he left for home with only one day's warning. When something like that happens the great distance seems a real misfortune. I hope that he found her improved, and that that will never happen to me. . . .

List of pictures sent with Bursell.

I. Still-life with a stuffed rhinoceros bird,
property of Denys Finch Hatton.

II. Head of old Kikuyu,
for Aunt Bess, if she would like it.

III. Head of young Kikuyu girl,
my own, and requested returned.

IV. Head of Somali boy (Farah's brother Abdullah),
green turban, property of Denys Finch Hatton.
V. Sketch. Head of young Somali with yellow turban,
for Thomas, if he wants.

Perhaps Aunt Bess would like to deal with all this shaurie, if you will explain it to her. You know she has always been the true patron of my art!

To Ingeborg Dinesen

Ngong. 13/4 24.

. . . Naturally it cannot be avoided that one looks at things many times quite differently, and I often think that one must give way in the belief that more is gained than lost by doing so, that is to say that letting one's people work with *enthusiasm* and in the hope of proving to one that they are right is of more value than having a window put in, or a piece of land harrowed in a certain way. In the long run people cannot work happily unless they are given free rein to a certain extent, or: without it they cannot put themselves into it personally, and feel more and more that it is personality that counts, even for definite work or tasks. . . . I think experience constantly shows that wholeness is the most important thing; it is only "prigs," the most abominable to me of all human types,—who will insist, in art, politics, or whatever form of life is concerned, on the details at the expense of the whole, and if one has faith in a person in general one must often force oneself to schwam über a great many details.

In "For Life's Sake" by Jakob Knudsen,—who was certainly no prig or pedant, whatever else one may accuse him of,—there is a passage toward the end discussing this, which you must read through, if you have the book, in which one of his old priests tells Thomas Viig, regarding his relationship with Karen, that if one believes in a person, one must have faith that what one does is right, *because one does it*, without concerning oneself over whether it is in fact in accordance with one's own view. This is not expressed very clearly, but I hope you can understand what I mean. In any case, in every sort of co-operation I think it is essential first and foremost not to damage one's subordinates' enthusiasm. For the sake of "speed" it is worth cutting out a lot of smaller details that might be desirable, and to shut one's eyes to many weaknesses, in order that: "Those remaining to you,—will flush at your name.". . .

I am obliged to trouble you over old Aarup's shauries. As you will see from the enclosed newspaper clipping, he died suddenly last Monday here on the shamba. . . .

As you see from the paper, it was I who found him; he was lying on the road leading up to my house. It was very fortunate that it happened there, because he was in the habit of going into Nairobi now and again and coming back when it suited him, and he had in fact spent ten days in Nairobi and had just returned. If he had dropped dead on the way out here,—he used to take a short cut across the plains,—months might have gone by before either his friends in Nairobi or I had got in touch with each other to find out what had become of him. I carried him up to his house; Kamante, my "Christian" toto, was with me,—we had gone out looking for mushrooms,—and he said that this was the third dead person he and I had carried, which was true; first the young Kikuyu girl who fell from the ox cart, then the toto who was shot, and now Aarup,—I hope he will be the last. Ten minutes afterward Rose Cartwright came out here in her car, and when the boys said that I had gone out into the shamba they drove after me; I am glad that it was not she who found him, because she is expecting a baby at any moment and it could well have given her a shock. So I gave them a message to give the police, and in the middle of the night three policemen came out here in a car with a coffin to fetch old Aarup. They wanted me to go out into the shamba with them to show them where I had found him, and as we were going out there in their car a storm suddenly came up such as I have never seen the like of; we had an inch in three quarters of an hour. I was standing in water above my knees on the road where he had been lying and where then there had not been a drop of water. While we were down at his house getting him into the coffin all the roads had turned into torrential streams, and I really never believed they would get into Nairobi with the coffin, which was very difficult to fit into the car; in the typically foolish way of the Nairobi police they had no chains with them and they were veering from one side of the road to the other like a ship in a high sea; all the while the lightning was flashing around us, the thunder was rumbling and the rain coming down "in sheets"—it plastered my clothes so hard to my body they were really hard to get off. It was like a chapter in a novel, and I could not help thinking how much Aarup would have enjoyed it; for he was always fascinated by anything out of the ordinary. Next day I heard that they had not got back to Nairobi until four in the morning.

I drove in next day to go to his funeral but my car broke down so I did not get there.

I miss old Aarup, who used to come up here and sit chatting, and who was of course the only person I could speak Danish with; but his death was a blessing for him. He was almost completely blind and

I think his general health was quite ruined; he had probably never lived in a very sensible way. He was always in good heart and still perpetually making plans for what he was going to do. He had a remarkable memory and could remember a great deal from his childhood and from country life in Jutland at that time, and he knew all the old Danish patriotic songs. But he had grown very bitter and was constantly harping on old insults that people had inflicted on him; in particular he had some enemies here called Brink and Andersen, toward whom he showed an implacable hatred, although I never discovered what it was they had originally done to him and I think he had forgotten it himself. The other day he came back from Nairobi boiling over with fury against old Nepken, our neighbor here in the Ngong Hills, whom you have probably heard about from Thomas, and who he thought had cut him in the street in company with Brink and Andersen. I tried to pacify him, because Nepken has really been a good friend to him; but he declared that he would never speak to him again, "and if it had been Jesus Christ who had passed me by in such a way I would not acknowledge him," he said. "Yes, but Jesus would never have done such a thing," I said. "Oh," said he, "if he had been with Brink and Andersen, you never know.". . .

If you can find Aarup's daughter, and she wishes it, I will get a stone or a cross put on his grave in Nairobi, with the inscription she suggests; but I will wait until I hear from her before doing anything, because I do not know his full name, nor do I know when he was born. It is very difficult out here to know what to do at all when things like this happen; I imagine that the English are very disorganized in such matters, and of course we have no Consul,—I have been to twenty different places about it. . . .

My typewriter ribbon is rotten because I have been writing away at my essay on marriage for Thomas,—but I am not making any progress with it partly because I have no one to discuss it with or to criticize what I have written, so I do not know whether it is not the most banal thing in the world, and partly because I cannot verify quotations to use as I have no books to consult. I am of the opinion that in reality there is no longer any such thing as marriage, or only in name, and that what has to be done is, either reestablish it on some basis or other that is clearly evolved,—or to teach people to practice free love, which they have so to speak jumped into completely unprepared for, with more dignity and beauty. Personally I believe that a new kind of marriage will be constructed on the idea of *race:* eugenics, birth control, etc. with a stricter idealism than that of the old form, but that free love will be entitled to exist without restraint, to be people's private shaurie. There is no prestige at all left in present-day marriage; this is certainly the case, anyhow, among the English, and I do not myself think that a marriage that is not upheld by some religious, moral or social idea in some way, and that can be dissolved at any time, for instance because of a single case of infidelity,—and that is entered upon with this assumption by both partners,—deserves to carry any prestige or is worth preserving.

I see that you are still letting yourself be upset over Tommy's flirtations. I am so sorry about this, but I have preached as much as I could to you on the subject and don't think I have any more to say. But as a conclusion may I put in a serious word or two without your taking me amiss? I think that to a certain extent all of your family lack the ability to "amuse themselves,"—or, to express it symbolically: "to enjoy the *wine* of life," and are inclined to think that happiness is to be found in a diet of bread and milk. But the greater part of humanity needs exitement [*sic*], some slight intoxication, pleasure, and danger too; I think that if it were in my power to do anything at all for humanity I myself would want to *amuse them.* I think it is wonderful that such delightful, peaceable people as you exist; but there is need for more than this, and I shall allow myself to make use of Shakespeare's words: "Dost thou think, because thou art virtuous, there shall be no more cakes and ale? Yes, by Saint Anne, and ginger shall be hot i' th' mouth too."—

Now, Thomas's small flirtations probably don't burn any one's mouth; but let him drink all the champagne and Asti Spumante he can get, and which he enjoys, even though all of you may prefer a cup of coffee. I think that one should be sincerely glad that Thomas, who had so little appreciation of it as a boy and a very young man, is now really able to *enjoy himself,* even though it may be through things that neither you nor I have any liking for; I think that, besides in my opinion being really sad when a man comes to say like J. P. Jacobsen: "I never experienced the life of a youth, I dreamed it away, alas, in the land of the shadows, I never was a youth, and now I am a man,"—it is *dangerous* for some types of character, so I will conclude by begging you most earnestly: let him enjoy himself, let him enjoy himself, let him enjoy himself,—and do not throw a shadow of any kind over his enjoyment. . . .

To Mary Bess Westenholz

Ngong 19/4 24

Dearest Aunt Bess.

Many thousand thanks for your interesting letter, which arrived on my birthday—in addition to two letters from Mother and one from

Thomas. Yours was so full of riches that I am afraid that my reply will not at all match up to it; but if for no other reason than to show you how highly I value your letters and how grateful I am that you really take the trouble to write to me at such length, I will try to answer it.

But I must say that I find it difficult to conduct a discussion by correspondence from such a great distance,—it is rather like playing tennis and sending the ball so high that one has to wait half an hour for it to come down again. This inevitably deprives the game of some of its style and charm, although it may perhaps gain a certain amount of dignity.

First I am going to try to deal with the inexhaustible old subject of the loss of trust.

I must start off by saying that I quite agree with you that in this case the conflict, in its time, was chiefly due to misunderstanding or lack of understanding,—which of course is the chief cause of almost every conflict among decent people,—and when all is said and done, probably to lack of clarity in the choice of words. It would not have been reasonable of us to complain, or to blame any of you because your faith in us had been weakened, because this can happen to the best of people; but it seemed to us that you thought we had disappointed you or been disloyal, or that we had deceived you, and this hurt us, and in particular made us feel insecure, because of course we had not consciously deceived you and we wondered when you would interpret what we thought, said, did,—wrongly, again, with the same deplorable results!

If Farah, for instance, whom I myself have taught to drive, and who I believe is an excellent chauffeur, suddenly turns out to be unable to handle the brakes and drives me into the river, it will probably be true to say that my faith in him (as a chauffeur) has been shaken, but it will not mean that he has failed my trust or cheated me. I could, by the very phrases or choice of words with which I address him after the accident, direct a reasonable reproach or an unjust accusation at him.

Then it would also be perfectly reasonable if, after having seen the paintings that I have sent home, you said that your faith in me as an artist had been weakened. Naturally it would be disappointing; but it would have been as much your error as my fault. And if in the same way you come to the conclusion that as regards virtue, self-sacrifice, efficiency, talent, the younger generation do not match up to what you had hoped and believed of them, you can probably say that your faith in the youth of Denmark has been weakened; but very probably this is something that with the best will in the world they cannot alter, and in any case cannot be expected to rectify out of regard for you. So the problem really only relates to cases where there is a question of their having made use of, or misused, your trust, when it becomes a question of integrity.

In my opinion we must distinguish here between: frankness, sincerity—and confidentiality. One may expect a certain degree of sincerity from everyone, but I do not think that any one person has the right to demand confidentiality from another.

Decent people don't sail under false colors but have the right to demand of their acquaintance that they know the flags. For a red, white and blue striped flag means nothing to the uninitiated. To an ordinary seaman it means that the ship flying it is French, and he probably attaches certain simple ideas to this; in wartime it indicates whether it is a friend or an enemy. To other people, who are educated and traveled, it is an immediate reminder of what the country stands for geographically, constitutionally, and culturally.

I think it is in one of Jakob Knudsen's stories that a young country bumpkin on coming to Copenhagen feels that he is surrounded by unreliable people, by liars, indeed, among other reasons because they tell the maid to say they are "not at home" to callers while they are quite calmly sitting behind their closed doors. They even lie in print, so to speak, by hanging a card saying "not at home" at the foot of the staircase in order to prevent visitors from going up and trying their luck by ringing or knocking. Now if this boy were to take the card home with him and hang it outside his father's door, where such habits were hitherto unknown, it would be taken literally at its face value, and people would be justified in saying that they had been cheated if the family were sitting inside; but if according to this premise he were to call the Copenhagen lady a liar, could she not legally make him retract this and make her an apology, even if he had the card in his hand and could prove that the whole family had been at home all day?

Now if similarly this young man or his sister were suddenly dropped into certain circles in London, Paris or even Copenhagen, where more or less every lady improves her appearance with the aid of creams, powder, and rouge, with false and dyed hair and false eyelashes, etc., it might well be that after such frightful disillusionment they would brand every woman in that layer of society as thoroughly dishonest people,—but would they be right? I even think that many elderly ladies would be considered absolute Jezebels by these young people, with their heads covered in false curls, painted and powdered, boldly proclaiming themselves to be far younger than in truth they are, but who in all their relations with God and man are as honest as the day. Would it not be in their own interest for these young Danes to come to understand and realize this? There is a description in Samuel Butler's book, "The Fair Haven" of how a truth-loving small boy has his faith in human beings shaken for the first time when he discovers that the impressive dimensions provided for his mother by crinolines and skirts are not actually her nether parts, but can be taken off. With a little more age and experience would not this little boy in all fairness have to reverse his judgment against his mother's honesty and veracity?

Or let us consider the fact that under the terms of the constitution the King of Denmark is committed to the Lutheran denomination. Now would a person who had privately come by the knowledge that the king did not believe in the Trinity have the right to call the King a liar and hypocrite?

In my view it is a misconception, or shortsightedness, or pedantry to talk of deception in all these cases. In actual fact all these people are in the literal sense lying and deceiving; but they are not sailing under false colors, they are not lacking in integrity. The reason for this is not merely that all those persons who might be thus said to be being deceived are completely aware of the real state of affairs and themselves practice the same system of "deceiving," have their hair dyed or "permanently waved," or anyway constantly walk past shop-windows displaying artificial curls, and read advertisements for rouge, belladonna and so on,—and allow themselves to be baptized, married and buried according to rituals of which they are probably ignorant. It must also be acknowledged that when all is said and done all these lies and deceptions are a kind of regard that people who are forced by society to live at close range mutually pay each other. They safeguard each other from inconvenient visits; they attend each other's dinner parties with the appearance, dress, and so on, that is more or less expected of them, and the King listens to sermons, attends the consecration of churches, receives communion, and so on, in order to aid the avoidance of the conflicts that varying confessions of faith and pronounced religious opinions in the chief representatives of the nation would lead to. In other words: in general there is not the slightest desire to get to the bottom of these lies and deceits, or to replace them with the complete and entire truth.

Therefore in my opinion you can say of your acquaintances that "they are insincere and made up from top to toe," and apply a similar judgment to the other examples I have mentioned; but if you say that they are sailing under false colors and that their whole way of life is lacking in integrity you do them injustice.

It is my conviction also that the same applies to the brides you write about in your letter. Their circle of acquaintance expect: not to be caused embarrassment by the arrival of illegitimate children or by unorthodox behavior in a young couple paying a visit, and at the wedding itself they expect to see the bride in a veil and garlanded,—and incidentally I think it is only a very few who attach any special significance to this,—just as at a funeral they expect to see the widow "in mourning" with a black veil, and as they expect to see the bridal pair kneel and hear them promise to live together till death do them part, even though they have deep misgivings about their religious convictions and know what percentage of marriages end in divorce, just as they expect to hear them sing that their house will be built "on the rock of the Word" although they know perfectly well that "the Word" has had a negligible part to play in the foundation of the home; but they have not the remotest desire to be made acquainted with their more intimate physical and spiritual qualities and would be utterly ill at ease if they had to listen to an account of them. They make no demand to be told whether the marriage at whose solemnization they are present has been entered upon in deeply felt love or out of regard to family and position, or perhaps because neither partner has been able to get anyone else,—and generally they certainly do not feel they have any more right to know whether a young unmarried couple are living together than whether a young married couple are not doing so, even though both cases do of course provide very intriguing themes for "gossip." I must say that I feel it is crude and vulgar of outsiders to set such store by the idea of the bride's physical "innocence," and I think that anyhow the whole of the masculine element in the wedding party think as I do in this. Apart from a few interested parties who have been concerned with this point and who may have assumed one thing or another, and have thereby been, so to speak, "deceived,"—I still think that the couple are justified in maintaining that this was their private concern, for which they are not accountable to outsiders. In the same way let us imagine a young married couple who for one reason or another postpone their married life for a year or two. It is quite likely that if their circle of acquaintance came to discover this later on they would recall certain arrangements, the odd joking comment, regrets that the young wife is still not expecting the stork, and so on, which had in a way made them look foolish but which could surely not justify them in saying they had been deceived! There are many aspects of life that are so intimate that no one can be expected to reveal information about them,—and that *no one would wish* to be acquainted with.

It is therefore my opinion that you are perfectly justified in saying, for instance, that in spite of her deep "mourning" with veil and black crepe, a widow may be infinitely glad to be rid of her husband, or that at the three last weddings you have attended the bride was not a "virgin,"—whether it is tactful to make such remarks is another matter,—but if you claim that they have been sailing under false colors and have tried to deceive the whole congregation, you do them injustice.

It was in this connection that we,—at that time,—young people were protesting, as I remember. Of course we could not object to the fact, regrettable in itself, that you found us to have looser morals, to be less patriotic, less well brought up, considerate, and so on, than your own generation; if I remember rightly we admitted to a good deal of this without prompting. But we felt that we had been unjustly treated when you felt that we had betrayed your trust, that we had no integrity.

Where the examples that you mention are concerned I think you have every right to be indignant. If you give money to a young man for the express purpose of using it to pay for a journey, and give your maid permission to be with her sweetheart until nine o'clock, her aunt on Wednesday, and her grandmother in church on Sunday, the person concerned must either assent to your decree or try to get it changed, or admit afterward that he or she has deceived you. To what extent his or her behavior was decent or sensible depends in cach case on the nature of your relationship with him or her and the character of the injunction.

But I don't think that these examples resemble any of the instances that made you accuse us of letting any of you down; I cannot remember any such. As far as I can remember the whole problem first arose on account of the casual moral attitude of certain of my girl friends. And it is in this respect that I feel, since I have never been hypocritical in expressing any particular respect for the sixth commandment, that the charge of deceiving you or abusing your trust was unjust.

I think that the question of confidentiality is quite a different matter. In this sphere one can be disappointed and hurt far more deeply than in things concerning one's wider circle of acquaintance, and if my best friend were to tell me that she has been conducting a love affair for several years, or my sister confides to me on her silver wedding anniversary that she has never had a married life with her husband, it will probably hurt me very deeply to realize how little I have participated in their lives; but I do not think there can ever be justification in *demanding* confidences, any more than love. Nor can there be a demand for reciprocity; rather, one must say sadly, like Heine: She was lovable, and he loved her, but he was not lovable and she did not love him,—and think: He inspired trust, and I gave him my confidence, but did not inspire trust and he did not give me his,—so much the more, as I feel, after all, that one is demanding just as much when one expects someone to be willing to receive my confidences as that he is to give me his own.

I think that most people have an urgent need to be able to talk completely frankly to someone or other and that those people who have the gift of winning and keeping the confidences of others are true benefactors. But it is a special talent and special conditions are attendant on it, and it is too large a subject to deal with here; but I must say something about it. To begin with, it is vital for the person who confides in someone else to be sure of his silence. On this point I must be permitted to say that I think our generation is morally superior to yours: we were more discreet. I can remember one occasion, when circumstances and some sort of crisis in my life had thrown me completely off balance, on which I talked to Aunt Lidda about intimate details of my life, and afterward discovered that she had, to put it plainly, blabbed about it right and left. I do not censure her for it in the same way as we would have judged one of our contemporaries, for I know that would be unjust; but she must have realized that she could never expect confidences from me any more. And we never could feel completely sure of any of you. I believe that in the Catholic Church, which has developed this point to the highest degree, it is an utterly unforgivable sin to reveal the secrets of the confessional and that a priest may be obliged to watch the execution of an innocent person with the entire confession of the guilty one ringing in his ears, and be unable to speak a word. Whether this in itself is right I don't know; but I am utterly convinced that this absolute silence is a necessity for confidentiality, if it is not to become quite meaningless. I have met three people in my life whom I could have unshakable confidence in on this point: Ellen Wanscher, Thomas, and Farah, and I can also say in all our time together I have never had secrets from any of them.

There is another factor that is necessary for complete confidence,—for which the Catholic Church can serve as an exemplar again: the *personal* relationship must not be too pronounced. So one can see that someone chooses a friend whose house he does not frequent,—nor the friend his,— or an elderly aunt or children's nurse, who has been washed up on the shores of some remote and peaceful institution, or a doctor he does not normally consult, as his confidant. It is not particularly comfortable to live at close quarters with someone who knows all one's thoughts and affairs. But there is also a purely practical aspect: one wants to be able to talk freely without running the risk of interference in one's plans. In any case no one can expect to receive confidences without the realization that he must not interfere, and I think it is this that so frequently prevents confidentiality between the young and the old.

For the older people do think, partly that they know best in all the eventualities of life, partly that in the last resort they are responsible for the welfare of the young, and the young generally find it difficult to give expression to their thoughts and feelings and have a certain degree of natural reticence in acting upon, and explaining and defending their ideas.

I can give an example here from my own early youth, when I was once reproached for insincerity, although I now wish that I had had the strength to act more on my own initiative. It was when I was quite young and once sent some flowers to Georg Brandes, who was lying ill in the city hospital. I had done this with all the fervent enthusiasm of a young heart for what was to me the first revelation of intellectual genius; I had been immersed in Brandes's books for a long time and I can say that it was he who revealed literature to me. My first *personal* enthusiasm for books,—for Shakespeare, Shelley, Heine,—came to me through him. From a purely objective point of view Brandes was of course one of the greatest minds of my country, and a sick old man. I took this step without the least element of bad conscience, but I was of course aware that it would not be approved of,—and after all, that is the kind of infatuation and romantic action that a young girl keeps secret from her family. I cannot remember how the whole thing did come to be discovered; but I can remember what a frightful blow it was to me when the whole family, including Aunt Thora, who must have been visiting us then, joined in an indignant discussion and what an extremely unpleasant episode the whole thing came to represent.

I was reproached with the fact that I had taken it upon myself to do such a thing behind your backs—but how else could I have done it, if I wanted to do it at all? as soon as you had anything to do with it, you put a stop to any further development; I never wrote to Brandes again, or heard from him, or saw him, which I would so much have liked to do. At least my cunning action had resulted in my writing to him this one time and "rendering him homage," and the thought of that often made me happy later on. I had neither the strength nor the ability to strike a harder blow then, and probably nothing would have come of it anyway, although my admiration for him never slackened.

This was a great grief to me then and now I consider it to have been a great misfortune. It would have been a chance for my youthful fervor for "intellect," which was after all rather "starved" in my everyday life; it is the only time in my life when there has been a possibility for personal contact with one of the great minds of Denmark, and I believe that Brandes might have made a writer or artist of me, as he did with so many,—indeed, probably none of the artists and writers of Denmark during the last fifty years have been without his influence to a greater or lesser extent,—and my youth might have been blessed with intellectual work and enthusiasm for art and "genius." If I had realized at that time how much was at stake I would probably, if I had not had the strength to carry it through openly, have had strength enough to deceive you, and I wish that I had had it. The first Christians,—otherwise sans comparaison,—did not have their divine service in the catacombs purely and simply out of fear of the arena full of wild beasts and so on, but in particular because they feared the prevention or stopping of their worship, which to them was of the utmost necessity,—and can one charge them with perfidy?

Well, after these considerations of integrity, frankness, confidentiality I will bring this letter to an end. I had in mind to continue it with an essay on the equally immortal topic of love, about which you write as well; but I imagine that by now you are worn out by my observations and that it would be better to give you a dose of it another time. Incidentally, I am in the course of writing a series of reflections on this theme to Thomas, and probably my witticisms will not bear repetition. So I will thank you for accompanying me this far so patiently,—if you have done so. I expect you have noticed that I am out of practice in this kind of discussion, which I do not get out here, so it is quite a challenge to get it down in print.

Many thousand greetings to you and all at Folehave. No doubt you will hear from Mother about what else is happening here; but I hope you are aware that I am breaking the ten commandments and finding much happiness in doing so.

Last night I dreamed that I was attending old Sanne's funeral, and that you said to me that you hoped I would follow in her footsteps. It is strange that one can dream like this; I can't have thought about her for thirty years.

Well, once again many, many greetings, beloved Aunt B.

Your Tanne.

Ngong 20.4.24.

. . . On the subject of Tommy's flirtations, which ought to have a mention in every letter,—Don't you think that much the same risk has always existed for a young man to be captured by an unscrupulous girl, if it comes to that? Perhaps in the past they did not have so much opportunity to practice their wiles; but then too a man was much sooner committed and in honor bound to lead them to the altar. When I was a child I heard that Uncle Gex was obliged to propose to Aunt Lidda as a man of honor, because he had seen her petticoats and white knickers through the slit in her dress when she lifted it up. That is how it was then, anyway, but I don't think one hears of many cases like that nowadays. And dearest Mother, isn't it just a little bit arrogant always to be wondering whether Thomas will get a girl who "is worthy of us"? Are we ourselves worthy to receive a lively, vigorous young girl, who would give him the whole of her life?—That is to say, have we enough heart to receive what *she will give* as a great joy, to acknowledge her personality and think of *her* happiness? In ten years' time I would have my doubts at seeing Mitten dedicating herself to such a "self-concentrated" family. . . .

To Thomas Dinesen

Ngong. 27.4.24

Dear old Tommy.

A thousand thanks for a letter which arrived on my birthday; it was so good to hear from you, and I hope you are still flourishing in Oxford and have met interesting people, and are enjoying yourself. Have you been to see Wells? I really think you should do that; I think that one is often hesitant about that sort of thing, because one feels that famous people get so much of it; but for one thing I am not so sure that they do, and for another they can probably never have enough of it, and also they are discerning about people. The only time I did anything of this kind, was with Georg Brandes and I was shown a touching interest and could have acquired much richness in my life if I had not been a fool,—and then of course your V.C. ought to provide you with a privileged position in this sort of situation. Are you reading Well's "The Dream," which is appearing in "Nash's Magazine"? It interests me enormously and I agree absolutely with his view of how life is regarded in our time. I have so often thought about what you used to say: that human beings could easily become more clever, more beautiful, and so on, but not happier. I think you are wrong there; I somehow think that the great idea of our time is education for happiness,—or as Wells says, in the art of being human,—and that this may well be the germ of a "Golden Age." The road to it has not really been clear until now; many things in our old view of the world had first to be eliminated, in my opinion first and foremost religion,—and then we had to a certain extent to liberate ourselves from the powers of nature, or deal with them, before we could make any progress. If "The Dream" has come out in book form would you please send it to me?—but it probably won't appear before it is finished in Nash's.

I am afraid that I overwhelm you sometimes with my worries; but now and again they do grow rather big, and you must remember that you are the only person in the world to whom I can write freely and really express myself. For I always have to write cheerfully to Mother, and there is no one at all out here who wants to bother to listen to my shauries or who can understand them at all. I seem to notice from Mother's letters that she has come more under the influence of the rest of the family at home, unless it is only that she has grown older, and worn down by her sorrows; but she no longer has her old "mobility of spirit," which enabled her to be sanguine even under difficult conditions. For instance, she is much more easily upset by differences of opinion between herself and us, so it is a shame to worry her with them.

I think that the sort of family affection or solidarity in a family that there has been in ours can be a bane; for Mother, for instance, it is her relationship with us, primarily, and then her relationship with her sisters and brothers and so on that fills her whole life, and although I am probably able to satisfy her on this score I cannot do so in a really honest fashion, and that is painful, because the whole of her heart and soul is in this relationship,—if you understand what I mean. I think it is impossible for Mother to realize that there may be relationships in our lives that mean more to us than the relationship with her or the mutual relationship among us as siblings. And she cannot understand that the tragedy of my marriage has been a greater sorrow to me than Ea's death; I don't think that she ever gives a thought any more to Bror or the whole of that shaurie, or thinks that I do, while she probably thinks now and again that I have got over Ea's death more easily than she can understand. But no matter how indescribably devoted I was to Ea, in reality she was never as close to me as Bror was in the years when we were really happily married and had started on a completely new life together.

If Mother should ever get to know that I cared for another person who meant everything in the world to me I believe it would be incomprehensible to her, indeed, that it would cause her pain. I think she feels like this about Elle, and that it is somehow a constantly recurring, unconscious disappointment or a kind of unconscious resentment,—or rather, that although she is satisfied in every way with Elle's circumstances, she herself is not really *happy* in her relationship with her and seeks a sort of substitute in the relationship with her other children. I don't think Mother ever realized how large a part Viggo played in Ea's life . . . or conversely that she has any idea of the proportions of the role that Anders plays in my life or I in Anders's. No matter how much we like each other nor how happy we will always be to see each other, there has been too much of an age difference and other factors for us ever to have been close,—heaven knows whether Anders thinks of me three times a year,—but I am sure that Mother imagines that Anders takes one of the first places among the people I care for and who give meaning to my life.

Mother and I have been carrying on a lengthy correspondence on the subject of your "flirtations,"—I don't know whether you have heard anything about this,—and I ended up by writing her an admonitory letter recently, partly because she is unable to stop grieving over this shaurie, partly because she keeps returning to her dread of your marrying a girl who "is not worthy of us." Quite apart from the fact that this is frightful arrogance, it is really not right that she should think of your wife primarily in relation to Mother herself, Rungsted, Folehave, Mitten, and me. If this point of view were carried through it could become a formidable obstacle to your marriage as a whole, and for your married *happiness,*—if you did marry,—and I must say that in fact if we were as Mother, Mama, and Aunt Bess believed us to be,—that is, as concentrated on family as they are themselves,—we would be completely and utterly *unfit* to marry anyone at all. . . . I do wish so much that Mother could find something else, if not to absorb herself in, then at least to occupy herself with, than her children and grandchildren, for example, music, good works, a little social life, or some such activity, just as Fru Wanscher occupies herself with and is interested in literature and the theater; but I know that that is out of the question.

So therefore I am somewhat anxious at the thought of Mother's visit here. . . . Just because I have been so far away that it has not been possible for Mother to be disillusioned, and because it has been so easy to give her what she was wanting to hear in my letters and to keep everything else out, I think that Mother has become absolutely convinced that she and I are all in all to each other,—at least that she is everything to me, and I don't think she is conscious of this, or that she could consciously be disappointed over it; but I think that if she *were* disappointed, even a very little, it would be a terrible grief to her,—indeed, she would feel as if the last sanctuary for her great love had been closed to her. She writes, for instance, that it will be for "both of us like being in heaven to celebrate Christmas together,"—and I am sure you will understand that I am afraid of not being able to live up to this,—while I think that if you were here it would be quite all right? . . .

To return to my own shauries, I have something else I want to ask you to help me with, namely concerning Bror. You see, I have had two letters, first one from Roy Whittet, who went out on safari with Bror, and next one from Bror himself, telling me that he is very ill in Arua in Uganda. There is little doubt as to what is wrong with him, he himself realizes that it is his old illness; he writes that to start with his whole body became covered with sores, and now he has a kind of inflammation in all his joints, which are quite stiff and swollen, as well as constant high fever and a kind of paralysis. Whittet wrote without Bror's knowledge to ask me to prepare Aunt Clara; I think they consider that there is very little hope. In these circumstances I have written to him and asked him, if he can be moved, to come here. He has no money and went off on this safari in the hope of shooting elephant, which came to nothing. I cannot let him lie there and die like a dog, and I have once and for all promised not to write anything to his family.

I do not yet know whether he can, or will want to, come, but if anything comes of it I want to ask you to talk to Uncle Aage about it. If he dismisses me for doing this, so be it. I do not think it could have any effect on our divorce, which is now practically through; the lawyers at home will have to take into account the fact that conditions out here are not as they are at home; there is hardly anything in the way of hospitals, and no sanatoria, convalescent homes, health resorts or anything like that. I cannot think of anywhere else for Bror to go; people would probably be afraid to have him, anyway for instance the Lindstrøms or the Bursells, who have children. I would only consider keeping him here for as long as he is very ill, and he will not be allowed to have any influence on the farm. I am of course most reluctant to involve Uncle Aage in any of my shauries, but if it is necessary, which you will have to decide, you can tell him everything quite frankly; but you must ask him not to tell anyone else. But you need not do anything before you have heard from me again; it may be that Bror is too ill to travel at all.

. . . I have been somewhat anxious about the farm because the rains stopped on the 5th of April and we then had three weeks of cool weather, exactly as usually happens when the rains are finished. Everyone was predicting an abortive rainy season and things were looking serious. However the day before yesterday it began to rain again and is still raining now. We have had fine blossom and if we get good weather we should have an excellent year.

I am still thinking about my purchase of the farm which in my opinion would be the best solution. I had been thinking of offering a certain sum and promising, if I should ever sell the whole thing, to share any profit with the old limited company. Mervyn Ridley, who has gone home, is going to try to arrange it for me. I am sure you can understand that I feel this would be a good piece of business for me. . . .

Denys has gone home to England; he was staying here when he had letters from his father and brother saying that his mother was very ill, and he left after only one day's warning. I do hope that I will come to see him again in this life, but don't know when he will be coming out again. You can imagine how much I miss him,—or merely knowing that he was in this country and that it was possible to meet him. If you should come across him you really must not tell him that you drove across the dam in the car; because he did it and was immensely proud of doing so, so I do not wish to deprive him of his game. I had one letter from him but have heard nothing since and do not expect to, as I think he is hopeless at writing.

I have sent my paintings home to get an opinion on them, and I have sent a couple of poems,—as Osceola,—to "Tilskueren" magazine; I don't know whether they will accept them so please do not say anything about it. They are: "Moonlight," "Following Wind," "Fortunio's Two Songs," "The early morning," "Song for Harp," and "Masai Reserve." I have one or two little stories that I may send them if they accept the poems. Do you know, I have never received your article in "Gad's Magazine" on lion hunting. It is really the limit.

I have a suggestion to make to you, although you must not be afraid of refusing it. I *must go home,* I am ill and need treatment; but I do not want to go to Denmark, particularly as things are. I would much rather be in Paris, where Rasch should be able to find a good doctor for me and where I could attend an art college at the same time. I think it might be next spring. I should be able to hold out for that long; I have been quite bad but am better now and do not think there is any great hurry. If it fits in with your plans, would you go with me? I am not particular with regard to Paris; it could equally well be Munich; only it must be somewhere with good opportunities for studying art, and preferably not London, I have spent so much time in the company of the English that I feel a change would be a good thing; but Florence or Rome would be excellent.

I think that it might be pleasant for you and me, as we are gradually severing so many ties with family and homeland, to have a spell like this together. I have been thinking that if you were to come out here with Mother, in October perhaps, and left again with her on the 1st of January or before that, and then spent three months in the Orient,—or are you thinking of a longer stay there?—we might meet, in some suitable place, in the middle of April, and stay for three months; I would in fact like to stay in Europe longer than that, preferably for six months, but for the later part of the time could travel around a little. Of course I am deeply grateful to you for your offer of financial assistance. I have actually been considering whether to ask you if I could come to China with you, but that may not be so suitable. But I *must* have a change. I really do want to try to get a clear idea of my future,—whether I should stay out here or get started on something quite different,—but that must wait awhile. You don't need to answer now, but please think about it. There might be plenty for you to study in Paris, for example; we could take a small flat on the left bank of the Seine and work hard during the day and then take a few tours now and again.

Well, I hope this long letter has not worn you out. Please tell me a little about modern intellectual life in England; I am so afraid of becoming a complete idiot out here. You know that I am writing a paper on marriage, but it is making very slow progress and will be terribly bad because I never have anyone to talk with about that sort of thing; I actually get a headache when I have to think. My view is: that there is no such thing as marriage any more, only the name remains, but that a stricter form of it will emerge, *for the race,* while *love,* as the inspiration for art and every kind of happiness, will remain a private concern,—and that humanity in any case is in for a thorough, ideal, "sexual education," which will consist not only of physical information and the control of physical relationships, but of training in loyalty, unselfishness, beauty in this particular human relationship. But more on this later on. . . .

To Ingeborg Dinesen

Ngong 11.5.24

. . . You really must not interpret what I wrote about your not coming out here if there were too many shauries as meaning that I feel I am not as close to you as before. But everyone has his own way of looking at things and perhaps my way is to be very reluctant to have people to whom I am close at my side in times of difficulty. For instance, I am sure I would not have recovered so well from my illness if at that time I had been surrounded by commiserating friends instead of completely (personally) indifferent doctors and nurses; I was enormously happy to be among them in the hospital and hope that if I should ever be seriously ill again it could be under the same conditions. . . .

You ask about my health, but it is not easy for me to reply. There are no doctors out here in whom I have real faith, and I think that when one has once had that disease they always start preaching and saying it is that, so I am reluctant to consult them. But I am actually somewhat better now and I think I can hold on until next spring and then I can get to a decent doctor. . . .

There is a tragedy going on around me at present, as Juma, my boy, Maho's father, as Thomas will remember, who had three months' leave recently, spent this time in gambling away his entire property, not only the money that he had saved but all his cattle and sheep. He was very well off for a native, he had been here in fact for seven years, and is now reduced to absolute penury. His wretched family does not even know where he is; he has taken all the sheep and cattle off with him and they have heard nothing from him for three weeks. I am having to support them, which is cheap enough with people who eat posho; but it really is a sad sight to see. . . .

To Ingeborg Dinesen

Ngong 18.5.24

. . . You know, I can remember that in the old days we celebrated your wedding anniversary, while Father was alive, with dancing around the dancing tree, and once, as far as I remember, with hot chocolate and tables set in the basement at Rungstedgaard, probably because it was raining. When one is so far away from all the old surroundings, changes that have taken place in them mean so little; in a way everything is as vividly present in its old form as in its present one. I always think that the 17th of May is the clou to early summer; for on your birthday we could never be sure of finding green foliage, but it was fairly certain for your wedding anniversary. . . . I have to thank you for two letters, in which you again inquire about my health and ask me to write about it, but that is not so easy. . . . I believe that if I had not gone into the hospital in 1915, it would not have been long before I had a complete collapse, and yet it cannot be said that I was terribly ill when I went in; it was even almost regarded as affectation. I have after all been worn down a good deal in recent years, and every now and again I get the feeling that I might suddenly drop down and give up the ghost; but until that actually happens I think I will go on feeling reasonably well, if you can imagine such a state. . . .

Berkeley Cole is probably coming out here to stay a few days. His father has died; but according to what I have heard the family see this as a great blessing. His father and mother could never get on together, and his mother always lived somewhere outside Florence; Berkeley says that she has an extremely interesting circle of friends there and he has always urged me to go and visit her when I am home some time. . . .

To Thomas Dinesen

Ngong. 22.5.24

Dearest Tommy.

Herewith I send you the first eight chapters of my treatise on love and marriage. The rest is to follow; but I thought it might be quite interesting if you had this while you are in Oxford and this is perhaps the last post that will reach you there.

Of course you will not be able to judge it properly before you have seen the whole of it, so don't trouble to write any criticism of it until later on.

I am quite aware that there is nothing special about this piece of work; and there would be little use in emphasizing the various extenuating circumstances, since the reader can rightly ask why, when conditions were so difficult, I took it upon myself to write at all. But to you, who after all I can take to be more interested in me than in my writings, I can at least give this explanation: that the moral commitment of rousing and conserving the energy to finish what I had started on, and to keep my thoughts clearly ranged, has been quite important to me here, where there is so little opportunity for abstract brain work.

One special difficulty has been the lack of access to the books I wished to quote from. Thus, I cannot remember the name of Martensen-Larsen's book, which I would like to ask you to insert, nor what Kormak said to Stengerde (the last two lines). I apologize for these omissions.

As I have not made a copy of the piece and this, therefore, is the only existing one, I have ventured to register it, which I hope will not cause you a lot of inconvenience, and must not be interpreted as if I attached any great value to it. But it would be sad if the results of my efforts were lost before they came into the hands of their only reader!

Many greetings and best wishes for your future success from your

Tanne.

To Ingeborg Dinesen

Ngong. Sunday 1/6 24.

. . . Berkeley Cole came for the weekend the other week; he is always a congenial and pleasant guest, but a typical Englishman of a certain class and period,—whom I like a great deal, but whose limitations in their view of life and humanity is almost comical. They are interested in perhaps ten among all the phenomena of life and on these subjects they are real "Fundees" ["craftsmanlike experts"], for instance, they enjoy wine, hunting, a certain kind of love with sincere understanding, but anything other than this is a closed book to them. And yet all the same they think they can rule the world,—and the odd thing is that they are not at all bad at it! Berkeley, like Delamere, is one of the old "Masai people," who have lived among and grown to know the Masai thoroughly, and have a great interest in and sympathy for this ill-fated race,—dying, as I believe, like the Indians in America, of shortage of living space; there is little doubt at all that they have been treated with gross injustice and that this is still continuing to this day. We drove out into the reserve when he was here and called on some of his old acquaintances; he has a number of medals from the war to distribute to them and wanted to come here and gather them together for this ceremony. . . .

To Thomas Dinesen

Ngong.20.6.24.

Dearest Tommy.

I am sending you herewith the last four chapters of my observations on marriage. God knows, they are not up to much; they are doubtless both banal and boring—but it is at least something to have got them finished, and they may perhaps amuse you, or Aunt Bess or Elle, who may, like you, be personally interested in my views, and who can read them if they wish.

The pagination is a bit muddled (2 × 69 and 2 × 77), which I hope is not confusing. I look forward greatly to hearing your opinion of it.

I also want to ask you a favor. I sent some poems,—seven in all—to "Tilskueren" magazine, but Dr. Levin only wants one of them ("Masai Reserve") and says that he has no room for more. However, he kindly offered to get them put in another journal if I wanted that; but I feel there is no need to trouble him with that. I thought that as you are in contact with "Gad's Magazine" you might try to get them to accept them. So I have asked Levin to send them to you and would be very grateful to you if you would do what you can to have them published there or somewhere else.

With many thousand greetings.

Your Tanne.

To Ingeborg Dinesen

Ngong 23.6.[1924]

. . . It is amazing to see how much England has changed during the last twenty-five years, and in particular since the war; when you read books from Queen Victoria's time it is as if it were a completely different country or a different race; but probably this is largely due to the fact that in old Victoria's time there had developed such extremes in the way of almost inhuman virtues and morals that they could not possibly be maintained, particularly because a lot of the "Victorian" thought and spirit was alien to the English nature and temperament, being influenced by the German, and therefore the reaction against it has been so much greater.

Now the whole nation is truly "in the melting pot," and it is remarkable to see how even the most conservative English people are quite calmly coming to anticipate not only the dissolution of the church, marriage, and the home, but even of "the Empire;" Queen Victoria must certainly be turning in her grave. I would think that something far better may very well emerge from all this, but just at the moment I think that actually the cultivation, anyway in theory, by the English in literature of love, "passion" as the absolute element in life, is a kind of "cant" in a different way; for in my opinion they do not really feel it. On the other hand I believe the modern worship of "beauty" is genuine, anyway on the part of the upper classes, and perhaps that may come to be the saving quality. . .

I have just been reading "The Forsyte Saga" with great interest and think that with all its deficiencies it is an important book. One drawback that Galsworthy has for me is that I never care for his heroes and heroines; I think the only really likable people in this book are Soames and Prosper Profond. "Nash's Magazine" is running a sequel to it at the moment, "The White Monkey," about Fleur's marriage, which is actually the best of them; I think he works himself up a great deal as the book progresses,—"The Man of Property" is the weakest part of it, and the last part, "To Let," the best. . . .

Unfortunately nothing has yet resulted from my school project. I went up to the Scotch Mission to try to get a teacher from them, but they had no one available at the moment. I myself would prefer one of the Catholic missionaries, but the beastly other missions have drummed such a truly demonic fear of the Catholic Church into their disciples! They write to me from the mission stations that I must not on any account have anything to do with "Rome," which has no "message" to give to the natives of this country! Now I am going to try to get a native teacher directly through Farah, whatever message he may have. . . .

To Ingeborg Dinesen

Ngong. Sunday 29.6.24

. . . I have been out every morning with my coffee pickers; people may think it strange that I find it an especially delightful occupation to go and pick coffee with them and listen to all their chatter. The coffee picked so far is of poor quality, but no doubt it will get better. . . .

It is beastly cold here at the moment and,—whether on account of this or not I don't know,—I am afflicted with a kind of lumbago that sometimes almost drives me mad. I think there is something the matter with my nerves; I do not mean that I am "nervy," but now and then I get such terrible pains, like a toothache, in various places, my heels, hands, ears,—but one must always have something wrong with one. . . .

To Ingeborg Dinesen

Ngong. 29.7.24

. . . A few days ago the toto who was shot just before Christmas was sent back to me; I think he is finding the change from hospital life, where they did everything they could for him, very hard. He is healed after a fashion, but does look rather terrible; he wants to be a houseboy here, but I am not very keen about that as he really is a pretty awful sight; but no doubt that is what it will come to. I am going to try to adjudicate in the case between his parents and the parents of the boy who shot him by accident, and who as you know disappeared and has not been seen since; I think all the Kikuyu customs in this kind of case are quite atrocious, all they want is to squeeze sheep and cattle out of the family of the killer, and in fact there is not the least justification for that; I tried to arrange it in such a way that the "murderer's" father would help this toto by giving him milk, because he cannot eat solid food, but his family flatly refused that; they wanted to bring a big "case" against him and their aim is naturally to squeeze as much restitution out of the others as as they can, so that the wounded boy's father can buy himself a new wife, and the boy himself will get nothing. However, I will do what I can to prevent this and am thinking of getting Kinanjui over here to help me to settle the case in a better way. I must say that I hate their "kiamas"; they consist of only the old Kikuyu who just want to sit chattering, drinking and eating endlessly, their judgments are completely worthless, I think they are absolutely fortuitous or dependent on bribery. . . .

I was interrupted here because I had to go out and act as doctor to a toto whom I diagnose as suffering from the plague, and also an old woman who had been, of all things, attacked by a snake that had spat in her face. There is a species of snake here that spits,—fortunately I have never come across one,—and although one does not die of it, one is blinded for a long time if it goes in the eyes, and judging from the old woman's squalling it must be very painful. I really did not know what to do about it; I bathed her eyes and mouth with permaganent [*sic*], I hope she will feel better soon. . . .

To Thomas Dinesen

Ngong 3.Aug.1924

Dearest Tommy.

Many many thanks for your letter which arrived the day before yesterday by a dreadfully slow post. I will reply as best I can to what you write about yourself in it,—partly because I have no shauries just at the moment, and God alone knows how long that will last, or when our letters will be purely concerned with them again.

But I know quite well that I can't hope to be able to advise or help you very much in any way. All the same, there is always the chance that something will come out of presenting one's view of the case and listening to what other people have to say about it.

I was almost on the point of writing the same sort of letter to you. I have been feeling so dreadfully down, so,—as you write,—"desperately unhappy" during the last few months, since Denys left, as you can no doubt understand; and then the uniformity of my life here and the impossibility of getting away or having a change is so inexpressibly against my nature that I writhe under it. I have felt it to be so utterly crazy and meaningless—in general: that I exist at all, in detail: that I was out here, that I was painting, getting up in the morning, etc., etc., and like Sabine I "was disgusted with life as with a dress that does not fit." But where I am concerned I find that when I am really in the depths of despair, what generally happens is that, why I do not know, I rise very slowly to the surface again. I think the reason for this is that I have in my nature unusually large resources of "joie de vivre" that in fact assert themselves against all the dictates of reason,—just as in the same way scratches heal on me quicker than on other people.

Now I know that it is not like this for you. But I think one can improve things quite a lot by adapting oneself and trying to create such conditions for one's life that the powers of this kind that one has can be most effective. I think that the climate here and the fact that I am a free agent, that no other people can interfere in my affairs helps me greatly, I believe, to feel strong and in possession of the ability to revive in spite of every sorrow. I do not think that you have adapted yourself properly in that respect,—and I will come back to that later.

If you were to ask me first whether I think the best thing for you to do would be to give up what to you is the highest thing in life, and settle down to, as you write: "sail with the old familiar cargo along the well-marked routes," I can only reply no, no, no. I do not think that one can run away from one's nature in this way. . . . Where "regular work" is concerned I think the same thing applies: it would be unprofitable for you,—and the only advantage it would have over marriage would be that you could give it up whenever you liked; but that is not worth much. I think there are not a few people calling themselves freethinkers, indeed even anarchists, who in reality have great respect for a contract, what is known as a "profession," and for a substantial regular income, but you are not one of those. I cannot imagine anything at all,—considering the state of mind you are in, the attitude toward such a position you would hold at the start of it,—that could bind you to it.

I can judge from myself; I would really like to be married and am tired of always being alone. If I were not as I am and so forth I could quite easily do it, for instance, get married to Jack Llewellyn or Berkeley Cole, I like him very much and enjoy being with him, and he is to get 150,000 acres in the north as a gift from the Government,—and that is always something! But as things are I realize it is impossible. Of course I could *do it* from the practical point of view, that is to say, I could go to a registry office with Berkeley and then drive off with him in his car to Nyeri. But I think it would come to seem just as meaningless and just as unnatural as if I suddenly said that I had got married to Banja. Perhaps, looked at impartially, this is "stupid," but if so, the stupidity lies in the fact that I am as I am, and it would be far more stupid to think that I could voluntarily change this, as much as to think that I could voluntarily make myself seventeen years old, or a man, or a dog.

I believe that for all time and eternity I am bound to Denys, to love the ground he walks upon, to be happy beyond words when he is here, and to suffer worse than death many times when he leaves. . . .

If I did not have the Somalis and natives to fall back upon here the middle-class English people I am forced to associate with would drive me mad. I like the aristocrats and bohemians, whom perhaps you do not; but on the other hand you as a man have more possibility for getting to know, or living among, the lower classes or proletariat. You once spoke of signing on as a seaman; I really think you should do that now. Or it might serve you equally well to spend a year in Somaliland and Abyssinia.

It is my conviction that to live among your own class, in well-being, in a comfortable well-ordered existence, is completely impossible for you at present, indeed, that it is poisoning you. When one has been really hard hit I believe that comfort, small pleasures, pleasant entertainments are the worst things one can be subjected to.

But right outside one's door there are starving, miserable, despairing, struggling people. I don't mean only the proletariat, but in Germany, Russia, Austria, all over the world, almost everyone. If I have any advice to give you it is to seek them out—or anyhow to seek situations where danger, and revolution, are the order of the day. . . .

You write as if there were nothing else in the world besides traveling, studying,—and then "the eight hour's office chair" and bourgeois marriage. It is all on much the same level and among the same kind of people. But there is a wild world outside that everyone seeks to avoid, but that I think could do you good. I for one, before I relinquish hope and declare that life is not worth living, would like to have known it.

I think I have a certain "faible" for giving advice; I have given a great deal, anyway, and when I come to think about it I don't think one person has ever followed any of it. Nor do I know why they should have; if one cannot directly see that a piece of advice is advantageous one would have to believe in some sort of divine inspiration or at least human superiority in the giver of it. But on the other hand I think there is some sort of deliverance,—when one has gone so far as to ask for advice,—in following advice, even if one cannot see much point in it.

I do not think that the sort of person you are,—I will say it, above all: so honest,—can fail to achieve results. And when one is as honest as you one must not give up, no matter how hard it becomes, as long as one *can* endure. If Erasmus Montanus had really been passionately enthusiastic about science, it would have been better if he had stayed in the Army rather than admitted that the earth was as flat as a pancake; for how happy would he really have been on the mountain and even married to Lisbet?—All the appreciation in the world from Per Degn [the Parish Clerk] and the Bailiff would have been but poor satisfaction to him. . . .

Regarding my paper on marriage, which you write so kindly about, you are welcome to show it to anyone especially interested, if you wish, but it was really written for you only. Much of it arose directly out of our discussions on the subject and you will find several of your own opinions in it. I have been thinking that it might be a help for you to write something yourself about the problem. . . .

I am looking forward more than I can say to seeing you out here again. I have been longing terribly for you.

A thousand greetings to all.

Your Tanne.

I am opening my letter again to add a few words in reply to what you write at the end of your letter: "What you have attained I can perhaps attain again as well some day—" indeed, I am sure that you will. One cannot have the capacity for love without sooner or later meeting the one to whom one can give it without reservation. Someone who has never loved may perhaps come to doubt whether he will ever be able to love; but I do not think that life ever gives us a flash of love once, and never again; it is there within one, and it will come to one as surely as death. I can speak from my own experience; I fell very, very deeply in love when I was quite young,—it was in 1909,—and I really believed that it would never happen again; and then nine years later, in 1918, it did,—and far, far more strongly and deeply than before. I once read a translation of a little Greek poem:

> Eros struck out , like a smith with his hammer,
> so that the sparks flew from my defiance.
> He cooled my heart in tears and lamentations,
> like red-hot iron in a stream

that I often think of. That is how I feel it is, and not at all the yielding tenderness that is so often described. Just you wait; that hammer will surely be raised for you again.

I think you have been mistaken in never having read any *older* literature. I think it would be good for you. Read the old philosophers and satirists, Rabelais, for instance. I think two things would help you just now: a sense of humor, and danger. And by the way, read Søren Kierkegaard, too, even though you may find him a little complicated (he may be a little old-fashioned to you, too!); I know that we have "Either-Or" at home, anyway. I do not think that anyone can read him closely without being gripped by him. He was an honest person and suffered for it; you may perhaps see something of yourself in his concept of "The Individual."

Please forgive this stupid letter. It is not at all what it ought to be. But once more I will shout what I really want to say: Endure.

To Thomas Dinesen

Ngong. 4/9.24

Dearest Tommy.

Mother's telegram came the night before last and you can imagine how tremendously happy I am at the thought of seeing her and you here before very long. I can hardly realize it, and I long to see you both so much, now that I really dare to think that you are coming I don't know how I will get through the waiting time.

I am sure I don't need to ask you to look after Mother in every possible way on the journey; I think you may not quite realize how ghastly it is for most people. I am sending little Abdullah,—who is here on holiday for the time being and has grown into a giant of enormous proportions, and is, I believe, something of a mathematical genius,—to meet you in Mombasa, and hope that you will manage otherwise. Farah really thinks that he ought to go down there, but I want to keep him here,—and come to the station at Nairobi myself!!. . . .

It is possible that you may be traveling out with Denys, as I hear that he is coming out on a French boat in October. If so it would be best if you ask Mother to appear as if she has never heard of him.

I had tea yesterday with Genessee, who spoke in a most friendly way about you and is greatly looking forward to meeting you again.

And now, welcome, welcome, dearest brother. Everyone here is looking forward more than I can say to seeing you again. Poor Singh, who has grown really beastly, by the way, Kamante, who is now our best football player, Abdullah, Farah—and not least your old, deeply devoted sister

Tanne.

You have all been quite hopeless at writing lately; I have not had a single word by the last three mails!

On 11 October 1924 Fru Ingeborg Dinesen left Denmark with Thomas Dinesen and traveled via Paris to Marseilles. Five days later they embarked on the S.S. "Chambord" *and sailed through the Mediterranean, past Port*

Said and along the east coast of Africa to Mombasa, where they were met by Farah on 3 November. Fru Dinesen stayed on the farm for over two months. In the diary that she kept during her visit to Kenya she recounts her meetings with most of Karen Blixen's English friends, Sir Northrop and Lady McMillan, Denys Finch Hatton, Charles Bulpett, Berkeley Cole, Hugh Martin, and Algy and Rose Cartwright, to name only a few. On Sunday, 11 January 1925, a big ngoma was held at the farm, at which, among others, the chief Kinanjui was present, and two days later Ingeborg Dinesen parted from her daughter at Nairobi Station. Thomas Dinesen accompanied his mother to Mombasa, and she arrived in Copenhagen on 7 February.

1925

To Ingeborg Dinesen

Ngong. 14.1.25

My beloved blessed Mother.

From the moment when I saw your beloved face disappear in the train I have been looking forward every single day to seeing it again on the veranda at Rungsted, and after all that is not so far off. Lady McMillan tore me away before you had quite vanished; it is probably an English superstition that one should not see the last glimpse of someone, and of course it was nice of her to go down there, but I feel it would have meant a lot to see you for one second more. She dragged me off with her to Chiromo, but I managed to get away quite soon.

When I got back here to the farm I felt that the sense of loss was almost too hard to bear; but as I turned the corner and the house came in sight a strange thing happened: I felt as if I were coming home to you,—and that is how it has been ever since, and still is. Now I can really understand what it means to say that the house where my mother has been is "forever blessed," and how true that is. You are on the veranda and on the stone bench. You are sitting in the drawing room sewing and coming out of your room to meet me. Everything that I have been attached to has taken on a wonderful new value because your eyes have rested on it and because you care for it. I can never be alone in this house again. All the boys came and said how sad it was that you had left and asked why you had not wanted to stay for six months, "Wataa yaate na penda Mama" ["We are so sad, because we like your mother so much"]. Tumbo, poor fool, had been crying all day long because you had left and he had not gone with you; he had achieved a certain degree of resignation when I got home and only said very dejectedly, "mimi kidogo" ["I am too little"],—which was the reason he had been given. Little Dragon came running joyfully to greet me but is still looking all over the house for you, and slept in your room last night.—On my arrival I found the animal part of the household had been augmented by a tortoise that Kamante had caught; it has dropped into the peaceful atmosphere without any difficulty.

When I got home I found a letter from Aunt Bess, which could not have come at a better moment or been more welcome, and also two letters enclosed from Aunt Lidda, from which I can see that things at Matrup have been very peaceful and harmonious lately.

I had a telegram from Repsdorph saying that I have obtained my divorce; strange that it should have been on the eleventh anniversary of my marriage.

I have nothing else to write about today. I want to thank you once more,—thousands and thousands of times,—for coming out here;—I will never, never forget that you did that. From the very first moment when I unexpectedly saw your face in the car to the final minute the hours and days seem like a huge rich treasure that I have gathered together and can never, never lose. Everything here has acquired significance, a kind of gleam like that the evening sun gives to the Ngong Hills; you have tuned all the various strings here and in my life with your light beloved hand so that they play together in harmony,—and for everything, for every word you have spoken to me and for each time you have looked at me I thank you more than I can ever say. Dearest, dearest Mother, now as I am writing and as I look up I seem to see you standing there, and hear your steps and your voice and feel that you *must* be in the house—and so you are; "The power of the spirit is great"—one knows that and yet one goes on thinking in doctrinal terms of physical conditions and suffers for it.

Of course Lady McMillan could not stop talking about how charming my mother is and that you personify "the most beautiful, lovely, and delightful type of woman."

Everyone here sends you their warmest greetings, including Lulu, Minerva, the house itself, and the hills; they will not and cannot give you up. I myself will not say goodbye for when I look up you are looking at me.

Thanks and thanks and thanks again, as long as I live, for coming.

Your Tanne.

To Ingeborg Dinesen

Ngong. 9.2.25

. . . Denys and Mclean came out here on the 28th and we decided to go up into the hills on the 1st. We had two tents and 25 porters as well as Farah, Kamau, Nduetti, and my little cook-boy as chef. It was absolutely lovely up there, green after the rains. The view was wonderful as you would know. We pitched camp where Thomas and Miss Miles had had theirs, at about the same height as we got up to when we went, but rather closer to the summits. The air was so wonderful. There were a lot of buffalo, but only cows with calves, which of course must not be shot. But Mclean got a fine bush-buck; I have never seen so many bush-buck, they came out early in the morning, we sat on the brow of a hill and counted twenty-nine. The nights were wonderful, with moonlight. Unfortunately we had to go down again early as Mclean had to go to Mombasa to meet his wife and sister, who are going on safari with him and Denys in the Masai Reserve.

Denys stayed on here and has just driven in. You will understand how happy I have been to have him here. He sent his kindest regards to you and was so sorry not to have seen you again. He won't be back from his safari before I have left, and you can imagine how sad I am not to be able to see him for so many months. . . .

On 5 March 1925 Karen Blixen, Thomas Dinesen, and Farah sailed from Mombasa Harbor on board the "Admiral Pierre". *En route to Marseilles the ship called at Aden, where Thomas Dinesen and Farah went ashore; they intended to go on safari for two months in Somaliland, Farah's native land. Karen Blixen continued the voyage and arrived at Marseilles at the end of March.*

To Ingeborg Dinesen

Marseilles.
Hotel du Louvre & de la Paix
28.3.25.

My dearest Mother.—

Well, here I am in Europe again: and will begin by thanking you for your letter and welcome to me here.—It is *lovely* to have got so far, traveling is always trying. . . I parted from Tommy at Aden and he was greatly looking forward to his trip, but as you no doubt know they refused him entry to Somaliland. It is really the meanest trick I could imagine, a man who was ready to give his life for them!—sometimes I get so furious with the English that I think I will never have anything to do with them again! I don't know what he is doing now; I am expecting to hear from him in Paris, you probably know more than I do.—

It was very hard to part from him, we had had such a happy time together. Farah went with him, I don't know at all what has happened with him. It was quite difficult to leave everyone at Ngong, too, especially Pjuske, who was so sad himself.—The natives were most touching, came in droves to say goodbye, and all said: "We will say thank you, thank you, thank you to you when you come back again."

The old woman, you may perhaps remember, who called me Mama, came crawling up on the last morning and said: "I have heard you are leaving, but I cannot believe it, God must have deserted us." She stayed outside crying. I had a great sorrow, Minerva died the day before I left; she had grown so sweet and amusing, you have no idea,—Thomas and I both loved her. Tumbo wanted to come to Europe to be with you, and they *all* asked me to give you their very warmest greetings, you have made a greatly loved name for yourself among the natives.—How can you think, dearest Mother, that I would find the house at home old and shabby! We love it just as it is. You really must be a little crazy to write that! I am looking forward more than I can say to everything that awaits me: buying clothes in Paris, looking at pictures and listening to music again, the countryside at home, fruit and rye bread and shrimp,—and please will you buy a *real Norwegian goat-cheese* to greet me with; I have been dreaming of that time and again. . . .

To Ingeborg Dinesen

E. Boyd Neel & Co.
21 Rue Daunou, Paris (2e)
April 1st 1925.

My own beloved Mother.

I have just been to the Legation, but unfortunately did not find any letters there. I came round here to see about my money, and received the news that Sir Northrup McMillan is dead; I feel so sorry for Lady M.M.; and so I will not see them in Paris. He died in Nice. I hope that this does not mean that she will not be going back to Africa.—It is disappointing that my pictures were not taken to Charlottenborg. Surely it cannot be that Fru Dorph had any objections; she could not have had the least grounds for that,—other than feeling they were not good enough, and after all there is nothing to be ashamed of in that!. . .

To Ingeborg Dinesen

Quai Voltaire 7.4.25.

My sweet beloved Mother.

A thousand thanks for your telegram about Tommy, which has just this moment come. I can't tell you how glad I am about it; I thought it would have been a disappointment hard for him to accept, if it had really come to nothing. . . . I can't tell you what a weight this has lifted from my heart, because the last thing I heard from him and

Farah was that they were going to hire a dhow and go fishing, so it is good to know that they are on dry land again.—I do so hate the idea of things going wrong for Tommy, he is such a dear person; I hope with all my heart that this trip will be a worthwhile one for him.—Farah is sure to do what he can for him but of course he is not such a brilliant personality in whom to put one's trust.—

. . . As I have been looking so ill groomed, with holes in my shoes and my clothes more or less in rags,—I think that has been the cause of Madame at the hotel here looking at me somewhat askance,—I have kept mostly to the left bank of the Seine, which I always find so charming. . . . Yesterday I went to the theater to see "L'Idiot,"—a dramatization of Dostoievski's book. I have not read the book, but, from what I have read of Dostoievski's works, I cannot think it has the slightest resemblance to it; but it gave the prima donna, Ida Rubenstein, who is extraordinarily beautiful, the opportunity to show herself off to advantage in some delightful outfits. . . .

To Ingeborg Dinesen

Hotels S^{t}. James 211, Rue S^{t}. Honoré
& D'Albany 202, Rue de Rivoli
Paris
16.4.25

. . . . Here it is still *beastly* cold, they say they have never had such a late spring, but I think it was the same when I was here in 1910. It is tiresome that they have stopped the heating in museums and exhibitions,—because of that I haven't been able to go to as much as I would have liked. I have been to see a very interesting play, "Henri IV"; it is by a new playwright, Pirandello,—I don't know whether he has been performed in Denmark. I found him absolutely delightful,—an Einstein in literature!—and then the performance was quite excellent. Tomorrow I am going to tea with the Polowtzoffs; I am looking forward very much to seeing them. . . .

To Ingeborg Dinesen

Hotels S^{t}. James 211, Rue S^{t}. Honoré
& D'Albany 202, Rue de Rivoli
Paris
20. April [1925]

. . . Now I am thinking of sticking to my own plans and leaving here on Friday or Saturday morning, traveling via Hamburg and so getting home on Saturday or Sunday evening, which I hope will suit you.—You may think it wrong of me to come home so quickly, but I think I will either have to do that or else really settle down in Paris and attend an art college for at least three months, and I think that is too much; and in some ways I think it will be easier for me to get started on my painting at home than here, where I do not know any painters and cannot get any recommendations, which means that they will only take me as a complete beginner.—There are two things that I want to do when I am at home: paint, and learn to cook. Do you think I could take lessons in the royal kitchens? Perhaps, if they still exist the Misses Nimb would take me on as a pupil for old acquaintance's sake. . . .

In May 1925 Karen Blixen arrived in Denmark on her third trip home since her departure for Africa. This time she stayed at Rungstedlund for almost eight months. The undated letter to Aunt Bess that follows must have been written before this period.

To Mary Bess Westenholz

[Rungstedlund, 1925?]

Dear Aunt Bess.

Like most people I am too slow witted to have my arguments ready at hand in a discussion and am therefore often obliged, if I am to be honest and not merely extemporize when my opponent pins me down, to resort to the excuse of saying: I haven't thought about it. But afterward, of course, one tries to give the subject serious thought and to clarify it, and then one may wish to resume the discussion, which happens all too seldom.

As a continuation of our discussion yesterday I would like now to try to express rather more clearly what it actually is that seems to me to be "un-English" in Victorian thought and philosophy. What I believe I really think is that it was *doctrinaire* in a sense that is alien to the fundamental character of the English. In Kenya it has often struck me—particularly in their agricultural methods—how incompatible it is to the English to rely upon theory, or in fact to make use of theory at all. In this country we probably tend to place too high a value on theoretical training, considering that when a man has undergone a course of study and succeeded in passing an examination he is equipped to deal with the tasks assigned to him; yet this system has enabled us to acquire great proficiency and competence. My experience has shown that the English take the least account of theory and rely far more on a kind of instinct—when selecting a candidate for a difficult post or assignment they are more likely to appoint a man whose intuition and sound judgement they trust than to give consideration to the applicant's training and qualifications. This is especially noticeable in comparison with young Swedish farmers and dairymen, for in recent years the Swedes have based their systems chiefly on those of Germany, and the Germans are doctrinaire and systematic theorists par excellence.

I believe that the same applies in the military sphere and was clearly apparent during the Great War, when, of course, the Germans—and the Swedes, despite the fact that they had no occasion to demonstrate it—had their affairs impeccably well-organized, calculated for every eventuality, while the English waged war by muddling through. They are only able to practice this system because of the enormous capital resources they have to fall back upon and the corresponding special resources in their character, so that miscalculations and setbacks have no material effect on them and in some ways they lack the ability to grieve or be chagrined over an error or a miscalculation.

So that when I try to look at the spirit and character of the English in the light of history, as I believe I have come to know it through, for instance, literature and art, through memoirs and cultural descriptions as a whole, it is then that I consider that the Victorian era, which had, like the Prince Consort himself, a predilection for memoranda and for "laying down rules," marked England with a concept of life and thought that is incompatible with its real and true life and character.

I would be the last to deny that Victoria's age also created much that was great; and of course it is only natural that those of you who became acquainted with England and chiefly with English literature and art precisely when it was marked by that spirit, should see these things as inseparably bound together. I myself support my theory—which I do not claim to be other than such—on personal experience, namely that I did not acquire a liking for, take any interest in, or understand the Victorian England that was presented to me in my childhood, but that later, through a knowledge of old England gained through history and literature, and through acquaintance with such English people as I take to be either a "throwback" to its characteristics or a continuation in line with its life and traditions—which I believe in a way to be true of the aristocracy, who seem in some degree to have "lain low" under Victoria—I have come to admire and to feel in deep sympathy with the English.

But for me now this English character is particularly bound up with the need and demand for human freedom.—When I read memoirs and history from the period before the French Revolution, when the French aristocracy so suddenly became attracted to and influenced by the English, I believe that this too was a return to what was free, human and natural, away from the conventional. It is surely symbolic that under this influence the great French noblemen converted their stiffly geometric gardens into parks; for to me there is no better expression of the English spirit than a park. Here nature is invested with dignity, and the noble with naturalness,—but no rules can be laid down for this; most probably there are numerous rules and regulations for the construction of a French garden, but for a park it is a matter of intuition and instinct. I also think that when throughout the ages Shakespeare has been taken up and performed again after, for instance, Racine, he has represented humanity and freedom.

Now it seems to me that in Victoria's time much of this ideal of human freedom was lost; in my opinion England under the great Victorians became in spirit less of a park; more rules were enforced, dead straight paths were laid down, one was forbidden to walk on the grass. We are not talking now of to what extent this can be called an improvement or the contrary, but of how far this is, or is not, true to the English character, in line with the rest of its development, and which I believe not to be the case.

When I read a Victorian writer, Dickens, for instance, whom I really love, and most of whose works I believe I have read—then it strikes me also that he is true, and thereby great and really charming when he is writing about those situations and people where no rules are enforced, where everything is permissible and where nothing matters provided it be lively, amusing, in some way or other free and delightfully human. One cannot help loving Micawber, Fagin and the whole mob including the artful dodger, indeed, there is even something engaging about Bill Sykes,—and his descriptions of them are in line with Swift, Hogarth, and the great humorists of old. But when he is occupied with those people and situations subject to definite rules and regulations, where the free play of impulses is restricted, then in my opinion he becomes completely lifeless—in Agnes and Doctor Wickfield, in the whole of that world into which, to my despair, Oliver Twist was drawn and assimilated, he really is, I think, utterly tedious.

The same is true, I feel, of Kipling, who is an excellent representative for the later Victorian period and who took the world they had created for granted; if the native world of India, which to him is outside the pale of law and order, did not sometimes intrude into his works he would be quite intolerable, but in his descriptions of that there is something that I would take to be truly English.

Closely allied to this sympathy with human freedom is, I consider, the English sense of humor. Now I am not saying that the Victorian age was completely lacking in humor; but it imposed a taboo on many situations that in my view is totally opposed and contrary to the true English character. I think that every kind of prudery was completely absent from the older England, and that the ladies whose portraits were painted by Gainsborough and Reynolds were in many respects more freely natural than their French counterparts.

When you characterize the English public schools before Arnold as pure chaos then I think it must also be taken into consideration that the English are probably perfectly content to exist in, and can make something out of, a state of chaos that would drive a German or a Frenchman to despair. I think that they very seldom organize their ideas into any kind of system and I have frequently been astonished to see how difficult they find it to carry out any sort of systematic division, even for instance the index of a book. Hindenburg would have probably wrung his hands in despair if he had had to assume command of the British army in the middle of the war. It is perhaps questionable whether Dr. Arnold really succeeded in making the English youth of his day less brutal and more chivalrous, such progress is naturally not achieved overnight; although he probably did bring about more respectable conditions in the schools, he is considered, by Strachey, among others, to have had a philistine influence—or according to my own view, rendered them intellectually and morally doctrinaire.

In passing I would say that I almost get the impression that the English idolization of the monarchy belonged in essence to the Victorian period and began with Victoria herself. I do not believe that they worshiped their Stuarts and Hanoverians any more than we did the Oldenburgs. It seems likely that the great English nobility never held them in any great esteem, considering themselves to be superior, and even though they were restricted in numbers, such an element has its effect on the life and opinions of a nation. In this country there were not enough to make any considerable impression; in Sweden, as in France, the aristocracy—until the royal family made themselves impossible there—were grouped around the Court. But my knowledge of this is insufficient for further comment.

Perhaps you will say that I do not know enough about the Victorians to express myself at all on them. Of course that's true; but unless one has a particular intention in mind it is difficult to involve oneself in the serious study of a subject for which one feels little sympathy. There are some of them, however, Tennyson, Rossetti, the Brontës, for example, that I think I probably know as well as you do. But when it is a question of comparison one's knowledge of the other periods or personalities must surely carry some weight, and there I have really studied English history and literature and art fairly thoroughly.

If an idea can be elucidated in one word, I will finally sum up what I mean by saying that the Victorians in my opinion asserted their influence by making the English into "people with a purpose"—(if you know the expression; Rathenau or Erichsen uses it and bases an entire view of life on it)—but in themselves they are not so.

I do not think to have discovered any new or absolute truth in what I have said here and will be very satisfied if you think or say there may be something in it.

No events of any particular moment occurred in Karen Blixen's life during her long stay with her mother at Rungstedlund in 1925, apart from a brief spell in hospital. The family news that overshadowed everything else was Thomas Dinesen's engagement to Jonna Lindhardt. On Christmas Day Karen Blixen bade farewell to her relatives and friends, and her brother Thomas traveled with her to Antwerp, where she embarked on the "Springfontein"*. On 1 February 1926 she was back on the farm.*

1926

To Ingeborg Dinesen

Ngong 4/2.26

My own beloved Mother.

I've been back here at Ngong for four days and have still not written,—but it is because I have such a frightful cold that I can hardly see and have to take half a dozen towels to bed with me to cope with a nose that runs nonstop,—I think it is a kind of inflammation of the brain. I have had it, in fact, ever since Antwerp and think it is about time it stopped; but it seems to get worse instead, with a temperature and vomiting. . . . I have been all around the farm and it looks *fine;* if we can hold out until the next harvest all right all should be well. I have been in to see Hunter, too, on my last legs. I had lunch with Lady McMillan, who sends her best regards to you; she looked terrible. I have a constant stream of black people of all ages filing through my bedroom, the old woman has been here too, shedding floods of joyful tears. . . .

To Thomas Dinesen

Ngong. 24.Febr.26.

My own dear Tommy.

I should have replied to your letter, which was a great joy, long ago, but I have had such a cold, or, rather, whatever I should call the state of fever, coughing, sneezing, headache, and so on with which I have been afflicted for the past seven weeks,—(I think myself that it is a nervous condition caused by my not daring to be seasick in the Bay of Biscay)—that I have not managed to get through other than the most necessary things,—and when one returns to another quarter of the globe after an absence of almost a year they are not a few!—and only now am beginning to hope that I am strong enough to write a fairly reasonable letter. I have written several of them to you in my mind in varying moods; but this should turn out fairly lucid as I am much better now and after having been back about a month should be able to give a quite comprehensive view.

With this mail I had a very sweet letter from Jonna, which I would reply to if I could think of what might be of interest to her to hear about from this part of the world which is so completely unknown to her. When anything like that should happen, for instance, that the lions drag Mr. and Mrs. Dickens and the baby out of their house and I find their half-devoured corpses on the plains I will write to her at once; but for the present you must give her my grateful thanks for her letter, it was really touching of her to write. . . .

First of all I must send you warmest greetings from all the natives here, Somalis and Indians, who are your most devoted friends. There is not one who has not asked whether you were not coming out soon, and sighed and groaned when they heard that there was no likelihood of that in the immediate future. When I say that you have "pattat Ndito" ["found yourself a sweetheart"], they ask: "Modja tu?" [Only one?"] and probably think you deserve ten. Farah said that you were "very good, very good, very good,—*all people* say this, and when I said yes, for you were not kali, he said in a very superior way: "Not this,—many other people not kali, but Thomas quite different, his *word* more good than big contract with other white men."

Poor Sing was very pleased with his watch, although he had a suspicion that it was not silver, much to Farah's indignation. Kinanjui was also bursting with gratitude for his baksheesh of 20 shillings. But I have not given Juma the 20 intended for him, because I suspected him,—indeed, that is putting it mildly,—of having stolen the shirt buttons I had promised you, and which now to my chagrin I have to admit I cannot send you. The case for them was here, but it was empty! I am most extremely annoyed , because they were really nice and I did want you to have them. I don't think Juma is really responsible for his actions in such matters; he can do the most extraordinary things. Of course it *may* have been one of Denys's boys,—if not he himself,—who has taken them; but I have lost a number of things like this before and think everything indicates a house thief. . . .

I see that "The Revenge of Truth" has still not appeared in "Tilskueren" magazine. I wonder if they have changed their minds and not accepted it after all? Please could you find out from them, and also tear "Jacques" away from Holstein,—he might have shown some sort of reaction to it, don't you think? However, *if* "T.R.O.T." does finally come out, would you please send it together with the enclosed letter to old Georg?—I would like him to see it and perhaps have a word from him about it. Even if it should have appeared in the March number I would like to ask you to send him the letter; you could then perhaps add a few words to it saying that I had sent it to you but that it had been unexpectedly delayed.

Unfortunately, I feel far from fit enough to get going on "Elmis Hjerte" or anything else; it is seldom that I have felt so devoid of energy for work and life as I do now, I don't really know why it can be. I must hope that it will soon be over, and that I will be able to send you both a new book and a painting that can at least to a certain extent remind you of this country, but it won't be for a while yet; just now I feel that I will never have the strength to walk down to the dam again. . . .

Denys is still on safari but I am expecting him soon. I have had a couple of letters from him; I think he was very pleased to be staying here, all his friends say they couldn't drag him away from Ngong. He is going home, because his father is ill,—it is so sad for him; it is two years since he went home and his mother died. He invited a great many people out here; at least they have the politeness to say that it "was always you we came out to dine with,—but it was ghastly without you, like a haunted house." Naturally I am very much looking forward to seeing Denys again, only I hope I will be better by the time he arrives. . . .

I can't tell you how much I should like you to have something to do with the "League of Nations" and perhaps in time take up the question of the natives' interests here. I am so angry with the English because they want to impose higher taxes on them, they are talking about a kopftax of 20 shillings; it is disgraceful when you think that the most a man can earn is about 150 shillings a year; if only people at home could get to know about it, but this country is so amazingly outside the bounds of law and justice. The upper classes have not improved in the least since the revolution; when they are not *afraid* of the lower classes they are really completely without shame; the natives can be starving here and dying of starvation, and the Governor is building a new Government House for £80,000, and the champagne flows in torrents at their races and so on.—Lord Delamere recently held a dinner for 250 people at which they drank 600 bottles,—and they just do not *see* it; the ladies here are quite capable of asking, when they hear that the natives cannot get posho, why they do not eat wheat or rice instead, just like Marie Antoinette, who asked why the poor did not eat cake if they could not get bread. One loses patience with them, and it is regrettable, because I think it is a pity that the concept of "ruling class" should vanish; but it has vanished already, of course, and not merely through their own fault.

Now and again I long for you so much, to talk to about all these things, that I feel as if I will burst,—I dare not talk to any of the English, I think my influence here as a woman and a foreigner must be strictly confined to being an example; if I start to preach I shall lose my power, which must be won through being a hostess and friend; even my glasses and my big cupboard must work in my mission for my "black brothers", but the "example" takes effect so slowly, and sometimes one feels like firing off a broadside right in their silly faces, when that typical English stupidity starts braying too loudly!

I have read a nice book: "The Constant Nymph," by Margaret Kennedy, which is also really amusing, a rare thing in a book, and a slim volume of poems, "A Shropshire Lad," both of which I recommend to you, if you can get them.

Please let Mother read some of this and explain to her that she will not be getting a letter this time because I don't feel up to it; I have had to stay in bed again for several days, but I don't think it has helped so now I have got up again. I have had a temperature of 104 and such a sore throat.

To end up with I will just write a few words about myself. I think it was true when you said that the right thing for me to do was to come out here,—meaning that I considered my future to lie here; because I had no alternative to coming out here. I belong here and should be here. Much, perhaps most, of my heart is in this country, and I must just get accustomed to loneliness and other things here; and the things that drew me toward home, being without shauries, uncertainty, and difficulties, being as it were wrapped in cotton wool, are not in fact the right things for me. But now I want to ask you,—without meaning that I expect anything superhuman from you,—to help me to manage to stay here, as much as you can. I *could not stand another transplanting* now, it would take far too much out of me,—I really believe that I would die, or what corresponds to dying, of the strain and suffering it would involve. If, when I was home this time, I had not considered the possibility of staying at home, it would not have been so hard for me to leave and such an effort to come back here; indeed, I sometimes still have the feeling that I *am* at home in Denmark, and that I am imagining everything here,—somehow my center of gravity has not yet really been transferred, though no doubt it will have been soon. But when I said that I "hated" it here, of course it was not the country or the people or the conditions I meant,—I don't hate them, I love them, as you know,—but the state of uncertainty that I have been living in out here, and that I really can't take any more. When my heart has once more been firmly rooted here it cannot be pulled up yet again.

You have understood me better and helped me more than anyone else in my life; now you must understand and help me so much again that you must realize and agree that I cannot be moved again merely because of exterior circumstances. You must concur with me, and if necessary support me in seeing that a bullet would be the more decent solution for me than becoming, in this earthly existence, like a fly in a bottle.

It is blowing from over the Athi Plains, and the hyenas are howling quite close by. Everywhere is green after the rains and the woods and maize fields are fragrant. The moon is rising from behind the coffee, the whole sky is filled with great white clouds,—I am sure you can remember this African night. Everything sends many many greetings to you who were once here too.

Always always your faithful old friend Tanne.

To Ingeborg Dinesen

Ngong. March 7th 26

My own beloved Mother.

Although I know it is disgraceful to be so preoccupied with the state of one's health I must begin this letter by reporting with much pleasure that I am better again and think that I have at last recovered from the mysterious disease that afflicted me in the Bay of Biscay and really made me extremely miserable up to now. It is marvelous to feel one's strength returning; it was beginning to be quite insufferable. . . .

You must know how much I am thinking of you just now. By the time you get this letter it will not be long before Tommy's wedding day, and I know how much that moves and delights you. . . . I think that it is strangely unreasonable that even though the human race has after all existed for many thousands of years and we ourselves are in possession of a considerable amount of human experience, we cannot accustom ourselves without pain to the fact that something is over and past, although one has always been aware that everything must come to an end and one's common sense tells one it should not be wished otherwise. When one goes to a fine concert one is not in a state of utter despair when it comes to an end and one gets up to go, and when one has eaten a really delicious meal one can see the coffee arriving without pain; but where certain things in life are concerned one's whole being rebels at the idea of an ending; and there is a built-in instinct that demands endlessness and will not accept compromise. Perhaps we will attain this infinity in the end. . . .

I have had the great joy and happiness of having Denys here for two days and so have nothing more to ask of life. . . .

The following letter, which was never finished, was not sent off immediately. Karen Blixen mailed it to her brother five months later, enclosed with her letter of 5 September 1926, to provide evidence of the crisis she had been through shortly after her return to the farm. Although printed chronologically in this edition, the two letters should preferably be read together.

To Thomas Dinesen

Ngong. 1/4.26

My own old Tommy.

Now I must start by thanking you for the telegram announcing your wedding, and wishing you with all, all my heart every possible happiness. My thoughts are constantly with you and Jonna; on this solemn occasion there can be no one who desires more fervently for you and her all the riches that life can offer, harmony and contentment, real, real love and understanding in all the eventualities of life, excitement and experience, to mature and grow older believing in and in concord with ever living poetry. There are so many people who love you, but not one of them to whom you have been more than to me; no one who thinks of your friendship, your understanding and help with more gratitude than I do. God bless you, my true brother, and Jonna,—may you have a long, bright future before you, and may you come to celebrate your silver, gold and diamond wedding anniversaries, filled with an ever richer, deeper and truer love, and with each year an increasing store of great and wonderful, vivid, marvelous inward and outward experiences and memories.

Thank you so much for your letter, which made me very happy. It is always good to hear from you, and except for the news of Jonna's illness, which was a great shame, but which I take it is now a thing of the past, all was joyful and happy, and it is lovely to have a letter like that. I only hope that all the letters I may get from you in the years to come,—and if we both go on living I hope there will be a vast number of them,—may be equally good. I am thinking of some of the letters from you that I have had in the past, especially one from Oxford two years ago, and rejoice so much at the comparison; not only because I am glad to know *you* are happy but because I can see that life can offer so much light after darkness; that the books that have a "happy ending" and reward virtue are not wrong; that there really can be hope for all those who now. . .look upon life with fear and despair, without hope.

And now, after that, I will go on to write about what you may perhaps be sorry to read. I shall begin by saying that when I received your telegram I had one here ready to send to you, which ran thus: "Will you help me to get to Europe, I shall die if remaining here."—and the only thing that stopped me from sending it was the thought that it would make an odd reply to your telegram. And then of course it is only pure despair that makes one send that kind of thing by telegraph; there is time enough, and it is more reasonable to send it to you in a letter, and by this time, when this letter gets to you, you will no doubt be at Rungstedlund again after a few lovely weeks with your young wife, to celebrate Mother's seventieth birthday; even though it may not be a particularly suitable occasion for such melancholy outpourings at least I know that you will be reading them in such happy surroundings that you will not find it too harrowing. I *must* write and I don't know whom else to write to, besides you; to whom can I speak sincerely if not you? To be forced to silence, as I am here, when one has great difficulties, as I have now, feels as if one is buried alive, and you must imagine me as if you saw me lying in darkness with the weight of the earth on my breast, and forgive me for this screaming.

When I was at home and we were discussing my plans I think that both of us were right: you in saying that there was no sense in my staying at home in Denmark, at Rungstedlund,—and I that there was no sense for me in coming back here. If either of us was *more right* than the other—it was *you;* it would have been madness for me to settle down at home with Mother. That I could think of this as a possibility at all can only be explained by the special circumstances: that I was at home on holiday after so many years and was in a mood that encouraged me to value comfort and peacefulness very highly; that I knew all the time it was not to be for long so that I was never in need of thinking ahead to some sort of work or in any way a continued existence; and even the fact that it was such a particularly lovely summer had a great influence on my view of Denmark and life there. But it was completely wrong. Now I am at a distance from it and have had time to think things over—and I can assure you that I have been struggling unceasingly, on the boat out and since I got back here, to come to a clear view, and I think I have achieved a more comprehensive one; I must try to write to someone to whom I can speak absolutely frankly and truthfully from my present standpoint,—that is why I am sending you this letter now.

You may remember that I said several times at home that I have constantly pondered upon *when* it actually was that I first got on to the wrong track that led me to the point where I am now, that is, at the end of my resources,—and that I could never decide on that; was it when I got engaged to Bror?—when we decided to come out here?—at some point out here? As I look at it now I can see that it was at none of these points in my life, but much earlier, I could almost say at my entry into this world.

I think it was a great misfortune for me to grow up and come to belong to the family, the milieu, the "outlook on life" into which I was born. You must realize that I say this without the least reproach toward any of them at home, and with no wish to criticize except as much as one can criticize everything and anything; I don't know of any better, nicer, sweeter people than everyone at home, it was just that they did not suit me. And their great unlimited goodness and love for me, all the kindnesses they showered upon me were only so many misfortunes the more. They made it impossible for me to show any opposition. You remember we have talked about the strange power that Mama,—probably especially in her time where her own children were concerned,—and Mother over us, had to render any criticism, any contradiction, impossible, to make impossible even one's private thoughts that Mother might ever make a mistake, so that it might have been better to dispute with her; this particular capacity has been a fatal influence in my life. If, for instance, you had grown up under the influence of Uncle Laurentzius, the moment would inevitably have come when your *convictions* would have driven you to emancipate yourself; this, which would have been the one right thing for me, was made impossible for me by the whole of that atmosphere at home. The weak attempts that I did make at it as a child and young girl seemed to me in the light of that air to be deeds of darkness.

I do not say that it made me unhappy, but all my abilities were destroyed by it; any possibility for me to live and act, achieve something *as myself* came to nothing because of it. Now, when I think that I can see and judge the whole situation clearly, I am left with an enormously great debt to all of them,—or rather: to that particular *spirit*, for a completely undeserved amount of love and indulgence,—but on the reverse side of the account: with a claim against it for that period of my life, childhood and youth, where there were possibilities for me to become something, especially to become self-supporting, independent of them,—of which they deprived me, and which I cannot see now how I am to make up for.

I think it is possible to live at home and be very happy there if one can, like the Merman with Agnete, "stop one's mouth and one's ears" against the whole of the outside world. I think that is what all of them at home do, with the greatest harmony. When Aunt Bess writes to me and talks about Mama, about Mother, about you and Uncle Aage as the noblest people in the world, about Magleaas, about Folehave,—then I can see that it is possible to live in this way and be happy, useful, develop oneself in the best way possible and thereby spread happiness and harmony around one. *It is just not possible for me.* (That

I believed for a moment last summer that it really would be possible, and felt tempted to do it, was an extremely odd, if perhaps understandable, illusion.)

Can you remember us talking about Lucifer in Knuthenborg Park?—Well, I am convinced that Lucifer is the angel whose wings should be hovering over me. And we know that the only solution for Lucifer was rebellion, and then the fall to his own kingdom. In Paradise,—if he had remained there,—he would have cut a poor figure. But Lucifer had greater stature than the undersigned, his humble servant who remained in Paradise and who cuts a poor figure there now, indeed, who has been annihilated in it.

Lucifer did have the advantage of being immortal, and possibly with him there could not be talk of lost time or neglected opportunities. Perhaps he neglected several opportunities for rebellion; but that did not matter. He did not grow too old, either to learn or study something, to "begin on something," to marry into different conditions, or actually to have the energy to get hold of something new.

Now I am able to see many opportunities when I ought to have made a break with that special Paradise, in which anyway I played my part so badly. For instance, I should have insisted on taking the Student Examination. That would not in theory have been directly against the spirit of the Paradise; But it would have turned out like that in practice *because of the way in which I wanted it.* (When I tried to get started in that direction, at the Academy, I was put in charge of the Plums, an offshoot of the Paradise, and I can remember how insecure and guilty I felt, for instance at our "Student Society Carnivals," which I ought to have greatly enjoyed.) Later on I ought to have got married,—or tried to, —to old Hoskier in Paris. Or I should have run away with some man or other in Rome. It was simply contemptible of me not to do so, and lack of Lucifer's vision; but at the time I could not see this, for I saw the whole of life as it is expressed in Captain Brun's simile of the matches,—which I think is the Paradise view of life to this very day. The same is true of my pathetic "authorship." I cannot, I cannot *possibly* write anything of the slightest interest without breaking away from the Paradise and hurtling down to my own kingdom. "The Revenge of Truth" is a miniature of that, you know; I wrote that in Rome. But the little African travel descriptions that the Flensburg newspaper is kindly waiting for are meant to be mimicry of the angels' hymns of praise, and I can't do this sort of thing anymore; they turn into mbuni ["coffee waste"] before my pen can touch them.

You can say two things to me as you raise your eyes from the paper having read this far.

Denys Finch Hatton on Poor Box, photographed by Karen Blixen.

In front of the natives' huts: in the center from left, Juma, Isa, Hassan Ismael, Abdullai, and Kamante (with the dogs) (photograph by Thomas Dinesen).

The African farm, 1923 (photograph by Thomas Dinesen).

Karen Blixen dressed for a party, about 1923 (photograph by Thomas Dinesen).

Kikuyus dressed for a ngoma, about 1923 (photograph by Thomas Dinesen).

Juma with children and young people on the farm (photograph by Denys Finch Hatton).

Dickens and his daughter Anne on Peter.

Ingeborg Dinesen, Karen Blixen, and Farah with Juma's son Tumbo on the farm, 1925.

Ingeborg Dinesen on the farm with the tame owl Minerva, 1925 (photograph by Thomas Dinesen).

Ingeborg Dinesen and Chief Kinanjui attend a ngoma, January 1925.

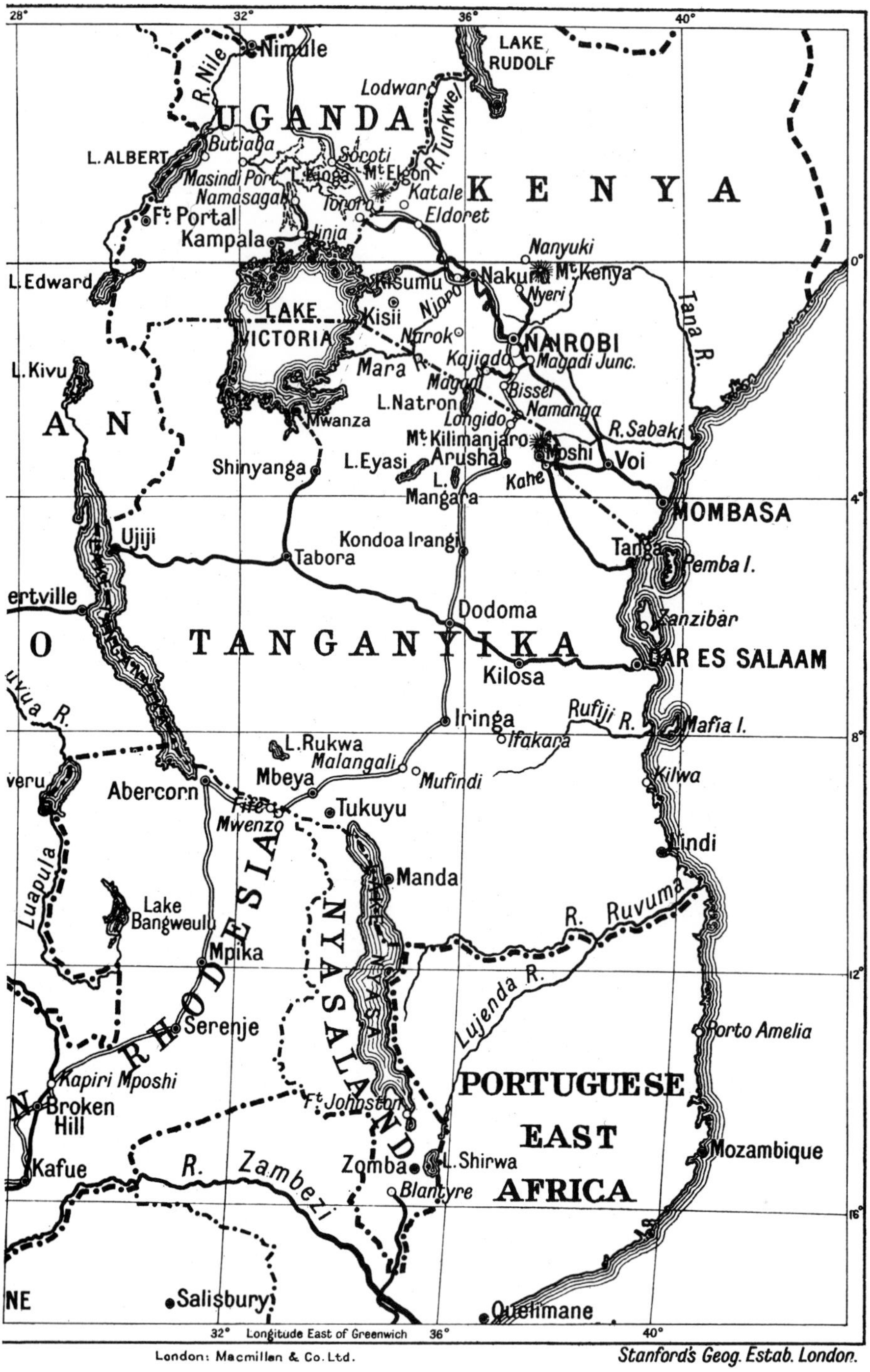

East Africa in 1926.

Lord Delamere, 1870–1931.

The farm office (photograph by Thomas Dinesen).

The future Delamere Avenue, Nairobi, in the 1920s.

Farah on board one of the ships in which Karen Blixen sailed home to Denmark (photograph by Thomas Dinesen).

Farah with his son Saufe.

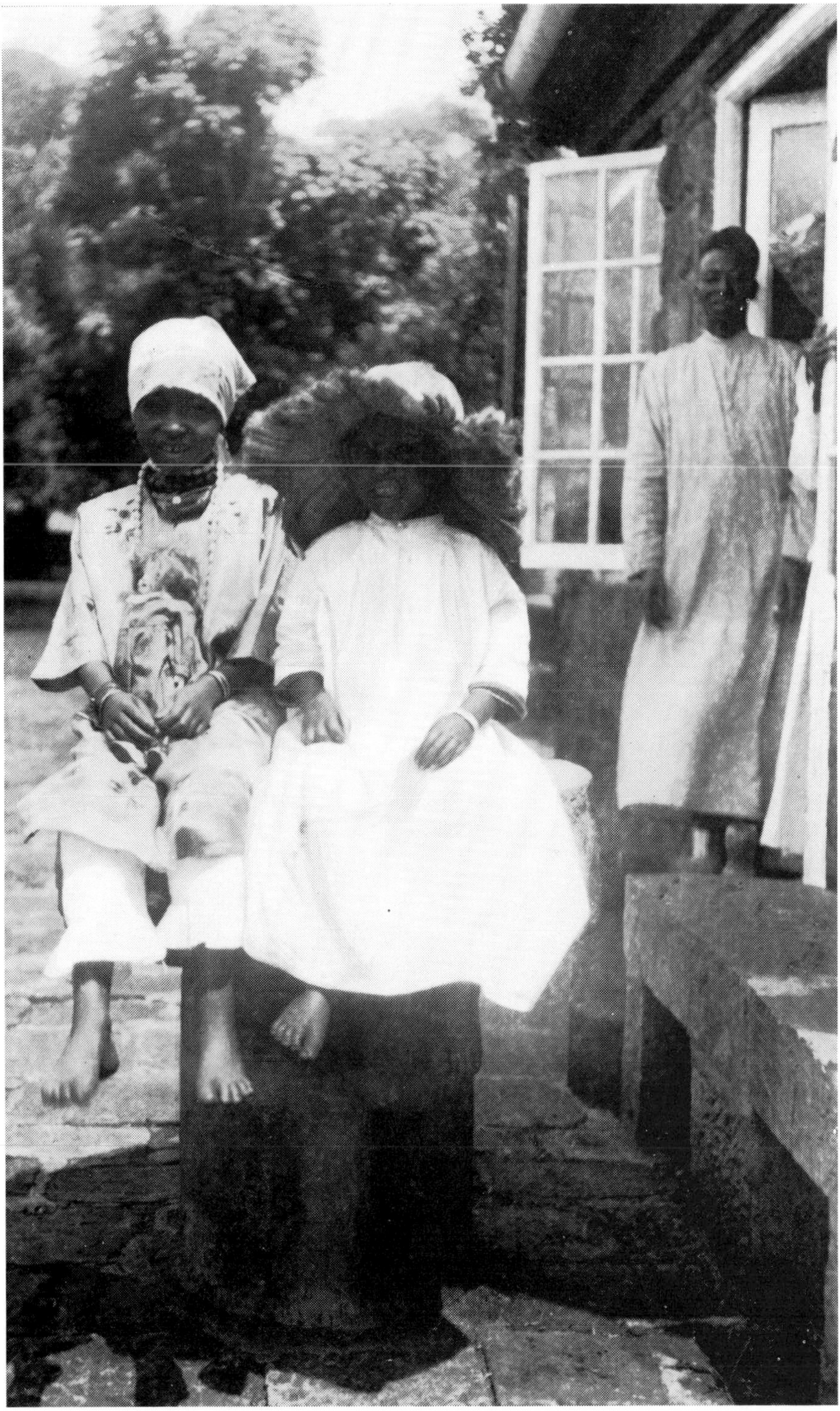

Juma's children Tumbo and Halima on the millstone in front of the farm. In the background is Juma himself (photograph by Denys Finch Hatton).

Karen Blixen and flowering coffee bush.

Denys Finch Hatton's car being pulled out of a river in which it had stuck.

Karen Blixen driving Finch Hatton's car (photograph by Denys Finch Hatton).

Denys Finch Hatton with Rose and Algy Cartwright.

Young people on the farm at the close of the 1920s.

The first is: You have been an incomparable idiot, a fool, a lunatic to such an extent that you really can be compared to that Lucifer you mention. With the spirit of Lucifer still alive in the Universe and represented on every side of you you have allowed yourself to be completely paralyzed by a pleasant, loving, infinitely kindly family milieu, certainly at most numbering some hundreds of thousands of people in amiable, most cordially tolerant Denmark. I have nothing to reply to this reproach except "amen, amen." It is true, I have never met such a foolish person as she who writes these lines; God preserve everyone from coming to see themselves in such a light of the purest idiocy and turpitude.

The other remark that you can make and that any honest person would have to make on reading this, is this: Cross out all your past idiocy and do immediately what you ought to have done long ago,—rise in that revolt that no longer is a revolt because in fact every sensible person assumes that at your age you are your own master, and go to hell, if that is where you feel you belong.

Yes, I would like to do it. But "that which I would, I do not, and that which I would not do, I do." And one of the reasons preventing me from doing it is that I cannot see the way. I am beginning to believe, with Sophus Claussen, that "there is no longer a staircase to hell," and that "the Devil is expensive to talk to, a sparkling glimpse of his fiery tail of stars costs more than most people can pay,"—or that, however it may be with "most people," I personally have squandered those assets of youth, of time, of work, of personality with which I could once have paid for it,—and am now left insolvent.

I seem to have waded rather too deep into similes and philosophy with all this. So now I will put down as clearly as I can how the situation looks to me at the moment, and ask you to give me some advice.

CONTINUED 3/4.26

Dear Tommy. I foresee that this letter may end up by being just as long and far less interesting than Rousseau's "Confessions," and I feel that it is wrong to demand that you read it. But I will continue nevertheless, because I feel real relief and a feeling of well-being,—which is unusual,—from having started on it and come thus far. Perhaps when I have come to the end of it I can quite simply not send it so that you are spared having to read it. But now while I write I must have the feeling of addressing my letter to someone, which in this case means you, as I know no one else to whom I could write so frankly and from whom I could expect understanding.

To begin where I left off I will try to give you an impression of my situation as it is at this moment, April 1926.

Denys has been here for a fortnight and is now going home to Europe, that is, I expect him to be here tomorrow and the day after tomorrow and then he is to leave from Nairobi on Tuesday.

During the time he has been here I have, as on similar occasions previously, been in a state of quite perfect bliss, mixed with a state of quite perfect despair, at the thought that he is leaving again so soon and that I may possibly never see him again.

The results of these varying states of mind is complete awareness that he is the only person who means anything to me in life and that my whole existence revolves around this relationship as around an axis, which means that it offers the possibilities of what is called heaven or hell, with very abrupt transitions.

But I will not and cannot continue to go on living in this way, with this single element in my life; it is an intolerable situation and I find it impossible to allow my immediate future to take the form of six months of utter desolation, emptiness and darkness, with the hope of seeing him again in the autumn, and being lifted up to the same unqualified happiness, only to be cast back into desolation and darkness—and so on and so on for infinity.

I know that you have said that it is worth being utterly miserable for some time and then having this followed by utter happiness. From the purely mathematical point of view this might well produce a balance, for instance if someone agreed to lie in a perfumed bath and listen to the loveliest music in the world for six hours, and then to be put on the rack for the next six (and so on); but in practice this is quite simply impossible as a modus vivendi because one cannot thus isolate oneself from past and future; before very long one's whole existence would turn into chaos and destroy one.

I doubt that it is feasible at all to "live on" a passion, as the saying goes,—I mean, that one can do it for more than a short space of time. But even if that were so, this relationship is not at all merely a passion; it should comprise and include far, far more. If this relationship should come to be my only possession in life, if I should come to it completely empty-handed, without any other interests, experiences, new ideas or impressions, then it would change from being the most joyful friendship, the loveliest sympathy and understanding I can imagine, into a purely physical hunger and its satisfaction, and I will not allow that to happen; and anyway it would never last only in that manner, it would burn out in no time.

No, you see, I must *be myself,* be something in myself, have, own something that is really mine, achieve something that is mine and is me, in order to be able to live at all, and in order to be able to have, and hope to continue to have, the indescribable happiness in my life that my love for Denys is to me. And I do not have that here, now,—I have and am nothing at all; I have betrayed my angel Lucifer and sold my soul to the angels in Paradise, and yet I cannot live in it; I don't belong, I have no place to be anywhere in the world, and yet I must stay in it; I hate and dread each minute and yet they come, one after the other; in short, it is sheer misery, and if I came to hear about it I would not believe it possible to live in such a manner.

You must not think that I am so spineless that I have not considered whether it would not be best if I were to take my life, and been prepared to do so if I really came to the conclusion that it was. Surely the greatest coward in the world would be prepared to do it to escape such a life as I have now. But I do not think that it would help. For what I long for is after all life, and what I fear and take flight from is emptiness and annihilation,—and what else can one hope to achieve by dying? I want so terribly to live, I want so terribly not to die.

But if I intend, or am going to try, to go on living, it has got to be in some way or other. Can I envisage, then, the possibility of leaving here and living,—what I would call living,—in some other place? Or can I envisage the possibility of living,—what I would call living,—here?

It occurs to me that I ought perhaps to explain in more detail what I mean by the symbolic expression Lucifer, so that it does not appear as if it means that I am longing for something wild and demonic, or be misunderstood in some other way.

I conceive of it as meaning: truth, or the search for truth, striving toward the light, a critical attitude,—indeed, what one means by *spirit*. The opposite of settling down believing that what one cares for is and must be best, indeed, settling into the studied calm, satisfaction and uncritical atmosphere of the Paradise. And in addition to this: work,—I think I can work longer and get less tired than most people,—a *sense of humor* which is afraid of *nothing*, but has the *courage of its convictions* to make fun of everything, and life, new light, variety.

And here I am living in an idyll which is only an idyll because I *want* to make it one!

Ah, do you think, do you think, Tommy, that I can still "become something," and that I have not thrown away all the chances life has offered me and have nothing left to look forward to but to fade and go to seed, have patience myself and hope that others will be patient with me for being an utter failure?

You must not reply just to comfort me by saying that I *have* "become something" and do *not* try the patience of my fellow men and so on—

that would be the worst thing you could say when I myself do know how things stand, and that I am on the verge of what is generally known as going to the dogs.

But if you can think of any way out for me, please write and tell me and I will be grateful to you all my life.

There are of course such terribly great, almost insuperable difficulties in getting me into any kind of profession or any sort of "job," because there is nothing whatsoever I can do.

But isn't it frightful that honorable people can allow someone to grow up,—merely because they belong to the female sex,—without learning *anything at all?* I believe that I was of above average intelligence as a child and I was *eager to learn,* mathematics, for instance, I really think I had talent for that; but while my family was eager to teach me moral conduct and unselfishness it never occurred to them to have me taught more arithmetic than Miss Zøylner could manage! Mama and Miss Zøylner were my teachers, and from the time we returned from Switzerland,—where we had learned nothing at all,—and I was fourteen, I learned absolutely nothing. Even though they knew,—which was never really clear to me,—that I would not be in such a position that would allow me to live without earning anything myself. Of course I should have decided for myself; but here again I met with that strange opposition to everything that was in any way outside the narrow circle of home, and that peculiar power they had of always making one feel in the wrong when one stood out against them. What were they thinking of? I suppose they really thought that our future lay in marriage. If only they had arranged that properly. I do not think it would have been at all hard to marry me off; I think that a good match, an estate, for instance, would have tempted me a lot. But I was given no chances. For we never met any good matches. . . .

But it would have hardly been possible to air the idea of a marriage of convenience at home. It is as if they seemed to put their trust in love. But should a person's future be left entirely to a feeling like that? And what if one never comes to fall in love? Or falls in love and is not loved in return? Or falls in love and is loved? Is it right to come to it entirely empty-handed, without resources of any kind, without oneself knowing, or having learned, anything? Even married life itself has a practical side. We knew nothing of housekeeping, accounts, how to entertain. And we were cut off so much from the world that we had nothing at all to hang on to that could give us a start; I went to Paris without a letter or a single introduction, and when I was staying with the Plums in Copenhagen I did not know of any other house except for Aunt Ida's and Aunt Ellinor's where I could go the evening. But of course all this is neither here nor there.

You will have to try to put yourself in my place—that is to say that at this moment you found yourself without money and without *any kind of* training, to be able to understand how I am feeling.

Do you think that from the purely practical point of view it is possible to rescue me from this situation? Do you think that it would be possible for me, at my age, with for instance a year's training, for which it should be possible for me to get help, to get into something that I could live on and that would be a profession that suited me and for which I could use the abilities that I have?

In spite of endless "draw-backs" I do have one advantage, that regard for convention is not of the slightest importance to me. I would be happy to go into the white slave trade if I saw an opening for me there; I would also gladly go to China as a missionary. I want to be where there is life and where I can make use of my strength and abilities, if I have any left. I know that you think I could write. And I think that I could, if I could come to find myself in circumstances where I could be open to impressions that would help me to be inventive again.

Will you give some thought to this? You must not think that I am so desperate,—although I am desperate,—that if you give me *hope* I shall go and hang myself because it will take a year before anything can be done. Even though time, time passes and *never* comes back;—alas, if only, instead of embarking on that cursed ship, I had taken the train for Paris at Antwerp and bought newspapers to sell on the street!

CONTINUED

To Ingeborg Dinesen

Ngong. 4th April. 26.

. . . I feel that I have no words to express what I wish when I think of you and everyone at Rungsted on your seventieth birthday. Congratulations, you beloved young Mother, on having lived so long and cast joy and blessings around you every single moment, on being surrounded now by so many for whom you are the clear light of life, and on being as you are, as charming with your white hair now as you were as a young girl and a bride at Matrup, ready to climb Africa's mountains and dare the heat of the Red Sea just as much as to play the hardest music and embroider the finest design, so filled with wisdom and experience, and yet so young that your daughters feel themselves old and dry beside you,—in short, just like the Master of Ballantrae,

A MASTER OF THE ARTS AND GRACES,
ADMIRED IN EUROPE AND AFRICA,
IN WAR AND PEACE,
IN THE TENTS OF THE SAVAGE HUNTERS AND THE CITADELS OF KINGS. . .

I have always felt that when I went into a beech wood it was as if I met and walked along with you; now I think that your whole life is like a wood, every year, each day a tree that you have planted and which stands straight and tall and shades us. I thank you and bless you for everything that you have been and are; my heart is at Rungsted, and my hand lifts a chocolate cup together with all the others who are feting you.

Greetings to all, including Malla, and feel my arms around you.

Your Tanne.

To Ingeborg Dinesen

Ngong. May 4th. 1926

. . . It is amazing that you are seventy,—but no doubt that is what everyone is saying to you,—and it is strange to think of all that a human life actually is, when on such a day as this one sees the whole of it at once, somehow gathered together; that you are so many people, the little girl who was born on the 5th of May at Matrup, without doubt to the great joy of the young Papa and Mama, and the young bride who celebrated her last birthday as a young girl forty-five years ago,—and Mitten's grandmother and Jonna's mother-in-law and Tumbo's Memsabo mesei. . . .

I have so often felt, when I heard that someone had died,—at that moment one feels that they have ceased to exist at a single, isolated point in their existence, but their life, their personality becomes a completed reality, and they are equally alive in every phase of it, something in the same way as when one is watching a play at the theater and is absorbed in the individual scenes and acts as they are being performed, but as soon as the curtain falls, regards and judges the play as a whole. And one can do this on such an occasion as your seventieth birthday, perhaps especially when one is so far away; one looks upon these seventy years as *a life*. . . .

I am annoyed because I have had to stay in bed again, and because I am really not at all well and have not been since I took ship at Antwerp. It is getting really tiring. I cannot say that I am actually ill, but so immensely tired, and not fit for anything at all. I have never felt anything like it before, it is as if it's too much trouble to live, and I can't tell how it is going to develop. Except for the time when Denys was here I have been feeling like this ever since I left home. . . .

My school is not going well, and if it were not a matter of honor toward Dickens and others I would be very inclined to give it up. I do not think that the natives here are sufficiently mature for this sort of education yet,—it is as if they have to jump over a stage that we in our long, slow development from barbarians to civilized people have had to go through; I sometimes get the feeling that through a kind of impatience we deliberately allow them to come into the world prematurely and then put them in an incubator, which would be a terrible thing to do in the flesh, and for which one would doubtless be punished. I am not certain that the kiboko is not healthier for them at present.

I have arrived at this view of everything connected with education not from a predilection for corporal punishment but in order to avoid what is worse, because what has always been most abhorrent to me is to "work upon" people's "feelings"; and if one wants to achieve any sort of result, change, or development, some means or other must be employed; the clay must be worked malleable before it can be formed. Let the realities take effect, primitive natures are able to understand them rather than the reasoning deduced by the far more highly developed races from the realities; to me it seems that to force these upon children or natives is like feeding them on predigested, regurgitated food. I think that this method of education is far from being more merciful; one imposes far more suffering on a child by driving it *into* him that he has made Mother terribly unhappy and so on,—if he really must be made to feel this, otherwise it is pure hypocrisy and insincerity,—than by the hardest slap.

When, for instance, I hear Father Bernhard proudly recounting that a group of boys from the English Mission came to him and declared that they wanted to join his mission because they had been reading the Bible, and could not possibly accept that the bread and wine only *represented*, and was not *transformed* into the body and blood of Christ,—I cannot help being really grieved that shortsighted people interfere in a completely superficial and irresponsible manner and confuse the really good, healthy, well-balanced native disposition, and spoon feed a spineless, artificial type that it will take generations to get rid of again. . . .

Ngong.13/5.26.

. . . I think that this especially, if you like "heroic,"—for this is what I believe Tommy's disposition is,—type of character can live and thrive very well and harmoniously in a calm, even, workaday life, outwardly exactly like any bourgeois, just as it is seen in scientists,—in contrast to artists; I don't think it works for them—and I would far, far rather see Thomas settle down and go on living a life like that than see him,—since he has chosen a girl like Jonna and must and will cleave to her as she to him,—playing with or,—well, it is not the right word but the best I can think of,—pandering to "adventure." By doing that I think he would do harm to himself and harm to Jonna by forcing her to do things that might upset her equilibrium. The fact, as you write that he mentioned, that Jonna dared to get engaged to him knowing neither what he "was," nor where he lived, does not in my opinion show an urge for adventure, but what any good, innocent, simple young girl might have shown: a deep trust in the man she had come to love; in this case I think too, faith in her innermost heart that he will also be satisfactory with regard to "being something" and finding her a place to live and arranging her life in the best way,—and I do not consider not getting a flat in good time, and setting off on a three-month honeymoon by car is of any importance.

Adventure—yes, what is it? It is no special caper, it can appear in a perfectly ordinary guise, as homely as the folksongs and the sagas, that grew out of the everyday life of the time; in its most hidden and noblest form it will always be at Thomas's side, because he is a "hero"; it may also come to show itself as clear as day at his right hand at the moment when his *conviction* drives him from hearth and home and country to take up some work or other that to him represents the highest that could be offered him; but I think that we who love him can be quite sure even when we see him living day after day in a Copenhagen apartment with birthday chocolates for the Rothe children and trips to the Deer Park when mother-in-law comes to visit,—that it will *always* be the glorious things of life that mean most to him. . . .

I think that Tommy "carries too heavy weight" to turn somersaults and has an intensely sober nature, which ought to shun "intoxication." I have often thought that I,—who can turn somersaults and love all kinds of intoxicating drink,—perhaps without knowing it, and quite definitely without wishing it, may have harmed him; but good Lord, then he was young and single, and one must make some mistakes in one's life, and anyway now I am far away and wiser. I think that now he is making a new start in life the most vital thing for him is to be true, to be *so* true that he will be resigned to giving up "being smart." I don't think it will be entirely easy for him,—for Tommy has been spoiled where this is concerned,—but I would dearly like to help him in this, because I think he will find real happiness in this school, and preserve and develop the best in himself.

As you can imagine, what you write about Mitten . . . has been much in my thoughts. . . . I think on the whole it is true of every side of upbringing that the behavior and effect of one individual is fairly hard for another to understand, and that all children, when they come to years of discretion, look back on much of the treatment that was handed out to them,—both thoughtlessly and after the deepest reflection on the part of parents and guardians,—with amazement and with no more apparent reason to them than that is how it was, and yet they cannot doubt that there was love and good will in the relationship. . . . With a beloved and especially precious little one like Missen one may certainly wish to keep the wind and the frost away from her and to stop the onset of night, and yet one knows that it is a *good* thing that one cannot do so; for even the wind and the frost and the darkness have a mission in the service of life and bring encouragement and benefit, so that if one did have the power one would come to restrict and harm the one one loves. . . . You must not feel guilty about all the love and richness that you pour over Missen at Rungsted, but let it bring joy to her life,—and then you must take into account that no upbringing in the world would escape criticism if watched with intense interest and concern by someone who loved the child deeply but was outside the sphere of the daily influence,—and quite rightly.

I think that life teaches one that one should not be too inclined to think that what is good, pleasant, sensible for oneself is necessarily so for others; not in such a way that one ends up by humbly acknowledging that the methods of others are better, but by taking it for granted that they are equally good and being able to see the good and the beautiful expressed in every possible different form; as for instance one can see,—something that is impossible immediately after one's arrival in this country, but perfectly obvious when one has learned to realize it,—that a ndito is beautifully and elegantly dressed for a ball when she has smeared red clay all over herself and just shaved her head. I think, if I may say so, that it is a great pleasure in life to be able to see its beauty, joy, and harmony expressed in constantly varying forms. . . .

I did not manage to write last Sunday because I have had such a bad cold and been confined to bed. If I am not extremely careful all the time,—and that is almost impossible in the rainy season,—I get a cold like the one I caught on the boat, and such pain in my head and ears. I think I must have a kind of chronic inflammation somewhere in the head, and if I were at home they would no doubt advise an operation; but I dare not on any account let them do it here, and no doubt it will pass in time. . . .

I went in yesterday to see four airplanes, the first that have been here, arrive from Kisumu,—two hours' flying time!! They landed at Dagoretti Junction; there must have been a thousand cars and countless crowds of people to see them arrive. They were *beautiful* when they came rushing past,—but the whole thing was quite spoiled for me because it was not until I got into Nairobi that I heard they were coming, and could not manage to fetch my totos in time to see them; we had been there the previous day in our best clothes, but they did not come. It says something for the kindness of the English that almost every European car was loaded with houseboys and totos. . . .

To Ellen Dahl

Ngong. 16th May. 1926.

. . . I want to reply at once to what you write about having "The Revenge of Truth" performed. Nothing would please me more. Both Poul Levin,—what is the matter with that sheeny, not printing it in "Tilskueren" magazine?—and Ludvig Holstein talked about it, but probably haven't the energy to get the plan realized. Of course, Johannes Poulsen would be best; you can say what you like about him, but he is an artist. In case you really should be able to get it put on I will give a couple of hints as the author's ideas regarding scenery and costumes.—It cannot be emphasized too strongly that it is a *marionette comedy* and as such not subject to the usual rules. So there need not be any uniformity of costumes and decor and it should be produced in quite a primitive manner; for instance, when Mopsus's bats come out of the sack and fly away they can be shown quite clearly being pulled on a cord. The setting: a room in an inn, fairly dark, as if lit by footlights or poor lamplight, picturesque but very simple,—something like the enclosed pictures could be used. The various characters as follows:

Abraham. Immediately recognizable as an *old Jew,* either in a caftan as a Polish Jew or like Fagin, but the caftan is probably best. Beard and curls, everything very dark and dingy in color.

Sabine. I would like her to be fairly magnificent, for instance in silver brocade. Should be quite modern, as in a "robe de style" from Lanvin, with padded hips. Short, permanently waved hair. She must have a fichu, because as far as I remember she talks about taking it off. Very young.

Mopsus. It does not matter what costume. Perhaps something from 17th-century Dutch paintings. The mask is the most important thing.

Fortunio. Likewise. I can see him in shirt and long trousers, something from the twenties or "The Maidens' Room." Perhaps an apron.

Jan Bravida is the most difficult to dress, as he is to play. Either very correct like a young soldier from one of Frans Hals's pictures or quite fantastic, for instance, in plus fours (Shepherd's plaid), sweater and sports hose, but these like mail stockings and the sweater like a coat of mail, right up to the neck. Frans Hals is probably best. In any case modern hair cut and clean shaven. He, Sabine, and Fortunio must all be quite young. Jan Bravida rather elegant.

Amiane. Like an old Dutch beggar woman, it should be easy to find a model in Dutch paintings. Fairly shabby, in black, with a touch of white. There might well be some scenic effects to emphasize her character as a witch or fairy, for instance, when none of the others are looking having her unfold a pair of bats' wings, or by means of lighting effects show her for a moment in a very magnificent, jewel-encrusted dress with heavy hip padding and with a tiara or fontange on her head. Apart from these tricks with the light she should keep to the darker corners of the stage.

There should really be some music to "The Revenge of Truth." A short overture, a theme for Fortunio's first song, and perhaps a kind of accompaniment to "Haul up the anchor,"—but that is probably difficult to get hold of. Is Jeppesen about and would he do it ? In any event "Come sweet sorrow" must be sung; but perhaps some old tune or other could be adapted for that.

It would really give me enormous pleasure if this play were put on, and I would be tremendously grateful to you for taking the trouble to get it done. . . .

Now I have to go around putting on a good face after Denys has gone and the scent faded from the roses and the light from the full moon,—but everything in this world must be paid for, even having one's own way. I am working on two new little marionette comedies to console myself, but it is poor consolation. . . .

Your article about Rosenborg Gardens has just arrived,—excellently written and very charming and intelligent. A thousand thanks for it.—

Ngong. May 23rd. 26.

. . . I have been to the Somali town to look for something or other to send to old G.B., for whom I still feel a warm regard; I am most grateful to you for helping me to meet him even though it is hard for you on that account to be put on a par with the lasses with bobbed hair; but I could not find anything worthy of him. I have had a letter from Miss Collin, Dixen's cousin, who wants some Kikuyu and Masai "curios" for the museum; it is very difficult to find anything at all interesting and I have advised her to look at Tommy's things at Rungsted and to let me know if she would like anything similar; without being sure of it I am loath to send big awkward things like spears and shields, but I am getting a collection of Kikuyu snuff boxes together for her; they are rather nice and could be sent in a cigar box.

Elle wrote that she thought there might be a chance of getting "The Revenge of Truth" performed; it would give me the greatest pleasure if it could be done, and perhaps it would be easier to understand on the stage! I am writing another couple of marionette comedies,—for Holstein wanted to have three to publish as a book,—but I find it hard to write when I have no one to discuss it with while I am composing; you know, Elle suffered a good deal in the part with the evolution of "The Hermits," "The de Cats Family," etc., while we were undressing in the evenings at Rungsted.

A subject that I have been thinking about and would very much like the chance of discussing with you again is the old one of "feminism," in its present-day form, which has come to mean something very different from what was signified by the term when it was first evolved three-quarters of a century ago. I think that one can see now that those who were at that time filled with horror at the thought of women being made eligible to take the student examination and thought that that would bring about the collapse of the whole existing state of things,—and who were laughed at by others for it, in fact showed clear-sightedness and foresight. They were right, it did collapse, and took very much more with it than they had thought possible; and that is what always happens whenever the very possibility of criticism and radical change in an area previously considered to be raised above it, or immune from it, enters the consciousness. When the idea of it being possible for the French intelligentsia to ridicule the king and the monarchy came into being it was followed by the entire French Revolution, and took their own heads with it. The same has happened with, for example, biblical criticism, and with the ownership of property. Can you remember how the priest in "Jerusalem" shudders,—quite unnecessarily as the others think,—at the school teacher's suggestion of starting up a parish hall? He, who is depicted otherwise as being of little account, is here much more farsighted than any of the others; for from this small seed grew the dissolution of an entire society,—the emigration to Jerusalem, and great misery.

I consider then that "feminism" or, if you will, the phenomena that were the basic cause of it, have had far more effect on and have far more radically divided the old society that was in existence when it arose,—that on the whole it should probably be regarded as the most significant movement of the nineteenth century, and that the upheavals it has caused are far from "done with" at the present moment; for it has not reached its goal by having made it possible for women to become lawyers, doctors, priests, etc., by a new marriage law and equal right of inheritance for women and for men; all these things are only manifestations of the far deeper rooted movement. If I were asked what this movement does consist of, I would reply that it is my opinion that women now,—in direct contrast to what was previously the case,—desire and are striving to be human beings with a direct relationship with life in the same way as men have done and do this.

I once said something like this at Folehave, and you answered me then by asking whether a "human being" was, or ought to be, sexless? You must forgive me for saying that in my opinion that was a somewhat specious reply, that evaded the meaning of my statement in an underhand manner. All the same, it certainly deserves a reply, and I would point out that "a human being" can certainly be thought of as sexless or as characterized very little as a sexual being, and that this is expressed, for instance, in pictures and statues of angels, which after all must be regarded to a certain extent as the highest idealization of the human form or concept, and which are as a rule portrayed as possessing a beauty that is a combination of what is noblest in both men and women without any particular sexual characteristics. But of course in reality it is impossible and undesirable to do this. But similarly at our present stage of development "a human being" cannot be thought of as not having a nationality or a profession, and yet it is possible that an earnest desire and resolution in, for instance, a German officer to put being a human being before being a German and a soldier would result in a great deal of the character of the German military force being disintegrated and radically changed. If a king should desire and decide to be a human being rather than, and in a more heartfelt manner than, a king, the monarchy and the idea of the monarchy could not long survive. One can sometimes actually see the conflict in a priest, who often has one foot in humanity and one in the religious life; Catholic priests do show more consistency here, since on no account will they regard themselves first and foremost as human beings, but feel themselves to be priests in the sight of God and the rest of humanity.

You once said that in your official conduct in public and abroad what you were consciously most aware of was yourself as Danish and as a woman. But was not the reason for that the fact that in both these situations you have a good deal to combat, namely, that you belong to a small nation, and that it is still an exception for women to assume official position? Would it be legitimate for some other participant in your congress in the same way to feel himself consciously to be, for instance, English and a man? Is it not in any case desirable that in such situations, when people meet to elucidate and make decisions on great questions that concern the whole of humanity, they should be able to meet as human beings and not, as in former times, first and foremost as members of a clan or a fraternity or as now, as members of a nation, a political party, or of one sex or the other?

I can imagine that you might then ask what I mean in this connection by "life" and by standing in a direct relationship with it. I ought to be able to reply to this, but do not find it easy—(what is life? the wind in the reeds)—and although the concept of the world covers much of what I mean, I think I would come closer to it if I reply that it is what you call God. And to illustrate the difference in attitude between that which women in previous times adopted or wished to adopt and that which we now adopt or wish to adopt, I would like to make use of two quotations, one from Milton, when he speaks in "Paradise Lost" of the creation of woman: "He all for God, and she for God in him" [*sic*], and a few words by Jakob Knudsen, when at the end of a story he has his old priest say to a young man who has been in great doubt over what he could and should do: "And you—you have begun to *live,* which means: to find your joy and your oblivion in the grace of God. Nothing better can befall a human being."

Naturally it is not women themselves as a body or a concept who have suddenly resolved to live and take their happiness in a different manner from before; conditions have brought them to it. Although I do not agree with Karl Marx that all the phenomena of life are caused by the economical situation, I think that it explains many of them. And in this connection—or perhaps what at root was the origin of the swing in economic conditions,—it is also noteworthy that society has developed in such a way that the chief original point of difference between men and women, pure physical strength, came to a great extent to lose its significance. And as this has gone out of fashion,—for today a gifted weakling who would have had only in an exceptional case a chance for power and honor in medieval times is on an equal footing with the most muscular athlete,—men as a *type* are really nearer to the old idea of women, than even the shortest-haired modern women in their audacious approach to the old idea of men. How many modern men feel a really deep urge to take part in fighting and bloodshed, in wild drinking bouts or blood feuds?—indeed, how many feel the need for bawling and great oaths?—they have probably come to speak exactly the same language as women. But because of the great advantage there originally was in possessing physical strength, so that no other qualities could have any influential effect unless they were in some way or other allied to it, all types of property were held by the men. Just as in "Two Cities" Dickens describes the situation before the Revolution by saying: "The earth and its riches belong to me, Monseigneur said."—so it was with the situation of men and women in regard to all the glories and possibilities of the world. No work, no talent, no form of productivity could pay women anything nearly so much as pleasing, or making themselves necessary to a man. It is not to be wondered at that they came to devote all their abilities to that and that their whole nature was characterized by it above all else. In my opinion "manliness" is a human concept; "womanliness" as a rule signifies those qualities in a woman or that aspect of her personality that is pleasing to men, or that they have need of. Men had no particular need for or pleasure from, and therefore no reason to encourage, women painters, sculptors, composers,—but they did have for dancers, actresses, singers, and it was the sensible and natural thing for artistically gifted women to adopt such careers. A man might well be attracted to and admire a woman who took a passionate interest in the stars, or who cultivated flowers with which to beautify his home; but she would be sinning against the idea of womanliness if she sought to establish a direct relationship with nature in these branches by taking up astronomy or botany,—for how could such ambitions have anything to do with him and his happiness?

I once read an article on feminism written by a man, in which he actually criticized women for their foolish efforts to acquire the glories of life on their own initiative when they could get them so much more easily through a man who loved them. In his argument he used the fable of a flying competition held among all the birds of the world in which as far as I remember the eagle mounted to a great height by means of great effort and then the little goldcrest,—which had hidden itself in the eagle's feathers and which, when the great bird had reached the uttermost limits of its capacity and was obliged to stop, flew a very little bit higher still—won the first prize. He felt that this illustrated how a woman could gain everything in the world for herself by allowing herself to be supported by a man and his work and efforts instead of in sheer foolishness attempting to take an independent part in life's flying competition. And he was absolutely right; one need only read history to see how much more easy it was for a charming woman to acquire wealth, influence, excitement, than for anyone else. After all, it is not so long ago that the only way for a woman to travel was through the invitation of a man. Not only would she have been murdered if she had gone down to Nyhavn to haggle with a skipper for a passage on his smack, or on the highways and in the inns; but unless she could get a man to give her money and a vehicle she had no means of getting there. And it was perfectly reasonable that her chances of travel should be dependent on her "charm," for when he had to pay for her and have the trouble of making the arrangements, no one could blame him for saying: if you are not nice to me I won't take you with me. Precisely the same thing applied to theaters, music, even to having a meal in a restaurant, which it is surely reasonable to expect that a woman might feel like doing; she was obliged to wait for, or provoke an invitation, she had to be obliging to a man. Her entire position, both economic and social, was dependent on her marriage, and do you not think that the desire to *get married*, that you feel you detect in present-day young women, is brought about to a great extent by the fact that now more than in the past they want to travel, to experience something, to have influence, and so far can most easily achieve these things through marriage? While she would have very limited possibilities if she had to work her own way up, there would be nothing at all to prevent a beautiful young girl from getting everything she had ever dreamed about, providing that a man fell in love with her.

The only way to reply to all this is: but what if we *want* to fly ourselves!? What if we love wings and the air rushing past us? What if we wish to own and drive our own cars along the roads which appeal to us? And if we show that we can do it,—then why shouldn't we?

It is often said that chivalry will disappear from the world if women start to *live* by their own efforts. To this I can only say that an "artificial mountaineering"—chivalry, in which one first binds fast the legs of the object of one's homage in order to serve her, seems to me of scant value, and that it would be more chivalrous to cut the bonds, and also that I think there ought to be,—and I hope this will come,—far more chivalry among people of the same sex, among friends and colleagues, than there is now, and that perhaps gallantry has stood in the way of development here.

I can't think of a more typical demonstration of the old world order than the shooting parties at Näsbyholm. The sport, the excitement, the experience, were for the men; for the women they were a kind of mystical rite from which they were excluded,—somehow they did not exist until the men came home from shooting and they could begin to be charming for them at dinner. I have heard Uncle Frederik and Bror say quite seriously: "Gentlemen do not like ladies to be at the butts,"—and that made it absolutely unquestionable that it would be stupid and reprehensible for the ladies to attempt to take part. It was really refreshing when Inger and Sophie came, and went out shooting themselves, coming home tired, stimulated, enthusiastic about the countryside, the game and their own proficiency. Father writes in similar fashion in "Hunting Letters": "—and however enchanting a well-formed feminine leg may be when revealed by an incautiously lifted dress, there is nothing in the least alluring in being presented with the whole leg, right up to the knee, because of a skimpy short skirt.—" no doubt presuming by this pronouncement to have demonstrated to all decent sensible women the reprehensible foolishness of these skimpy skirts, as if it were unthinkable for us really to *want to run* and be free of clothes impeding our movements.

As if we could never want to have the whole of life,—nature, art, science, open-air life, sport, and our own destiny,—before our eyes without having to see all this through our relationship with men, *any more* than they should see all this through their relationship with us.

It is often discussed how much influence the feminist movement exerts on women's morals, and these very discussions generally show to what a great extent women are regarded as sexual beings, to what a small extent as human beings. A woman's "morals" are understood as something purely sexual just as a woman's "honor" always has to do purely with sex. An "honorable man" is in general thought to be a man who understands and follows such clear and simple, human concepts as honesty, reliability, loyalty, fearlessness; an "honest woman" is a woman who maintains certain traditions in her relationship with men,—indeed, in the end, as Harald Nielsen defines it: "A woman who can be had only through marriage," without regard for the moral value of that marriage. It is my opinion that the young women of today are more courageous, more truthful, less inclined to intrigue, more loyal, than "the women of bygone days"; they are more "gentlemen," this can be seen in, for instance, women's relationships with each other,—and is that not one of the highest universally human ideas?—and their morals should not be judged in one sphere only.

We have talked so much about sexual morality, you know,—I think that there should not be such a concept as sexual morality at all, any more than political, diplomatic, or military "morals"; for I think that the same ideas of decency should hold true for all the affairs of human beings.

Where the relationship between men and women is concerned, a French author I have read says: To love a modern woman is homosexuality,—and I think he is right (apart, of course, from the physical unnaturalness that gives the word an ugly connotation). But I believe it is possible to think that such a "homosexuality,"—sincere friendship, understanding, delight shared by two equal, "parallel moving" beings,—has been a human ideal that conditions have prevented being realized until now. In ancient Greece, when some of the most beautiful and noble relationships occurred between men and youths, may it not have been because their women were so handicapped by their sex that all their interests, the whole of their existence lay in spheres that were completely alien to the men? There is another French quotation which runs: "L'amitié uni au désir ressemble tant à l'amour"—in my opinion it not only resembles, it *is* l'amour. And I think that the morality existing between friends is something higher and more human than that between lovers has usually been,—perhaps just because it cannot be bound by promises and vows. For it is a fact that in all other relationships, if one becomes aware that what one promised was without all rhyme or reason, one must then try in the nicest, most honorable and considerate manner to escape from it; for "the letter killeth, but the spirit giveth life."

Well, this has become a good deal longer than I had intended; that is what usually seems to happen when I am writing from out here. I hope what I have said is reasonably clear so that it can be understood as it is meant, and that it hasn't tried your patience too much. I would like to make one or two remarks in closing:

I can very well imagine that everything I have written here is *unacceptable* to you, that it does not appeal to you or is distasteful to you. And "taste" is the one thing that I defer to more than most others; for the taste of one person is almost always as legitimate as that of another, and one cannot change it or expect or wish to change it in others. I would likewise admit that all human forms of living can possess great value, particularly where beauty is concerned, and that it is sad when this disappears. It was so with the "Church," with the feudal system, with absolute monarchy. So it was as well, to a very high degree, with the relationship between men and women who remained more or less of a mystery to each other, and in the expressions taken by that relationship.

It is just that to make one's "taste" synonymous with the only right thing for everyone is what I find dangerous and "immoral." Every human being has the right to say that he cannot stand sweet soups and will not have them in his house; but unless he really has science and experience on his side he should be cautious in forbidding other people to use them, or even to oppose their increasing use.

The other thing I want to say is this, that when certain phenomena impress one as being dangerous and destructive, one should try to elucidate whether they are so according to an eternal law or according to temporal circumstances. As I have postulated before, a "heretic's" friends and relations were perfectly right to point out to him that by speaking ill of the Pope he risked his life, ruined his good name, his family's future, and so on; for they were able to illustrate all their arguments by showing him the heretics being burned at the stake on all sides. But time has shown that there was no real or eternal necessity for it to be so then or later. Later Vilhelm Beck could stand in the pulpit at Ørslev and call the Pope that old donkey in Rome without anyone thinking of putting a match to his trouser leg.

Well, dearest Aunt Bess, I can almost believe that we have been sitting on the veranda at Folehave having a really heated discussion,— except, it's true, that my poor opponent has not had a chance to get a word in! if only I could fly over there for an hour. Now the cherry trees must be in bloom and the forget-me-nots underneath them, and the forest green. I so often dream about Folehave, and about Mama; from here Denmark and all of you are a little vague with regard to time,— it seems to me that Thomas is still at home with us both as a little boy in a striped pinafore and as a young husband, and that I could expect to see Mama coming out into the courtyard with her red parasol, if I could be coming up from the forest. . . .

To Ingeborg Dinesen

Ngong. Sunday 13.6.[1926]

. . . Thank you for "The Revenge of Truth,"—it is entirely wrong and impertinent that Levin has put my name to it; it is absolutely contrary to agreement, and I emphasized to him that if I sent him some descriptions of Africa he could print them under my name, but not this kind of fictional writing. It was not in the proof. However, I am so far away that in perspective the annoyance is reduced. . . .

I have planted maize behind my house where I want to grow grass during the next long rains; it was so thick with bush and roots that I could never have made a nice lawn of it without plowing and cultivating it thoroughly and I did not feel I could let the company go to that expense without getting something for it. It is bringing Lulu with two daughters, one grown and one a baby, up to the house every evening; they are so delightful to watch. The whole wood is full of the little blue monkeys; one is not permitted to shoot them, I don't know why as they do a fair amount of damage, especially in the native shambas. . . .

To Ingeborg Dinesen

Ngong Sunday 27/6.26.

Dearest Mother.

I have just been at the school, which is going much better; I think I have been really lucky with my teacher this time. I find it really hard to keep a straight face, especially during the hymn singing, which it is the fashion at the moment to carry on in such a bleating manner that it would satisfy even Per Degn. The teacher began with a sermon, and I am ashamed to admit that I didn't understand a word of it; I sat there hoping that he was not preaching wild rebellion to my totos, when I realized that he was telling them how good I was and how depraved they were not to come to school every day. Both the address and the singing were interrupted from time to time by Rouge, whose stable adjoins the schoolroom, you know, and who was obviously excited by the noise so that every now and then he gave the wall a kick. I think the teacher chooses terribly hard tunes for the children to learn; when one is as bad at Swahili as I am it is of course harder to learn by heart, it is fairly easy for them and one must hope that he is in sympathy with their taste and ideas; the title of the hymn they learned today was translated "There is life in a look at the Crucified One," which to my mind does not make sense, but it was sung with much enthusiasm; there was a good deal in it about "damu a Gondoa," which I assume must be translated as "the Blood of the Lamb,"—I myself have only come across the expression "gondoa" from sheep trading, but they may not have any other word for lamb. . . .

On Wednesday when I was working in my garden,—which gives me much pleasure,—a message came from Dickens asking me to take a sick toto to the hospital. So I drove him in, and as there was a "matinee" in the afternoon by some Italian singers,—from the Papal Choir in Rome,—I stayed in to hear them. They have really lovely voices and sing with such perfection. They had chosen a rather too popular program, but anything else probably doesn't go down well with an English audience,—but included a lot of really lovely things as well: "The Barber," "Bohême" and some old Italian songs; it was marvelous to hear them . . . how different the Italian are from the northern peoples, and how *gifted* they are, artists in a completely different manner; the danger with these was that they were so over-dramatic and became theatrical at the least opportunity, for instance in a duet between Faust and Mephistopheles; the little fat Mephisto turned completely demoniacal with rolling eyes and fiendish laughter and masses of wild gestures,—it was quite irresistible. . . .

To Mary Bess Westenholz

Sunday 4th July 26.

. . . Mother writes in her letter that she is considering whether it would not be better to use the money intended for her journey out here for a trip home to Europe for me. As I think it is an advantage to take some sort of firm stand or other on the subject of these plans I will begin by saying that in no possible way and under no circumstances will I go home before the spring of 1928. It is partly because I can see that things *cannot* go so well and methodically here when I am away, and partly because I will not *break up my life* in such small pieces. Besides the considerable amount of time that goes in travel preparations and in the journey itself, which I consider to be utterly without value, it takes one,—or anyway it has taken me this time,—three or four months before one gets used to affairs and conditions out here again. After my return this last time it is only just now that I am beginning to feel really at home here again. . . .

I think that the really decisive factor must be whether Mother wants to make this trip, and that you think it will do her good, and that other considerations must give way to this *most important* one, even the anxieties that I know we must all feel, and that all the plans must be made with this in mind despite any difficulties involved. At present these may be quite considerable; but I always think that when later on in life one looks back on difficulties they are diminished in perspective to the vanishing point, and one wonders how one could ever have worried about them in contrast to what was "essential": what you call the "fullness of life." I think that so many errors and mistakes are made in life because when one is confronted directly with things one cannot get a comprehensive view of them,—and just as I have come to feel that in building up this country, it is important when considering the natives to adopt a historical view, so I think that we can most easily make the right decision regarding these plans if we imagine ourselves in many years, perhaps after Mother's death, looking back on this great wild plan of hers and our attitude to it. . . .

Ngong. Sunday 1.8.26.

My dearest Mother.

I probably won't get much written today as I have a lot of preparations to make for Lady Grigg's confounded fete tomorrow; among other things they have asked me to make roasted almonds for their tea pavilion, and I am not sure whether my cook remembers the art of doing them, which I taught him once. To me the whole festival seems pretty crazy and so barbaric that in a hundred years' time I think such phenomena will seem utterly incomprehensible; of course it is in aid of a good cause to which any profits will go, but with such enormous costs,—not to speak of the trouble,—I think direct begging would be much more profitable. Now every member of the community here, which is not very large, as you know, so that it will be hard to find enough purchasers, has been pumped and badgered to give to the utmost, and the arrangements for putting up booths and tents have cost several hundred pounds, and so,—besides the fact that a lot of things like vegetables, fruit, flowers, butter, poultry, etc. that are sent from up-country must suffer and be reduced in value,—most of it will presumably be sold off cheaply, which must be annoying to the donors, while it cannot really pay the purchasers either, since normally they would not buy these turkeys, angora goats, guinea fowl, or "native curios" at all and in any case can only get them with the additional costs of hotels, car and train journeys, entrance fee, new hats and dresses, all of which they could save if they were left in peace to make their purchases where they live. The whole thing is based on the sort of economy one reads about in Madame de Sévigné's letters when, during one of Madame Montespan's journeys through France the maire of a provincial town had a gilded ship made to carry her down a river, at a cost of more than 100,000 livres for the boat, its silken sails and other equipment,—which the province no doubt had to meet,—"but this was certainly not money wasted; for the Marquise was so delighted with the magnificent vessel and Monsieur de Tourvel's attentiveness that on her return to Versailles she obtained the King's consent for Tourvel's nephew to be appointed to the command of one of the very best regiments." It is to be hoped that it did not go to war. . . .

My profession of, rather like what Anders called "professor of—every type of menagery," has developed so much that I don't have time for much else, especially as I am now called out to minister to the most serious cases. If I may be permitted to boast about it, I think I have a certain talent as a doctor and quite a good eye for illness and sick people, and so far I have been lucky with my cures. But the

Kikuyu have in their nature, and one could say, as part of their view of the universe, such a deeply rooted lack of trust that only a small percentage of the sick come for treatment, and there have been many deaths in the last few months, especially among the old people. Then of course they keep to their old custom of putting out their dead, and the hyenas drag them around wherever they like, so I have had the pleasure of finding a couple of corpses in the wood and in the maize behind my house. Dickens and Farah,—burial is important to Muhammadans,—want me to order them to bury all the dead in the future; but I can't really bring myself to do this because actually I am in sympathy with the Kikuyu on this point and would rather like my own transition to a skeleton,—which takes such a short time out here with the aid of sun and wind and animals and birds,—to take place in the dry grass and the open air and under the stars, and before the eyes of my friends and acquaintances, as it were. . . .

To Thomas Dinesen

Ngong. Aug. 5th 26.

. . . Following these tardy thanks I send you my warmest wishes for joy and happiness in every way in your daily life in your new home, which I look forward to hearing more about. May it prove for both of you, as Jakob Knudsen writes about his: "the home of my soul, of my heart,"—as I myself have so often felt about this house at Ngong. I also wish for you that it may be the base from which you set out for a real profession, what is known as "a calling"; that here you may see your personality expressed in action. Holger Drachmann has a poem,—which many have laughed at, it goes something like:

> In the night I hear
> from silent woods
> a cry like: help me,
> my God!
> I rise, listen,
> cannot sleep.
> Who am I?
> How do I
> look?

I think that he says something real, true, there. In a way this is what one is always searching for in life. By trying to look into oneself one can somehow only glimpse it, or one can see the drawing of, the model of the house or ship that is to be built; in one's work, one's profession, the impression one makes, the relationship one has with the outside world,—its people and ideas—one comes to know it, one somehow sees it face to face. One often has to laugh at it, it is so remote from what one had thought it was, many times surprising to oneself; it is my old simile of the man who "fell into a ditch, up again,—and there was,—a stork"; so different too from what one felt it ought to be,—like my primitive young Wakamba artists' sculptures of "Nuggos" and "Ngoroas"—and yet they have given a glimpse of themselves as "they are, this is how they look." It is usually satisfying, strange as it may seem; it is,—forgive me for repeating myself,—the assignats, which are for 100 francs and are exchanged in gold for the sum of 10 francs,—to the complete satisfaction of everyone. Reality converts dreams according to its own calculations, and far from the "face value" but it "sounds true, like a good Sovereign," and one has to accept the exchange and acknowledge it, even give thanks for it. May you now in your new home,—for which I still do not know the address,—gather such a collection of genuine gold, of Jan Bravida's bread, for yourselves, which will be more satisfying than a cookery book. . . .

I hope that you are still interested in hearing about my life here and myself, and so I must tell you that I am *very* happy; indeed, sometimes when I let Pjuske out at night,—in great fear of a kali leopard that is playing havoc here,—and stand on the stones outside and look at the starry sky and the shadow of the Ngong Hills against it, I feel that I am completely happy and can almost see the "stork." I think that despite all the shauries, which actually have nothing to do with this, one has freedom and peace out here; perhaps that really means that I myself am in harmony with my life here. You see I have come to realize,—something that in itself is extremely strange and just as ridiculous as the Wakamba animals,—that the really great passion of my life has come to be my love for my black brother; never mind that he causes me a great many anxieties and troubles, he also gives me great satisfaction and tremendous joy. And then too I can write to you that my great devotion to Denys fills my whole life with indescribable sweetness, in spite of constantly missing him. If things can continue as they are now I will never wish for greater happiness. Now, we have discussed marriage so often that there cannot be much more to say about it, and I will certainly not speak against it to a young husband in his honeymoon days; but for myself, it does not seem to me that I am suited to it. I have advanced the theory, to Elle and possibly to you too, I am guilty of constantly repeating and harping upon the same ideas in my old age, of modern love as "homosexuality",—understood as meaning the same as homogeneous,—which takes the form of passionate sympathy, a mutual love of ideas or ideals rather than a personal devotion to and giving of oneself to each other, and I do not think that such a feeling is so easy to maintain and flourishes in,—I will not say a life together day in, day out throughout life, for I think this is perfectly possible,—as in conditions where each partner does not have, as it were, his own existence, in the same way as would be the case with the most devoted friends of the same sex. Aldous Huxley has an expression: "The love of the parallels," which he uses in a somewhat tragic context, it is true, but which I must surely be permitted to construe as I like,—which to a certain extent expresses what I mean by this: one does not "become part of," become "devoted to," the other; perhaps one is not as close to the other as in those partnerships that are able to encompass such merging, and there is no question of each being the aim and goal of the other's life, but while one is oneself and striving for one's own distant aim one finds joy in the knowledge of being on parallel courses for all eternity.—You must not show this to Jonna; partly because I do not want to talk about Denys to anyone but you, partly because it is not good for a young wife to hear such immoral relationships discussed and commended.

I want to tell you that I am very grateful to you for insisting, when I was last at home, that the right thing for me to do was to return to Africa. But I want to explain how it was possible for me to see any conflict in this; when I talked to you about it I do not think I saw my own attitude and ideas on the matter as clearly as I do now. What I was afraid of, with a fear that sometimes approached real horror, was not conditions here in themselves but the insecurity of everything and the calamitous possibility of once more, and as it were irrevocably, putting one's life into, and abandoning one's soul to something that one might come to lose again. Everyone in Denmark seemed to me to live in such security; they ran no risks, and it was for this,—and not the particular conditions in which they were able to do this,—that I envied them. And the presentiment, the conviction, that my return to my life here, particularly to that which is *my life* here, could not be made as an experiment, but was in truth decisive, made the decision as serious as anything ever could be for me. Surely there must always be one moment in life when there is still a possibility of *two* courses,—and another, a next moment, where there is only the possibility of a single one. Now I am fully aware of this: this time I have burned my ships. "—No retreat, no retreat,—they must conquer or die who have no retreat,"—but it is childish to be alarmed over this certainty, and it was probably only because for a moment the choice was so exceptionally clearly materialized in the departure itself that it affected me so strongly; in reality this is doubtless something that happens to everyone.

Something has happened that I think has infuriated me more than anything else ever could: one day, when I just turned my back for a short while to drive into Nairobi to talk to Hunter, my boys let a beastly shenzie [wild] dog get in and mate with Heather. When I think of everything I have done to get her, and get her out here, indeed, that I risked y life for her on board, and that this is the result, it almost suffocates me. I have not even brought myself to write home about it; I suppose it is more like what is called "chagrin" than a real sorrow, in that one cannot give it expression in any way,—it eats into one and poisons both one's own soul and the whole of life. When I heard about it and went out to talk to my boys about it I found to my astonishment that I was unable to utter a word. When I found my tongue again I fired them all wholesale,—with the exception of Farah, who had probably had no more sense of responsibility than the others, but who happened to have been to Nairobi with me. Now they have all promised to be good and as you can imagine have persuaded me to let them stay, and they have invented a story to boot that actually Banja had got in before the other dog; of course that is not impossible, and we can only await the course of events,—I will be able to see at once who has been responsible for the puppies. . . .

Finally, I will report on the farm. As you no doubt know, we have been very disappointed in the blossom and so will only get a mediocre harvest. You probably remember that in 1922 something similar happened after a dry year, and in spite of really good rains, and that this,—I am quite sure,—sent me to hospital in Nairobi. Ever since I came back I have been afraid that this would be repeated this year; we are too high up here for our trees to be able to pick up right away after a drought. However, I must say that I think the farm is looking fine; there has been progress in all directions, and I am convinced that we can look forward to a good harvest next year, if the climate does not present us with too many obstacles. . . .

To Ingeborg Dinesen

Ngong. Aug.8th.26.

Dearest Mother.

I am very grieved to have to tell you that Abdullai, whom I had with me in Denmark, died the day before yesterday. There is so much sickness everywhere here at present; this was "black-water," following malaria. He died in the hospital in Nairobi. It is a tragedy because he supported his mother so much; she has a bad husband and now she is left with two small children. The poor thing was quite wild with grief and disappeared for two days, although she has come back again now. Some time ago when I heard that Abdullai was ill I went to visit him in the Somali town, I cannot remember if I wrote about that; he sent his regards to everyone at Rungsted,—he and his mother were so sweet together, and I was always so fond of him and had such a homely relationship with him. Today Farah has gone to a Muhammadan ceremony that is held following the funeral,—all I have been able to do is send his poor mother something toward it; all Muhammadan festivities on any occasion chiefly consist of philanthropy, for of course they do not drink and are also very abstemious about food. Abdullai was to have been married next week; now the young bride who had never seen him is coming from Mombasa to his funeral ceremony. . . .

The other Abdullai, Farah's brother, is taking his final examination next month; it is high time for me, as in the course of time I have paid more than 1200 shillings on his education—I hope it will be of use to him. He is indescribably big and fat, but his face is exactly as it was when he was six years old; he is a remarkable young fellow with his passion for learning, particularly for anything to do with mathematics; he is highly esteemed among the Somalis, especially because he is never kali, and Farah says that even old Somalis ask his advice in their disagreements. Perhaps he is going to turn into a kind of Solomon.

This week has been under the sign of Lady Grigg's charity fete and I might say as my old Christian cook did recently: "By God's good grace it is now Wednesday," when it was over and done with. It was one of the most exhausting things I have ever experienced. . . . In my brief free periods from the trading I had to walk around the other stalls and get a whole lot of rubbish foisted off on me, the sort of thing you can truly describe as something you can't "ever rid of be." What cheered me on the most was the cocktail bar, which was run by Keith Caldwell, which gave one instant strength, but I think not a lot of good in the long run, because they were mixing their cocktails with the wildest flights of imagination; if you went late in the day you were given a glass put together from about twenty different leftovers. . . .

To Ingeborg Dinesen

Ngong. August 22nd. 26.

. . . There is so much sickness on the farm it is really frightful, and all over the country, too,—it is really like the plague in "Kristin Lavrandsdatter,"—and my experiences in this sphere have again convinced me that Sigrid Undset's *despicable* view of life is completely wrong, in this respect also. I think on the whole it is fear of the Devil, or some or other fear of hell that is still in her blood, inherited from the Norwegian Middle Ages; I think I have seldom come across anyone who had such a horror of all the phenomena of life; horror of any form of love or passion, horror of every kind of experience, and the frightful horror of darkness and death.

In the end one feels that spiritually speaking her characters huddle together like people in a terrible storm, close all the windows and doors and hardly open their mouths except to scare each other.—I don't think reality is like this; there is most probably always a certain amount of jollity even during an outbreak of plague and among people who are to go to the guillotine next day. When, for instance, I think of the final episode in "Kristin," in which she carries the dead women to the consecrated ground, I think it is very reminiscent of my burying the young girl who was run over here, which I think of without the remotest shudder of horror,—but as I said, it is probably belief in the Devil or in something fiendish that causes the difference; of course it was revolting that they wanted to bury the child alive, but the natives could easily do something much worse without there being that element of the gruesome horror of darkness that marks this chapter,—the Devil, the Devil! . . .

Denys sent me an interesting book, "China under the Dowager-Empress,"—a frightful old hag, but extraordinarily interesting, and strange conditions, a mixture of a culture that far surpasses our own in refinement, and barbarism. . . .

The following letter was sent by Karen Blixen to her brother together with the uncompleted letter of 1 April 1926. These two letters should be read at the same time.

In a letter to the editor dated 14 March 1978 Thomas Dinesen states that the incident mentioned by Karen Blixen on page 277, which led her, as she puts it, to take stock of herself, was her conviction, at some point during the spring of 1926, that she was pregnant.

To Thomas Dinesen

Ngong. Sunday 5th September 26.

Private

Dear old Tommy.

It is with a certain amount of hesitation that I write to you today. It was all very well to bring every kind of shaurie to you, both material and spiritual, in the old days, when you were a free agent, and one did not feel too conscience stricken about clinging on to you then; for it could not be the cause of your neglecting anything, as it were, and one never knew whether some or other of the shauries one loaded upon you might not turn out to lead you to an interest, a meaning, that you were searching for. (That was what I thought, for instance, in 1920 when I more or less chucked the whole of Africa, with blacks and whites, farming, politics, hunting and so on, at you). Now you are a man with absolute responsibility for another person's happiness, perhaps soon for several people's,—who can presumably no longer put off the decision to settle down into something or other, and on your own account have need of all your abilities, strength, money, and time. You must not think that I regret this at all; it has been my heartfelt wish for you not only to find happiness in the normal way, but just this: the devotion of your whole personality and your whole life,—and I, more than anyone else, ought to be able to resign those demands for your "complete attention," that I used to make so often, but should now, quite poli-poli ["softly, gently"] leave out of our otherwise eternally unchanging friendship.

But on the other hand: just now I am pining for someone I can talk to completely openly and honestly about everything, with whom I can discuss all my difficulties and worries, and from whom I can ask advice and help,—and even if he may well reply that he is unable at present to do any of these things, yet there is something uplifting in at least having someone to ask,—and who else in the whole world have I but you to whom I can talk or write in such a way? As long as you don't get kali over it, it can do no harm, and I am relying on you not to do this even though you may put the letter down when you come to the end of it with the thought: she is getting crazier than ever. I can't think of anything that you could write to me that would have the effect of making me "lose my patience with Thomas,"—and experience has taught me that I may have high hopes of your patience with me.

I know that in the past I have been rather bad about "complaining" or, rather, raging or storming at fate in general and at every lesser affliction—but I believe I have cured myself of this almost better than most people; if I sometimes still give way to an outburst of this kind it is probably partly because I am on my own to an unusual extent as far as intimate confidences are concerned. I am not getting on very well with Dickens at the moment, he is really being rather rude and unpleasant, and when Farah has been in his sulky mood I have come to realize to what an extent I am reduced here, not merely as regards the normal congenial exchange of opinions but even the modest encouragement provided by what one calls "a kindly word." The "Jambo Memsabo" of my little totos has taken on unnatural significance, and I have been looking forward to my little get-together every Monday with your friend Mohr at the Stanley Hotel for a vermouth,—when we usually lend each other books,—to an unwarranted extent merely because he offered me ordinary kindness and sympathy. Bear this in mind and make allowances for what I may write in this letter; if nothing else you can shout a "Jambo Memsabo" back to me from Denmark and that in itself will be quite satisfactory.

This time it has been pretty hard for me to come back here from Europe and find my feet and my equilibrium again (I must say, of course, that it has been pretty hard for me to find my feet and my equilibrium all my life, but I won't go into that now but restrict myself to this particular case),—so that I feel very hesitant at the very idea of ever going home again; conditions are so different that it takes it out of one to change from one to the other. I have been, if I may say so, the victim of a completely meaningless see-sawing in my view of life itself, and for someone who has retained at least a modicum of sense there is really something extremely depressing in such an experience. I do not think it was produced by the particular external circumstances only, but, rather, by that stage in life in which I happened to be: when one no longer looks forward to a whole range of various possibilities but must accept what life has given one for good and take stock of oneself, as it were,—and I think this is always difficult and one is inclined to take a very bright view of one's position at one moment and an unreasonably dark one the next; and this is no doubt natural, for it *is* a difficult thing to judge, and one of the advantages of youth, for many people, is that then, as long as one has all these possibilities before one, one has no need to take stock. But it is bound to become relevant for everyone who reaches my age; and the reason for not everyone doing it is partly because so many people mentally speaking live from hand to mouth without ever coming to grips with their active and passive attributes, partly because in marriage or family life or in any kind of intimate relationship whatever, they back each other up by convincing themselves mutually of the significance and superiority of their particular attributes,—and I am excluded from this sort of encouragement,—and in a really happy marriage there is no need for any stock taking, since it far surpasses any evaluation!

I am enclosing a letter that, as you can see, I wrote two months after I came back to Africa. At least at the time I had the sense in spite of everything not to send it off,—and when I realized that it should not be sent there seemed little satisfaction to be had in finishing it, so it has remained incomplete. Now, when I have gained a rather different view of things, I am sending it to you to explain the situation,—of one phase, at least, that I have gone through. I am not saying that I feel I was wrong in what I wrote then; where the facts are concerned I think that I described them more or less correctly,—but I have, if I may put it like this, come to accept them in a different way,—and probably with good will this is something one *can* always attain in life. Have you read Stevenson's "New Arabian Nights"?—and can you remember how there Prince Florizel of Bohemia, after having been banished from his kingdom, ends up running a "Cigar Divan" in Piccadilly and finds that he is far happier than when he was a prince?—According to the description, he is perfectly right in that; but it is equally certain that he would never voluntarily have resigned his regency and settled down to a cigar divan. Similarly I believe that someone who had, for instance, lost both legs in the war, could come to realize that it is possible to live without legs, and that through the loss of them he could achieve a higher appreciation of literature or thought, the observance of nature, music and so on, and would be able to conclude that he was happier than before; but he would be quite aware that he could never have reached this view immediately.

Some time after I wrote this letter to you something happened to me that caused a climax in my situation, that is, forced me to take stock. I believe that in the spring I found myself in the same situation as A. . . . last year in August. I do not know for certain if it was really so, and will never know, but that is beside the point, and the real crux of this experience,—which also brought a great deal of unpleasantness,—lay elsewhere. After it had become quite clear to me that I did not want to have a child,—and it *was* clear, even though there might be moments when I imagined it would be, why, almost "a great joke," and amused myself with the thought of what it would have been like if circumstances had been different, if, for instance, you had not married, or if Daisy had been alive, while there have been times when I would have regarded it as a great happiness,—what then was the reason?

I have always felt that to resort to "living in one's children" after having oneself "failed in life,"—and thus to have no faith or substance to give the children,—was one of the most pitiful things one could fall back on. . .and to me it seems both morally despicable and logically utter nonsense. But was this my own position? Had I an unconscious conviction of having failed, either purely externally, in uncertain or hopeless conditions,—or more deeply, in having come to see that life is not worth living?—

If there is to be any proportion in it this letter is going to be far too long after six pages of introduction. But let me imagine that we are never going to meet again, for instance,—then at least it would have a certain amount of interest for you, like the last chapter of a book, of which a few chapters had once absorbed your attention.

When one sets about evaluating or measuring one's own life one of the difficulties is that one is involuntarily affected by the viewpoints and yardsticks of other people. Especially when one has had to admit so many times that one is an idiot, and has lost most of one's original self-confidence, without wanting to one comes back to trying to evaluate with other people's eyes, and one forgets that each one of them too judges things and circumstances from a more or less personal view and standpoint. But of course what it is important to clarify is how the case stands for oneself,—for the human being of particular inclinations and characteristics with which one is dealing. Have I, as regards myself and my own point of view, failed?

I think it would sound strange to most people,—but less so to you, who have yourself experienced something somewhat similar,—when I say that what struck me or affected me when I was at home and what I have since found difficult to connect with conditions here and my life here, was this, that it seems to me that people in Denmark aim at making life happy, and that they really are happy. For so many years my life had been a struggle either to keep myself going or to carry something through,—first because of my illness, later because of Bror's paranoia and the difficult conditions here,—that I had forgotten about this view of life. One could be happy when a shaurie had succeeded or was over, until the next one cropped up, but to be happy in oneself, from day to day, to plan one's life for the purpose of being happy and to place its significance in this,—that had not occurred to me for such a long time. So that now when I seemed to see it being realized you will understand how greatly it appealed to me, not only because it promised rest but because it seemed so beautiful to me.

What had previously caused me pain in regard to my own life was nearly always the fact that I did not feel that I had achieved what I ought to have, that my abilities or talents had not been put to full use,—I think I looked at this purely objectively even though it might appear as colossal overestimation of self! But we have often talked of what a sad phenomenon this is; that, for instance, it was not distressing, even though actually quite painful, to see a gun dog whipped in order to make it retrieve, or a racehorse to do its utmost, but that it was tragic to see a gun dog chained up, a thoroughbred before the plow, a wild bird in a cage, a coffee tree planted in poor soil. Now, for instance, when I have paid for Abdullai's education, or cannot give up hectoring my natives here in the hope of making them a bit more human,—which is probably not at all in my own interests, to do,—indeed, when I lie awake at night pondering how to teach my chef to make really good éclairs, or replant my cinerarias twenty times in different sorts of soil, I am being driven by the same conviction: the feeling of the immense value of the divine,—in talent, in character, in beauty,—and the fear of seeing it destroyed or wasted. And then I often felt that I myself had had ability and a great capacity for work, but for some reason or other or in some way or other had not brought these to fruition; these two things had not worked together, I had not had the opportunity to use my abilities; my work,—and I do think that I have slaved at it,—had come to resemble a gun dog barking and keeping watch in its kennel,—without purpose in "spirit and truth," indeed, *against* any purpose,—and was extremely mediocre!

But when I was last at home it seemed to me that I should stop mortifying myself in this way, and that there was even something restless, inharmonious, and almost ugly in this whole viewpoint, when I saw with how much harmony and beauty people there,—without reservation!—directed the whole of their lives toward being happy and content. Everyone I met there and was so happy to be with: Elle, Koosje, Sophie,—they were not striving to attain "the ideal" but to see the ideal in the things they cared for and had attained, in what they were suited to. If you talk about an ideal horse or dog or garden, you are not trying to train a Derby winner or a mathematical horse at Elberfeld or a prize police dog, but you are maintaining that Trimse and Faithful are ideal pets. To walk through the woods from Rungsted to Folehave, to make a cup of tea and some toast, to plant a new row of hyacinths,—that gives meaning to life, that is worth doing, because one enjoys it, feels contentment in doing it, is happy in it. The "ideal, spartan, patriotically minded home"—that is the Magleaas that one has decorated to one's taste and where one feels oneself, at ease. How beautiful and smiling it all was,—as if they were walking up and down in a garden or a wood, while I myself had been climbing panting up to the top of a stony and dangerous mountain summit!—and how much more did they not achieve—seeing gardens, children, and friends flourishing around them, without effort,—while I, who felt that I had been ready to stake everything, and in some ways had been beaten as black and blue as someone who has staked everything, had never been in gear, had ended up by giving my life to making both ends meet on a remote coffee farm whose future continues to be extremely dubious!—

I imagine that you are very happy now, or that anyway,—for in your life and future there must inevitably be a number of problems,—you were completely happy on your honeymoon in France. I know you will not think that I am dictated by envy when I say that I have absolutely no recollection of having experienced anything remotely approaching such happiness!—Perhaps when I was with Daisy in Rome our rides to Frascati might have sparkled with something of the same luster; but they held no perspective, we knew all the time that they would soon come to an end. It has been the same when I have been out driving with Denys in the Reserve, and my holiday at home had to suffer the same fate; it was going to be cut short, one could see the dividing line from where one was standing. I have probably told you that it has become a kind of habit or fixed idea with me to be continually anticipating like this and calculating how much is left of anything, even if it is just driving in to Nairobi,—"now there are only ten, twenty minutes left,"—I think it is because most of my experiences during the last ten years have been of such a kind that one clung to this thought. When I went on board ship I entered the right element for me as far as this way of thinking is concerned; in the Bay of Biscay there was plenty of opportunity to find comfort in this kind of calculation.

But as I say: other people's lives compared with one's own for the most part only serve to enlighten. For I am not Elle, Koosje, or Jonna; I don't think myself that I am generally oppressed by envy, and if I should envy them then it must be for their personality or inclination, and I don't think that anyone, even those most gifted at envying, would go so far as that.

I have read true piety defined as: loving one's destiny unconditionally,—and there is something in it. That is to say: I think that in a way this sort of "religiousness" is the condition for real happiness. Neither do I think that what preys on one's mind, obsesses one, drives one,—gives one no peace when once one is trapped in it,—is so much disappointment over wasted chances or, as I said, envy of those for whom things have gone better, as the thought: how shall I make the best of this life, which perhaps, in spite of everything, I nevertheless love "unconditionally"; just as the question has previously been put: "how shall I manage it with the intelligence,—the time of life, the appearance, the house, the circle of acquaintances, the future, the possibilities,—that I have?" "What are, given my situation and my present circumstances,—and as I have said, I do not know how or when, even if I had had the possibility, I would have been able to change or improve them, and in any case it is no use crying over spilled milk,—my qualifications for, my difficulties in achieving either development or happiness?"

I will not begin to divide them into those arising from outward circumstances and those that may be said to originate from my own temperament; for I think that in reality these two categories form part of each other. If, for instance, I am cold, it can be said that this is a result of my own constitution or of the surrounding temperature, but whichever is the case my feeling is the same, and figuratively it would take a very clever man to decide whether I ought to take a tonic or light a fire. I do not think that any two people feel the same in regard to the same external phenomenon, and age teaches one to be truthful or unprejudiced regarding both oneself and others in these matters. Those people who, if they were to read this, would blame me for being spineless about something that to them seemed a lesser misfortune should then remember that I had borne a greater one perhaps with more fortitude than they would have. If it did not sound so beastly I might say that, the world being as it is, it was worth having syphilis in order to become a "Baroness"; but I certainly do not think this is applicable to everyone.

I prize my freedom above everything else that I possess; of course it is somewhat limited by circumstances, but the limits are widely spaced, and there is no one who has the right to criticize me for my appearance or my thoughts or,—outside the bounds of business,—my speech and actions. It has been bought with my "lack of relationship," I know, and sometimes I suffer greatly because of this, which you, who now enjoy the light and warmth of a secure relationship, can no doubt understand; but even though it has been dearly bought it has not been too costly. I know that my love of freedom is real and very deep, —for in theory I do not estimate freedom so highly,—but in practice I think that whenever I am faced with a choice I am most influenced by the thought of this. If I had felt a greater need for a "relationship" I could have decided on loving Geoffrey Buxton, which would have given me a really safe anchorage, or developed a passion for The Empire; the reason for my giving up my life to loving the independence-seeking Denys and the black race so boundlessly must be because this is a necessity for me; I cannot be possessed and have no desire to possess,—it can be cold and empty, God knows, but it is not cramped or stifling. I know that I must accept this aspect of my life "unconditionally" too, for however much I may long for something more secure and intimate in my life, when the crunch comes I back out of it, and this recurs continually. You know that I have said that I would like to be a Catholic priest, and I still maintain this,—and I am not far from being one,—but he would have to be more than human if he did not sometimes heave a deep sigh on seeing the lights lit in the windows and the family circle gathered together. I will not say that I am, like Shelley: "One, whom men love not and yet regret"; they do like me, I am pretty sure of that, but they do not want to or cannot get really close to me,—no closer than Farah or Pjuske,—and surely that is rather remote from real relationship, such, for instance, as you are experiencing now? I can write all this to you without being afraid that you will grow impatient or misunderstand me because I believe that you have sometimes felt the same. I can remember Daisy talking to me about the same problem,—she was a much beloved Catholic priest, as it were; as soon as she met anyone at all she would fall into a personal relationship with him,—waiters, cab drivers, people she only met once or twice, who now many years later still talk about her,—but no one could anchor her, and I think she felt the lack of this at the end of her life. . . .

But you will understand that although one can resign oneself quite cheerfully to being without really close intercourse with others, or with one other person, still one can miss and long for more superficial sympathy and understanding so much that it is almost suffocating. Now that Berkeley is dead and Denys at home I have hardly anyone to talk to at all, and I find myself longing for you and for our discussions so much that I feel as if my longing must pull you like a magnet over land and sea here to me. If you find it wearisome to get such a long letter, you must ascribe it to this. The mental reciprocity one gets from being with people who share one's interests and care about one is so hard to do without day out, day in, without giving one a feeling of being starved,—so much so that one can get in a panic and think one will die of hunger and become completely empty and "stale" in the end. At this distance correspondence moves at a completely unnatural and unbearable tempo; I feel as Ea did about a priest she had listened to, who "speaks so slowly that you cannot follow him." And even though I may have just as real a relationship with heaven and the saints as the Catholic priest, still I have no relationship with the *Church;* I get no pastoral letters from the Bishop and can not look forward to an audience with the Holy Father. And besides the fact that this really is a great lack and in the end can well bring about spiritual death, it is the kind that tells on one's nerves; one can get into a completely desperate mood about heaven and earth, that five minutes' conversation with some decent person or other would evaporate totally.

Then I am sure you can see that the uncertain situation that continues to exist regarding this company and myself with it does come near to breaking one's heart. It was exiting [*sic*] at one time, but now it has become an exhausting joke. I myself believe that if we get through this year our difficulties will be at an end; but of course we have believed that before, and also I am not sure if we will get through this year. And this: never daring to make a long-term plan, never daring to look further into the future than a few months, absolutely no further than to February or March, is not good for one; one ends up like the prefect's wife in "The flags are flying,"—who "gradually lost her footing out of uncertainty, so that her mind and thoughts were hopping about like a bird,—until one day her strength gave out."—I won't enlarge upon this, it could easily turn into a discussion backward and forward, backward and forward, and quite unprofitable; one ends up where one started, just slightly dizzy.

But everything I have detailed here is not going to break me. I think it might well break others, just as the Bibi's faggots and harness could break us, while they keep their balance under them. This lack of relationship that I have described,—loneliness from day to day,—the wildest uncertainty in every practical circumstances of every day,—is nevertheless a load that is in the right position for me; I can take it quite lightly even when it really gets rather too much of a good thing. But now I am going to write something that is, if not exactly despicable, at any rate horribly banal, and that I think you will frown upon, or even utterly despise,—but it can't be helped; when I write to you it must be as it has always been when I am talking to you: completely honestly,—otherwise there is no sense in it all.

When I say that conditions that would seem perhaps very trying to others do not actually oppress me, it must be because after all they are in accord with my nature, and that of course is always the decisive factor that determines how unpleasant or unbearable conditions and vicissitudes are felt by each and every one of us. In the end it depends on whether they allow us to go on being ourselves, and whether the reaction produced in us by the pressure of circumstances is an expression of our own personality. For instance, my illness was not so terribly "repugnant" to me; many shauries that might seem completely intolerable to some people, to me are quite stimulating, such as the difficulties that my "pro-nativeness" land me in with the English. Do you remember that we once talked about the actual possibility or difficulty that ruling circumstances present in "being oneself" and that you said that it would be extremely difficult if not absolutely impossible for an eminent professor of mathematics, for instance, to be himself among savages on a desert island; the conditions for expressing what is really his personality would be missing, the roots, so to speak, would be cut off, and it would be a far worse deprivation for him than it would be for a practical man,—just as it would be a far greater misfortune for a virtuoso on the violin than for a big shipowner to lose two fingers from his right hand.

Last year, when I was trying to arrive at an accurate assessment of my own position and life as a whole, in conditions where it was particularly necessary to apply thoroughness and honesty, and was studying my situation here and my possibilities for development or happiness, I came to the conclusion that what was making life so hard for me was the fact that I am so poor. It sounds so despicable and it took some time before I could really admit the truth of it; but now I know that it really is so, and I don't know why it should be so terribly despicable, in fact. Of course one has been brought up to regard such thinking as wrong, as banal, unintellectual, and unidealistic, about the lowest level to which one can sink. And it is of course true enough that the people who do not bother about money (because they have something greater or higher to bother about) are superior to and more worthwhile than others. But this superiority is something that they have in themselves; it is not the love or the contempt for money that is decisive, and the lowly or inferior kind of person would be not a scrap better or more superior just because he could get rid of his avarice. It is greater to be Einstein than to be able to do artistic embroidery or to act; but if these should be the things that one *can* do, through which one expresses one's personality, then one does not improve oneself by throwing away one's embroidery silks, or turning one's back on the stage in contempt.—

I myself feel that a certain kind of shape and color in my surroundings, a certain amount of "showing off," for which I was rebuked by Elle in the past, is the expression of my personality, is what is called a natural necessity for me; without these things I am,—not by any means a gourmand who cannot get hold of pet dishes,—but an actor without a stage, a violinist without hands or at least without a violin, indeed, your professor of mathematics on the desert island,—I am not myself. Of course, one may be constrained to do without them, just as, for instance, one can be forced to do without exercise if one is put in prison; but one cannot be without them without being miserable. I would consent to lose a leg in order to have £5,000 a year; not because I think it would make life more comfortable or easygoing,—I would gladly accept that a condition for the contract would be that I give the £5,000 away,—but because I think I could be myself without a leg, but it seems to me to be so extraordinarily difficult to be myself without money. I have felt my illness, I feel my loneliness as inconveniences, that is true enough, but still as misfortunes that in the course of time have become part of myself,—like my nose, for instance, which I could certainly wish to be more beautiful, but which doesn't constantly prey on my mind; but I feel my poverty like a foreign body inside me, like the broken-off point of a spear or point of a needle or perhaps a jigger, that I cannot accustom myself to, indeed, against which my whole constitution is constantly in revolt.

God knows I feel it is contemptible to write this, but is it any good to live completely according to what is contemptible or virtuous,—without any consideration of one's nature and inclinations,—does that not bring an element of untruthfulness or prejudice into one's life? Is it worse to admit that one suffers through poverty than that one suffers through loneliness or fear?—(which *I do not;* I really believe that I have developed an unusual degree of fearlessness, I can almost take to myself the quotation you once wrote to me: "Nothing bites me any more, lice as little as enemy bullets"—I have even ceased to be afraid of snakes and have killed two with a stick,—but I am naturally afraid of poverty)—and to be able to judge a person's weaknesses accurately surely one must regard them in the light of his whole personality and his virtues? For instance, when you caused yourself and others a deal of suffering through your penchant for what Aunt Bess called wenching, wasn't it to a certain extent the fault of life, society, circumstances, and wasn't the cause something in you that was also of value, indeed, that when you had the good fortune to be able to alter circumstances somewhat could turn into happiness and meaning in life for you and another person?

My craving for money is partly due to the fact that for me material or physical and visual things, I think more than for most people, are the expression of something spiritual, but is that a bad attribute or a fault?—it is certainly what enables me to paint a little myself and in any case take the greatest delight in art. I once saw it stated that "'Michelangelo's dome possesses far greater moral and educative value than a whole library of moral doctrine"—and that rings true to me, for I have always thought that one might be as severely judged on the Day of Judgment for having juxtaposed the wrong colors as for having borne false witness against one's neighbor. My clothes, for instance,—I don't throw away such vast sums of money on them to make an impression or to be favorably compared with other women, but because for me, more I think than for others, they are the expression of my personality. I can go about in rags, as you know, but to go out to dinner or the races in a dowdy outfit is as unnatural to me as it would be for you to walk down Bredgade in a pair of white embroidered ladies knickers. . . .

But it is not,—if you still have the patience after all this to go on listening to me,—only my desire for "good things" that makes my poverty so oppressive to me; you know, for instance, that in my relations with the natives, which mean so much to me, it is almost impossible for me not to do things for them on a grand scale, far grander than my position really allows. Of course that is wrong. But it is what gives so much of my happiness here and so much meaning to my life. Of course it can be said that one can help them with other things besides money, and I think that I do that; I give up a great deal of my time to them, with my doctoring, for instance, and of my strength,—and yet here again it is money that represents the violinist's hands; he may well be just as great an artist without them, only God can know that, and who else has any joy of it? The natives have been so hard up this last year; the money that I have lent them here and there,—1,600 shillings,—I have not the heart to demand from them now.

It is probably still contemptible but when I was thinking about my problems in May it seemed to me as if I,—if, for instance, I had won the Calcutta sweep or pulled off a scoop somehow or other,—would have wanted to have that child. It was not only because I myself was afraid of having to economize and so on, but for its own sake.—When one has suffered so much from poverty oneself one does not feel that one can expose another person to it with one's eyes wide open. I believe that everyone would condemn me when I say,—what I *am* saying to you,—that it would have seemed of less consequence to me if I had known that the child's health would have been endangered through my illness; to judge from my own experience I think, as I have said, that it hampers one less than poverty does in being oneself. But however that may be, it is done with.

But now in my relationship with Denys,—which in spite of everything is, as Stuckenberg writes, "the joy of my life,"—you can understand that there too it oppresses me or restricts me, prevents me from being what I would wish to be, as it would seem natural for me in such a relationship? It is not that I want to "put on airs" in front of him or butter him up like some aging mistress who has to ply him with delicacies and comfort in order to make an impression; but when I feel that, as I wrote in my previous letter, I sometimes come to him empty-handed, it is largely due to the fact that I have no money. If I could come back to it after a trip to China, or now when I was last at home, had had a round tour like yours and in Italy, which he loves as much as I do, or in Egypt, which he knows so well,—yes, if I could keep up my knowledge of music with a pianola,—then I would not feel so dependent only on him and my feeling for him, and this makes me unhappy over the very thing that could make me completely happy. You will probably say that these are trifles when one really loves someone; but I would liken it to how you would feel toward

Jonna if you were to lose some of your athletic strength or were to become short-sighted. That you can take her out in your car, go skiing, even that you can carry her upstairs if that should be necessary,—these things may be trifles, but they express your personality, perhaps particularly in your relationship with her.

When I say that I feel poverty as a "foreign body" it is because I think it is not an expression of anything in myself; it is not my own fault. My "exile" with regard to people, my loneliness,—those are my own fault; wherever I was and however I were situated I would probably be assailed by these in some form or other; but where poverty and money as a whole are concerned I have been "taught wrong on purpose," as Bernard Shaw's Mrs. Warren says. I believe that those who had charge of my upbringing and education were quite aware that my nature would not let me be in accord with them, but they *wanted* me to be so; I myself was not aware of it, and so cannot be too sternly reproached for being different and for not acknowledging it. I remember Aunt Bess saying when I got engaged to Bror that the only good she could see in it was that he was a poor man; now I can say that in the whole wretched affair that was the only really miserable thing! I should have made myself realize that when money really did mean so much to me, and as I had none myself, I would have to get myself some in order to be happy, and if I had really tried in earnest it would after all not have been impossible in some way or another. It seems to me that this is where I made my mistake and where I was "misled" and that now I have to suffer for it.

I have written about this at such length because I think that this whole way of thinking is very foreign to you and therefore needed explaining, and also because my ideas have changed since we last talked together;—but it does seem to have got a little out of proportion! The problem does not take up quite as much room in my life as it does in this letter! But if these are to be my "Confessions,"—and this will be the last time I write to you in this fashion,—it must all go down as clearly as possible!

Then after all it is not out of the question for this concern to go well and provide me with the money that I need; it is not such a huge amount. And now that I have taken "stock" of my situation, my happiness or unhappiness here, I think I can end up by saying that if I knew that this would happen, so that I could stay on here enjoying success in the enterprise that through the strange windings of fate has come to be my life work, and that Denys would go on coming here—and the relationship between us remain as it is now,—then I would be as happy as it is possible to be in this life, that is to say, whatever is meant by happiness. Can you remember that we said once that the best way to judge one's happiness or unhappiness in any situation was to imagine it as lasting forever?—and that one would then very often come to the realization that conditions that at that moment did not seem particularly hellish were in fact bad enough to mean that one was "in hell."

However, generally one's circumstances are characterized by the fact that they are not infinite. If I had been told in the middle of the Bay of Biscay that I was to be thrown about like that, while being responsible for Heather, for all eternity, I should undoubtedly have been just as despairing as the damned in Michelangelo's Day of Judgment; but as it was, it was almost an enjoyable experience. And the reverse, like a mirror image, applies to my situation here: if I can only be sure that it will go on, then in spite of everything, through a great deal of doubt and troubles of various kinds, many of which I have now told you about, I am aware that I am very close to Paradise. Of course not in the same way that you are now in Paradise, for I am, as I have said, the child of Lucifer, and the angels' song is not for me, but as close to happiness and balance as with my nature I can approach.

In my last letter to you I wrote that when, like this evening, I stand outside here looking at the moon and listening to a distant ngoma,—and looking back: at my departure from Naples, my shauries with Mrs. Birkbeck!—my illness, my first meeting with Denys,—I sometimes think that I can "see the stork." It is true. I can see it or glimpse it,—by that I mean that I believe in it. Perhaps one day I will really see it. It is still possible that I may find myself here, not so far from all of you and everything at home in comfortable circumstances, because I can take a trip home to you when I feel like it, with success on the farm, with Denys as my trusted old friend, with successors of Pjuske and Heather, with Farah's son as my butler,—with more wisdom, harmony, and balance in my life than ever before. And then I will admit, what I would be willing to acknowledge now, that I have received more than I deserve, and that falling into the various ditches and the wild chase around the lake was worth doing for a sight of the beautiful and perfect contours of the stork!—

I have written too much, but I am justified by the Christian principle: Be unto others etc.—I would be very happy if you would write about yourself as I have written to you. Even if you should not be too pleased with me now you must be tolerant when you consider that it was a necessity for me to write in this way before I could get started on something else, my marionette plays, for instance, which I really must get on with now. I was feeling so uncertain and could not do anything about it until I had heard my own voice, seen myself in that mirror that is the person to whom one is speaking,—taken stock of myself. Now I feel that a weight has lifted from me, and thank you in advance because you are reading this.

I have often thought it desirable that someone should talk or write completely honestly to one; even if one had no special interest in him his life would be bound to be illuminating. When one is reading a book one often thinks: yes it is all very well for it to go in such or such a way, or that it ends in this manner; but I don't believe it. And in life one thinks often: if only those who have been through something similar to my experience would tell me really honestly how it ended.—Of course I cannot say how it ended, time will tell that; but however it turns out, when you come some day to look upon the conclusion of it this may perhaps have some interest as a document to clarify the principles underlying the ditches and the trip around the lake and that produced this particular stork.

I know of no other address than home to send this to; if you get it when somebody else is there you had better say it is a manuscript!—You will certainly be getting one in the fairly near future now that I have unburdened my heart in this letter.

My very best greetings to you, my own old Tommy. I promise not to write like this anymore. And now we get up from the stone seat and go,—you straight in to Jonna, feeling happy if slightly exhausted!

My love to all.

Your Tanne.

To Ingeborg Dinesen

Ngong. Sunday 12/9.26.

. . .I drove out to see Abdullai's mother,—I think Tommy knows her. I cannot describe how heart-rending and tragic it was; she looked like Niobe or one of the women by the Cross, and one can give her no comfort. Abdullai was so good to her; I went to see him shortly before his death, after I heard that he was ill, and he and his mother were so sweet and touching together; they looked at each other really radiantly, like a pair of lovers. Now she is completely broken. It seems hard to believe, but this unhappy mother has lost eleven children. I think they are tuberculous,—they are such nice, fine-looking children, but when they grow up they die off. . . .

Denys is coming back about the 1st of November. . . .

Farah is going to take over Hassan's duca ["grocery store"] here at the end of the month, but will remain in my service. I am glad about it; it will mean that I can get all my stores and meat from him, and now his duca at Thika takes him away so much. Fat Abdullah is to work in the shop for a year when he leaves school. Farah has bought himself a Chevrolet lorry and is very excited, as you can imagine. . . .

To Thomas Dinesen

Ngong. 22.10.26.

. . . I have thought several times of writing to you on the subject of "sexual morality," and as I have some time today I am going to make a few statements which I hope you will take as well-meant advice, and anyhow not take amiss.

I think that one of the most dangerous "moves" to make when one is starting out on a career,—as a politician, social worker, or any kind of writer,—is: "to flog dead horses." It can easily handicap one in people's estimation and brands one, no matter how forward-looking one may be, as having fallen behind. I think that this has weakened the Unitarians, for instance; if they had started out by saying that they brought a message to a more and more godforsaken world they would probably have had quite a different hearing, but they have concentrated their efforts on fighting backward against dogma, orthodoxy, and so on, so that I think whatever they may say now will receive scant attention.

Now I believe that Denmark and Scandinavia, which take the lead in so many directions where progress is concerned, so that a man who is in the lead there will be in the forefront all over the world, in questions of sexual morality and birth control are *officially* surprisingly far behind. This is possibly because we are in fact so liberal that this whole problem has actually been solved without blows being struck, so that there has been no necessity for arguments and these are heard only as faint echos from without; possibly we are conservative about this,—I cannot judge of this since I am not conversant with "intellectual life" and conditions at home at all. But whatever the reason may be I am certain that the battle now being waged on this point at home is a thing of the past in the world at large, and that Thit Jensen's and Dr. Leunbach's war cries will not affect a single soul there. I have talked with Denys about this and he said that he was astonished to hear that we, whom he considered to be very advanced in all kinds of social problems, were still discussing this matter at all. Similarly I,—when I observe the situation out here and see how people with the greatest equanimity and social success conduct themselves—I am certain that the old, negative "sexual morality" has long since had its day. It may be of course that to a certain extent this country is outside the normal bounds of law and order; but English people do not come out here and change their views and consciences the minute they set foot in the country, and there is quite simply nothing that one cannot freely undertake in this direction providing one does not directly irritate and provoke others. I believe this to be the normal state of affairs in every intellectually liberated circle in Europe, more or less *expressly* stated: sexual morality is a private matter, and, birth control, according to their own understanding and capacity, the duty of decent people.

I do not mean that there is no need for a real *ideal* regarding this question; on the contrary, I think the soil is ripe everywhere for the proclamation of a gospel, as it might possibly be for a religious gospel or for a positive social ideal. But it is my conviction that we have no use for any campaign against the old morality, for any criticism of it or judgment of it. What the English people here are fighting against, insofar as they are fighting, is their old *marriage law,*—and they are fighting it because they want to abolish a law that is contrary to the working of conscience of every cultivated human being,—but here the battle takes on other forms, because, when it is a question of law and legislation, even the most old-fashioned, most *"reactionary"* opinion, which is not worthy of consideration in *moral* problems, carries some weight. I think that such an opinion is supported by everything that one reads about it in modern English literature. If you have not already read it I recommend to you a book by Bertrand Russell: "Principles of Social Reconstruction"—already quite an old book, in fact, written during the war, but a really good one in many ways, in my opinion. I would send it to you if it were mine; but I have borrowed it myself.

Naturally, for a man with direct influence on practical life, who has a seat in parliament, for example, there will frequently be occasions when he feels obliged to fall back several centuries in his arguments, for instance, in this matter I am discussing,—when there is a strong Catholic element in the population, that influences legislation,—to concentrate his discussion on the divine institution of marriage bestowed on Adam and Eve in the Garden of Eden, or St. Peter's attitude toward birth control. This can also happen to us others in practical life; Knud might decide to say to Elle that he will not have a Jew in the house, and out here it can be difficult for a lady to have any influence in the "E. A. Woman's League" because she has Dutch blood.

But no one trying to listen to the pioneers working on these problems would emphasize such things in their writings except as curiosities or in a historical survey; for it is obvious that a subject "can be found existing as a part of life and be of interest in life after it has disappeared from literature," and the work of the reconnaissance patrol has little to do with the whereabouts of the baggage train in the rear.

I believe your discussions with Aunt Bess on this subject can be and have been rather dangerous for you. Of course Aunt Bess is not a "reactionary"; but partly because in her own life and among her circle of acquaintance she has no opportunities for coming to understand this matter from a personal point of view, and partly because by nature she has an aversion to it,—although, strangely enough, at the same time it interests her,—she has had no desire to become acquainted with the most elementary literature on the subject; a number of her theories are completely absurd,—for instance, she believes that venereal diseases are caused, irrespective of any other party, by wild erotic life,—and in these discussions with her one has to take account of what is personally distasteful to her,—as when you dared not mention that the abstention from women practiced by the young men at Oxford often led to more or less erotic relationships among themselves,—so that the entire discussion is utterly valueless. These discussions do have a meaning and a value to us because we are so fond of Aunt Bess, because she meant so much to us in our childhood and youth, because she is so gifted, warm, so interested in us; but from the abstract point of view they are in reality only the repetition of a battle that has already been fought and won, and if they were printed they would not be of the remotest interest or relevance concerning the problem,—whatever they might later have, considered as literature!! . . .

If one wants to be one of the best people it follows that one must seek out and associate with the best people; if one wants to be a leading figure one must seek out and get to know leading figures,—not necessarily by mixing with them personally but in thought and intellectual life. I have always regretted the way in which you seemed chiefly to seek out people who were inferior to you or anyway equal. Even though it might have been more difficult for you to find your superiors than for most people,—they were after all somewhere to be found and some of them would have been very close to you. I think I have said before that I longed to see you listening at the feet of a master or a brilliant friend. But if you have an element in your personality that makes it hard for you to associate with these people,—then at least you should always try to follow them in literature, in theories, in the world of ideas. This is not to say that participation in one's own private circle may not be very beneficial, providing one realizes that it is of no importance outside; it is not to say that a conservative politician is not just as effective or even more so than a revolutionary,—but one can only be a Danton on the Mountain and in the Jacobin Club, and an agitator who thinks he is a revolutionary because he carries out a revolt in the editorial offices of "Berlingske Tidende," and a Titan because he can "shock" the Queen Dowager's sewing circle,—he is neither flesh nor fowl; he may possibly be able to help a few individuals but he does not help any ideas.

Therefore as far as this question of sexual morality is concerned I believe that what is needed is far more something positive than something negative, and to criticize and condemn orthodoxy is scarcely necessary; it has already taken such a beating that one feels that in all normal Christian decency it should be left in peace. Freedom . . . in my opinion we have it, and if we may not always have had it, the generation that follows us can be assured of it in full measure. But what are they going to do with this freedom, and where is the star that should shine upon it and them? I must say that I don't know. Eugenics may very well be a fine light to steer by; but I would think that if our descendants' descendants are to voyage with an eye to their descendants' descendants in turn, they might grow somewhat tired of it. This predilection for the continuation of life when that life has no absolute value in itself has always seemed a weak argument to me.—But I will not begin on all that now or this letter will be too long. I myself am inclined to think that in future sexuality as a whole,—for a time,—will come to have less importance when its rights and freedom have finally come to be established and confirmed; this is, after all, what has happened to many forces that have been fettered, indeed, people of today must give hardly a thought to the ideas that lay behind those "human rights" that they would have sacrificed their lives for in the past, and that seemed as necessary as light and air. As you know the sexual element,—physical as well as mental,—in a relationship between man and woman has never seemed the most important to me, there must be more; and from the social point of view there must be more than the relationship between employers and workers, between labour and capital,—but we are still waiting for a prophet to clarify that for us, and perhaps the best thing to do at the moment is to join a party and put one's best efforts into that, or to mind one's own business. . . .

To Ingeborg Dinesen

Ngong. November 7th.1926.

. . . Something has happened to me that I can only call a miracle in miniature. You know that I have often enlarged upon and taken comfort in my theory of "the stork"—that is to say that it happens to one in life as it did to the man in your old illustrated story, who heard the water rushing out of the lake and ran to stop it, fell into a ditch and so on—and next day discovered—the most unexpected result of all: a stork! The day before yesterday, precisely as I was sitting outside by the stone table and thinking,—in connection with Thomas, I think,—over this philosophy of life, I looked up, and there was a stork!—one of the real European or Danish kind, exactly as if it had come down from a roof at Ølholm or out of H. C. Andersen's fairy tales. It is completely tame, walks about on the veranda and comes when it is called, and makes no attempt at all to go away. I do not know where it can have come from; it gives the impression of being familiar with human beings. I am feeding it on frogs, which the totos bring in buckets for 3 cents a piece, and rats caught in the store, it is amusing to watch it eating; it does everything with great dignity. At this moment it is standing on the lawn just outside looking at me gravely. Lulu, with a married daughter and her baby, is keeping it company. I think I have quite a gift with wild animals,—do you remember how tame the owl became, too, in quite a short time? It must be the same ability I have for getting on with the natives,—and the same which gives me my aversion to marriage, if you understand what I mean! I have no desire to capture and shut in and appropriate them, and they can feel that. In any case I care deeply for "the forest's light-footed sons" of all kinds, at whom "the herds bellow," and will,—in conclusion to this dissertation,—put in a word for what all of you call my "snobbery," in the words of old Aarestrup, when after talking of

"—peasants or bards,
with pen and with cockade,
minister or cook,
in rags and in robes
still workers to a man—
Your health, you tame flock!"

he switches over to

"The wild creatures of the forest
and the birds of the air above,
who loves not them?
Ah, aristocrats are the same
as the wild among the tame,
A mighty cheer for them!

etc.

. . . For me the natives, without being in any way commensurate with the aristocracy of humanity, have the same wild charm, and can doubtless feel my sympathy toward them, in the same way as do Lulu and my stork, which Kamau considers to be msei kabisha ["a very old man"], and Farah, who is very well up in A Thousand and One Nights, probably suspects of being the Caliph in disguise. . . .

To Ingeborg Dinesen

Ngong. Sunday 14.Nov.26.

. . . You know that I have been hearing a great deal from home about your trip and what you and the others are thinking about it. But it has all of it been from the point of view of how good or how dangerous it would be for you,—and certainly there is much to be thought of and talked over there. . . . But besides the problems of your health and strength, the circumstances you are leaving behind at home and the difficulties of your journey, there is also to be considered the question of the circumstances you will be coming to meet with here, and where they are concerned I feel that I am responsible, at least with regard to giving you advice. I really thought that I had already written about this long ago; but as to getting a reply to what I wrote I have not heard them *mentioned* or dealt with at all in a single one of any of your letters from home,—it is as if the question did not exist. Now I know well enough from experience that something mysterious happens to letters on their way from Africa to Denmark and vice versa during the long journey; whether it is the climate or the time it takes or the ghosts of old pirates in the Red Sea who have something to do with it I do not know, but there is no doubt about it, what would be absolutely clear and plain in a letter sent from Vejle to Rungsted, or from Njoro to Ngong, on the long journey from one part of the world to another is subjected to some mysterious influence and rendered unclear and obscure,—indeed I even believe that sometimes whole sections disappear. . . .

Now I would like to try to write in such a way that you too can form a fairly accurate judgment of conditions here and take this into account in your future decisions; I would prefer you to have a really clear picture of how things are, and then for all of you to come to a decision according to your own understanding of the situation.

To begin with, I can be quite definite about *some* things:

We have everything in good order here.

The farm itself is looking better than I have ever seen it.

We have more blossom on the trees now than we have ever had before during the short rains, and I think I can say than we have ever had at all.

The sum of this is: that we will have come through all our difficulties and will at last see our work crowned with success, if only:

1. The climatic conditions are favorable,—and

2. Our present harvest is big enough to see us through until the next harvest is ripe.

It is these two factors, on which we are utterly dependent, that are the cause of my doubts. . . .

I am quite aware that when I am assessing these various points the shadows of the past often exert far too much influence. During the six years that I have had responsibility for this concern we have so often teetered on the edge of the abyss that my occasional attacks of dizziness now are a trick played by my nerves, similar to when after a long sea voyage they make one feel as if one were still rocking long after one is safely on land. In 1923, just after Thomas and Viggo had left here, I can remember that I used to heave a sigh of relief on Saturday evening because then I was safe from any decisive and shattering telegram from home for 36 hours. I think that kind of experience sets its mark on one's mentality completely unconsciously and emerges when one least expects it.—Even the prosperous appearance of the farm and the sight of the trees so thickly covered with buds can "upset" me,—and that is really all wrong.

And in addition to this, the possibilities of the success or failure of the farm have gradually come to affect me with the added weight of the years and the strength and the love that I have put into it. . . . For I am not now the same person who boarded the Admiral in Naples in 1914; not only have thirteen years set their mark on me, but all the possibilities open to one between 27 and 41 and *never* again in life have been gathered together in my life here at Ngong. . . .

But now, no more about this. As I said, please let Aunt Bess and Thomas read it, and let them advise you.

I will only write one small thing more. If you do come, please bring some music with you; I can get hold of a piano. Beethoven's piano concerto, "A Midsummer Night's Dream," "The Marriage of Figaro," and some Schubert and Grieg, and "Orpheus.". . .

To Ingeborg Dinesen

Ngong. 27th November 1926.

. . . Everything is looking so good here after the rains. Lulu and my stork are walking about on the lawn that has at last been properly mown in anticipation of your arrival. Of course it is not really Christmas-y here; but you know how balmy it is here after rain, like Bödtcher's poem:

> "The sweltering night has bestowed its gifts,
> fresh as a glass of water is the morning air.
> In through the open window pours the scent
> from Ngong's gardens rich in oranges—"

or from the woods, where everything is in flower. There are masses of mushrooms on the plain, just as when you were here last year.

Denys was out here yesterday and is coming again this afternoon. He wrote to me from Mombasa that he was very glad to be in Africa again and not on his way to England, and added this, which you will understand made me very happy: "Homeward bound I feel that I am, for now Ngong has got more of the feeling of Home to me than England." He may be staying here over Christmas. . . .

To Thomas Dinesen

Ngong. November 29. 1926.

. . . As long as I do not collapse completely into raging against fate I would rather get myself through difficulties without commiseration from fond participating friends,—and I pray fate to preserve everyone I care for from being present at my collapse.

However,—if Mother really wants to come out here, and all of you at home think that it would do her good, I expect I can manage to cope with the situation with good humor and promise you that she will not be made to suffer.

But I must lay down as an absolutely definite condition for her setting out from Denmark at all that no decisive decision regarding the Karen Coffee Co. will be taken while she is here. If such a decision is ever to be made I must be in a position of complete freedom at the time and not under the obligation of paying regard to anyone at all. . . .

On 2 January 1927 Ingeborg Dinesen, then aged seventy, set off on her second journey to Kenya. Thomas Dinesen accompanied her as far as Marseilles; from there her ship sailed on 6 January, and on her arrival at Mombasa on 23 January she was met by Farah, who went with her on the train to Nairobi, where Karen Blixen, Denys Finch Hatton and Tumbo were waiting at the station to greet her. The following letter was a first greeting for Ingeborg Dinesen when she left the ship at Mombasa.

1927

To Ingeborg Dinesen

Ngong. 19.Jan.1927.

My own beloved snow-whitest lamb.

That was a deed of valor!—I always knew myself that my mother was a heroine, but that now it is proved to two continents gladdens my heart.

And now the whole of Africa lies before you with open arms, proud and grateful for your love. The wind, the sun, the shade, the great mango trees, the black children, the game in the Reserve, the white peak of Kilimanjaro and your own Ngong Hills, when you see them from the train,—all of them say "Welcome, welcome"; you are riding straight into the open heart of Africa. . . .

I am sending Farah to meet you and hope he will be of help. I hope you will not mind that Denys is staying here at present. He has been very ill with dysentery and fever, and is just getting over it, so I am reluctant to send him away to Nairobi, where sickness and death are lurking. He has offered to take himself away when you come, but I said that I did not think you would have any objection to his being here; he is so much looking forward to seeing you again. . . .

To Ellen Dahl

[1927]

. . . I dream so frequently about you, and often that we are little girls again,—the other night that we wanted to run away and live in a forest! One's childhood seems so strangely remote when one can never talk about it; I often have to laugh when I am sitting here all alone at the thought of things that one's mind was so full of then. Do you remember when we used to sing to the frogs in the pond? Do you remember the "Frederiksborg dresses,"—I think they were blue calico with white spots,—and what really great experiences those trips to Frederiksborg were, just like the first windflowers and primroses?—I don't actually feel that all that is so much further away now than our last walk to Folehave in the snow on Christmas Eve, when we talked about,—or I expounded upon,—how we were in no danger of corruption because we had already long since been some sort of mummies!. . .

To Thomas Dinesen

Ngong. January 29.1927.

. . . I think myself that, as far as possible from ever having encouraged Mother to make this visit, on the contrary from the outset I emphasized the difficulties of it and toward the end, although perhaps indirectly, advised against it. . . . When I telegraphed a definite cancelation at the end of October, surely you could all understand that I felt the whole plan was inadvisable, and at Christmas I telegraphed you: "prospects doubtful," and later at New Year to Mother herself: "prospects very uncertain."

Denys, who was staying here and who saw all my telegrams, said: "Your people must be quite mad if they let your Mother start after this." But I know that that isn't so; on the contrary, you probably see the situation more clearly than I do. But as I have said, it is hard to understand from halfway around the world. . . .

If you had given any thought at all to *my* point of view wouldn't you have realized that there must be a reason for this standpoint, probably that I was afraid that the situation here would prove too difficult? Then in your discussions on the matter didn't one of you ever say: It will be too much for Tanne?

The reason for my not being able to say anything more definite earlier was that circumstances have a habit of changing so much from one day to another, something that you, who are familiar with them, can surely understand. Now you write: that you have allowed Mother to start in spite of everything I have told you about times being hard; that you cannot help me to get through them, but that I must not let Mother feel them. That is the sort of advice the English give when they say; "Don't be an ass,"—there is nothing to object to in the advice itself; the only drawback is that you are given no instructions on how to implement it!—

However, I do believe that you have all done your very best to arrive at the best decision; now you must believe that I will do my very best to make the best of it.

Please show this to Elle; this will be my last word on the subject. Tender love to you all.

Your Tanne.

To Thomas Dinesen

Ngong.Sunday 27.3.27.

. . . It is such a pleasure to see how much Mother loves this country, and also the black people of all ages; she in turn is worshiped by all. It is not always so easy with the whites; European standards of behavior are so quickly forgotten out here, and I do take so much delight in having Mother get to know the people I know and associate with here, but when we invite ourselves to tea with Charles and Honour Gordon and then hear that Idina and her current husband are staying there I am obliged to try to recall my civilized way of thinking and out of consideration for the dignity of an elderly, distinguished Danish lady, to postpone the visit. Madame Gliemann is never one for keeping anything back, and Mother appreciates her conviviality. . . .

Denys and Mother took a great deal of pleasure in each other's company while both staying here for the first month of her visit. Technically I have not been entirely honest in this situation, although I have often thought of being so,—mostly for the following reasons: first I thought that Mother would get a more *really* true impression if she apprehends the relationship between Denys and me as friendship, because then she will see it as a joy for me, while otherwise, given Mother's background and philosophy of life, it would be difficult for her not to regard it as something of a misfortune,—and it *is* a joy,—partly because it would upset me so much to have this relationship frowned upon or criticized as it upsets other people to have their marriages criticized. I think that very often in life one has to ask with Pilate: "What is truth?"However, if some time when you are talking to Mother you should feel that it would be better to give her a different view of the relationship, you are authorised to do so, and to show her this letter or explain my point of view to her. For that matter it may very well happen that I will manage to confide the situation to Mother before her departure, and it is possible that it will not make the slightest impression on her.

It is so touching and pleasurable for me to have Mother sitting here in the living room and on the veranda sewing cot sheets and pillowcases for your baby. The stork has been stalking around the house all the time and we are sure that it wants to make the acquaintance of the family before setting off for the north to deliver the little one. I would so much like to see it before it grows too big; to me it does not seem very long ago at all since you were a little boy in petticoats stumping around shooting foxes in the woods at Folehave, and I think it would be nicest for us old aunts if it is a boy, although a little girl who took after her sweet mother and grandmother would naturally be irresistible to all of us. . . .

It is awful to think that soon I will be into the last month of Mother's visit; I think she might stay until September, but she won't agree to that. I will go with her to Mombasa where we will stay for a day or two with Ali bin Salim. I do hope she will have a good journey home. I really do not feel she should think of this as her last visit here,—much more that this country should come to be her normal winter resort. She is sitting here sewing and I really feel it is as if she had been born here and that everything out here is her work and property. . . .

After spending more than three months in Kenya, with various visits to different parts of the country to see friends of Karen Blixen and many welcome guests at the farm, Ingeborg Dinesen set sail from Mombasa on Sunday, 1 May, bound for Marseilles. On 24 May Thomas and Jonna Dinesen met her at the central station in Copenhagen. So ended another successful journey.

To Ingeborg Dinesen

Ngong. Saturday. 14.5.27.

. . . As I was coming home from Mombasa, without realizing it I was thinking all the time that you would be standing at the door when I drove up to it. And it has been the same all day; when I am up at the office or out riding I have the same feeling: "Mother is at home, she will be there to meet me when I get back." Perhaps after this last visit of yours I will go on feeling like this for the rest of my days; for it really was almost incredible that you did come, and now that it has happened, it is perfectly reasonable to hope that you will come again, or stay here always. My people and children are always talking about you and are so sympathetic; when I got back on Monday I was very tired and went to bed, and suddenly all the women came in, wearing their Sunday best, looking like a great bouquet of flowers, and ranged themselves quite silently by the door; they had come to greet me and to help me not to grieve too much over the old lady's departure. . . .

Kanuthia was at Nairobi to meet me, with a big parcel of mail, including Elle's telegram, which I replied to immediately. Also a letter from Aunt Bess, which was a great comfort and consolation to me, and several letters from Denys, who is coming out in the first week of June. He was well and had found his father fit and very glad to see him, and he has had a lovely spring in England, but was longing for Africa; he wrote: "I bless you whenever I think of you, which is very often."

I was hoping to get some money cashed before the bank closed to pay the boys but the train was late and I could not bear the thought of staying in there until they opened again, so I put it off until next day and drove straight out. . . . All my boys were standing outside the house to receive me and ask for news of you. Old Pjuske was happy to see me, but very ill; I don't think he has much time left, but he is not suffering and is still himself, so sweet and gentle and keeping his old sense of humour despite his weakness. . . .

As I expected, Banja died this morning. 18.5.

To Ingeborg Dinesen

Ngong. 24. 5. 27.

. . . I know you'll understand that my thoughts this week have chiefly been occupied with old Pjuske's death, I feel as if I had lost the best friend in the world. . . . In fact, I just can't take in the fact that he is dead; the whole time I have the feeling that he must be in the house,—and that if I should take the wings of the morning and dwell in the uttermost parts of the sea, etc., there too his right paw would hold me.

I wrote to Aunt Bess last Sunday, she has been so faithful in writing to me since you left, so I did not get my usual Sunday letter to you written. In the afternoon I managed to get myself thrown from Rouge, because I was so annoyed with Heather for not wanting to go with me when I go out riding, so I thought I would teach her to come by putting her on a lead. But the lead wound itself around my fingers so that I couldn't let go, and cut into one of my fingers, and both Heather and Rouge started to leap about in the greatest excitement and in the end I fell off right on my head, which highly amused some totos who happened to be up by the house. I am still quite tender. . . .

Thomas and Jonna Dinesen's first child, a little girl who was named Anne, was born on 2 June, 1927.

To Thomas and Jonna Dinesen

Ngong. 20.6.27.

My own dear Tommy and Jonna.

Many, many congratulations on the birth of your little girl,—may she "grow and thrive, charm and be charmed," resemble her mother and father, be happy and spread joy around her from her first breath and throughout a long rich life. You may be sure that your telegram set many thoughts in motion in this far country; a whole series of pictures unroll themselves on the receipt of such a message, and it is strange how it somehow turns the future into reality; how many remote and shadowy developments of our problems will be everyday reality for this child, who will be a young woman by the start of the second half of this century, and when she reaches Mother's age will be living in the year 2,000!—and for whom we old aunts and our leben und treiben will come to seem like people from a dark, confused age of legend. And not only I have been affected by the news, but the rumor of a toto for Bwana Thomas has spread out into wide circles and been discussed everywhere; and your little Ingeborg has faithful friends of many shades out here, who will follow her course through life with the greatest interest.

I meant to have written much sooner, but have had so much to do, and now for my sins am writing this in bed, where I have been for a week with what the doctor calls malaria but I myself consider to be pneumonia. So you will only get a short letter but many, many thoughts by night and by day, and good wishes to all three of you.

As you must realize I am longing to hear all about the event; it was a good thing that Mother arrived home in time and had a little while to recover from her journey before the great experience. When you get this perhaps the whole little family is at Rungsted, and little Ingeborg can be wheeled around in the shade under the trees where Grandmother as a happy young wife wheeled little Thomas, and Malla is able to renew her youth. May you come together there for many, many years to come, with myself in a not all too distant future as one of you.

With many many many greetings from Farah, Juma, Ali, Abdullai, Hassan, Kamante, Kamau, Kinanjui, I am and remain your faithful sister and little Ingeborg's sincerely devoted old Aunt

Tanne

To Ingeborg Dinesen

Ngong. 10.7.27.

. . . Thaxton wants to leave on 1 December; I had actually been expecting this, as he has some land in Tanganyika and will lose it if he does not occupy it before the end of the year. In my contract with Dickens, which I am just about to renew, I will stipulate that he is not to have any outside interests in Africa; it is pretty ruinous with farms in other places like this. . . . .

We have had a frightful murder on the farm, probably committed by a Kavirondo who is working in Farah's duca.

Criminals have an extraordinary and interesting way of thinking; this one asserted that he had seen another man committing the crime,—Jerogi, Tommy will probably remember him, the boy who is considered to be a great Don Juan, and who used to go about wearing my cast-off artificial curls to ngomas,—and in court he gave a detailed account of what he had seen, which was completely in accordance with the established facts, so that when it was proved that Jerogi—as usual,—had been taking part in a ngoma in a completely different place on the day of the murder, it was clear that he had in fact been giving evidence against himself. As yet sentence has not been passed, but the case has been referred to the High Court and Abdullai is staying in Nairobi so that he can give evidence. . . .

I am expecting,—more or less, as you can imagine,—Denys here today on his way from south to north with his safari. They are coming from a place where they were chiefly hunting lions, there are a lot there, it is said; Ritchie, who came out and saw me when I was ill, was very concerned about the damage they have caused to the Masai's cattle and the Masai themselves in the Game Reserve; for they have confiscated the Masai's weapons, and now the lions are devouring them, and he thought that if people at home came to hear of it they might well completely give up the whole reserve. Obviously they must do something for the unfortunate Masai. . . .

To Mary Bess Westenholz

Ngong. 13th July. 1927.

My own dearest Aunt Bess.

In the hope that this will reach you in time for your day of celebration I send you many, many felicitations with heartfelt thanks for those of your seventy years in which I have had the joy of knowing and loving you. I am so sad that I cannot join with everyone else in feting you, for I am among those who have most to thank you for, and to whose life you have brought so much significance. From Mrs. Drost's children and the Court at Nusve, throughout all our discussions,—even when trust was most severely shaken,—to your letters to me here, which always bring such great joy, I have looked up to you and realized how much meaning and light and warmth you have brought into the lives of all who knew you; it is not always so much a matter of peace, for you yourself do not want this,—but I wish we could express what you have been to us and how much we love you, then you would feel yourself at Folehave surrounded by a great blossoming of admiration and love and fond thoughts every day.

It is a grief to me that you will probably never get to see my establishment out here; I would so much like to know that your eyes had rested on it just once. I think it is so sad that distances on this diminutive planet still carry such weight for us. But in my heart I feel certain that you are sometimes here, just as on this solemn occasion I am at Folehave.

When I imagine that I really am there, looking first at one of you, then at another, I realize how enormously much I would want to say and get to know, things that are hard to express properly in letters. I can see that I would have to have a discussion with you on marriage; I have thought so much about it after all your letters on the subject and I have started on quite a long dissertation, but it is so much more satisfactory when one can talk about these things. I have been thinking that that is one subject on which I really would be able to speak as an expert, for when Mother says that "no one has tried both things," I must probably be the rare exception to the rule; I really think that,—on average,—I can be said to have been very happily married for a time (and then of course I have emerged safely from the wreck in possession of the title of married woman and my linen cupboard with which to brighten up my present solitary state)—I really do not think that it is a personal feeling of rancor or bitterness against the married state that makes me unable to see it as the only,—or even most,—saving relationship in life. I think that it is hard to preserve one's *humanity* in marriage, or probably actually in this: that one's whole life is passed in relation to just a few people; as well as finding one's whole happiness in this, it is hard to maintain a broad view of life, and without some kind of wide outlook people of my type find it completely impossible to be happy; everything gets "out of proportion" and out of harmony for us.

I can test my belief in this point of view in practice, for instance, when I always prefer an unmarried man as manager on the farm, and am reluctant ever to work with married people in any kind of undertaking. You must not think that I feel it means more to have a coffee farm or a school or a shipbuilding business than wife and children; most probably it can be said to mean less, but it does not to the same extent take possession of one's whole personality, and even if one should put one's whole heart and soul into it in the same way as a happy spouse into his marriage and parents into their children, in my opinion such concerns do not intrude between oneself and the world in the same way that marriage and family most often do; on the contrary, they are, or should be, a means of increasing one's understanding of social conditions, for instance, and other people in general, or of such abstract concepts as justice. Here I might refer to the Apostle Paul himself, when he writes: "He that is unmarried careth for the things that belong to the Lord, how he may please the Lord; but he that is married careth for the things that are of the world, how he may please his wife—" (although to express my opinion properly I would have to change the words *Lord* and *world* in his epistle.)

I think that married happiness very often consists in one's purchasing the continuous,—and unreasonable,—approbation and admiration of the other with a continuous,—and unreasonable,—admiration and approbation of him; in the end neither partner can manage without this, but what has been achieved by it? I do not think that this situation arises in cases where one or both partners have a calling or an occupation outside marriage, when the marriage acts as a haven where they can find rest or strength for their work; but in many cases, of course, such a calling brings conflict into the happy marriage, or this ends by dulling it or making it less valuable than it ought to be. A friendship, in my opinion, no matter how passionate, or a "free relationship," is not in this kind of danger, because these do not encroach upon or have any authority over one's everyday life, tastes, interests, or principles in the same way as marriage; on the contrary, it is most usually mutual work, taste, or interests that bring friends together and condition the friendship, and that remain its chief constituents. . . .

Incidentally, in connection with advising, helping, or looking after other people in general, I want to write something that I have thought of saying before in answer to something in your letters, and that is that I cannot think where you picked up the implicit belief,—which it seems to me you have,—that, when all is said and done, what everyone is striving for, and what, when all is said and done, is what makes them happy, is *bourgeois* happiness,—secure, accepted, normal, domestic happiness. In theory I cannot say anything definite against it; but it has not been my experience that it is either what people are searching for in life or that which satisfies them in the slightest degree. On the contrary, I believe that most people, if they could manage it, would be happier traveling around from one fair to another with a monkey, if that would enable them to gain some experience and have new impressions and movement, than sitting with a secure income in an insured house, where one day is just like another. When you feel that Helene Prahl takes such a wrong view of herself and human nature in general by declaring that she prefers to "have admirers" rather than living for her home and child, then

I have to say that,—while quite agreeing with you that it is extremely silly actually to *say* that kind of thing,—that I think it may very well be that she really has arrived at a knowledge of the truth. Of course it is rather tiresome that in present-day society adventures almost always mean "adventures of the heart," when far from everyone has the inclination for that kind of experience; in our way of life that sort of adventure has gradually come to be about the only one people have the chance of getting. But I think that most people have an unconscious feeling that there is more nourishment for soul and spirit in danger and wild hopes, and in this: in hazarding everything, than in a calm and secure existence, and that they are extremely undernourished in this respect, and would give almost anything to the one who can get them this nourishment.—

This love of adventure and experience is particularly in evidence in my Somalis; every member of that race is happy, *whatever* happens as long as *something* is happening; the thing that makes them quite desperate is an uneventful life,—actually, the same can be said about almost all natives. On this topic I think that among other great writers the brilliant author of "Stankelben" shows his deep understanding of life and human nature; when one has read his book one feels that the wild lions of the wilderness, burning ships, pirates, the coldness of the North Pole, and whales, are the slightest of misfortunes, if they can be called misfortunes at all; but what was really intolerable, what drove him to flight, despair, suicide, was his sister Stine, in many ways such an excellent woman, who wanted to do everything for him, take care of him in every way, save him from the wrath of the pirates, even dive down to the bottom of the sea after him, but who neither could nor would show the remotest understanding for his one great passion, his life's adventure and meaning. . . .

I am very glad to hear that you are reading "Homeless" again with so much interest; it was a favorite book of mine when I was young. Like you I think it has many shortcomings; but the expression that Goldschmidt uses so often about his characters, that he or she "has spirit," can be applied to their creator himself to such an extent that all the rest is of no great consequence. And as I grow older I find myself applying this criterion more and more to the people I meet; of course one cannot say that those people who have no "spirit" may not very well be excellent and useful people, but I think that one gets so little out of being with them, while one is somehow always captivated or moved by those who do have it; here I do not at all mean culture, for many natives, for instance, and people who are hovering on the verge of lunacy "have spirit" in my opinion.

Have you read "The Silver Spoon,"—the last part of "The Forsyte Saga" to be published? As a novel I think it is quite simply bad; I find it impossible to believe in the story, but it is so interesting to go along with Galsworthy,—who is a writer of great spirit, I think,—and follow his exploration and description of modern society. He does not stand still or settle down into one particular phase, but is driven onward by his own great interest in the development of his period, and for historians "The Forsythe Saga" is bound in the future to have great value as a document humain and a really truth-seeking depiction of the thought and mores of a certain class over the last fifty years. Then one has gradually become really interested in Soames, Fleur, and Michael, and I am longing to see how things turn out for them in the third and final part. . . .

Now I will end where I began, by wishing you every possible kind of happiness and good fortune in the year to come, and sending many many greetings to Folehave and to all of you there on the 13th of August. I find it impossible to realize that you have both reached such an age; somehow I feel that you are always so young, indeed, almost younger than we are. Such people as you and your generation we will not see again; I think you preserved yourselves and your generation at such a high standard; and the world has allowed it to decline sadly since. On the last Christmas Eve that I was at home, and Elle and I were walking to Folehave, we spoke of how grateful we were to you because you had taught or inspired us to live in such a way that we could not be "messed about with." I have noticed it with Mother out here,—among people who do not know anything at all about her, and in her great unpretentiousness and modesty, and without ever thinking of her own dignity, she draws a circle around herself that makes it completely impossible for the biggest cad in the world to treat her with nonchalance. Neither is this possible with me; even though I have found myself in circumstances where I could have been thoroughly messed about with, something prevents it, and for that I am indebted to you. You are probably not aware yourself of how great an example you have been to all of us, and when you now have so much homage and gratitude bestowed on you on this your jubilee day, you must not think that it is something produced in us by the solemn mood of the occasion, but that it is sincerely true and the most fervent expression of our hearts, that for once we have the courage to utter.

With thanks for everything, and many many loving greetings from this far country, where something of your spirit and your presence is alive.

Your Tanne.

To Ingeborg Dinesen

[17 August 1927]

. . . My cold is worse than the one I had at home during the summer of 1925, and is hanging on and on, so finally I drove in to see the doctor at the European Hospital,—I dare not go to Burkitt,—and he says that I have what in medical language is called frontal sinusitis, for which he recommends an operation. As you can imagine I am not very keen on letting the local doctors mess about with me, but on the other hand I can't stand the state I am in any longer; I have pain in my head, nose, and ears practically the whole time, and my eyes are running continually, so I have decided to let him do it at the end of this month.

After he had examined my head,—it is one of life's puzzles how they can stick such long steel instruments so far up a person's nose without them coming out at the back of the head,—I had such terrible pains in my head that I really could neither hear nor see, and what did I do on the way home from Nairobi but drive Denys's car into the ditch in the Forest Reserve and smash it up. It was a frightful shock; I had brought René Bent with me from the hospital, too, to give him a few days rest cure here before he had to go back to Nanyuki, he was sitting beside me, and is as you know almost paralized, so I felt great anxiety for him at the very moment of the accident; and also the back was full of boys and totos,—but we had a very lucky escape, only I got a blow from the steering wheel. I am hoping to get the car put right before Denys comes back, and it is sure to be insured. The windows broke when we crashed and made a horrible noise so I thought we were smashed to pieces. René took it like a true hero, and I couldn't help laughing once I had recovered from the first shock; how one could do such an idiotic thing on a good, straight road was quite unbelievable. After we had been pushing and tugging for several hours trying to get it up, one of the big Indian buses came by and they helped us to get it on its feet again, and the engine was still working well enough for me to be able to drive home, although it was hard to steer.

I drove the car in next day in a very dignified manner; it looked pitiful and I was terrified that Denys might turn up unexpectedly. As I was driving in I saw a boy sitting at the side of the road opposite the hanger, he put up his hand to stop me, but I did not dare have him in the car with the steering unsafe. Afterward I sent a note round to Judge Creene, who lives in Coney's house, to ask him to give me a lift out, which he kindly did, and when we went past the boy was still sitting there. I got out to see what was the matter with him, and you cannot imagine anything so frightful as his feet; he had burned or scalded them, but it must have been done a long time ago, they were terribly inflamed and black. The good-natured Creene turned around and we took him in to the hospital, where the doctor said it was very bad; he was quite unable to speak, and I cannot understand how he can have got to the place where he was sitting, or who could have left him there; if we had not picked him up the hyenas would have got him during the night,—it was already getting late. I went to visit him in hospital yesterday, he was very ill, they may have to amputate his feet. It is terrible that such things can happen, who can he have been working for, or where did he come from. . . .

It is dreadful to have as many foster children as I have. Now I have got Tumbo back, but the next thing is that Halima's father wants to send her to Ngong to Jama's wife because she is not learning to speak Somali with us. She is boarding with Maura, Ali's young wife, whom she loves more than anyone else in the world, and she is an intelligent, lively little thing; she hates the idea of leaving here,—after her father had spoken to her, she hit on the idea of saying she could not travel because she had a bad leg, and walked around with her leg bandaged, limping and very pale, so I thought it was something serious; but when I took off the cloth I found absolutely nothing wrong and she roared with laughter at my finding her out. She always reminds me of Missen; she is so upright and graceful and has the same straight look.

Ali and Maura continue to be very happy; yesterday I found them spooning beside the duck pond. Kamante, inflamed by this romance, has resolved to marry a big blooming ndito; at present he and Kinanjui, Tommy's old cook, are employed in my kitchen department and are doing really well, I have just taught them to make sauce bearnaise. . . .

To Ingeborg Dinesen

Ngong. Sunday 21 August 1927.

My own beloved Mother.

Enclosed I am sending you an everlasting flower that I picked on the summit of the Ngong Hills, when I was up there with Ette and Nisse and Ingrid's two eldest girls last Thursday. It is so strange, I always feel that the Ngong Hills, and especially the desert landscape you can see toward the west, actually belong to you; I felt you were with us the whole time, and I wonder whether you by any chance had the feeling of being in the mountains that day. Strangely enough at this dry season there were masses of flowers up there; whole slopes were completely yellow with these everlasting flowers, and then there was a little white clematis climbing about over everything, that I had not seen before.

We had a really lovely day up there. We had arranged to meet at nine o'clock by my corner on the Ngong road, and at that time it was drizzling and there was such a thick fog that you could not see your hand before your face; but as I had dragged them right out from Kiambu, and the girls were very keen about going up, we decided to go nevertheless. It grew worse as we ascended the mountains,—one could not see where one was driving at all, and there was no question of a view. . . . As we were driving the fog started to spread out over the valley, and then we came into the finest, clearest weather with sunshine,—in fact most like a September day at home. I parked my car, with the lunch, Farah, and Juma, in the same place where we once had a meal, but we had decided to climb one of the real peaks before lunch, and Nisse wanted to see how far he could get in his car; actually it was a dress rehearsal for my funeral, for he has given me his word of honor to get me buried on top of the Ngong Hills, if I should die out here while he is in this country!

The grass was still soaking wet when we got out, but of course it dries up so fast here when the sun comes out, and there was a nice light breeze,—it almost seemed up there that one could feel the earth flying off through space. But it certainly is high,—the rest of the party were driving, and I wanted to try if I could run as fast as the car; it is no strain at all to run when one is up there, but when I came to a stop I could hear my heart beating so loudly they must have been able to hear it down in Nairobi. . . . When one gets right up on to the ridge a path made by animals follows the crest, trampled hard down and easy to walk on; it is pleasant to visualize the buffalo, eland, and other animals strolling along it, attracted by the enormous view on both sides. A flock of eland had left it just ahead of us, and as we were ascending the summit,—which is very steep,—we saw them on their way up the next peak, like flies on a wall. There is something special about the Ngong Hills, almost like a dream, at one and the same time so immeasurably huge and free and yet like a toy. Eland are certainly very large animals, like the biggest bulls in Denmark, but from one peak to another they looked quite small, and yet we could see them absolutely clearly as they walked up the path in the short grass, turned and looked at us, and the whole scene, with the blue air and the small trees that you know, looked rather like a gigantic Noah's Ark. We also saw a lot of bushbuck, and at a great height a large number of eagles, as there always are. But we did not get a glimpse of any giraffe. We sat there on the summit for a while and felt we were on the peak of the whole world, and then we went back for lunch, which the boys had been setting out in the meantime, and around it had gathered hundreds of Masai sheep and their shepherd boys. . . .

Yesterday I went out toward Orungi and shot an eland for my Wakamba totos, who pester me to get meat for them. . . .It is a very beautiful sight to see a flock of eland, that do not suspect one's presence, grazing; and then the sun was just setting and was shining on them—there were over 50. I shot one that was quite close to me. But we only had two Wakamba totos with us as we had not had much faith in getting anything, and so we had to send one of them back to fetch the rest of the troops, and meanwhile it grew quite dark. We portioned out all the meat ready for their arrival. . . . The Kavirondo get intoxicated on meat as more civilized folk do on spirits and cannot bear to miss a chance of some. The Wakamba totos appeared, as Tommy can no doubt remember them, like a flock of young vultures, in utter ecstasy, and divided up the meat among themselves, and then I started off for home in the dark with a train of heavily loaded youngsters of all sizes behind me. Around us on all sides we could hear hyenas, and, before we got home, a lion on the remains of our eland. As I was walking along I thought how much I have come to love this country; being out with a gun in the fine, clean air, that penetrates right to bone and marrow after sunset, with the dogs and the happy puffing boys around me, and the stars coming out and growing clear, reminded me of the safaris of my youth. Venus is still shining above the hills, as when you were here,—Tommy will know if it is Venus or not. We thought we had lost Pedro with his enormous load and had to wait half an hour for him by the river; then, when I got to the place where you let down your hair for the Kikuyu nditos, my own boys came to meet me with a lantern; they had grown worried about me, it was past nine o'clock. And the schoolmaster had been waiting in vain for his pupils, too, who had been raising their hymn of praise over their fire and their fat meat instead, in deepest gratitude to Providence, I imagine, for sending them such a baksheesh after long privation. . . .

Ngong. 22/8/1927.

You really must not feel that you are obliged to reply to what I wrote about, what you call "the problem of morals versus beauty." . . . I have given the wrong impression if I made you think that I was talking about *beauty* alone or to a particular extent; for I intended it to include much more: spirit, humor, genius, for instance—indeed, it was altogether so little my intention to uphold one concept to the detriment of another that I think on the contrary that all of these, as the expression of a striving toward an ideal, are in reality one and the same; and if I may so express myself to you, who believe in a *personal* god, when so many religious people make morals into our Lord's speciality and allow great areas of human existence and consciousness,—nature, art, science, for instance,—to remain a kind of No Man's Land, they make it impossible for people of my own type to love or take any interest at all in their idea of God. We know that Kant said that he could never cease to wonder over the glory and wondrousness of two things: the starry sky above him and the moral law within him,—and naturally he had a right to say and think that; but one must surely then also believe in the sincerity of people who do not see any essential difference between the glory and wonder of the starry sky and of the sea or the desert or a forest, any more than between that which one terms the moral law and the invincible striving for the ideal in all its manifestations; being very unversed in philosophy I am not sure whether by his "moral law" Kant meant only what is generally understood by "morals,"—are not the Pythagorean theorem, or the law of perspective, or the rules of harmony in music, for instance, equally representative of "moral law,"—Nemesis, if you like, in another way,—as, for instance, the commandment: Thou shalt not steal?—or is it not the same moral law or instinct, conscience, "the voice of God," that made the Dukhobors refuse, even at the cost of their lives, to fight in a war, and Beethoven to work, without regard for anything else at all, toward the highest perfection he could attain in his symphonies, or Heine to rewrite "Atta Troll" nineteen times, or Einstein to wear himself out by his astronomical investigations?. . . .

To Ingeborg Dinesen

Sunday 9th September, 1927.

. . . On Thursday morning I drove in to Dr. Sorabjee. . . . He dripped cocaine into my eyes, which did not hurt in the slightest, but I am constantly amazed to see what long instruments they can put into one's head; after he had cut me, he put in two steel pins in order to widen the "tear ducts" and they were really like the longest knitting needles and were only just sticking out of the corners of my eyes. I seem to remember Elle describing this operation on an old woman, from when she was at Frederik's Hospital. So I drove away like Christian IV with a blood-stained bandage over my eyes, much to the horror of people I knew who saw me; I was in my own car, as Denys does not like Farah to drive his. . . .

In spite of all the privations I am happier here than I ever believed it possible to be. For after all I am free,—would be completely free if we could overcome our economic problems, and there is so much here that I love. And then, you know, my relationship with Denys makes me very happy. I wrote to Ellen Wanscher recently that I can really understand how King Valdemar felt when he said that Our Lord was welcome to keep the kingdom of heaven if he could remain in possession of Gurre. I should not repeat this statement after I had seen the terrible consequences that followed it for him, but I imagine that he did not make it out of arrogance, but as a kind of acknowledgement; he was declaring himself to be satisfied with what he had received from life and demanded no more. And that is how I feel with regard to Ngong and all that it represents to me. No doubt it is impossible for it all to last forever, and perhaps in fifteen years' time I may come home and keep house for Anders, if he has not married by then; but if I had to leave here now I believe, as I have said, that I would die.

When you are thinking about me, you must not dwell on my loneliness and my difficulties, but on this lovely country, my dear natives, my horses and dogs, on the feeling I have of being in the right place for me, of being able to achieve something, and then on the great joy I have of being with someone here whom I really do love. It will turn out well, you will see, and we will have far fewer difficulties in the future and will meet again with gladness in the spring of 29; of course I long for Denmark and for all of you, and especially for you, but after all one must pay for everything in this world, and I am not paying too dearly here,—if only I may stay on here.

Goodbye, my dearest snow-white lamb.

Your Tanne.

To Thomas Dinesen

Ngong. 18th September 1927.

. . . You can imagine how much it interested me to read your article, dealing as it does with some of the questions that interest me most of all, and that we have discussed so often. Of course a number of your opinions and arguments have developed since my time. I think it is *absolutely excellent*, in some ways the clearest and most intelligent view I have ever read on this subject. It is so concise as well. You have included everything and related it all so well; you are neither too brief nor too wordy,—I always have difficulty in avoiding the latter.

And then I must say that what I particularly admire in you,—as also often in oral discussion,—is your consideration for your opponents or for anyone holding opinions that differ from yours at all. You show them both great understanding in their views and opinions, and much patience in presenting your own. I know that I am lacking in these things, as on the whole most polemicists are. The majority of people speak *for themselves* in a discussion,—and the more excited they get, the more this is so,—they are neither interested in listening to or allowing themselves to be enriched by their opponent, nor to try to enrich him. Therefore discussions so often are pointless. On both sides the person speaking feels he is the more important, and if he is not raging at the views of the other or holding them up to ridicule, his courtesy seldom goes further than to ignore them, while his entire interest is concentrated on his own. . . .

You most probably owe a good deal of this good will toward your opponents to the discussions with Aunt Bess that I described in my letter as being a possible danger for you. Well, it may also be that because you are so much younger than I am and a man as well you find it easier than I to avoid a feeling of bitterness where the old laws and ideals are concerned. It is easy to judge a defeated opponent with impartiality and appreciation, one can even come to have some fondness for him and see his regime as something poetic or idyllic; but while he held the power he was still just as unbearable for all that. For instance, where the case of the emancipation of women is concerned, I myself feel, despite my affection for much that was beautiful and graceful in the old ideals, despite my gratitude toward those old women who struck the first blow for our freedom and independence, that the accounts have not been quite settled with a world, a system (not, of course, with any individuals at all), that with a perfectly clear conscience allowed practically all my abilities to lie fallow and passed me on to charity or prostitution in some shape or other. . . .

Regarding the problem that has been keeping me from writing to you because I could not decide whether there was any point in discussing it with you or not,—I myself have been very preoccupied with it, but it may be quite another matter for you,—it is all bound up with this:

When Denys came out here last November he took passage on an Italian ship and had spent a few days en route in Italian Somaliland,—in Mogadishu and Kismayo,—and the accounts that he gave of the Italians' treatment of the Somalis shocked me very greatly, and he himself was severely shaken by conditions there. He had stayed with an old acquaintance, a Conte Capallo, I think, who had been employed there for many years and who was attached to the people, and who was now in absolute despair over what was happening; he had supplied him with a lot of details and stories that sounded utterly incredible to me, but that were apparently quite true. From what I understood they have a new governor, who is a kind of little Mussolini,—and is under his protection,—but who sounds as if he has an even greater degree of folie de grandeur, and it seems to be the fundamental aim of himself and his subordinates and with all the aid of all possible means, to subjugate and crush a proud nation thoroughly. What Denys told me about completely systematic massacres, about dues and fines for quite imaginary offenses, which laid waste whole districts, of the ruthless abduction of Somali women and young boys by utterly coarse and brutal petty Italian military personnel and officials for their harems,—the trafficking in boys seems particularly prevalent,—was more than frightful. Torture is made use of quite openly,—Denys told me that his friend there had described to him how four Somalis of good family who had protested against the Italian injustices had been subjected to torture for a theft that everyone concerned knew they had never committed; two had died under it, and Denys had seen their clothes and those of the survivors himself, and said that they were completely covered in blood. Meanwhile the Governor is building himself a palace and living like a king. Denys said: "If I have ever seen a region in need of the intervention of the League of Nations, it was there."

I asked him why he did not do something about it himself, but in further conversations it became clear to me how different from ours the English,—and probably that of every great nation,—view of politics is. They are far more disciplined. And this is probably right, seen from their point of view,—because of the far-reaching effects that may be caused by the political action of a member of a great nation, in general their politics must be left in the hands of those elected to be responsible for them. Anyhow, I was given to understand it thus,—for instance, through what Denys said about the best course of action here being to get France to take up the matter, since the French hate the Italians and resented them getting more of Somaliland; but then England's relationship with France and Italy would come into play.

But then one thinks: can it not be that small nations should feel it their duty to make a stand in favor of the purely human ideas of right and wrong, since they would not be suspected of being led by their own political interests?

I have really been thinking of the possibility of taking this matter up personally,—although I haven't got further in my plan of campaign than thinking of learning Italian. But for one thing I cannot desert my work here with a good conscience,—not so much for the farm, but for the natives of this land,—and for another, such a task is after all more difficult for a woman to undertake,—even if I did go to it wearing Elle's trouser suit. . . .

Well, but now I have written to you about it. . . .

To Ingeborg Dinesen

Ngong. Sunday 2nd October 1927.

. . . I have in fact received Tommy's article on birth control and think that he has written it extremely clearly and concisely. . . I myself believe that there is no possible way of ignoring the idea of birth control any longer, whatever the twenty-five million Catholic women may say,—that is to say, that we must inevitably go forward to education and choice where that subject is concerned,—but of course, as one goes through life and feels one comes to understand it better, one acquires numerous new views,. and I am in the process of reshaping my ideas about individuality and democracy quite a lot; I have to confess that I believe it is necessary for there to be an élite,—that is, people who not only *are* something, but *represent* something, and I can foresee that it might well happen that while a love affair remained an individual matter, breeding the future stock could become a special and important task for the sake of society, and that marriage thereby might take on a new form or rather return to something much more akin to the well-considered matches of former times made for the sake of the family, the property or the dynasty; but as I said, all this is not yet completely clear to me.

I fail to see how there can be anything more ideal nowadays in living together in order to have children than for the individuals' own sake, for clearly no one these days grows fruitful and multiplies for the sake of name, country, or God, or for anything at all apart from or more important than themselves, but because the idea of a family is attractive to them, or because they may wish to feel themselves surrounded by beings who are dependent on them or whom they can influence, or who are bound to love them, when they cannot get anyone else to do so, which I do not think is in the slightest degree more ideal or moral than what the partners in a love affair strive for and live by, and where the goals are mutual love, satisfaction and development. Of course I do not know how the situation is among genuinely believing Catholics but I do not think there are any other people who produce large families nowadays with a really good conscience,—that is to say *with a feeling of vocation*—(except perhaps in old military German families, if any of those still exist); and in my opinion it is the idea, the ideal *of uncontrolled births* that is lacking, while the protagonists of birth control have, if not exactly an ideal, then at least a number of arguments of practical value, and consideration for the child, to put forward. . . .

For my sins I was dragged off to a dinner and dance with the Steeles last week, horribly trying and they are the sort of people I find completely uncongenial; undoubtedly very good, nice people, but I would rather spend my time with bandits in the mountains. But of course life does become simpler as one gradually comes to understand oneself and so avoids wasting time trying to combine what *cannot* be combined. . . .

To Ingeborg Dinesen

Ngong. Sunday 16th October.
1927.

. . . If we pull through I will not forget Dickens and how he has kept up his hopes and spirits during these trying months. Running a farm under such conditions is probably much like leading an army in retreat, and I have been thinking a lot about Napoleon on the retreat from Moscow; he has my heartiest sympathy. But Dickens has been my Marshal Ney who was complimented by the Emperor because he presented himself each morning every bit as carefully shaven and immaculately turned out as if he were attending a review outside Paris,—and that *is* something to be commended; not that shaving is actually Dickens's strong point, but his strength and fortitude, expressed in his own way, have been of inestimable value to me. . . .

I took Tumbo to his boarding school at Pangani, much against my will; I cannot hold out against Juma's ambitions to have him taught learned pursuits any longer. It was really sad to have to leave him there with his little bundle in his hand and to see him gazing after the car, I am going to see him again on Monday. I bribed all the totos and the schoolmaster with costly presents to make them treat him well; but it is such a beastly place up there, you get covered with dust and dirt, and I feel Tumbo is too small to be able to look after himself. Halima, my other foster child, has been taken to Embu where I can never get to see her,—she and Maura, Ali's wife, have a really touching relationship; there was a rumor the other day that Halima was in Nairobi, and Maura walked all the way there barefoot in order to see her. I asked her if she had talked to her,—no, but she had seen her standing in a doorway. She did not want to talk to her as she was afraid that Halima would be so upset that she would start crying, and that would annoy her foster parents.—Not many young men in love could match up to Maura. . . .

I am so happy that I can write to you about Denys, and it is beautiful and generous-hearted of you; I know you understand how far I am from having any feeling of bad conscience over the matter,—but it is of course a little outside the bounds of the law. . . .

To Ingeborg Dinesen

Ngong 1st November 1927.

. . . Denys is staying here for the time being; he arrived a fortnight ago and will stay, I hope, until he goes out on his next safari just after Christmas. It is not only, as you can imagine, a delight, but so immeasurably stimulating for me to have him here; indeed, I must say that life could not be more happy for me than when he is in my house. . . .

Before I forget, in answer to your question I can tell you that the grass has grown well on my lawn on the west side, but of course it will be a little while before it becomes a real lawn, it will have to be cut a few times first. My gramophone is working extremely well and Denys brought a lot of excellent records back with him, among them the Kreutzer sonata which really sounds so lovely,—although no doubt you people who are able to listen to real music, despise gramophones. Tumbo is back at his school, I can't stop Juma's ambition for him, but he comes out here for weekends and then is made a great fuss of by the whole establishment, and actually I think he is quite happy "at Eton," as Denys calls it. Tumbo is such a sweet, frank and honest, friendly little person, and he seems to have a lot of friends at Pangani too, where he is probably the youngest boarder. . . .

As you know, Thaxton has left, he was really a bit crazy in the end, I think, so that it seems quite a relief, particularly for the new man Nisbit, who appears to be getting on well with Dickens, which is one of the most important things, and to be sensible about labour. . . now the Nisbits are moving into Thaxton's house, which is indescribably filthy; Madame Nisbit is slaving away getting it clean, and I will probably have to spend a bit on painting for them; otherwise they are very happy to have come out to Ngong from the scorching region around Donya Sabuk. . . .

Last night I had a fearful shaurie, I was called out to a boy who had come here to get quinine when I was out, and who had been given two corrosive sublimate tablets by my new dog toto on his own authority, which he had eaten; I had to go out to him in the pitch dark, and as was to be expected he was very ill, vomiting great streams of blood and in great pain; I have him here now and am hoping that I will be able to pull him through. I am getting a medicine cupboard made now that can be locked, as the present situation appears to be too dangerous. Denys gave the toto a beating for me.

I am tremendously satisfied with my kitchen department, which has never gone so well before, and really provides me with much relief. I think Kamante has a great talent for cooking; yesterday he made some really fine croustades all on his own and is really good at mayonnaise and sauce hollandaise and bearnaise. The trouble is that the temptation to spend my time in the kitchen teaching him is so great that I neglect more important things, which shows that the definition of "a vice" as: "a sin that has become a habit" is wrong; for after all being in the kitchen can hardly be called a sin. . . .

To Thomas Dinesen

Ngong. November 19. 1927.

. . . I am sure you both know that I send many loving thoughts to you every day,—when one is as close to someone as I am to you, that person's happiness means so much in one's life; and as we are probably not the easiest people for Our Lord to dispose for, and there have certainly been times, as for instance when you were out here, when the problem seemed hard to solve, I think He has shown both imagination and resolution in His dealings with us, and that we both have reason to take off our hats. May we both still be standing holding them in our hands by the next New Year. . . .

You write that you have not heard from me for a long time. I hope that you have since received my letter thanking you for your paper on birth control. I have in fact been giving a good deal of thought to it,—or rather to that part of it that deals with sexual morality as a whole, and now I have a few things to say about it.

I think that your paper reveals itself to have been written by a young man,—that is to say, for him the sexual problem has been concentrated on the problems of young people forced either to comply with abstinence or surrogates, and with the solution of their problem he feels that the whole problem has been solved. Most older people will probably agree with me in thinking that this is only one aspect of the matter. No matter how fervently I may hope that you will not be confronted with the difficulties of "marriage,"—you will still, if this be the case (whatever Aunt Bess with her blind faith in the saving power of marriage, may have to say), be an exception. Read Strindberg, read Bernard Shaw, read, indeed, old Shakespeare,—Othello was a perfectly respectable person, with an unusually generous nature in the bargain; nothing on earth would have induced him to suffocate a defenseless person in bed except for one reason,—and you will see the shoe pinches the one who wears it!

I must say that actually I speak without much *personal* experience here. Polowtzoff told me that he had never known "anybody so sensual and so little sexual," and that was probably not far wrong. The breakup of my marriage was caused by the sort of thing that could have brought about the breakup of a friendship or a company, not the sort of passion that causes Strindberg's "Father" to take leave of his senses or that, as I said, drove Othello to murder. I have emerged from any love affairs that I have had as the very best of friends with my partner. What has captivated or infatuated me, or however you like to put it, has been a human personality or some kind of mutual interest that we have shared,—or else the whole relationship has been, if I may so express it, like a game or a dance. I don't think I am capable of treating a sexual relationship in itself with any great seriousness. And although I think it is delightful to go out hunting or to the ballet or to travel with a person I am in love with, I find it intolerable to "be an object." Never in my life have I been able to sit and gaze adoringly into somebody's eyes; I just don't think I could do it. I do not in the least like being caressed, I just can't stand being called by pet names and made a fuss about.

But I have in fact seen enough of other people to know that this is not the usual state of affairs. On the whole when all is said and done the other partner in the relationship and his or her actual human personality is fundamentally of minor importance and may be chosen purely accidentally; what moves them, delights them, enchants them, destroys them (etc.) is the force of erotic feeling. I think one can go so far as to say that the majority of happily married people find happiness in marriage because *they enjoy being married,* much more than because they like their particular spouse, and because marriage or the marital relationship attracts them, even though he may not always do so. They are blissfully happy in his arms because they like to be fondled and paid court to,—and this happiness makes them care for and feel deep affection for the person who pays court to them and caresses them.

This can also lead to the most intimate, the most fateful relationship between two people who hardly know each other—(it was that very fact: that he did not know her, that Iago played on with Othello in his relationship with Desdemona)—and are completely unsuited to each other. A person whom you may have met quite by chance, a woman you have seen for two days and never spoken intimately to, may, because to you she represents one of the greatest and most violent of life's forces, inspire you, make you happy, torture, destroy, drive you out of your mind far more easily than a long-tried friend, indeed, in a way in which he could never begin to do it.

There *must* be something out of proportion in the purely personal relationship between people who are in this way "possessed," in the power of a power. You write that "far the greatest majority of people will have to admit that the most unworthy of their actions are in the sphere of sexual relationships." But on the whole the majority of people have known ecstasy only in these relationships, known what it is to be "beside themselves."

In fact a great deal of what could be stamped as really tangible lies, but that in this connection is not so, but is a displacement, a transference of concepts, is an almost inevitable part of a sexual relationship, which can be ascribed to the same phenomenon. It is (sorry) my old simile of the assignat transferred to gold in another manner. It is hardly possible, it is unnatural, it is not at all decent at the zenith of an "erotic situation" to make use of ordinary human, normal and truthful forms of expression. The situation requires the language to be elevated on to a completely different plane. The lover groans in the beloved's arms: "I have never loved anyone but you. I will die for you. You wonderful woman, I want nothing in life but you." Does he mean it?—Yes. Must he make good his utterances and be held to account for them next day?—In no way. He was not compos mentis, and his greatest confusion of ideas was the error of mistaking an individual for one of the strongest forces of life. He could truthfully have said: I cannot live without love ten minutes longer; but in the circumstances that can neither be thought nor said, it is expressed as: I cannot live for ten minutes without Caroline. It takes a Bienen to talk,—and then not in cold blood,—of "a little of what you fancy," and it is probably doubtful if Bienen's partner, however much he had renounced romance in the relationship and however much they were in agreement, appreciated his honesty.

Say what you will, these are dangerous circumstances. (And grow still more so through the much discussed children whose only means of getting into the world to date is through these circumstances.) There is actually not a little to be said for the sensible views of the old folk, who tried to protect themselves in every way they could and equip themselves with both safety valves and fireproof walls; this perilous power was necessary to life, but no one should be permitted to set it free, play with it without being under control or run around with it by themselves.

Naturally you may assert that neither the law nor the police can prevent the occurrence of personal tragedies here as in any other sphere. But one is not thinking of those when one talks about "morals."—What is needed is a code, to provide instructions for exchanging currency, an opinion. I have the impression that most people at the moment are in a state of absolute confusion about everything concerning rights and duties in the field of sexual relationships, marriage included. I think one exception is to be found in a small advanced minority, the "smart set" in the larger countries (and to a certain extent my circle of acquaintance out here), where a sexual relationship is more or less regarded as the normal social convention among young people, in which no one,—spouses, parents, or former lovers not excepted,—have a right to interfere, and where everything is all right, providing neither partner looses [*sic*] his temper or in any way pretends to take it seriously.

When people talk about "old days" they are generally thinking of a period that ended fifty years ago, and treating it as if it had been going on since the beginning of time. Most people who discuss sexual morality at home and in this connection refer to the old days as preferable, are reckoning with the last seventy-five years of the nineteenth century and are not thinking of the ancient Egyptians, not even of the time preceding the French Revolution. But the very period they are upholding,—let us say from the fall of Napoleon up to the World War,—far from being a solid established order, in my view forms a very brief and myopic period of exception in the history of man where sexual morality is concerned, since it appears to me to be the only era that has reckoned to build really practical and concrete situations in life,—home, family, economic conditions,—on this dangerous and unreliable force: eroticism.

Presumably this came in with Romanticism which took a serious view of love as passion in an entirely new manner; but I do not know enough about this to be able to express myself. In my view the system could not last and in fact did not last; it has pulled a lot down with it—(and in my opinion together with a number of other factors has contributed in breaking down the position of women. At a pinch it is possible to retain one's human dignity in having to earn one's keep by one's efficiency in brewing and baking, bringing up a large family, running a beautiful large house or taking a post at Court, but not by one's good figure and capacity to please)—and I think that by confusing realities and feelings in a hitherto unknown manner it has done much to muddle up a code that was probably none too clear previously.

But all the same, in an age where at any rate in theory and according to the law and the prophets a sexual relationship outside the bonds of marriage was in itself "immoral," marriage in itself "moral," there were more guidelines than there are now and the partners concerned had a better idea of where they stood. A husband could demand and expect faithfulness, a certain degree of obedience, and legitimate children from his wife, a wife support for her lifetime and a certain respect from her husband. To offend against these expectations was to commit a breach of contract affirmed by official opinion. A girl who had been seduced had not much in the way of secular rights to insist upon but she could invoke the indignation of heaven; a married lady's lover was a free lance who had to have an eye for the main chance of what he could get out of the affair.

It seems to me that nowadays the moral demands, obligations and rights in a sexual relationship depend entirely on the personalities concerned, and that people who are lacking in personality and personal convictions are pretty much "at sea" in this situation,—indeed, no matter how much sexual education they may have only the very few have the slightest idea of what they are letting themselves in for when they embark on a sexual relationship.

You may be right in saying that general moral laws are as valid here as elsewhere and that unselfishness, consideration and honesty will stand the test just as well here as in every other kind of human relationship. But in practice conditions are seldom so clearly defined to obviate the necessity for a more exact exposition of these ideal rules of life. After all, they exist for most other forms of human intercourse. But at the moment I think that a great deal of uncertainty and disagreement prevails over a great many situations connected with sexual morality.

To what degree does one take it upon oneself to be faithful when one embarks upon a love affair,—marriage included? Is absolute honesty regarding this point a generally acknowledged demand? Does a love affair or marriage bring with it any obligation, unless by specific agreement, in the matter of children? Is it, as I have frequently heard it said, a "dirty trick" on the part of a woman who allows herself to become pregnant without the man's expressed assent, either in a marriage or a free relationship, or is it a breach of contract on the husband's side to deny her this? Does a sexual relationship imply a certain obligation toward the actual sexual life of the other partner, or is the general conception of morals solely on the side of the woman who breaks off marital intercourse but maintains the other aspects of the relationship?

I think that there is far from any real understanding of such questions, and very many more that I could mention.

In my opinion it is impossible for any agreement to endure that can only, in the event of divergences of opinion, seek a solution by saying: well, then, we can always break it off. But I really think that for the time being that is what most marriages and love relationships resort to when things go wrong. It is certainly very difficult for the person feeling himself wronged to point to anything in the way of a foregoing agreement to hold on to. I recently heard of a conflict like this from a young wife. Her husband had in no small degree neglected to observe what in the old days was held to be the duty of fidelity in marriage, and when she remonstrated he suggested that she was perfectly free to do likewise; he would have no objection. This was completely unsatisfactory to her as she had no such desires. All right, then, they could get divorced, and what more could she want?

I really do not know whether according to the generally prevailing moral rules she could ask for anything more. I assume that nobody would base his practical life on anything so uncertain,—for instance, marry out of his country and class on such a loosely constructed basis. And apart from the fact that a sexual morality like this would "do away" with marriage, not the worst thing that could happen, it would also discourage people from putting very much at all into their sexual relationships. As I have already said,—and here I really can speak with a certain amount of experience,—in those circles where this kind of view of sexual relationships is the prevailing one these relationships are those that are least long lasting and are regarded the least seriously by everyone. A friendship or a partnership of any kind whatever carries quite another kind of weight.

I am quite aware that no one, whether he holds views in either one or the other direction, can work miracles or change human nature. But some ideal or other can be set up and striven for. Where it is a matter of a *relationship,* where therefore it is a matter of more than one person's happiness or well-being, there must be a certain clarity, a certain understanding; otherwise you may find yourself playing football with a partner who does not know what it means to be offside. Either a "sexual relationship" means something in itself and carries a certain weight, a significance outside itself, and a mistake here is really a misfortune or as they used to say "a fall,"—or it exists entirely for the pleasure of the participants, and is entered upon and dissolved in accordance.

 I don't really think that your marriage, based on experience and experiment, in itself possesses more powers of resistance than, for instance, Luther's, instituted as acceptable to God,—among other reasons because the experienced and tested spouse may well choose an entirely inexperienced partner, and yet will be little inclined to let marriage be that partner's first experience, which later of course may benefit him or her.—

This letter is far from being what it should be, partly because I have been interrupted the whole time by Denys, who has now driven off to Nairobi, thank God. I have considered not sending it; but I have so many Christmas letters to write that the result would probably be that you would get nothing at all, and this letter, stupid as it is, will let you know that it brings very many greetings and loving thoughts to you and yours, and so I am sending it.

Give Jonna and Anne a hug each from me; so much deep love and sympathy goes with you along all your paths, not least from Africa and your faithful old sister

Tanne.

To Anders Dinesen

Ngong. 22nd November. 1927.

Dear old Anders.

Merry Christmas, and very best wishes for a really happy 1928. You know, we clodhoppers understand each other and must stick together,—if only the good God had a sense of liberty, equality, and fraternity and could have let me have a bit of your downpour in 1927; you would have been heartily welcome to some of my drought. Now your crops will be gathered in, and I hope it turned out to be better than expected, and I am busy getting off the trees what coffee I can that has not dried up and fallen off already, and think I will not do too badly after all; but it is heartrending to see the bushes covered with little dry, black berries after being lovely white blossom in the spring and which could have grown into big red coffee berries at £140 a ton, if the heavens had not been so utterly contrary. All the same I still think it is the only kind of work that is really worthwhile, this clodhopping, and I shall go on with it until I am forced to hop off myself.—

Apart from good weather and bounteous harvest and full barns and good prices I don't know what to wish you,—in general, I mean,—oh, yes, and that Thyra may make a full recovery; it is really terrible for you that she has been so ill, and I imagine that it is difficult for you to manage without her,—I like her so much and think she suits you well. If you are thinking of following the usual example and entering the state of matrimony and so on, I wish that you may be just as blissfully happy as the two Thomases. But if you can get on without that sort of thing be sure that I will come and keep house for you in 1948. But you must come out here before then. I know quite well that Karen Coffee Co. have got the idea into their heads that they are going to be bankrupted, but no such thing as that is going to happen. And here there are miles of unrestricted plains, green marshes and fine thorn forests, huge flocks of zebra and wildebeest gallop along, elephants stroll and lions roar for you and your peers, but no one knows how long it will last; for there are not so many places left in the world where nature is still undisturbed and that have not been marked by the hand of man. You will be more welcome than almost any other person, and my black folk, guns, and dogs will be at your disposal with whatever help I can give you. So then it remains for me to send many greetings and good wishes and thanks for everything in the old year.

Your faithful sister Tanne.

To Ellen Dahl

Ngong. 22.11.1927.

. . . It always makes me so happy to hear from you about everything at home, for we understand each other, and your letters say more to me than other people's.—I do feel a great longing for you all and can't tell you what I would sometimes give to see you or Tommy or Malla coming through the door, or to be able to walk over to tea at Folehave, and of course each year something vanishes from the world that one knew at home; it even makes me sad not to be able to go by bus to Villa Vesta. Sometimes I pine so dreadfully for Danish nature, and I know you will sympathize with me over that!—But it is a part of life that something grows up where something else has gone,—not only in the small person of Anne and the new young home in Serridslevvej, but for us as well, who have no fleshly descendants to leave behind us in this world,—although something of our spirit must remain and grow green here and there.

This letter is being written by a very happy person, which I am sure will gladden your loving, sisterly mind. We have had wonderful rains, and because of various circumstances I myself feel like a tree that is blossoming and bursting into leaf. . . .

Ngong. 1.12.1927

. . . I realy think that what is anyway part of the underlying cause of the present-day "women's movement" is the fact that men have lost their prestige, and this is probably not entirely their own fault but due to the fact that conditions of life have changed with the advance of civilization; physical strength has not the importance it once had, and with comparative peace and security for moving about women too are able to acquire insight and experience in many spheres that were once the exclusive preserves of men. Aunt Bess writes that what in her opinion is woman's greatest happiness in life, and what she would wish most for herself, is to serve an (excellent) husband,—but of course she was not able to find one for herself. To serve a Napoleon, Gustaf Adolph or General Booth,—as far as that goes everyone would be prepared to do, men as well as women; but the question here is: is the average woman to serve the average man? and I cannot find the least reason for that, and I am sure the average woman and average man would agree with me. . . .

Denys is here, but is not well; he himself thinks it is something to do with his heart, and I think it probably may be that from what I know of it from Elle, he has the same sort of restlessness and is horribly thin. He is supposed to be taking a safari out just after Christmas and is very worried in case he is not up to it. . . .

To Ingeborg Dinesen

Ngong. 5.12.1927.

. . . Horrible things have been happening on the farm. On Friday evening we had a murder, a little Kikuyu girl,—Monyu's daughter,—was strangled with a strap out in the maize field. I can't remember whether I wrote about the murder, almost exactly similar, that was committed here seven months ago while Dickens was in South Africa. It was a little girl who was murdered then, too, at the same time of day and almost on the same spot. They arrested a Kavirondo who was working for Farah in his duca and who tried to throw the blame on Jerogi, whom Thomas can no doubt remember and perhaps you as well; he was the one who was so enchanting that no woman could resist him,—but on that occasion he had an alibi as he had been at a ngoma near Kikuyu. I think that in the meantime they have hanged the accused Kavirondo, but have heard from the other side that he has lodged an appeal which was to be heard yesterday. I think everything indicates that the same man committed both crimes, so I have let them know about this as quickly as possible, as it would be a great shame if they hanged an innocent man,—if they have not already done so.

Jerogi is certainly not guilty this time either as I took him to hospital with pneumonia last week, and he died there the same evening the child was killed. But most people think that the criminal is Lori, Mrs. Dickens's garden boy, whom you often saw down in my garden with Muthaiga. Strangely enough, if he really is the murderer, I must have spoken to him just before he committed the crime and again immediately afterward. For I happened to be down in my garden on Friday afternoon about five to give Muthaiga a message; he was not there, and I called Lori and explained it to him. He left the garden at the same time as I did, and I went up along Hemsted's boundary and sat and smoked a cigarette and looked around for partridge, which I had seen around there a couple of days before. I must have been there while the murder was being committed, not 500 yards away. Then I walked up to Dickens's house to talk to him about a shaurie, and when I was crossing the plain along by the ox boma Lori came up behind me and said something about rain and we talked for a couple of minutes. On Saturday morning, which by the way was little Anne Dickens's birthday, Dickens came in very upset and told me that they had found the murdered child, and then I drove to Nairobi and reported it to the police, and they came out here at once and have been here every day since.

One can quite understand that the Dickenses and everyone with children are very distressed to feel that we have that kind of person on the farm, whether it is Lori or not. My evidence is considered to be of the first importance; it is very unpleasant, and one cannot be completely accurate about time because of course under normal circumstances you don't keep track of it so exactly. I hate to take part in a manhunt of that kind whatever the circumstances and feel no excitement at the hope of being able to help in catching the guilty person although it is a revolting crime and I would like to see him hanged for it. It is terribly hard to get anything resembling the truth out of the Kikuyu, or any kind of native; their minds do not work like ours. . . .

To Ingeborg Dinesen

Ngong. Sunday 11.12.27.

. . . The police officer from Nairobi was out here last Wednesday and I had to go with him over the places where I had seen Lori and take the time very exactly. It is impossible of course to say at precisely what minute, what time one was here or there; but as far as I can see it is *possible* that Lori murdered the child between the time when I talked to him down in the garden and then when he came up to me again and talked when I was on my way to Dickens. His behavior was strange in many ways that evening, among other things he did not go back to his hut but spent the night with some Kikuyu where he had never been before, and when I recall it now he was also very odd when he came up and talked to me; he crept up behind me so quietly that it made me jump when he started to talk, and what he said was pure rubbish,—it seems likely to me that he saw me and came after me in order to get himself an alibi. But all this is too vague to form any judgment on, or actually even to suspect a man for. They think they have found a stick that belongs to him, and that has bloodstains on it; but I haven't a great deal of faith in the intelligence of the local police, and they are mad on playing Sherlock Holmes. I was chiefly put in mind of the trial in "Alice in Wonderland" when he questioned me: "Can you remember what Lori was wearing?"—"No, not at all." "Can you remember whether he had a stick in his hand?" "No, not at all."—"It is very important". Gets out his book and writes: Baroness Blixen has no remembrance at all of what Lori was wearing, etc.—and so on in the same key. . . .

I have been thinking so much about what you write of your relationship with Aunt Bess. . . . I so often get the feeling that the proximity of Magleaas has contributed to making Aunt Bess's old age less happy, and that this also affects your feelings for each other. It seems to me as if the ideal she sees there has made her less satisfied with what she herself has achieved in life and somehow given her the view that marriage and children to such a great extent represent "happiness" in life, that those who have attained it are always, "eo ipso,"—and of course often undeservedly,—"The Rich Ones," and she herself diminutive in relation to them. . . . There is something morbid about this and in my opinion something really sad in the case of Aunt Bess, who in fact in many ways is so rich and so beloved and admired, and who ought to feel pride in just being "a glorious strongminded old maid of old Denmark," and I can understand that it must be very trying for you at times, as when one hears the lower classes in the same bitter tones harping on the fact that of course they are "proletarian" and have no "education and upbringing" at the very moment when the wretched "upper classes" feel they are most burdened with taxes and demands etc. . . .

Farah can fall into the same type of fit and harp on his privileged misery as "only a coloured man," until I have to say "Stop that nonsense, now, Farah; you are much better off than I am,"—but he is easier to attack as I'm convinced that he would not change places with me for anything, while I think it goes deeper with Aunt Bess. I myself have come to the conclusion that it is no use at all to start discussing these things with her; perhaps she may come to change her views,—for they are so very different from those she held, as I remember, in my childhood and early youth. Until then you have my sympathy, and then of course I do know that between you and Aunt Bess there is so much love, fidelity and understanding that one little fixed idea can be accepted without too much trouble. . . .

1928

To Ingeborg Dinesen

Ngong. 3rd January. 1928.

. . . . Denys and I had a quiet repetition of our Christmas dinner with lights and spruce boughs but decided not to sit up until midnight to say farewell to the old year. I must really say that it has been a lovely year, with your visit, and despite all the worries a pretty satisfying result from the farm, and Denys's long visits, and good news from home.

Now I'm going to tell you about something really exciting that happened on New Year's Day. Very early in the morning Denys and I made up our minds to try to drive out along the new road from Ngong to Narok and catch up with the safari in question to take them some guns and binoculars he wanted to lend them. We had not driven that way before and it turned out not to be finished more than half way, so we didn't meet the safari. It was the most beautiful clear morning, and it is a very fine road,—it goes down where Thomas went out shooting with Palme, and is very well made; I felt sorry to think it was not there when you were out here, it would have been such a good trip for you. We saw masses of game, eland, zebra and grant. Then, when we had driven fifteen miles from the house, Kanuthia pointed to the right and whispered "Simba," and sure enough,—on top of a huge dark mass, which later on proved to be a dead giraffe, a big lion was towering with its face straight toward us. Now the Masai have been suffering a lot from lions, and Denys had earlier been asked by the Game Department to try to shoot lions there, so of course we felt it was a good opportunity. Denys shot it with two shots, at about 250 yards—an old lion, not a particularly good mane, but how big and magnificent they are, and how interesting it was to see them again.—

Then we covered it up with thorn branches intending to skin it on the way home, and drove on to find, as I said, six miles further on that the road came to an abrupt end, so we had to turn round and drive back. I had to keep a lookout for the giraffe so that we did not drive past it, and when I caught sight of it I could hardly believe my eyes: another lion was standing on it looking toward us,—an absolutely splendid, big black-maned lion, I think the best I have seen. I think it must be one of the most beautiful sights in the world. We sat there for a while considering whether to shoot it or not, but came to the conclusion that we had to have it, so just as it was about to take itself off Denys shot it; it leaped high up into the air and fell straight down. Denys says it is the best skin he has ever had; the mane was completely black and grew right back over the shoulders.—We then skinned them both and then, very proud and happy, had a New Year's breakfast of bread and cheese, raisins and almonds, that we had with us, and a bottle of red wine, in the lovely clear air, with the Ngong Hills and the bright green plains around us; I don't think I have ever had a more delightful New Year's morning. Then we drove to Nairobi with the skin,—incidentally we have kept the place where we saw the lions secret from everybody, so that the whole of Nairobi doesn't go out there to shoot. You have no idea how huge a giraffe looks when it is lying on the ground like that,—or how it can stink! Kanuthia got four bottles of fat from the lions, and Denys bought one bottle from him for Poor Singh; I expect Tommy can remember how keen he was to get hold of lion fat. If 1928 continues to be so enjoyably exciting there will be a lot to look forward to.

Tomorrow Denys is leaving on his safari. . . .

To Ingeborg Dinesen

Ngong. Sunday 8.1.28.

My beloved Lamb.

The strangest thing that happened here this week was that we had an earthquake on Friday night. It is true that it was only a footling little one; but for someone who has not experienced an earthquake before it was a special sensation all the same. I was in the bathroom getting ready to go to bed and my first thought was that a leopard had somehow got up into the loft; but when the whole house began to rock there had to be another explanation. Despite the fact that it is an uncanny feeling there is something, if I may say so, intoxicating about it, that something one has regarded as lifeless can start to move. You feel as if you want to pat the earth and talk to it: Well, so you are alive after all, old Earth!—Juma says he has experienced it before in Uganda, and then King Edward died the same day!—so now we must be prepared for great events. . . .

The police are keeping watch around the house as it is thought that we have a band of bandits here on the farm; they killed an Indian and a native in Limoru day before yesterday. Yesterday an Askari came up and said a Kikuyu would show the police their hiding place if we would give him 20 shillings, and asked me to give the money; but I felt it was such a mean affair that I would have nothing to do with it. Anything that is captured fills me with horror, and when I saw the policemen carrying handcuffs I would have been prepared to send a message to warn the murderers. If I knew where they were and that they would not kill me, I would really like to meet them; there is always something fascinating about people who are absolutely desperate. . . .

Farah's wife has arrived and is very sweet; it is hard for the poor little thing in such utterly strange conditions, she cannot speak a word of Swahili,—Ali's young wife is giving her lessons in it,—and Farah I am sure is a terrible martinet. Most Somali women have a certain dignity that is attractive; this one is not beautiful, but they are finely formed with beautiful hands and feet, and carry themselves well.

Tell Tommy that I now have Kamante's little brother Titi as a dog toto,—I imagine Tommy can remember him. He had lost his job because Kamante sold all the goats and calves that he used to look after in order to buy his ndito; the other day when I was out for a walk with Heather and Titi he met some of his own calves in strange hands and burst into tears at the sight of them. This marriage has put Kamante so deeply into debt to me that I think he will have to be considered a slave for the rest of his life. . . .

To Ellen Dahl

Ngong. 13.1.1928.

. . . To begin with, many, many thanks for the little harlequin you sent me for Christmas; I am really delighted with it, I have wanted it so long. It and Columbine are standing on Mama's old chest of drawers in my bedroom, but on Christmas Eve they made their appearance on the mantelpiece in the dining room behind a row of candles, and it looked so charming, as if they were dancing on a stage. Besides being so sweet in themselves they stand in a way for a great deal of the old Copenhagen spirit,—Tivoli and the ballet and Deer Park Hill,—that with the years and the distance I have come to hold so dear, for the sake of its charm, straightforwardness and conviviality; indeed, I have always had a passion for both "The Midsummer Night Play" and for "Christmas Fun and New Year Jests," and of course Harlequin appears in both of them. I think that this whole age has a longing for fantasy and the marvelous in art, I myself read H. C. Andersen's fairy tales with deep admiration,—I see that you are celebrating his Jubilee this year and wish I could join you; I would very much like to have his collected works if they can be bought in bound copies at a not too exorbitant price. Denys and I actually said on New Year's Eve what an incredibly great joy and experience it would be if your harlequin would make just one pirouette,—that the unexpected would happen, even if it were in miniature. . . .

I particularly wish you well with your hostel for the homeless, of which Mother has written, and which interests me enormously. Can you remember that once, in the summer of 1925, we were sitting in Skodsborg Station,—incidentally, it was probably the day, just after Tommy's engagement, when we had walked there from Springforbi, and we had a balloon like a stork on a string,—talking about what passions one continues to hold through life, when gradually one comes to relinquish so many, and I said that with the years my greatest passion had become "the lower classes"?—Then you did not agree with me; but now perhaps you are not after all able to escape your fate. It is true that for me out here it is the natives who have won my heart, but that is of minor importance; for they are the same people: "The wronged and the oppressed" in one way or the other. Father writes in "From the Eighth Brigade" that "one loves soldiers as one loves young women,—fiercely, uncontrollably,"—and I myself have come to take the view that the general impression of the *personal* passions and relationships as being the strongest and most important in life is quite wrong; it is true of these, as Stuckenberg writes to his beloved, that: "The joy of my life, the joy is your picture,"—but the really fierce, uncontrollable passion is reserved for other things: art, for instance, the soil, soldiers (young women), my black brother, or the unemployed. . . .

It is hard to say whether the young people in this life will find it easier or harder; but probably in a way life, as well as dress and menus, has become simpler since our youth. I think this has brought about a great change, that can be regarded according to how one views it as a relief or a void, in that so extremely few, if any people at all, now feel themselves, toward other people or themselves, to be *representative* of anything whatsoever apart from their own mere humanity and personality. The enthusiasm, pride, and feeling of responsibility of representing some nation or other seems, however strong may be the love of country and people felt by individuals, for most people to be a thing of the past, and class consciousness and pride may perhaps be found in those who consider themselves to represent the proletariat,—even though in that class there is too strong an element of practical interest to allow of much idealism,—but quite certainly no longer in the upper classes or the military, for instance. I think that Uncle Mogens still confronted life first and foremost as:

a Frijs, who represented Frijsenborg and his family, and felt both the privilege and the responsibility of that; but don't you think that this whole view of life followed him to the grave and is now only to be found in the museums?

The reason for these phenomena is probably that the old ideas that certainly the generation that preceded ours lived with and for, had outlived themselves and with the years and the effects of wind and weather had become somewhat brittle,—they could stay alive still in fine weather, but could not survive the Ragnarok of the war; but the question remains as to whether they can ever be resurrected in other forms and names, and whether our contemporaries' children and grandchildren will ever come to do battle under a coat of arms and device, whatever color that might be?

I think there has been another great change, that perhaps people are still not conscious of, in that the idea, so to speak, has disappeared from womanliness, of what it is to be a woman. I think that the women of the old days, and especially the best of them, felt themselves to be representatives of something great and sacred, by virtue of which they possessed importance outside themselves and could feel great pride and dignity, and toward which they had a weighty responsibility. Neither the arrogance of the young and beautiful girl or the majesty of the old lady was, after all, felt on their own behalf; they were without any element of personal vanity, but were borne as something to take pride in, a shield or a banner. Where a personal affront might well be pardoned, a violation of that womanliness whose representatives they were could never be forgiven; a blow might perhaps be overlooked, but never a stolen kiss. I think very few young women in our time feel any of this.—

In one of Blicher's stories the heroine is given the choice between her young brother's life and the sacrifice of her (womanly) honor to the enemy commander, and neither she nor her brother entertain a moment's doubt: —it is his life that must be sacrificed. In a modern story,—by Jakob Wassermann,—a Bolshevik officer gives a young lady the promise of sparing a company of refugees if she will come to his quarters at night; she hesitates no longer than Blicher's brother and sister, but replies: "Yes, of course,—here I am." I think there are very few young women whose conscience and moral sense would not bid them give the same answer. For they no longer feel their "womanliness" to be the most sacred element in their nature, and the concept of "womanly honor" is of no importance to them, hardly any meaning.—Likewise Blicher's young nobleman would have chosen death rather than hang his escutcheon round the neck of a pig, while I am pretty sure that nowadays no nobleman in the world,—anyway in any of the civilized countries,—would not be prepared to do so with a perfectly good conscience if thereby he could save his friends' lives, or even his own; for his highest duty is on a different plane. However deeply outraged a young woman might feel against an assailant who tried to rape her,—in the same degree as against a person who had burned down her house, for instance,—I think she would feel an even greater fury towards the people involved who assumed that she would feel herself degraded and "dishonored" by it.

However much beauty and grandeur there may have been in the ideals of the old days, the proof that the salt has lost its savor is this: that nowadays it is,—in some way or other, intellectually or morally,—the people of no account who still air them. Of course it is true that some English people still lead "The Empire" and expand on "we Englishmen," but *never any* of the best of them, and no doubt the same is true of other nations. . . .

And those women who most exploit their sex, and ascribe importance to their "womanly" virtue rather than to their purely human honesty and frankness, in my opinion in our time are far from being the feminine élite of humanity.

All the same there can surely be no doubt that there has been some loss of values that strengthened people and gave meaning to their life, and that presumably in many cases made the individuals themselves happier and brought ease to social intercourse. The consciousness of being: a German, a Reventlow, a member of the honest fraternity of tinkers, an "honnête femme" has no doubt kept many people up to scratch and filled them with proper pride, with which the young of today who "have nought but their sheer humanity to rely on" cannot compete. I also think that it was to a great extent the conventional sacredness and importance of "womanliness" that made marriages in the old days, if not exactly happier, then anyway easier. A young bride gave her bridegroom immeasurably much more than her purely personal value; she brought something eternal and invaluable to his home, the sacrosanct merit and dignity of a "wife," and the essence of their life together consisted less of their individual sympathy and antipathy than in the actual relationship between "man and woman,"—her sewing basket, and his pipe and newspaper, were insignia,—and in their marriage the two of them met, so to speak, as the ambassadors of two great powers, in fully mutual consciousness and recognition of the powers and values that lay behind them.

Nowadays cohabitation between two purely human personalities has a different basis and a different content (if any). Now I for one do not know whether it is possible for people in general to live profitably in such a completely human and personal way without any given role in life. In heaven, I have heard tell, there will be neither taking nor giving in marriage, and there, no doubt, a Reventlow will have to sit beside Tom, Dick, and Harry. But it must surely be assumed that there will be some special arrangement or a distinctive spirit that will serve to ease intercourse among them; otherwise I think that both the old Reventlows and old-fashioned married couples will find themselves pretty much at sea.—It cannot surely be said that it is entirely from free choice that young people nowadays have taken upon themselves, in one particular direction, the modus vivendi of the millennium, but they will not escape having to pay for it; for it is bound to demand of them more imagination, more strength and idealism than the way of life of bygone days.—May God be with them, for although I don't know them particularly well I have great confidence in them. . . .

You write that it can't have been easy for me to have Denys and Mother here at the same time.—Between ourselves: has Mother given you that impression or is it your own idea? I did not think that Mother felt it like that and I was glad that she got to know Denys. Mother knows all about this relationship, you know, and so does everyone else out here, naturally, and I cannot see what difference it could make in their view of, or feeling for, me, whatever these may be.

Well then, I shall just send many, many greetings, my own dear Elle, and greet Knud warmly from me,—and Miss Møller and Ella too. Everything good for the New Year both in Sølvgade and on Mols, and wherever you find yourselves in the wide world. Greet the King's Garden and Langelinie, the Deer Park and Ellemandsberg; it is all so far away, and yet I don't think that nature and life out here are as different from Denmark as from many other places,—sometimes I think that many of the old Danish folksongs could have been written out here: "So softly drove the shepherd his flock in the cool of evening, and wrote tracks in the dew."—"Ride softly through the grove, my dearest dear,"—and Lulu "gambols in and out, on the farm and out through the forest,—each of her hairs shone like red gold." And after rain: "The forest blooms, the twigs burst into leaf, while smoke falls on the grass."

So now, take care of yourself, and write now and then.

Your Tanne.

To Ingeborg Dinesen

Ngong. Sunday 22.1.1928.

. . . Mohr and I have been discussing,—with due respect to Kierkegaard,—"'the concept of angst," really arising out of my bandits here; I think that I myself have come to the conclusion in life that all fear in reality is nervous, because there is nothing to be afraid of. That is to say: naturally one may be afraid of being killed, of getting pneumonia, driving one's car into the ditch and so on—all these risks naturally exist in life,—but one must not be *terrified* of them,—because there is nothing in life to be terrified of (unless one believes in the Devil in which case one has the right to be afraid always). For instance, when I am not terrified of natives and would not be so even though I could be imagined to be aware that they were outside my door planning to put me to death, and even though I thought they would succeed, that is because they themselves would not be terrified of killing me, that is: neither they nor I believe in the Devil, and the whole situation would much more resemble a hunting episode, such as driving a bear out of its lair, which does not seem anything terrifying to the hunters even though they know there is a risk of their getting killed, nor probably to the bear, however enraged it may be and determined to put up a fight. All terror is more or less terror of the dark: bring light, and it must of necessity pass, because it will be shown that there is nothing to be feared. But for so many years we have believed in hell and the Devil and worked each other into a state in which so many things inspired us with fear that there is a hellish pusillanimity in our very blood, and it can raise its head on the most unreasonable occasions. . . .

On Thursday I went out to the Fjæstads' for lunch, I had arranged to meet Mohr there and drive out with him to his farm in the afternoon; he has asked me to help him to buy curtains and other things for his house, so we had to go out there first to take measurements and look at the colors. I enjoyed seeing his farm, I think he has a very interesting post for such a young man,—there are over 11,000 acres, with 6,000 acres of sisal and probably 500 acres of coffee; he has four white men, four fundees and 500 natives under him. . . .

It was quite late when I got home and to my great joy found Denys here; he is staying for a week before going out on safari again. . . .

Do please send me the "Revolution of Youth" that you write about; I would so much like to learn more about modern young people than I have the opportunity to do. I think people make far too much fuss about many of the upheavals of our time; things need to change and develop, and it is obvious that you can't make an omelette without breaking eggs. . . .

Ngong. Sunday 5.2.1928.

. . . I cannot give you any more information about the murder as they have not been able to prove anything against Lori but have let him go again. We have sent him away from the farm, as, whether he is guilty or innocent, there is too much hostility toward him, so for the sake of peace he has returned to his own tribe at Meru. After that the police stopped making any effort so probably nothing more will come of it.

Nor have they made any progress in their search for the bandit Muange, who they think is hiding out with his band somewhere around here. Last Sunday when, as I may have written, we were having a big ngoma, a police officer from Nairobi came out here in his car hoping to find him, as he is said to be very keen about ngomas. But the policeman made not the least effort to catch him but spent his time in the house here drinking beer and boasting of his exploits, so it would have been strange if Muangi's friends did not warn him in time, if he really was at the ngoma. I think it would have been very "sporting" of Muangi if he really put his life in risk in order to come to a ngoma,—the police have orders to shoot him on sight if they catch sight of him,—so Dickenson, Denys's friend and second in command on safari, who has been staying here this week, and I were thinking of arranging a ngoma for him and giving him safe conduct, with lookouts posted along the road to let us know if the police were coming; but it is unlikely that he would trust us enough to come. Anyway, I feel sure that he is no longer in the area. . . .

On our arrival home [Wednesday] we found to our great surprise that Denys was here; he had broken the magneto on his one lorry 30 miles the other side of the Tanganyika border and had come back without a stop to get a new one. He had dinner with us and went to bed, as he had to get up again at one o'clock to start back again, in the pitch dark. I would have driven him for a stretch, as he was so dead tired and sleepy, if I had known how to get back again,—everything about safaris is so indescribably fascinating to me, even starting in the dark in the cold, clear night air; but I went with him, in my nightgown and a coat, to the dam and walked home, the stars were so bright and the air so soft. . . .

To Ingeborg Dinesen

Ngong. Sunday 12th February 1928.

. . . Last Sunday, after I had written to you I had a visit from a pathetic personage, a Swede, Casparson, who was for a time maître d'hôtel at the Norfolk and who is now completely without any means of subsistence. He came walking out here through all the dust so he looked absolutely wretched and was a pretty hopeless case in every way. It seems that he has been in some sort of trouble with the police, and the Swedes here, who of course are never particularly anxious to help anyone, will not have anything to do with him after that, so his prospects are black. And then he is pretty useless in this country; he is not in the least practical, cannot drive a car or use any tools, has no knowledge of farming or business of any kind, and does not seem to be able to make friends, either. He was—an actor! when he was in Europe; his best parts were Armand in "The Lady of the Camellias" and Osvald in "Ghosts," he says,—whatever use that may be out here. I like him very much; he is a really thorough "sponger," and they are always charming people,—pretty much of a toper too as befits the part, but what can you do with him? I gave him 25 shillings, but that didn't go far. . . .

On Monday I was in Nairobi,—as usual: lunch with Bent, shauries with Hunter and Milligan. . . . Tea at the Stanley Hotel with the wretched Casparson. . . .

On Friday I was on the farm all day, partly with Dickens. I came home late and when I arrived found Casparson, so help me God, standing outside the house like a shadow. "Yes, here is a tramp, Baroness!" and he looked like one, unshaven and pitiable. He was on his way to Tanganyika,—on foot! It is an absolute impossibility, it is 230 miles, most of the way without water,—and when he does get there he hasn't the least opportunity of finding anything, does not know a soul and of course has no money. But what can you do with people like that?—Of course I gave him dinner and he stayed the night here and it was really very pleasant, but it was no use, my trying to make him give up his plan and go back to Nairobi and look for another job there; he had got the idea into his head to try his luck in that way and there was nothing for me to do but send him off quite early in the morning, so at least he could get some way before it got too hot. I drove him to Farah's duca at half-past five and gave him a parcel of food and a bottle of beer, ten shillings, and my blessing, but he looked pitiful when he started off along the road; he did not even have a blanket, only a big overcoat, and no luggage at all. I sent him to Nepken and doubt if he will get any further than that; surely Nepken will be able to explain to him that it is impossible. I really think there is too much danger from lions on the road; of course I could have driven him to Nepken, but I thought it wiser to let him get some experience of walking tours in this country before he got there so that he can change his mind before leaving the last human habitation behind and going off into the desert. As I said, I like him very much and will follow him with interest and sympathy; he kept on saying that anyway things could not be worse for him than they were now, and in the midst of all the misery he was cheerful and entertained me with his experiences, which are fairly extensive. He is married to a Danish Miss Kofoed-Hansen, poor girl. . . .

To Ingeborg Dinesen

Ngong. Sunday 19th February. 1928.

. . . Everything that has to do with Elle's hostel for the homeless interests me in the very highest degree. . . . Regarding the question of entertainment that you write about,—and that seems to have been solved in the best possible way with the assistance of kind people,—I have been thinking a lot about it,—I would really *love* to be at home and taking part in the enterprise,—and I think that one should get the audience themselves to contribute, by suggesting that since they consisted of so many different types of person and had such a variety of experience among them, they should take the opportunity of learning from each other, and then encourage those who were forthcoming to recount the worst thing they had experienced, for example. I did that once with my people on safari and although some really awful things came out they ended up with laughing so much at each other's sufferings that one felt that at least that gave them the courage to face what else was in store for us. Perhaps you could get some white people,—excuse me: I mean, what corresponds to that,—to start off, Elle with her fire, Tommy with some of the horrors of war; of course I would be able to offer something, too, so that it might become: "By your right hand, O King of Erin, and by my own, if it were free, then I was worse off than I am now in your prison and with your threat of death before me.". . .

On Saturday I rode over the whole of MBagathi in the morning. . . . In the afternoon I drove,—as you can imagine, with a car full of totos,—to a big Air Rally. Lady Carbery has come out with her new little machine which she flew herself from Mombasa to Nairobi, and three other airplanes took part in various races, difficult landings, takeoffs and so on. Lady Carbery did very well in the competition; it looks delightful to see these small planes playing in the air, and it must be something that we can do just as well as men. Of course there were crowds of people, among others I met Mrs. Bursell who had just come back from Tanganyika, and who lifted a stone from my heart by telling me that she had met Casparson driving in style on top of a lorry and in great high spirits. The image of his lonely and pathetic figure starting off on that hopeless walk had been weighing on my memory and I have had a pretty bad conscience over letting him go. I had tea at the airfield and then had quite a lot of trouble getting my totos collected for the drive home; they had had a marvelous time. . . .

To Ingeborg Dinesen

Ngong. Sunday 4th March 1928.

. . . . It is really amazing how quickly everything here grows green after rain; there is a tinge already on my desert-like lawns and a new shade on the coffee. I will be glad to have it looking well when Denys arrives this week, he grieved so over it last time. There is more water in the dam and the little green bushes are beginning to come out. . . .

On Tuesday Dickinson left very early in the morning, and I went riding on the farm. In the afternoon Lady Grigg and Lord and Lady Islington came to tea here. It was the Islingtons' last day in this country so it was nice of them to come out here. I met them by the turn and drove them over MBagathi; they are very keen about getting that house. I think Lady I. and Lady G. were quite terribly sad at heart at the thought of Lady Islington's departure, and these mothers and daughters who are about to be parted are almost more than I can bear to be with; after tea they went for a long walk in the woods and I entertained Lord I. Everyone is accusing us of loving each other, and in a sense they are quite right, he is really a charming old man.

We talked politics and were exactly of the same opinion regarding this country and the natives here; he said that he would put forward his views in the House of Lords, and that I must go to London and stay with them next May, and he would introduce me to people who are interested in these questions, so that I could talk to them. That would be really interesting and probably more effective than writing to such apathetic creatures as Inge and Wells; I rather think that any influence I may have the opportunity to exert must be carried out orally. Lady I. teased us about our agreement. "What will bring me back to Kenya first of all—" began Lord I., meaning the sun.—"Yes, we all know that," she said, "it's Baroness Blixen." "Yes," he said, "you're quite right, it has been my greatest experience out here." I have now come to the conclusion that actually gentlemen only become really charming when they are seventy.

Then on Wednesday, all due to that confounded Milligan's fault, I had to go to Nairobi to get some money. It was so hot that I have never known anything like it. I met Idina's husband there, Joss Erroll,—his father died the other day, so he is not Lord Kilmarnock any more,—and asked him if he would like to come out here for a "bottle" in the afternoon, and he asked if he could bring Alice de Jancé,—you know, the one who shot Raymond de Trafford and who has been ordered to leave the country. I thereby acquired a tea party which was really so comical that I lay in my bed that night laughing about it. Now there is at the moment an American cruise ship at Mombasa; the passengers have spent three days in Nairobi and of course have been tearing around looking at all the sights. So while I was sitting in the office paying the boys I could see a car drive up to my house, but I thought it was Joss and Alice and considered that they could wait. However Titi came to me and said that this Memsabo could not possibly wait, so I asked Dickens and Nisbet to finish paying and went back to the house to find Lady McMillan, Mr. Bulpett and two really huge and corpulent old American ladies, who were from the cruise ship, waiting for me. They were taking a drive in the hope of seeing a lion, for it would be such a source of pride if they could go back to the other passengers and tell them about it.

Then they started to discuss all the dreadfully immoral people there were in Kenya, Americans too unfortunately, and as the worst one of all they mentioned Alice, and I, who of course knew that she was about to turn up, let them go into great detail about it. So when their car drove up and I went out to receive them, and came in and presented Lord Erroll and Comtesse de Jancé, I don't think that the Devil himself could have had a greater effect if he had walked in; it was undoubtedly better than the biggest lion and has given them much more to talk to their fellow passengers about! Lady McMillan must really be very grateful to me,—I invited Alice to come and stay out here if she has to come to Nairobi to put her shauries in order before her deportation. . . .

I had a letter from Moshi from the foolish Casparson,—nothing about how he had got there, but only about how it had been such a "deliverance" to "speak with the Baroness."—However, at least it proves that he is alive and has reached as far as Moshi.

To Ellen Dahl

Ngong. 13th March. 1928.

. . . There cannot be many people who are fonder of Aunt Bess than I am, and it upsets me so terribly to hear she feels unhappy,—also to think that many times I have contributed to this. But I do not really regard Aunt Bess in the way that you do in your letter and can't agree with you that she is a type of "the women of bygone times,"—and I do not think that her difficulties in life have been brought about solely through her upbringing and outward circumstances, but through something peculiar to her own nature; perhaps one could call this, if one wishes, something of the primitive woman, but I have in fact seen it in men as well. If you are going to talk of a type for the women of the old days I think it would be more accurate to cite "Aunt Arnette" or Aunt Ida Bardenfleth, and they had, in my view, according to both their womanly predisposition and through what you call their "millennium-style upbringing," the capacity to adapt themselves to circumstances, and also, without bitterness, probably without giving much thought to it, to put themselves in the background and be, as the bailiff says in "The Family at Gilje": "invisible and yet always present as a gentle spirit" in the house, the family or in society when circumstances required it of them, and if only those whom they loved were happy.

You write: "Aunt Bess denies herself so completely that for her nothing is of value an sich"—but I cannot see the logic of this idea and think that for a self-denying person innumerable things in fact must be of value an sich; I believe that if one took as an example of such people, who have "denied themselves" and in a way renounced all desires of their own, a nun or a philanthropic doctor or a prophet, one would find that not only God, the Church, science, humanity were of value to them an sich but that very often those very people, animals, or things, that seem to us others completely insignificant or valueless,—publicans and sinners, idiots and sick animals, the trees St. Francis wept for when they were to be felled, and the fishes he preached to,—for them are of the greatest value "an sich."

Neither is "self-denying" the word I would apply to Aunt Bess, although I think that she is capable of sacrificing herself for others perhaps more than any other person I know.—I think that many of Aunt Bess's difficulties arise because she is to such a great extent *personally* disposed,—she can only get something out of them, indeed, they can only come to exist for her at all, if the circumstances are felt by her to be personal circumstances,—and then also because she demands too much of relationships: I mean, that there must be more giving and receiving and taking on than other people find possible, indeed, in any way in actual normal human life. Even though it is indescribably tragic when you write that Aunt Bess can compare herself to an ownerless dog,—and I cannot think that this was anything else than a passing mood of hers,—I must still express my opinion that if a human being in any way wants to feel like a dog then he will come to be like an ownerless dog; for very few other people will have the ability or the will to take on the opposite role in the sort of relationship they are seeking. Actually, I myself, to a quite different degree from Aunt Bess, who is loved and appreciated, in so many ways really indispensible to those around her, could make use of that comparison; I have not thought of that before, but if I am to be a dog, I would prefer to be an ownerless one.

Never mind that since Mama's death there is no one in Aunt Bess's immediate circle who as a matter of course necessarily demands that she give them her time and energies, the world is certainly not perfect, neither are all the people in it happy, neither is there, even in the small circle surrounding Folehave, any lack of people in need of support and advice. My own experience there is that one has no need at all to seek them out; not only do they come knocking on the door at all times, they break it down,—particularly, most probably, if one lives on one's own and is considered, being without husband and children, to have one's time at one's own, and their, disposal. But it is true that what she could find in this way would not satisfy Aunt Bess, she would not get anything out of it,—of course, it would be more accurate to say: she *does not* get anything out of it, for as we know there are many people who come seeking her advice and support,—because they are "out of proportion" to the needs and demands of her own nature; there is no one who needs her whole life, her complete devotion, and so she will never again receive anyone's complete confidence and subjection. . . .

Now you must not think that I do not have great sympathy for Aunt Bess now that she is feeling miserable. That is to say: I don't think there are any grounds for complaint in Aunt Bess's outward circumstances; of course I have not her passionate faith in the infallibility of marriage as the source of bliss, and I think there are few people who in their capacity of sister, aunt, friend, employer and so on are so loved and admired. But I do think that hers is a tragic temperament. And I am also aware that Aunt Bess, even in the sort of circumstances that would be considered by other people to be exceptionally harmonious and happy, for instance in her relationship of sister-in-law to Koosje and partly as aunt to us, has suffered bitter disappointment. It causes me great grief, as I wrote, to think I have brought sorrow to Aunt Bess. But if you can bear in mind that all that unfortunate business of "loss of trust" arose through Aunt Bess's despair over my relationship with Daisy,—and to this day I cannot see what there was in that to grieve over,—you surely must admit that judged according to ordinary human relationships, in the view of ordinary people who take it for granted that an aunt cannot in this way control a young niece's choice of girl friend, it must be ascribed as being a "self-created torment"—that is to say, a torment not caused by circumstances but by the viewpoint of the person who does not follow the norm.

Of course it can probably be said that this kind of need for devotion and such demandingness in human life are best suited to the relationship between man and woman and in a mother's relationship with her children, and that it is tragic that Aunt Bess has not solved the problem of her own nature by the simple means of getting married. But I think that part of the reason for Aunt Bess not getting married was: that she never found anyone who had need of her gifts and could offer her what she had need of, and part the fact that I think one can say that if these feelings flourish best in marriage and the relationship with children, it is in fact also there that they can lead to the greatest unhappiness. "Let us picture a man," who might have satisfied Aunt Bess,—"there are some who can, but not many, and far from each and everyone," anyway, I cannot do so, even with the help of the whole of history.

I have probably spoken before of my view that one can "live for" humanity, or for the poor children of Sengeløse, but one cannot "live for" Mr. Petersen, at least without spoiling him or making him unhappy, usually both. I do not think any human being will accept or can tolerate another person "living for" him in this way; it is only possible, I think, when both,—one person directly, the other through him,—live for an idea. As I have (also previously) said: not a single one of the soldiers to whom Florence Nightingale dedicated herself could in decency have borne the acceptance of her sacrifice in a personal and private capacity; they could only do so with such great enthusiasm because the sacrifices were brought through them to Queen Victoria's Army, or England, or whatever it was that represented their idea and ideal to them.

For two thousand years human beings have felt gratitude to Christ because he "sacrificed himself" for them; but I really think there would be very few who would not, if they were offered the chance of having the crucifixion carried out for their own personal salvation, this very afternoon,—even if they were directly confronted with flaming Hell and eternal damnation,—rush up and say: for Heaven's sake do not take that upon yourself. I could actually imagine that some artist might be prepared to accept Aunt Bess's whole life for the sake of his art; but then I think it would be very difficult for Aunt Bess to adopt such an impersonal attitude towards his art that she could leave it in peace and not try to get even Shakespeare to abstain from his worst crudities, or Michelangelo from his nude writhings.

I have come across the same temperament out here in Eric Otter, whom I may have talked about. I think I made him very unhappy, but it would have been impossible for me to have made him happy, and the worst thing that could have happened to him would have been my marrying him, for I, like the majority of human beings, am incapable of "living for" one person and still less of letting another person "live for me," and could not possibly have done it for him. . . . The English have an expression: "to call your soul your own," which fits this situtation very well; this is exactly what those people who want to give their soul to others and can be satisfied with nothing less in return will not allow one, and in this, for me and other ordinary people, there is something utterly unbearable and intolerable. . . .

Can you remember "Svend Dyring's House"?—There Ragnhild's tragedy is really, in the lyrical style, as deep as can be imagined. A lovely, well-born, proud woman, an impressive strength that is rejected at the very point when she is prepared to give her all,—it cuts one to the heart; one feels that it just *could* not happen. Now I do really think that Knight Stig from the purely legal point of view had a plain duty to marry Ragnhild; when one has behaved so foolishly in such an ill-fated affair one should at least do what one can to improve the situation, and I think too it is obvious that if he had not had the good fortune to bring about her death it would have been the best thing for his own sake; for it would have been quite intolerable for him and Regisse in their marriage to have run the risk of Ragnhild turning up and demanding her rights at any moment.—

But ignoring this aspect, one may ask whether this would have helped Ragnhild, and I do not think that it would. For here there was more than the human element (I mean the runes) supervening; ordinary human life could not possibly meet the demands that were made there. Perhaps Knight Stig could not feel more than the mild infatuation upon which he and Regisse could presumably base a marriage of trivial happiness; he could do nothing at all for Ragnhild and the demonic forces that were set in movement here. The unhappy Ragnhild could really talk of feeling like an ownerless dog, but her misery did not lie in outward circumstances, and as far as the reader can see and understand, her misery would have continued into eternity even if Stig Hvide had led her to the altar at once; for he would not and could not be master, he had no wish for her to go to war with him and sleep at his feet in the open, and one can well ask which of them would have suffered more in a marriage,—if it is possible to compare the sufferings of a passionate and a nonpassionate person.

Now you must not think from this that I am splitting hairs in order to show that Aunt Bess is not to be pitied. . . . I really have,—together with, as I'm sure you know, the deepest love for and admiration for Aunt Bess,—great sympathy for her if she is feeling lonely and miserable. But I think that one comes to develop a deep aversion to orthodoxy,—and also to the orthodox view of what, for instance, makes up happiness or unhappiness,—and then I admit it may well be that I sometimes come near to the "Griffen's" [*sic*] heartless view of both the Mock Turtle and the Queen: "It's all his fancy that; he hasn't got no sorrow, you know."—

I think it has been "bad luck" for Aunt Bess to come in her old age to live in a milieu,—fostered particularly by the proximity of Magleaas and Aasebakke, but also in a way by Tommy's marriage,—where family life and happiness are so predominant, indeed, almost made to monopolize the wealth and content of life; there are after all so many other things in the world that give value to life. . .I myself think that one can,—to be slightly banal,—compare life to a game, like bridge, for instance, in such a way that it is not the cards: the outward circumstances, but the game: one's own judgment of how to live, which is the decisive and central thing; and at least one can say of the person who, because he picks up a rotten handful of cards, throws them indignantly away, that he has not grasped the spirit of the game.—I myself can say that I have experienced many things that according to the ordinary view must be reckoned as misfortunes, and on which I can look now, if not as pleasure, then yet as a lucky turn of events.

I do think it can be said that Mama in her time was in error, and perhaps even that she wronged Aunt Bess, by making her world such a little one. Naturally, I cannot properly judge of that since I only knew Mama in her old age, when the world grows smaller for most people; but I have the feeling that in fact for Mama only her children and grandchildren really *existed,* and just a few other people,—yes, and then Gladstone or Stead, or other such great and distant beings. But don't you think that Aunt Bess herself must have something of this in her nature in order to be able to tolerate it at all without breaking out?. . .

If one limits oneself in this way so as to concern oneself only with those to whom one is nearest, surely the result must be that not only does one cut oneself off from much in life, but one becomes terribly dependent on those people, and when they become occupied with other things one feels deserted. It has always seemed strange to me that Aunt Bess, who has so much interest in and understanding of literature, has read so terribly little. Not only is the whole of Classical, French and German literature an utterly closed book for her but also far the greater part of English and Danish literature, Holberg, Oehlenschlæger, Søren Kierkegaard, Drachmann,—and many more that I could name; I almost think that throughout the whole of our youth I can only remember Aunt Bess being really absorbed in Selma Lagerlöf and then "Their Silver Wedding Journey," wherever she may have got that from. Now I think that if you or Thomas or Uncle Aage suggested to Aunt Bess that you should study philosophy together, this would interest and absorb her a great deal, and you would have a lot of enormously interesting and entertaining discussions over it; but if for some reason or other you were obliged to give it up, I don't know how long Aunt Bess would be able to keep her interest in it alive, and there is something slightly out of proportion about that when with the best will in the world you or Thomas could hardly be compared with Plato or Spinoza.

Of course, this may well be, as you say, something particular to women. And yet I think I know many women, even of the old-fashioned type, who are able to get a great deal out of things like flowers, music, needlework, "an sich," or else, if they really want to have to do with human beings, can take such a lively interest in people they meet with whom they are completely unconnected, for the children of their childhood friends or for the poor, the sick, talented young artists, school children. I think that Mrs. Wanscher has had quite as much interest from many of the young people who have visited her, from the Poulsens and their art, and Aunt Ida from Sybille and the Misses Gad, as they have had from their own children.

. . . When, for instance, Mother is more harmoniously happy in her relationship with us, this is not entirely due to the fact that we are her children, while we are only Aunt Bess's nephews and nieces, but far more because Mother can also transform conflicts to harmony through her whole nature and view of life. It would not have gone so easily and happily if, for instance, I had told Aunt Bess about my relationship with Denys, indeed, there might have been "loss of trust" or some other horror as a result, and yet really it might have been easier for her to take it than Mother, who among other things was in the same house with him, and who gained such a good and happy friendship thereby. . . .

And now about life or fate as a whole, as these powers show themselves to all human beings. Here it is not so easy to determine what is happiness and unhappiness as one thinks when one is a child and young person. Here I may again quote "Stankelben" which Missen has kindly lent me for the last two and a half years; no reader of that book, and they must surely number many thousands, can doubt that pirates and the cold of the North Pole, whales and even such quite exceptional misfortunes as the world itself catching fire are as nothing compared with Stine's uncomprehending tyranny and persecution, although in reality that was very self-sacrificing. "Stankelben" can hardly have gained its immense popularity if there were not something in this viewpoint that attracted everyone's sympathy.

The things that I myself have experienced, that according to the orthodox way of thinking are "misfortunes,"—illness, poverty, loneliness, being "let down" to an extent that can only have happened to the fewest people,—I really do not look upon now as things I would wish not to have happened. I may also say that the greatest ills and misfortunes that I have suffered have been imposed on me by people with so-called good intentions. It is difficult to estimate a human life; it is quite impossible to do so according to definite rules, and as time goes by one grows very cautious about it. The things that happen do not have the same value for everyone. In the end there is probably *something* for every individual that he cannot renounce; but I also think somehow that it is my experience that most people manage to do this in various ways, as in Goldschmidt's story of Mephistopheles and the photographs, and that what they pay for it with, is "life." That which I have achieved, and which is costing me and will cost me life, is not in detail what I would have imagined for myself when I was seventeen,—it is probably not so for you either, or for any one we know, with the exception of such steady and orthodox characters as Else, and no doubt she would have been happy in quite different circumstances as long as they had been marked and approved by the world as valid "happiness,"—but I, and probably you as well, are willing to give our *lives* for it.

One can say that it has cost Aunt Bess her life to be an old maiden aunt at Folehave, and that seems a wretched fate for such a highly gifted person. But then it would be a very superficial view to regard my existence as that of a poor coffee farmer with a load of worries. But one can say as well that her life has been, in accordance with her nature, spent in loving and exerting influence on the people with whom she has been concerned, and so she has been able, to a far greater extent than most people, to avoid everything that was distasteful to her, to be able to have "a clear conscience," which for Aunt Bess with her extraordinarily pronounced and scrupulous moral attitude could not have been easy. If it were not that in her old age, in a moment of weakness, as it were, she had come to take account of the yardstick of other people, which in reality is alien to her nature, I think that she would see it this way herself. . . .

Ngong. Sunday 18th March. 1928.

. . . Denys arrived on Friday after a very successful safari, accompanied unfortunately by his slave Dickinson, who is a bit of a bore, particularly because he seems to think that he can take up his abode here whenever he likes and for as long as it suits him; I have put up with it chiefly as a favor to Denys, but as Denys turns out to object strongly, I will have to give Dickinson a hint sooner or later to the effect that he might think of staying at Muthaiga. . . .

On Monday I went to Nairobi; as we were driving past the airfield the four airplanes that had been here for a few days en route from Kisumu to the Cape, took off and rose into the sky like four great shining swans,—just like the day we saw them land here. In Nairobi I got my new records; they are not exactly what I had ordered, but there are a lot of delightful things, among them Max Bruch's concerto, which is so good and reminds me of Thornberg and our youth.

In the evening Juma came in very aufgericht and told us that one of Kaninu's sons, who takes milk in to Nairobi on his bicycle, at about six o'clock had seen an airplane, which he thought was the one we had seen the Memsabu flying, crash with two people in it who were killed instantly. Of course we were hoping this was the natives' normal habit of exaggerating when something disastrous happens; but when we were driving in next day,—Denys was going to take his party up to Rejaf from where they are starting off down the Nile, and I drove in with him in order to bring the car back,—we saw the airplane lying on the ground near the road and could see that it was impossible for anyone to have escaped alive from such a crash; it looked like nothing but a pile of old iron and fragments of wood. They had both been killed on the spot,—Maia Carbery and a young Cowie, a neighbor of ours here, whom she had taken up in order to teach him to fly.

Nobody will ever know what actually happened; the machine had dual controls, but probably she did not have the strength to take control at the last moment, if he had made some mistake. I was talking to her the day before and she was so happy and pleased with her new little plane. Both she and Cowie were 24. . . . She was married to Lord Carbery and had a little girl of three years old. They were both buried in Nairobi the day after the accident; of course there has been a great deal of sympathy expressed, and it is really tragic. Carbery, and Cowie's mother and brother, were at the airfield and saw them crash. . . .

I have been enjoying the contents of your parcel,—Denys asked me to thank you very much indeed for the shawl, he was awfully pleased with it; he was going to write, but he had so little time and he wanted to take some photographs here of the dogs, the horses and so on, to enclose with his letter. . . . I think Byskov's book is very interesting, but uneven; in my opinion parts of it are sheer rubbish, parts really brilliant. "Birds around the Lighthouse" is interesting and well written; it is very nice to be able to keep up a little with Danish writing.—Maho and the other children were thrilled with the presents, Denys could hardly bear to give up the sparklers to Tumbo. . . .

I would so much love to have some of Grieg's songs, preferably "Thought of my Thought," "A Swan," and "The First Meeting"; I seem to remember hearing them on the gramophone sung by Ellen Bech, but perhaps that is my imagination. But on the whole it would be nice to have some Danish music to play to English people and myself; I would also like to have some choral music, "Summer Lightning" or "Wide Sails," and the sort of thing I listened to in my youth. They should be the new, electrically made records, they are so much better than the old ones; but as I have said, if I could have a catalog I could arrange myself to have them sent out. . . .

Lady McMillan wants me to go with them on a trip to Uganda, but I will not go, partly because I would have to take my own car which I can't really afford, and partly because I do not want to go away when Denys is coming back. Of course this sounds pretty stupid, I see him often enough, but I am so much happier with him than with any of the other people here; after all, it is something rather special, when one lives "among strangers," to be with someone who has tastes so similar to one's own, and with whom one is so much in sympathy. . . .

To Mary Bess Westenholz

Ngong. 30th March. 1928.

. . . I should be most grateful if you would send me the issue of Scribner containing the last installment of "The Forsyte Saga"; I cannot get it here and and am longing to read about the course of events. Since you write that it deals with Irene, I can foresee that it will arouse my irritation; because I can't help thinking that she is the weak or dead point in the entire saga. Of course, up to a point I can understand your view that she should not be regarded as realistic character description, but as a kind of symbol; but I can by no means allow that the author is right in, or has the right to, treat one individual character in this way in what is otherwise such a realistic and humanly conceived novel.

Partly I find that it completely breaks up the style of the book and think that here one can blame Galsworthy in the same way that Goldschmidt (in "A Jew") castigates Oehlenschlæger for letting the genius of the lamp in "Aladdin" mix together Greek and Scandinavian mythology in one breath in his usual oriental fairy-tale jargon; this may perhaps be legally defensible because of course the spirit may very well be thought to have knowledge of all the mythologies in the world,—but aesthetically it is indefensible because it grates on the reader's ear and breaks up the whole spirit and style of the work.

Partly it is my personal view that Irene,—and particularly seen in this light,—is a failure on the author's part, and this is by virtue of a just nemesis, for Galsworthy is a realistic author, and no artist has the right to do as he likes with his work in such a way.

If she is supposed to represent "beauty" it is regrettable that one, or at any rate I, get no impression at all throughout the book that she was in fact beautiful.—Stevenson has commented on this phenomenon; he says: "Readers can not fail to have remarked, that what an author tells us of the beauty of his creatures goes for nothing, that we know instantly better, that the heroine cannot open her mouth but what, all in a moment, the fine phrases of preparation fall from her and she stands before us, self-betrayed, as a poor ugly sickly wench or perhaps a strapping market woman. Authors, at least, know it well, a heroine will too often start the trick of getting ugly, and no disease is more difficult to cure—" I for one cannot get away from the impression that Irene was pasty-faced and very tightlaced. But let us not dwell on her outward beauty, of which other readers may have quite a different view; as to her being possessed of a beautiful mind,—as the intention seems to be that she is,—against her being attributed with that I protest most strongly; she was on the contrary an unusually silly, sulky, and vulgar person. Can you imagine anything more stupid and indelicate than when, in the scene where Soames comes to see her after a gap of twelve years, she says to him: "I am alone here. You won't behave as you once behaved?"—?! In real life,—if one can imagine anything like this being said in real life,—this would be interpreted as an invitation!—in any case, no one who knew Soames could possibly imagine this entering his mind in those circumstances; for of course he was far from being a criminal, but had been provoked into that unfortunate act, which she had to rub his nose in, by quite particular circumstances and by Irene herself; and she, who thought that she understood what a great passion was, and what under its influence one can be driven to do, ought, if she had not been such a coarse and vulgar female, to have had enough generosity of heart and understanding to show some feeling for what he had suffered and forgiven him,—or if she could not do that at least she might have had the simple tact to keep quiet about it. Perhaps her lack of loyalty to June can be forgiven, but not her total want of kindly human sympathy toward her,—and how, in the last section, can she protest that she has never opposed Jon and Fleur's marriage, after she has allowed Jolyon in his letter to dig up old unhappy circumstances which were quite unnecessary for Jon to hear about, in minutest detail, with the sole view of hindering it?

Throughout the book Irene appears only in the light of the other characters in the novel,—through the impression she makes, the effect she has on them; as far as I recall, the author does not once let us know directly what she is thinking and feeling, and the few remarks she does make really are, to put it mildly, pauvre. This is an artistic tactic that can be extremely effective,—I will use an example to show what I mean: Sigrid Undset treats Erlend in the same way; while we are generously regaled with every phase of consciousness in Kristin, Simon, Ragnfrid, there is hardly one instance where she condescends to let us know directly what is going on in Erlend's mind; we see him through the eyes of the other characters. But Sigrid devoted a great deal more effort to making Erlend's character convincing, he "carries weight"; no matter how much he is used as a symbol, in himself he is no symbol, but a human being, we believe in him, and one can quite well imagine Erlend on his own, in his own right,—while in my view this is not possible at all with Irene; when the other human characters shift their attention from her she collapses completely, like a puppet when the puppet master relaxes his hold on it.—There is in fact proof of this in that she, who does have such a colossal influence on all the characters in the book, so that she cannot show herself without causing the most appalling havoc, lives for twelve years,—(outside the scope of the book) without any kind of experience or acquaintance at all. This suits the author's plan; in real life it would be quite unthinkable.

In short, I don't think that there is any redeeming point for Irene in the entire book, as either a human being or a symbol, and I find it hard to forgive her for marring a monumental work; I look forward eagerly to meeting the other characters again.

What a frightful idea of yours, to publish my letters; if I knew this was going to happen I think it would be impossible for me to write.

I am really very grateful to you for taking pleasure in reading my letters, and it interests me just as much to write to you as it has always done to discuss life's problems with you orally,—but I do not have sufficient self-confidence to feel that my observations can be of any interest except to someone who, like you, takes a benevolent interest in me for my own sake.

When I write to you about art, morals, women's affairs, and so on, it is not in the least because I consider myself to be possessed of the highest knowledge regarding these things, and not at all like Erasmus Montanus, in order to "triumph in the argument," but because I think that it may mean something to you personally to have me explain and expound what I personally have come to understand by them and think about them, and what through them I have gathered together and clarified for myself. But I think it is too much to expect the Danish reading public to accept them in the same way.—You are welcome to give my letters to whoever you like; for then they will anyway get them through you, which may give them a certain weight and interest, but they must be regarded in the light of contributions to a personal conversation, not as dissertations, for I do not consider that I have the slightest aptitude for that sort of intellectual exercise.

However, as in fact I am constantly finding, when it happens that I become convinced about or change my view of the various problems of life, that I think: I would like to talk to Aunt Bess about that,—something that I have in common with all my siblings, and with so many other people who have come to know you,—I have actually had the idea of trying to deal with some of them and thus to give you something of a "philosophy of life"; if one makes the effort to be completely honest, surely such an attempt must always be of some interest. I feel that out here I have come to understand the value of distance or perspective,—(it is true to say that something of this dawned on me when I attended the Academy and learned to draw perspective, which I count as one of the experiences of my life, but whose significance I only recently understood how to apply to practical life) - I think you will have a better chance of understanding my views more easily when they are written from Africa than if they were expressed in the living room at Folehave. So many factors come into play when people are together in person,—for instance, to what extent the other person's view and conduct of life can be thought to intervene in one's own or one's surroundings' existence,—which can be left out of account completely when one is separated by a distance of many hundreds of miles, and I think this provides the possibility of a more impartial and purely human opinion. Then one says,—or anyway I do,—a good many things that are unconsidered in a conversation, that one would not embark upon in writing a letter, and which cannot do other than confuse both myself and the person I am talking to.

My letter has been neglected all this time, and I have got no further with my "Religion and my View of Life," nor will I get any further with it this time, but I will do something about it later on. In this letter I must content myself with thanking you very much for your letter for my birthday; I am always so glad to get a letter from you, and there was so much of interest in this one.

It was interesting to hear about Merete's home, and I agree with you that modern comfort is in no way synonymous with cosiness; but there are probably two things that can be said here: partly that with the years what has vanished forever acquires a special tinge of poetry, so that one can even feel moved on seeing again those upholstered chairs with velvet and silk covers and fringes and tassels with which people decorated their homes in the seventies, and which are only to be found now in guest rooms, and which were really not so very poetical even when they were brand new,—and that is no doubt because people have sat in them, thought and talked, written love letters and made baby clothes and so on, and thus have bestowed on them some kind of spirit or element of human life that is not directly discernible in the things produced yesterday,—and then too, that when "modern conveniences" can be picked up just around the corner, then there may well be an element of "artificial mountaineering" in doing without them at all, which probably in practice and detail may resemble bygone times but which in its actual spirit, is very remote from them.—

Just after I had arrived in this country, a man who had previously been in India said to me,—and I have often since thought about it,—that: "India is a Thousand and One Nights, and Africa is Robinson Crusoe."—they must therefore be judged from completely opposite points of view; for although it must have been wonderful for Aladdin to be enabled to erect a royal palace, complete down to the last detail, with the aid of the genie of the lamp, there must also have been an indescribably special charm for Robinson Crusoe, in the sweat of his brow and after many abortive attempts, to produce one loaf that he might perhaps have criticized severely if it had been handed him in a baker's shop at home,—and just as many readers have been held in suspense and rejoiced over his efforts as those who have reveled with joy in the riches of Albondocani. It is true that life out here has this character, and that to a great extent is what gives it its charm,—although at the same time one complains about it. When you see how as soon as all the women here get together the first thing they talk about is gardening, and exchanging flower and vegetable seeds, and when I think how proud I am after many unsuccessful attempts finally to have managed to grow lavender in my garden, one can understand how the flowers we have succeeded in nurturing have in a special way become a part of our life; but of course it would be just as stupid to compare these modest specimens with the beautiful blooms to be seen in European gardens as to try to collect seed and give time to one's flowers in the same way at home, where one can achieve so much better results with such infinitely greater ease.—

Life here, you know, has many features in common with life in Denmark two hundred years ago; the huge flock of utterly superfluous servants that somehow inevitably cluster around one, the roads that at certain times of the year become completely impassible, which restricts one's whole world to the house and its immediate surroundings,—and the fact that the roughness of the conditions shows up the difference in the physical capacity of men and women in quite another way from that apparent in a civilized country, where in fact there are no tasks beyond the power of a woman; here there are some things that one cannot join in, but the men come in, tired out after their safaris or from plowing and working our shambas, and place quite a different value on a comfortable living room, flowers, conversation, than can in any way be expected of their brothers at home who come in from an office chair,—and take us out hunting or driving on trips that we could not undertake by ourselves, not even I, who do not consider myself to be naturally timid.—

In a few years, when all this has vanished, I think much of it will be recalled with special affection and a particular feeling of loss; but at the same time it is quite impossible not to set all one's energies into changing all these conditions; to improve the roads, to educate people so that one of them will be able to carry out a job it now takes between five and ten of them to do,—in every way to get: "the landscape that lies around us,—threatens with desert and with peak,—slow to smile and unyielding"—to become, as in Bjørnson's poem, "The giant that must be tamed,—so that we may have our will. He must carry, he must pull,—he must hammer, he must saw,—mill light in the waterfall. All the roaring, the defiance,—will between the fjord and mountain,—build for us a realm of beauty."—and it is in this that we truly resemble, and live in the same way as people of former times.—

I understand so well what you write about "novel reading," even though at present I am more inclined to read other things, preferably either poetry or philosophy, and so am afraid I do not know any good books to recommend to you. There is an English writer called Aldous Huxley whom I like very much and have thought of recommending to Elle; but I don't think he would be to your taste. Have you read "Olav Audunsson"?—it was given me by the faithful Katla last Christmas. I admire Sigrid Undset, but her nature and philosophy of life is so remote from mine that it costs me some effort to read her. It would be hard to find another such gloomy world as that in her books; you start off thinking that what she wishes to demonstrate in her books are the strict moral laws of life,—nemesis in other words,—but you find this impossible when you see that things turn out equally badly for everyone, and that basically it makes no difference whether one "plunges into a wild life" or enters a monastery; one is bound to be utterly miserable either way, and you end up realizing that it is quite out of the question to live in such a world. But she has flashes of great beauty and harmony all the same; in the last part of "Olav Audunsson" there is a description of a half-crazy young man and a depraved old woman and their life together in the woods far from other people, that is one of the most beautiful "idylls" I have met with in any book. And everything she writes makes a great impact,—but how one can thirst for a glimpse of humor in just a single one of her characters!. . .

To Ingeborg Dinesen

Ngong. Tuesday 24.4.1928.

. . . To begin with, we have had rain,—almost three inches in a week. Of course it has put quite a different colour on things, both by the direct good it has done us and because it really does look as if the year will pull itself together and be fairly normal, even with a month's delay. . . .

Then I must tell you about something really exciting that happened yesterday. Early in the morning Dickens came up here and told us that two lions had been in our old ox boma,—you know, the one near Farah's house—and taken two fine young oxen; that was anything but good news. Denys and I followed their tracks through the coffee in drizzling rain up to the little wood near Thaxton's house, but lost it there. Then we went back to the dead oxen and pulled them a little way into the coffee, to try for a chance in the evening. We were in Nairobi during the afternoon. . .and returned at dusk, when we spent some time in the coffee shamba measuring out along which rows we could get a shot at the lions on the oxen, and worked out directions and distances with little bits of Americani tied to the trees. Dickens was in despair and very bitter because we would not put strychnine in the remains of the oxen,—one was half eaten, the other not touched,—but we did not feel we could do that and lose the chance of some real sport.

There was a small moon, but it went down too early to be of any use to us, so our shooting-party consisted of, besides Denys with a 350, Farah and me each carrying a flashlight; these were not as good as they should have been, but still gave us quite a good light, and Denys had a third flashlight tied in his belt. We started out at 9 o'clock, left the car near the school and then walked softly, softly, in single file, first some way along the Kilimanjaro road, and then up between two rows of coffee trees, where our little white cloths shone faintly in the darkness. Then we saw the kill straight in front of us, but had not gone very far,—we moved forward very slowly and stopped to listen every other stride,—when we heard a lion's deep warning growl out to the right. Then there was complete silence again, but after a minute or two it came again, more strongly. Denys signaled to me to shine the light in that direction, and as it shone out white down between the rows of coffee, it showed us first a brightly illuminated little jackal that stared at us in utter bewilderment, and a moment later, as I turned it a little more to the left, almost supernaturally large, his Majesty Simba himself, at a distance of about 25 yards, lying on the ground with his head on his paws and his eyes fixed upon us.

I can't tell you how huge he looked, and so light against the darkness,—everything seems possible when night on a coffee shamba can reveal something like that! Now it is not very easy to pinpoint and keep the light on an object with a flashlight; he was clearly about to move and would probably next moment have glided off out of sight, but Denys shot immediately, and he sank down with one of their deep roars or grunts that are like an echo of the shot. Like lightning Farah and I swept the nearest area of the shamba with our torches,—and there, somewhat further away, stood the other lion, not quite so clear, but still light and with two shining green eyes. He had time to turn and vanish behind a coffee bush,—on the whole a coffee shamba is not at all the ideal terrain for shooting in, because when they go behind a bush they change the entire direction of the shot,—but we jumped into the next row and got the light on him again, and he fell at once from a lightning shot. Then followed some very tense minutes because we could not in fact be certain that they were dead or mortally wounded, or anything at all other than that they were both within 50 yards of us and we could only give ourselves a limited circle of light in the great African night!—We had to keep the flashlights trained on one with the possibility of getting the other on our backs, and the second one needed two more shots, but the first had died immediately.—

They were two young male lions, both with some black in their manes and enormous paws; they looked beautiful even when they were dead, and I will never forget the picture they made while still alive and in movement in the midst of the black night. As you can imagine, the whole school came rushing up in the greatest delight. We skinned them and came back, just as from the wildest adventure, at 11 o'clock,—the whole thing had taken two hours,—to a bottle of champagne. . . .

To Ingeborg Dinesen

Ngong. Sunday 20.5.1928.

. . . Denys left for Mombasa on Tuesday; I would like to have gone with him, but was obliged to stay here, as I was going to a dinner for Princess Marie Louise,—if you know who that is, a daughter of Princess Christian and I think the grand-daughter of Victoria,—and the Governor, that I did not dare refuse to attend, and then there is Lord Delamere's wedding that I have promised to go to. Actually, the Princess dinner was enjoyable; I sat beside Tom Cholmondeley and played an exciting game of bridge with him and Lord Francis Scott, who is considered to be the best bridge player in Kenya, and the Governor. Lord Francis and I inflicted five grand slams on the others and won a fortune. . . .

I have Halima as a handmaid at table; there is always something about her that reminds me of Missen, she is just as straight and graceful and has the same way of looking one straight in the eyes, and then there is something special about her, she is not like other children. She is a great actress, she can tell stories and quite unconsciously mimic everyone she is talking about. Since her Mother's death she has been so afraid of people dying; she has been sitting in here and "watched over me," she says, "so that I do not die"—"You are not going to die?" she keeps saying. . . .

Denys is in absolute despair because he has been asked to take the Prince of Wales, who is coming out here in October, out on safari. I laughed at him for taking it so hard, but he says that I don't know what English royalties are like, or the "fuss" that is made about them. I can quite well imagine it, already now people are thinking and talking of nothing but this visit. . . .

To Ingeborg Dinesen

Ngong. Sunday. 27. 5. 1928.

. . . I had the pleasure of getting a letter from Casparson, which even enclosed the money I had lent him without the slightest hope of seeing it again. He was in good spirits and hope, and it is really interesting to follow the fortunes of someone one has seen in such dire straits. He wrote that on his way to Tanganyika he had been warned in one place by the natives not to go further on because there were so many lions.—"After having given the matter serious consideration," he writes, "I went on my way, since I thought that it was morally right to give my family this chance of getting rid of me. Although I did not succeed in carrying this through, I do feel myself in possession of a good conscience and will now do no more for them."—He felt that the natives had been touchingly helpful toward him and also thanked me in the nicest possible manner for my,—extremely small,—support and my sympathy, which really was sincere. . . .

The Governor has demanded £7,500 to complete the ballroom at Government House on the occasion of the Prince of Wales's visit. I suppose it is possible that they can get the country to fork out for this rare occasion, otherwise they would probably never have got it to consent, as Government House is most unpopular out here; I must say that I think it is a lot of money, as after all the building itself is there, and we really don't need antique tapestries and so on.—The Prince is only going to stay for three weeks in all and will no doubt want to be out shooting a lot of the time, so it may well mount up to £1,000 a day for each day he spends at Government House. . . .

To Ingeborg Dinesen

Ngong. Sunday 3rd June. 1928.

. . . Incidentally, I wonder if I ever sent you,—or perhaps it was Tommy,—a letter from an old gun-bearer, addressed to Lioness von Blixen,—and that began: Honourable lioness—? This is how I am now generally addressed and I think it is rather grand.

. . . The MBagathi house is causing us anxiety; the tenants there have given notice because the rain comes in, and it is generally in a bad state, but of course we have no money for repairs to it. We agreed to go over there together to look at it, and I took Farah's wife and Halima with me in the car for a joy ride.

Halima is the funniest little thing; I really don't know how she will "fit in" in the more respectable Muhammadan female world; she is a real gypsy. She plays the harmonica and sings and dances to it at the same time with a quite astonishing lightness and, if I may say so, power,—more than grace; she imitates people and acts out whole plays about her life,—for instance, the obviously lamentable conditions at Embu, where she was living for a time, and where the vice of drunkenness must be prevalent,—to the greatest delight of Tumbo, who falls about laughing, and a mixture of indignation and admiration on the part of Farah's young wife, who herself is the epitome of womanly dignity. In the afternoon I tried to go for a walk on the farm; it is so long since I have seen the actual effects of the rain, but I arrived home so exhausted that I could neither eat nor sleep. On my walks I always have Tumbo and Titi as my companions and to look after the dogs; they are exactly like two puppies themselves, rush about all over the place bubbling over with laughter over everything. Tumbo has grown into a real boy, with a catapult and "gruesome cries at night," he is a bright kid. . . .

On Friday morning Choleim Hussein came out in his car and asked me if I would receive the Indian High Priest, who is on a tour of inspection in Kenya, for tea. He had very providently brought cakes and fruit with him. So I got up in time for tea and was quite overwhelmed to see eight cars driving up, with altogether seventeen high priests accompanied by Jevanjee and others from among the Indian élite of Nairobi. We had to lay the tea table in the dining room. They were all in long white robes and looked picturesque all around the house; the High Priest, a very old man with a delicate face, like wax, was wearing the most beautiful raiment of the very finest, handwoven white wool one can imagine,—almost competing with you! He could speak neither English nor Swahili, so we expressed our mutual esteem and goodwill in pantomime. He presented me with a pair of earrings.—He is a Muhammadan, I think from a particular sect, but esteemed over the whole Muhammadan world, so you can picture Farah dressed up in his best clothes, and all my boys on their toes. . . .

To Ingeborg Dinesen

Ngong. Sunday 10th June 1928.

. . . I can well understand what you write about Tommy wanting to get rid of his boat, and generally that it is a little sad to see how that luster of brave deeds that was around him as a young man is fading; but if his marriage has given him something different, then that is really the right way of development for him, and after all sailing races and so on are more the province of youth. Well, of course, Tommy is not exactly an "old man"!—and yet I think that actual youth comes to an end at 35. . . .

The longer I live, I think that what matters most to me is *truth;* I do not think that anyone can be happy except in conditions that, consciously or instinctively, they have chosen as the expression of their true nature, and many of the difficulties of one's youth are the result of one's having chosen or had ambitions about things that one admires theoretically, and that "must be" right for one too, but that in reality one does not love or belong among. Most people probably have quite a lot to overcome or resign themselves to in order truly to recognize, and acknowledge, their own true nature. . . . Perhaps a few years in this solid bourgeois atmosphere may clarify and concentrate much in him that could not have come to full growth in a life filled with adventure, and that in the fullness of time may emerge as something greater and more true in his nature than he himself,—or we, for all our admiration and love,—have known before. . . .

To Mary Bess Westenholz

Ngong. 18th June. 1928.

. . . There is so much that I would like to write to you about or, rather, talk to you about, for I don't care for the monologue form that letters are, especially at this distance, but think that the reciprocity engendered through conversation is of greatest benefit to both sides. . . . However, as so often in life, this is a case of "si on n'a pas ce que l'on aime, il faut aimer ce que l'on a—," and although I consider myself to be a better conversationalist than correspondent, I must be satisfied with paper and try to get as much as possible into it. And as I think that the trivia of practical life sometimes illuminate a problem just as well as weighty arguments, I am going to tell you about a little episode that may perhaps have some relevance to our numerous discussions on the subject of "marriage," or my view of it.

You have probably heard through Mother about a nocturnal lion hunt that we had on the farm. It started with two young lions, with hitherto unknown audacity, taking two young oxen out of our boma, and Dickens coming down here in the morning to tell me about it and to ask if I would agree to his putting strychnine in the remains of the oxen.—But this idea was so repugnant to me that I refused, and said that I thought lions should be shot. However, he thought that we could ill afford to risk the lions getting more oxen for the sake of a little "fun," and of course he may have been right in this. But he then went on to say that he himself had thought of building a boma and sitting up at night in order to shoot at the lions, but that he had come to think that he was a married man, with one child and another on the way, and had reached the conclusion that it would be irresponsible and wrong of him. Yes, I said, I understood that perfectly, but I myself and Denys Finch Hatton, who was staying here, would go after them. This completely reassured Dickens and he declared that of course that was all right. "Come now then," I said to Denys, "and let us go and risk our entirely worthless lives."

However, if I give some thought to Dickens's point of view I have to allow that he is right. It is really quite immoral for a "married man" to risk life and limb unnecessarily, and if it had ended with his being eaten by the lions and his wife left with one unborn child and another two years old without a halfpenny or any possibility of earning a living, it would not only have been a tragedy but a wrong and foolish action, quite unscrupulous behavior, resulting in misery and hardship for all concerned.

Of course this applies particularly to people in his position, who have nothing other than their personal work from day to day to rely on or fall back on in life; but if one really thinks about it the situation is actually more or less the same for everyone who has shouldered the obligations of marriage and family.

Now, naturally I don't think that to renounce shooting lions is any great sacrifice, and probably one can say too that people who have reached years of discretion could leave it alone as well. But the lions here signify or represent something, and as I was thinking it over I felt that I had arrived at the understanding that this was really a matter of a choice in life, and that at least those people who are considering taking the step of marriage would do well to make clear to themselves whether they will choose the lions or family life.

I think that conscientious people who get married must realize and decide that from now on consideration for their wives,—(and perhaps,—children) takes precedence over all others. I have always believed that one could not expect to get much out of life if one were not able to clarify for oneself what was "essential" for one, and that when this demanded it of one to let everything else go, and that it is not quite playing the game to get married if one does not feel that home and family are now and will go on being what is essential; in my opinion, anyhow, that would be to go against the true spirit and meaning of marriage. In my view it is wrong for a married man to risk or destroy the life of his wife and children for the sake of a conviction, an idea, or a passion, and I cannot find any enthusiasm to support the people here who want to put up a monument where Maia Carbery crashed in her airplane, to "A Pioneer of Flying"; for I consider there is something irresponsible in the mother of a little girl of three gallivanting around in the sky as a pioneer for the art of flying until she crashes and kills herself.

In other words this means that by embarking on marriage one renounces an enormously great wealth, of activity, of experience, of new impressions in life, and acknowledges, declares oneself satisfied with and determined from now on to nourish one's spirit and one's brain through a specific diet and in a specific relationship.

I am certainly not going to say that it is not very possible that this is what suits the great majority of people best,—indeed, it is possible that they may get married without reflecting upon it and never ever come to experience this conflict. But I think that with each year that passes it becomes more difficult to get over it so lightly. In the old days, when people had ten children and were old when they were fifty, then family life could occupy, not only their "life and soul," but their entire time and their talent and strength from day to day. I can say with Wells: "The whole adult life was consumed by sex and its consequences; the business of the family, of making it and toiling for it, of weeping over the dead and beginning again, was the complete circle of life. Man was almost as sexual as a cat with its ever-recurring kittens. In the past the normal existence fell wholly into the frame of the family. Man was a family animal. Now this is no longer the case. Now family life becomes merely a phase in an ampler experience. Human life escapes beyond it."

It may well be possible to find examples that defy this view, but I for one cannot find any that do not to a certain extent have their roots in the past, when the family had a different meaning from that of today. When the Duke of Orléans marries in order to preserve the ancient dynasty of France for happier times, then marriage for him is undoubtedly bound up with everything that means something to him and has value and importance in life: with honor and justice, with God himself and "la grâce de Dieu," with history and fatherland,—and for the Duchess of Orléans, provided that she is of like mind, it may very well be the highest moment and fulfillment of life to bring the Count of Paris and the Duke of Chartres into the world. But this is not the case with the majority of mankind in 1928, and if religion, science, art, social problems, fatherland, history, or education of the people mean anything at all to them, their significance is completely independent of and unconnected with their marriage and family. And they have the opportunity of coming in contact with them and acquiring an understanding of them, and time to devote to them, in quite another manner than was the case in older times.

It is then quite conceivable that there are many people for whom the unconditional freedom to seek out and take what at each phase of their lives must represent to them the highest and best, that which is most necessary for them, must greatly exceed in importance the earlier undertaken relationship to a certain task or person. And there may be people for whom this freedom or frankness in regard to what they love may be of such great importance that they cannot at all imagine giving it up. (From the purely legal point of view, of course, people can be married or unmarried without changing this factor in the least.) And since we know that it takes all sorts of people to make the world, so I think that there is need and room for a class of unmarried and free people in the world we find ourselves in today, just as much as for a stable population of family men and women, and that it is impossible to prove that the married state, if one takes the whole of humanity into consideration, is the natural and normal one.

Naturally, it may well be that this situation will come to change to a greater or lesser degree in the future. Birth control, and the independent employment of women,—or similarly, for example, the institution of the communist state, or a change in education, a sexual liberation for women,—may change the pivotal point of the whole problem, and Mrs. Dickens may wish for and approve of Dickens taking on the lions of life; now she would not even, when he heard us shooting down in the shamba and got out his car to drive down to find out what was happening, allow him to do that. As it is now, Dickens, who put the car away again,—I am sure with the greatest reluctance, for he is certainly no coward,—is really an ideal and model husband and father, and I could raise a monument to him just as well as the Flying Club can raise theirs for Lady Carbery. But as long as conditions are like this, there must be many men who cannot or should not take on the role of Mr. Dickens, and women,—I know this for certain,—who must at all costs avoid the character part of Mrs. Dickens!—

You must not think that I cannot see the beautiful and valuable element in the other type and life. As I have probably written before: I can,—in the same way as the Archbishop of Canterbury, when he was going to discuss some matter with Lord Melbourne, said to him: "My Lord, it will save our time if we to begin with agree that everything and everybody is damned,"—begin this discussion, as well as any other, by admitting that there is something great and beautiful in every one of the ideals that through the ages humanity has set up and been uplifted by and rejoiced in, in the Valkyrie as in the nun and the housewife,—and something dangerous in every one of them. Of course I am only saying this so that those who have a longing to shoot lions may be respected for their motives to an equal extent as those who keep the midwives occupied may have theirs acknowledged. I myself will never forget the lion's short, muted, somehow warning growl as we approached, or the sight of it like a flame against the great African night. But I believe and can well understand that Mrs. Dickens gets just as much out of, sees "the highest and greatest" in Anne's first tooth and evening bath. Nor do I bear her any grudge because she cannot take the slightest interest in or sympathize with my views.—But I would really like to feel that you understand what I think and feel about these things,—and I hope I have succeeded in conveying at least some impression of them.

And so goodbye, dear Aunt Bess, and again all my good wishes and thanks for many old years. When I think of our various discussions I feel there is much more to unite us than there is to separate us; may we come to meet in steadily greater understanding and constant friendship!—When I think of your spirit and influence throughout our childhood and youth, it is very remote from representing to me any expression of the "everlasting bourgeoisie" that you are a little infatuated with at times. There was a little too much moralizing for me personally, but far, far more enthusiasm, light, and warmth, for which I am *eternally* grateful to you.

Your Tanne.

To Ingeborg Dinesen

Ngong. Sunday 24.6.1928.

. . . I'm sure you would find everything unchanged,—I even still have the stork; it causes some conflict in my life because it eats baby chickens. It can fly all right, and the other day I met it when I was out riding, right out at Wangatta, you know, where the pink and white flowers were; and it is quite tame; I was able to ride right up to it,—but in the evening it comes back and walks solemnly into its house. I have a tame egret as well, by the way; it lives in a tree on the lawn and sits on the same branch every evening; during the day it walks about on the lawns.—The boys say my gander is a great success, and I hope to have goslings, which are about the sweetest things in the world.

I was interrupted by a company of seven Somali ladies in the most beautiful colors, who had come on a visit to Fathima and came to greet me. They always nearly kill themselves laughing at everything I say,—not, I believe, on account of my wit, but probably because they think I'm incredibly comical. I suggested that I should teach them to drive a car; they just couldn't get over that but burst into cascades of laughter and kept repeating it to each other. One of them presented me with an exceptionally beautiful head scarf of the kind they wear, black cloth richly embroidered with gold; I hope she doesn't regret it. In the end they fled away in the greatest horror because I said I wanted to photograph them. For Denys has given me a small camera and innumerable rolls of film, so now I'll try to take some pictures here to send you. I'm afraid I am not very gifted at it, but it's worth a try. . . .

I don't seem able to get better, but continue to have a temperature of over 100, now they are going to try a new kind of injection which is supposed to be an excellent tonic; I don't like the idea, but it is so tiresome to drag oneself around feeling that everything in the world is insurmountable. . . .

I have such a horror of everything to do with childbirth; the other day, when I went with Lady Grigg to her Native Maternity Home, I went in to see a very young native woman, with such a sweet face, taken into the "labor room,"—they said that she would have her baby in half an hour; of course in some ways it is so natural, but I think it is an awful method and could wish they could discover another one,—think how nice it would be if one could sit on an egg. . . .

To Thomas Dinesen

Ngong. Monday 25th June. 1928.

. . . There is only one thing that I am going to ask you to do for me about this,—and that is to explain to Mother that in these circumstances I cannot go home in the spring, and explain this shaurie to her. I had been counting on Aunt Emy's money for my traveling expenses, and now that I have to use it for other things, I will have to wait until 1930. Naturally I am terribly disappointed, but it is not such a long postponement, and I am sure Mother will be able to understand; anyway it can't be any worse than when I had to tell her that you wanted to go to war!. . .

To Mary Bess Westenholz

Ngong. 29th June. 1928.

Dearest Aunt Bess.

In continuation of my previous letter:

It must be of value to clarify for oneself in this connection whether one really thinks that the life of the family man and woman in itself really is of more value than that of the unmarried. I think, as I wrote, that it is often, or at least usually so, more necessary to safeguard them and more irresponsible to expose them to risk; but this cannot be used unconditionally as a yardstick for their actual value.

What in my opinion must be considered here is first that a concept like this: the value of a person's life, must be judged from other viewpoints than the immediate situation, and next that what is at stake is not only the trouble and unhappiness one can cause by dying, but also the benefit and happiness one can bring about by remaining alive.

To illustrate my first point I will adduce something that I have heard, that it made very little impression, indeed, was hardly noticed outside certain narrow circles, when Spinoza died, and that Corot effected the very first sale of a picture shortly before his death,—(and then remarked that he was reluctant to part with it because until then he had been in possession of a complete collection of Corot, which uniquely valuable idea it would be impossible ever to experience again)—and even if these examples should prove to be wrong,—because it is difficult for me to check the truth of such things since I have no books to consult,—everyone knows that it has often happened that the value of great personalities' work has only been realized by the rest of humanity after their deaths. It has even gone so far that society has felt it necessary and in its interest to put an end to certain human lives and executed such people as criminals whom they have later canonized as saints or acknowledged as great benefactors of mankind. The immediate anxiety and sorrow at a deathbed is by no means an accurate measure of the real value to the world of the individual life.

Next: I may very well cause a great deal of confusion, trouble, and despair at my death without ever having achieved, and without having had the possibility of achieving, an approximately corresponding amount of benefit or joy for the sake of another human being while I am alive.—Let me "for argument's sake" say that I have hidden an infernal machine somewhere in a big ocean steamer in a place known only to me. It would then be in the vital interest of a great number of people to keep me alive until I could take it away again, and the message that I had jumped overboard would be greeted with general despair; but it could not be asserted that such a deed as this would impart any real value to my life.

Now it could be possible for a woman to acquire ten children, who were so wild that no other person than herself could manage them, or, for instance, were deaf and dumb and could only make contact with the world around them by means of a system known to her, and obviously then those around her would do all they could to keep her alive, and would be very alarmed at the news of her death,—and yet her existence cannot be taken as a model of a particularly valuable human life.

Aunt Lidda wrote to me once that she thought that as long as one could let in a dog that was whining out in the cold night, one's life could not be without value. I am not sure whether that can be maintained as a matter of course.—Perhaps, if the dogs do happen to be there, and one is doing something to improve a regrettable situation, or if it should concern, in some way or other, some specially valuable examples of the canine race, it may well be said; but if one has procured and acquired the dog for one's own pleasure and put it outside or inside the door, then I do not think that the effort of letting it in can be regarded as anything else than carrying out a duty one has brought upon oneself. For to acquire a number of not clearly defined dogs and then let them in and out cannot, I consider, be called a very valuable task for a human being.

Now I think that many married people, especially those with large families, often in this manner make a wrong judgment of the *value* of their own lives in relation to those of unmarried and childless people.—They undertake various obligations solely for their own pleasure or in their own interest, and then think that by fulfilling these they have provided life or society with new values.—And here I think, as I say, that it may very well be beyond doubt that their surroundings would be worse off if they took these obligations lightly, but that this is no proof that it would have been equally good or better in every way if they had never embarked upon them.

If one does not think it is a good thing that, without regard for quality, as many people as possible should be brought into the world, or has a purely orthodox respect for marriage in itself, then one must assess family life, just like everything else in the world, according to the results. The fact that marriage partners, or parents and children, hold each other in mutual esteem above everything in the world does not alter their value for the rest of humanity, and they cannot possibly demand acknowledgment from it of their private yardsticks.

Admittedly I feel that human *happiness,* when it occurs, is of great value and well worth conserving, and I also think that the person who can be said to have created something beautiful and harmonious has given the world something of value, even if this is apparently only to be found, and is effective, in his own sphere. (I think on the whole that a very long intervening distance is necessary before one can judge of what can be called useful or beneficial.—Probably one can say that all beautiful, noble, or brilliant works are of use, or that everything that proves to be useful or beneficial has its own beauty. Whether Ramses [?] would have done better to build a plague hospital to relieve the momentary hardship in Egypt than to erect a pyramid that for centuries has been an inspiration and interest to humanity is impossible to determine offhand, and probably not even if it were put to the vote.)

But who can judge whether Dickens is actually happier than Finch Hatton, or Mrs. Dickens happier than I? I myself think that I am much happier and get far more out of life than Mrs. Dickens, who is always pretty sulky. Dickens gives me the impression that he was more cheerful before he got married, but of course so many things that I know nothing about may contribute to this.—And who can come and say that they know that the Dickenses' home, that is concentrated solely on Papa and Mama and the little three-year-old, in itself is a better or more beautiful or more harmonious concern than my own house, which is not self-sufficient in that way but which has windows and doors open to the world of the natives and the wayfarer?—I do think that it is easier for me to have a clear perception of human rights in general and to act accordingly; I have seen the otherwise decent Dickens forget all reasonable standards of behavior toward the natives and toward their wretched old Danish nurse when they had been unlucky enough to upset Mrs. Dickens.

I am aware that all respectable people rush for the midwife when it is necessary, and show the greatest consideration for a lady who is expecting. It is of course a right and vital human instinct that would detract from life were it absent. Mrs. Dickens is now in a nursing home in Nairobi having her baby, and we are deeply interested in the event; we would put our cars at her disposal with the greatest alacrity and presumably in the event of an earthquake we would save her life before our own. But I have no illusions as to the result of this entire undertaking; I don't think that Mrs. Dickens's (dreadfully spoiled) brood have any great possibilities for exhibiting any qualities in the future beyond—Mrs. Dickens's own. A repetition of Madame Dickens down through the centuries may be a highly respectable undertaking,—but in all sincerity I don't think that it will affect the balance on one or the other side of the human scales to any great extent.

So:—as I've already said, I take my hat off to Dickens, who drove his car in again when he heard us shooting in the shamba, and I quite agree with him that as a married man and a father etc. he should not risk his life unnecessarily. But I do not think that this is any yardstick to measure the *value* of his life. And in any case: this is not the sort of value that I personally aspire to. I take no satisfaction whatsoever in the exaggerated estimation that I might win from another individual in a personal relationship,—and pay for with an exaggerated estimation of his or her character. Let me have that worth accorded me by God and other people with no magnification, out of proportion, brought about by the momentary interest or necessity occurring in a small circle of my acquaintance. A good deal of that worth, if it exists at all, is due to the fact that I—shoot lions. Or that: it is possible for me to live on a free footing and do what I like with my life. There are many people of this kind in the world and I consider that they are just as entitled to their rights and their place in it as family men and women. I myself am very happy to be numbered among them.—

Your Tanne.

P.S. Naturally I have often seen the phenomenon where a person who has been personally unable to get any content or happiness out of life has found his raison d'être in this: making another person happy. Or he produces some children to whom he believes he can bring happiness, and feels he has added value to the world in this way and fully justified his existence.

Whether this is a line of reasoning that can be defended in itself is a question that ranges too widely and is too complicated for me to be able to go into more deeply. Actually, of course, when one comes to think of it one can say that if two people who both take this view of life, meet and "make each other happy," they have not in fact gained anything else or more than if they had managed to achieve happiness on their own, and the world has not acquired any greater value than if they had succeeded in this; and similarly: that a person who has not personally succeeded in adopting an attitude to, in reaching any understanding of life, cannot be regarded as having any great possibility of imparting a better view of it to his children, or giving them proper contact with it,—but one should probably not isolate an individual relationship like this, and can always hope and partly rely on other influences and in the wealth that lies in the nature of all reciprocity.—

I believe that what can be said about this relationship in *practice* is that it is very often built on pure illusion.

I think that it is true of an exceedingly large number of married people (and parents) who thus base their lives and happiness on *what they are to others,* that they would be extremely surprised,—(whether happily or sadly is not easy to determine, in many cases it might bring a feeling of relief)—if they were suddenly told, or suddenly realized with certainty that they themselves are not "more to"—their spouse than she or he is to themselves. The average human being who has no particularly strong feelings or any particularly strong urge of any kind often calculates, in order to create a balance in life, much stronger feelings than his own in the people with whom he is in a relationship; and while, if one were to press them, they might come to realize that their husband, wife or children are not absolutely necessary to themselves, they work up a conviction that they themselves are absolutely necessary to their relatives.—I think that very often a marriage comes about or is kept going, indeed, achieves a certain amount of harmony and happiness, because both partners independently believe they have sacrificed their own happiness for the sake of the other, "made him happy," and feel their own worth to lie in the fact that the other partner "cannot live without" them, and it is obvious that this evaluation is rendered invalid when it is mutual.—I really believe that by far the greatest majority of happily married people would be astonished, and pretty shaken, if they were told that their spouse had no greater love for them than they themselves nourished for that partner. . . .

To Ingeborg Dinesen

Ngong. Tuesday 3rd July. 1928

. . . I enclose some photos which, although not specially good, as they're the first I have taken with the camera that Denys gave me, will perhaps be of interest to you even so, as you know every inch of this place. . .Halima and Kanini are in the one with the geese, and Titi is holding Heather,—you can see David in the background. The bull is from Geoffrey Buxton's farm; you can see the sort of landscape it is up there, it is like an old painting or tapestry.

Perhaps next time I may have some better subjects to send you, because I am thinking of going off on a little safari tomorrow for a fortnight with Denys, who wants to photograph lions down toward Tanganyika.—I have not been able to get over the influenza or whatever it was I had; the other week I tried a new kind of injection,—quinine,—that the doctor thought would be good, but it merely made me utterly wretched, and I think a change of air would be the best thing. . .

To Ingeborg Dinesen

Ngong. Sunday 22nd July. 1928.

. . . When Denys and I were out riding the other morning we found 25 goats in our maize and drove them back here, so the owner had to come and fetch them; Holmberg used to "fine" them one goat for that kind of offense, but that can soon develop into an abuse, so I have stopped it, and now Dickens usually gives the toto who is in charge of them a spanking; but this is not a really good system either, for if one does not get hold of the guilty toto actually in the act, it is always the very youngest member of the family, who has no one smaller to fall back on, who gets sent up for the beating,—this time

Ingrid Lindström and Karen Blixen at Njoro, about 1928.

Picture from The Strand Magazine, *September 1934: from the left Bror Blixen, the Prince of Wales, and Denys Finch Hatton, photographed during the prince's visit to Kenya, 1928.*

Karen Blixen with Juma and his family, 1930. She is holding Farah's son Saufe in her arms (photograph by Carl Søgaard).

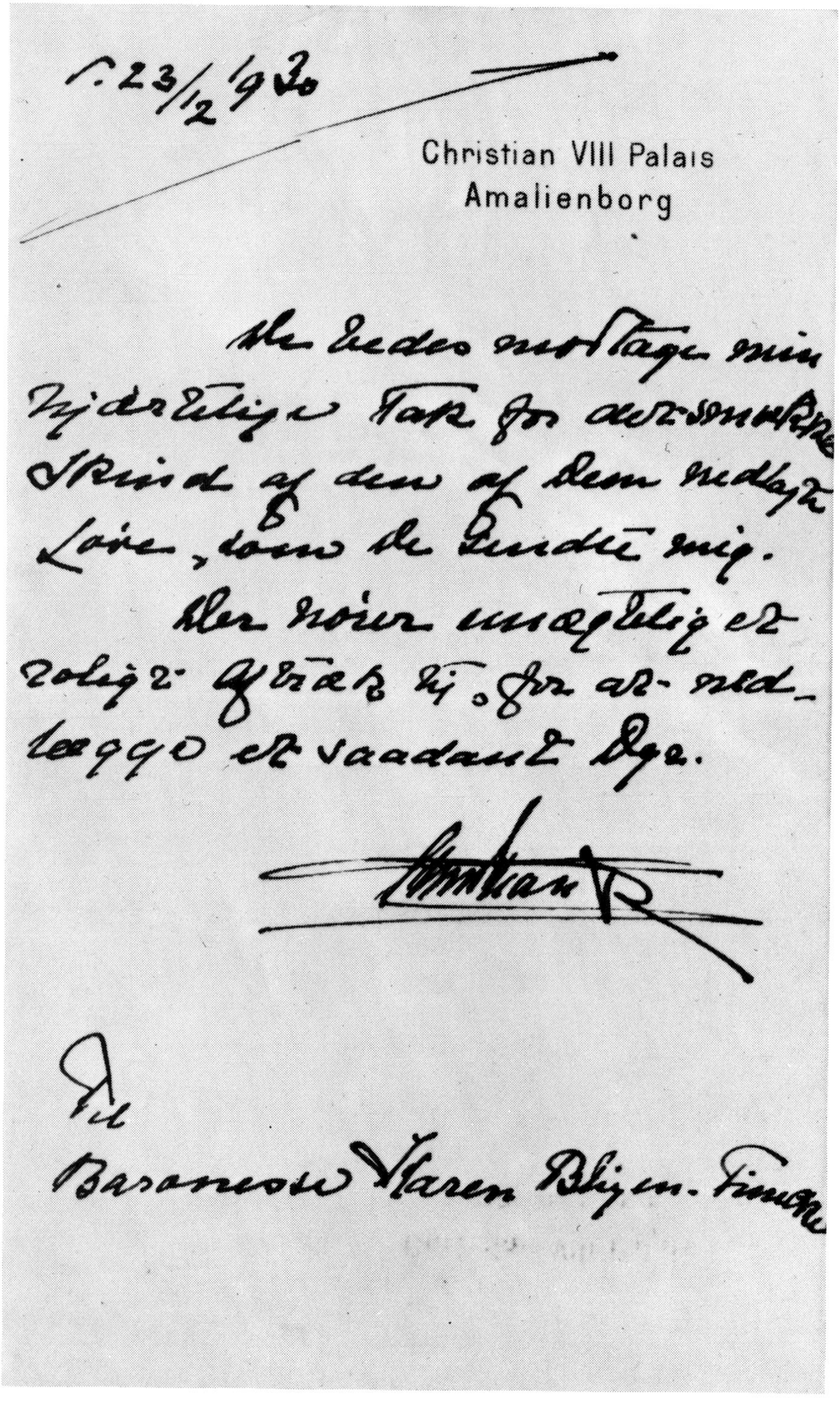
r. 23/12 930

Christian VIII Palais
Amalienborg

De bedes modtage min hjertelige Tak for det smukke Skind af den af Dem nedlagte Løve, som De sendte mig.

Den vidner unægtelig et roligt & sikkert Sigte for at nedlægge et saadant Dyr.

Christian R.

Til

Baronesse Karen Blixen-Finecke

Christian X's letter to Karen Blixen thanking her for the lionskin, December 1930 (mentioned in Shadows on the Grass, *1960).*

Denys Finch Hatton ready for a trip in his airplane.

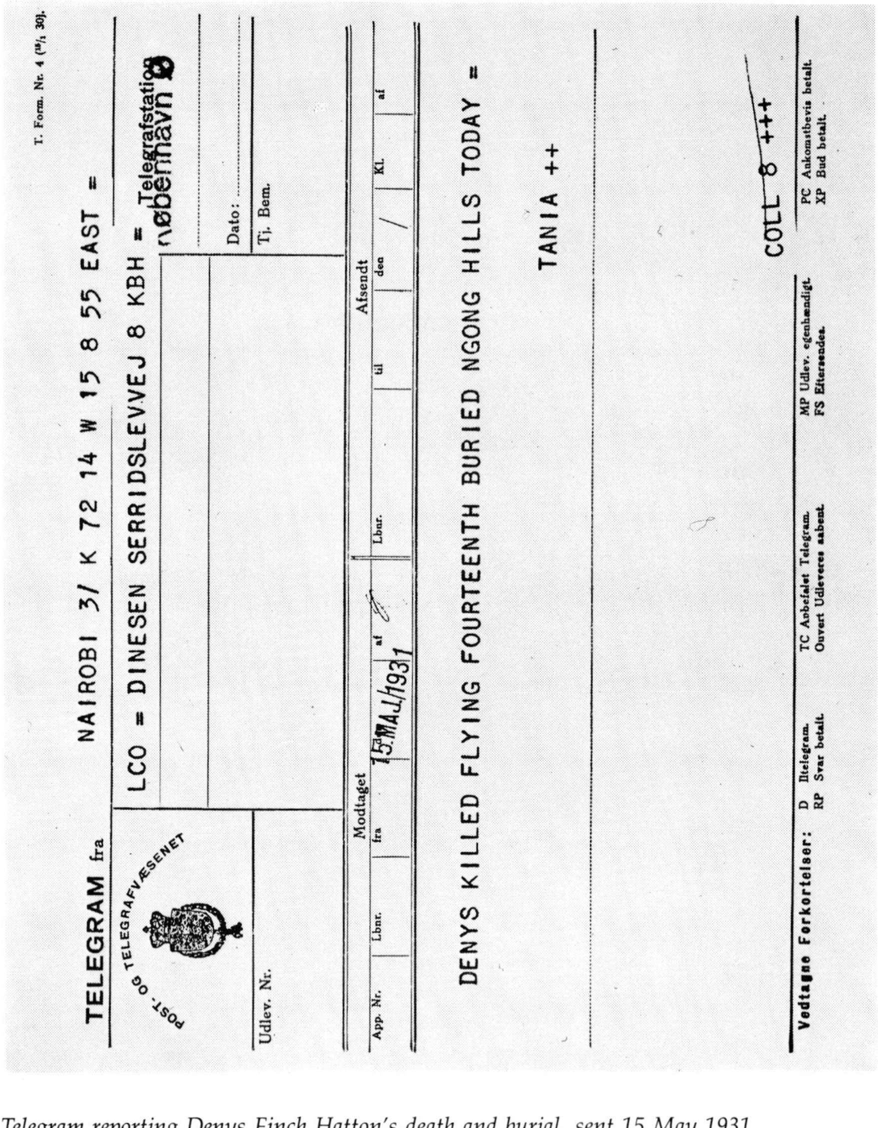

T. Form. Nr. 4 (18/1 30).

TELEGRAM fra

POST- OG TELEGRAFVÆSENET

NAIROBI 3/ K 72 14 W 15 8 55 EAST =

LCO = DINESEN SERRIDSLEVVEJ 8 KBH =

Telegrafstation København Ø

Udlev. Nr.

Dato:

Tj. Bem.

Modtaget				Afsendt			
App. Nr.	Lbnr.	fra	af	Lbnr.	til	den	Kl.	af
		15 MAJ 1931				/		

DENYS KILLED FLYING FOURTEENTH BURIED NGONG HILLS TODAY =

TANIA ++

COLL 8 +++

Vedtagne Forkortelser: D Iltelegram. RP Svar betalt. TC Anbefalet Telegram. Ouvert Udleveres aabent. MP Udlev. egenhændigt. FS Eftersendes. PC Ankomstbevis betalt. XP Bud betalt.

Telegram reporting Denys Finch Hatton's death and burial, sent 15 May 1931 from Nairobi to Thomas Dinesen in Copenhagen.

Denys Finch Hatton by his airplane.

The railway station in Nairobi (photograph by Thomas Dinesen).

Karen Blixen and her seventy-nine-year-old mother at the reception for "Isak Dinesen" in the hall of the Civil Engineers' Society, Copenhagen, 1935, on the occasion of the publication of the Danish edition of Seven Gothic Tales.

it was a little girl of at most five, dissolved in tears, whom Denys and I declined to punish. . . .

When things are going well here I think no human being could be happier than I am. Of course many things are lacking in the kind of life I lead here; but then most people lack something or other, and I have so much that does not merely satisfy me but really delights me. I have just had a letter from Katla in which she asks me: How can you be so happy and see so much in life?—which has made me consider what it really is that does make me so happy here. Naturally one can point to many things and say: it is this or that; but what is the reason for the richness they bring one? Indeed, the longer I live I feel that *truth* is the most important thing for me, and in the same way that you say: Love comes first, I say: Truth comes first.—And here I can be true, I can be myself.—

What is it then "to be oneself"? It is not as easy as one might think. For everyone who is not an absolute exception, there must probably be an element of luck to enable them to do it. I have just written to Elle about it and emphasized that it is not done by "having one's freedom" to a greater or lesser degree, but that one must be in contact with one's surroundings,—so that a professor of mathematics on a desert island or among the Hottentots or la belle Otero among Russian Dukhobors with the best will in the world *cannot* manage to be themselves, or to be anything at all; first they must go out into other surroundings, and they can breathe again and develop their true personality when they get back to the study or the lectern, or to the boulevards of Paris. Many people find it hard to be themselves because there really is not anything in them to be, and when one says to them: "Come on, show your flag,"—they look anxiously around them for something to show; it is really too much to ask of them, and the best they can do is to find some scraps of philosophy and understanding they have picked up here and there,—a bit from Miss Zahle's school, from "Politiken," from Elinor Glyn,—to hoist and fly. To "be true" is something positive and by no means merely to refrain from lying,—indeed, it has nothing whatsoever to do with that, in fact.—

Professor Wicksteed says, in "Four Lectures on Henrik Ibsen": "What is it to be one self? God meant something when he made each of us. For a man to embody that meaning of God in his words and deeds, and so become, in a degree, a 'word of God made flesh,' is to be himself.—But what if a poor devil can never make out what God *did* mean when He made him? Why, he must feel it. But how often your feeling misses fire! Ah, there you have it. The Devil has no stauncher Ally than want of perception."—

But out here I anyhow have nothing to do with this devil. I think that here it comes naturally to me to be myself, to be what I believe that "God meant when he made me." In my relationship with the natives, with white people,—that is to say, to those who are somebody, not to the "middle class," and that is why I can get nothing at all out of being with them,—particularly with Denys, I believe that I am "myself as the whole man, the true, with God's sigil upon my brow"—(I have no Norwegian edition of "Peer Gynt"). And that, I believe, is to be happy, to feel like a fish in the water or a bird in the air.—And then I think that unless one is oneself one cannot do anything much for others. With the best will in the world and even with a great deal of effort, one will always to a certain extent give them stones instead of bread,—and both sides know it.

And so goodbye, my dearest Mother, and give everyone at home many, many greetings from me. I feel so very sorry for old Uncle Fritz and his daughters, such an illness, probably hopeless, is hard to bear, and it is sad when the old generation goes; even in the greatest weakness and misery they give shelter from the wind, and a special world lives around them, and that kind of person will never come again. . . .

To Ingeborg Dinesen

Ngong. Sunday 5th August. 1928.

. . . The day before yesterday poor Mrs. Bruce Smith was going down Van de Weyer's horrible hill when a truck driven by a native driver, and with native passengers, came down the hill on the other side of the bridge and drove into the river,—turned right over and she says there was screaming, blood and smashed fragments of the truck everywhere. It was late in the evening. However, no one was killed, but a few were badly injured. She said that she asked one of the casualties who seemed least injured how many had been in the vehicle, as she was afraid there might be some underneath it. He stared at her blankly, so she asked again how many there had been when they set off in the morning. "There were eight of us," he said. "Eight! —she said in horror after having counted them, "Then there are three of them under the truck, we must get it up at once."—She says that she worked like a slave with the help of the natives and at last they got it up, but there was nobody underneath it. "But you said there were eight of you," she said to the one who had given her the information. "Yes," he said, "there were eight of us when we started off this morning, and that was what you asked me. But three got off at Kajado."—that is typical of native intelligence.

The mail came yesterday, but brought no letter from you. . . . But there was one from Bror telling me that he is getting married this month to Cockie Birkbeck. He wrote that he expected I had heard rumors of it, but I haven't. I imagine that they must care for each other; for of course this affair began many years ago, and perhaps she may be the right kind of wife for him. . . .

Everything is now beginning to revolve around the Prince of Wales; all the roads in Nairobi are under repair, so that driving around there is very difficult, and all the shops are advertising the advent of new hats, dresses, and so on for the royal visit. The Ngong road has been repaired too, which is very pleasing. You can imagine how much rivalry there is in Nairobi concerning who is to be asked to Government House, attend the various festivities, and generally share in some of the glory. The English are completely crazy over their royal family; they really seriously believe that the current reigning monarch and his family are something absolutely unique,—and yet you couldn't find anyone much more uninteresting than George and Mary. Audrey Coates, about whom I have probably written before, who was here a few times last year and is generally considered to be a princely favorite, is coming out on the Prince's boat; I think that is like Louis XIV, who traveled about with Madame Montespan, [*sic*] but that is his affair. . . .

To Ingeborg Dinesen

Ngong. Sunday 26th August. 1928.

. . . I have had a lovely trip up to Naivasha and Njoro; it was actually a wedding trip for Heather, but as I had gone so far I took the opportunity to drive up and visit Genessee Long and Ingrid. It was the most marvelous weather up there, and it was nice for me because I had Denys's new Hudson. . . . I think few places in the world are more lovely than Njoro, and then they are such extremely delightful people to be with [Ingrid and Gillis Lindström]—well, Tommy can describe it all to you. I love Ingrid,—she is a little like Sister Folsach, but with more sense of humor; there is, as I have always said, a bit of the madame about her, but the kindest and jolliest sort, and something really poetical. I think this is why the English like us, because they think we are poetic, in contrast to their own practical females, who have to get something out of everything.

Anything more happy go lucky than Ingrid's housekeeping is impossible to conceive; the three little girls came home on vacation the next day, and they and Ingrid all slept in one room and Gillis on an old legless sofa in the living room, which was really most inconvenient for the poor man, who could not get to bed at night because Ingrid and I were sitting on it talking far into the night, and it really resembled the "Karindehutte" in "The Constant Nymph,"—except, of course, that the genius was missing. The three little girls went around with bare legs and in the shabbiest outfits imaginable, indescribably happy over being home and busy with all their animals and chicken run; meal times are completely vague, and the whole time I was there they had neither butter, milk, nor sugar in the house; their car was such an utter wreck that it was even something unique out here, and Gillis has hammered most of their furniture together himself out of old packing cases. But in spite of all this they are about the happiest family I have seen out here. It is all due to Ingrid, and they do appreciate that; I think that Gillis and the children all adore her.

And then it was such a tremendous pleasure to see how well everything is going for them this year. Everywhere else is dry, but on their farm the maize was looking brilliant, and Ingrid says that this year it has seemed as if she could just press a button to get rain. She is really very clever; she has a huge kitchen or market garden, which has doubtless helped to keep them alive the last few years. I went down there with her a lot, and twice a week she sends 25 baskets of vegetables off to her various customers, private clients and hotels and clubs. We worked in the stable packing them,—it was like the Vegetable Market! . . .

To Ingeborg Dinesen

Ngong. Sunday 2nd September. 1928.

My own beloved Snow-white Lamb.

To begin with, many, many thousand thanks for H. C. Andersen's "Fairy Tales," and the cosmetics. Some books are an experience as well as a pleasure, and I always think this about Andersen. What a wonderful, delightful attribute imagination is,—indeed, as I grow older I think it is truly divine, the foundation of everything else,—(and therefore I think that it is so pleasurable and interesting that modern science has allowed it a part of, or allied itself with, imagination, to such an extent as it has: look at Einstein, Haldane, etc.)—It is people without imagination who are "the worst," because they have no understanding, like the aldermen in "Clumsy Hans"; only those who possess it can see the true nature of things, every door is opened to them.—I have been sitting out here alone in the evening laughing at the top of my voice over "In the Duck Yard",—I *must* have met "the Portuguese one" somewhere or other at some time, but can't think where. And then Andersen can be so indescribably simple and touching in other places, it is like a violin,—he is a great magician. . . .

Unfortunately I have had to take Juma to hospital, very ill with pneumonia. I knew that he was ill and had given him medicine, but I did not think he was so very ill, and his wives, beastly hags, could not be bothered to send for me; native women are revolting, quite without feeling. Then on Sunday night I heard someone coming in through the house bumping against everything,—I thought whoever it was must be blind drunk, but it was Juma who revealed himself, looking like death, he could hardly speak. So I took him into the hospital on Monday morning, by which time he was very ill. Then he sent for me on Friday; he was certain he was going to die, and wanted to make a kind of will, which was chiefly to consist of his bequest of Tumbo to me. Tumbo came with me and is here now; he is so quiet and sorrowful, but the wives, heartless creatures, quite uncaring. I do hope Juma will recover, but he is old and thin for a serious illness. . . .

I have had a letter from Casparson, so we know he is alive. He has written two articles (in the biweekly edition of "Aftonbladet") of the 9th of June, entitled: "Tramping through East Africa",—in which I appear, I hope fairly respectably.

Regarding the letter to the King, I know quite well what I want to write but not how to sign it, so you must get that out of Uncle Torben and let me know, as of course the letter must be written here. The lion skin is in London ready to be sent off. . . .

To Ellen Dahl

Ngong. 13th September. 1928.

. . . Otherwise I think that Mother has reason to be happy in most of her relationships,—and she seems to be of that opinion herself. In the course of my long life I myself have come to the conclusion that happiness does not depend on exterior circumstances but is a state of mind,—but at the same time: in any case until one is completely certain about one's faith certain exterior conditions must obtain,—or perhaps, rather, there are certain exterior conditions that must be avoided in order to enable one to arrive at and remain in this state of mind. It is best to get rid of,—even at one's own and others' expense,—whatever lies in the way of this; for unless one is in this state one can become or achieve but little. . . .

I think in my last letter to you I wrote about this: being oneself,—and will not touch upon it here. But there are some situations in which it is so excessively difficult "to be oneself" that it is not worth the trouble of remaining in them; although it is quite possible that when one has been away from them for a while and become strong in the art, one can return from them so immune that there is no longer the slightest difficulty in overcoming obstacles.—

I believe that Mother is by nature "light in mind"—(I do not in the least mean: light-minded in the sense of irresponsible!)—and that, in order to feel happy she must be able to believe or be certain that *life is light,* sweet, and delightful in itself,—in short, like the equally "light-minded" Nora, to believe that the wonderful is close at hand. If she can hold firmly to this belief then nothing is hard or terrible to her. I sympathize with her most deeply in this, for it is and I believe always has been my own striving and my goal in life to hold more and more strongly to the feeling that there is nothing bad and frightful in the world, but millions and billions of possibilities for beauty and glory. I would gladly sell my soul to a bold and jolly devil in order to obtain sundry things I really want; but not for anything imaginable would I ever believe in the real Devil, "in evil." "So far" I have not seen or met "evil," although I have met with a few unpleasant beings, and I don't believe in it. . . I am extremely reluctant to have anything to do with people who believe in the Devil and all his works and all his tribe,—or to live constantly among them; for it can be quite curious for a short while, and in fact I can well imagine that the time may come when I can live among the very worst invokers of the Devil, even indeed meet the Devil himself, without being in the least affected. As it is now I am always afraid that they will "cramp my style" that is to say: prevent me from being myself.

I think that this was how Mother, for the period of her marriage, could be herself and feel that life was easy, and no doubt this was largely due to Father; because of course Mother could have had a much better and more secure husband in many ways, but for the author of "Hunting Letters" and "From the Eighth Brigade"' life was light and enjoyable.—But it seems to me that Mama and Aunt Bess and their tribe and their works have a frightful capacity for making life difficult. I don't think they give this impression to everybody, but they gave it to me. One was surrounded by dangers of the blackest and most extensive kinds: of becoming worldly and vain, of hurting Madame Jensen's feelings, of getting into debt, of not thinking of others, etc.—not to mention the quite dreadful dangers and horrors inherent in everything that had to do with sexual relationships. And probably Madame Jensen would have greatly enjoyed hearing a small oath or seeing a young man slightly merry!

I don't think Mother feels like this, but I am always a little worried by the thought that she is so close to Aunt Bess's ideas of "loss of trust" and Aunt Lidda's fearful moral hairsplitting, and if she is tired and out of tune with her everyday life, then she may fall from "grace" and start to lie awake with the thought of Madame Jensen and grow quite convinced that the Devil does exist.—I don't think the kind of family colony that has developed in the district at home is a good thing; if one is not in perfect harmony or can emancipate oneself from it, it can easily hinder everyone concerned from being themselves. Otherwise Mother, with Malla and the rest of her good staff, should be able to have a milieu in her own home where she really can be, "a word of God made flesh," and be without too much difficulty; she does not mind the kind of mess in a house that I could not put up with, and in her hands it really does become more like a meadow, where "no one has plowed and no one weeded, but thousands of bees have sipped the honey."—

As the years go by one learns to understand and sort out the minor phenomena of life, that are necessary to enable one to be oneself. For instance, I know that I must not get fat; it is preferable for me to suffer the pangs of hunger, because being overweight "cramps my style." I also know, as I wrote to Mother, that, like Aunt Emy, I am God's chosen snob, and if I cannot be with the aristocracy or the intelligentsia I must go down among the proletariat or, what corresponds to that out here, the natives, because I cannot live with the middle class.—The real aristocrats, where they exist, or the proletariat, have nothing to risk. But the middle class always has something to risk, and the Devil is there among them in his very worst, that is to say, his very pettiest, form. . . .

Regarding Muhammadanism, which I gather interests you, I must admit that I cannot speak of it with any authority, for I actually know too little about it. I find it impossible to get any benefit from reading the Koran, and the Muhammadanism that I see in practical life is probably the most primitive type.—I think that Muhammadanism makes the people who embrace it or have been brought up to it clean and proud and gives them a kind of heroic or stoic view of life, but also that it makes them, to us, quite intolerably doctrinaire and intolerant. As a whole, in my view, it is a *dry* religion or philosophy of life, and its dangers lie in either becoming purely external and consisting of an endless number of formal rules and ceremonial, or else in leading to fanaticism.

As far as I am concerned it contains the unattractive element of making the position of women so bad, although this can no doubt be argued: in many ways Muhammadan women are honored and esteemed, and I can quite appreciate the oriental element that is also to be found in our western European chivalry, which was probably acquired during the crusades, and it has colorfulness and something noble in character; but it makes women solely sexual beings, and such real prisoners of this situation, without even a view of the world outside. To me this protective role played by men has something artificial or unbalanced about it; if, for instance, from the outset one maintains and educates the race to believe that it is utterly frightful to let one single hair of a woman's head be disordered, there will naturally be plenty to do for the rest of her life running about with parasols or shields of every kind; but in my opinion it would really be more chivalrous to latch on to the hair a little less, and neither am I at all certain that the most perfectly set hair in itself is really more beautiful than freely flowing locks, or a coiffure à la coup de vent. But all my life I have cared more for Diana than Venus; I am both more attracted to her type of beauty, as I have seen it portrayed in statues and paintings, and also I myself would prefer Diana's life to that of Venus, however many rose gardens and dove-drawn coaches she might have. . . .

To Ingeborg Dinesen

Ngong. Sunday 16th September. 1928.

. . . Denys is coming home today and the totos have decided to bathe all the dogs in his honor, so I can hear howling coming from the lawn.

Farah's child is expected to arrive any day now; because of this he is praying and fasting so zealously that he is not much use to me. I hope all goes well, Fathima is so slim and fragile, but of course this does not necessarily mean anything, it is often easier for them. Juma is better, but is looking so old and emaciated.

We have the great robber captain Mongaj on the farm again, last night he took two sheep from Kaninu. It is rotten of the police in Nairobi not to have caught him; several times they have been to the places in the woods where he camps and devours his stolen meat, but I think they are afraid of him. Naturally the Kikuyu know quite well where he is, but are partly terrorized by him and have partly a kind of sympathy for or admiration of him, and anyway will always try to hinder the police when they have a chance. . . .

To Ingeborg Dinesen

Ngong. Sunday 30th September. 1928.

. . . So the Griggs came out here to lunch last Sunday; they were both rather done up by the preparations for the Prince of Wales's visit, but they are always so tremendously pleasant. I gave them a risotto, chicken à la marengo, which Kamante makes to perfection, cauliflower au gratin and those black berries, you know, that I have in the garden, with cream,—I hadn't actually had much time to prepare the luncheon. They invited me in to stay at Government House while the Prince of Wales is there; I think it will be fun. . . .

After the Griggs had gone I went out into the Game Reserve with the dogs; you can't imagine how dry it is, the whole plain is like the floor of a room. To my surprise I found Denys here when I returned; he only stayed one night, as he had to take his party to Uganda next day. . . . Denys was very tired after hunting through the Kijabe forests for bongo,—without results,—for two days; I feel like David with Saul when I am playing the gramophone for him, and gave him a Schubert evening with the Unfinished Symphony and "Der Tod und das Mädchen,"—yes, you may well laugh when I talk about my gramophone as if it was real music, but you know it is all we have out here. . . .

On Tuesday morning Farah came and said that Fathima had had a terrible night and was very ill, and as she had been ill since Wednesday of the previous week, I decided to drive in to fetch a doctor for her. I did manage to get hold of Dr. Sorabjee but he could not come until later, so I left Farah with him and drove out to the show grounds to see where Poorbox was going to be. . . . Then I drove home by the French Mission; from there you come out by Dagoretti Junction on the Ngong road; the show grounds are at Kabiti, on the other side of the railway, five miles from Nairobi.—The doctor had still not arrived, but came just after I did, and we were both met with the good news that the child had just been born at that very moment,—so said Halima, who had been employed as errand girl throughout the event,—when I turned up to the house. . . .

To Ingeborg Dinesen

Ngong. Sunday 14th October. 1928.

. . . On Wednesday I drove into Nairobi early in the morning to meet Denys, who arrived on the train from Kisumu at eight o'clock. They had had a successful safari and got three sitatunga; Denys came down now to be on hand if the Prince of Wales wanted to go out shooting. . . .

On Thursday Denys drove into Nairobi, but came back at half-past one at great speed because Lord Delamere, with whom the Prince was staying, had sent him a message telling him to go up the same day to make plans with them for a shooting trip; they had an airplane ready at the airfield at two o'clock to take him up there. I drove him to the airfield so that I could bring his car back and felt exactly as if I were in a film; we tore along there at a colossal rate to find the machine ready for takeoff with its propellers turning, so that Denys could jump in and start without delay. He was not allowed to take any luggage whatsoever except what he could pack in a handkerchief; they said he was already too heavy himself. They flew up there in one hour, right over the Longonot crater, which must be interesting to see in that way, and Lake Naivasha. . . .

Denys came home on Friday; he had had an excellent trip, was most enthusiastic about the view from the airplane, and had had an enjoyable evening with the Delameres; the Prince of Wales is extremely reluctant to go shooting, so it doesn't look as if there will be a safari, but they wanted Denys to go with them when they go south in case there should be a chance of getting some shooting on the way, and that may be interesting for him.—We went to dinner at Government House with the Prince of Wales, who came back the same day; in the evening they showed Martin Johnson's new film, "Simba,"—but I find I have no feeling for films, not even with animals, which are otherwise the best ones, in that they at least are natural and not posed. There were some quite interesting films of galloping giraffe, which were taken unnaturally slowly, so that one could really follow their movements; I don't know whether you have ever seen that sort of film, they are really very curious. Otherwise it was an enjoyable evening, for the Prince of Wales *is* really absolutely charming, and I am so much in love with him that it hurts. And then it is pleasant for me to go out to dinner with someone else and not be obliged to drive the car myself, but to have someone to talk to on the way home, and you know that normally Denys will never go out. . . .

To Ingeborg Dinesen

Ngong. Sunday 4th November. 1928.

. . . I have been really worried about Heather all this week, she has been very ill and is still poorly. She began to be ill early on Monday morning; I was obliged to go into town but was hoping to find her with a litter of puppies when I got home, but things went wrong. Not until late on Monday evening did she have one little puppy, and then another early on Tuesday morning, so I spent most of the night in the dog kennel. . . .

This morning I have been out riding with Denys, a long ride, and we rode hard,—I always wish Elle could go for a ride on the plains on Rouge, I think she would really enjoy it. We were so exhausted afterwards that the Bruce-S.'s, who came over to afternoon tea, found us fast asleep each in our chair, and were about to leave again without waking us, when I woke up. . .

I am reading a book: "Disraeli," by a French author, André Maurois. If you can get hold of it you should read it, it is very enjoyable. I think I would have been completely happy if I had been married to Disraeli, but so of course was his wife; you know I have always been mad about Jews, and he was an exceptionally brilliant and charming Jew.

It is amazing to think that Christmas is so close that I will have to send Christmas cards by the next post. I wish I had something to send you, but there is nothing to be had here. I do so wish, too, that I had got my article on "sexual morality" finished for Tommy, but I have had my hands so full recently, just now with Heather, so if I don't manage to get it off before Christmas he must forgive me, and it will arrive later on. . . .

To Ingeborg Dinesen

Ngong. Sunday 11th November. 1928.

. . . Last Sunday, after I had written to you, Denys and I drove over to tea with Crean, and afterward for a drive along the new road to Kajado that they are in the process of making.—It runs roughly parallel to the road to Nepken, but up in the hills to avoid "the black cotton soil," which is so impossible in the rains. I am not happy about this road because it makes the beautiful wild country up in the hills so civilized and cuts it, as it were, right through the middle, but in itself it is absolutely lovely; I think it is about the most beautiful drive one can take out here,—and that means in the whole world. And now everything is so wonderfully green and fresh, all the slopes and gorges up there where they have burned the grass are covered with the finest short new grass, and you know how green it is out here, as if transparent, and the light was actually streaming out from the grass itself, or as if the air and the sky were reflected in green, in the plains and the slopes,—and then the shadows of the great clouds running over it, and the game grazing and resting on it,—the whole scene is an "ideal landscape," like a dream. We came home around by the waterworks, just at sunset. . . .

At lunchtime [Tuesday] a car came out from Government House bringing me an invitation to a dinner that the Prince of Wales was giving in his private dining car at the railway station the same evening; he was going to travel to the races at Nanyiki and probably felt that would be convenient for him.—So Denys and I drove in to the dinner; it was rather strange to go into a station wearing evening dress, and a dining car is never particularly comfortable, of course; and then it was a frightful dinner, but still, it was very congenial. We were only sixteen people, and sat at four small tables, and then after dinner went out on to a kind of open veranda on one of the coaches. The whole train is very tastefully appointed, by the standards of this country, with a very comfortable sleeping car, and a bathroom.—Just as they were about to leave, the Prince of Wales came up and said that he, Lascelles, and Leigh would like to come to dinner here on Friday and if possible see a ngoma.

It is not so easy to make a good ngoma at this time of year because the actual dancing season is over, and I was not able to do anything about it on Wednesday because I was expecting the Mohrs; but I sent Farah out with the car on Wednesday morning, to Kinanjui and Kioi, to ask them to come with their young ladies and cavaliers on Friday evening. And they promised to come. . . .

On Thursday I drove into town to shop for the Prince of Wales's dinner here on Friday, and in particular to try to get hold of some ladies, which of course is not easy out here. It is such an extremely great help that Denys pays for the drinks and cigars on these occasions; partly because it saves me a lot of money and partly because he is so knowledgeable, so I know I will be getting the right kinds. . . .

Then on Friday of course I had a lot to do with my dinner and ngoma; when one has only a dog toto as "chef" who can do absolutely nothing apart from what I have shown him myself, one does not feel very secure unless one is watching over him,—and the ngoma gave me a lot to do as well, with firewood for the bonfires, food and drinks for the chiefs, and so on.—I really love cooking, and I love giving dinner parties, but I don't love combining the two and could wish that other people would do the cooking for my parties and that I could go out as a cook for the parties I am not invited to; it is a strain to have to fulfill both roles.—

However, I think I can say that the dinner was a great success; the Prince of Wales said it was the best he had had in this country, and Denys, that he had never had a better, so all honor is due to Kamante. I gave them: clear soup with marrow,—fish from Mombasa, a kind of turbot, with sauce hollandaise,—ham, that Denys had given me, with Cumberland sauce, spinach, and glazed onions,—partridges with peas, lettuce, tomatoes with macaroni salad and cream sauce with truffles,—croustades with mushrooms, a kind of savarin and fruit,—strawberries and grenadillas.

My dancing guests began to arrive early, in the afternoon, and I had to go out now and then to see to the preparations and compliment the chiefs. We had the ngoma among the boys' huts, which had been freshly whitewashed for the solemn occasion, and there was a big fire in the middle and a lot of small fires in a big circle around it; I had also made a series of small fires alongside the road through the wood, and it looked really lovely. Then I had Berkeley's green and red lanterns, that Aunt Lidda gave me, alight in front of the house.

I was "short of" one lady, as I had only been able to get hold of Vivienne de Watteville, whom I have probably written about before,—incidentally, she is very like Jonna, although a coarser version and with better color,—and Beryl, who was in Nairobi on her way to Mombasa and home, and looked absolutely ravishing that evening. I had sent a message to the Prince of Wales saying that I had left one place free in case he wished to bring a lady with him, but he did not do that, so we were only seven,—seated thus:

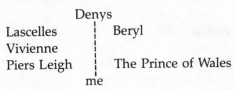

	Denys	
Lascelles		Beryl
Vivienne		
Piers Leigh		The Prince of Wales
	me	

We had a coffee cocktail before dinner out at the ngoma, which was in full swing and really the best ngoma I have seen; it looked really magnificent with all the fires. Then we had dinner before going out to the ngoma again, and the Prince of Wales greeted all the chiefs and talked to them in Swahili, which they must have greatly appreciated.—I think the Prince of Wales has a great deal of charm, and I think everybody thinks so, and he was quite particularly charming here, really pleasant and very much at home, as if he had known me all his life. So I enjoyed myself enormously and was very satisfied with my party.

On Saturday I was in my garden, and went home via the Bruce-Smiths', it is such a nice walk. After dinner I drove in to a dance at Muthaiga; Denys didn't want to go, and I meant to go home early, but one never does that from Muthaiga, I didn't get back until half past five.—Lady Delamere behaved scandalously at supper, I thought; she bombarded the Prince of Wales with big pieces of bread, and one of them hit me, sitting beside him, in the eye, so I have a black eye today, and finished up by rushing at him, overturning his chair and rolling him around on the floor. I do not find that kind of thing in the least amusing, and stupid to do at a club; as a whole I do not find her particularly likable, and she looks so odd, exactly like a painted wooden doll. . . .

Ngong. 20th November. 1928.

Dearest Tommy.

Merry Christmas!—and may the New Year bring you much happiness. I know that you are expecting a new little wonder in March and wish it the happiest of entrances into the world; it will be greeted with much love even from distant climes. I hope as well that you are making good progress with your book and that you are generally feeling possessed of a superabundance of power, and that "the flames, the fire,—have re-erected the fallen altars of your youth,—in the grass, by the spring."

I am sending you a picture of this house that I hope will fill you with kindly remembrances.

I have been wanting to send you a rather lengthy paper on your "sexual morality," which I have been pondering over for some time, but I have had so much to do that I have not had time to collect my thoughts, so it will have to wait. Some of the difficulty for me probably lies in the fact that I myself have not thought the subject through completely clearly, and then also that it is unavoidably fairly personal, which of course results in its making special demands on the reader's understanding and discretion.

I know that you will be glad to hear that it is pouring with rain; we have had more than six inches during the short rains, since it started, and it is as lovely here as you know that it can be.

I would have liked to send you a book by Professor Haldane: "Possible Worlds." But they did not have it,—of course,—out here, and when you have to order it from home you never know whether they really send it or not, so all I can do is to advise you to get it for yourself. In my view, since the last century a change has taken place in science, in that it has accepted the existence of imagination to a far greater extent than before, which has had the effect of giving it completely new life, as it were. Can you recall that we talked out here of how the priests always maintain that *belief* is higher than *knowledge*,—and so it is, in my opinion,—but that in fact it is they who say that they *know* that things are like this or like that, while the scientists say only: we think.—I now think about myself that I have always unconsciously been an Einsteinian; for instance, I have always been convinced in my heart that time was an illusion, and that "hier c'est demain," and during the trials of life it is an enormous comfort to me to be aware that although it is true that two and two appear to make four, in different circumstances they may come to be something quite otherwise, and that while line A-B is much longer than line B-C, on the other hand line B-C is twice as long as A-B. I think that imagination is one of the qualities,—if not *the* quality,—to which humanity owes most in its development; without it nothing would have been created, I still believe, as you know, that the concept of dog was created before individual dogs,—and in general: create a concept, and the dog will be sure to follow.

Incidentally, I think it is quite remarkable how slow human beings are to apply the theory of evolution to the more intellectual world, for instance, to what is known as morals. I can understand that people who believe in a Fall,—if any such exist,—can still adhere to the old morality with its negativity: "Thou shalt not,"—"'do not," but not that those people who believe that we have fought our way to our present standpoint through a series of daring experiments can find it so hard to take this line in their own life. If the saurians had not made the effort to try to fly, even with the risk that it might go wrong, or the apes to come down out of the trees, or the hoofed and clawed animals to remodel their hooves and claws,—we would probably still be floundering around among the meadow grasses and been about forty feet long. If it turns out not to work, then one must just become a penguin, for example, and again give up the idea of using wings. But probably quite a lot of good things have emerged in the meantime. Have courage!—have courage!—I think that is what everything in the world preaches, except, that is, the very pedagogues and priests.—I expect you will laugh at this and think that I am what I myself abhor, a sciolist, and really I have no pretensions at all really to understanding the theory of evolution, for instance; but yet I may perhaps have gained a glimmering of truth, and in any case I have a burning desire to *understand*.

Talking of development, if you were to come out here again you would probably notice a great difference in the natives' way of life and "education";—they have an astonishing ability to imitate and adapt themselves to new conditions. I think it will be interesting to see if it is really feasible for a race to step straight out of the Stone Age into the era of the airplane, and, for instance, to find and adopt the modern, tolerant, and undogmatic form of Christianity without having had to go through artisanship and road making and saints and burning at the stake. If it proves to be possible it will show that we have actually wasted a terrible lot of time over Gothic and le roi soleil and the abolition of adscription. Now you see all the little totos who look after the cows, with primers in their hands, and the ngomas are becoming rare events; instead they hold a sort of prayer meeting with singing. . . .

Ngong. 20th November. 1928.

. . . As I have no doubt written before, I always feel there is so much that I want to discuss with you, and I had thought of putting it all together in a reasonably lucid form one day; but that will not be this time. But as usual there are a few things that I want particularly to enlarge upon and explain to you, and I will try to deal with one or two of them in this letter. And once again it is poor old marriage that is to be the victim. . . .

Now there are two statements of yours on the subject that I want to try to answer. One of them is in your last letter, where you maintain that the essential happiness in marriage lies in the fact that one no longer lives "for oneself alone," but that through marriage one's life and actions acquire value and meaning for the sake of another.—The other is from an earlier letter to me. You say there: "As far as I can see the difference between you and me is that you would rather *be* an artist, leader, statesman etc., while I would rather serve the man I loved in whatever of these qualities he excelled."

Having pondered over this, I now think that there is a *fundamental difference* in our view, not only where these questions are concerned, but of life as a whole, which can perhaps be expressed by saying that you are more personally disposed than I am,—that is to say: individuals and relationship with them is the essential thing in life to a far greater degree for you than for me. Like Aunt Lidda, I have a real horror of being "an object" and am moreover quite incapable of letting an individual person be "an object" in my life. I believe that I am conditioned by nature in this, but it may perhaps have been emphasized in me through having been transplanted as I was, partly because of what happened to my marriage and relationship with Bror; I have become hesitant about staking a great deal on a personal relationship.—However, I would not have it any other way; I am quite against having an idol or, rather, seeing an idea or an ideal solely represented in one single individual, and can say with Ambrosius Stub that I will not kneel to any person. Although, for instance, I have come to realize that one of the greatest passions of my life is the relationship with my "black brother." I also know that there are no representatives of this race that I personally could not do without, without the relationship being radically changed,—besides which I am quite convinced that the natives here are just about the most ungrateful race on earth, and that there is no point in expecting to receive anything in exchange for this feeling. This sort of predisposition in emotional temper and view of life can probably be taken, as one wishes, as a talent or as ineptitude, wealth or poverty; but,—strangely enough,—

as a rule one would not wish to exchange one's view of life for anyone else's.

Then, regarding your first point, I must say that I cannot see at all why marriage should be the only relationship in which one "does not live for oneself alone," and through which one's life, actions, and speech have meaning for other people. If this were so it would follow that, for instance, a nun or (Catholic) priest would be precluded from living for others, and after all it is just that they believe they do. Nor does it agree with my experience at all; I do not in the least believe that unmarried and childless people are on the whole greater egoists than married couples and family men and women. Neither do I think, honestly speaking, that I live more for myself than do the married women in the neighborhood. I think that it often happens in marriage and family life, in the same way as for instance in a social, artistic, or literary "set," that one acquires a completely unreasonable and exaggerated appreciation of one's own abilities by evaluating and appreciating those of the other members in a completely unreasonable and exaggerated way. . . . In my opinion one can really only be something to others by being, and giving, the highest that one "according to one's nature is capable of," and the real artist lives for, and serves, humanity through scorning "his clients"; but the family circle is almost always in danger of becoming its own clients, whose appreciation is based on a kind of reciprocity and is in itself an illusion. It is as if I felt my own aspiration to be more greatly satisfied through another person looking at me through a magnifying glass.

I really think it would have been a terrible shame if Mother, even while she was unengaged, had broken her nose by running down the hill at the World's End. Of course, "for argument's sake" one could imagine that Father had quite unusual taste and thought a broken nose was charming, but would this absolve the lovely young Ingeborg Westenholz from her duty toward the rest of young Denmark?—In the same way I think that respectable people in general should be able to button their gloves (boots, trousers, etc.) almost perfectly without the consciousness of another person's admiration, devotion, or dependence causing them to feel themselves elevated to a higher standing in life. Don't think that I am not aware that admiration and recognition on the part of people one loves, and particularly from those whose judgment one trusts, is a great joy and happiness, but nevertheless it does not change anything in the ability itself. Or does an artist live more for others because he can sell his pictures for a good price, and don't you think that all human talent, beauty, wealth, warmth and power lives and works and "never dies" without engagement announcements having to be sent out?—

Coming to the second point, your thinking here is really so alien to mine that I have been obliged to think about it for a long time before I could take up any standpoint toward it, and I am still not sure that I fully understand you. For it is a fact that if one occupies oneself with music, politics, science, or religion, and has a bent for these subjects, one will end up by becoming a musician, statesman, scientist, or prophet; but probably no one starts out with the idea of "becoming" any of these things.—I for one certainly have no ambition of this kind. My burning devotion to this farm has brought,—among other things,—a certain position, but God knows that it has never been my aspiration or my hope in life to "become" a coffee farmer. And while I know well enough that in the case of a Napoleon or a Wagner it is not only the women but the men as well who generally flock to serve and work alongside the genius, I see no reason why one should consider, for instance, music, science, or social justice expressed better indirectly in the figure of a man, who moreover is gifted similarly to oneself, than directly in its own character, or in other words: any reason for,—if one does not from the outset assume that men are necessarily superior to women,—the average woman having to serve the average man. I think that this is something about which I would always feel: that—I could not love you, dear, so well, loved I not honour more,—or else, as Frau Wagner would put it:—so well, loved I not music more. However deep was my love for Wagner, and however greatly I admired his music, surely there would be moments when I felt I had had enough of it and would rather listen to some Chopin. Then would I be unable, if one to begin with assumes that I myself am a musician of genius, for instance a pianist, to play Chopin with the very greatest enthusiasm and delight, just because I loved Wagner? Of course it must be a very great *joy* for a musical wife to be married to a musical husband; but personally I cannot imagine that it would be ideal, or even possible, to see music, art, science so expressed and compressed in one personality that it no longer had any other existence in itself for me. I regret that I did not study medicine when I was young, for I think it is such a tremendously interesting science and has such a great mission; but even though I could imagine that I would be enormously happy married to a doctor, this in itself would not at all satisfy me or make up for this lack, unless, of course, he made me conversant with his science and work, and that is something entirely different.

It is, no doubt, for the majority of average human beings, men as well as women a joy or an ideal to serve a genius and a great personality. But obviously there are not enough geniuses to go around, and besides, I would think it is an awfully indirect way to serve, for instance, music through being married to even the greatest of musicians,—in practice it would no doubt be very similar to the way in which a wife serves and helps the director of a bank. Probably if one loves him it can be the most satisfying thing in the world, but it can hardly be the normal aspiration toward and love for music, or normal ambition and striving, before one has even met the man. I believe that the greatest of happiness is to be found in meeting and being united with another person in love for an ideal, or for ideals, in life, but just as I would not wish to serve him rather than them, so I would not want him to serve me at their expense,—and in this I do not think that I am dictated by either vanity or egoism, but by my belief in the divine element in the world, without which it would hardly be possible for me,—who have called myself a pantheist from my early youth,—to see any coherence in life. . . .

Reading through my letter, I see that I have not really expressed what I wanted to and have perhaps given the impression of being rather heartless, as if I did not in the least set any value on the close and deep relationship between human beings in life. I do value it, although I must admit that there is something repugnant to me personally in the way in which Danes in particular always have to lean up against each other.—I don't think there is anything more wonderful than feeling in sympathy with people, and I have the most heartfelt belief in reciprocity, where two people who understand each other can achieve things that would be quite impossible for either of them alone. (And here I think that hospitality and social life have their great mission). But I think: first, that one does not need to be in a marital or any other familial relationship with people to be able to do something for them; I think that one must have had the feeling of wanting to do one's best, for the sake of other people as well, even before the day of one's engagement.

Friendship,—Wahlverwandtschaft,—in the end that is the highest human relationship for me. I believe that a human being has far greater influence through the mind than through "the family," and that Absalon in his capacity as a monk bequeathed more to his own time and the future than Esbern Snare with a large family. If one were only able really to love husband, children, siblings, etc., then I would have nothing to love in my life here, and yet of course I feel that I have. Next: one does nothing for other people by spoiling them, and that is what I so often feel happens in marriages and family life,—a mutual and, so to speak, holy or canonized kind of spoiling. One becomes something for others by being the best one can, and making the best out of them. But that is seldom the aspiration in marriage. I think it is more likely to be found in friendship, collaboration, in the relationship between a master and his disciples.—Naturally I don't think that married people cannot be friends, siblings cannot work together, fathers and sons cannot be like teachers and disciples to each other. But I do not think that it is a universal remedy to provide someone of such a barren character that he has never, until for instance his twenty-fifth year, experienced the glory of any of these human relationships, with a spouse, and succeeding children. Of course one can to a great extent rely on Nature here; but Nature's way in these matters is often merely an extensive, ravenous egoism that includes husband and children at the expense of everyone else. Forgive me if this is very vague, it has been written in the greatest haste. Summa summarium: there is so much in life to love, so much to live for, that to me there is something blasphemous about this monopoly of love and cooperation between human beings by marriage and family life.

Your Tanne.

Happy Christmas again!

To Ellen Dahl

Ngong. 21st November. 1928.

. . . Thank you for your card from Mols, I feel that I know your house so well. I have frequently dreamed that you were showing me around it, and once that you said that you had tried to make it look like something out of Blicher's stories; I wonder if it does. I find myself reading them so often, and I think that when he refrains from the completely idiotic "intrigues" that were more or less obligatory in his time he is almost perfect. In, for instance, "The Journal of a Parish Clerk," "Gypsy Life," "The Priest at Vejlby," "The Robbers' Cabin" you have first-class masterpieces.

There are some artists, and in fact human beings in general, and no doubt usually those who possess marked personal charm, or charming personality, who have the gift of "making myths"; their personalities remain alive in people's consciousness as well as their works, and the particular kind of poetry that they have represented or expressed goes on gathering or maturing around them; people continue to add to it. Such are, in Danish literature, Wessel,—about whom Brandes says that every good joke that was told in the whole of the eighteenth century, and every diverting story, was attributed to him,—St. St. Blicher and Drachmann. "Drachmann's Inn,"—there is something in the very name, even probably for people who have never read a line of Drachmann, that is poetical, festive, devil-may-care; you know right away where you are, you can paint a frieze of decoration in an inn with his figure as the center, and people love and know it, with cloak and white hair and beard, they feel relationship with it, it is a symbol; the light nights, burgundy, music and song and pretty girls,—and it is probably doubtful whether you could find any other Danish poet who could go on living in the festivity and fun of the Danish people.

So it is with Blicher; there is a whole class of people,—countrymen, hunters,—for whom his figure, with spectacles and gun, and the heath as a background, is both almost holy and a good and intimate friend who means something in their lives and with whom they have a personal relationship, and every story that is told about him is listened to with interest and love; new ones grow up around his image quite naturally. So it is in private life with Daisy,—I have met some English people here who knew her, and can feel the impression she made on them, although it is now a long time since she died, and actually one can't really say that she did anything especially great or good in her life. They know so many stories about her, some of which are true and some not, although they might be; she has become the expression, the representative of a certain kind of romanticism that somehow goes on renewing itself and centering around her personality.—So it was too in ancient times with Olav Trygveson, who in fact was probably not a particularly great king, but who somehow could never really be put to death; he turned up again at Miklagaard, he was not dead, he appeared in visions to his men, and can rise again even in modern poetry and song in "Wide Sails over the North Sea fly," so that modern readers can feel it as a personal horror, a personal sorrow, that "fallen is Olav Trygveson."—I think this is true of Father too in a way; I have met so many old gentlemen who when they grew really mellow began to recount with great pleasure and admiration: "Then Wilhelm said,"—"Then Dinesen did"—and God knows if it is always true, but it is truth in a higher sense, it is myth.—

And incidentally I may say that some of this applies, I think, to the Prince of Wales, whom I have had the pleasure of meeting. This is surely how royal personages ought to be, and they should have a good chance of it, but there is precious little about King George to stimulate anyone's imagination; Queen Alexandra was lovely and gracious but not much else, and there is little scope; Queen Victoria was certainly the right sort, she was monumental, but she "war nicht liebeswurtig, und sie liebte er nicht" (that is probably misspelled),—but of course the little Prince of Wales expresses above all something they love; he is "a good sport" and then I think he is a very determined young man who does what he likes, and then he has such a special little personal charm, somewhat childish or shy; all this combines to create the impression of a definite personality. I am not considering the English here, for they are stupid about royal persons, but the natives; small myths have begun to grow up from the one evening he was here,—"then ille Sultani went right up to Kinanjui and said—," —and no people have more sense of and talent for mythmaking than the natives,—prestige means everything to them,—and they would certainly have loved Daisy and Olav Trygveson and Drachmann and St. St. Blicher too.

Missen looks so big in the pictures I get of her,—has she changed much? I wish I had as many chances of seeing her as you have and could share in her development. Now she is probably as big as you were when you played little Marguerite with such great success.—Can you remember other things from that time, by the way? Naturally I can remember things from my childhood if I try; but it does not seem close to me, and I am so often surprised when I hear other people,—particularly those from an earlier generation, and perhaps it is something that comes back with age,—dwell on their childhood as if it still existed or had done so yesterday. . . .

To Ingeborg Dinesen

Ngong. Sunday 16th December. 1928.

My beloved Snow-white Lamb.

I am so distressed, Heather died last night. I was not even here, but the boys told me when I got home from the Danish reception at Clairmount House.—Farah and I had just said a couple of days previously that she was so much better and was probably over the worst when she fell ill again the day before yesterday, with big sores on her head and around her eyes, and would not eat. I sent her in to the vet in Nairobi with Farah and he gave her some new medicine, but she was really ill in the afternoon; but as I did not think that it was worse than before, I went to the dance. . . .

So I was at the party at Clairmount House; I had been dreading it rather, and then it turned out as it always does for me when I actually do go out, and I really enjoyed myself greatly. There were a lot of speeches and songs and decorations of portraits of the Danish colony here, among them also one of me seen driving an enormously big car, which must be Denys's, with an enormously small black toto, obviously Tumbo, beside me. . . . These young Danes are really nice, pleasant people, but when I am with them it strikes me how little *youth* there is about them; I don't mean that they are particularly mature, or that they cannot be quite childish, but they are like little old people, so strangely stolid and tame, somehow dry, with neither any indomitableness nor defiance nor longing nor imagination about them, nor anything that goes with youth. There is more go in old Nepken than in these amazingly old-womanish von Huths, Schlichtkrulls, Harpøths, and what's-their-names, who when they are with him seem like a shoal of little cod beside a sporty old flounder. And yet those who come out here ought to be among the most enterprising of the younger generation, and one asks oneself if there is any real youth left in Denmark. You can hardly believe that it was the Danes who composed in their time: "There is a lovely country," "King Christian," etc. and sang them last night.—You may perhaps remember Clairmount House; we had lunch there on the way home from Donya Sabuk.

I forgot to tell you that last Sunday I had a visit from Choleim Hussein with a whole car full of Indian women, magnificently dressed, like a huge bed of colorful flowers. All their customs, going veiled, seclusion, the harem system, and the rest, repel me so much that I find it hard to appreciate the really interesting and fascinating aspects of this world. . . . I said to Choleim Hussein that I thought he ought to give his wife a car, and then I would teach her to drive; I don't think he could have been more horrified if I had said that I thought it was time that his wife boiled him up for soup. His wife was nearly dying with laughter,—but all the same perhaps it will not be so long before she gets the car. I let Farah give them tea as I had promised to go over to Crean, and I walked over there with the dogs, and at Ducan I met Kinanjui in his car, and we had a long conversation,—a situation one would never have imagined ten years ago.

Well, goodbye now, a thousand greetings. I am well, if it were not for little Heather's grave, which I can see from the stone bench now. . . .

1929

To Ingeborg Dinesen

Ngong. Sunday 17th March. 1929.

Beloved Snow-white Lamb.

I am enclosing a picture of my house that Denys took from the air; Ali and I and some of the dogs can be seen outside the veranda to the south, and a mixed group of boys sitting on the wall on the other side. It all looks like a toy, doesn't it?—I think it would be suitable for enlarging, but don't know whether you would like that, or I would send you the film. Denys took another one from the airplane which I think is better because it is taken from higher up, so that one can see the surroundings like a map, but I haven't got that; I will send you a print of it when he gets back. . . .

Denys left on Tuesday morning and expects to get back again about the end of the month.

On Wednesday morning all the male members of my household drove into Nairobi to church, as fortunately Ramadan is over. They set off before daybreak and I was up to see them leave, all in their finest array; Tumbo had so many clothes on that he looked like a stuffed pig; they really have beautiful things when they are dressed up, and it was like a Christmas morning at home to see people getting up and sprucing themselves up for church by lamplight,—I had a cup of tea with cardamom in it, something I have come really to enjoy, in Farah's house with the whole company. The women were not going, that would not have been seemly. The ideal way of life for a really respectable Somali woman is probably never to venture outside the house. Of course I can see that there is something quite poetic in the Muhammadan view of woman and her position in life as its crown and greatest treasure for man; they do spend almost all their money on their wives and in a way value them highly; and then they are not subjected to many of the nightmares that oppress European women,—I don't think it would be possible for a Muhammadan woman not to be looked after,—the title of married lady, the linen cupboard, bridal veil, and children are things they can be sure of; but it gives me the same feeling that I get with people who assure me that bull fighting is the finest sport and display of courage and dexterity and so on,—in a way I would gladly believe them, but I am instinctively against it all to such an extent that I have to give up any idea of getting much out of it from the outset; it is not merely that I would not go to a bull fight for anything in the world, I also think I could not live in a society that was so much concerned with it, and I cannot resist trying to get my Muhammadan women a little way out of their cage.

I think it is frightful that Halima, who is a little younger than Missen, I think, has to be sacrificed on the altar of propriety to such an extent that she is never allowed to come out with Titi and Tumbo and me when we drive down to fish in the dam or go over the river to look at game. The house and wretched little kitchen is all the world that is open to the poor child, otherwise she would not be a really nice young Somali girl,—and she is so lively and intelligent, would doubtless love to ride and romp as Missen does. . . . No fortune could compensate for my rides, journeys, safaris; not even if in the eyes of the world I could become as lovely as the Virgin Mary herself would I give up the freedom of my relationship with nature and people and be confined to four walls and get the whole of life at second hand through one man.

On Thursday I drove Fathima, Halima, and the baby over to tea with Mrs. Bruce Smith, who shows much understanding and interest in my various protégés. It was a great success; they came home and told the men that they had had a much better Christmas than they had, and Shimbir, who is the baby,—it means bird, and they have named him that because he lies in his cot and smiles and babbles and sings,—behaved in an exemplary manner and charmed everyone. I think Mrs. B-S. is going through a difficult time; her husband seems to get on her nerves, which I can well understand, and she doesn't know how to cope with life at all. She and Mrs. Steele rode over here the other morning and sat talking about how unreasonable marriage is; and yet I think that in some ways they are both in love with their husbands and that the men do what they can for them; but they take it for granted that they can dump them into a life that is quite unsuitable for them, but that has been chosen entirely by the men, and that they will adapt themselves to it and be happy by making their husbands happy.

There will have to be a change, and I think it will be entirely dependent on the women to decide what it is to consist of; I think one difficulty lies in the fact that as a rule women will not acknowledge to themselves how much more, on the whole, it means to them than to men to be loved and admired, to have someone who makes a fuss about them and is grateful to them and cannot do without them, etc.; when it comes to the crunch they can't really renounce that, and yet modern women don't want to pay the price of it but think that it can be done, and the only justice lies in their being able to eat their cake and have it. In many women's view of life there is something dishonest, as when they think they can get the finest hat in a shop for the price of the cheapest, and actually get angry when they cannot beat the milliner down. . . .

In March 1929 Ingeborg Dinesen, who was then 72, fell gravely ill. The doctors did not hold out much hope, and the family in Denmark reported the situation to Karen Blixen. She left the farm as soon as it was possible and went to Denmark to be with her mother at Rungstedlund; meanwhile her mother's condition improved, and by the time that Karen Blixen arrived on 18th May, her mother had almost recovered.

Karen Blixen remained in Denmark for almost half a year before she set off on 25 December 1929, traveled by train to Genoa, and a few days later sailed for Africa on the S.S. "Tanganyika". *She was back at the farm on 16 January 1930.*

1930

To Ingeborg Dinesen

Ngong. Sunday 19/1.1930.

. . . Then I arrived at Mombasa on Monday evening and met Farah there, which is always so comforting, and he was extremely useful to me. Lady Colville came on board to say hello, and as I felt it was too late to go over to Ali bin Salim, I stayed the night at her hotel. The next day I worked on getting my furniture through customs, with final success, and went for a drive with Lady Colville around the island, and then went to Likoni for dinner. Ali was as sweet as ever and asked me to greet you many times, I stayed there the next day,—Wednesday the 15th,—and drove with him up to Kalifi and to Denys's land, where Ali and I had lunch from a lunch-basket in his house; it is really lovely there, with cliffs and a long sandy beach and a long line of surf,—the whole of the Indian ocean beats in there, cornflower blue. There are a lot of old ruins. On Thursday afternoon I came up by train. . . .

One very troublesome thing happened just after I arrived, with the very best intentions of getting the better of Dickens where the natives' ngomas are concerned; the night before last they held an (illegal) ngoma here during which a man was killed,—now of course we have the police all over the farm, and the dangers of ngomas painted in the most horrific colors; Kamante was arrested this morning, although I think only as a witness. If only they had managed to toe the line until I got back!. . .

To Ingeborg Dinesen

Ngong. Sunday 2nd March. 1930.

. . . Last Sunday, just after Denys had left, the Prince of Wales came out here on a visit, very charming, which of course he is; he talked about meeting Tommy and his charming young wife; he sounded very pleased with his safari even though they did not get any elephant. He thanked me in the most charming way for offering to lend him my house,—but I think everybody is satisfied with the arrangements for him to stay at Government House; they seem to think there would have been quite a scandal if he had not gone there. I was glad to have met the Prince; he is in Nairobi for such a short time, and as it is impossible for me to go to Government House now it was a pleasure to see him. . . .

On Monday I was in Nairobi and met Mohr, who gave me two fine trout,—I drove back for lunch, and Denys came out here and enjoyed them immensely. He left, with the Prince of Wales and the whole of their safari, on Tuesday morning. They intend chiefly to photograph for the next fortnight and were also hoping to be able to watch a lion hunt with spears in the Masai Reserve. . . .

On Wednesday I had Dickens down here as usual. Something tiresome has happened, which I have not yet written to Uncle Aage about as I want to wait until I get the situation a little more clear: Dickens has warned me that he may not stay on here after his contract expires, that is, after 1 July. . . .

To Ingeborg Dinesen

Ngong. Sunday 23rd March. 1930.

Beloved Snow-white Lamb.

It has become a regular habit for the Wakamba totos to come up here on Sunday morning to listen to the gramophone, so I have had a rather big concert; special favorites are "The March of the Björneborgers" and "Tommy's Tunes,"—the latter is the finale because it ends with a hip, hip, hurrah in which the audience joins. There is something touching about their reverent attitude and at the same time complete trust; in some ways I think they regard my house as theirs, but I don't think they would dream of taking anything, although they examine it all with great interest and apparent admiration. . . .

On Monday Charles Taylor came to lunch. I had arranged for him to come out here to put an end to the Dickens problem and am prepared to take his advice; now he is going to see Dickens in the course of the week and then come out to tea here today and let me know what he has achieved, and then the decision will have to be made. . . .

To Ingeborg Dinesen

[1930]

. . . An enormous ngoma has just assembled on my lawn; it is really good to see them in their proper dress again; there is no doubt that before long it will all have vanished. Alas and alack, I grieve about what we have done and are doing with this country and about the "civilization" we are bringing to it. I was thinking about it on the boat; when people are imagining themselves to be going out with the treasures of culture to the savage land; not one word was spoken during the seventeen days I was on board, not one thing discussed, not one forethought expressed that was not the most deadly ignorance and stupidity. Well, the Germans do at least sing sometimes. . . .

It is strange, and to me completely unexpected, to hear of the effect Tommy's book has had. I had no idea that Denmark was so pacifist. I thought myself that the tone of his book was jaunty and free and easy, and yet not to the same extent as a good deal of Danish literature and press; it sounds now as if Valdemar Rørdam is talking with real knowledge of the feelings of the Danish people when he says that they would like to forfeit the author of "No Man's Land" his honor and estate, if not his life. I wonder if this hasn't been a surprise to Tommy himself?—I think in a way it may suit him better than homage would have done, but it is not really good for him; in his time of life he should be standing *together with* other men or others' movement and effort; this is an easily bought sort of unpopularity that gives me no joy. . . .

To Ingeborg Dinesen

Ngong. Sunday 13th April. 1930.

. . . At long last Fathima had a little girl on Sunday; I was almost about to believe that it was all a false rumor. She is so delighted with the baby and is well;, I think she is specially pleased that it is a girl. In the conditions of the Muhammadan world, where men and women are so far away from each other in work, interests, and life in general, and really only come near each other when, as Goldschmidt says, they are: "either to dance or be united in wedlock,"—and anyway I am not at all sure that Somali men and women do dance much together,—I think that the women gradually grow unable really to feel anything for the male sex,—not even for their sons. The men's whole world is too incomprehensible to them; I do not think that they actually have any respect for it at all, except insofar as it provides them with food; but the real, actual, and reasonable world is that of the women, and with a little girl they feel that they have something that really actually and reasonably is close to them and belongs to them, while a boy will sooner or later be drawn into the strange and irrelevant existence of men. I think you can see something similar in sailors' wives, for instance—when they get letters from Rio Janeiro [*sic*] or hear about cargoes for Singapore and signing on and so on, they listen with a kind of disbelief or superciliousness or complete indifference; but the laundry, or the children's socks, or childbirth, these are real things that one respects.

Fathima's baby has been named Amina, but is called Kinsi,—they always give them some nickname or other meaning something that is particularly beautiful and good, like a flower or an ornament, but Farah explained to me that the name Kinsi means "some person who is not really rich, but nearly rich"; why they should be so modest when they have free choice, I cannot think. It is terribly sweet; little newborn Somali children are exactly like little dolls and don't have that oddly unfinished look that white children of the same age have, and then they paint blue eyebrows on them right away, so they look like Elle's old Algerian doll.

On Monday my faithful friend Mohr came out to lunch here and devoted his entire day to walking around the farm with me, and only went home after dinner. He has been the only one in this Dickensian dilemma who has "acted and not talked," and I will not forget what he has done. . . .

I have taken to reading Dickens, which I find cheering during the rains, and have read both "Pickwick" and "Bleak House." I think "Our Mutual Friend" is his best book, but I admire all his books; it is astonishing what a gallery of characters he has, unlike any modern author almost,—perhaps Tolstoy approaches it in "War and Peace," but even the suspense he does offer is a dying art too. Some passages in "Bleak House"—for instance, when the horrific old Krook goes up in flames or Lady Deadlock's flight,—keep one utterly breathless, and who else can do that nowadays?. . .

To Ingeborg Dinesen

Ngong. Sunday 11th May. 1930.

. . . I really rather like living like this, it's like being behind a closed-up drawbridge, one day like another passes, and then it is so good for the farm to have so much rain. I went to town on Monday, lunched with Mohr, and visited Lady Colville, who is very ill and not clear in her mind; she told me a long story which she forbade me to breathe a word of to anyone, and which would have been impossible for me to repeat a word of; among other things she said: "Nobody knows about it, but one Christmas Eve my father's cook slapped King Edward on the side of his head."—It's like Bienen with the Queen Dowager in the chandelier, and although there is something sad about it, it is hard to keep a straight face.

I have always rather enjoyed being with mad or slightly dotty people; there is something liberating about being able sometimes to get away from the unspeakably worn-down, conventional paths, for the mind as well. I understand so well how it was that great folk in the old days felt their ménage to be incomplete without a jester, who should preferably not be quite all there, and this is what gives me such pleasure in being with the natives; at present I hardly talk to anyone else and feel no desire to. In my opinion really respectable, sensible, conventional people are the only ones who one *cannot* stand in the long run, and they have such a beastly habit of monopolizing the whole of life so that you really forget that such people as jesters and madmen, publicans and sinners, exist, and fall into the deepest melancholy, from which you are happily released by the Dowager Queen in the chandelier.

We have had some entertainment lately from what Farah is convinced were three attempts to murder him. For a long time he has been at loggerheads with Hassan and his tribe and says that they have constantly threatened to kill him, and the other day when we were in Nairobi and Farah was waiting for me outside the Somali Hotel, one of them knocked him down with a stick and stabbed him in the back with a knife. The other night the dogs suddenly started to kick up a fearful din in the middle of the night, and when I went out to see what was the matter, I saw,—there was faint moonlight,—two shadows running away from the neighborhood of Farah's house. He said they had been shaking the door. This was repeated the following night, so I then gave Farah a gun and told him to fire off a shot if they came again. In the middle of the night the dogs started barking again, so I grabbed a pair of shoes to run out in,—bang went Farah's shot. Then there was a shout, but no one was lying on the battlefield when I went out, no blood was to be seen, but footprints of people in shoes all around Farah's house. There is great excitement among the whole of my ménage, and Fathima is taking it quite calmly, almost as a joke; I think Somali women must be accustomed to this kind of war situation from childhood. . . .

No doubt you will be visiting Ellen in her new home, and please do tell me how she is getting on. Ellen has so many friends that she should not feel too lonely; but in some ways life is not easy for her; she feels things so deeply. It is strange how some people, especially women, have the ability, without any outward insignia, to surround themselves with a special kind of dignity, so that everyone really feels it an honor to be with them. Ellen, who as we know is neither beautiful nor rich nor really talented (nor married!) and certainly not particularly kind or obliging to her friends, is still in some special way welcome everywhere, as if it were a particular honor for those on whom she bestows her presence. And so it is, actually. . . . If I were a man I could not possibly fall in love with or marry a woman who did not have this talent,—but in fact they often prefer it so, the wretches. Incidentally, I think both Thomas and Anders have probably been a little in love with Ellen. She is one of the people I most look forward to seeing every time I go home.

Juma has just come in with three new-born goslings, I got one the day before yesterday and have two hens sitting on eggs. I think they are some of the most enchanting creatures that life has to offer. On the whole geese are a very attractive race and must command respect from everyone. They lead such a charming family life, and I have the deepest regard for ganders, although I can't say that I am fond of them; one of them bit me in the leg the other day, it was just like a pair of pincers. But when he was walking with his wife and the one child along the road, and I came along in the car, he would not leave the child but walked right up to the car with his neck stuck out, hissing, and really held me at bay, and one really must take one's hat off to that.

I have sold my bookcase to the Bruce-Smiths and am getting a big bookshelf made by an Indian, a friend of Poor Sing, to go along the whole of one wall. Denys is paying for it so that I can house his books; he has six crates in Nairobi, and I have been to fetch two of them, he has a lot of beautiful old books that I think belonged to his mother. He has also asked me to bring out twelve crates of very fine old port, which he sets great store by, but I don't want to do this as long as the road is in the state it is now; you bump up and down several feet, and that cannot be good for it at all. I don't myself drink port, so I wish it were something else. . . .

To Ingeborg Dinesen

Ngong. Sunday 18th May. 1930.

. . . It is this truly frightful tension that I constantly live under and that affects my whole future that makes it difficult to concentrate on producing anything like an interesting and entertaining letter from here. You say you are sorry for me because I am alone, but you really mustn't be; it suits me really well and never seems hard; but I really need my nerve to cope with this eternal balancing on the edge of the abyss, and even that has to be treated with care under the circumstances. . . .

This farm, or the milieu here, is as you know the only thing that I have produced in my life, and I do think that it is of value, quite apart from the pecuniary side of things,—and for the entire time that I have been occupied with it it has hung by a thread. The great trust that all the black people place in me, and in my ability to arrange everything for the best for them, and my own awareness of the appallingly insecure basis of it, use up all my mental powers, as it were; when it eventually improves they will gush out on all sides with unlimited energy, and then I will really write. They must not stop writing to me on that account; letters give me such joy, but they must be patient.—

However it may have come about, it is clear to me by now that my black brother here in Africa has become the great passion of my life, and that this cannot be changed. Even Denys, although he makes me tremendously happy, carries no weight in comparison. It is lovely for me that he exists, I am always happy when I am with him; but he can do just about anything he likes for me and still not greatly affect my feeling of happiness or unhappiness in life,—although I made a scene of the first water because he had taken on Bror as second white hunter for the Prince of Wales, and even that ended up with my laughing, and in general I find it hard to take anything concerning Denys really seriously; but with my black brother it is something quite different; it is a matter of life and death. I don't think I have it in me to allow one individual to be of such great importance to my life. For instance, when I find myself longing for Denmark now, as I have done so much since I came back this last time, the longing for nature is more heart-rending than for people, at least with only a few special exceptions. The rondo from "Sonate pathétique," that reminds me of you in a lovely, gracious way, but of a Danish spring evening, with dew on the grass, cowslips, and the sound of waves from the Sound, in a way that sends me completely wild.

By the way, I should have heard from Tommy about the King's lion skin. I sent him Dolle's letter about it and will have to reply to her sooner or later. It is a wretched story, but of course it has been my own fault from the start, and I really cannot think that Tommy cares so much about a lion that he has not shot himself (any more than I have, although this must for ever be the most strictly kept secret); if he does, I can get another skin for him. . . .

To Ingeborg Dinesen

Ngong. Sunday 22nd June. 1930.

. . . First: regarding the lion skin I gave to Tommy. Shortly after I had arrived back here, I had a letter from Dolle saying that she had told the Queen about it, and that she had been very interested, and

Dolle begged me to let His Majesty have it, and said that she thought it would bring great happiness; of course, having once mentioned it, she was really obliged to take some steps about it. So then I wrote to Tommy and sent him Dolle's letter and gave it as my opinion that he was now obliged to give it to the King; and it was not particularly nice for him to be in possession of a lion that he had not shot himself. I also wrote what I felt should be written to the King on my behalf and sent to the King with the skin. Since then I have not heard a word about all this and am afraid that my letter to Tommy may have been lost; will you please let me know what is happening about it?. . .

To Ingeborg Dinesen

Ngong. Sunday 10th August. 1930.

. . . On Tuesday evening I went to the pictures,I don't think I have been for six years, and it was really entertaining; it was "Beau Geste," with beautiful pictures of the Foreign Legion and fights with the Arabs in the desert, with a lot of horses, which is refreshing, because they are not affected like actors; but they were actually not bad, and there was no love element, which is a blessing,—I am probably like the audience at the marionette theater in H. C. Andersen: "Children don't like long rubbishy love scenes, what they want is: something sad but quick."—

I really like Government House so much; it is beautiful with its large rooms and very high veranda, and I actually thought it was at its most pleasant at lunch time on Wednesday, after the others had left and the Governor and I had a really interesting chat. I think he is glad to be leaving, and God knows whom we will get now; I don't think anyone knows yet. If only we could get someone who is a statesman, who can take a comprehensive view of things; but they are not to be found two for a penny. . . .

To Ingeborg Dinesen

Ngong. Wednesday 10th September. 1930.

. . . First of all thanks for the records with your and Missen's voices. Of course it is true that something like this is really interesting, but as far as I am concerned it is overwhelming, and then at the same time it seems like a sort of trick; I don't really know how to take it. Of course it is exactly as if you were in the room,—and what wouldn't I give to have you here!—and yet I know that the whole thing is purely mechanical. It was wonderful to hear your voice. But the world is beginning to grow a little too strange.—

It gave great joy to all my people. When their names were mentioned they could not stop themselves from saying: "Jambo Memsabo, Jambo Memsabo." Farah showed his higher cultural standing by being frightened and very moved; Tumbo was grinning, as Malla says, like a cracked clog. Kamante came in later and asked why you would not say hello to him; I think he thought I had kept it back because he was in disgrace. Poor Singh was extremely moved and asks me to thank you very much. . . .

It was a joy to come home to Farah's little boy; he is the most enchanting thing you could imagine; he will be two on the 25 of September and must be at the culmination point of delightfulness, from which he will come to descend for the rest of his life. His chief interest in life is ngomas, of which we have had a whole lot on the farm recently; he can dance both Kikuyu and Wakamba and sing as well, also the banned Ngoma, which is said to be very indecent, but I don't imagine he can understand that. Tumbo is his ideal and enjoys this position. . . .

For the time being I am going through a phase of finding it difficult to stand the English; if I did not have the natives to stick to, I would become a real hermit. I think really intelligent English people must suffer terribly from the general English spirit or lack of spirit; I am sure they do. As you grow older you get a better idea of what it is you look for in your fellow human beings, and what you cannot tolerate; I think that what is most indispensable for me is a certain kind of poetry, I don't mind if otherwise they drink, murder and don't give a damn for me, but I can't stand really prosaic people. I think I resemble Anders in this, while both Elle and Thomas can thrive on mere prose and be quite happy. For me the natives always have something deeply poetical about them, like nature itself; but there is a certain class of English, and they are the great majority of the nation, who are so frightfully prosaic that they really cannot be stomached. . . . The mere fact that the English are always so skinny shows their uncongeniality; it was clever of Shakespeare to be able to hit on Falstaff, and must have been enjoyable for himself and beneficial for the sensitive souls who might have existed in England then. . . .

To Ingeborg Dinesen

Ngong. Sunday 14th September 1930.

. . . I think that many of Denys's books that I have here now, would make Knud's mouth water, for instance, a first edition of Voltaire's "Dictionnaire philosophique" in sixteen volumes, and a very beautiful edition of Racine,—but of course he really has so many himself that it is a good thing he can't have these as well. I also have an edition of H. C. Andersen with illustrations by Dulac, but think that the old Danish illustrations are much better; I have not got them in the fine new reproduction, but even as they are they have far more of H. C. Andersen's spirit. I have always thought H. C. Andersen resembled Voltaire, but thought I was alone in this; now I have just read a letter from Andersen in "Tilskueren" in which he says "that the big Parisian work, 'Dictionnaire des Contemporains,' ends an article about me very flatteringly with the words: avec un esprit qui rappelle celui de M. de Voltaire Andersen a tout le sentiment des peuples du Nord."—Aunt Lidda wrote that she agreed with Vilhelm Andersen that H. C. A. was a "priest of the same church for which Ingemann had written the hymns."—I can't really agree with her there; I do not think that Andersen is in any way a priest, although it is true enough that his tales are some of the most edifying that have ever been written. I read them very often.

I have to go into town to dinner tomorrow, to the Welbys, unfortunately; it doesn't suit me at all well when I have to go in in the morning as well. I had just accepted their invitation when I was asked to Government House on the same day; I would have preferred to go there, as it is always pleasant to meet Grigg, and of course he is leaving soon,—I hope he will ask me another day. He is such a great devotee of Shakespeare, so we always talk very enthusiastically about him,—also very well up on the Old Testament, two interests that often go together, although not where I am concerned, for I can get nothing whatsoever out of it and think they were a lot of scoundrels. . . .

To Ingeborg Dinesen

Ngong. Sunday 21/9.1930.

. . . I am sending you a couple of pictures from Rongai,—Fridtiof Mohr and his wife and me, with Tumbo in the background. . . . I don't remember whether I wrote that Mrs. Mohr's grandmother is thought to have been a siren who came down from the mountain, married a young farmer on his farm, and lived there for many years, until one day, long after she had become a grandmother, she said to the family: "Now Grandmother must go back to the mountain,"—and left them leaving no trace behind her. I won't say whether this is true; I don't myself feel confronted with anything supernatural, although there is something alien, to which I don't react sympathetically; it seems most like: a relic of slavery in their blood,—they are not free-born. They would no doubt *like* to be honest, but they *can't*, they get up to tricks, they play act; the serfs have to please and have to discover how they can please, just as the wind blows. All the same I can see that Mrs. Mohr is charming, after all a slave girl can be that, but I really like him better. Did I tell you that the grandfather of these Mohrs was a son of Carl XV of Sweden?—they do rather resemble the Bernadottes. I think they are gifted people; I don't think I have ever met anyone who can get through so much or get so much out of his time as my "little" Mohr; it is a quality for which I have the greatest admiration. . . .

I myself have had a few of the loveliest days, for Denys came last Thursday and left again yesterday. It is a magical effect that he has upon me; never have I ever known such a feeling of happiness as I have in his company, it is as if I get light and air after having been long confined in a room. I went up flying with him yesterday, and I think it is doubtful whether a greater happiness could exist for me than to fly over Ngong with him. We stayed up for an hour and part of the time flew along the ridge of the Ngong Hills, a few times almost down to the ground, so we could see flocks of impala and zebra down there, and then again up to a couple of thousand feet above the summits.

One ought to see Africa from the air, that is certain; then you really see the enormous expanses and the play of light and shadow over them. There was a shower of hail while we were up, it really stung the face, like when the princess in "The Traveling Companion" flew to visit the troll; it grew dark around us, and yet at the same time you could see the sun shining on the Kedong Valley. Denys wanted to try various maneuvers and turned the machine on its side once or twice, so I was glad I was strapped in; it must be marvelous fun to be able to fly. He says he has brought this machine out here for my sake, and I am hoping we will be able to go for many trips in it; now he is out again for two months, but after that should be able to stay here for at least as long as that. . . . Ali, Tumbo, and Sirunga came with us to the airfield and enjoyed it immensely, even if they seemed a little disappointed that I had not fallen out. We flew right over this house once, and there have been a lot of old Kikuyu up here this morning to interview me on my flying.

My dog David died yesterday. . . .

To Ellen Dahl

Ngong. Sunday 12th October. 1930.

. . . I have been up almost every day with Denys, who keeps his airplane in Nairobi but can land here on the farm. There is great excitement among all my totos when they hear him in the sky. "Bedar's bird, Bedar's bird," [Bedar: the bald one] they shout with all their might and watch it with delight when it circles over the house and comes down; I have a train of black folk of all sizes behind me when I go out over the plain where it lands, to see me go up. I have not been up for more than an hour at a time, as Denys has a lot to do at present; I am hoping we shall go for a longer trip later on. But even in an hour one can see a great deal.

I don't think there could be any greater happiness for me in the world than to fly over the African plains and the Ngong Hills with Denys. Here I must say with Father Daniel (?) in "Jacques," that God has far more imagination than we have, something that I don't consider he shows a great deal of in everyday life. Because by myself I could have discovered neither Africa nor Denys,—perhaps I might have imagined myself flying, that is surely a normal human desire, and aren't we supposed to have been birds at one stage?—and now I can really picture to myself what it must be like to be an angel. There is anyway something absolutely natural and reasonable about it, like a dream come true. I am constantly brought in mind of H. C. Andersen when we are in the air; the first time we went up it was showery, with icy cold showers lashing us at a height of 9,000 feet, and dark clouds sweeping around us,—it was like the princess's flight to the troll in "The Traveling Companion"; last time, in the evening, with a clear high sky and blue clouds, it was like "The Wild Swans." But now imagine great wide, endless green plains below, with flocks of zebra, gnu, giraffe, and long chains of green mountains, and light and shadow changing over it all, and then one's own speed high above everything.

All the same, in my opinion, it is neither the speed nor what one can see that is the really intoxicating thing about flying, but this: that one is moving in three dimensions. Even to move in two, as when one is riding cross country or motoring over the plains here, and anyway has escaped from the narrow road, from the *line* possesses a delight of its own, and the thing that most nearly approaches flying is in my opinion skiing, where one does enter a third dimension as well. And yet that has such difficulties for me when it comes to going up, and also brings with it a good deal of anxiety going down; when you fly you lift up your head and whirl up into space just as easily as when you are on the level. There is actually no longer any up or down; when the machine leans right over on its side in the turns you can see the whole landscape beneath you face to face. It is the most divine *game* imaginable; you cannot prevent yourself from laughing when you streak down from on high and chase, quite low down above the plain, a flock of madly galloping zebra, and see your own shadow over them and the grass, in this light, light air,—when you steel yourself against the strong daylight, cut through the air, occasionally make just a couple of brisk, quick turns, fling yourself headlong down, lurching, turning, climbing, beating down like a dragon caught by the wind almost to the earth,—spinning, rushing, writhing through the turns!—

Then, flying suits Denys so perfectly. I have always felt that he has so particularly much of the element of air in his makeup,—(sanguineous, wet, and warm, or how does it go?)—and was a kind of Ariel. There is a good deal of heartlessness in this temperament,—where the heart predominates, the character feels most at home on earth where things grow and blossom; a garden and a cornfield can be so full of heart,—and Ariel was in fact rather heartless, as you can see if you read "The Tempest" again, but so pure, compared with the earthly beings on the island, clear, honest, without reservation, transparent,—in short, like air. I think, too, that what partly appealed to me in Denys from the beginning was this: that he moves, spiritually, in three dimensions.

And this is actually what I want to write about, and if possible provide Paracelsus with material for consideration and for a parable, that we have to get ourselves up into three dimensions. Let us leave Einstein to develop them in the physical world, where it is quite hard to understand them; I think that in the spiritual world everyone, and in any case those who have reached our age, ought to have had a glimpse of them. I definitely believe that people who think wings are one of the attributes of the blessed are right, or: the capacity of moving in three dimensions is a part of bliss, or at least of transfiguration. If human beings would only try to achieve it, instead of all the other things they slog away at, they would see.

I am really excited to hear that you are writing another book. Please do write and tell me what it is about. I am so much looking forward to it, and I enjoy the picture of you there at Mols filling page after page, like a silkworm; I hope that inspiration will go on brooding over you. Let me know what other people who have read it have said about Paracelsus. Out here I have only been able to show it to Mohr, who was most enthusiastic,—please remember to send it to him, I think he would treasure it greatly.—

It doesn't surprise me that it has not made any particular impression on the family; it is partly because when people get to Mother's age the impact of their impressions depends so much more on the manner in which they are imparted to them than on the actual content,—I saw that so clearly that time when I had to let Mama know cautiously about Aunt Bess's appearance in Parliament, which I think she never really saw as anything of import.—If you go to them with a horrified face and say: The cat has died,—they will never get over it; but with other things they can react like the chamberlain's wife at Ruggaard: "Were the children burned too?" [The rest of this letter is missing.]

To Ingeborg Dinesen

Ngong. Sunday 23rd November 1930.

. . . I am sending you a picture of Saafe to make up for the shortness of this letter.—You may think you have had enough of him by now, and perhaps the pictures do not show how really enchanting he is; but he plays a big part in my life and is a great joy. He hasn't really got such a stomach as he appears to have in the photograph, but he is an Askari and has adopted a military stance; he is an incredibly funny mimic; now that he has had his head shaved he is Denys and comes in saying: "Good-morning, good-morning, and is ready to die laughing over his roles. Farah is still having trouble with Hassan, who he thinks wants to murder him, it is really sickening, because it is upsetting him;—I cannot say how much reason he has for his suspicions. Last night he fired off a shot because he thought he could see his enemy at the door, and of course his wife is terrified, particularly that they may take revenge by stealing Saafe. . . .

1931

To Ingeborg Dinesen

Ngong. Sunday 8th February. 1931.

. . . You will only get a few words today, because I came home from the hospital in Nairobi yesterday and am rather worn out after a couple of injections they gave me there. Mohr came out here on Tuesday with Dr. King, whom I had consulted in Nairobi, and they both begged me earnestly to go into the hospital for just two days so that he could have me under observation there. . . . I really like the doctor, who is not attached to the hospital in any way apart from being allowed to have his private patients there, and I think it is possible that he knows what he is talking about. Anyway he was quick to come to a definite result and said at once that what was wrong with me was chronic dysentery and very severe, perhaps pernicious anemia. . . .

Saafe was so terribly sweet when I came home yesterday, deeply moved, he held my face in both his hands and would not let me go; they said he had been in utter despair when he came into the house and did not find me. This is a very happy love affair. . . .

1930 was the year that decided the farm's fate and the lives of its inhabitants. The shareholders in Denmark came to the decision that they wished to sell Karen Coffee Company, Ltd. *Well-intentioned suggestions to sell part of the land for building plots were met with hostility by Karen Blixen, and accordingly the farm was sold in one piece to a purchaser who naturally invested in the plantation with a view to speedy development. At an extraordinary general meeting in Copenhagen in November 1932, the company was liquidated in accordance with company law clause 67, on which occasion the board was obliged to reveal that the previously held forced sale had not raised sufficient funds to cover the costs of liquidation.*

By agreement with the new owner, Karen Blixen stayed on at the farm to direct the work of getting in the last crop of coffee and arranging for the future of her African staff.

Ngong. 17th March. 1931.

. . . I know I should have answered the telegram from you and Tommy. But the fact is that everything is so uncertain; it is almost impossible for me at the moment to deal with my own plans at all, let alone take any decisions. There are still so many shauries about the farm, with meetings in Nairobi and so on, and then there are my black folk here. Until arrangements have been made for them,—as far as they can be made, and I don't know how good they will be,—I have neither the strength nor the time to manage to do anything for myself. You understand, they stay here the whole time and come running after me when I am walking or riding on the farm; they say: "Why do you want to go away? You mustn't go, what will become of us?". . .

Then I have got to help Farah and his family, Abdullai, and my houseboys. Farah does not want to stay in this country, but he has his duca and various other shauries that have to be wound up. Juma wants to go back to the Reserve,—the Masai Reserve; it was fortunate that I arranged for him to have his registration changed and for him to become a Masai some time ago,—and build himself a house there, which I have promised to help him with. In short: I have enough to do.

You must not think that I feel, in spite of it having ended in such defeat, that my "life has been wasted" here, or that I would exchange it with that of anyone I know. I feel, like Aunt Lidda, that in fact it is astonishing how much, given my abilities, I have been able to achieve. Aunt Lidda did not say this as applying to me in particular, but to herself in comparison with Aunt Bess, who did not feel she had got what she should have had out of life.

Of all the idiots I have met in my life,—and the Lord knows that they have not been few or little,—I think that I have been the biggest. But a certain love of greatness, which could not be quelled, has kept a hold on me, has been "my daimon." And I have had so infinitely much that was wonderful. She may be more gentle to others, but I hold to the belief that I am one of Africa's favourite children. A great world of poetry has revealed itself to me and taken me to itself here, and I have loved it. I have looked into the eyes of lions and slept under the Southern Cross, I have seen the grass of the great plains ablaze and covered with delicate green after the rains, I have been the friend of Somali, Kikuyu, and Masai, I have flown over the Ngong Hills,—"I plucked the best rose of life, and Freja be praised,"—I believe that my house here has been a kind of refuge for wayfarers and the sick, and to the black people has stood as the center of a friendly spirit. Lately it has been somewhat more difficult. But that is so all over the world.

Farah is *very* helpful, as you can imagine, and has put all his nonsense behind him and is a great comfort to me. Saafe is a great joy; I cannot describe how sweet he is. I have been suffering from such terrible nightmares that I have been quite terrified and have had him to sleep in my bed; it is so big that he quite disappears into it. I could not have the dogs, they make such a noise. . . .

It is an irony of fate that we have had such good, early rains. When I think how often at this time of year I have gone outside gazing for the rain that would not come, it is strange to lie and listen to it pouring down now, and know that it doesn't make the slightest difference.

Now there is a lovely time coming for you at home; I think early spring, with all its disappointments, has an utterly matchless delight and charm.

Give a thousand greetings to everyone, and all, all my love to you, my own beloved, charming Mother.

Your Tanne.

To Thomas Dinesen

Ngong. 10th April. 1931.

Private.

This letter is written in haste to catch the post, but I hope the meaning is fairly clear.

Dear Tommy,

You must be feeling that it is strange and wrong of me not to have written before, but the reason is that I have been quite unable to look ahead in any direction. I have had so much to do making what arrangements I could for my squatters and my boys and hope to work things out reasonably well for them; but I have not been able to see any way forward whatsoever for myself, and in that situation one does not know what to write.

But you must not think that I am frightfully depressed and see everything in a tragic light. That is not at all the case; on the contrary, I think that these difficult times have helped me to understand better than before how infinitely rich and beautiful life is in every way and that so many things that one goes around worrying over are of no importance whatsoever. The wider one can manage to get one's overall view of life to become,—and that is about the most vital thing to aim for in life,—the more one comes to see the magnificence and multitudinous facets of existence. But this also involves a real and true freedom from prejudice, so that one does not at the same time try to go on maintaining that this or that is of immense importance, for it is not. For instance, it seems to me that it would in no way be terrible or sad if I, after in many ways having been more happy here than it is by far the majority of people's lot to be,—and there is not one single person I would change with,—were now quite calmly to retire from life together with everything that I have loved here. What I imagine a great many people would think of that: for instance, that it was terrible for Mother and so on, is something I cannot take into account. It may perhaps be just as hard for Mother to lose me as for me to lose Ngong; but when one comes to realize the whole nature of life, which is: that nothing lasts, and that in that very fact lies some of its glory, the sadness of this is really not so terrible. To me it would seem the most *natural* thing to disappear with my world here, for it seems to me to be, to quite the same extent as my eyes, or as some talent or other I might have, vital parts of myself, and I do not know how much of me will survive losing it. Generally: the continuance of life is in my opinion often misunderstood, for how much of oneself does in fact go on living? How much is there left, under present circumstances, of that person that I, or you, were fifteen years ago?—

But when all the same I am going to write what follows to you today it is because both Denys and Mohr, who have been such true friends to me, think that I ought to, and so it is partly due to them. They think that on account of such a long wearing period of trouble and one-sided work on the same shauries I now cannot take a correct view of things and that what I ought to do is to have another try and attempt to make a plan. And they think that I should put this to you, since I am so far from being independent as to be able to carry through any kind of plan whatsoever, and find out whether you might be in agreement with them and willing to assist me. You must regard what I am now going to write from this point of view. It is, as I say, very unnatural for me, and I would much rather not say that in any case at all I think I am able to carry it through or feel myself bound to even try.

As far as I can see from the letters I have received, everyone who has any interest in this affair at all is reckoning on my going home and staying at home. From my point of view this is quite out of the question. Quite apart from the fact that the atmosphere at home has never suited me and that I got married and put all my efforts into emigrating in order to get away, and that it would suit me infinitely much less now,—insofar as the divergences in outlook that made it difficult for me to live at home have grown far more pronounced during these seventeen years,—it would be completely and utterly unnatural for me, rather as it would be for you if you had to go back to Rungsted Boarding School as a pupil, and I doubt whether either I or you would be able to find any level in such a situation. I do not say this as a criticism of anybody, not even of Rungsted School; but what suits them does not suit me. At home I lose that capacity for taking an overall view that it has cost me so much to attain. I am quite aware that during my visits home, particularly the last two, I have fostered in Mother, perhaps in everyone, an inaccurate impression, both as regards my own nature and the relationship between us. This is almost unavoidable when one is at home for a few months and cannot tell when one will be together with people again, and in any case it was done from the best of motives; but it is not the real state of affairs, and if I were to be permanently at home I would be unable to maintain it.—

I am putting this so strongly in order not to express it too weakly and so give you a wrong impression. Summa summarum: I am no more acquiescent than I was before; on the contrary; I cannot come home with remorse and contrition no matter what has happened to me and what I have been doing; I still feel that death is preferable to a bourgeois existence, and in death I will confess my faith in freedom.

This does not mean that I wouldn't be terribly happy to stay at home for a few months; but if I am to make plans I suppose I must look further ahead. I know quite well that it would only be fair for me to say that I would stay at home and try to be something for Mother during the years that are left to her; but you see, those are the very years in which, if I am ever to get started on anything, I must do something about it.

In all sincerity, it is really very difficult to see what if anything I can do in this world. As I have probably written, I have wondered whether I could learn to cook in Paris for a year or two, and then perhaps get a post in a restaurant or a hotel. But I really don't know; there are probably not many posts in these hard times. So, during these difficult months, I have begun to do what we brothers and sisters do when we don't know what else to resort to,—I have started to write a book. I have been writing in English because I thought it would be more profitable, but as I was afraid that the language would prove a great difficulty, I sent a section of it home to a friend of Mohr's, a publisher called Morley, and asked for his opinion. He was encouraging,—(the leisurely style and language are exceedingly attractive),—so I am inclined to think that it should be possible for me to write in English, and thereby I would have a chance at various openings, for instance in journalism. But if this should be so I would have to have time in which to finish writing my book, and I think, from what I understand of conditions in English publishing, I would have to publish the first book I wrote,—all supposing there should be more!—at my own expense. But in general: in order to be able to earn anything at all I will really have to have one or two years in which to train myself; for everyone knows that I can't do anything.

This brings us to the question of money. I understand from Mohr that you have written to him saying that you think you could let me have enough to live on to keep me satisfied. But this does not remove the difficulty of making a plan, because I don't know whether you mean, like the others, to live on at home at Rungsted, or to be in some place where I could learn and which would of course involve expense. You know that I have never done anything on my own initiative in Europe; I don't know, for instance, what it would cost to live in Italy. And if I were to try to write, then I would need to be able to go to England and talk to people there. It is no use for me to try to put forward ideas to be acted upon without taking everything into account, and it would come to cost a good deal. Would you, for example, be prepared to take a job,—that is if you can get one; I know nothing at all about conditions at home,—for two or three years in order to help me to educate myself or get started on something or other? You know me so well that I don't need to tell you that I am not cheap. There are many things that I can do without perfectly well; I can live on bread and water quite easily, but that doesn't alter the fact. I think we must get this quite clear because it would be terribly upsetting if there should be misunderstandings later on. I can't live without *fun* in life; *fun* is what I am in need of even now. I must have £250 to get away from here (that is, to get back to Europe)—and I do not know how much more it will cost after that; but I do know that there are many people who can manage with much less money than I can.

They have the idea here that I am very ill. It is true that I am not at all well, and how can anyone expect me to be when sorrows and worries completely prevent one from eating and sleeping for six months.—But I think this is of completely minor importance. I might have to stay somewhere or other for a month or two, but I don't really think so. I am sure it will all clear up and will not cause lasting trouble.

Now you must not, and I am sure you will not, take this as a sort of threat; help me and sustain me, or I will die. As I said I am writing chiefly because I promised Mohr and Denys that I would. But you must give it consideration from the following point of view: as far as I myself am concerned, the most reasonable and easy thing to do would be to die. But if you feel, and this is something that I can't really see for myself, but that other people seem to think, that there is some meaning in making yet another attempt to live, then give it some thought and decide,—whether you think you can help me to live the kind of life that would suit me, a happy life. There must always be one thing that is more important than anything else to a person and I think that for me this is freedom, or space. I cannot and will not live in a situation where I feel myself incarcerated. Naturally no one can tell how it will go; but please consider whether you think that you can and want to advise and help me to live happily.

I know that I can die happily, and if you are in doubt, let me do that. Let me take Ngong, and everything that belongs to it, in my arms and sink with it, and it will be without complaint, but with immense gratitude to life. There is so infinitely much that I love out here and also at home; I love you all and thank you for so enormously much.

Will you please reply to this letter by telegram? If it should turn out like that your offer to meet me in Genoa would be accepted with joy.

Many many greetings. Everyone and everything here send greetings as well.

Your Tanne.

To Ingeborg Dinesen

Ngong. Sunday 12/4 1931.

My own beloved Snow-white Lamb.

Many thousand thanks for your letters; I am so terribly glad to get them and I know you will forgive me for not writing myself, for there is so much to do. I ought to be getting on with my own plans and trying to work out some scheme or other; but first I must get all the people who are dependent on me here and expect me to help them, off my hands. Now I am going to describe the various items so that you can get an idea of it all and see that it is not so easy to start on personal plans while I am burdened with all this, and of course every shaurie with natives always develops, because of their nature, into an endless affair.

I. is my squatters. There are 153 families here on the farm, some of whom were living here before the land was even allotted to white people, and who counted on being able to end their days here and leave their cattle and shambas to their children. As I thought that it was going to be Andersen, that cad and bounder, who was to be in charge of the farm, I went and saw him about it and he said straight away that they would all have to leave immediately. I said he could not do that as they all had contracts and would have to be given six months notice. He tried to bluff me by saying that he himself had been both to the Native Affairs Department and to the D.C. in Nairobi, and that it was all quite in order and that I did not need to bother with it myself. However, when I went to those authorities they said that they had never so much as heard from Andersen and that there was no question of his giving them notice to quit in under six months. Some time after that came a message from the police (from Andersen) saying that if one drop of tembo [palm wine] was found on the farm after 1 April, the person guilty of possessing it would have to leave the farm immediately and his contract would be void. This too was pure bluff as I discovered when I went to the D.C.; he can certainly ban tembo brewing and report it to the police, but contracts cannot be annulled because of it, although a fine may be imposed.

So far everything was in order,—especially as Andersen is not now to have charge of the farm's affairs,—but it turned out to be a far greater problem to find land for these squatters to go to when, as will happen in any case, they receive notice to leave in six months' time. The Reserve cannot take them,and there is no land to give them. I have been countless times to see the Native Affairs Department, and the D.C.s in Nairobi and in Kiambu, about this, and I have had to draw up lists for every single family stating how many wives, cows, and sheep it owns, where it comes from, how long it has been here, and who was the chief and subheadman of the district they lived in previously. As you can imagine, this is an interminable business with natives, and just as I had got the whole thing finished, divided up according to different districts and stating the numbers of cattle, they came to me again and again telling me that some man or other had been put on the wrong list, or that the number of sheep was incorrect, or that they had settled here in quite a different year than had been stated, and I had to do the whole thing again. But now I have got these lists finished,—they take up twelve typed pages and are just as bad as lists of prisoners, and I have taken copies to the Native Affairs Department, the D.C. Nairobi, the D.C. Kabete, the D.C. Kiambu, the D.C. Dagoretti, the D.C. Fort Hall,—Nyeri and Machakos. Then there is also every possible kind of shaurie with them, this one or that one wants to go with his father-in-law and not to his own district; one is too old to work or to pay tax and so on, and they are also trying to settle their own mutual shauries over unpaid debts or wives and raking up ancient matters like the accidental shot at Thaxton's house seven years ago, for me to get finally settled before I leave. As I may have written, I had the D.C. from Nairobi out here one day to see about these things, and he is very obliging; but they prefer me, because they know me, and there is really no end to it when one once begins with the natives.—

I think it is quite scandalous that the government has given so little foresight to getting land for these people to live on. They have been planning to abolish the squatter system (which I think is far the best if only it could be made secure in some way or other) without having the least idea about what they are going to do with the squatters they are sending away from white people's land. As far as I understand from the officials I have spoken to, it is a much larger problem than that affecting only my black people here. They say there is no possibility of getting shambas for them sooner than six months and very doubtful then. I think the poor D.C.'s themselves are going through a great deal because of it and are very indignant over the Government's attitude.

This is probably a matter you could kick up a row about in England, and I have even thought I might go and visit my friend Lord Islington and get him to help me with it,—and that is really an effective threat to people out here,—but in reality I do not feel very inclined to do it because the people one would have to work with would probably not be very attractive,— press men and politicians,—and it is doubtful whether it would come to benefit my squatters; it might just as easily harm them in the end. It is unlucky for me that Grigg has left, he was such a friend. I have been promised a personal interview with the new governor in the near future. All the D.C.s I have been in contact with over this matter think it would be so much better if I stayed and saw the thing through; they say that once I have gone nothing will be done, but that means staying more than six months and I don't really know what to say to that.

Then come my own people.

I. FARAH does not want to stay in Kenya but to go to Somaliland; but he has so many and varied interests here that must be wound up first. He has a big case on in Nairobi, which I have probably written to you about, but I think this is actually nearing a settlement now; but in connection with it my enemy Hemsted has contrived to have the permission for Farah to run his duca here withdrawn. I have been into Nairobi about that at least ten times. It is Hugh Martin who has the final say in this matter and it is never possible to get hold of him. In the end I ran him to earth at his house at eight o'clock in the morning, so that he couldn't escape, and I think it is in order now as far as the government permission is concerned, but now it remains to be seen what attitude the new owners will adopt toward it. It is unfortunate that when something collapses, like my ménage, it pulls so much down with it: Farah and Abdullai have had a row, and

Abdullai has gone away without anyone knowing what has become of him, so I must set that to rights before I leave. In addition to all this we got involved in a cattle-robbing shaurie the other evening,—we caught some thieves as I was driving home after going to the farewell evening at the school,—which looks like taking up some time, and which Farah cannot get out of, although of course he is not suspected. Of them all it is Farah I am most deeply concerned about; he has been so extremely good in helping me with all kinds of shauries, but he has after all counted on his future being a part of mine, and I do want to help him and his family as much as I can.

JUMA wants to go back into the Masai Reserve as a Masai, and so had to be re-registered as such. This we managed to do after some difficulty. He has acquired an excellent shamba out there and I promised him help in building himself a house, but it really is quite incredible how stupid the natives are. Of course I should have supervised the building a little and given him some advice, or found a proper fundee for him, but I took it for granted that he would be able to build a house for himself,—after all they build houses all the time and have done so for many thousands of years,— but I grew rather worried when I discovered how much timber,—which was what I had first promised him,—was going into it, so last Thursday I drove out there to have a look at it and found to my horror that he has built up the walls for a house 65 feet square. I really grew quite depressed as I sat there looking at it; I cannot imagine how they are going to get a roof on that house, and just the iron for it will cost 800 shillings, according to my calculations!—And I think it will collapse on top of them in the first gale. Juma could have been so comfortable if he had had a little common sense; but who would have thought he would be so crazy. Now I am going out there again today,—it is out near the Ngong Boma,—with Farah and Juma and a fundee to look at it; I think they will just have to take the whole thing down again. I have promised Tumbo a cow, and my geese.

ALI wanted to learn to drive a car and get his license before I left, so I have taught him to drive and he got his license last Thursday. I don't think it will be difficult for him to find a job, although nothing is certain in these hard times. His father has a shamba in the Forest Reserve,—weren't we out there once?—and sounds well off. I intend to give Ali a cow as well.

KAMANTE will of course lose his post and his shamba here, and despite his indisputable genius for cooking I am doubtful whether he will get another post; he is really rather lacking. But he is not so badly off; he has saved enough money here both to get married and to buy a couple of cows, so if only he finds somewhere to live,—like the other squatters,—he should be able to manage. He has two children of whom he is very fond. Titi is very miserable over my leaving; I think I shall give him a little bull that I have, to console him.

CHOTHA, my blind boy, is litigating a case in Dagoretti, I am going over there to help him with it tomorrow; otherwise there will never be a settlement. He was shamefully cheated by some Kikuyu from whom he had bought a ndito. It is sad for him, he will probably go completely blind; I must arrange to get him to an optician before I leave, though I do not think there is much hope for him.

KAMAU, the syce, is going to Fort Hall, where he seems to have made quite satisfactory arrangements for himself, strange as his relationship in his marriage to Tumbo's grandmother may be. I have promised to try to get him a job as a syce.

MAHAA is going to be married next year to a schoolteacher and I hope she will be happy with him.

LITTLE HALIMA causes me anxiety. Her beastly father has promised her in marriage to a man here in Kenya who is said to be unpleasant. She is so attached to Farah's family and has grown so sensible since she has been with them; I think she will be in utter despair if they go without her and leave her alone, but it is terribly hard to interfere in the Somalis' life and decisions and I do not even know where her father is. There is much that is good in Halima but she is wild; if she is deserted now there is no knowing what she will become.—

Then there are so many others that you don't know, for example the pathetic little Sirunga, my clown; I just do not know what will become of him. He has become so deeply attached to me, and life isn't easy for him, because he is not quite all there. He suffers from a kind of epileptic attack; the other day when we were in the middle of a game with Saafe, he suddenly stood quite still and said: "Mimi na take kufa" [I want to die]—I did not understand what he meant, but it was clear that he was terribly frightened; he clung to my legs and began to tremble and then fell into one of his attacks, which are really dreadful to see. One feels so strongly that this kind of toto ought to be shot, just like a little dog with a broken leg that one has to go away from. But like most living creatures he does have many pleasant and happy hours in between.

Now I'm sure you can understand that with all this on my shoulders I haven't managed to make any plans for myself. As soon as I can do it I will be sure to let you all know. It is unfortunate that I am unwell; it makes one so much slower about everything than one would be if one were fit, and sometimes, in the middle of a talk with the D.C. or some other important person, I cannot remember what I wanted to say. But now at least we have finished with the farm shauries which have certainly taken up a great deal of time, with inventories and outstanding bills and half-finished tickets, and every day I do manage to get something or other dealt with.

Denys has been staying here but is in Nairobi at present, as he wanted to finish up all the things that are always awaiting him after a safari. He is probably coming out again tomorrow. It has been really lovely to have him. The other day he came and took me up in his airplane to look at a whole flock of buffalo out in the hills. It was quite marvelous to see them, more than twenty, and some very large bulls, on the green slopes.

And then Mohr has also been a true friend and really taken so much trouble to help me in every way he could. I shall always be deeply grateful to him.—Rose Cartwright has been out here for a few days; she is an extremely sweet person and so understanding. In fact everyone is so nice. . . .

The letter that follows is the only one in the collection not written by Karen Blixen. But in its sympathetic understanding of Karen Blixen's true nature and the immediate situation in which she found herself, it provides an invaluable glimpse of Ingeborg Dinesen's human stature and shows the rare personality of Karen Blixen's mother.

The letter from Karen Blixen to Thomas Dinesen mentioned at the beginning of the letter below is on pp. 417–21.

Ingeborg Dinesen
to Thomas Dinesen

Rungstedlund. 9/5.1931.

Private. To Tommy.

My own beloved boy,

I was aware of the risk I was taking in opening Tanne's letter to you,—the chances were high that it would contain things that I ought not to read,—but it was such a great temptation to find out as soon as possible what plans she might be making. You must not say that you forgive me,—you would say that anyway and I do not even think that you would be angry with me. I do not think I could be angry with you, in any case, if you were to do something like this. Anyway, it looks as if I have had my punishment by reading this letter, which was certainly not intended to be made known to me. But I shall give no more consideration to that,—the vital thing is that Tanne *must never suspect* that I have read it.

As it happens I think it will be easier for you to know that I am aware of Tanne's plans and ideas. You know that for the whole of my life with you I have tried my best to understand you, and you may be sure that I understand what Tanne is going through now. For I have always known that the environment I offered her here was not suited to her character and talents,—this has caused me great pain, but it has not been possible for me to change it so much that it would make her happy. Perhaps she has not really been willing to make the attempt to find happiness in this environment; but no matter how much violence she might have done to her nature she would never have been able to feel at home in what she rightly calls a bourgeois existence, and so much of the value in her would have been wasted.

It is not at all incomprehensible to me that Tanne can write of death so calmly. I know that I have talked so little to you all about Father's death,—perhaps I really should have been more outspoken to you, but it has seemed like holy ground to me, that no one must walk on without being able to understand what had happened. To Father the thought of having to live as a sick and stricken man was intolerable, and when I felt,—especially during the initial painful period,—as if he had failed me, it immediately grew clear to me that it would have been impossible for him to live like that,—and so he chose the only solution available to his nature. Many times have I thought that it would have been harder to see him growing old and feeble; speed and movement were essential factors of life to him, he had to be experiencing something, whether it were joy or sorrow, anything but stagnation, "respectability." How he could ever have come to choose me, and during all the years we lived together show me,—and feel, as I know that he did,—the greatest love and understanding, has always been a riddle to me,—it must have been something in him that needed another side to life, perhaps during a period when he needed more peace and quiet after a stormy spell. I have no doubt that he was happy here in his home,—happier than Tanne has ever been.

I know,—and I know that you believe it to be true,—that I will be able to give Tanne complete freedom to do what she thinks is best for herself,—I will not hold her back if she thinks life is too hard for her, I will not for one moment put her under an obligation to "be something" to me in these years,—when I wrote that to her it was mostly so that she should take it as the suggestion for an undertaking. The sole consideration for me is that she should live according to her nature,—I neither can nor will demand anything else of her. She has often caused me anxiety, probably more than any other of my children, but she has filled my life with so much love, so much festivity, I have been,—and am,—so proud of her, that whatever she may come to do I will always love and bless her. I would rather never see her again than that she should feel herself "incarcerated." I should know that in a life where she did not feel that, she would love me more than if she were caged in here at Rungsted.

You know that when I first began to reconsider, after Tanne told me that you wanted to go to war, I was fully aware that it was necessary for you to have my complete approval and blessing before you went,—that was what I owed you, and the only thing that I have been able to do for all of you is that, to try to understand and help you to follow your own natures. Whenever I felt something in you that was alien to me I was always afraid lest it should be impeded if I did not take the trouble to support it. Those rich years that I spent with Father taught me to understand other aspects of life than those to which I was drawn. I have had so many qualms of conscience because I allowed Folehave to bear down on you with its loving but heavy weight to such an extent,—and naturally most on Tanne, to whom the whole of that atmosphere was most foreign. I make no excuses for it,—it arose from love, but it was wrong.

As far as practical considerations regarding Tanne's possible plans are concerned, you know I will do everything that I possibly can. It is better that she should have some money now, when it can perhaps help her, than inherit it. You *must* not say,—as I know you will,—that I really must not give her any more,—it is of such vital importance for her and thereby for me that she should be given the possibility of starting life again. If she had been able to consider living here with me it would in any case have been a good deal more costly for me than it is now, and I must be allowed to give her that money. It will not do for her to accept too much from you,—you have other responsibilities now, so you must not leave me out of account.

In one way I am glad that I have read Tanne's letter. You would probably not have let me see it, and it is far, far better for me to have a clear idea of what she is thinking. I think the worst possible thing that could happen would be to lure or push her into a situation that oppressed her, and I know full well that she would feel oppressed by life here with Bess and me, Countess Ahlefeldt, Mrs. Funch, Ulla, and the others,—nothing but bourgeois existence in pleasant backwaters.

My own dearest boy, you must not harbor any hard feelings toward Tanne because she despises what I have to offer her, and perhaps, too, makes too great demands on us. She is cast in such a completely different mold,—and I am glad that I have realized in time that we were wrong in thinking she had changed. She has been through a hard school, but this in itself has not changed her nature,—the development that these years have brought her has not turned her into a more commonplace person than she was, and if we have thought so we have been wrong, I see that very clearly now, and I see that we mistook the situation chiefly because it would have been easier for us.

I cannot imagine how you could possibly reply to Tanne by telegram,—how could you do that?!

I don't know how much of this you will make known to Jonna,—for my sake, anyhow, I only ask that you take care never to let Tanne know that I have read her letter.

I am sending you the letter I have had myself from Tanne today; please be sure to let me have it back at once. I have written this immediately after reading yours; I will put it aside until tomorrow,—perhaps I may need to rewrite it completely, I must sleep on it and see. In any case I will write a letter to you both about the children.

You know that I love you.

Your Mother.

To Ingeborg Dinesen

Ngong. 13th May. 1931.

. . . I am sending you a letter from Joanie Grigg, partly because I think it is very sweet, and partly because she writes about Valmont, where she thinks that she recovered in a miraculous manner from much the same thing that they say is wrong with me. They specialize generally in tropical diseases and are apparently known all over the world. . . . I know that Elle is very enthusiastic about Solsana, but I myself feel most drawn to Joanie's,—which is called the Clinique Valmont, Glion,—because it is so important, if one goes for a cure, to get hold of the right people, and these must anyway have a great deal of experience. The doctor in Nairobi says that there is not the slightest doubt that what is wrong with me is what they call amoebic dysentery but as I have said before, I think I will get better when I leave all the shauries behind me.

I shall send a telegram this week with further details of my plans, so you should get that long before this letter arrives. I am thinking of leaving here on the 9th of June, on an Italian ship, partly because it is cheaper than the others, and partly because it goes to Venice, and I think it would be pleasant to land at a different place from the other times. Then I would very much like to spend a week in Venice and then travel quite slowly, so that I could see a little more of my dear northern Italy, to whichever clinic I decide upon, either Valmont or Solsana. . . .

I haven't time for much today as I have advertised my furniture for sale and have a lot to do. The prices one gets at the moment are really disgusting; you are lucky if you get half what things cost at home, discounting freight, but all the same it is no doubt best to sell it; it would be much too expensive and difficult to take it home. I will be taking the silver and linen with me and a few other things, the little chest of drawers from Folehave, and Father's old Bornholm clock, and then my books which have been on a short pleasure trip to the tropics; but in a way I think it is quite amusing that the old classics: Oehlenschlæger, Blicher, Heiberg, and so on have been in Africa; perhaps it will increase their value for Anders when he comes to inherit them. . .

On 14 May 1931, Denys Finch Hatton's airplane crashed near Voi, and he was killed instantly. He was buried in the Ngong Hills next day.

To Thomas Dinesen
Telegram from Nairobi Received 15th May 1931.

LCO = DINESEN SERRIDSLEVVEJ 8 KBH =

Telegraph Station
Copenhagen Ø

DENYS KILLED FLYING FOURTEENTH BURIED NGONG HILLS TODAY =
TANIA**

To Thomas Dinesen

Ngong. 7th May [June] 1931.

My own dear Tommy,

I would have thanked you very much for your letters and check for £200, but I was expecting a telegram from you in reply to my letter of the 10th of April and therefore did not write. Now I understand from Mother's letter that you have been away on a trip to Germany or Austria. Please forgive the delay; of course I am terribly glad about the money, and it arrived all right.

At the moment I really cannot foresee what I will, or can, do, so I will not begin to write about it. I still think it was sensible for you not to come out here; I don't think you could have helped me with the actual practical shauries I have, because you are not conversant with them,—at the moment they chiefly consist of selling my furniture, which is a real curse because people come out here at all hours and I have to show them around; you get absolutely nothing for them these days and I can't say that I am in a condition to take much interest in it, but it must be done, since I can neither leave them in the house nor put them out on the Ngong Road,—and in trying to arrange things for my boys, and there is no peace in which to do anything else. I am sure you know that the fate of my boys, especially Farah's, is something that I feel perhaps unreasonably deeply about. It is especially hard for them now, for if Denys had been alive they could always have turned to him and known that he would help them, both for my sake and because in a way he counted them as his own; his death means they are completely deserted here. Times are hard for them as well, particularly for the Somalis, who are so unpopular with the class of white people we have in this country now; all their old friends: McMillan, Berkeley, Galbraith, Charles Gordon, the Northeys have gone, and they feel they are up against it. Whatever comes to pass, please will you remember that Farah has been my best friend out here, and Saafe is the apple of my eye?

If you had come out and had the time and the means to go for a month's safari, it would have been a different matter. I would so much like to do that, to get a parting smile from Africa, now there have been so many shauries during the past year. It would have been like old times. If I still feel strongly enough about it and it seems possible I may do it, and no doubt you would help me to go. I do not want to shoot, but to sit by a camp-fire. I would only need Farah and one or two other boys and would go out for a month, somewhere where nobody would know where I was. Mohr does not think it is a good plan, but he cannot be expected to understand how it all seems to me at the moment,—I don't think it would do any harm, even if it is pretty silly; there cannot be any great risk involved and I feel that it would do me good, and I can't think of anything else that would.— But of course I must get all the shauries with the farm and the house settled first. I may possibly telegraph to you about it later on.

Many many greetings to you and everyone.

Your Tanne.

To Thomas Dinesen

Ngong. 5th July. 1931.

Dear Tommy.

This week I am sending about 25 crates containing partly such things as I have been unable to get rid of out here, partly things that I really want to take home with me,—some of it personal luggage, so that I do not need to take them with me. . . .

I am very tired, I have had so much to do. If you should think that this is either a bad arrangement, or that when the things arrive they seem a peculiar selection, and that I ought to have sent other things, and anyway not these, you must just realize that this was all I could manage, to get things in some sort of order.

Please do not discuss it with the others or there will be so much discussion over it.

Many many greetings to you all.

Your Tanne.

Thomas Dinesen was at Marseilles to meet his sister when she arrived on 19 August 1931 on the S.S. "Mantola". *After a few days at Montreux, where Karen Blixen recovered a little of her strength at the Clinique Valmont, they continued their journey through Europe. On 31 August she rejoined her mother at Rungstedlund, the house that was to become Karen Blixen's home for the rest of her life.*

Notes

Each note is preceded by the number of the text page to which the note refers.

1. "Fara the Warrior" alludes to a Danish children's song that is invariably misunderstood because of its syntax, which is beyond the understanding of children.

2. Charles William Hobley, 1867–1947 was acting senior commissioner in the East African Protectorate, 1907. His writings include *Kenya from Chartered Company to Crown Colony* (1929).

4. "The whole world disgusts you like an ill-fitting dress": from Karen Blixen's marionette play *The Revenge of Truth.* In scene 4 the girl Sabine says, "I loathe life here in Edam as much as an ill-fitting dress."

7. Kavirondos: Africans from the Nile region and Bantu people from the east coast of Victoria Island.

9. J. H. Patterson, *The Man-Eaters of Tsavo and other East African Adventures* (1907). An account of the man-eating lions that harassed builders and engineers during the building of the new railroads from Mombasa to Uganda.

9. In Karen Blixen's time, one rupee, a unit of currency in Kenya, was worth about twenty pence.

10. Ea's deportation: "Karen Blixen's sister had a great affection for German-occupied north Schleswig, and in the spring of 1914, she and another girl went down there on a concert tour to sing at private gatherings. The program was chosen with the greatest care in order not to offend the German authorities, but nevertheless one evening the two girls were arrested by a gendarme during a banquet at a private house. Their host earnestly entreated that he be permitted to drive them to the railroad station, but the gendarme demanded that they obey him and—in thin evening dresses and light shoes—accompany him and his lantern on foot. He went with them on the train as far as the border, and not until then were they able to change their clothes" (Th. Hauch-Fausbøll, *Slægten Dinesen gennem 300 Aar* [Three hundred years with the Dinesen family] [1934], pp. 86–87). The Danish critic Georg Brandes later mentioned this incident when lecturing in Norway, according to an unpublished letter of Karen Blixen's.

11. " . . love soldiers as one loves young women, without limit." See Wilhelm Dinesen, *From the Eighth Brigade* (1889): "One loves soldiers as one loves young women: blindly, uncontrollably" (p. 47).

13. On 3 August 14, Germany had declared war on France, and in the course of a few days World War I was in progress. For Bror Blixen's participation as a volunteer and Karen Blixen's oxen transport (mentioned in the letters that follow), see the chapter entitled "A Safari in Wartime" in the fourth section of *Out of Africa.*

13. *Posho* (Sw.), supplies. In other letters, used to describe a kind of thin maize porridge.

14. Hugh Cholmondeley, third Baron Delamere, 1870–1931. English pioneer and leading personality in the construction of the British East African Protectorate, later the Crown Colony of Kenya. He arrived in Africa in 1903 and became chairman of the Farmers' and Planters' Association and a member of the Legislative Council. An un-

ceasing advocate of white rule in Kenya, after 1920 he came to oppose strongly the government in London that urgently wished to promote the interests of the Africans. Delamere was owner of the farm Soysambu on Lake Elmenteita and a great deal of other property.

16. "The lake": Lake Victoria.

17. *Arda Volaja: Adhama Ulaja,* "Majesty of Europe," "Greatness."

19. *"Boma"* (Sw.), enclosure. In the story *Kongesønnerne* [The kings' sons] written in 1946, printed in *Blixeniana 1978,* Karen Blixen described a night in a boma, clearly deriving from the description in this letter.

23. It appears from Karen Blixen's letters that, during the period 1914–31, Farah was married to at least three Somali women.

23. Karen Blixen's maternal grandmother, Mary Westenholz, died 7 September 1915 at Folehave, at the age of 83.

29. Censor: the English censor in Nairobi, whose task was to read all letters sent during the first world war from British East Africa.

32. In 1916 both her sisters were married. On 14 July Ellen Dinesen married Knud Dahl, a barrister who had been courting her for many years, and on 24 August the wedding of Inger Dinesen took place; she married Viggo de Neergaard, who owned the estate Valdemarskilde in central Sealand.

36. Sir Joseph Baynes, born in England in 1832, died at Nelsrust near Pietermaritzburg in 1925. A pioneer of South African dairy farming and a large-scale farmer in Natal, in 1868 he took over his father's farm and made it into an agricultural model comprising finally no less than 24,000 acres.

38. The *Königsberg* was a German warship sunk by the English off the Rufiji River south of Dar-es-Salaam in July 1915.

41. Karen Blixen's closest girlhood friend, Daisy Grevenkop-Castenskiold, whose husband was the Danish ambassador in London, died suddenly on 12 January 1917.

45. Carl's boy: Baron Carl Fredrik von Blixen-Finecke, 1903–50, later owner of Näsbyholm. He was the son of the previous baron, Major Carl Emil von Blixen-Finecke, 1874–1940, eldest son of Karen Blixen's father-in-law.

45. Hans's boy: Baron Hans von Blixen-Finecke, born 1916, son of Baron Hans von Blixen-Finecke (1886–1917), Bror Blixen's twin brother.

48. "If one does not set life at risk, then life is never won," from the finale song in Schiller's play *Wallensteins Lager* [Wallenstein's camp] (1798) which runs as follows: "Und setzet Ihr nicht das Leben ein, / Nie wird euch das Leben gewonnen sein." Karen Blixen probably learned the quotation from one of her favorite books, M. A. Goldschmidt's *Hjemløs* [Homeless] (1857), 2:1019, where Otto Krøyer cites it.

52. "Erling had the longboats launched against the king": from one of Sigvat Tordsson's plays about Erling Skjalgsøn's battle with King Olav of Norway in *Olav den Helliges Saga* [The saga of King Olav the saint], translated by Gustav Storm in Snorre Sturlason's *Kongesagaer* [Sagas of the kings] (Kristiania, 1900).

54. Johannes Poulsen's book: the travel book *Gennem de fagre Riger* [Through the fair kingdoms] (1916) by the eminent Danish actor Johannes Poulsen.

57. "In the Masai Reserve—": from Karen Blixen's poem "Ex Africa" (1915), published in *Tilskueren* magazine April 1925.

58. The Swedish Baron Carl Erik August von Otter, 1889–1923, went to British East Africa in 1914. During World War I, he served in the East African Mounted Rifles. A captain in the King's African Rifles in 1916, he became commander of all the troops in Turkana and a memorial tablet was erected to him in All Saints Church in Nairobi. Von Otter married Helga Maria Stenborg in 1911, and they were divorced a few years later. Two daughters survived him.

58. "High on the quarterdeck in the morning": from the first stanza of Bjørnstjerne Bjørnson's poem "Olav Trygvason" whose first line runs, "Wide sails over the North Sea fly."

59. Neither the poem nor the accompanying letter seem to have been preserved.

64. Hans Hartvig Seedorff's collection of Danish poems, *Hyben* [The rose hip], was published in 1917 and soon republished in several editions.

66. Daughter of the previous Governor: either Miss C. E. M. or Miss G. S. E. Belfield, daughters of Henry Belfield.

68. Musset's poem to Victor Hugo: the sonnet "A M. Victor Hugo," written 26 April 1843, the three last lines of which run as follows: "On s'approche, on sourit, la main touche la main, / Et nous, nous souvenons que nous marchons ensemble / Que l'âme est immortelle, et qu'hier, c'est demain."

69. "Lived a woman wonderful": first line of Rudyard Kipling's poem "South Africa" (1903).

70. "The same beeches and light nights": from the Danish poet Johannes V. Jensen's poem "Envoi" (1910).

71. The idea of allotting free or cheap land to ex-servicemen was officially mooted by the English as early as 1915. Bror Blixen took the initiative in an attempt to procure Swedish capital to finance the plan, but both his calculations and his personal motives were deemed unacceptable. The plan was resumed and carried out on a purely English basis in 1919.

71. Land Commission: this commission made decisions regarding rights of use and grants of natives' requests for land and administered the laws relating to native reserves. On 2 March 1917, a commission was established for the parceling out of land and its function was to investigate the possibilities of granting land to soldiers of European origin who had served under the English flag during the war, either in East Africa or elsewhere.

74. Maude Windinge's first son, Erik Christian Windinge, was born 11 March 1917. Her second child, named Søren, was born 1 January 1919.

75. "Face to face should eagles do battle": retort to Erling Skjalgsøn from Sole to Olav the saint in the skald Sigvat Tordsson's poem about the fight between Erling and King Olav that ended with Erling's death on 21 June 1028. The poem is in *Olav den Helliges Saga* [The saga of King Olav the saint].

76. I have written some stanzas which I am sending you: "Vuggesang. En Moder synger for sin i Krigen faldne Søn" [Cradle song: A mother's song to her fallen son], published in Gyldendal's Christmas book *Osceola* (Copenhagen, 1962).

78. ". . . the god, your fathers' god": from the story *Isbjørnen* [The polar bear] in Hans Kaarsberg's *Stort Vildt* [Big game] (1901). The original runs thus: "The God is above me, the God of my father. This was ringing in his ears when the sea took him—the heathen."

78. "Goulash": the term used for certain people in Denmark who grew wealthy in the first world war by exporting canned food, especially to Germany.

82. Leerbæk: manor farm at Grejsdalen, Vejle, in Jutland. From 1874 to 1925 it was in the possession of Georg Sass, the agricultural commissioner, and his wife Karen Sass, née Westenholz, sister of Ingeborg Dinesen. In 1925, Leerbæk was taken over by Karen Blixen's younger brother Anders, who had been assisting his uncle in running the farm since 1920. Georg and Karen Sass stayed on at the manor house until their death, while Anders Dinesen preferred to live at the so-called Hopballehus, a much more modest residence on the estate. In 1956, Thomas Dinesen took possession of Leerbæk, which since 1962 has been owned by his youngest son.

82. The old man in the armchair: Karen Blixen's paternal uncle, Laurentzius Dinesen (who possessed the courtesy title of Master of the Royal Hunt), lived at Katholm. In 1910, he suffered a stroke and another in 1915.

84. The harbor at home: the small harbor on the Sound at Rungsted, now a large pleasure boat marina.

85. "Veldt sores": chronic sores; a South African term for desert sores, painless but difficult to heal, appearing on the arms and legs, affected by various types of bacteria, including diphtheria.

88. "Victory in your hand and victory in your foot": from the Danish folk song "Svend Vonved," also cited in Christian Richardt's libretto for Peter Heise's opera *Drot og Marsk* [King and lord high constable] (1878).

90. Thomas Dinesen was awarded the Victoria Cross on 26 October 1918.

91. "Le superflu, chose très nécessaire" (Voltaire, *Satires, Le Mondain,* 9 November 1736).

93. Our neighbor Johnnie: Johnnie van de Weyer, a farmer.

94. Alfred de Musset's sonnet about Beatrice Donato (1838) is included in his story "Le fils du Titien"; it contrasts fame unfavorably with life.

94. "Alles geben die Götter": from Goethe's poem "An Auguste Stolberg" (1777).

95. Thomas Dinesen was awarded the French decoration on 27 September 1918.

95. I am sending you a clipping from one of our newspapers: this must be the article in *The Leader,* 21 December 1918, with the heading "Baroness Blixen's Brother Gets V.C."

98. "Nun, armes Herz": from Ludwig Uhland's poem "Frühlingsglaube," set to music by Franz Schubert (1820).

99. The Polowtzoffs: the Russian General Peter A. Polowtzoff and his wife. They fled during the revolution and lived in Monte Carlo for many years, as described in his book *Monte Carlo Casino* (New York and London, 1937). His other book, *Glory and Downfall—Reminiscences of a Russian General Staff Officer,* appeared in Russian in Paris in 1927 and in English in London in 1935.

99. During the rapid advance into eastern Europe by the Bolsheviks shortly before peace was signed in 1919, Aage Westenholz, brother of Ingeborg Dinesen, was the leading figure in the formation of a voluntary Danish corps that went to aid the Baltic countries in their struggle against Communist occupation. The establishment of the corps was not greeted with unanimous enthusiasm in the Danish press, and when the first Danish losses were reported from Estonia, criticism broke out in earnest, particularly in *Politiken.* A protest meeting called by the Radical Youth in Copenhagen movement resulted in the reporting to the police of Aage Westenholz and the other organizers concerned, charged with unlawful recruitment of Danish mercenaries. The dispute about the corps lasted for several months before dying down.

111. During his visit to the farm, the company chairman, Aage Westenholz, wanted Karen Blixen to move into an extremely modest, primitively furnished house, "The Grass House," to show her willingness to save money, but this Karen Blixen categorically refused to do.

116. ". . . je mourai si de cette hauteur": from act 3, scene 6 of Rostand's *Cyrano de Bergerac* (1897). In the original, Cyrano's reply runs as follows: "Et vous me tueriez si de cette hauteur / Vous me laissiez tomber un mot dur sur le coeur!"

118. Gerda Møhl-Hansen, 1878—1962, daughter of Mary Westenholz's brother, Octavius Hansen, a barrister. In 1903 she married the painter Karl Kristian Møhl-Hansen; her daughter Ida was born in 1904 and her son Ulrik in 1908.

119. "Here he is, where he longed to be": from Robert Louis Stevenson's poem "Requiem" (1884), used as an inscription on his own grave. The two stanzas of the poem run thus:

> "Under the wide and starry sky
> Dig the grave and let me lie.
> Glad did I live and gladly die,
> And I laid me down with a will.
>
> This be the verse you grave for me:
> Here he lies where he longed to be,
> Home is the sailor, home from the sea
> And the hunter home from the hill."

124. An English lady: Jacqueline ("Cockie") Birkbeck, née Alexander.

134. The church: Hørsholm Kirke, in Sealand. Ea Neergaard was buried beside other members of the family in Hørsholm churchyard.

134. Grandfather's "quick eye and quick wit": from Wilhelm Dinesen's inscription for his parents, Chamberlain A. W. Dinesen and his wife, on their tombstone. A. W. Dinesen's inscription reads, "Strong of soul, of arm, of voice, / carried not his sword in vain, / quick of eye and quick of wit / one of Denmark's fine men." Dagmar Alvilde Dinesen's inscription reads, "Thought only of others good / tender of heart and mild of mind / strong in adversity, compliant in good fortune / noble, faithful good woman and true."

135. The little poem I sent to Thomas during the war, about the star above the trench: the poem, "En Stjerne" [A star], was printed in Thomas Dinesen's war memoirs, *No Man's Land* (1929).

138. I have been reading a book by Wells about the Washington Conference: H. G. Wells, *Washington and the Hope of Peace* (London, 1922). The Washington Conference, 12 November 1921 to 6 February 1922, was attended by representatives from the United States, England, France, Japan, Italy, Belgium, China, Holland, and Portugal. Treaties were signed regarding the island possessions of the first four powers in the Pacific, as well as the limitation of their naval forces and the use of submarines in wartime, and forbidding the use of poisonous gas as a weapon.

141. After the death of Ea de Neergaard on 17 June 1922, Viggo de Neergaard needed a change from the sad situation at home, and late in the year he left Denmark with his cousin, Peter de Neergaard, Master of the Royal Hunt, to stay for a month or two as Karen Blixen's guests on the farm.

146. "The Indian question" was aggravated in 1923 when the government in London planned to give the franchise to some 35,000 Indians in Kenya. So much opposition was raised by the 10,000 Europeans that the government was forced to drop the proposal.

150. Zahrtmann's letters: the Danish painter Kristian Zahrtmann's letters to Benedicte Frölich, a selection published by M. K. Zahrtmann in *Tilskueren* magazine, March 1923.

150. Those one-acters by Otto Benzon: the dramatic trilogy *Forældre* [Parents], consisting of "Interiør" [Interior], "Landskab med Figurer" [Landscape with figures] and "Genrebilled" [Genre picture], first performed at The Royal Theater in January 1923.

152. Cellini's autobiography was published in Danish in 1900 in two volumes.

153. Mama's biography: memoirs of her life at Matrup, Folehave, and Rungstedlund written by Mary Bess Westenholz, printed in *Blixeniana 1979*.

154. "Say then, what is the *spirit* of Jesus's teaching?": one of Saint Peter's many questions to the soul in the first act of Johan Ludvig Heiberg's play *En Sjæl efter Døden* [A soul after death] (1841). The original reads, "Say then, what is the spirit of Christ's teaching."

155. The poem about "The divine serpent": The Dane Sophus Claussen's poem "Man," written on Capri in 1903, was published in 1904 in the collection *Djævlerier* [Diableries].

162. "Offered in a crystal goblet," "offered in a golden goblet": from Ludvig Bødtcher's poem "Høstminde" [Harvest remembrance] (1865).

163. "Il n'y a que le premier pas, qui coûte," written by Madame du Deffand (1697–1780) in a letter dated 7 July 1763.

164. The Land Department was established in 1903 and controlled all the land in British East Africa belonging to the Crown. It specified the conditions for the conveyance of land and the collection of purchase money and rents. In addition, it supervised the parceling out of agricultural and urban plots, temporary occupation (in the country) and improvements in agricultural methods. The department was responsible for valuation of country areas and authorization of building plans.

164. All applications for land had to be made directly to the Land Inspector in Nairobi; these had to supply information as to the size of the area and the type of land required—whether it was to be used for farming, removal from town, or pasture.

166. Nøddebo Vicarage is featured in Henrik Scharling's Danish novel *Ved Nytaarstid i Nøddebo Præstegaard* [New Year at Nøddebo Vicarage] (1862), later dramatized by Elith Reumert.

167. "Death is nothing, winter is nothing": from Sophus Claussen's poem "Røg" [Smoke] (in Kulrøg [Chimney smoke] [1899]), penultimate stanza. The remainder of the stanza reads, "For the flames, the fire / have reerected the fallen altars of my youth /in the grass by the spring." See Karen Blixen's letter to Thomas Dinesen dated 20 November 1928, p. 388.

170. Managing director: Karen Blixen's position in the Karen Coffee Co. from 19 June 1921, when the agreement for her appointment was signed by Aage Westenholz and Karen Blixen and witnessed by Thomas Dinesen.

173. "What concerns respectability": from Trop's reply to Ledermann in J. L. Heiberg's Danish vaudeville comedy *Recensenten og Dyret* [The critic and the beast] (1826), scene 14. The original reads, "Those who are against political economy, public utility, what concerns respectability. . . ."

174. Legislative Council: an assembly consisting of officials and private individuals that had authority to promulgate laws, establish the necessary law system and offices, and administer the laws necessary for the maintenance of public order and administration in the protectorate, later the Crown Colony of Kenya.

175. A little piece on sexual morality: *Moderne Ægteskab og andre Betragtninger* [Modern marriage and other observations], an essay containing twelve chapters, the manuscript of which was sent to Thomas Dinesen in May–June 1924 and printed in *Blixeniana 1977*.

180. Audhild: Aashild, a character in Sigrid Undset's novel *Kristin Lavrandsdatter.*

181. Young Jocelyn: young Jolyon in Galsworthy's novel.

184. Fru Slott-Møller's book: *Folkevise-Billeder* [Pictures from folksongs], by the Danish painter Agnes Slott-Møller (1923).

188. Without "a shade of irony in the voice": from the Danish author J. P. Jacobsen's *Breve og Strøtanker* [Letters and jottings], printed in *Digte og Udkast* [Poems and drafts] (1886). There it reads, "No educated person in our time can utter the word 'touching' without a shade of irony in the voice."

191. Peter M. Aarup, ca. 1860–1924, came from an old Danish family of fishermen and was in youth himself a sailor and fisherman. He went to Africa around the turn of the century, where he made a living as an excellent boatbuilder in East Africa; among other things he built pleasure boats for the sultan of Zanzibar. As he grew older he became almost blind but never ceased working on big new projects. He was the first person to succeed in finding and catching fish in the great Athi River near Nairobi—thus instituting the large-scale fishing in this river that still today supplies Nairobi with fresh fish. In 1924, the government decided to reward his efforts with a monthly pension for the rest of his life, but shortly afterward he died. In 1887, Aarup became the father of a daughter born to a Danish girl and remained in contact with his daughter's family.

194. "—I have relatives in abundance": from Ragnhild's speech in Henrik Hertz's Danish play *Svend Dyrings Huus* [Svend Dyring's house] (1837), act 4, scene 3. The original reads, "Yes, it is sad, one has relatives in abundance; / they see how one's cheek pales with affliction. / But it never occurs to them that one is suffering, / unless the dead send pity from the grave."

197. My old "Owl": Karen Blixen's painting "Still Life with a Stuffed Owl," which Aunt Bess had on her wall at Folehave (reproduced in *Karen Blixens tegninger* [Karen Blixen's drawings], published by Frans Lasson [1969]). The painting is now in the possession of Thomas Dinesen's youngest daughter, Ingeborg Michelsen.

198. Countess Anne of Winchilsea died on 24 June 1924.

199. "Those remaining to you will flush at your name": from the last stanza of the Danish poet B. S. Ingemann's poem "Til Dannebrog" [To the Danish flag], whose first line reads, "Fly proudly on Codan's waves." The reference reads, "See those remaining to you / They flush at your name / For your honor they will go / With joy to death's embrace. . . ."

201. Old Nepken: the Dane who spent his life in Africa, Johan Dobi Nepken, 1870–1966. Born on the Danish island of Lolland, he emigrated to South Africa in 1895 and went to Kenya in 1912. After World War I, he built a waterworks for the Magadi Soda Company and was later appointed manager of the works and inspector of the 160 kilometer waterpipe from the Ngong Hills to Magadi Lake. Nepken was a first-class hunter; because of the lightning speed of his reactions to game, the natives called him *Bwana Chui* ("Mr. Leopard").

202. "Dost thou think, because thou art virtuous": from Shakespeare's *Twelfth Night,* act 2, scene 3. The sentence blends both Sir Toby Belch's and the fool's speeches, freely cited from memory, a habit of Karen Blixen's.

202. "I never experienced the life of a youth": from the second stanza of J. P. Jacobsen's poem "Der hjælper ej Drømme" [Dreams are no help], in the collection *Hervert Sperring* (1867–68, published posthumously in 1886 in *Digte og Udkast* [Poems and drafts]). The orginal reads:

> I own I had a childhood sweet and rich,
> But childhood is naught but smoldering life,
> And I never experienced the life of a youth,
> Alas, I dreamed that away in the land of shadows,
> Never came to grips with the world,
> Have never been a youth—and now am man.

206. "On the Rock of the Word": from the hymn "Ye Shall Build Your House on the Rock of the Word" (1878), by Jakob Paulli, dean of Copenhagen cathedral (1844–1915).

208. "She was lovable and he loved her": epigraph to chap. 1 of Heine's *Ideen: Das Buch le Grand* (1826) (Danish translation by Sophus Claussen, 1901).

212. ". . . mobility of spirit. . .": from the Danish poet Carsten Hauch's *Minder fra min Barndom og Ungdom* [Memories of my childhood and youth] (1867), p. 203.

215. He had a letter from his . . . brother: Guy Montague George Finch Hatton, later fourteenth earl of Winchilsea.

215. Your article in "Gad's Magazine" on lion-hunting: "Paa Løvejagt i Østafrika" [Lion-hunting in East Africa] by Thomas Dinesen, (Gad's Danish magazine), 1924, pp. 51–64.

218. His father and mother could never get on together: Lord and Lady Enniskillen.

218. Martensen-Larsen's book: *Tvivl og Tro* [Doubt and faith] (1909).

218. What Kormak said to Stengerde: the quotations in Karen Blixen's essay originate not from *Cormac's Saga* but from J. P. Jacobsen's saga-pastiche *Kormak og Stengerde* [Cormac and Stengerde], written about 1868 and published in *Digte og Udkast* [Poems and drafts] (1886). The text in Karen Blixen contains a few divergences. See *Moderne Ægteskab og andre Betragtninger* [Modern marriage and other observations], chap. 7, p. 31.

226. The individual, a concept in Søren Kierkegaard's thought, is mentioned, e.g., in the foreword to *Two Edifying Discourses* (1843) and *The Viewpoint from Which I Write* (1859).

232. Yesterday I went to the theatre to see *L'Idiot:* Fernand Nozières and J. Wladimir Bienstock's dramatization of Dostoievski's *The Idiot,* had its premiere at the Vaudeville in Paris in April 1925.

233. Karen Blixen stayed in Paris during 25 March–1 June 1910, partly in order to attend a French art college.

240. Henry Stormont, thirteenth earl of Winchilsea, died on 14 August 1927.

243. Thomas Dinesen was married to Jonna Lindhardt on 7 April 1926 in Aarhus, Jutland.

245. "Stop one's mouth and one's ears": from the Danish folksong *Agnete og Havmanden* [Agnete and the merman]: "He gagged her ears, he gagged her mouth. . . ."

247. ". . . that which I would, I do not, and that which I would not do, I do": variation of "the good that I would, I do not, but the evil that I would not do, I do." Rom. 7:18.

247. "There is no longer a staircase to hell": from Sophus Claussen's poem "Trappen til Helved" [The staircase to hell] (1904).

247. ". . . the Devil is expensive to talk to": from Claussen's poem "Djævlerier" [Diableries], published in 1904 in the collection of the same title. In the original, the second line of the quotation reads, "a boastful flash from his fiery tail of stars."

251. Ingeborg Dinesen was seventy years old on 5 May 1926.

252. "A master of the arts and graces": from Robert Louis Stevenson's epitaph to J. D. (James Durrisdeer) at the end of his novel *The Master of Ballantrae.* In the original, the second line reads, "admired in Europe, Asia, America."

254. The Rothe children: Pastor Oluf Rothe's children were Jens Vilhelm Rothe, born 1911; Nina Rothe Friedberg, 1916–70; and Bendt Rothe, born 1921. Oluf Rothe's second wife, Lilli, née Lindhardt, was the sister of Jonna Dinesen.

257. Your article about Rosenborg Gardens: The Society for the Improvement of Copenhagen held a competition in 1925. Ellen Dahl's entry won a prize and was also published in the society's magazine *Forskønnelsen* [Improvement] 16, no. 2 (1926) under the signature "M."

258. Old G. B.: Georg Brandes.

260. What is life? the wind in the reeds: from the penultimate stanza of Adam Oehlenschläger's poem about a Danish king and his housecarls "Bjarkemaal" (1804). The whole stanza reads in the original,

What is life then?
A puff of air in the reeds,
That sinks down;
A waste of strength
That yearns upward
Toward an eternity.
To Eternity
So morning-red
The road down here
Goes only through death.

260. "And you—you have begun to live": from the end of the Danish author Jakob Knudsen's story "Gamle Andersen" [Old Andersen], in *Jyder* [Jutlanders] (1915).

261. The fable of a flying competition: "The Wren," from Grimm's fairy tales (the Danish edition by Carl Ewald was in Karen Blixen's library).

263. "—and however enchanting a well-formed girl's calf": from Boganis, *Jagtbreve* [Hunting letters] (1889), p. 146.

263. "Women of bygone days": from the introductory words to chap. 6 of Selma Lagerlöf's novel, *Gösta Berling's Saga*.

264. ". . . the letter killeth, but the spirit giveth life": 2 Corinthians 3:6.

266. "There is life in a look at the Crucified One": from an English missionary hymn by Amelia Matilda Hull (ca. 1825–82), entitled "Life in Christ." Norwegian translation by Eveline Heede (1820–83), the first lines reading, "There is life in a look at the bleeding lamb, / there's salvation, O sinner, for thee" (hymnbook of the Danish Inner Mission [1945], no. 503).

269. After their honeymoon, Thomas and Jonna Dinesen moved in at Serridslevvej 8, in the Østerbro district of Copenhagen.

269. "The home of my soul, of my heart": from Jakob Knudsen's autobiographical story "Bortliciteret" [Contracted], in *Jyder* [Jutlanders].

269. "In the night I hear / from silent woods": first stanza of Holger Drachmann's poem "Jeg hører i Natten" [In the night I hear]. The three last lines in Karen Blixen's version are taken from the final stanza of the poem; in the original, the first stanza ends, "I am called, I am coming out there."

270. Assignat: security issued by the French government from 1789, originally a mortgage deed on sequestrated church property, later functioning as a kind of paper money.

270. My old simile: refers to a favorite story of Karen Blixen's, "The Roads of Life," told to her as a child and described in *Out of Africa*, sec. 4, "From an Immigrant's Notebook."

271. "The Loves of the Parallels," pt. 3 of Aldous Huxley's *Those Barren Leaves* (1925).

277. A cigar divan: a small booth selling cigars where customers could sit on sofas and smoke.

279. "Spirit and Truth": John 4:23–24.

282. "One whom men love not and yet regret": from Shelley's "Stanzas Written in Dejection, Near Naples" (1818), stanza 5.

283. "Gradually lost her footing out of uncertainty": from Bjørnstjerne Bjørnson's novel *Det flager i byen og påa havnen* [The flags are flying in town and harbor] (1884), sec. 4, chap. 2. The original text reads, "From jealousy and uncertainty she had gradually lost her footing, so that she hopped about in her thought and body like a bird; she wanted to appear so overjoyed, so absorbed in brilliant subjects and music. . .until one day her strength gave out, she sank down."

283. Bibi's faggots: the Swahili word *bibi* is used here as a term for an elderly married native woman.

286. "The joy of my life!": from Viggo Stuckenberg's poem "Ingeborg,"1, in the collection *Sne* [Snow] (1901).

291. East African Women's League: founded 14 March 1917, its objects were to stimulate women's interest in the duties of citizens; to further unity, cooperation, and charity for the public good; to found district libraries and set up classes for Red Cross lectures; and to further the welfare of women and children throughout the colony.

294. "The forest's light-footed sons. . . the herds bellow": from stanza 2 of the Danish poet Johannes Ewald's ode "Rungsteds Lyksaligheder" [The delights of Rungsted] (1775) that begins, "Where the herds bellow / to the forest's light-footed sons."

294. "—Peasants or bards": from the Danish poet Emil Aarestrup's poem "Skaaler ved et Barselgilde" [Toasts at a christening party], written in 1833, published in *Efterladte Digte* [Posthumous poems] (1863). Presumably written out from memory. The two stanzas are cited in transposed order, abbreviated, and with some divergences from the poet's original text.

297. "The sweltering night has bestowed its gifts": first stanza of Ludvig Bödtcher's poem "Piazza Barberina" written in Rome in 1830, published in 1866. In the original, the fourth line reads, "From Rome's orange-rich gardens."

298. My own beloved snow-whitest lamb: an expression taken from eight-year-old Karen Neergaard's birthday poem for her grandmother Ingeborg Dinesen's seventieth birthday, 5 May 1926, which reads, "A snow-white lamb has seen its chance. . . ." Karen Blixen later used various versions of this expression to address her mother in letters.

300. Sigrid M. Gliemann: in her journal from her stay in Kenya, Ingeborg Dinesen states that she met this lady several times. She was Danish born but taught English at the Aga Khan School in Dar-es-Salaam.

300. "What is Truth?": John 18:38.

302. "Take the wings of the morning": Psalms 139:9.

302. "Grow and thrive, charm and be charmed": from Emil Aarestrup's "Skaaler ved et Barselgilde" [Toasts at a christening party], stanza 2. The original reads, "May you blossom and thrive, charm and be charmed."

304. High Court: in Karen Blixen's time the legal system of the colony consisted of the high court, whose jurisdiction covered all persons and all cases and which dealt with all serious criminal and civil cases; lower courts, presided over by magistrates (classes 1–3); lower courts for natives in the coastal areas, presided over by Arabic *liwali'er* and *kadhis* (their jurisdiction covered the coast dwellers in most civil cases); and native tribunals, generally traditional tribal courts, whose jurisdiction covered the members of the tribe in minor civil and criminal cases, under the supervision of the local magistrates.

304. Your day of celebration: Aunt Bess was seventy years old on 13 August 1927.

304. Mrs. Drost's children and the Court at Nusve: probably titles of now unknown stories, either written by Karen Blixen in childhood or told to the children at Rungstedlund by Aunt Bess. *Nusve:* "Venus."

306. "He that is unmarried careth for": 1 Corinthians 7:32–33.

307. *Mr. Stankelben's Strange Journeys and Adventures on Land and Sea* (1845), by the Swiss writer Rodolphe Töppfer (1799–1846); first Danish translation 1847. This in the typescript, referred to "Daddy Longlegs," but that translation of *Stankelben* was given up. This translation was in the possession of the Dinesen children. Karen Blixen was reminded of the book when Thomas went hunting butterflies in Africa, as Mr. Stan-

kelben was a lepidopterist who, in the picture book, was always trying to escape from his tormentor and sister Stine.

314. In the summer of 1927 Thomas Dinesen sent his sister the manuscript of an article he had written on birth control.

327. The two Thomases: Thomas Dinesen and Karen Blixen's cousin Thomas Westenholz, both married in 1926.

328. Gustaf Adolph: Gustaf II Adolf, king of Sweden, 1594–1611–1632.

334. Farah's wife has arrived: the young Fathima.

336. In one of Blicher's stories: "Den sachsiske Bondekrig" [The Saxon peasant war], first printed in *Nordlyset* [The northern light] (1827). Steen Steensen Blicher [1782–1848] was one of Karen Blixen's favorite Danish authors.

336. In a modern story—by Jakob Wassermann: the tale called "Golowin," in *Der Wendekreis* (1920); Danish translation by Carl Gad in *Den ensomme Gæst* [The solitary guest] (1924).

338. On Mols: Ellen and Knud Dahl's summer residence, Neder Strandkjærgaard, was in Mols, the peninsula in east Jutland.

338. "So softly drove the shepherd his flock in the cool of evening": from the Danish poet Thomas Kingo's love poem "Chrysillis" (1669), stanza 6.

338. The quotations from folksongs in this letter seem to have been composed freely from memory, and Karen Blixen's chief purpose in using them was to convey an intimately Danish mood. Some lines from well known folksongs are recognizable, e.g., from "Ridder Stigs Bryllup" [Childe Stig's wedding]. Karen Blixen possessed a copy of *Udvalgte danske Viser fra Middelalderen* [Selected Danish ballads from the Middle Ages], edited by Abrahamson, Nyerup, and Rahbek, vols. 1–4 (1812–14), which she had with her on the farm.

342. When Karen Blixen's younger sister was twenty-one, she suffered an accident. She was ready to go to a party and was standing in front of the stove at Rungstedlund in evening dress when the draft swept her dress into the fire. She was very severely burned and for some months the doctors feared for her life; the worst burns were on her shoulders and neck. Deeply shocked by the experience, Elle lost some of her confidence in life and the future (information supplied by Thomas Dinesen to the editor).

349. "It's all his fancy that": from Lewis Carroll's *Alice's Adventures in Wonderland*, chap. 9, where the Gryphon says, "It's all his fancy that: he hasn't got no sorrow, you know."

350. The Poulsens: the two brothers, Danish actors Adam and Johannes Poulsen.

352. Max Bruch's concerto: Violin Concerto in G. Minor, opus 26, 1866.

353. Byskov's book: *Talt og Skrevet. Foredrag, Artikler, Afhandlinger* [Spoken and written: lectures, articles, papers] by Jens Byskov (1927).

357. *Albondocani* (Arabic: *Al-Bunduqani* = "person of Venetian origin"), one of the names of the Caliph Haroun al Raschid, when he appeared in disguise. See the story "Albondukani" in *A Thousand and One Nights*, published in Valdemar Thisted's Danish rendering (Copenhagen, 1895–96), vol. 4. Perhaps used by Karen Blixen with a hidden allusion to *The Merchant of Venice*, the story of which she had told to Farah.

358. "The landscape that lies around us": first line of the Norwegian writer Bjørnstjerne Bjørnson's poem "Tæmme eller tæmmes" [Tame or be tamed]. The whole poem runs:

> The landscape that lies around us
> and threatens with sea and mountain,
> winter cold and summer pale,

slow to smile and never yielding,
that's the giant that must be tamed,
so that we may have our will.
He must carry, he must pull,
he must hammer, he must saw,
he must mill light in the waterfall,—
all the roaring, the defiance,
will between the fjord and mountain
build for us a realm of beauty.

361. The heir to the English throne paid an official visit to Kenya in the autumn of 1928. His stay was interrupted by the sudden serious illness of King George V, which necessitated the prince's return home in the middle of December.

364. "Si on n'a pas ce que l'on aime": the French writer Count Roger Bussy de Rabutin (1618–93) in a letter to Madame de Sévigné.

369. Karen Blixen had received a portion of "Miss Emy Dinesen's Family Trust Fund," created 17 December 1925 for the benefit of descendants of Chamberlain A. W. Dinesen, Katholm. The trust fund, which still exists, was to be allotted principally to women in the family. Emy Dinesen died on 25 January 1927 in Randers, Jutland.

376. "Myself as the whole man": English translation from the Norwegian of Peer Gynt's words to Solveig in the final scene of Ibsen's *Peer Gynt* (1867): "Where was I, as myself, as the whole, the true? / Where was I, with God's stamp on my brow?"

376. Master of the Royal Hunt Fritz Ræder, two of whose children were Cæcilie and Thyra Ræder, died on 24 November 1928 in Copenhagen at the age of eighty-four.

379. The lion skin that Karen Blixen wished to present to King Christian X, was not delivered to Amalienborg Palace, the royal residence in Copenhagen, until 1930. The king wrote her his personal letter of thanks on 23 December 1930. This letter was the factual background to Karen Blixen's saga about *Barua a soldani* ("Letter from a king"), and for many years the lion skin lay in the banqueting hall in the palace building in Amalienborg built for Christian VIII (1786–1848), where Christian X lived; but now it no longer exists (information from a letter by Sybille Bruun, private secretary to Queen Ingrid of Denmark, to Karen Blixen dated 8 January 1960).

381. "A word of God made flesh": John 1:14.

383. Before the Prince of Wales's visit to Kenya, Karen Blixen was training her horse Poorbox for a spring race meeting in Nairobi arranged for the special occasion.

387. Vivienne de Watteville, who died in 1957, was daughter of the Swiss natural historian and big game hunter Bernard Perceval de Watteville of Bern (1877–1924), whom she accompanied on his travels. After his death she presented his large collections to the Natural History Museum in Bern. In 1930 she married George Gerard Goschen (1887–1953). She was author of *Out in the Blue* (1927) and *Speak to the Earth: Wanderings and Reflections among Elephants and Mountains* (1935).

388. Your book: *No Man's Land*, that Thomas Dinesen was writing during these months with material from his own notes and letters about his active service in World War I.

390. And can say with Ambrosius Stub: in Chr. K. F. Molbech's Danish play *Ambrosius* (1878), act 4, scene 5, Ambrosius Stub says to the Baron, "No, Sir Baron! Once I forgot myself and kneeled to an idol. . .I will not do so again. From now on I will bend the knee only to my God and maker."

391. "Never dies": from Ludvig Bödtcher's poem "Skjulte Kræfter" [Hidden powers] (1867).

396. "Little Marguerite": probably a character in a comedy written and performed by the Dinesen sisters in their childhood at Rungstedlund.

398. I am enclosing a picture of my house that Denys took from the air: the photograph is reproduced in *The Life and Destiny of Isak Dinesen,* collected and edited by Frans Lasson, with text by Clara Svendsen (Chicago, 1976), p. 137.

401. Denys's land: Denys Finch Hatton owned a piece of land on Takaungu Bay, 50 kilometers north of Mombasa.

401. The heir apparent visited Kenya again in February 1930, intending among other things to go on safari. Presumably through Denys Finch Hatton, who was to lead the planned expeditions, Karen Blixen offered to accommodate the prince on the farm during his stay. However, her offer was not accepted. Later on a rumor arose in the family that Karen Blixen had refused the prince's request to stay at her house, an insinuation that she indignantly refuted.

404. "Acted and not talked": variation of "he does not talk but acts," from the fifth stanza of the Danish author Peter Faber's poem "Den tappre Landsoldat" [The brave soldier] (1848).

408. "Children don't like long rubbishy love-scenes": from H. C. Andersen's story "The Puppet Master," originally printed in his travel book *In Sweden* (1851). The original text reads, "Little ones don't like long rubbishy love scenes, what they want is something sad but quick."

410. *Dictionnnaire des contemporains = Dictionnaire universel des contemporains:* international French biographical dictionary, vol. 5, 3d ed. (Paris 1865), p. 43. This states that H. C. Andersen has been mentioned also in previous editions.

412. "Bedar's bird": the natives' name for Denys Finch Hatton's airplane, a De Havilland Gypsy Moth, which he bought in 1929 and had transported by sea to Kenya. The registration letters of the machine were G-ABAK.

413. Paracelsus: pseudonym used by Ellen Dahl for her first book *Parabler* [Parables], Copenhagen (1929).

413. I am really excited to hear you are writing another book: Ellen Dahl's *Introductioner* [Introductions] appeared in 1932, again under the pseudonym "Paracelsus."

414. "After the Alberti affair on 19 August 1909, when Parliament was discussing national defense at an extraordinary session, suddenly a lady who had managed to gain entry to the house came in, took the chairman's bell, rang it, and began to speak. The lady was Mary Bess Westenholz, who, according to newspaper reports of the time, said, 'In this assembly there sits a man who has brought shame on Denmark' (here Miss W. pointed to the ministerial bench, and was understood to be indicating J. C. Christensen). 'Here you sit, you Danish men, bargaining and bartering the welfare of the country in overweening ambition and self-interest, but it will be said from this place that the women of Denmark despise you and brand you as a mob of hirelings without a country, who are selling the honor of Denmark.'. . .The chairman, Anders Thomsen, disconcerted, rang the bell loudly but only managed to stammer out in his very weak voice, 'She took my bell.'—The scene gave rise to much attention and comment, also since at that time it was unheard of for a woman to speak in Parliament." From T. Vogel-Jørgensen, *Bevingede Ord* [Winged words] (1963), col. 406.

416. "I plucked the best rose of life": from stanza 2 of "My Helmet for Me is Too Bright and Heavy," the skald's song in act 4 of Adam Oehlenschläger's tragedy *Hagbarth and Signe* (1814).

422. The Native Affairs Department (Nairobi): it dealt with inspection of work and administration of and census of Africans. The department issued regulations and determined conditions of work for the natives.

Index

The index does not include references to Karen Blixen, Ingeborg Dinesen, or Thomas Dinesen. Ngong as a letter-heading is not listed. An asterisk following a page number indicates that there is a note to the name or subject in question (see notes pp. 433 ff.).

Aage, Uncle. *See* Westenholz, Aage
Aarestrup, Emil (1800–1856), Danish poet and doctor, 150, 294*
Aarup, Peter M. (ca. 1865–1924), Danish-born boat-builder in Kenya (appears in *Out of Africa* under the name of Old Knudsen), 191,* 193, 200
Aasebakke, property at Sjælsø, Høsterkøb, North Sealand; belonged to Lennart Grut (1881–1949), 349
Abdullah Hassan, also known as "the Mad Mullah," leader of the Dervishes in Somaliland, 69, 174
Abdullahi Ahamed, relative of Farah, Somali servant to Karen Blixen on the farm, 43, 46, 48, 66, 104, 152, 199, 226, 273, 278, 289, 303, 304, 416, 424
Abdullai, ca. 1907–26, young Somali taken by Karen Blixen to Denmark during 1919–20, 54, 83, 138, 272, 289
Aberdaire, i.e., Aberdare, chain of mountains to the north of Nairobi, 30
Absalon (1128–1201), Danish archbishop, 94, 163, 393
Academy of Art (Copenhagen), 246, 356
Acting governor. *See* Bowring, Sir Charles
Abyssinia, north-east Africa, 224
Adam (biblical), 291
Adam Homo, contemporary Danish verse novel by Frederik Paludan-Müller (1841–48), 175
Aden, 1, 23, 29, 38, 85, 106, 230
"*Admiral*," German steamship on the Naples to Mombasa route, xlii, 58, 296
"*Admiral Pierre*," steamship plying between Mombasa and Marseilles, 230
Africa, 16, 32, 33, 37, 43, 100, 101, 104, 125, 126, 133, 144, 145, 174, 227, 231, 233, 251, 252, 265, 271, 275, 295, 297, 298, 304, 356, 357, 400, 407, 411, 412. 416, 430, 431
Aftonbladet [Evening News], Swedish daily newspaper, 379
Agriculture Department (Nairobi), 147
Ahamed Fara Aden, known as Saufe, born 1928, son of Farah Aden, 382, 383, 399, 409, 414, 417, 431
Ahlefeldt-Laurvig, Christine, née Musaeus (1863–1936), countess; lived at Flakvad south of Rungsted, 428
Aimable, one of Karen Blixen's horses on the farm, 13
Aladdin, Danish comedy by Adam Oehlenschläger (1805), 354
Albert, Prince (1819–61), 234
Alberti, P. A., 1851–1932, Danish minister of justice (1901–08), found guilty of extensive fraud in 1910, 114
Alexander the Great, (356–323 B.C.), 75
Alexandra, queen of England (1844–1925), 33, 395
Alfred, Uncle. *See* Grut, Alfred Walter
Ali bin Hassan, Somali, 43, 303, 319, 334, 397, 411, 424
Ali bin Salim. *See* Seyyed Ali bin Salim
Alice in Wonderland (1865), 330
Almannagjaa, a ten-kilometer-long ravine north of Tingvalla in Iceland mentioned several times in the Icelandic sagas, 58
Alvernia Mountain, 144
Amanzimtoti, locality near Durban, 35
America, 48, 72, 112, 176, 219
Amina, known as Kinsi, born 1930, daughter of Farah Aden, 403,404
Anemia, 415
Anders. *See* Dinesen, Anders
Andersen, Dane living in Kenya, 201

Andersen, H. C. (1805–75), Danish fairy-tale writer, 334, 378, 408, 410, 412
Andersen, P. E., Danish Consul in Nairobi, 421, 422
Andersen, Vilhelm (1864–1953), Danish literary historian, 410
Anderson, doctor in Nairobi, 154
Anker, Thomas Dinesen's Norwegian traveling companion in Kenya, 145
Anna Karenina, 87
Anne. *See* Dinesen, Anne
Antwerp, 238, 251, 252
"Aphrodite's Vapors," poem by Sophus Claussen, printed in *Tilskueren* magazine (1903), 136
Apothecary. *See* Scheel, Paul
Arcadia, 54
Archer, Sir Geoffrey (1882–1964), governor and commander-in-chief in Uganda 1922-24; in 1920 led the operation against "The Mad Mullah" in Somaliland, 174
Armistice Day (11 November 1918), 90, 132, 138
Arnette, Aunt. *See* Tegner, Arnette Margrethe
Arnold, Thomas (1795–1842), 236
Arras, Battle of (October 1914), 57
Askari (Swahili), native soldier in East Africa, 62, 333, 414
Askari (Swahili: *askari polisi* = police officer), one of Karen Blixen's dogs on the farm, son of Dusk and Dawn, 45
Assignat (security document), 270,* 322
Assisi, 42
Athi Plains, area in the neighborhood of Nairobi, 242
"Atta Troll," poem by Heinrich Heine (1843), 313
Australia, 72
Austria, 224, 429

Back to Methuselah, play by George Bernard Shaw (1921), 171
Bagatelle, i.e., le Parc de Bagatelle, in the Bois de Boulogne outside Paris, 32
Bakkehus og Solbjerg, descriptions of Danish intellectual and cultural history in the nineteenth century by Troels-Lund (1920–22), 153
Balfour, Lord Arthur James (1848–1930), British statesman, 82
Ballet, i.e., the Tivoli Ballet performed in the Pantomime Theater, Copenhagen, 334
"*Balmoral Castle*," steamship on the England-Africa route, 34
Banja (Swahili: panya = rat), one of Karen Blixen's dogs in Africa, son of Dusk and Dawn, 45, 84, 223, 272, 302
The Barber of Seville, 266
Bardenfleth, Ida, née Meldal (1856–1946), wife of Rear-Admiral, Chamberlain Frederik Bardenfleth (1846–1935); mother of Else Reventlow, 251, 345, 350
Bartels, Anna, 155
Baynes, Sir Joseph, (1842–1925); large-scale farmer and pioneer in the dairy industry in South Africa, 35,* 36
Bazaar, native business area of Nairobi, dominated by Indian merchants, 65
B.E.A. *See* British East Africa
"Beatrice Donato," sonnet by Alfred de Musset (1838), 94*
Beau Geste, French silent film by Herbert Brenon (1926) from the manuscript by Percival Christopher Wren, 408*
Bech, Ellen (1873–1953), Danish royal court singer, 353
Bech Frijs, Baron. *See* Beck-Friis, Carl Augustin
Beck, Vilhelm (1829–1901), clergyman and founder of the Danish Inland Mission, 265
Beck-Friis, Carl Augustin (1869–1927), Swedish baron; counsellor at the Legation in Paris, later envoy extraordinary in Rome, 31
"Bedar's Bird," the natives' name for Denys Finch Hatton's airplane, 412*
Beethoven, Ludwig van, 296, 313
Beethoven's piano concerto, No. 5 in E flat major, Opus 73 (1808–9), 296
Beira, sea-port in Mozambique, 37
Belfield, C. E. M., or G. S. E., daughter of Governor Henry Belfield, 66
Belfield, Lady Florence, wife of Governor Henry Belfield, 7
Belfield, Sir Henry Conway (1855–1923), governor and commander-in-chief in

Kenya 1912–17; husband of Florence Belfield, 2
Belgium, 37, 86
Bent, René, 309, 341
Benzon, Otto (1856–1927), Danish author, 150, 181
Bergen, Norway, 32, 48
Bergson, Henri (1859–1941), 64
Beri-beri, 76
Berlin, 166
Berlingske Tidende, Danish daily newspaper, 51, 293
Bernhard, Father, head of the French Catholic mission in Kenya, 253
Bernstorff-Gyldensteen, Agnes Louise ("Sophie"), née Lady Krag-Juel-Vind-Frijs (1892–1975), Danish countess; daughter of Count Mogens Frijs, 100, 263, 279
Beryl. *See* Markham, Beryl
Bess, Aunt. *See* Westenholz, Mary Bess
Bible, 36, 63, 136, 253
Bienen. *See* Krag-Juel-Vind-Frijs, Frederik
Birds around the Lighthouse, novel by Jacob Paludan (1925), 353
Birkbeck, Cockie. *See* Blixen-Finecke, Jacqueline von
Birth control, 176, 187, 201, 290, 291, 314,* 318, 320, 367
Biscay, Bay of, 238, 242, 280, 288
"Bjørneborgers' March, The," poem by J. L. Runeberg in *Ensign Steel's Tales* (2: 1860); known as song to an an old French folk-tune, 402
Bjørnson, Bjørnstjerne (1832–1910), Norwegian author, 40, 358
Blackie, Ingeborg Dinesen's Scotch terrier, 119
Black-water, complication following on malaria, 166
Bleak House, 404
Blicher, Steen Steensen (1782–1848), Danish author, 336,* 394, 396, 430
Blixen-Finecke, Bror von (1886–1946), Swedish baron, farmer and safari leader; Married (1) Karen Dinesen (1914; marriage dissolved 1925), (2) Cockie Birkbeck (1928; marriage dissolved 1935), (3) Eva Lindström, 1, 2, 3, 4, 6, 7, 8, 10, 11, 12, 13, 14, 15, 17, 18, 19, 20, 21, 22, 27, 29, 30, 31, 32, 34, 37, 38, 39, 40, 41, 42, 43, 44, 45, 46, 48, 49, 50, 51, 54, 55, 56, 60, 62, 63, 67, 68, 69, 70, 71, 78, 80, 81, 83, 84, 86, 87, 88, 89, 91, 93, 100, 102, 103, 104, 105, 108, 113, 115, 117, 122, 123, 124, 125, 132, 137, 153, 158, 182, 183, 193, 212, 214, 244, 263, 278, 287, 377, 390, 407
Blixen-Finecke, Carl Emil von (1874–1940), Swedish baron and major, owner of Näsbyholm; eldest son of Frederik von B.-F., Karen Blixen's father-in-law,45
Blixen-Finecke, Carl Fredrik von (1903–50), Swedish baron, owner of Näsbyholm; son of Baron C. E. von Blixen-Finecke, 45
Blixen-Finecke,Clara von, née Lady Krag-Jeul-Vind-Frijs (1855–1925), baroness; wife of Baron Frederik von Blixen-Finecke, Näsbyholm; Karen Blixen's mother-in-law, 31, 51, 192, 193, 214
Blixen-Finecke, Frederik von (1847–1919), Swedish baron, Master of the Royal Hunt, owner of Näsbyholm in Skaane, South Sweden; Karen Blixen's father-in-law, 8, 55, 192, 193, 263
Blixen-Finecke, Hans von (1886–1917), Swedish baron; twin brother to Bror von Blixen-Finecke, 45
Blixen-Finecke, Hans von (born 1916), baron, lieut. colonel; son of Hans von Blixen-Finecke, 45, 193
Blixen-Finecke, Hilla Brita von (1894–1943); wife of Baron Hans von Blixen-Finecke (1886–1917), 193
Blixen-Finecke, Jacqueline ("Cockie") von, née Alexander (1892), baroness; married (1) Ben Birkbeck, (2) Bror von Blixen-Finecke, 124, 288, 377
Blixeniana 1978, the third yearbook of The Karen Blixen Society in Copenhagen, edited by Hans Andersen and Frans Lasson, 30, 100
Blohm, Elisabeth, née Lady Ahlefeldt-Laurvig (1888); daughter of Count Theodor Ahlefeldt-Laurvig and Christine A.-L., née Musaeus; in 1920 mar-

ried Thomas Blohm of Viecheln in Mecklenburg (1885–1944), 110, 136
Blokken, the northernmost part of the Rungstedlund grounds, between the grove and Rungstedvej [Rungsted-road], 102
Blood-poisoning, 100
"Blossom Like a Rose-garden," Danish hymn by N. F. S. Grundtvig (1837), 107
Blue Post, The, hotel in the neighborhood of Nairobi, 65
Bödtcher, Ludvig (1793–1874), Danish poet, 297
Bogani, the main building on the second farm acquired by the limited company, Karen Coffee Company, in 1916; Karen Blixen's home in Africa from 1917 to 1931, 32, 44, 54, 60, 64, 66
Bohême, La, 266
Bombay, 100
Booth, William (1829–1912), general and founder of the Salvation Army, 328
Borre, one of Karen Blixen's creditors in Denmark, 111
Bostrøm, Erland (1876–1954), High Groom in Waiting, companion to Prince Wilhelm of Sweden on his visit to Kenya 1913–14, 2
Botha, Louis (1862–1919), South African general and politician, 36
Bowring, Sir Charles (1872–1945), chief secretary, East African Protectorate 1911–20, colonial secretary 1920–24, acting governor of Kenya 1917–19, 51, 97
Boyd Neel & Co. (Paris), 231
Brandes, Georg (1842–1927), Danish literary critic, 144, 209, 210, 211, 239, 258, 394
Bret Harte, Francis (1839–1902), 40
Brinck, A., Dane living in Nairobi, with whom the blind Peter M. Aarup lived for a time, 201
Brita. *See* Blixen-Finecke, Hilla Brita von
British East Africa, 3, 12, 27, 38, 50, 66, 85, 90, 100, 104, 108, 116
British Somaliland, 173
Bromhead, editor of the newpaper *The Leader* in Nairobi, 51
Brontë, Charlotte (1816–55), 236
Brontë, Emily (1818–48), 236
Bror. *See* Blixen-Finecke, Bror von
Bruce-Smith, friend of Karen Blixen, a neighbor in Kenya, 385, 387, 399, 406
Bruce-Smith, Felice, 376, 385, 387, 399
Bruch, Max (1838–1920), 352*
Brun, Alf (1866–1932), captain, adjutant to King Frederik VIII of Denmark 1909–12, 246
Buch der Lieder, collection of poems by Heinrich Heine (1827), 136
Buchanan, manager of the East African Syndicate farm at Gilgil, Kenya, 41, 42
Bulpett, Charles W. L. (1851–1939), globe-trotter, lived with the McMillans at Chiromo in Nairobi, 56, 87, 179, 193, 227, 344
Burkitt, Rowland Wilks, Irish surgeon; went to East Africa in 1912; resided in Nairobi, 73, 86, 154, 165, 309
Bursell, Mrs., wife of Åke Bursell, 342
Bursell, Åke Ernest Hjalmar, Swedish farmer living in Kenya from 1913, 12, 39, 40, 104, 197, 198, 214
Butler, Samuel (1835–1902), 205
Buxton, Geoffrey Charles (1879–1958), English major and farmer in Kenya; lived at Naivasha, 96, 97, 101, 103, 104, 150, 197, 282, 374
Byrne, Sir Joseph (1874–1942), brigadier-general, governor and commander-in-chief in Kenya 1931–37, 423
Byskov, Jens (1867–1955), Danish head of High School, minister and author, 353

Cabell, James Branch (1879–1958), 164
Cairo, 67, 70
"Calcutta sweep," international lottery in connection with the Derby in Calcutta, 286
Caldwell, Keith, 273
Camelias, Lady of the (1852), 341
Canada, 54, 58, 60
Canterbury, Archbishop of, 131, 367
Capallo, Conte, 316
Cape Town, 32, 34, 352
Carbery, Lady Maiä Ivy, née Anderson (1903–28); daughter of Alfred Anderson, Nairobi; in 1922 married John Ev-

ans, tenth baron Carbery, at Nyeri, 342, 352, 365, 367
Carbery, John Evans Carberry, tenth baron (1892–1970); lived at Seremai, Nyeri, in Kenya, later in South Africa; in 1922 married Maiä Ivy Anderson (died 12 March 1928), 352
Carl. *See* Blixen-Finecke, Carl Emil von
Carlton Hotel, London, 32, 49
Carlyle, Thomas (1795–1881), 63
Cartwright, Algernon ("Algy") Richard Aubrey (died 1947), English officer; owner of the farm "Melewa," Naivasha, 65, 66
Cartwright, Rose, née Buxton 1898, sister of Geoffrey Buxton; married Algy Cartwright, 1923; Lives at Naitolia, Gilgil, Kenya; their daughter Prudence married a son of Galbraith Cole, 200, 227, 426
Casparsson, Otto (1888–1941), Swede living in Kenya (appears in *Out of Africa* under the name of Emmanuelson); married Astrid Harriet Kofoed-Hansen from Korsør in Denmark (1923), 340, 341, 342, 343, 344, 361, 362, 379
Casse, Christine Bothilde Petrea, Née Winding; died 1917, 169, 170
Casse, Peter (1837–1920), high court attorney, 170
Catholicism, 138, 141, 208, 221
Cellini, Benvenuto (1500–71), 152*
Censor, i.e., the English censor in Nairobi during the first world war, 29, 94
Central Station, Copenhagen, 301
"*Chambord*," the, steamship on the Marseilles-Mombasa route, 226
Charlie's House, on the farm, 158, 177, 191
Charlottenborg, Copenhagen, site of the annual spring art exhibition, 184, 231
Chartres, Robert, duke of (1840–1910), son of the Duke of Orléans, 366
Cheops's pyramid, 14
"Children's Samaritan," 73, 76
China, 216, 251, 286
China under the Empress Dowager, by J. O. P. Bland and E. Backhouse (London, 1911), 274
Chinde, sea-port in South Africa, 34
"Chiromo," property of the McMillans in Nairobi, near Westlands, 86, 228
Choleim Hussein, Indian timber merchant in Nairobi, 363, 397
Cholmondeley, Thomas ("Tom") Pitt Hamilton, born 1900; son of Lord Delamere; fourth baron Delamere after death of father (1931), 361
Chopin, Frédéric (1810–49), 392
Chotha, Karen Blixen's blind gardener, 425
Christian IV, Danish king (1577–1588–1648), 314
Christian X, Danish king (1870–1912–1947), 379, 407
Christianity, 9, 57, 64, 140, 141, 154, 210, 389
Christmas Fun and New Year Jests, Danish comedy by Johan Heiberg (1817), 186, 334
Church, National, 154
Churchill, Sir Winston Spencer (1874–1965), 131
City Hospital, Copenhagen, 209
Clairmount House, hotel in Nairobi, 396
Clairvoyant, The, novel by Jonas Lie (1870), 142
Clara, Aunt. *See* Blixen-Finecke, Clara von
Clara van Haag's Miracles, Danish novel by Johannes Buchholtz (1916); continuation of *The God of Egholm*, 64, 89
Claussen, Sophus (1865–1931), Danish poet, 136, 247*
Clinique Valmont, Glion, Montreux; health resort in Switzerland on the north shore of Lake Geneva, 429, 432
Coates, Audrey, friend of the Prince of Wales, 377
Cole, Lady Eleanor, née Balfour, wife of Galbraith Cole, 82
Cole, Galbraith Lowry Egerton (1881–1929), son of the earl of Enniskillen; went to Kenya in 1903; owner of the farm, "Keekopey" at Elmenteita; brother of Berkeley Cole, 41, 42, 49, 66, 69, 82, 85
Cole, Reginald Berkeley (1882–1925), English officer and farmer in Nyeri; son of the earl of Enniskillen; fought in the Boer War in 1900; member of the

Legislative Council of Kenya; brother of Galbraith Cole, 174, 176, 179, 218, 219, 223, 227, 282, 387, 431
Colenso, town in eastern South Africa, 35
Collet, Holger (1864–1943), Chamberlain, Master of the Royal Hunt, owner of Katholm in Jutland, 92
Collett, Camilla (1813–95), Norwegian author, 163
Collier, Englishman on safari, 80, 81
Collin Hedvig (1880–1964), Danish painter and illustrator of children's books, 258
Colville, Lady, née Olivia Spencer-Churchill, wife of Arthur Edward William Colville (1857–1942), 401, 404
Company. *See* The Karen Coffee Company, Ltd.
Concept of Angst, The, by Søren Kierkegaard (1844), 338
Confessions (Rousseau), 247
Congo, 129, 153
Conscription, 43
Constant Nymph, The, novel by Margaret Kennedy (1924), 241, 378
Copenhagen, 30, 91, 118, 137, 184, 204, 227, 250, 301, 430
Corot, Camille (1796–1875), 370
Coryndon, Sir Robert Thorne (1870–1925); born in South Africa; governor of Uganda (1917); governor and commander-in-chief of Kenya (1922–25), 133, 135, 153, 174
Country Life, novel by Fritz Reuter (1862–63), 2
Covent Garden Opera House, London, 102
Cowie (died 1928), 352
"Cradle Song. A Mother Sings to Her Son Fallen in Battle." Poem by Karen Blixen, printed in Osceola (1962), 76
Crean, B. A., judge, occupied Coney's House on the farm for a time, 310, 385, 397
Crighton, staff member of J. W. Milligan & Co., Nairobi, 137
Croix de Guerre, 95*
Croz, Michel, French mountaineer; Died on the Matterhorn (July 1865), 56
Cæcilie. *See* Ræder, Auguste Cæcilie
Dagoretti Junction, rail junction on the ourskirts of Nairobi, on the road to Ngong, 60, 67, 158, 256, 383, 422, 425
Dahl, Ellen ("Elle") Alvilde, née Dinesen (1886–1959), author (under the pseudonym "Paracelsus"); Karen Blixen's younger sister; in 1916 married the barrister Knud Dahl, xlii, 10, 24, 29, 32,* 53, 58, 59, 90, 108, 109, 114, 128, 129, 131, 134, 139, 143, 162, 184, 197, 213, 219, 256, 270, 279, 280, 284, 291, 298, 300, 301, 308, 314, 317, 327, 328, 334, 342,* 344, 357, 375, 379, 384, 394, 404, 409, 411, 429
Dahl, Knud (1876–1945), barrister, director of "The Silk House" in Copenhagen; owner of the estate Sandbjerg, Als, an island off the coast of North Schleswig in Jutland, 53, 59, 113, 127, 156, 291, 338, 409
Daisy. *See* Grevenkop-Castenskiold, Anne Margrethe
Dallund, estate on the island of Funen, in the possession of the Blixen-Finecke from 1792 to 1915, 45, 55
Danish Love Poems, collected by Kai Hoffman (1916), 155
Dar-es-Salaam, sea-port in Tanganyika; Seat of the German East African government until the end of the First World War, when it was taken over by the English, 10, 16
Darwin, Charles, (1809–82), 171
David, one of Karen Blixen's Scottish deerhounds on the farm, 374, 411
Davis, H. Home, major in the King's African Rifles; chairman of the Kaimosi Farmers' and Planters' Association; magistrate in North Kavirondo, Kenya, 67
Dawn, one of Karen Blixen's Scottish deerhounds, 46
Deerslayer, The, novel by J. F. Cooper (1841), 61
Delamere, Lady Gladys, wife of Lord Delamere (1928–31), 384, 387
Delamere, Hugh Cholmondeley, third baron (1870–1931); pioneer and leading personality in Kenya; owner of the farm "Soysambu" near Lake Elmenteita, 14,* 15, 42, 49, 65, 66, 69,

71, 73, 77, 80, 81, 83, 85, 88, 98, 132, 133, 174, 219, 240, 361, 383
Denmark, xlii, 24, 26, 30, 32, 55, 100, 110, 117, 118, 124, 144, 146, 151, 153, 184, 186, 195, 198, 203, 210, 215, 226, 233, 244, 247, 265, 271, 272, 276, 278, 290, 295, 297, 314, 338, 358, 397, 400, 403, 407, 415
Devil, 274, 339, 344, 380, 381
Diableries, collection of Danish poems by Sophus Claussen (1904), 136, 155
Diana (mythological), 382
Dickens, Anne, daughter of W. H. Dickens, 329, 367
Dickens, Charles (1812–70), 235, 261, 404
Dickens, Mrs., wife of W. H. Dickens, 329, 365, 367, 372
Dickens, W. H., born in South Africa, for some years manager of the farm (appears in *Out of Africa* under the name Nichols), 131, 140, 145, 161, 165, 167, 177, 191, 239, 253, 266, 269, 275, 303, 318, 319, 329, 330, 341, 343, 359, 364, 367, 371, 372, 374, 401, 402
Dickinson, Finch Hatton's assistant on safari, 340, 343, 352
Dictionnaire philosophique (1764), 409
Dictionnaire universel des Contemporains (1865), 410*
Dinesen, Adolph Wilhelm (1807–76), Chamberlain, owner of Katholm, Grenaa (1839–76); Karen Blixen's paternal grandfather, 32, 134*
Dinesen, Adolph Wilhelm ("Boganis"; 1845–95), captain, author, owner of Rungstedlund, Rungstedgaard, and Folehave from 1879; Karen Blixen's father, 32, 52, 58, 90, 94, 95, 110, 111, 114, 117, 130, 134, 177, 217, 263, 335, 380, 391, 395, 427, 428
Dinesen, Anders Runsti (1894–1976), second lieutenant, owner of the manor farm, Leerbæk (1925–56); Karen Blixen's younger brother, 68, 82, 100, 101, 104, 115, 129, 171, 186, 195, 213, 268, 314, 326, 406, 409, 430
Dinesen, Anne Arendse, born 1927; eldest daughter of Thomas and Jonna Dinesen; wife of Erik Kopp (1950–75); owner of Folehave since 1958, 302, 303, 326, 327
Dinesen, Dagmar Alvilde, née von Haffner (1818–74), wife of Chamberlain A. W. Dinesen; Karen Blixen's paternal grandmother, 52, 134,* 173
Dinesen, Emilie ("Emy") Augusta (1851–1927), sister of Wilhelm Dinesen; lived at Villa Vesta, Randers, 115, 369,* 381
Dinesen, Inger. *See* Neergaard, Inger de
Dinesen, Jonna, née Lindhardt (1902); married Thomas Dinesen in 1926, 237, 239, 243, 244, 252, 254, 269,* 271, 280, 287, 289, 301, 302, 303, 326, 387, 401, 429
Dinesen, Wentzel Laurentzius (1843–1916), Chamberlain, Master of the Royal Hunt, owner of Katholm in Jutland (1876–1916); Karen Blixen's paternal uncle, 56, 82,* 177, 245
Disraëli, Benjamin (1804–81), 385
Disraëli, biographical novel by André Maurois (1927), 385
District Commissioner, 14, 140, 167, 422, 423, 425
Dixen. *See* Knudtzon, Benedicte
Djibouti, capital and sea-port of former French Somaliland, 169
Doctor, in Nairobi. *See* King, Alfred
Dombey & Son, by Charles Dickens (1848), 1
Donya Sabuk (Buffalo Mountain), 80 km from Nairobi, 67, 131, 320, 397
Dorph, Bertha (1875–1960), Danish painter, 139, 184, 197, 198, 231
Doubt and Faith, by H. Martensen-Larsen, Danish author (1909), 218
Douglas, Lord Francis, English mountaineer; died on the Matterhorn, July, 1865, 56
Doune, Lord Francis, 112, 116, 124
Drachmann, Holger (1846–1908), Danish author and painter, 166, 269, 349, 394, 396
Drachmann's Inn, in the establishment, Lorry, in Frederiksberg, Copenhagen, 394
Draga, queen of Serbia (1867–1903), 49
Dragon, the little, presumably a dog on the farm, 228
Dream, The, novel by H. G. Wells (1924), 211, 212

Dukhobors ["The Champions of the Spirit"], Russian religious sect established in the eighteenth century, 313, 375
Dulac, Edmund (1882–1953), 410
Durban, sea-port on the east coast of South Africa, 1, 32, 34, 35, 36, 37
Dusk, Karen Blixen's first Scottish deerhound in Kenya, 13, 14, 24, 45, 46, 48, 65, 80, 81, 82
Dybbøl, in Sønderjylland, North Schleswig, where the battle between the Danes and the Germans took place in the war of 1864, 78
Dyrehaven [the Deer Park], Klampenborg outside Copenhagen, 3, 50, 338
Dyrehavsbakken [the Deer Park Hill], Klampenborg, 334
Dysentery, tropical, 298, 415, 429

Ea. *See* Neergaard, Inger de
"Early Morning," poem by Karen Blixen (1924), 215
East African Protectorate, 38
East African Syndicate, 41
East African Women's League, nonpolitical welfare organization in Kenya, 291*
East London, seaport in South Africa, 34
Ebbe Skammelsøn in the Wedding Courtyard, painting by Agnes Slott-Møller, 184
Eden (biblical), 291
Edmund, Uncle. *See* Grut, Edmund Hansen
Edward VII, king of England (1841–1901–1910), 36, 333, 404
Egede, Hans (1686–1758), Danish priest and missionary to Greenland, 151
Egholm, The God of, Danish novel by Johannes Buchholtz (1915), 64, 89
Einstein, Albert (1879–1955), 116, 126, 133, 136, 164, 232, 284, 313, 378, 413
Either-Or, philosophical novel by Søren Kierkegaard (1843), 173
Ejnar Tambeskælver, great Norwegian nobleman of Trøndelagen, died c. 1055, 75
Ekman, Swedish financier, 104
Ekstra Bladet, Danish morning paper, 164
Elberfeld, industrial town in Germany, 279
Eldoret, town on the railway line from Nairobi to Uganda, 146
Elisabeth. *See* Blohm, Elisabeth
Elkington, Major, 87
Ella. *See* Taube, Ella
Elle. *See* Dahl, Ellen
Ellemandsberget, i.e., Ellemandsbjerg, the highest point on the peninsular of Helgenæs in Djursland, Jutland, 338
Ellen. *See* Wanscher, Ellen
Ellen, Aunt. *See* Plum, Ellen
Ellinor, Aunt. *See* Knudtzon, Ellinor
Elmenteita, town on Lake Elmenteita north of Naivasha in Kenya, 49
Elmenteita, Lake, 83
Elmis Hjerte, incomplete and unpublished marionette play by Karen Blixen (manuscript in the Royal Library, Copenhagen), 240
Elmorans, young Masai warriors, 16, 20
Else. *See* Reventlow, Else
Elvestad, Sven (1884–1934), Norwegian author (also wrote under the pseudonym Stein Riverton), 164
Eminent Victorians, by Lytton Strachey (1918), 119
Empire, 146, 220, 281, 337
Emy, Aunt. *See* Dinesen, Emilie Augusta
England, 36, 56, 57, 59, 89, 96, 99, 100, 153, 162, 176, 185, 195, 215, 220, 234, 235, 236, 297, 302, 316, 347, 409, 420, 423
English Magazine, The, 99
Enniskillen, Charlotte Marion, countess of, died 1937; married fourth earl of Enniskillen in 1869; mother of Berkeley and Galbraith Cole, 218
Enniskillen, Lowry Egerton, fourth earl of (1845–1924); father of Berkeley and Galbraith Cole, 218
Erichsen, Erich (1870–1941), Danish author, assistant chief constable in Sønderjylland, 237
Erling, Skjalgsøn (ca. 975–1028), Norwegian chieftain in Sole; mentioned in *Olav the Holy's Saga* and in Bjørnstjerne Bjørnson's poem, *Olav Trygvason*, 9, 52,* 75, 78

Erroll, Idina, countess of; died 1955; married to the twenty-second earl of Erroll from 1923–30, 343
Erroll, Josslyn ("Joss") Victor, twenty-second earl of (1901–41); farmer in Kenya; name until his father's death in 1928 Baron Kilmarnock; 1923–30 husband of Countess Indina of Erroll, 344
Esa, old houseboy and cook on the farm, 43, 46, 83, 139, 160
Esbern Snare, died 1204, Danish chieftain, 393
Escorial, i.e., San Lorenzo del Escorial, 131
Esmail, Somali, Karen Blixen's first cook on the farm, 12, 14, 25
Esman, Somali from the Habr Yunis tribe; Bror Blixen's gun-bearer on safari, 19, 20
Eton, 67, 319
Ette. *See* Fjæstad, Henriette
Eugenics, 293
European Hospital (Nairobi), 119, 122, 272, 309, 415
Eve (biblical), 291
"Ex Africa," poem by Karen Blixen, 1915, printed under the pseudonym Osceola in *Tilskueren* Magazine (April 1925), 215, 219

Fägerskiöld, Helge (1871–1926), Swedish baron and railway engineer, 30
Fair Haven, The, novel by Samuel Butler (1873), 205
"Fair Wind," poem by Karen Blixen, printed in *Norden's* yearbook (1943), 70, 215
Family at Gilje, The, Norwegian novel by Jonas Lie (1883), 132, 345
Fangen, Ronald (1895–1946), Norwegian critic and author, 180
Fanø, island off the west coast of Jutland, 35
Farah Aden, born c. 1885, died during the second world war, Somali from the Habr Yuni tribe; Karen Blixen's butler on the farm from 1914 to 1931, 1, 2, 4, 9, 12, 14, 20, 21, 23,* 30, 31, 38, 39, 41, 42, 43, 46, 49, 51, 54, 60, 65, 71,* 74, 76, 81, 83, 91, 104, 124, 126, 152, 156, 158, 159, 161, 165, 167, 174, 178, 179, 199, 203, 221, 226, 229, 230, 232, 269, 273, 275, 288, 290, 295, 298, 303, 304, 311, 314, 328, 330, 334,* 341, 359, 360, 362, 363, 383, 396, 398, 401, 404, 405, 409, 414, 416, 417, 423, 424, 431
Father. *See* Dinesen, Adolph Wilhelm
Fathima, married to Farah in Mombasa in 1918, 71, 83
Fathima, Farah's young wife, who arrived at the farm at New Year, 1928, 334, 363, 368, 382, 383, 399, 403, 404, 405, 414
Faust, the opera by Charles Gounod (1859), 102
Ferasi, native kitchen boy, 12
Fernanda, parlor-maid at Folehave, 161
Figaro, The Marriage of, opera by Mozart (1786), 296
"Fils de Titien, Le," short story by Alfred de Musset (1838), 94
Finch Hatton, Denys George (1887–1931), English officer, trader, and safari leader in Kenya, second son of the thirteenth earl of Winchilsea, 66, 67, 69, 77, 89, 98, 100, 103, 106, 124, 139, 142, 148, 150, 151, 167, 169, 170, 174, 176, 179, 185, 191, 196, 197, 198, 215, 224, 226, 227, 230, 239, 240, 242, 248, 253, 257, 270, 274, 280, 281, 286, 287, 288, 289, 290, 297, 298, 299, 300, 301, 304, 309, 314, 316, 319, 326, 328, 332, 335, 338, 339, 340, 343, 350, 352, 353, 359, 360, 361, 364, 374, 375, 377, 383, 384, 385, 386, 387, 396, 398, 401,* 402, 406, 407, 409, 411, 412, 413, 418, 420, 426, 430, 431
Finse, skiing resort in Norway, 52, 57
Firman Åbergsson [The Åbergsson Firm], novel by Erik Fahlmann (1914), 24
"First Meeting, The," poem by Bjørnstjerne Bjørnson, 353
Fjæstad, Henriette, née de Maré (1899); sister of Ingrid Lindström; married Nils Fjæstad (1926), 310, 339
Fjæstad, Nils, (1890–1964); plantation owner in Kenya, married Henriette de Maré (1926), 13, 310, 339

Flags Are Flying in Town and Harbor, novel by Bjørnstjerne Bjørnson (1884), 283*

Flensborg Avis, Danish daily newpaper in Flensborg, published since 1869, 246

Florence, 215, 218

Fog, Mogens, born 1904, professor at Copenhagen University and chief surgeon at the neurological department of the National Hospital (1938–74), 30, 100

Folehave, property at Hørsholm, Sealand, in the possession of the Dinesen family since 1879, 68, 82, 102, 110, 210, 213, 245, 259, 265, 279, 299, 305, 308, 327, 346, 351, 356, 428, 430

"Folksong Pictures," by Agnes Slott-Møller (1923), 184

Folk songs, 184

Folsach, Dagmar Alvilde von, née Dinesen (1874–1950); wife of Christian Caspar von Folsach, 377

Fontainebleau, 54

Forest Reserve, 158, 309

For Life's Sake, Danish novel by Jakob Knudsen (1905), 199

Forsyte Saga, The, novel by John Galsworthy (1906–1928), 181, 220, 308, 353–55

Fort Hall, town to the north of Nairobi, 422, 425

Four Lectures on Henrik Ibsen Dealing Chiefly with his Metrical Works, by Philip H. Wicksteed, (1892), 375

France, Anatole (1844–1924), 24, 175, 180

France, 53, 57, 58, 70, 72, 78, 86, 87, 88, 89, 90, 95, 110, 143, 150, 162, 195, 236, 268, 280, 316

Frascati (Italy), 280

Frederik, Uncle. *See* Blixen-Finecke, Frederik von

Frederik VI, Danish king (1768–1808–1839), 118

Frederik's Hospital, hospital in Copenhagen until 1910, 314

Frederiksborg Castle, Hillerød, Sealand, 298

Frederiksen, Mrs., Slettemose House, Hørsholm, Sealand; worked at Folehave for Mrs. Westenholz, 68

Free State, the Orange Free State in South Africa, 37

French Mission, in Kenya, 10, 141, 177, 383

French-German War, The (1870–71), 53

French Revolution, 99, 240, 258, 261, 323

French Somaliland, 189

Frijs, Frederik. *See* Krag-Juel-Vind-Frijs, Frederik

Frijs, Mogens. *See* Krag-Juel-Vind-Frijs, Mogens

Frijsenborg, castle at Hammel near Århus, Jutland; family seat of the Krag-Juel-Vind-Frijs family, 160, 336

Fritz, Uncle. *See* Ræder, Johan Carl Fritz

Fritze, Aunt. *See* Krag-Juel-Vind-Frijs, Frederikke

From the Eighth Brigade, by Wilhelm Dinesen (1889), 11,* 335,* 380

"From the Journal of a Parish Clerk," story by S. S. Blicher (1824), 394

Frydenlund, [Delightful grove], name for a short time for the house on the second farm, which was later called Bogani, 37, 40, 42, 44

Funch, Johanne Frederikke Louise, née Andersen (1868–1936); wife of Dr. Frederik Funch, Hørsholm, the Dinesen family doctor at Rungstedlund, 428

Funen, the large island between Jutland and Sealand, 55

Fyfe, Henry Hamilton (1869–1951), English journalist, author and war correspondent, 99

Gad, Misse. *See* Madsen, Emilie

Gad's Danish Magazine, monthly literary periodical (1906–53), 215, 220

Gainsborough, Thomas (1727–88), 236

Galsworthy, John (1867–1933), 220, 308, 353, 354

Game Department, 332

Game Reserve, 172, 280, 304, 383

Garman and Worse, novel by Alexander L. Kielland, Norwegian author (1880), 177

"*Garth Castle, The,*" steamship on the Marseilles-Kilindini route (Mombasa harbor), 100

Genoa, 400, 421
George, boy at Naivasha, 84
George V, king of England (1865–1910–1936), 36, 377, 395
Gerhardt, Uncle. *See* Lichtenberg, Gerhard de
German East Africa, 16, 37, 43, 46, 56, 58
Germany, 32, 43, 58, 136, 143, 224, 234, 430
Gethin, on the staff of the Swedo-African Coffee Co. Ltd., Ngong, 13
Gethin, Mrs., 16
Gex, Uncle. *See* Sass, Georg
Ghosts, play by Henrik Ibsen (1881), 341
Gilgil, town on the railway line Nairobi-Uganda, 40, 41, 42
Gilliats, i.e., John K. Gilliat & Co. Ltd., 7 Crosby Square, London. One of the oldest established firms handling coffee and other products in England, 147
Gillis. *See* Lindström, Gillis
Gladstone, William Ewart (1809–98), 349
Glion, one of the small towns constituting the health-resort of Montreux in Switzerland, 429
Glyn, Elinor (1870–1943), 375
Gösta Berling's Saga (1891), 112
Goethe, Johann Wolfgang von (1749–1832), 87
Goldschmidt, Meïr Aron (1819–87), Danish writer, 180, 186, 307, 351, 354, 403
"Golowin," story by Jakob Wassermann, published in *Der Wendekreis* (1920), 336
Gordon, Charles, lived for some years in Kenya, later secretary of the Traveller's Club in Paris, 190, 300, 431
Gordon, Honour, wife of Charles Gordon, 300
Gorringe, Captain (Ngong), 67, 90
Goschen, Mary, 70
Gothenberg (Sweden), 32
Government House, seat of government in Nairobi, 99, 101, 153, 172, 240, 362, 377, 383, 384, 402, 408, 410
Government Sale, 41
Grandfather. *See* Dinesen, Adolph Wilhelm
Grand Hôtel Louvre & Paix, Marseilles, 102
Grandmother. *See* Dinesen, Dagmar Alvilde
Grass house, on the farm, 111,* 121
Greece, 264
Greswolde-Williams, Francis ("Frank") Wigley, English farmer in the Kedong Valley, went to East Africa in 1907, 56, 96
Grevenkop-Castenskiold, Anne Margrethe ("Daisy"), née Countess Krag-Juel-Vind-Frijs (1888–1917), Karen Blixen's girlhood friend; in 1910 married Henrik Grevenkop-Castenskiold, Danish ambassador, 41,* 42, 277, 280, 282, 346, 395
Grevenkop-Castenskiold, Henrik (1862–1921); Danish ambassador to London; married Daisy Frijs in 1910, 33, 42
Grieg, Edvard (1843–1907), 74, 296, 353
Grigg, Sir Edward William Macleay, later ennobled to Lord Altrincham, first baron Tormarton (1879–1955); governor and commander-in-chief in Kenya 1925–30, 240, 361, 362, 383, 408, 410, 423
Grigg, Lady Joan ("Joannie") Katherine, née Dickson-Poynder, daughter of Lord Islington; in 1923 married the later governor Edward Grigg, 268, 273, 343, 369, 383, 429
Grut, Alfred Walter Hansen (1859–1928), factory owner; son of Alfred Hansen, merchant, brother of Mrs. Westenholz, 117
Grut, Edmund Hansen (1831–1907), Danish doctor, professor of ophthalmology, 114
Grut, Torben (1865–1952), major-general, chamberlain, 379
Grøn, Ada Louisa (1855–1939), daughter of Ludvig Grøn, merchant; lived in Copenhagen, 118
Guaso Nyiro, river in Kenya, 12, 15, 18
Gustaf 2. Adolf, king of Sweden (1594–1611–1632), 328
Gustav, Prince, 1887–1944, fourth son of King Frederik VIII of Denmark; owner of Egelund, Fredensborg, Sealand (1912–17), 56

"Gypsy Life," Danish story by Steen Steensen Blicher (1829), 394

Haarek of Thjotta (ca. 965–1036), Norwegian chieftain, 9
Haldane, John Scott (1860–1936); English physiologist and writer of philosophy, 378, 388
Halima, daughter of Juma bin Muhammed, 310, 319, 361, 362, 383, 399, 425
Hals, Frans (ca. 1580–1666), 257
Hamburg, 232
Hamilton, Gustaf (1880–1935), Swedish captain of horse 1917; Major and head of riding school 1926; husband of Tyra H., sister of Bror Blixen-Finecke, 32, 37, 40, 49, 50
Hansen, Ulf (1867–1926), barrister; son of the barrister Octavius Hansen, brother of Mrs. Westenholz, 117
Harlequin, 334
Harley, i.e., Harley-Davidson motorcycle, 135, 136, 137
Harrison, one of the solicitors in the law practice of Harrison, Creswell & Hopley, law practice in Nairobi, 164
Haslemere, town in southern England, 101
Hassan, a play in five acts by James Elroy Flecker (1922), 196
Hassan Ismail, Somali in the service of Karen Blixen, as cook and other functions, 39, 74, 198, 289, 303, 405, 414
Heartbreak House, play by George Bernard Shaw (1919), 171
Heather, one of Karen Blixen's Scottish deerhounds in Kenya, 272–73, 288, 302, 334, 374, 384, 396, 397
Heiberg, Johan Ludvig (1791–1860), Danish poet and critic, 186
Heiberg, Johanne Luise (1812–90), Danish actress, 118
Heidenstam, Verner von (1859–1940), Swedish author, 40
Heine, Heinrich (1797–1856), 209,* 313
Heise, Peter (1830–79), Danish composer, 74
Helene, Princess (1846–1923); daughter of Queen Victoria of England; wife of Prince Christian of Schleswig-Holstein, 361
Helleholm, the southern point of the island of Agers in the Great Belt, the channel between Sealand and Funen, Denmark, 67
Hellstern, shoe shop in Paris, 46
Hell, 247, 288, 339, 347
Hemsted, Henry, doctor, district commissioner in Dagoretti, 167, 174, 329, 423
Henri IV, i.e., *Enrico IV*, play by Luigi Pirandello (1922), 232
"Hermits, The," early story by Karen Blixen, printed under the pseudonym Osceola in *Tilskueren* magazine (August 1907), 239
Hero-Worship, i.e., *On Heroes, Hero-Worship and the Heroic in History,* by Thomas Carlyle (1840), 63
Herredet, [The District], novel by Thorkild Gravlund, Danish writer (1919), 186
High Court, in Nairobi, 304*
"Hill at the World's End, The," a favorite object of excursions on the Matrup estate in Jutland, 391
Hindenberg, Paul von (1847–1934), 236
Hobley, Charles William (1867–1947), acting senior commissioner in the East African Protectorate 1907; member of the Legislative Council 1912–20, 2*
Hogarth, William (1697–1764), 235
Holberg, Ludvig (1684–1754), Danish author and historian, 349
Holbæk Ladegaard, i.e., Holbæk Castle Home Farm, in Sealand; in the possession, 1913–39, of Paul Dahl, (1886–1939), brother of Knud Dahl, 109
Holmberg, Emil, farmer in Kiama, Thika, 374
Holmberg, Olga, died 1962, wife of Emil Holmberg, 16, 74, 104
Holstein, Ludvig (1864–1943), Danish poet, 239, 256, 258
Homeless, Danish novel by Meïr Aron Goldschmidt (1853–57), 186, 307
Homosexuality, 264, 270, 316
Hopcraft, J. N., farmer and hunter at Naivasha, 40

Hoskier, Emil (1830–1915), banker, Danish consul-general for Paris, 246
Hostel for the homeless, Ellen Dahl's 335, 342
Hôtel du Louvre & de la Paix, Marseilles (previously Grand Hôtel Louvre & Paix), 230
Hôtel du Quai-Voltaire, Paris, 232
Hotel Edward, Beach, Durban, 35, 36
Hotel Washington, London, 101
Hôtels St. James & D'Albany, Paris, 232
Hougaard, Alice Laura (1882–1933), owner of Rungstedgaard, 133
House of Commons, 131
House of Lords, 343
Hugo, Victor (1802–85), 68
Humlebæk, town on the Sound (Øresund) between Rungsted and Elsinore, Sealand, 67
Hunter, W. C., proprietor of the law practice in Nairobi, 71, 137, 148, 151, 158, 168, 179, 238, 272, 341
Hunting Letters, by Wilhelm Dinesen (1889, 1892), 263, 380
Huth, Erik Wilhelm Tancredo von (1895–1952), bookkeeper on the farm 1918–20; later lived at Ruiro, Kenya, 44, 80, 81, 82
Huxley, Aldous (1904–63), 271, 358
Hørsholm, town in northern Sealand, 137
Hørsholm Church, 134
Hørshom Churchyard, 119

Ibanez, Vincente Blasco (1867–1928), Spanish author, 164
Ida, Aunt. *See* Bardenfleth, Ida
Idina. *See* Erroll, Idina, Countess of
L'Idiot, play in six scenes by Nozière and Bienstock, from the novel by Dostoievski; produced in Paris 1925, published 1931, 232*
Ignatieff, Madame. *See* Polovtsoff, Elena Vladimirovna
India, 16, 112, 146, 357
Indian High Priest, who visited Karen Blixen on the farm, 363
"Indian question" (in Kenya), 146,* 156
Inge, William Ralph (1860–1954), Dean of St. Paul's, London (1911–34), 343
Ingemann, Bernhard Severin (1789–1862), Danish poet, 52
Inger. *See* Wedell, Inger
Ingrid. *See* Lindström, Ingrid
"In the Duck Yard," fairy tale by H. C. Andersen (1861), 378
Isa. *See* Esa
Isle des Pingouins, novel by Anatole France (1908), 175
Islington, Lady Anne, wife of Lord Islington, 343
Islington, John Poynder Dickson-Poynder, first baron of (1866–1936); governor of New Zealand (1910–12), 343, 423
Italian Somaliland, 316
Italy, 108, 152, 156, 286, 316, 429

Jacobin Club, 293
Jacobsen, Jens Peter (1847–85), Danish author, 202
"Jacques," Karen Blixen's story, "Uncle Théodore," published in *Carnival* (1977), 239, 412
Jama, Somali, servant of Berkeley Cole, 310
Jancé, Alice de, 344
Jensen, Mrs., 380, 381
Jensen, Thit (1876–1957), Danish author, 176, 290
Jeppe on the Mountain, Danish comedy by Ludvig Holberg, 66
Jeppesen, Knud (1892–1974), Danish composer and music historian, 257
Jesus Christ, 154, 201, 253, 347
Jevanjee, A. M., wealthy Indian merchant in Nairobi; leader of the Indian delegation that went to London in 1906 to discuss the Indian question with the British Government, 363
Jew, A, Danish novel by Meïr Aron Goldschmidt (1845), 354
Jews, 139, 154, 256, 385
Jogona, groom on the farm, 60
Johnson, Martin (1886–1937), American photographer and writer of animal books, 384
Jonna. *See* Dinesen, Jonna
Judgement Day (Sistine Chapel), 288

Juja, Sir Northrup McMillan's coffee farm, 30 km from Nairobi, on the road to Thika, 56
Juma bin Muhammed, houseboy on the farm 1916–31, 43, 46, 132, 138, 145, 161, 198, 217, 239, 303, 311, 318, 319, 333, 352, 379, 382, 406, 416, 424
Jurgen, novel by James B. Cabell (1919), 164
Jutlanders, two Danish short story collections by Jakob Knudsen (1915–17), 142
Jutland, 201
Jørgensen, Marie ("Malla"), died 1931, children's nurse at Rungstedlund from 1894; in service of the Dinesen family until her death, 110, 128, 177, 252, 303, 327, 409

Kabiro, son of the squatter Kanino, 179, 182
Kabiti, i.e., Kabete, locality on the road to Naivasha, in the Nairobi district, 67, 383, 422
Kadidja, first wife of the prophet Mohammed, 69
Kaffir, South African language, 36
Kaiserliche Schutztruppen, Die, in Dar-es-Salaam, 10
Kalifi, i.e., Kilifi, coastal town north of Mombasa, 401
Kamante Gaturra, born ca. 1910, Kikuyu, Karen Blixen's dog toto, later cook on the farm, 141, 178, 181, 182, 200, 226, 228, 303, 310, 320, 334, 386, 401, 409, 424
Kamau, Kikuyu, who took care of Karen Blixen's horse, Rouge, for many years, 44, 229, 295, 425
Kanini, native boy on the farm, 374
Kanino, squatter on the farm, father of Kabiro, 179, 182, 221, 352, 382
Kant, Immanuel (1724–1804), 313
Kanuthia, Kikuyu, Denys Finch Hatton's chauffeur in Kenya, 301, 332
Karen Blixen Society (Copenhagen), founded 3 April 1975, 30
Karen Coffee Company, Ltd., 32, 36, 37, 41, 70, 93, 105, 112, 120, 124, 137, 147, 148, 157, 164, 169, 182, 187, 265, 282, 297, 327, 415
Karen Estates (Nairobi), 109
Karl (Charles) XV, Swedish-Norwegian king (1826–1857–1872), 411
"*Karoa*," steamship on the Durban-Mombassa route, 34, 37, 38
Katholm, estate to the south of Grenaa, Jutland, in the possession of the Dinesen family 1839–1916, 45, 82, 90
Katla, one of Karen Blixen's Danish friends, 359, 375
Kavirondos, tribe in Kenya, 7,* 11, 15, 60, 68, 85
Kebri, nandi, toto employed by Karen Blixen on the farm, 44
Kedong Valley, ca. 50 km to the west of Nairobi on the borders of Ukumbu, the largest administrative province in Kenya, and Naivasha; an agricultural region where there were also successful experiments with vineyards, 14, 56, 96, 100, 411
Kennedy, Margaret (1896–1967), 241
Kenya Colony, British Crown Colony (1920), 1, 32, 72, 108, 135, 137, 182, 183, 198, 200, 233, 241, 343, 344, 361, 416, 423, 425
Kenya, Mount, 29, 56, 115, 131, 145
Kenya Nursing Home (Nairobi), 86, 129
Kiama, native court, 167, 222
Kiambu, Kikuyu district in the neighborhood of Nairobi, on the road from Nairobi to Naivasha, 191, 311, 422
Kierkegaard, Søren Aabye (1813–55), 225, 226, 338, 349
Kijabe, town on the railway line from Nairobi to Uganda, 12, 13, 14, 15, 22, 383
Kikuyu, town to the west of Nairobi, 81, 328
Kikuyu language, 182
Kikuyu Reserve, 8, 422
Kikuyu Station, nearest railway station to Ngong, 80
Kikuyus, tribe in Kenya, 5, 11, 15, 38, 44, 73, 74, 77, 140, 156, 174, 182, 198, 200, 221, 222, 258, 269, 312, 328, 329, 330, 334, 382, 409, 411, 416, 425
Kilimanjaro, 298
Kilimanjaro road, 259
Kilindini, sea-port for Mombasa, 100
Kilmarnock, Lord. *See* Erroll, Twenty-Second Earl of

Kinanjui, Kikuyu Chief in Kenya; his village was near Dagoretti in the Kikuyu Reserve, 5, 107, 167, 222, 227, 239, 386, 396, 397
Kinanjui, Thomas Dinesen's cook in Kenya, 303, 310
King, Alfred Charles, doctor in Nairobi, trained in England, 415, 429
"King Christian Stood by the High Mast," Danish national anthem by Johannes Ewald (1779), 396
King's African Rifles, the African regiment in Kenya, 64, 166
King's Garden (Copenhagen), 338
King's New Marketplace (Copenhagen), 184
Kinsi. *See* Amina
Kioi, native chief, 386
Kipling, Rudyard (1865–1936), 40, 69, 235
Kismayo, coastal town in what was at that time Italian Somaliland, at the mouth of the Juba River, 316
Kisumu, town in Kenya on Lake Victoria, 256, 352, 383
Kjellberg, J. Mbagathi, 13, 44
Knud. *See* Dahl, Knud
Knudsen, Jakob (1858–1917), Danish author, 199, 204, 260,* 269*
Knudtzon, Benedicte ("Dixen"; 1889–1943), 258
Knudtzon, Ellinore, née Hansen Grut (1859–1935), daughter of Professor Edmund Grut; in 1882 married Christian Knudtzon, director of the Bank of Denmark, 251
Knuthenborg Park, on the Knuthenborg Estate on the Danish island of Lolland, south of Sealand, 246
Kofoed-Hansen, Astrid Harriet; in 1923 married Otto Casparsson, 342
Kolbe, Dutch farmer, 49
Kolding, town of Jutland, 191
Koosje. *See* Westenholz, Ellen
Koran, 58, 64, 92, 381
Krag-Juel-Vind-Frijs, Frederik ("Bienen") (1882–1926), count, Master of the Royal Hunt; owner of Halsted Monastery, near Nakskov, Island of Lolland, 150, 322, 404
Krag-Juel-Vind-Frijs, Frederikke ("Fritze"), née Danneskiold-Samsøe (1865–1949), countess of Frijsenborg; wife of Count Mogens Frijs, 100, 105, 114
Krag-Juel-Vind-Frijs, Mogens (1849–1923), count of Frijsenborg, Jutland, politician, xlii, 12, 14, 56, 99, 114, 160, 335
Kreutzer Sonata, by Ludwig van Beethoven, opus 47 (1805), 319
Kristin Lavransdatter, Norwegian novel in three parts by Sigrid Undset (1920–22), 130, 141, 180, 181, 273, 274
Krohn, Mario (1881–1922), Danish art historian, director of the Thorvaldsen Museum (1916–21), 159

Ladysmith, South Africa, 35
Lagerlöf, Selma (1858–1940), Swedish author, 40, 112, 350
Lakepea, i.e., Laikipia, a nonnative district administered from Rumuruti, 100 km to the north of Naivasha, 30
Land Commission, 71,* 96
Land Department (Kenya), 164*
Land Office (Nairobi), 164*
Lanvin, French couturier, 256
Lascelles, Sir Alan Frederick, born 1887; private secretary to the Prince of Wales 1920–29; later private secretary to George V, George VI and Queen Elizabeth II, until 1953, 386, 387
Laura. *See* Hougaard, Alice Laura
Laurentzius, Uncle. *See* Dinesen, Wentzel Laurentzius
Leader, The daily newspaper in Nairobi, 51
League of Nations, 240, 316
Leerbæk, manor farm in the Grejs Valley, Vejle, Jutland, 82,* 109
Legation, the, i.e., the Danish Legation in Paris, 231
Legh, Piers Walter (1890–1955), second son of Baron Newton, Lieutenant-Colonel, adjutant to the Prince of Wales, later Master of the royal household until 1953, 386, 387
Legion of Honor, French decoration, 32
Legislative Council (Kenya), 174*

Lettow-Vorbeck, Paul von (1870–1964), German general, 2, 10, 43, 57, 58
Lettres d'un Soldat, unidentified book about the experiences of a young French artist at the front during the first world war, 87
Leunbach, Jonathan Høegh (1884–1955), doctor in Copenhagen from 1925; co-founder of the World League for Sexual Reform, 1928; author of publications on birth control and sexual education, 290
Levin, Poul (1869–1929), Danish author, editor of *Tilskueren* magazine, 256, 265
Lewenhaupt, Claës Gustaf August C: son (known as the count of Aske; 1870–1945), Swedish count, naval officer and landowner, 2
Lichtenberg, Gerhard de (1845–1927), landowner, husband of Wilhelm Dinesen's sister Anna Ulrikke Dinesen, 191
Lidda, Aunt. *See* Sass, Karen
Life Recalled through Recollection, A, memoirs of the Danish actress Johanne Luise Heiberg (1891–92), 185
Likoni, Kenya, coastal area south of Mombasa Island, 401
Lilian, friend of Thomas Dinesen, 97
Lille Kongensgade, Copenhagen street, 54
Limoru, i.e., Limuru, locality and railway station ca. 20 km north of Nairobi in the Kiambu district, 145, 333
Lindhardt, Jonna. *See* Dinesen, Jonna
Lindhardt, Theodora, née von Bülow (1860–1931), wife of Archdeacon Vincentz Lindhardt, Aarhus, Jutland, 254
Lindström, Gillis (1882–1958); Swedish lieutenant; living in Kenya from 1920; owner of the farm "Sergoita", Njoro; married Ingrid de Maré, 1911, 108, 115, 131, 214, 377–78
Lindström, Ingrid, née de Mare, 1890; Swedish farmer at Njoro Kenya; lived in Kenya from 1920, 108, 115, 131, 214, 311, 377–78
Lindström, Nina, daughter of Ingrid and Gillis Lindström, 115, 311, 377–78
Lindström, Ulla, daughter of Ingrid and Gillis Lindström, 115, 311, 377–78
"Lion-hunting in East Africa," article by Thomas Dinesen in *Gad's* magazine (1924), 215*
Llewellyn, Evan Henry (1871–1948); brigadier general, brother of lt.-colonel John Malet Llewellyn, commander of The King's African Rifles, 67, 97
Llewellyn, John ("Jack") Malet (1885–1945), lt.-colonel, brother of Brigadier General E. H. Llewellyn; went to East Africa 1911, 97, 185, 223
London, 31, 32, 33, 34, 43, 100, 101, 103, 147, 155, 162, 197, 204, 215, 343, 379
Long, Gennessee, wife of E. Caswell ("Boy") Long, Elmenteita, who was from 1912 to 1927 manager of several of Lord Delamere's properties in Kenya, 377
Longonot Crater (2777 m. high), extinct volcano in the Rift Valley near Naivasha, 384
Longonot Ltd., agricultural supplies firm, 83
Lori, Mrs. Dickens's native garden help, 329, 330, 340
Lorrain, Claude (ca. 1600–82), 59
Louis XIV, (1638–1643–1715), 377
Love Poems, by the Norwegian poet Herman Wildenvey (1922), 155
Lucerne (Switzerland), 144
Lucifer (Latin: light-bringer), 246, 247, 249, 288
Lugano (Switzerland), 10
Lulu (Swahili: pearl), tame antelope who arrived at the farm in July 1923, 160, 265, 294, 296, 338
Lumbwa, district south of the railway line to Kisumu, 41, 60
Lund, Troels. *See* Troels-Lund, Troels
Luther, Martin (1485–1546), 326
Lutzen, the Misses. *See* Lytzen, Elisabeth and Mathilde
Lytzen, Elisabeth (1851–1934), Miss; for many years lived with her sister Mathilde Lytzen in the grace and favor residences at Hørsholm, Sealand, 118
Lytzen, Mathilde (1853–1925), Miss; sister of Elisabeth Lytzen, 118

Machakos, town southwest of Nairobi, 161, 422
Mackenzie, Lady, American woman on safari in Kenya, 20
McLean, participant in one of Denys Finch Hatton's safaris, 230
McMillan, Lady Lucie, née Fairbanks Webber (1869–1957); in 1894 married Sir Northrup McMillan, 56, 86, 87, 131, 135, 179, 228, 231, 238, 344, 353
McMillan, Sir William Northrup (1872–1925); born in the U.S.A., went to East Africa 1904; farmer, member of the Legislative Council; ennobled 1918; lived at Chiromo, Riverdale in Nairobi, 2, 56, 86, 87, 131, 135, 179, 228, 231, 431
Madsen, Emilie ("Misse"), née Gad (1884–1957), wife of Dr. Thorvald Madsen, for many years director of the Serum Institute, Copenhagen, 350
Magic Flute, The, opera by Mozart (1791), 65
Magleaas, Aage Westenholz's property at Sjælsø, Høsterkøb, North Sealand, 245, 279, 330, 349
Mahaa or Mahu. *See* Mannehawa
Malaria, 4, 10, 12, 31, 154, 272, 303
Malla. *See* Jørgensen, Marie
Mama. *See* Westenholz, Mary Lucinde
"Man," poem by Sophus Claussen, Danish poet (1904), 136, 155*
Man-Eaters of Tsavo and Other East African Adventures, The, by J. H. Patterson (1907), 9*
Mannehawa, daughter of Juma bin Muhammed, born 1918, 138, 145, 161, 175, 425
Man of Property, The, part 1 of John Galsworthy's novel, *The Forsyte Saga,* (1906), 220
"*Mantola,*" steamship of the Mombasa-Marseilles route, 432
Marie Antoinette (1755–93), 240
Marie Louise, Princess of Schleswig-Holstein (1872–1956), daughter of Prince Christian and Princess Helene; grandchild of Queen Victoria, 361
Maritzburg. *See* Pietermaritzburg
Marjama, one of Esa's young wives, 160
Markham, Beryl, née Clutterbuck, writer; wrote the memoirs *West With the Night* (1943), 387
Marriage, 47, 113, 117, 122–23, 124, 125, 159, 168, 181, 182, 188, 189, 201, 206, 210, 211, 213, 216, 219, 223, 225, 243, 250, 254, 262, 263, 270, 276, 294, 305–6, 321, 323, 324, 325, 330, 337, 346, 348, 364, 365, 366, 367, 370, 371, 372, 373, 374, 390, 392, 393, 394, 399, 418
Marseilles, 32, 100, 102, 103, 169, 198, 226, 230, 297, 301, 432
Martensen-Larsen, H. (1867–1929), dean of Roskilde Cathedral, Sealand, 218
Martin, Betty, daughter of Hugh Martin, 164, 167
Martin, Florence, née Northey, daughter of Governor E. Northey; wife of Hugh Martin, 164
Martin, Humphrey ("Hugh") Trice (1888–1931; head of the Land Office in Nairobi; educated at Oxford; arrived in East Africa 1917, 164, 227, 423
Marx, Karl (1818–83), 260
Mary, queen of England (1867–1953); wife of George V, 377
Mary, Virgin, 189, 399
Masai, tribe in Kenya; nomads and cattle breeders, 5, 9, 11, 15, 18, 20, 22, 23, 29, 30, 49, 73, 88, 174, 179, 182, 258, 304, 332, 416, 424
Masai Reserve, 5, 18, 49, 57, 79, 88, 98, 124, 219, 230, 402, 416, 424
Master of Ballantrae, The, novel by Robert Louis Stevenson (1889), 252
Matrup, estate near Horsens, Jutland, owned by the Westenholz family since 1853; Ingeborg Dinesen's childhood home, 61, 109, 229, 251, 252
Maturri, native boy, 178, 179
Mau, The, hill to the west of Lake Naivasha; forms the southern slope of the The Great Rift Valley, 100
Maura, Ali's wife, 310, 319, 334
Maurois, André (1885–1967), 385
Mbagathi, name of the first farm and its main building; Karen Blixen's home in Africa from January 1914–March 1917; the Karen Coffee Co. owned both this and the second larger farm, Bogani, 4,

6, 7, 8, 10, 11, 12, 13, 17, 23, 24, 26, 29, 39, 41, 45, 168, 342, 343, 362
Mecca, 4
"Mephistopheles and the Photographers." *See* "The Photographers and Mephistopheles"
Melbourne, Lord William Lamb (1779–1848), English statesman, 367
Merete. *See* Finsen, Merete
Meru, mountain to the southwest of Kilimanjaro in what was then Tanganyika Territory, 340
Merwede, Ida van der (1836–1917), lived at Bjerre Mill, belonging to the Matrup Estate in Jutland, 61
Michelangelo Buonarotti (1475–1564), 288, 347
Miles, Miss, one of Thomas Dinesen's friends in Kenya, 229
"Milking Time," poem in Robert William Service's collection, *The Rhymes of a Red-Cross Man* (1916), 75
Milligan, J. W., Karen Blixen's business connection in Nairobi; the firm of J. W. Milligan & Co., founded in 1912, dealt in real property, leasehold, and an extensive export-import business, 102, 137, 147, 168, 341, 343
Milton, John (1608–74), 260*
Minerva, Karen Blixen's tame owl on the farm, 229, 231
Missekatten (Puss-cat), Missen, Mitten. *See* Neergaard, Karen de
Modern Marriage and Other Observations, essay in 12 chapters by Karen Blixen, written 1923–24, published in *Blixeniana*, 1977, 175,* 181, 216, 218, 219, 225
Mogadishu, capital and largest sea-port of what was then Italian Somaliland, 316
Mogens, Uncle. *See* Krag-Juel-Vind-Frijs, Mogens
Mohammed (570–632), 62
Mohr, Fridtjof Lous (1888–1942), Norwegian forestry graduate, farmer and author; brother of Gustav Lous Mohr; married the painter Joronn Sitje in 1928; from 1928–39 lived at Rongai, Kenya, 386, 410, 411
Mohr, Gustav Lous (1898–1936), farmer in Kenya; born in Norway, son of Olaf Eugen Mohr and Jeanette Lous; brother of Fridtjof Mohr, the painter Hugo Lous Mohr and Professor Otto Lous Mohr, 145, 164, 276, 338, 402, 404, 411, 413, 415, 418, 419, 420, 426, 431
Mohr, Mrs. *See* Sitje, Joronn
Mols, in Djursland, Jutland, 338, 394, 413
Mombasa, sea-port in Kenya, 1, 2, 31, 39, 48, 71, 99, 100, 104, 152, 226, 227, 230, 273, 297, 301, 342, 344, 361, 386, 387, 401
Mombasa Island, coral island, site of the town of Mombasa, 401
Mongaj, native robber captain, 382
Montague, Lady Mary Wortley (1689–1762), English letter-writer, 173
Monte Carlo, 100
Montessori, Maria (1870–1952), 159, 163
Montreux (Switzerland), 432
Monyu, native, 328
"Moonlight," poem by Karen Blixen, published in *Norden's* yearbook (1943), 215
Morley, Christopher (1890–1957), 419
Mortimer, A. F., and Mrs. (Naivasha), 85
Moscow, 318
Moshi, town at the foot of Kilimanjaro in what was then Tanganyika Territory, 344
Moss and Soil, Danish collection of poems by Ludvig Holstein (1917), 64
Motherwell, Miss, nurse, 67
Mountain Health Resort, "Kijabe Hill," British East Africa, 12
Mourier-Petersen, Alvilda (1832–1911), wife of the landowner Ferdinand M.-P., 413
Mourier-Petersen, Ferdinand (1825–98), politician, chamberlain; owner of Rugaard, Grenaa, Jutland, 119
Movoroni, Uasin Gishu, 66
Muhammed Juma, called Tumbo (Swahili: stomach), born 1921; son of Juma bin Muhammed, 161, 175, 228, 231, 252, 297, 310, 318, 319, 353, 363, 379, 396, 398, 409, 410, 411, 425

Mullahen. *See* Abdullah Hassan
Munich, 215
Musset, Alfred de (1810–57), 68,* 94*
Muthaiga, i.e., the Muthaiga Club in Nairobi; founded 1914; white-only membership; in 1919 had about 250 members, whose chairman was Lord Delamere, 142, 150, 151, 174, 352, 387
Møhl-Hansen, Gerda, née Hansen (1878–1962); married to the Danish painter Karl Kristian Møhl-Hansen, 118*
Møller, Miss, 338

Näsbyholm, Blixen-Finecke estate, xlii, 192, 263
Nairobi, capital of Kenya, 3, 7, 17, 27, 29, 30, 31, 35, 37, 41, 44, 45, 54, 65, 66, 67, 73, 77, 86, 87, 90, 96, 97, 109, 131, 132, 139, 141, 145, 150, 154, 158, 161, 164, 168, 172, 174, 179, 181, 186, 193, 195, 200, 226, 227, 248, 256, 272, 280, 297, 298, 301, 304, 309, 311, 319, 329, 333, 340, 341, 342, 344, 352, 359, 363, 372, 377, 382, 383, 387, 396, 398, 402, 404, 406, 410, 415, 416, 422, 423, 426, 429
Nairobi Station, 227, 385
Naivasha, town on Lake Naivasha in Northern Kenya on the railway line from Nairobi to Uganda, 11, 40, 42, 50, 78, 79, 80, 83, 84, 86, 92, 99, 100, 377
Naivasha, Lake, 50, 78, 83, 84, 95, 384
Naivasha Station, 81
Nakuru, town on the railway line from Nairobi to Uganda, 71, 80, 81
Nakuru Hotel, 81
Nanyuki, town at the foot of Mount Kenya, 309, 385
Napoleon I (1769–1821), 75, 318, 323, 328, 392
Naples, xlii, 288, 296
Narok, town in the Narok region to the west of Nairobi, 332
Narok, high-lying region south of the Mau, to the west of Nairobi, 14
Nash's Magazine, English periodical, founded 1909, 211, 220
Natal, province in British South Africa, 36, 39
National Gallery (London), 162
National Hospital (Copenhagen), 30, 48, 100, 114, 217
National Museum (Copenhagen), 238
Native Affairs Department (Nairobi), 422*
Native Hospital (Nairobi), 178, 181, 221, 266, 272, 310, 329, 379
Native Maternity Home (Nairobi), 369
Nduetti, native servant of Karen Blixen on the farm, 229
Neergaard, Inger ("Ea") Benedicte de, née Dinesen, Karen Blixen's elder sister; concert singer; in 1916 married Viggo de Neergaard, of Valdemarskilde, Sealand, 6, 10,* 32,* 47, 50, 65, 74, 109, 114, 126, 127, 128, 129, 132, 134, 136, 137, 143, 159, 212, 213, 282
Neergaard, Karen Christence de (1917–50), daughter of Ea and Viggo de Neergaard, 55, 66, 127, 129, 130, 131, 132, 159, 211, 213, 252, 255, 310, 361, 396, 399, 408
Neergaard, Peter de (1871–1931), Master of the Royal Hunt, Groom in Waiting; owner of Taarnborg, Slagelse, Sealand; cousin of Viggo de Neergaard, 141*
Neergaard, Viggo de (1881–1965), owner of the estate, Valdemarskilde, Sealand; married (1) Ea Dinesen (1916), (2) Elisabeth Perrochet (1925), 47, 65, 84, 113, 114, 128, 130, 132, 136, 139, 141,* 145, 148, 153, 159, 213, 296
Nel, maternal grandfather of the South African General Louis Botha, 35
Nel's Rust, Sir Joseph Baynes's property in South Africa, 35
Nepken, Johan Dobi (1870–1966), Africa-Dane, lived in the Ngong Hills, 201,* 341, 385, 397
New Arabian Nights, by Robert Louis Stevenson (1882), 227
New Stanley Hotel (Nairobi), 276, 341
New Testament, 126
New York, 52, 75
Ney, Michel (1769–1815), French marshal, 318
Ngong, 51, 67, 90, 93, 98, 102, 148, 230, 240, 269, 296, 310, 314, 320, 332, 411, 418, 421

Ngong Boma, 424
Ngong Hills, 3, 83, 90, 98, 108, 135, 144, 185, 201, 229, 269, 298, 311, 312, 332, 385, 411, 412, 418, 430
Ngong Road, 377, 383, 431
Nice, 231
Nielsen, Harald (1879–1957), Danish literary critic, 263
Nightingale, Florence (1829–1910), 347
Nile, 69, 99, 352
Nimb, Henriette (1863–1919), restaurant owner, 233
Nimb, Serina Emilie (1865–1939), 233
Nina. *See* Lindström, Nina
Nisbet, factory manager on the farm after H. Thaxton, 319, 344
Nisbet, Mrs., wife of Nisbet, 319
Nisse. *See* Fjæstad, Nils
Njoro, town on the railway line from Nairobi to Uganda, 81, 108, 121, 295, 377
Njoro Station, 81
No Man's Land, reminiscences of the first world war by Thomas Dinesen (1929; English edition: *Merry Hell,* 1930), 403
North Sea, 101
Norfolk, i.e., The Norfolk Hotel, Nairobi, 341
Norway, 196
Northey, Sir Edward (1868–1953); major general, governor and commander-in-chief in Kenya, 97, 121, 130, 133, 164, 431
Northey, Lady Evangeline, died 1941, wife of Governor Northey, 121, 133, 141, 431
"Now It Is Chiming for the Christmas Feast," Danish hymn by N. F. S. Grundtvig (1817), 177
Nyeri, town in the vicinity of Mount Kenya, 223, 422
Nyhavn [New Harbor] (Copenhagen), 54, 262
Nørre Fælled (Copenhagen), 177

Oehlenschläger, Adam Gottlob (1779–1850), Danish poet, 150, 349, 430
Olav Audunssøn in Hestviken and *Olav Audunssøn and his Children,* Norwegian novel in two parts by Sigrid Undset (1925–27), 359
Olav the Holy's Saga, 52, 57
Olav Trygvason, king of Norway (995–1000), 395
"Olav Trygvason," poem by Bjørstjerne Bjørnson (1862), 58, 75, 353, 395
Old Testament, 410
Olga. *See* Holmberg, Olga
Orfeo ed Euridice, opera by Christoph Willibald Gluck (1762), 296
Orléans, Philippe Ferdinand, duke of (1810–42), 366
Orléans, Hélène, duchess of (1814–58), 366
Orungi, plains in the neighborhood of the Ngong Hills, 158, 312
Osceola, pseudonym, used by Karen Blixen when publishing her first stories and poems, 1907–25, 215
Otero, Caroline ("La belle Otero"; 1868–1965), well-known demimondaine, 56, 375
Otter, Erik von (1889–1923), Swedish baron and officer; went to British East Africa 1914, 58,* 62, 66, 67, 90, 166,* 190, 347
Our Mutual Friend, novel by Charles Dickens (1865), 404
Out of Africa(1937), 32
Oxford, England, 211, 218, 243

Palme, Swede who lived for a time on the farm, 191, 332
Painting, Karen Blixen's practice of, 37, 43, 130, 135, 139, 150, 151, 152, 174, 184, 197–99, 203, 215, 233, 240
Pangani, district in the northeastern urban part of Nairobi, in the vicinity of Muthaiga, 318, 319
Papa. *See* Westenholz, Regnar
Paracelsus, pseudonym used by Ellen Dahl when publishing her books, 413
Paradise Lost (1667), 260
Paradise, 246, 249, 288
Parents, three Danish one-act plays by Otto Benzon (1923), 150*
Paris, 31, 32, 38, 46, 53, 76, 78, 90, 100, 101, 102, 103, 110, 127, 151, 163, 195, 204, 215, 226, 231, 232, 233, 246, 250, 251, 318, 375, 419

Paris, the count of, i.e., Louis Philippe Albert (1838–94), son of the duke of Orléans, 366
Paul the Apostle, 306*
Pedro, wakamba, toto, 312
Peer Gynt, play by Henrik Ibsen (1867), 376
Pegasus, English warship in the first world war, 38
Penholder, The, novel by Elin Wägner, Swedish author (1910), 24
Persia, 112
Peter. *See* Casse, Peter
Peter, Saint, 291
"Photographers and Mephistopheles, The," Danish story by Meïr Aron Goldschmidt (1863), 351
Piccadilly, 33, 101, 277
Pickwick Papers, by Charles Dickens (1836), 404
Pietermaritzburg, town ca. 75 km west of Durban, South Africa, 35, 36
Pilate, Pontius, 300*
"Pine Hills, The," area south of Rungstedlund, originally owned by the Dinesen family, 68
Pirandello, Luigi (1867–1936), 232
Pjuske. *See* Banja
Plato (427–347 B.C.), 350
Plum, Ellen (1836–1913), daughter of A. N. Hansen, wholesale merchant in Copenhagen (Karen Blixen's great-grandfather); wife of Peter Plum, 114, 163, 246, 250
Plum, Peter (1829–1915), Danish chief surgeon, professor, 246, 250
Politiken, Danish daily newpaper, 51, 99, 375
Polowtzoff, Elena Vladimirovna, née Ochotnikova; wife of (1) Count Alexei A. Ignatieff (1877–1954), Russian officer and diplomat, on the staff of the Russian legation in Copenhagen from 1908–1912; and (2) General Peter A. Polowtzoff, 99, 232
Polowtzoff, Peter A., born 1874, Russian general, refugee from the Revolution, 99,* 190, 232, 321
Polytechnic Institute (Copenhagen), 32
Pontemolle, Danish ballet by August Bournonville (1867), 49
Pooran Singh, Karen Blixen's Indian smith on the farm, 226, 239, 333, 406, 409
Poorbox, one of Karen Blixen's horses on the farm, 383
Port Said, 54, 226
Posma, Dutch farmer, 49
Possible Worlds and other Essays, by John Scott Haldane (1927), 388
Poulsen, Adam (1879–1969), Danish actor and theater administrator, 350
Poulsen, Johannes (1881–1938), Danish actor and producer, 54, 62, 85, 256, 350
Prahl, Helene, friend of the three Dinesen sisters, 306
Principles of Social Reconstruction, by Bertrand Russell (1916), 291
Professor Umbrosus, by Sven Elvestad, Norwegian author (1922); historical-political satire in the style of *Gulliver's Travels*, 164
"*Pundua*," steamship on the Mombasa-England route, 100

Rabelais, François (ca. 1494–1553), 225
Racine, Jean (1639–99), 235, 409
Ragnarok, 75, 168
Ralli, wealthy European on safari, 19
Ramadan, the Islamic month of fasting, 15, 71, 73, 398
Rameses II, king of Egypt (1292–1225 B.C.), 371
Randers, town in Jutland, 119
Rasch, Carl (1861–1938), professor, chief surgeon at the National Hospital in Copenhagen, Department of Dermatology and Veneral Diseases (1911–31), 30, 31, 47, 100, 151, 195, 215
Rathenau, Walter (1867–1922), German-Jewish statesman and social philosopher, 237
Red Sea, 198, 251, 295
Rejaf, Africa, 352
Rentz, Uncle. *See* Dinesen, Wentzel Laurentzius
Repsdorph, Halfdan (1868–1941), Danish barrister, 182, 229
Reserve, the. *See* Masai Reserve

Reventlow, Anne Sybille (1888–1918), countess; sister of Eduard Reventlow, 350
Reventlow, Eduard (1883–1963), count, diplomat, later Danish ambassador to London, 33
Reventlow, Else, née Bardenfleth (1884–1964), countess, wife of later ambassador Eduard Reventlow; Karen Blixen's childhood friend, 33, 41, 118, 350
Revenge of Truth, The, marionette play by Karen Blixen, published in *Tilskueren* magazine (1926), 5,* 6, 165, 222,* 239, 246, 257, 258, 265
Révolte des Anges, La, by Anatole France (1914), 24
Reynolds, Sir Joshua (1723–92), 236
Ridley, Merwin, farmer, Chania Bridge, Thika, 215
Rio de Janeiro, 403
Ritchie, Archie, chief game warden, Kenya, 304
Riverton, Stein. *See* Elvestad, Sven
"Robbers' Cabin, The," Danish story by Steen Steensen Blicher (1827), 394
Robinson Crusoe, by Daniel Defoe (1719), 357
Rolin, Belgian businessman, 37
Romanticism, 323
Rome, 215, 246, 265, 280
Rongai, locality ca. 3 km west of Nakuru, 410
"Rosenborg Garden," article by Ellen Dahl, published in *Improvement* 16 (1926), under the signature "M," 257*
Roskilde Monastery, Sealand, 163
Rossetti, Dante Gabriel (1828–82), 236
Rothe, Oluf (1880–1966), Danish clergyman, 254*
Rôtisserie de la Reine Pédauque, La [Queen Goosefoot], novel by Anatole France (1891), 175
Rouge, one of Karen Blixen's horses on the farm, 172, 266, 302
Rousseau, Jean-Jacques (1712–78), 247
Royal Highlanders of Canada, Canadian regiment in the first world war, 54
Rubenstein, Ida (1885–1960), 232
Rugaard, manor farm estate near Katholm, Grenaa, Jutland, in the possession of the Mourier-Petersen family from 1857, 119, 414
Rundgren, Ture, Swedish member of staff at the Swedo-African Coffee Co.; later an independent coffee farmer in Kenya, 13, 22, 40
Rungsted Boarding School, founded 1900, 419
Rungsted Church, 119, 129
Rungsted Harbor, 84
Rungstedgaard (Rungsted Farm), neighboring property to Rungstedlund, in the possession of the Dinesen family 1879–1920, 217
Rungstedlund [Rungsted grove], 24, 32, 39, 100, 102, 110, 134, 141, 143, 213, 233, 237, 244, 251, 255, 258, 273, 279, 295, 303, 400, 420, 426, 428, 432
Russell, Bertrand (1872–1970), 291
Russia, 99, 138, 224
Ræder, Auguste Cæcilie, née Ræder 1888; wife of Johan Georg Jacob Ræder, Norwegian consul at Johannesburg, S. Africa, 29
Ræder, Johan Carl Fritz (1843–1928), Master of the Royal Hunt, owner of the Palstrup estate in Jutland; husband of Thyra Valborg Ræder, née Dinesen, sister of Wilhelm Dinesen, 375*
Ræder, Thyra, née Ræder (1877–1957), sister of Cæcilie Ræder; housekeeper to Anders Dinesen for many years, 326
Ræder, Thyra Valborg, née Dinesen (1847–1929); wife of Fritz Ræder; mother of Cæcilie and Thyra Ræder, 155
Rørdam, Torkil Skat (1876–1939), Danish nonconformist minister, 154
Rørdam, Valdemar (1872–1946), Danish author, 403

Saafe. *See* Ahmed Farah Aden
Sagas, 52, 75, 254
Sahara, 17, 30
Said, Somali boy, friend of Abdullai, 83
Salvation Army, 48
St. John's Night Play, Danish play by Adam Oehlenschläger (1803), 334
Sanna, i.e., Susanna Ovesen, children's nurse at Matrup, 210

Sass, Georg (Uncle Gex; 1851–1943), owner of the manor farm Leerbæk in Jutland 1874–1925; husband of Ingeborg Dinesen's sister, Karen Westenholz, 82, 117, 211
Sass, Karen (Aunt Lidda), née Westenholz (1861–1949), sister of Ingeborg Dinesen, 2, 82, 114, 208, 211, 229, 370, 381, 387, 390, 410, 416
Saufe. *See* Ahamed Farah Aden
"Saxon Peasants' Battle, The," Danish story by Steen Steensen Blicher (1827), 336*
Schubert, Franz (1797–1828), 74, 296, 383
Schumann, Robert (1810–56), 74
Scots Guards, 93
Scotch Mission, i.e., Church of Scotland Mission, Kikuyu, founded in 1898, 87, 140, 141, 220
Scott, Lord Francis George Montagu-Douglas (1879–1952), English officer and farmer in Kenya; arrived in East Africa in 1920, owned 3,500 acres at Rongai; member of the Legislative Council from 1925; husband of Lady Eileen Scott, daughter of the earl of Minto, viceroy of India, 142, 361
Scott, Lady Margaret; niece of Lord Francis Scott, 142
Scribner's Magazine, American periodical (1887–1939), 353
Seedorff, Hans Hartvig, born 1892, Danish author, 64*
Sengeløse, village between Copenhagen and Roskilde, Sealand, 347
Sévigné, Marie de Rabutin Chantal, Marquise de (1626–96), French letter-writer, 268
Sexual morality, 176,* 181, 263, 264, 290, 293, 323–25, 385, 388
Seyyed Ali bin Salim, sheik in Mombasa; liwali (official Muslim leader) on the coast; grand vizier to the sultan of Zanzibar; member of the Legislative Council of Kenya, 301, 401
Shakespeare, William (1564–1616), 36, 202,* 209, 235, 321, 347, 409, 410
Shaw, George Bernard (1856–1950), 171, 287,* 321
Shelley, Percy Bysshe (1792–1822), 209, 282
Shimbir. *See* Ahamed Farah Aden
Shoreham-by-Sea, town on the south coast of England, near Brighton, 60
Show grounds, Kabiti, outside Nairobi, 382
A Shropshire Lad, by A. E. Housman (1896), 241
The Silver Spoon, fifth part of John Galsworthy's novel cycle, *The Forsyte Saga* (1926), 308
Simba, animal film by Martin Johnson (1928), 384
Singapore, 404
Sirunga, epileptic half-Masai, 411, 425*
Sjögren, Åke, owner of the Swedo-African Coffee Co. until 1913; Swedish consul in British East Africa, xlii, 2, 5, 43, 45, 101
Skodsborg Station, on the coastal railway line in East Sealand, between Klampenbord and Rungsted, 335
Skaane, region in South Sweden, xlii
Slagelse (town in South Sealand) Music Society, 65
Slettemose House, near Folehave, 68
Slott-Møller, Agnes (1862–1937), Danish painter, 184*
Small pox, 88
Sofie. *See* Bernstorff-Gyldensteen, Agnes Louise
Soldier Settlement Scheme, 71,* 82, 96–97
Solsana, health resort, 429
Somali language, 69, 310
Somaliland, 4, 20, 23, 69, 224, 230, 316, 423
Somalis, 4, 5, 8, 9, 11, 15, 17, 21, 23, 26, 30, 43, 48, 51, 54, 64, 67, 71, 74, 76, 81, 95, 97, 138, 158, 165, 174, 199, 224, 239, 273, 307, 316, 368, 398, 403, 404, 405, 416, 425, 431
"Sonate pathétique," piano sonata in C minor by Ludwig van Beethoven, Opus 13 (1799), 407
"Song for Harp," poem by Karen Blixen, 215
"Songs for Little Brother," children's songs for Anders Dinesen composed by Ea Neergaard, 47
Sophie. *See* Bernstorff-Gyldensteen, Agnes Louise

Sorabjee, Elchi, Indian doctor at the European Hospital, Nairobi; trained in England, 313, 383
Soul after Death, A, Danish comedy by Johan Ludvig Heiberg (1841), 154*
South Africa, 5, 69, 72, 328
Spanish influenza, 87, 100, 126, 145
Spinoza, Baruch (1632–77), 350, 370
Spoken and Written, lectures, articles, and papers by Jens Byskov Danish writer (1927), 353
"*Springfontein,*" steamship on the Antwerp-Mombasa route, 237
Springforbi, station on the coastal railway line, Sealand, between Klampenborg and Rungsted, 353
Stanley Hotel. *See* New Stanley Hotel
"Star, A," poem by Karen Blixen, printed in Thomas Dinesen's *No Man's Land* (1929), 135*
"Star and Garter" Fund, Nairobi, 87
Stead, William T. (1849–1912), English journalist, 349
Steele, A., Major, lived at Kiambu near Nairobi, 318, 399
Steele, Mrs., wife of Major Steele, 318, 399
Stelling, paint merchant, 139
Stevenson, Robert Louis (1850–94), 40, 119,* 150, 277, 358
"Still Life with Stuffed Owl," painting by Karen Blixen (1922), 198*
"Stork, The," children's story known from Karen Blixen's version in *Out of Africa,* chapter entitled "The Roads of Life," 49, 270, 288, 294
Strachey, Lytton (1880–1932), 236
Strindberg, August (1849–1912), 180, 321
Stub, Ambrosius (1705–58), Danish poet, 390*
Stuckenberg, Viggo (1863–1905), Danish author, 286,* 335
Suez Canal, 13
Suicide, 249, 418, 420, 421, 427
Svend Dyring's House, play by Henrik Hertz, Danish dramatist (1837), 348
Swahili language, 4, 8, 11, 27, 266, 334, 363, 387
Swahili tribe (Kenya), 15
"Swan, A," poem by Henrik Ibsen, ca. 1865, set to music by Edvard Grieg, 353
Sweden, 26, 55, 85, 100, 153, 236
"Swedo," name of the Swedish-owned house acquired by the limited company, Karen Coffee Co. in 1916, later called "Bogani," 9, 13, 27, 32, 34, 39, 40
Swedo-African Coffee Co., Ltd., H'ruru Estate, Ngong, coffee farm purchased by Bror Blixen in 1913, xlii, 11
Swift, Jonathan (1667–1745), 235
Sybille. *See* Reventlow, Anne Sybille
Syphilis, 30, 31, 47, 48, 100, 103, 114, 119, 121, 127, 151, 165, 195, 197, 214, 215, 216, 217, 221, 278, 283, 284, 286, 288
Sølvgade, no. 26, Copenhagen; Ellen and Knud Dahl's property overlooking the King's Garden, 338
Sønderjylland, (North Schleswig), 84

Tabora, town in Tanganyika Territory, on the railway line from Dar-es-Salaam to Kigoma, 1
Tale of Two Cities, A, novel by Charles Dickens (1859), 261
Tana, river with source on Mount Kenya, running out to the sea through extensive lowlands, Tana Plains, 59
"*Tanganyika,*" steamship on the route from Genoa to Mombasa, 400
Tanganyika, governor of, 130
Tanganyika Territory, British mandate comprising the greater part of the earlier German East Africa, 303, 340, 341, 342, 362, 374
Tanne, My Sister Karen Blixen, reminiscences by Thomas Dinesen (1974; English edition: *My Sister Isak Dinesen,* 1975), 32
Taube, Ella, née Ekman-Hansen (1884–1966); daughter of Professor P. Hansen, Danish author; in 1911 married the Swedish actor and painter Mathias Taube (1876–1934), 337
Taylor, Charles, Major, of the Survey Department (Nairobi), 148, 177, 179, 402

Tegner,Arnette Margrethe, née Hage (1847–1938), wife of Jørgen Henry August Tegner, bank director (1843–1911), 118, 345
Tennyson, Alfred (1809–92), 236
Tempest, The, (Shakespeare's), 413
Thaxton, H., Karen Blixen's American factory manager until the autumn of 1927 (appears in *Out of Africa* under the name of Belknap); later farmer at Naivasha, 147, 165, 178, 179, 319, 359, 422
Their Silver Wedding Journey, novel by William Dean Howells (1899), 350
"There is a Lovely Country," Danish national anthem by Adam Oehlenschläger (1819), 397
"There is Life in a Look at the Crucified One," English mission hymn by Amelia Matilda Hull (ca. 1825–82), 266*
Thika, town to the northwest of Nairobi, 289
Thompson, Alan, 67
Thora, Aunt. *See* Westenholz, Victoria Christiane
Thornberg, Julius (1885–1945), Danish violinist, 352
Thorvaldsen's Museum, Copenhagen, 66
Through the Fair Kingdoms, by Johannes Poulsen (1916), 54
Thyra. *See* Ræder, Thyra
Thousand and One Nights, A, 74, 295, 357
Tilskueren magazine, Danish literary periodical (1884–1939), 150, 158, 215, 219, 239, 256, 410
Times, London, 92
Titi Gaturra, Kamate's little brother, Karen Blixen's dog toto, 334, 363, 374, 399, 425
Tivoli, famous pleasure park in Copenhagen, 334
"Tod und das Mädchen," string quartet in D flat by Franz Schubert, composed 1824–25, 383
To Let, third part of John Galsworthy's novel, *The Forsyte Saga* (1920–21), 220
Tolstoy, Leo (1828–1910), 24, 156, 404
Tommy's Tunes, collection of soldiers' songs, marches, and musical parodies, collected and arranged by Frederick Thomas Nettle-Ingham (1917–18), 402
Torben, Uncle. *See* Grut, Torben
Tours (France), 162
Tourvel, Monsier de, French mayor, seventeenth century, 268
Trafford, Raymond de, 344
Tramping through East Africa, reminiscences by Otto Casparsson in *Aftonbladet* (1928), 379
Trench, Mr., agricultural expert in Nairobi, 155
Troels-Lund, Troels (1840–1921), Danish historian, 153
Tumbo. *See* Muhammed Juma
Turkana, area to the west of Lake Turkana in northern Kenya, 166
Turner, William (1775–1851), English painter, 162

Uasha Nyero. *See* Guaso Nyiro
Uasin Gishu, district in western Kenya around the town of Eldoret; known for maize farming, 42, 64, 93, 103, 116, 147, 148
Uganda, 129, 135, 174, 214, 333, 353, 383
Ulf. *See* Hansen, Ulf
Ulla. *See* Lindström, Ulla
Ulla, Aunt. *See* Westenholz, Ulla
Undset, Sigrid (1882–1949), Norwegian author, 164, 180, 274, 355, 359
Unfinished Symphony, No. 8 in B minor by Franz Schubert (1822), 383
Unitarians, 290

Valborg, Aunt. *See* Ræder, Thyra Valborg
Valdemar Atterdag, Danish king (1320–1340–1375), 314
Valdemarskilde, manor farm estate between Sorø and Slagelse, Sealand, owned by Viggo de Neergaard, Karen Blixen's brother-in-law, 127, 130, 134
Valmont. *See* Clinique Valmont
Vejle, town in Jutland, 295
Veldt sores, 85*
Venice, 429
Venus (Roman goddess), 382
Venus (planet), 135, 138, 312
Verdun, 90

Versailles, 268
"Vicar of Vejlby, The," Danish story by Steen Steensen Blicher (1829), 394
Vice-Governor. *See* Hobley, Charles William
Victoria, queen of England (1819–1837–1901), 17, 220, 234, 235, 347, 361, 395
Victoria Cross, English decoration (the Maltese Cross), instituted in 1852 by Queen Victoria; awarded for outstanding courage in battle, 90,* 91, 94, 95,* 194, 211
Viggo. *See* Neergaard, Viggo de
Viking era, 52
Villa Vesta, property at Randers, Jutland, belonging to Emilie Augusta Dinesen, 327
Vimmelskaftet, part of Strøget (pedestrian street) in Copenhagen, 65
Vivienne. *See* Watteville, Vivienne de
Voi, town in southeast Kenya, on the railway line from Mombasa to Nairobi, 16, 430
Voltaire, François-Marie Arouet (1694–1778), 409, 410

Wagner, Cosima, née Liszt (1837–1930), 392
Wagner, Richard (1813–83), 392
Wakambas, tribe in Kenya, 158, 177, 270, 312, 402, 409
Wales, Edward, Prince of (1894–1972); son of George V; king of England Jan.–Dec. 1936 under the name of Edward VIII, thereafter duke of Windsor, 361,* 362, 377, 382, 383, 384, 385, 386, 387, 395, 401,* 402, 407
Walter the Potter, Danish marionette play by Johan Ludvig Heiberg (1812), 186
Wangatta, locality on the farm, 368
Wanjangiri, native boy, 178, 179, 181, 221
Wanscher, Ellen (1883–1967), Karen Blixen's childhood friend; later married Mogens Lassen, Danish architect, 65, 186, 208, 314, 405
Wanscher, Johanne Margrethe, née Hage (1850–1929), wife of Professor Oscar Wanscher, chief surgeon (1846–1906); mother of Ellen Wanscher, 213, 350
War and Peace, novel by Leo Tolstoy (1864–69), 404
Washington and the Hope of Peace, by H. G. Wells (1922), 138
Washington Conference, held in Washington 12 Nov. 1921 to 6 February 1922, 138*
Wassermann, Jakob (1873–1934), German author, 336
Waterworks, supplying the soda district of Magadi southwest of Nairobi with fresh water from the mountains, 385
Watteville, Vivienne de, died 1957; Swiss author; daughter of the natural scientist, Bernard de Watteville, 387*
Webb's Store, 15
Wedell, Inger, née Countess Krag-Juel-Vind-Frijs (1885–1975); countess of Frijsenborg and Wedellsborg; wife of Count Julius Wedell, 263
Welby, E., assistant district commissioner at Narok, 410
Wells, H. G. (1866–1946), 126, 138,* 211, 343, 366
Wessel, Johan Herman (1742–85), Danish satirist, 394
Westenholz, Aage (1859–1935); civil engineer and plantation owner; brother of Ingeborg Dinesen; chairman of the Karen Coffee Co. Ltd., 1916–32, xlii, 39, 40, 45, 61, 99, 105, 106, 107, 110, 111, 118, 132, 141, 144, 151, 155, 157, 167, 168, 213, 215, 245, 350, 402
Westenholz, Ellen ("Koosje"), née Grut (1875–1951); wife of Aage Westenholz, 279, 280, 346
Westenholz, Mary Bess ("Aunt Bess"; 1857–1947), sister of Ingeborg Dinesen; cofounder of the Unitarian union in Denmark, the Free Church; wrote "Recollections of Mama and her Family" (published in *Blixeniana* 1979), and published "From my Lumber-Room" under the pseudonym Bertel Wrads (1895), 4, 61, 109, 110, 111, 112, 114, 119, 127, 128, 130, 136, 138, 141, 153,* 160, 163, 166, 171, 175, 177, 190, 197, 198, 199, 202, 210, 213, 219, 229, 233,

245, 258, 265, 267, 285, 287, 292, 296, 301, 302, 304,* 313, 315, 321, 328, 330, 331, 344, 345–47, 348–51, 353, 364, 368, 369, 380, 390, 414,* 416, 428
Westenholz, Mary Lucinde ("Mama"), née Hansen (1832–1915), the Chamberlain's wife, married to Regnar Westenholz, owner of Matrup; later lived at Folehave with her daughter, Mary Bess Westenholz, 23,* 68, 85, 110, 132, 153,* 161, 190, 213, 245, 250, 252, 265, 334, 346, 349, 380, 413
Westenholz, Regnar Lodbrog (1815–66), landowner, businessman, and minister of finance; owner of the estate, Matrup, Horsens, Jutland, 252
Westenholz, Thomas Eiler (1891–1963), landowner; son of Asker Westenholz (died 1925); married Ingeborg Grøn in 1926; owner of Matrup 1925–63, 327
Westenholz, Ulla, née Hansen Grut (1860–1940); wife of Asker Westenholz of Matrup, 117, 428
Westenholz, Victoria ("Thora") Christiane (1858–1935); daughter of Rolf Krake Westenholz, brother of Karen Blixen's maternal grandfather, Councillor of State Westenholz; closely bound to the family at Matrup, 209
Weyer, Johnnie van de, officer, farmer at Ngong, 26, 42, 66, 67, 69, 74, 92, 93, 98, 376
The White Monkey, fourth part of John Galsworthy's novel, *The Forsyte Saga* (1924), 220
Whymper, Edward (1840–1911), English explorer and mountaineer; conquered the Matterhorn in 1865, 56
Wicksteed, Philip H. (1844–1927), English sociologist, 375
Wilde, Oscar (1856–1900), 40, 150
Wildenvey, Herman (1886–1959), Norwegian author, 155
Wilhelm, Swedish prince, duke of Södermanland (1884–1965), son of King Gustav V; author, 2, 101
Wilhelm, German crown prince (1882–1951), 35
Wilhelm II, German kaiser (1859–1941), 35, 86
Wilkes, safari hunter, 19
Winchilsea, Anne Jane, countess of, died 1924; daughter of Admiral Sir Henry Codrington; mother of Denys Finch Hatton, 198,* 240, 406
Winchilsea, Guy Montagu George Finch Hatton, fourteenth earl of (1885–1939); brother of Denys Finch Hatton, 215
Winchilsea, Henry Stormont, thirteenth earl of (1852–1927); father of Denys Finch Hatton, 240*
Windinge, Erik Christian, born 1917, lived in Copenhagen, 74
Windinge, Maude, née Bauer (1891–1978); in 1916 married Christian Windinge, engineer; lived in Kenya 1916–21 and again some years later, 74*
Windinge, Søren, born 1919; chartered surveyor, Aarhus, 74
Wisnes, A. H. (1889–1972), Norwegian literary scholar and historian of ideas, 164
Women's Movement, 163, 176, 258, 259, 260, 261, 262, 263, 328, 356, 399
World and We, The, Danish weekly periodical (1911–31), 51
World War I, 16, 23, 26, 27, 32, 33, 35, 43, 46, 48, 49, 51, 53, 57, 70, 75, 76, 77, 78, 79, 86, 87, 89, 90, 91, 92, 99, 136, 143, 146, 194, 220, 234, 336, 428
Wronged and the Oppressed, The, novel by Dostoievski (1861), 335

Young Ladies' Room, The, operetta by Heinrich Berté (1916), 256

Zahle's School, in Nørrevold, Copenhagen; founded 1851, 48, 375
Zahrtmann, Kristian (1843–1917), Danish painter, 150,* 155
Zanzibar, 38
Zanzibar, sultan of, 38
Zurich, 127
Zøylner, Maria (1876–1952), governess to Karen Blixen and her sisters at Folehave; in 1917 married Herman Heilbuth, director, 250

Ølholm, village ca. 20 km west of Horsens, Jutland, south of the estate of Matrup, 294

Ørslev, village near Slagelse, Sealand, where Vilhelm Beck, founder of the Danish Inland Mission, was the incumbent from 1874–1901, 265